ADTs, Data Structures, and Problem Solving with C++

SECOND EDITION

Larry R. Nyhoff

Calvin College
Department of Computer Science
Grand Rapids, MI

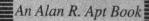

An Alan R. Apt Book

PEARSON

Prentice Hall

Upper Saddle River, NJ 07458

Library of Congress Cataloging-in-Publication Data

CIP DATA AVAILABLE.

Vice President and Editorial Director, ECS: *Marcia J. Horton*
Publisher: *Alan Apt*
Associate Editor: *Toni Dianne Holm*
Vice President and Director of Production and Manufacturing, ESM: *David W. Riccardi*
Executive Managing Editor: *Vince O'Brien*
Managing Editor: *Camille Trentacoste*
Production Editor: *Irwin Zucker*
Director of Creative Services: *Paul Belfanti*
Creative Director: *Carole Anson*
Art Director: *Heather Scott*
Cover and Interior Design: *Susan Anderson-Smith*
Managing Editor, AV Management and Production: *Patricia Burns*
Art Editor: *Xiaohong Zhu*
Manufacturing Manager: *Trudy Pisciotti*
Manufacturing Buyer: *Lisa McDowell*
Executive Marketing Manager: *Pamela Hersperger*
Marketing Assistant: *Barrie Reinhold*

© 2005, 1999 Pearson Education, Inc.
Pearson Prentice Hall
Pearson Education, Inc.
Upper Saddle River, NJ 07458

Pearson Prentice Hall® is a trademark of Pearson Education, Inc.

Printed in the United States of America

ISBN 0-13-140909-3

Pearson Education Ltd., *London*
Pearson Education Australia Pty. Ltd., *Sydney*
Pearson Education Singapore, Pte. Ltd.
Pearson Education North Asia Ltd., *Hong Kong*
Pearson Education Canada, Inc., *Toronto*
Pearson Educación de Mexico, S.A. de C.V.
Pearson Education—Japan, *Tokyo*
Pearson Education Malaysia, Pte. Ltd.
Pearson Education, Inc., *Upper Saddle River, New Jersey*

Preface

The first edition of this text grew out of the author's experience teaching an introductory data structures course (commonly referred to as CS2) for nearly two decades. It has served as a sequel to the widely used *C++: An Introduction to Computing* by Joel Adams and Larry Nyhoff, which grew out of their many years of teaching a first programming course (CS1) in C++. But computer science curricula change as do teaching pedagogy and methodology. In keeping with these changes, the introductory C++ text underwent revisions and has recently appeared in a third edition.

The content of the second course in computing also has changed, with the broadening of the traditional study of data structures to a study of abstract data types (ADTs) being one of the major trends. Consequently, there is an increased emphasis on ADTs in this new edition and a name change thus seemed appropriate: *ADTs, Data Structures, and Problem Solving with C++*. And as one might expect, there is a corresponding increased emphasis on object-oriented design.

In addition, the author's pedagogy has been honed over many years of successful teaching.[1] Reflecting this, the presentation in this new edition has been improved by reordering some topics, rewriting several sections, and adding new material. Many suggestions also came from those who diligently and thoroughly reviewed the manuscript and its several revisions. Their constructive comments and positive evaluations were very encouraging and much appreciated.

To Instructors

If you used the first edition and liked it, I trust you will like this new edition even more. Scan the overview and list of new features that appear later in this preface to see what some of the improvements are. Those of you who haven't used or who stopped using the first edition and are looking at this edition as one of several candidates for your course will, I hope, give it serious consideration. I have tried to preserve the best features of the first edition and made changes based on feedback from many CS2 teachers and users of the previous edition.

Approach   As an illustration of the approach that has worked well in my classes, take a look at Chapter 7 on stacks. Some examples of real-world phenomena that are best modeled by a LIFO structure lead to abstracting from these examples the common features, yielding a stack ADT. But ADTs must be implemented with data structures provided in some language, and so we build a stack class. (Incidentally, while we are doing this in class, my students are working on building a queue class in their lab period.)

---

[1] *Publisher's Note*: Professor Nyhoff's prowess as a teacher was acknowledged when he received the Presidential Exemplary Teaching Award for the academic year 2002–03 after being recommended by Calvin College colleagues along with current and former students.

Once this new `Stack` type has been created and tested, we use it to solve one or more of the original problems and usually at least one new application. I also believe in starting with a simple implementation—e.g., using a static C-style array—and get a working version. Then, emphasizing the need to preserve the public interface of an ADT, we refine it—e.g., use a dynamic array so the user can specify the stack's capacity; then use a linked list so an a priori capacity specification is not needed; and finally, convert it to a template so the ADT can be used with arbitrary type elements. This spiral/successive-refinement approach demonstrates clearly the "abstract" part of an ADT—that it is independent of the implementation.

I also cover many of the containers provided in the C++ Standard Template Library (STL), because several of them such as `vector` are very useful and powerful, and it does not make sense to reinvent the wheel by building our own versions. Others, however, such as STL's stacks and queues, are adapters of other containers and waste a lot of the horsepower of these inner containers. For these it makes sense to build our own "lean and mean" implementations, using lower-level data structures such as arrays and linked lists. It also provides practice for students with building customized container types for problems for which none of the standard containers is really suitable.

How to Use this Book   There is considerable flexibility in the kind of course that can be taught from this text. In particular, many of the topics can be covered in an order different from that used in the text. The diagram on the next page shows the major dependencies of the various chapters. An arrow running from one box to another indicates a significant dependence of the material in the second box on that in the first; for example, the material in Chapter 9 draws on the material in both Chapters 7 and 8. A dashed arrow indicates that the material in the first box may have been covered in a first course and might be omitted or assigned for review. Boxes not connected are, for the most part, independent of each other (for example, Chapters 7 and 8).

To Students (and Other Users of this Text)

You probably don't read prefaces of most textbooks unless your instructor assigns them and then perhaps only if you will be quizzed on it. For this text, however, you should at least read the section "Overview of the Text," because it is intended to provide an orientation to what the book is about, what its major themes are, and how they fit together. And you should also look through the Table of Contents for this same reason.

The topics covered in this text are typical of those in a course that follows a first course in programming. The aim of these two courses together is to provide you with a solid introduction to computing. You develop the skills to write substantial programs for solving non-trivial problems but are also introduced to important concepts and techniques in computing. These two courses should provide you with a solid base for using the computer as a problem-solving tool in whatever areas of study you pursue. If you do more coursework in computer science, it is important that you work hard at mastering the material of this second course, because the topics covered are fundamental to several upper-level courses. In fact, at many colleges and universities, this course is a prerequisite for intermediate and advanced courses in computer science.

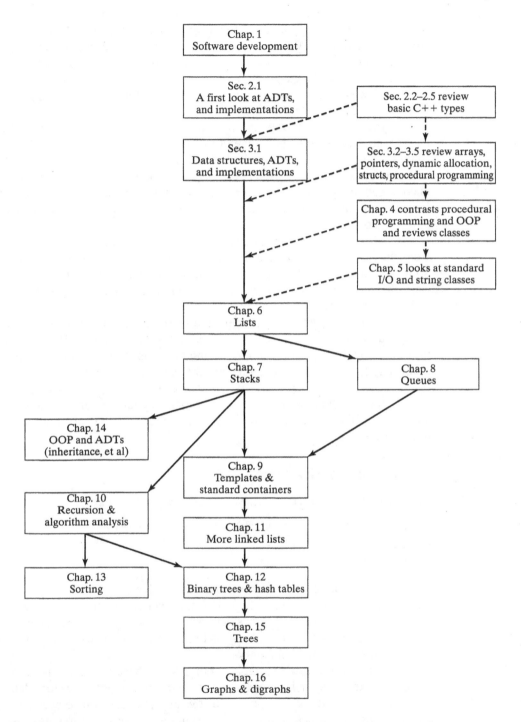

This text assumes that you have had an introduction to programming, prefera-
bly using C++ or Java. Appendix C (*Basic C++*) reviews the basic features of C++
that are typically covered in a first programming course, and Appendix D (*Other
C++ Features*) covers some features that are more advanced. Students in my classes

have found these two appendixes to be handy references when they need to look up something about the C++ language. If your first course was in Java, you should study Appendix E (*From Java to C++*), which provides a comparison of the main features of the two languages. It has been used successfully in my classes to get students with a background in Java up to speed with the basic features of C++ in the first couple of weeks.

As you read through the text, you should by all means use the Quick Quizzes to check your understanding of some of the main ideas from the reading. The answers to these can be found in Appendix F. These self-test quizzes are usually followed by sets of exercises, some of which your instructor may assign for homework. You are encouraged to try some of these on your own, even if it isn't required, because it will increase your mastery of the material. The same is true of the programming problems at the end of each chapter.

All of the C++ code in the program examples of this text can be downloaded from the author's website for the book: http://cs.calvin.edu/books/c++/ds. So if you see a particular function in an example that you can use in a program or class library you are writing, feel free to download and use it—unless your instructor forbids it, of course!

Hopefully, you will enjoy reading and learning from the text. Several hundreds of my students have used earlier versions of this text with very few complaints. But they do enjoy finding errors and informing me about them! I hope that you too will report any that you run across; they are there, in spite of long hours of "debugging" the manuscript before it goes into print. I can't offer you bonus points on your course grade for finding them, but I will recognize your contribution to the improvement of the book by adding your name to the list of other error detectors on the book's website.

Overview of the Text

As the title suggests, there are three main themes in this text:

1. Abstract data types (ADTs)
2. Data structures
3. Problem solving

Abstract data types consist of collections of data elements together with basic operations on the data. Nearly every chapter of this text deals with some aspect of ADTs—defining an ADT such as a list, stack, or queue; studying some application of it; implementing the ADT or studying its implementation in some library; looking at ways to improve the implementation.

Classes play a key role in implementing ADTs because they make it possible to encapsulate the data and the operations so that objects not only store data but also have built-in operations. This is one of the key properties of object-oriented programming and is emphasized from the beginning. Data structures provided in C++ (such as arrays) or that can be built in C++ (e.g., linked lists) play important roles in providing structures to store the data elements of an ADT. These key data structures along with the up-to-date and powerful containers from the Standard Template Library (STL) are studied for this purpose.

The third theme is problem solving. Chapter 1 describes some of the software engineering methodologies used to develop a solution to a problem, and the text emphasizes the use of object-oriented design (OOD) in the design phase. This is a natural continuation of the object-centered design (OCD) approach used in *C++: An Introduction to Computing* and which is similar to that used in many other introductory programming texts. The text has many examples, including several case studies, that show the roles that ADTs play in problem solving.

Implementing the operations of an ADT involves designing algorithms to carry out the operations. This means that the study of algorithms must also play a significant role in a study of ADTs, and this text has many examples of algorithms. These include searching and sorting algorithms along with the powerful algorithms from the Standard Template Library (STL). Analyzing the efficiency of algorithms is also introduced and illustrated, thus providing a first look at important tools used in later courses in computer science.

Algorithms must be implemented in a programming language. Thus this text includes some coverage of C++, especially the more advanced topics not usually covered in a first course and which students need to learn. These include recursion, function and class templates, inheritance, and polymorphism. The C++ features presented conform to the official standard for C++. In addition, some of the C-style topics appropriate in a data structures course are included for several reasons: many students will get jobs as C programmers; many libraries and operating system utilities are written in C or C-style languages; data structures provided in C are usually implemented very efficiently and they are often used to implement some of the more modern standard data types.

Another feature of this text is that it continues the portrayal of the discipline of computer science begun in *C++: An Introduction to Computing* by including examples and exercises to introduce various areas of computer science and thereby provide a foundation for further studies in computer science. The topics include:

- Descriptions of software development methods
- Introduction to data encryption schemes (DES and public key)
- Data compression using Huffman codes
- Doubly-linked lists and large integer arithmetic
- Random number generation and simulation
- Lexical analysis and parsing
- Postfix notation and generation of machine code
- Simple systems concepts such as input/output buffers, parameter-passing mechanisms, address translation, and memory management

New and Improved Features

- Revised first chapter:
  - Introduces other software engineering methods besides the waterfall model.
  - Introduces UML

- Describes top-down design and object-oriented design in detail
- Relates some of the "horror stories" of bad software design

■ More use of OOD and OOP in examples

■ Uniform method of displaying ADT specifications in a UML-style diagram

■ Improved pseudocode in algorithms

■ Naming conventions that are consistent with common recommendations

■ Complete source code for nearly all of the ADTs

■ Many improvements to diagrams and several new diagrams

■ Expanded and improved discussion of C++'s I/O and string classes (Chapter 5)

■ Earlier introduction to pointers and dynamic allocation, including an expanded discussion of the new operator (Chapters 2 and 3)

■ Earlier presentation of lists (Chapter 6)—before stacks and queues—and revised to include array-based (static and dynamic) list classes, an introduction to linked lists, and more standard symbols in diagrams

■ Array-based and linked-list implementations of stacks (Chapter 7)

■ Expanded treatment of queues, including array-based and linked-list implementations, and a revised simulation case study (Chapter 8)

■ New chapter on searching, including modified and expanded treatment of binary search trees and hash tables (Chapter 12)

■ Added discussion of heaps, priority queues, and radix sort (Chapter 13)

■ Revised chapter on inheritance (Chapter 14)

■ Chapter objectives and end-of-chapter summaries

■ Several case studies

■ A new appendix *From Java to C++* for those making a transition from Java to C++

Other Key Features

■ Self-test Quick Quizzes with answers in back of text

■ Large number of written exercises and programming problems

■ Chapter notes, programming pointers, and ADT tips at the end of each chapter

■ More conformance to the C++ standard than many other texts

■ Solid introduction to the C++ Standard Template Library

■ A review of C++ in the appendixes for handy reference (Appendices C and D)

■ Boxed displays to set off important concepts

■ A new design that makes the text more readable and attractive

■ Effective use of color to highlight important features and not simply for decoration

■ Icons that point out key features, special things to note, and warnings:

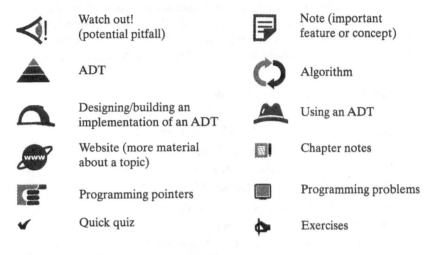

Watch out! (potential pitfall)		Note (important feature or concept)	
ADT		Algorithm	
Designing/building an implementation of an ADT		Using an ADT	
Website (more material about a topic)		Chapter notes	
Programming pointers		Programming problems	
Quick quiz		Exercises	

Supplementary Materials

A number of supplementary materials are available for this text:

■ An online solutions manual containing solutions for all of the written exercises. Access to these solutions is available to those who adopt this text for use in a course. Solutions to many of the programming problems are also available to them upon request from the author.

■ Author website (`http://cs.calvin.edu/books/ds`) and Prentice Hall website (`http://www.prenhall.com/nyhoff`) contain the following:

  ● Downloadable source code for text examples
  ● Solutions to case studies including source code
  ● PowerPoint slides
  ● Other supplementary material

■ A lab manual with lab exercises and projects (sold separately and also available as a value pack option). It is coordinated with the presentation in the text, reinforcing and expanding what students read there and hear in class.

■ Also available are software value pack options that include:

  ● Microsoft Visual C++
  ● Metrowerks CodeWarrior Learning Edition

Acknowledgments

I express my sincere appreciation to all who helped in any way in the preparation of this text. My gratitude for friendship, perceptive suggestions and directions, and unflagging support and encouragement goes to Alan Apt, a publisher highly respected throughout the publishing and academic communities, and to my editor Toni Holm; their friendship over the past several years has made textbook writing for Prentice Hall an enjoyable experience. I must also thank art director Heather Scott, production editors Chirag Thakkar and Irwin Zucker, and all the others who did such a fantastic job of designing this attractive book and actually getting it into print. Their attention to details has compensated for my lack thereof and their cooperation and kind words were much appreciated. I also appreciate the management of reviews and other details handled by Jake Warde. And I appreciate the many valuable observations and recommendations by the following reviewers of the manuscript; they have strengthened the presentation significantly:

Ping Chen (University of Houston)
Joe Derrick (Radford University)
Eamon Doherty (Farleigh Dickinson University)
James Durbano (University of Delaware)
Eduardo Fernandez (Florida Atlantic University)
Christopher Fox (James Madison University)
Mahmood Haghighi (Bradley University)
Oge Marques (Florida Atlantic)
Mark McCullen (Michigan State University)
William McQuain (Virginia Tech)
Jim Miller (Kansas University)
Jim Richards (Bemidji State University)
Robert Schneider (University of Bridgewater)
Joseph Shinnerl (University of California, Los Angeles)
Michael Stiber (University of Washington)
Al Verbanec (Pennsylvania State University)
John M. Weiss (South Dakota School of Mines and Technology)
Rick Zaccone (Bucknell University)

And, of course, I must once again pay homage to my wife Shar and to our children and grandchildren—Jeff, Dawn, Rebecca, Megan, and Sara; Jim; Greg, Julie, Joshua and Derek; Tom, Joan, Abigail, Micah, and Lucas—for their love and understanding through all the times that their needs and wants were slighted by my busyness. Above all, I give thanks to God for giving me the opportunity, ability, and stamina to prepare this text.

Larry Nyhoff

Contents

Appendixes

A   ASCII Character Set   A1

B   Number Systems   B1

C   Basic C++   C1

D   Other C++ Features   D1

1

Software Development

CHAPTER CONTENTS

Chapter Objectives

- Introduce some of the popular approaches to software development and investigate the basic phases of software engineering.

- Contrast software development in an introductory programming course with that in the real world.

- Study two of the basic approaches to software design: top-down design and object-oriented design.

- Introduce two basic aspects of design: select or build data types to organize the data and develop algorithms for the operations on the data.

- Look at some common guidelines for developing good source code and study an example of such code.

- Investigate the basic kinds of errors in software and methods for locating their sources.

- Emphasize the importance of testing software by means of some examples of serious consequences of bad software.

- Note the large amount of time and effort devoted to software maintenance.

Problem solving with a computer requires the use of both hardware and software. The **hardware** of a computing system consists of the actual physical components, such as the central processing unit (CPU), memory, and input/output devices that make up the system. **Software** refers to programs used to control the operation of the hardware in order to solve problems. Software development is a complex process that is both an art and a science. It is an art in that it requires a good deal of imagination, creativity, and ingenuity. But it is also a science in that it uses certain standard techniques and methodologies. The term **software engineering** has come to be applied to the study and use of these techniques.

Although the problems themselves and the techniques used in their solutions vary, software development always involves at least the following phases:

- Problem Analysis and Specification: The problem is analyzed and a specification for the problem is formulated.

- Design: A plan for solving the problem is formulated.

- Coding: The plan is implemented in some programming language, producing a program and, for some problems, one or more libraries.

- Testing, Execution, and Debugging: The program is tested and errors (*bugs*) are removed.

- Maintenance: The program is updated and modified, as necessary, to keep it up to date and/or to meet users' needs.

The names and number of these phases and how they are carried out varies, however, from one model of the software development process to the next. One of the earliest strategies for developing software is known as the **waterfall model** and is commonly pictured as shown in Figure 1.1. It consists of carrying out the preceding phases sequentially; when each step is completed, the development moves on to the next step.

Figure 1.1 Waterfall Model

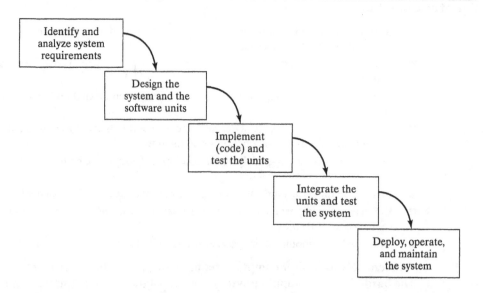

Although this model of software development has been widely used, it does have its disadvantages, chief of which is the difficulty of going back and revising something in an earlier phase. In reality, it may be necessary to go back from any one phase to an earlier one, as shown in Figure 1.2.

Figure 1.2 Realistic Waterfall Model

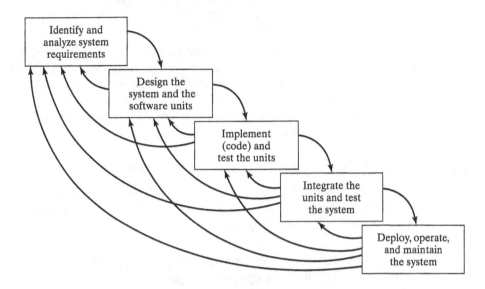

Thus, a variety of new alternative approaches have been developed, including the following:

- **Prototyping models**: A *prototype* (an early approximation of the final system) is built. It is then repeatedly evaluated and reworked as necessary, until an acceptable version is obtained from which the complete system or product can be developed. It is an iterative, trial-and-error process that takes place between the developers and the customer and that works best in situations in which not all of the requirements are known in detail ahead of time.

- **Spiral models**: These methods combine features of the prototyping model and the waterfall model and are intended for large and complicated projects. A preliminary design for the system is developed and a first prototype is constructed from this design. The result is usually a scaled-down system that only approximates the characteristics of the final system. This process is repeated, and prototypes that better approximate the final system are developed until the customer is satisfied. The final system is then developed.

- **Agile Methods**: As the name suggests, these methods adapt and change as necessary. Basic principles include the following:
  - Welcome changes in requirements, even late in development.
  - Working software is the primary measure of progress. Deliver working software to the customer frequently.
  - Developers and customers should work together daily.
  - Motivate developers by giving them the environment and support they need, and trust them to get the job done.
  - Face-to-face conversation is the most efficient and effective method of conveying information among developers.

One agile method that has received a lot of attention is **extreme programming** (**XP**). Developers, working in pairs, write and test code, integrating it into the design structure as the project develops, with much face-to-face communication among team members.

Because this is not a software engineering textbook, we will not describe these various software development methodologies in more detail nor concentrate on a particular one. Rather, in this chapter, we will focus on the five aspects of software development listed earlier. We will illustrate them and describe some of the questions and complications that face software developers and some of the techniques they use in dealing with them.

1.1 Problem Analysis and Specification

The assignment sheet in Figure 1.3(a) is typical of programming problems given in an introductory programming course. The exercises and problems in such courses are usually quite simple and clearly stated.

Figure 1.3 (a) A C++ Programming Assignment
(b) A Real-World Problem

CPSC 112 - C++ Programming Assignment 4

Due: Wednesday, November 12

The financial aid office at Universal University has decided to increase the amount of each financial aid award to students by 10 percent. The financial aid record for a student consists of the student's id number (an integer), name, the number of financial aid awards received, and an array of financial aid awards, each of which contains the source of financial aid (e.g., scholarship, grant, on-campus work), and the amount of financial aid (a real value).

Assuming that this information in stored in an array of student financial aid records, write and test a function to update these records by increasing the amounts by 10 percent. Execute the program with the following 3 financial aid records and then with 5 records of your own:

   12345 John Doe 1 (Scholarship 1250.00)
   22222 Mary Smith 1(Grant 555.50)
   31416 Peter Pi 2 (Loan 500.00 Grant 900.00)

(a)

To: Bob Byte, Director of Information Technology Center
From: Chuck Cash, V.P. of Scholarships and Financial Aid
Date: Wednesday, November 12

Because of new government regulations, we must keep more accurate records of all students currently receiving financial aid and submit regular reports to FFAO (Federal Financial Aid Office). Could we get the computer to do this for us?

CC

(b)

This often makes a description of the behavior of a program unit to solve such problems quite straightforward:

> The function should receive an amount representing a percentage increase in financial aid, the number of student financial aid records to be modified, and an array containing these records. It should then update these records by increasing all of the financial aid awards in each record by the specified percentage.

Such a description is also called a **specification** (or **contract**) for the problem. As a software developer, however, we would probably write this in a more formal way such as:

Purpose: Increase by a specified percentage the financial aid award in each record stored in an array of student financial aid records.

Precondition: The financial aid records are stored in an array of student financial aid records, each containing a student's id number and name, the number of financial aid awards, and a list of these awards (each consisting of the source of financial aid, and the amount of aid).

Postcondition: Each record in the array has been modified by increasing the amount of each financial aid award by the specified percentage.

Preconditions describe the state of processing before a program unit—a program or subprogram (a C++ function, a Java method, a Fortran subroutine, a Pascal procedure, etc.)—or a collection of program units is executed. Typically, these are assumptions made about a program unit, often one or more restrictions on what constitutes a valid input or received value. In a similar way, **postconditions** describe the state of processing after the program unit is executed.

For most real-world problems, however, formulating a specification is not so easy and straightforward, as the memo in Figure 1.3(b) illustrates. The initial descriptions of such problems are often vague and imprecise. The person posing the problem often does not understand it well and does not understand how to solve it or what the computer's capabilities and limitations are. Formulating a behavioral description of what is needed to solve the problem may take considerable time and effort: asking questions, gathering information, clarifying ambiguities, and so on.

For example, one of the first steps in formulating a specification is to give a complete and precise description of the problem's *input*—what information is available for solving the problem. Often the problem's statement includes irrelevant items of information, and one must determine which items will be useful in solving the problem. Usually, additional questions must be answered. For example, what information is available for each student? How will this information be accessed? What data will the user enter during program execution?

Analysis of what is needed to solve the problem requires determining what *output* is required, that is, what information must be produced to solve the problem. It may be necessary to find answers to many questions to determine this. For example, what must be included in the reports to be submitted to FFAO? Must these reports have a special format? Must similar reports be generated for any other government agencies or university departments? Must reports be prepared for mailing to individual students? Must computer files of student records be updated?

Additional information may also be required before the specification of the problem is complete. What hardware and software are available? What are the performance requirements? For example, what response time is necessary? How critical is the application in which the software is being used? If fault-free performance is required, must a proof of correctness accompany the software? How often will the software be used? Will the users be sophisticated, or will they be novices, so that the software must be extra user friendly and robust?

For some problems, decisions must be made regarding the feasibility of a computer solution. Is it possible to design software to carry out the processing required to obtain the desired output from the given input? If so, is it economically feasible? Could the problem better be solved manually? How soon must the software be available? What is its expected lifetime?

If it is determined that a computer-aided solution is possible and is cost-effective, then the problem's specification becomes a blueprint that guides the development of the software, and it serves as the *standard* or *benchmark* to use in validating the final product to determine that it does in fact solve the problem. Consequently, this specification must be complete, consistent, and correct.

When software is being developed under contract for a company or agency, it may be necessary to argue, perhaps in a court of law, that the software does (or does not) perform according to the specification. In such cases, the specification must be stated very precisely, and for this reason, a number of **formal methods** such as Z, VDM (Vienna Development Method), and Larch have been developed for formulating specifications. These methods are usually studied in more advanced software engineering courses, and in this text, problem specifications will be stated somewhat less formally.

1.2 Design

Once the specification of a problem has been given, a plan for developing a program or a system of modules, libraries, and programs that solve the problem must be developed. This design phase is the most challenging phase of software development. Because the computer has no inherent problem-solving capabilities, designing a plan for solving a problem with the aid of the computer requires ingenuity and creativity on the part of the programmer. Various design methodologies have been developed over the years, and here we will describe two of them: *top-down design* and *object-oriented design* (*OOD*). The main idea in each approach is **modularization**, that is, considering certain aspects of the problem separately, which together solve the original problem. They differ in how this modularization is achieved.

Top-Down Design

Whereas programs written in introductory programming courses rarely exceed a few hundred lines in length, software developed in real-world applications often consists of many thousands of lines of code and, in some cases, several million lines.[1] In

---

[1] Windows 2000 and Red Hat Linux are estimated to have over 30 million lines of code, and Debian Linux more than 50 million lines. At General Motors, it is estimated that more than 2 billion lines of code had to be checked and repaired in connection with the Y2K problem.

developing such systems, it is usually not possible to visualize or anticipate at the outset all the details of a complete solution to the entire problem.

One popular approach to attacking such problems has been the **top-down** approach in which the original problem is partitioned into simpler subproblems, each of which can be considered individually. Some or all of these subproblems may still be fairly complicated, and this modularization can be repeated for them, continuing until subproblems are obtained that can be solved. The solutions to these problems make up a system that solves the original problem.

As a simple illustration, consider again the financial aid problem in Figure 1.3(b). Recall that the statement of the problem as posed by the vice president of scholarships and financial aid was quite vague, stating only that accurate records of all students currently receiving financial aid must be maintained and that regular reports must be submitted to the FFAO (Federal Financial Aid Office).

Some obvious subproblems of this larger one are the following:

1. Get the student records
2. Process the records
3. Prepare the reports

We might picture this modularization with the **structure diagram** in Figure 1.4.

Figure 1.4 A First Structure Diagram for the Financial Aid Problem

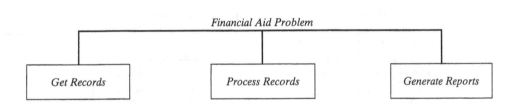

Typically, one or more of these first-level subproblems are still quite complex and so must be divided into smaller subproblems. For example, after consulting with the scholarships and financial aid staff, we might find that some of the information needed comes from student records maintained by the Financial Aid Office and other information comes from student records in the Registrar's office. So the first problem can be divided into two. Similarly, the process-records problem might be split into three subproblems: retrieve a student's financial aid record, read an update for it from the user, and then modify this record, as shown in Figure 1.5.

And, of course, some or all of these second-level subproblems might be split into smaller problems. For example, modifying a record might involve searching a collection of records to find it and then changing it with the update information entered by the user, as shown in Figure 1.6.

This process may continue for several more levels of refinement until each subproblem is sufficiently simple that designing a solution for it is reasonably easy and straightforward. This solution will consist of *storage structures* for the data and *algorithms* to process the data. For example, for the search problem, the collection

Figure 1.5 A Refined Structure Diagram for the Financial Aid Problem

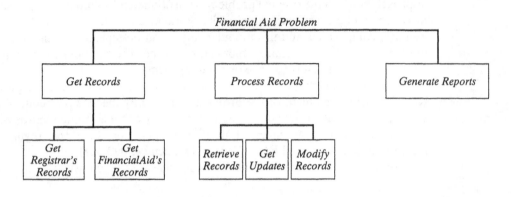

Figure 1.6 Additional Refinement in the Structure Diagram for the Financial Aid Problem

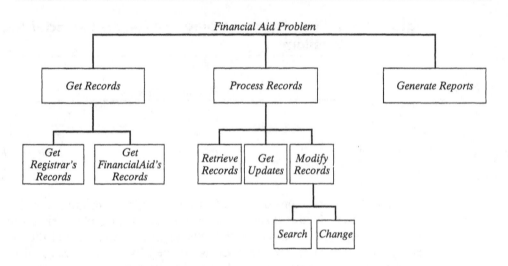

of student records to be searched might be stored in an array, ordered so that the key fields in these records (e.g., the students' id numbers) are in ascending order, and the algorithm might be a standard binary search algorithm that should be in every programmer's toolbox (see Section 1.4).

Object-Oriented Design

Another design methodology that has become increasingly common with the growing popularity of object-oriented programming is **object-oriented design (OOD)**. Whereas top-down design focuses on the tasks that have to be performed to solve a problem and the algorithms that carry out these tasks, OOD focuses on the "real-world objects" in the problem.

Modularization is achieved by identifying a collection of **objects**, each of which consists of data and operations on the data, that model these real-world objects and that interact to solve the problem. For example, in the financial aid problems in Figure 1.3, one central object is a financial aid award. It might consist of the following data items: an amount, a source (e.g., scholarship, grant, loan, and so on), qualifications for receiving it, length of time for which it is awarded, and so on. The operations might include retrieving the amount, the source, the qualifications, the time period; displaying the amount, the source, the qualifications, the time period; changing the amount, the source, the qualifications, the time period. Another central object is a student's record maintained by the financial aid office. It might store information about a student such as an id number, name, address, and age along with one or more financial aid awards. The operations on this data might include retrieving and displaying the id number and the student's name, retrieving and displaying the financial aid awards, modifying these awards, adding new financial aid awards, removing some of the financial aid awards, and so on. Another object is a student's record maintained by the registrar's office; it too would have specific data members and operations.

A collection of objects of the same type is called a **class** and each particular object is called an **instance** of that class. For example, the collection of financial aid awards make up a class that we might call *FinancialAidAward* and each specific financial aid award is an instance of this class. Similarly, all of the student financial aid records make up a class that we might call *StudentAidRecord*; Mary Doe's financial aid record is an instance of this class. And the student records from the registrar's office make up a class that might be named *StudentRegistrationRecord*.

In object-oriented design and programming, the word *object* refers to an instance of a class; that is, an entity whose type is a class. Every object has two parts: **data members** that store the data and **function members** that operate on the data; we say that the object **encapsulates** its data and the operations on that data,

In addition to encapsulation, object-oriented programming has two other characteristics:

- **Inheritance**: A class (called a *derived class* or *subclass*) can reuse all the attributes and operations of another class (called a *base class* or *parent class*).

- **Polymorphism**: The behavior of an object that can take on different forms at different times.

We will look at these properties of OOP in more detail in later chapters where we will see how they make it possible to extend OOD to large problems in which we can encapsulate common features of objects in base classes and then reuse these features in classes derived from them.

We will use a simplified *FinancialAidAward* class to illustrate encapsulation. Each *FinancialAidAward* object will have two data members that we name as follows:

- a real value *amount*
- a text string *source*

It also will have function members to carry out the operations that we listed earlier:

- *getAmount( )*: access the *amount* data member and return the real value stored there

- *getSource( )*: access the *source* data member and return the text string stored there
- *display( )*: display on the screen the values stored in the *source* and *amount* data members
- *setSource( )*: modify the *source* data member
- *setAmount( )*: modify the *amount* data member

(We use parentheses in function member names to distinguish them from data members.) We might picture a *FinancialAidAward* object with a diagram like the following:

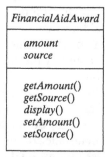

The preceding diagram is a simple form of **class diagram** used in the **Unified Modeling Language (UML)**, a visual modeling language used in object-oriented design that is becoming increasingly popular.[2] Note that the name of the class is in the top section, the data members are in the second, and the function members are in the third.

In UML, we can also provide additional information in a class diagram about the data members in the class, such as

- whether they are
  public (+): can be accessed both inside and outside the class
  private (–): can be accessed only inside the class
- their type (including integer, floating point, string, and boolean)
- a default value

More information about each function member can also be included:

- the kind of access to it: public or private (as described for data members)
- the parameter(s) of the function along with their types
- the function's return type (if it returns a value)

---

[2] UML grew out of the work of Grady Booch, James Rumbaugh, and Ivar Jacobsen, working separately from the 1980s through 1994. The "Three Amigos" joined forces in 1994 at Rational Software Corporation, where they have continued to develop the language.

Figure 1.7 UML Class Diagrams for *FinancialAidAward* and *StudentAidRecord* Classes

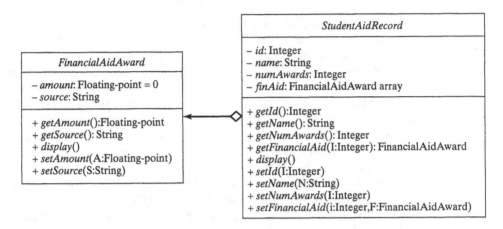

For example, a more complete class diagram for the *FinancialAidAward* class might look something like that in Figure 1.7. Also shown is a class diagram for a *Student-AidRecord*. The arrow indicates that a *StudentAidRecord* contains an array of *FinancialAidAward* objects. We will use diagrams similar to these UML class diagrams to define ADTs (abstract data types) in this text.

In addition to class diagrams, UML provides other graphical elements to describe object-oriented design, including

- *object diagrams*: to represent instances of a class
- *use case diagrams*: to describe from a user's perspective how the system behaves
- *state diagrams*: to show the different states a system may be in and transitions from one state to another

These are combined with other graphical elements to provide a collection of diagrams of the system being designed.

Since this text focuses on abstract data types and implementing them with data structures rather than on designing large systems, we will leave a detailed study of UML features to a software engineering course. (See the website for this text for some sources of additional information about UML.)

Design in the Small

For small problems such as those commonly assigned as programming projects in introductory programming courses, we can design solutions using methodologies similar to those we have described for large problems. Modularization like that produced in top-down design might consist of identifying program units such as C++ functions to carry out specific tasks, with their execution controlled by some higher-level program unit, with the main program at the top level.

Here we will assume that this has already been done and that we want to design a subprogram (a C++ function, a Java method, a Fortran subroutine, a Pascal procedure, etc.) to solve a small problem. In particular, we will consider the programming assignment in Figure 1.3(a), in which a C++ function is to be designed to modify student financial aid records. Our approach will be one that focuses on the problem's objects as object-oriented design does.

Data Types The most important attribute of each data item in a problem is its **type**, which determines what values it may have, what operations can be performed on it, and what these operations produce. In a first programming course you learn about the **simple data types** provided in the programming language for single entities. For example, in C++, int (or one of its variations such as unsigned, short int, and long int) is used for a single integer such as 123; double (or float, or long double) for a single real value such as 3.1415926535898; char for individual characters such as 'A'; bool for a single logical value true or false; enum for a single enumerated value; and *pointer* to store a single memory address. (All of these data types are reviewed in the next chapter.)

However, some objects are collections of values, and most programming languages provide **structured data types** (also called **data structures**) to store these collections. The most common of these, and one with which you may already be familiar, is the **array**. (They are reviewed in Section 3.2.) Nearly every high-level programming language provides arrays and also perhaps other more modern extensions such as valarrays and vectors in C++ (see Chapter 9). Arrays are used to organize data items that are all of the same type; for example, the array described in the financial aid programming assignment in Figure 1.3 is used to store financial aid objects.

The type of a financial aid object, however, must be a structure that can store items of different types: a real value for the amount and a string for the financial aid source. Similarly, the structure for a student financial aid object must store an integer id number, a string for the student's name, and a financial aid object. And most programming languages do provide a mechanism for building such types—e.g., structs and classes in C++, classes in Java, structures in Fortran, and records in Pascal. A large part of this text, beginning in Chapter 4, is devoted to studying in detail how to design and build such types—called *abstract data types* (*ADTs*)—and how to implement them using the data types provided in C++.

Algorithms In addition to the data members of an object, there are operations on this data that must be considered in the design process. For example, for the financial aid problem, we identified operations to retrieve the financial aid source and the amount, to set the source and the amount to particular values, and to display the financial aid. We will see in the next section how these operations can easily be implemented as function members of a class using predefined C++ operations.

Other operations will require some additional work. For example, another operation in the programming assignment in Figure 1.3(a) is to update the array of student financial aid records. Since this is not a predefined operation in C++, we will have to implement this operation ourselves by designing a function to perform it.

In the preceding section we formulated a specification for this function that spelled out its purpose, preconditions that hold before the function is used, and postconditions that spell out the result that the function must produce. We next must develop a sequence of operations, called an **algorithm**, that will produce this result. For example, the following might be a first version of an algorithm for updating the array of student financial records:

For each student financial aid record, do the following:

1. For each of the *numAwards* financial aid awards in this record, do the following:
   a. Set *aid* = the next financial aid award.
   b. Set *newAmount* = the value stored in *aid*'s *amount* data member.
   c. Add (percentage rate) × *newAmount* to *newAmount*.
   d. Change the value of *aid*'s *amount* data member to *newAmount*.
2. Change the financial aid award in this record to *aid*.

As we will see in the next section, each of the operations in these steps of the algorithm can be implemented with C++ operations.

Algorithms + Data Structures   We see that data and the operations on that data are parts of an object that cannot be separated. Stated differently, the way in which the data is organized and the algorithms for operations on the data are inextricably linked; neither can be carried out independently of the other. Quite a few years ago, Niklaus Wirth, the originator of the Pascal language, realized this when he entitled one of his texts

Algorithms + Data Structures = Programs

The word *algorithm* is derived from the name of the Arab mathematician, Abu Ja'far Mohammed ibn Musa al Khowarizmi (c. A.D. 825), who wrote a book describing procedures for calculating with Hindu numerals. In modern parlance, the word has come to mean a "step-by-step procedure for solving a problem or accomplishing some end." In computer science, however, the term algorithm refers to a procedure that can be executed by a computer, and this requirement imposes additional limitations on the instructions that make up these procedures:

- They must be *definite and unambiguous* so that it is clear what each instruction is meant to accomplish.
- They must be *simple* enough that they can be carried out by a computer.
- They must cause the algorithm to *terminate* after a finite number of operations.

In view of the first two requirements, unambiguity and simplicity, algorithms are usually described in a form that resembles a computer program so that it is easy to implement each step of the algorithm as a computer instruction or as a sequence of instructions. Consequently, algorithms are commonly written in **pseudocode**, a pseudoprogramming language that is a mixture of natural language and symbols, terms, and other features commonly used in one or more high-level programming languages. Because it has no standard syntax, pseudocode varies from one programmer to another, but it typically includes the following features:

- The usual computer symbols +, -, *, and / for the basic arithmetic operations.
- Symbolic names (identifiers) to represent the quantities being processed by the algorithm.
- Some provision for indicating comments—for example, the C++ convention of enclosing them between a pair of special symbols such as /* and */.

- Key words that are common in high-level languages—for example, *read* or *enter* for input operations; *display*, *print*, or *write* for output operations; *if* and *else* for selection structures; *for* and *while* for repetition structures.

- Indentation to set off blocks of instructions.

The last property of an algorithm requires that it eventually halt. For example, if an algorithm includes a set of statements that are to be executed repeatedly while some condition is true, then these statements must eventually cause that condition to become false so that repetition is terminated. Also, when an algorithm terminates, we obviously expect that it will have produced the required results. Thus, in addition to demonstrating that a given algorithm will terminate, it is also necessary to verify its correctness (see Section 10.6).

As a practical matter, simply knowing that an algorithm will terminate may not be sufficient. For example, a scheduling algorithm that requires 2^n operations to schedule n events will eventually terminate for large values of n but will require too much time to be of practical value. Useful algorithms, therefore, must terminate in some reasonable amount of time.

Also, we may have to decide between two or more algorithms for the same problem that perform differently. As a simple illustration, consider writing a function that accepts an integer n and then computes and returns the value of the sum $1 + 2 + \cdots + n$. Here is one algorithm for this function:

Algorithm 1

1. Accept an integer for n.
2. Initialize *sum* to 0.
3. For each integer i in the range 1 to n:
   Assign *sum* + i to *sum*.
4. Return the value of *sum*.

Another algorithm is based on the following well-known formula from mathematics for the sum of the first n positive integers:[3]

$$1 + 2 + 3 + \cdots + n = \frac{n \times (n + 1)}{2}$$

---

[3] Carl Friedrich Gauss (1777–1855), one of the greatest mathematicians of all time, amazed his teacher by using this formula to solve a problem when he was seven years old. One day in school, the students were asked (perhaps as punishment) to sum the integers from 1 to 100. Gauss produced the correct answer (5050) almost immediately, perhaps by observing that writing the sum forward and then backwards,

$$sum = 1 + 2 + 3 + \cdots + 98 + 99 + 100$$
$$sum = 100 + 99 + 98 + \cdots + 3 + 2 + 1$$

and then adding corresponding terms in these two equations gives

$$2 \times sum = 101 + 101 + \cdots + 101 = 100 \times 101$$

Thus, $sum = \dfrac{100 \times 101}{2} = 5050$. A similar approach gives the general formula.

Algorithm 2

1. Accept an integer for n.

2. Return the value of $\dfrac{n \times (n+1)}{2}$.

This second algorithm is better than the first because it solves the same problem *in less time*. For example, to compute the sum of the integers from 1 through 1000, Algorithm 1 must repeat the loop in step 3 1000 times, which means that it must perform 1000 additions, 1000 assignments, 1000 increments of i, and 1000 comparisons of i with n, for a total of 4000 operations. For an arbitrary value of n, $4n$ operations are required. We say that the number of operations performed by Algorithm 1 *grows linearly* with the value of n and denote this in **big-O notation** by saying the growth rate of Algorithm 1 is **O(*n*)**. By contrast, Algorithm 2 does 1 addition, 1 multiplication, and 1 division, for a total of 3 operations, regardless of the value of n. Thus, the time taken by Algorithm 2 is *constant*, no matter what the value of n. We say that its computing time is **O(1)**.

This is a first look at an important area of computer science called *analysis of algorithms*. We will consider it, along with big-O notation, more carefully in Chapter 10.

The analysis and verification of algorithms and of the programs that implement them are much easier if they are well structured, which means that they are designed using three basic control structures:

1. *Sequence*: Steps are performed in a strictly sequential manner.
2. *Selection*: One of several alternative actions is selected and executed.
3. *Repetition*: One or more steps are performed repeatedly.

These three control mechanisms are individually quite simple, but together they are sufficiently powerful to construct any algorithm. Algorithms that use only these control structures are called **structured algorithms**.

Structured algorithms are much more readable and understandable and hence can be analyzed and verified much more easily than can unstructured ones. To illustrate, consider the following unstructured algorithm:

Algorithm (Unstructured Version)

/* Algorithm to read and count several triples of distinct numbers
  and print the largest number in each triple. */

1. Initialize *count* to 0.
2. Read a triple x, y, z.
3. If x is the end-of-data flag then go to step 14.
4. Increment *count* by 1.
5. If $x > y$ then go to step 9.

6. If $y > z$ then go to step 12.

7. Display z.

8. Go to step 2.

9. If $x < z$ then go to step 7.

10. Display x.

11. Go to step 2.

12. Display y.

13. Go to step 2.

14. Display *count*.

The "spaghetti logic" of this algorithm is vividly displayed in Figure 1.8(a).

In contrast, consider the following structured algorithm. The clarity and simple elegance of its logical flow are shown in the second diagram in Figure 1.8(b).

 ## Algorithm (Structured Version)

/* Algorithm to read and count several triples of distinct numbers and print the largest number in each triple. */

1. Initialize *count* to 0.

2. Read the first triple of numbers x, y, z.

3. While x is not the end-of-data-flag do the following:

   a. Increment *count* by 1.

   b. If $x > y$ and $x > z$ then
       Display x.
       Else if $y > x$ and $y > z$ then
       Display y.
       Else
       Display z.

   c. Read the next triple x, y, z.

   End while

4. Display *count*.

1.3 Coding

Coding is the process of implementing the design in some programming language such as C++. If the design phase has been carried out carefully, some parts of this translation process are often nearly automatic.

The first decision that must be made is what programming language to use. This obviously depends on the languages available to the programmer and those that he or she is able to use. Also, the problem may have characteristics that make one language

Figure 1.8 (a) Unstructured Algorithm (b) Structured Algorithm

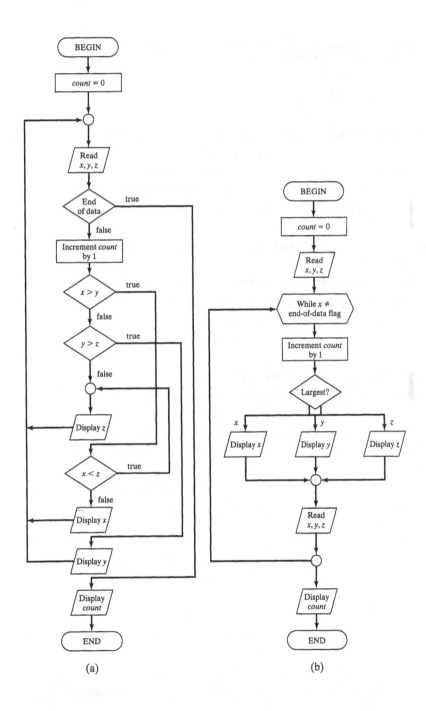

(a)

(b)

more suitable than another. In this text we will use C++. Figure 1.9 shows a C++ function that implements the algorithm for the financial aid programming assignment in Figure 1.3(a).[4] A program to test this function is given in Figure 1.10.

Figure 1.9 Financial Aid Update Function

```
#include <cassert>

void updateFinancialAid(int numRecords, StudentAidRecord studentRecord[],
                        double percent)
/*--------------------------------------------------------------------
  Increase the amount of all financial aid awards in an array of
  student financial aid records by a specified percentage.

  Precondition:    numRecords > 0 and percent > 0 is expressed
        as a decimal.
  Postcondition:   Each record in finAidArray has been modified by
        increasing the amount of each financial aid award in each
        record by the specified percentage.
  ----------------------------------------------------------------*/
{
  assert (numRecords > 0 && percent > 0);
  for (int record = 0; record < numRecords; record++)
  {
    int awardCount = studentRecord[record].getNumAwards();
    for (int count = 0; count < awardCount; count++)
    {
    FinancialAidAward aid = studentRecord[record].getFinancialAid(count);
    double newAmount = aid.getAmount();
    newAmount += percent * newAmount;
    aid.setAmount(newAmount);
    studentRecord[record].setFinancialAid(count, aid);
    }
  }
}
```

▲

---

[4] See the summary of basic C++ features in Appendix C if some parts of the C++ code in this section are unfamiliar or unclear to you.

Figure 1.10 Test-Driver for Financial Aid Update Function

```cpp
//-- Test driver for updateFinancialAid() function

#include <iostream>
#include <string>
using namespace std;
#include "FinancialAidAward.h"  // Financial aid awards
#include "StudentAidRecord.h"   // Student financial-aid records

//-- Prototype of updateFinancialAid(); definition follows main()

void updateFinancialAid(int numRecords, StudentAidRecord studentRecord[],
                        double percent);

int main()
{
  const int NUMBER_OF_RECORDS = 3;
  StudentAidRecord arr[NUMBER_OF_RECORDS];
  double percent = .10;
  int id, awards;
  string name, source;
  double amount;
  for (int i = 0; i < NUMBER_OF_RECORDS; i++)
  {
    cout << "\nEnter student's id, name: ";
    cin >> id;
    getline(cin, name);
    arr[i].setId(id);
    arr[i].setName(name);
    cout << "Enter number of awards for " << id << ": ";
    cin >> awards;
    arr[i].setNumAwards(awards);
    for (int a = 0; a < awards; a++)
    {
      cout << "Award " << a + 1 << "'s amount and source: ";
      cin >> amount;
      getline(cin, source);
      FinancialAidAward finaid(source, amount);
      arr[i].setFinancialAid(a, finaid);
    }
  }
  updateFinancialAid(NUMBER_OF_RECORDS, arr, percent);
```

Figure 1.10 (continued)

```
  cout << "\nUpdated Financial Aid Records:"
    "\n==============================" << endl;
  for (int i = 0; i < NUMBER_OF_RECORDS; ++i)
  {
    arr[i].display();
    cout << endl;
  }
}


//-- Insert contents of Figure 1.9 here.
```

Execution Trace:
```
Enter student's id, name: 12345 John Doe
Enter number of awards for 12345: 1
Award 1's amount and source: 5000 Merit Scholarship

Enter student's id, name: 22222 Mary Smith
Enter number of awards for 22222: 2
Award 1's amount and source: 1200 Grant in Aid
Award 2's amount and source: 3000 Presidential Scholarship

Enter student's id, name: 31416 Peter Pi
Enter number of awards for 31416: 3
Award 1's amount and source: 1000 Grant in Aid
Award 2's amount and source: 1200 Loan
Award 3's amount and source: 2500 Computer Science Prize

Updated Financial Aid Records:
==============================
12345   John Doe
 Merit Scholarship: $5500

22222   Mary Smith
 Grant in Aid: $1320
 Presidential Scholarship: $3300

31416   Peter Pi
 Grant in Aid: $1100
 Loan: $1320
 Computer Science Prize: $2750
```

▲

In this example, FinancialAidAward is the class defined by the **class library** in Figures 1.11 and 1.12. The **header file** FinancialAidAward.h stores the class declaration containing public declarations (prototypes) of function members and declarations of the private data members. The **implementation file** Financial-AidAward.cpp stores the definitions of the function members. Similarly, Student-AidRecord is a class declared in StudentAidRecord.h with definitions of function members in StudentAidRecord.cpp. These files can be found on the website for this text. We will study C++ classes in detail in Chapter 4, but the code is included here for those who have studied classes already and to provide a preview of them for those who haven't.[5]

Figure 1.11 Header File for the FinancialAidAward Class

```
/*- FinancialAidAward.h ---------------------------------------------------
   Header file of the class library for the class FinancialAidAward
   that models student financial aid records.
   ----------------------------------------------------------------------*/


#ifndef FINAIDAWARD
#define FINAIDAWARD

#include <string>

class FinancialAidAward
{
 public: // Function members

   //-- Constructors
   FinancialAidAward();
   /*------------------------------------------------------------------
     Default constructor
     Precondition:  None.
     Postcondition: FinancialAidAward object has been constructed in which
        idNumber is 0, name and source are empty strings, and amount is 0.
     ----------------------------------------------------------------*/
```

---

[5] This definition is intended to reflect the structure and form of a class definition you may have seen in a first programming course and is not as well designed and efficient as it could be. We will show how C++ class definitions can be improved, beginning in Chapter 4.

Figure 1.11 (continued)

```
FinancialAidAward(string src, double amt);
/*-----------------------------------------------------------------
   Explicit-value constructor
   Precondition: id > 0 and amt >= 0
   Postcondition: FinancialAidAward object has been constructed with
       idNumber = id, source = src, amount = amt.
 ----------------------------------------------------------------*/


//-- Accessors
double getAmount() const;
/*-----------------------------------------------------------------
   Postcondition: Value stored in amount is returned.
 ----------------------------------------------------------------*/


string getSource() const;
/*-----------------------------------------------------------------
   Postcondition: Value stored in source is returned.
 ----------------------------------------------------------------*/


//-- Output
void display() const;
/*-----------------------------------------------------------------
   Precondition:  None.
   Postcondition: FinancialAidAward object has been output to cout.
 ----------------------------------------------------------------*/


//-- Mutators
void setAmount(double newAmount);
/*-----------------------------------------------------------------
   Precondition:  newAmount >= 0
   Postcondition: amount has been changed to newAmount.
 ----------------------------------------------------------------*/


void setSource(string newSource);
/*-----------------------------------------------------------------
   Precondition:  None.
   Postcondition: source has been changed to newSource.
 ----------------------------------------------------------------*/
```

Figure 1.11 (continued)

```
private: // Data members
   string source;      // source of financial aid
   double amount;      // amount of financial aid

}; // end of class declaration

#endif
```

▲

Figure 1.12 Implementation File for the FinancialAidAward Class

```
/*- FinancialAidAward.cpp ---------------------------------------------
    Implementation file of the class library for the class
    FinancialAidAward that models student financial aid records.
    ----------------------------------------------------------------*/

#include <iostream>     // cout
#include <string>       // string
#include <cassert>      // assert
using namespace std;

#include "FinancialAidAward.h"

//-- Default constructor
FinancialAidAward::FinancialAidAward()
: source(""), amount(0)
{ }

//-- Explicit-value constructor
FinancialAidAward::FinancialAidAward(string src, double amt)
{
   assert(amt >= 0);   // check preconditions
   amount = amt;
   source = src;
}


//-- Accessors
double FinancialAidAward::getAmount() const
{ return amount; }

string FinancialAidAward::getSource() const
{ return source; }
```

Figure 1.12 (continued)

```
//-- Output
void FinancialAidAward::display() const
{
   cout << source << ": $" << amount;
}

//-- Mutators
void FinancialAidAward::setAmount(double newAmount)
{
  assert(amount >= 0);
  amount = newAmount;
}

void FinancialAidAward::setSource(string newSource)
{ source = newSource; }
```

▲

 Regardless of the language that is used, *source code should be correct, readable, and understandable.* Of these three properties, correctness is obviously the most important. No matter which of the other qualities a piece of code has—it is well structured, is well documented, looks nice, and so on—it is worthless if it does not produce reliable results. Code testing is therefore an important step in software development and is reviewed in more detail in the next section.

It is often difficult for beginning programmers to appreciate the importance of the other characteristics, that is, of developing good programming habits that lead to code that is readable and understandable. They have difficulty because, as we noted in Section 1.1, programs developed in an academic environment are often quite different from those developed in real-world situations, in which programming style and form are critical. Student programs, subprograms, and libraries are usually quite small (usually less than a few hundred lines of code); are executed and modified only a few times (almost never, once they have been handed in); are rarely examined in detail by anyone other than the student and the instructor; and are not developed within the context of budget constraints. Real-world software, on the other hand, may be very large (in some cases, millions of lines of code); may be developed by teams of programmers; is commonly used for long periods of time and thus requires maintenance if it is to be kept current and correct; and often is maintained by someone other than the original programmer. As hardware costs continue to decrease and programming costs increase, the importance of reducing these maintenance costs and the corresponding importance of writing code that can easily be read and understood by others continues to increase.

A number of programming practices contribute to the development of correct, readable, and understandable code. Because good programming habits are essential, we review some of these guidelines here. One principle is

> *Programs and subprograms should be well structured.*

The following guidelines are helpful in this regard:

■ *Use a modular approach for a complex problem.* Rather than writing one large program, develop individual modules—classes, subprograms, libraries—that handle part of the problem and that are relatively small and self-contained.

■ *Use the basic control structures—sequential, selection, and repetition—when writing code to implement operations.* Any program unit can be written using these structures. They should be combined to form nested blocks of code that are entered only at the top and normally have only one exit. The control structures provided in C++ are:

  • *Sequence*:   **Blocks**, also called **compound statements**, that consist of a sequence of statements enclosed in curly braces ({ and })
  • *Selection*:   `if` and `switch` statements
  • *Repetition*:   `for`, `while`, and `do-while` statements

■ *Use local variables within subprograms.* Variables used only within a subprogram should be declared within that subprogram. For example, the variable `newAmount` in the function `updateFinancialAid()` in Figure 1.9 was declared in the body of the function because it was used only to calculate the new amount of financial aid. It exists only while this function is being executed and is therefore accessible only within the function's body.

■ *Use parameters to pass information to and from subprograms.* Avoid using **global variables** for this purpose, which are declared outside all subprograms and are thus accessible from their declarations to the end of the file containing them. Although they provide an easy way to get information into and out of a subprogram, their use destroys the subprogram's independence. It can be difficult to determine the value of a global variable at some point in the program because it may have been changed by any of the program units.

▣ *Ensure that arguments that should remain unchanged are not modified unexpectedly by a subprogram.* Associating an argument with a reference parameter, for example, makes it possible for a subprogram to change the value of that argument. For example, in the function `updateFinancialAid()` in Figure 1.9, `numRecords` and `percent` are **value parameters**, which store copies of the actual arguments; modifying them within this function will not affect the corresponding arguments. In contrast, array parameters are automatically **reference parameters**; thus, modifying `finAidArray` in the function will change the corresponding array argument. Preceding the declaration of a reference parameter by the keyword `const` makes it a **constant reference parameter**, which prevents the function from modifying it. (See Appendix C for more information about parameters.)

■ *Use symbolic constants instead of literals for any constant values that may need to be changed in later versions of a program. This can also improve readability.* For example, the following statement illustrates what has been termed the "Houdini principle" because it allows numbers to arise suddenly without explanation, almost as if by magic:

```
popChange = (0.1758 - 0.1257) * population;
```

The literals 0.1758 and 0.1257 should be replaced by constant identifiers (or variables whose values are read or assigned during execution), as in

```
const double BIRTH_RATE = 0.1758,
             DEATH_RATE = 0.1257;
```
.
.
.
```
popChange = (BIRTH_RATE - DEATH_RATE) * population;
```

The second assignment statement is more readable than the first. Also, if these numbers must be changed, one need only change the definitions of BIRTH_RATE and DEATH_RATE rather than conduct an exhaustive search of the program to locate all their occurrences.

Similarly, declaring an array finAidRecords with

```
FinancialAidAward finAidRecords[100];
```

in a program to update 100 financial records is not good programming practice. If this program needs to be used with 250 records (or any number different from100) we must change the constant 100 in this declaration and in all other statements where it is used:

```
for (int i = 0; i < 100; ++i)
   // process finAidRecords[i]
```

Instead, we should name this constant

```
const int NUMBER_OF_RECORDS = 100;
```

and use this name throughout the program:

```
FinancialAidAward finAidRecords[NUMBER_OF_RECORDS];
for (int i = 0; i < NUMBER_OF_RECORDS; ++i)
   // process finAidRecords[i]
```

Changing the size of the array later requires only one change to the program:

```
const int NUMBER_OF_RECORDS = 250;
```

The C++ libraries climits and cfloat contain declarations of names for various constants associated with the basic integer and real data types, respectively, that are machine dependent. For example, the largest int value may be $2^{15} - 1 = 32767$ in some versions of C++ but $2^{31} - 1 = 2147483647$ in others; using the constant identifier INT_MAX from the climits library will select the correct value for the version being used. (See Appendix C for more information about these C++ libraries.)

■ *Strive for simplicity and clarity.* Clever programming tricks intended only to demonstrate the programmer's ingenuity or to produce code that executes only slightly more efficiently should be avoided. The savings in computing time will almost always be offset by the increase in programmers' time and effort studying the code to understand it well enough to use it and/or modify it.

■ *Identify any preconditions and postconditions a program or subprogram has and check them.* The assert() mechanism from the C++ library cassert, which evaluates a boolean expression and terminates execution if it is `false`, can be used for this. For example, we used the statement

```
assert(numRecords > 0 && percent > 0);
```

in the function `updateFinancialAid()` in Figure 1.9 to ensure that the values received by the parameters `numRecords` and `percent` were positive.

A second principle is

> *All source code should be documented.*

In particular,

- ◼ *Each program should include opening documentation.* This is in the form of comments that typically include the following:
  - A brief description of what the program does
  - Preconditions and other assumptions
  - Input to the program, output it produces, and postconditions
  - Notes about special algorithms it implements, classes it uses, and references to books and manuals that give additional information
  - Information about the programmer(s) such as their name(s), the date the program was written, when it was modified (and in programming courses, other information required by the instructors)

- ◼ *Each subprogram should be documented.* In particular, it should include (at least) a brief description of what it does, preconditions, and postconditions.

- ◼ *Comments should be used to explain key code segments and/or segments whose purpose or design is not obvious.* However, don't clutter the code with needless comments, as in

```
counter++;    // add 1 to counter
```

It is also common practice to precede key sections of source code with an opening comment that explains what this block of code is doing:

```
// Search for duplicate entries and if any are found,
// remove all duplicates after the first occurrence.
```

A practice followed by some programmers is to include the actual pseudocode descriptions of algorithms in the code that implements these algorithms.

- ◼ *Use meaningful identifiers.* For example,

```
wages = hoursWorked * hourlyRate;
```

is clearer than

```
w = h * r;
```

or

```
z7 = alpha * x;
```

Don't use "skimpy" abbreviations just to save a few keystrokes when entering the source code. Also, resist the temptation of what has been called the
"Shirley Temple principle" to use "cute" identifiers as in

```
bacon_brought_home = hoursWasted * pittance;
```

A third principle has to do with a program's appearance:

> *Source code should be aesthetic; it should be
> formatted in a style that enhances its readability*

In particular, the following are some of the guidelines for programming style
that are used in this text. They are by no means standard and are not intended to be
followed rigidly. The important thing is that a programmer's style be consistent and
enhance the code's readability.

■ *Put each statement of the program on a separate line.*

■ *Use uppercase and lowercase letters in a way that contributes to program readability.* In this text we will use the following naming conventions that are
used by most C++ programmers:

- *Names of variables and functions will be in lowercase, but with the first
  letter of each word after the first capitalized;* for example, `totalHours-
  Worked` and `updateFinancialAid()`.
- *Names of constants will be in uppercase with words separated by underscores;* for example, `TAX_RATE`.
- *Names of types will be in lowercase, but with the first letter of each word
  capitalized;* for example, `FinancialAidAward`.

■ *Indent and align the statements in a block and align the curly braces that
enclose the block:*

```
{
    statement₁
    statement₂
        .
        .
        .
    statementₙ
}
```

■ *Two-alternative* `if` *statements will be formatted as*

```
if (boolean_expression)          if (boolean_expression)
    statement₁                   {
else                                 statement_list₁
    statement₂                   }
                                 else
                                 {
                                     statement_list₂
                                 }
```

and multialternative if statements as

```
if (boolean_expression₁)
    statement₁
else if (boolean_expression₂)
    statement₂
        .
        .
        .
else if (boolean_expressionₙ)
    statementₙ
else
    statementₙ₊₁
```

■ switch *statements will be formatted as*

```
switch (expression)
{
    case_list₁:
            statement_list₁
            break;          //or return
    case_list₂:
            statement_list₂
            break;          //or return
            .
            .
            .
    case_listₙ:
            statement_listₙ
            break;          // or return
    default:
            statement_listₙ₊₁
}
```

Alternatively, each $statement\_list_j$ may be positioned on the same line as $case\_list_j$.

■ for, while, *and* do-while *statements will be formatted as*

```
for (...)                       for (...)
    statement                   {
                                    statement_list
                                }

while(loop_condition)           while(loop_condition)
    statement                   {
                                    statement_list
                                }

do                              do
    statement                   {
while (loop_condition);             statement_list
                                }
                                while (loop_condition);
```

■ *When a statement is continued from one line to another, indent the continued line(s).*

■ *Align the identifiers in constant and variable declarations, placing each on a separate line;* for example,

```
const double TAX_RATE = 0.1963,
             INTEREST_RATE = 0.185;

int employeeNumber;

double hours,
       rate,
       wages;
```

■ *Insert blank lines between declarations and statements and between blocks of statements to make clear the structure of the program.*

■ *Separate the operators and operands in an expression with spaces to make the expression easy to read.* For example,

```
cout << "Root is: "
     << (-b + sqrt(b * b - 4 * a * c)) / (2 * a) << endl;
```

is easier to read than

```
cout<<"Root is: "<<(-b+sqrt(b*b-4*a*c))(2*a)<<endl;
```

■ *Declare constants at the beginning of a function. Declare variables near their first use.* This makes it easy to find the constant declarations when they must be modified. It also reduces the tendency to declare unused variables, since declarations are deferred until they are needed.

■ *Label all output produced by a program.* For example,

```
cout << "Employee # " << employeeNumber
     << "  Wages = $" << employeeWages << endl;
```

produces more informative output than

```
cout << employeeNumber << "   " << employeeWages << endl;
```

1.4 Testing, Execution, and Debugging

Errors may occur in any of the phases of software development. For example, the specifications may not accurately reflect information given in the problem or the customer's needs or desires; the algorithms may contain logic errors; and the program units may not be coded or integrated correctly. The detection and correction of errors is an important part of software development and is sometimes referred to as verification and validation. **Verification** refers to checking that program documents, modules, and the like are correct and complete and that they are consistent with one another and with those of the preceding phases. **Validation** is concerned with checking that these products match the problem's specification. Verification is sometimes described as answering the question "Are we building the product right?" and validation as answering the question "Are we building the right product?"

Because errors may occur at each phase of the development process, different kinds of tests are required to detect them: **unit tests**, in which a subprogram or other code segment is tested individually; **integration tests**, which check whether the various program units have been combined correctly; and **system tests**, which check whether the overall system of programs, subprograms, and libraries performs correctly. These correspond to the various phases of software development we listed in the chapter introduction as indicated by the diagram of the "V" Life Cycle Model in Figure 1.13.[6]

Figure 1.13 "V" Life Cycle Model

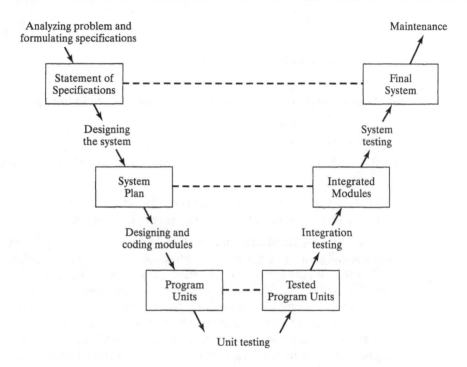

In this section we restrict our attention to some of the techniques used in unit testing, probably the most rigorous and time consuming of the various kinds of testing. It is surely the most fundamental kind of testing, since incorrectness of an individual program unit implies incorrectness of the larger system of which it is a part.

Only in the rarest cases is the first attempt at writing a program unit free of errors. There are a number of different points at which errors can be introduced. Three of the most common are

■ *Syntax errors*: Violations of the grammar rules of the high-level language in which the program is written

■ *Run-time errors*: Errors that occur during program execution

---

[6] Additional information about the "V" Life Cycle Model and about software testing can be found in Dorothy Graham, *Software Test and Debug: Techniques and Tools* (Manchester, England: A National Computing Centre Limited Technical Report, 1989).

- *Logic errors*: Errors in some aspect of the design—most often an algorithm—on which the program unit is based

The process of finding such errors is called **debugging** the program.

Syntax errors occur when the source code violates the syntax (i.e., the grammar rules) of the language. As the compiler translates code into machine language, it checks whether the source code it is translating conforms to the syntax rules of the language. If any of these rules is violated, the compiler generates an error message that explains the (apparent) problem. For example, if we forgot to type the semicolon at the end of a statement in the tenth line of some program and entered

```
double amount
cin >> amount;
```

instead of

```
double amount;
cin >> amount;
```

the compiler might display a diagnostic message like the following:

```
Error:  ';' expected
finAidProgram.cpp line 10
```

A different compiler might display a less precise diagnostic for the same error, such as

```
finAidProgram.cpp: In function 'int main()':
finAidProgram.cpp:11:  parse error before '>'
```

This compiler displayed the number of the line it was processing when it detected that something was wrong, which is the line following the line containing the error.

Run-time errors are so named because they are not detected until execution of a program has begun. They include such things as attempting to divide by zero in an arithmetic expression, attempting to compute the square root of a negative number, generating some value that is outside a given range, and attempting to dereference a null pointer. Error messages are usually displayed on the screen but are generally less helpful than those for syntax errors because they only display *what* happened but not *where*, that is, what part of the program was being executed when this happened.

Logic errors are the most difficult to locate because the program executes but does not produce the correct results. These errors may be due to inaccurate coding of the design or in the design itself.

There are many kinds of tests that can be used to locate sources of run-time and logic errors. One classification of testing techniques is into black-box tests and white-box tests. In a **black-box test** or **functional test**, the outputs produced for various inputs are checked for correctness without considering the structure of the program unit itself. That is, the program unit is viewed as a black box that accepts inputs and produces outputs, but the inner workings of the box are not examined. In a **white-box** (or **glass-box** or **clear-box**) **test** or **structural test**, the performance of the program unit is tested by examining its internal structure. *Test data should be carefully selected so that all parts of the program unit are exercised and all possible paths that execution may follow are checked.*

To illustrate some of the testing techniques that can be used to detect logic errors, let us consider a function to perform a binary search for some item in an ordered list stored in an array. The specification for this function is

Specification For Binary Search

Purpose: Perform a binary search of an ordered list.

Precondition: The list elements are in ascending order and are stored in array *a*. The list has *n* elements, where *n* is a positive integer. *item* is the value to be found and has the same type as the array elements.

Postcondition: *found* is true and *mid* is the position of *item* if the search is successful; otherwise *found* is false

It has been estimated that 80 percent of all beginning programmers will not write a binary search algorithm correctly the first time. One common attempt is the following:

Binary Search Algorithm (Incorrect Version)

1. Set *first* = 0.
2. Set *last* = *n* – 1.
3. Set *found* = false.
4. While *first* ≤ *last* and not *found* do the following:
    a. Calculate *mid* = (*first* + *last*) / 2.
    b. If *item* < *a*[*mid*] then
        Set *last* to *mid*.
      Else if *item* > *a*[*mid*]
        Set *first* to *mid*.
      Else
        Set *found* to true.

A C++ function that implements this algorithm is

```
//---------------- INCORRECT FUNCTION ------------------------
void binarySearch(NumberArray a, int n, ElementType item,
                  bool & found, int & mid)
/* ------------------------------------------------------------
   Perform a binary search of an ordered list stored in an array.

   Precondition:  Elements of array a are in ascending order
       and the first n elements are to be searched for item.
   Postcondition: found is true and mid is the position of item
       if the search is successful; otherwise found is false.
   ------------------------------------------------------------*/
```

```
{
   int first = 0,        // first and last positions in
       last = n - 1;     // sublist currently being searched
   found = false;

   while (first <= last && !found)
   {
      mid = (first + last) / 2;
      if (item < a[mid])
         last = mid;
      else if (item > a[mid])
         first = mid;
      else
         found = true;
   }
}
```

This function might be tested using a black-box approach with n = 7 and the following array a of integers:

$$a[0] = 45$$
$$a[1] = 64$$
$$a[2] = 68$$
$$a[3] = 77$$
$$a[4] = 84$$
$$a[5] = 90$$
$$a[6] = 96$$

A search for item = 77 produces the values true for found and 3 for mid, which is the location of 77 in the array. Testing with item = 90 and item = 64 also yields correct results. These tests might lead one to conclude that this function is correct.

Experienced programmers know, however, that *special cases must always be considered when selecting test data, because it is often these cases that cause a program unit to malfunction*. For collections of data stored in some data structure, we must always check **boundary values**. For example, in processing lists like that in this problem, try searching at the ends of the list. For function binarySearch(), therefore, we should test it with values of 45 and 96 for item as well as with values less than 45 and values greater than 96. For item = 45, the function sets found to true and mid to 0, as it should. A search for item = 96 fails, however; the search procedure did not terminate and it was necessary for the programmer to terminate execution using "break" keys (e.g., Ctrl + c) on the keyboard.

White-box testing would also detect an error because in this approach, we *choose data to test the various paths that execution can follow*. For example, one set of data should test a path in which the first condition item < a[mid] in the if statement is true on each iteration so that the first alternative last = mid is always selected. Using values less than or equal to 45 will cause execution to follow this path. Similarly, values greater than or equal to 96 will cause execution to follow a path in which the second condition item > a[mid] in the if statement is true on each iteration so that the second alternative first = mid is always selected.

Once it has been determined that a program contains an error, locating the error is one of the most difficult parts of programming. Execution must be traced step by step until something happens that is different from what was expected. To help with this tracing, most implementations of C++ provide a debugger that allows a programmer to execute a program one line at a time, observing the effect(s) of each line's execution.

Another common approach is to trace the execution of a program segment by inserting temporary output statements to display values of key variables at various stages of program execution. For example, inserting the statements

```
cerr << "DEBUG:  At top of while loop in binarySearch()\n"
     << "first = " << first << ", last = " << last
     << ", mid = " << mid << endl;
```

after the statement that assigns a value to mid at the beginning of the while loop in the preceding function binarySearch() results in the following output in a search for 96:

```
DEBUG:  At top of while loop in binarySearch()
first = 0, last = 6, mid = 3
DEBUG:  At top of while loop in binarySearch()
first = 3, last = 6, mid = 4
DEBUG:  At top of while loop in binarySearch()
first = 4, last = 6, mid = 5
DEBUG:  At top of while loop in binarySearch()
first = 5, last = 6, mid = 5
DEBUG:  At top of while loop in binarySearch()
first = 5, last = 6, mid = 5
DEBUG:  At top of while loop in binarySearch()
first = 5, last = 6, mid = 5
           .
           .
           .
```

One must be careful, however, to put such temporary output statements in places that are helpful in locating the source of the error and not use so many of these statements that the volume of output hinders the search for the error.

One can also manually trace an algorithm or program segment by working through it step by step, recording the values of certain key variables in a **trace table**. This technique is known as **desk checking** the algorithm/program segment. For example, tracing the while loop in the binary search algorithm using the preceding array *a* with *item* = 96, recording the values of *first*, *last*, and *mid*, gives the following trace table:

Step	first	last	mid
Initially	0	6	—
4a	0	6	3
4b	3	6	3
4a	3	6	4
4b	3	6	4
4a	4	6	5
4b	4	6	5
4a	5	6	5
4b	5	6	5
4a	5	6	5
4b	5	6	5
4a	5	6	5
4b	5	6	5
.	.	.	.
.	.	.	.
.	.	.	.

Either manual or automatic tracing of this procedure reveals that when *item* = 96, the last array element, *first* eventually becomes 5, and *last* becomes 6, and *mid* is then always computed as 5, so that *first* and *last* never change. Because the algorithm does locate each of the other array elements, a beginning programmer might "patch" it by treating this special case separately and inserting the statement

```
if (item == a[n - 1])
{
    mid = n - 1;
    found = true:
}
```

before the while loop. The function now correctly locates each of the array elements, but it is still not correct, as searching for any item greater than a[6] will still result in an infinite loop.

 Attempting to fix a program unit with "quick and dirty" patches like this is almost always a bad idea because it fails to address the real source of the problem and makes the program unnecessarily complicated and "messy." The real source of difficulty in the preceding example is not that the last element of the array requires special consideration but that the updating of *first* and *last* within the while loop is not correct. If *item* < *a*[*mid*], then the part of the array preceding location *mid*, that is, *a*[*first*], . . . , *a*[*mid* – 1], should be searched, not *a*[*first*], . . . , *a*[*mid*]. Thus, in this case, *last* should be set equal to *mid* – 1, not *mid*. Similarly, if *item* > *a*[*mid*], then *first* should be set equal to *mid* + 1 rather than to *mid*. The corrected version of the `binarySearch()` function is thus as follows:

```
//--------------- CORRECT FUNCTION ------------------------
void binarySearch(NumberArray a, int n,  ElementType item,
                  bool & found, int & mid)
/* --------------------------------------------------------------
    Function to perform a binary search of an array.

    Precondition:  Elements of array a are in ascending order
        and the first n elements are to be searched for item.
    Postcondition: found is true and mid is the position of item
        if the search is successful; otherwise found is false.
   ------------------------------------------------------------*/
{
   int first = 0,       // first and last positions in sublist
       last = n - 1;    // currently being searched
   found = false;

   while (first <= last && !found)
   {
      mid = (first + last) / 2;
      if item < a[mid]
         last = mid - 1;
      else if item > a[mid]
         first = mid + 1;
      else
         found = true;
   }
}
```

Testing of a program unit should be done several times using a variety of inputs, ideally prepared by people other than the programmer, who may be making unwarranted assumptions in the choice of test data. If any combination of inputs produces incorrect output, then the program contains a logic error. Thorough testing of a program will increase one's confidence in its correctness, but it must be realized that it is almost never possible to test a program with every possible set of test data. No matter how much testing has been done, more can always be done. Thus, *testing is never finished; it is only stopped.* No matter how extensively a program unit is tested, there is no guarantee that all the errors have been found. Obscure "bugs" will often remain and will not be detected until some time later, perhaps after the software has been released for public use. As these bugs turn up, the cycle of testing and correction must be repeated and a "fix" or "patch" or a new release sent to the users. There are cases in which apparently correct programs have been in use for more than ten years before a particular combination of inputs produced an incorrect output caused by a logic error. The particular data set that caused the program to execute the erroneous statement(s) had never been input in all that time!

The effect of errors in a program written for a programming assignment like that described in Figure 1.3(a) is usually not serious. Perhaps the student loses a few points on that assignment, or she may be lucky and the grader doesn't even notice the error. For real-world problems, however, instead of a course grade, much more may be at stake: money, jobs, and even lives. Here are a few examples selected from a plethora of software horror stories (see the website for this text for URLs of others):

- In September, 1999, the Mars Climate Orbiter crashed into the planet instead of reaching a safe orbit. A report by a NASA investigation board stated that the main reason for the loss of the spacecraft was a failure to convert measurements of rocket thrusts from English units to metric units in a section of ground-based navigation-related mission software.

- In June, 1996, an unmanned Ariane 5 rocket, developed by the European Space Agency at a cost of 7 billion dollars, exploded 37 seconds after lift-off on its maiden flight. A report by a board of inquiry identified the cause of the failure as a complete loss of guidance and attitude information due to specification and design errors in the inertial reference system software. More specifically, a run-time error occurred when a 64-bit floating-point number was converted to a 16-bit integer.

- In March of 1991, DSC Communications shipped a software upgrade to its Bell customers for a product used in high-capacity telephone call routing and switching systems. During the summer, major telephone outages occurred in these systems in California, District of Columbia, Maryland, Virginia, West Virginia, and Pennsylvania. These were caused by an error introduced into the signaling software when three lines of code in the several million lines of code were changed and the company felt it was unnecessary to retest the program.

- On February 25, 1991, during the Gulf War, a Patriot missile defense system at Dharan, Saudi Arabia, failed to track and intercept an incoming Scud missile. This missile hit an American Army barracks, killing 28 soldiers and injuring 98 others. An error in the guidance software produced inaccurate calculation of the time since system start-up due to accumulated roundoff errors that result from inexact binary representations of real numbers. And this time calculation was a key factor in determining the exact location of the incoming missile. The sad epilogue is that corrected software arrived in Dharan on February 26, the next day.

These are but a few examples of program errors that are more than just a nuisance and can lead to very serious and even tragic results. In such cases, careful software design, coding, and extensive and thorough testing are mandatory. In safety-critical situations where errors cannot be tolerated, relying on the results of test runs may not be sufficient because *testing can show only the presence of errors, not their absence*. It may be necessary to give a deductive proof that the program is correct and that it will always produce the correct results (assuming no system malfunction). Correctness proofs are described in Chapter 10.

1.5 Maintenance

Once a program and possibly a collection of subprograms and libraries developed for solving a problem have been validated and verified, they begin their useful lives and will, in many cases, be used for several years. It is likely, however, that for a variety of reasons, they will require modification.

As we noted in the previous section, software systems, especially large ones developed for complex projects, will often have obscure bugs that were not detected during testing and that will surface after the software is released for public use. A study by the National Institute of Standards and Technology (NIST) published in May, 2002, estimated that software errors cost the U. S. economy $60 billion annually.[7] (It also found that more than a third of this cost could be eliminated by better testing.) Fixing such flaws in software is thus a major and costly part of system maintenance.

It may also be necessary to modify software to improve its performance, to add new features, and so on. Other modifications may be required because of changes in computer hardware and/or system software such as the operating system. External factors such as changes in government rules and regulations or changes in the organizational structure of the company may also force software modification. These changes are easier to make in systems that are developed in a modular manner with well-structured program units than in poorly designed ones, because the changes can often be made by modifying only a few of the units or by adding new ones.

Studies have shown that a higher percentage of computing budgets and programmer time are devoted to software maintenance than to software development and that this percentage continues to increase:

1970s	35–40%
1980s	40–60%
1990s	70–80%
2000s	80–90%

A major factor that has contributed to the huge amounts of money and time spent on maintenance is that many programs and systems were originally written with poor structure, poor documentation, and poor style. This problem is complicated by the fact that maintenance must often be done by someone not involved in the original design. Thus, it is mandatory that programmers do their utmost to design programs and systems of programs that are readable, well documented, and well structured so they are easy to understand and modify and are thus easier to maintain than is much of the software developed in the past.

✔ Quick Quiz 1.5

1. The term _____ refers to the study and use of certain standard techniques and methodologies in developing software.
2. List the five key phases of software development.
3. One of the earliest models of software development in which the phases are carried out sequentially, moving from one phase to the next, is known as the _____ model.

---

[7] This report is available at http://www.nist.gov/director/prog-ofc/report02-3.pdf.

4. A description of the behavior of a program for solving a problem is called a _____ of the problem.

5. Formulating a specification for most real-world problems is usually quite easy and straightforward. (True or false)

6. _____ describe the state of processing before a program unit is executed. _____ describe the state of processing after a program unit is executed.

7. In the _____ design approach, the original problem is partitioned into simpler subproblems, each of which can be considered individually.

8. _____ (Top-down design or OOD) focuses on the real-world objects in a problem.

9. _____ is a visual modeling language used in object-oriented design.

10. A class has _____ members and _____ members.

11. Algorithms are commonly written in _____.

12. What three control structures are used in developing structured algorithms?

13. _____ is the process of implementing a design plan in some programming language.

14. Using global variables to share information between subprograms is a good programming practice. (True or false)

15. Distinguish between verification and validation.

16. Name and describe three kinds of programming errors.

17. Distinguish between black-box and white-box testing.

18. Testing can show only the presence of errors in a program, not their absence. (True or false)

◆ Exercises 1.5

1. Name and describe the five phases of software development.

2. What are some of the ways in which problems in introductory programming courses differ from real-world problems?

3. Name and describe two design methodologies.

4. What are the three characteristics of object-oriented programming?

5. What are structured data types? Give an example from C++.

6. Define an algorithm, naming and describing the properties it must possess.

7. What is pseudocode?

8. Name and describe the three control structures used in developing structured algorithms.

9. What are some of the ways in which student programs differ from real-world software?

10. Name three kinds of programming errors and give examples of each. When during program development is each likely to be detected?

11. What are some situations in which maintenance may be required?

12. Find some other examples of "software horror stories" and write brief reports for each, describing the error and what harm or adversity resulted from it.

SUMMARY

▣ Chapter Notes

- Five basic phases of software development are:
  1. Problem Analysis and Specification
  2. Design
  3. Coding
  4. Testing, Execution, and Debugging
  5. Maintenance
- Top-down and object-oriented are two important design approaches.
- Choosing or building data structures and developing algorithms are two important aspects of design in the small.
- Some basic programming guidelines are:
  - Program units should be well structured.
  - Source code should be documented.
  - Source code should be aesthetic.
- Verification and validation are two important aspects of program testing.
- Common kinds of programming errors are syntax errors, run-time errors, and logic errors.
- Check special cases when testing a program, because it is here that errors often occur.
- There are many examples where software errors have had very serious and even tragic results.

☞ Programming Pointers

1. Always formulate a *specification* for the behavior of a program for solving a problem and develop a *design plan* for it before beginning to write code.

2. Use *top-down* (or *modular*) *design* to partition a problem into simpler subproblems, each of which can be considered individually. This modularization may continue for several levels until subproblems obtained are simple enough to solve.

3. Use *object-oriented design* (OOD) to modularize a problem by identifying a collection of objects, each of which consists of data and operations on the data, that model the real-world objects in the problem and that interact to solve the problem.

4. Some algorithms for solving a problem may be much more efficient than others.

5. Source code should be *correct*, *readable*, and *understandable*.

6. Make all programs and subprograms *well structured*. (See Section 1.3 for guidelines.)

7. *Document* all source code. (See Section 1.3 for guidelines.)

8. Make source code *aesthetic*. (See Section 1.3 for guidelines.)

9. Consider *special cases*—e.g., *boundary values*—when selecting test data, because they often cause a program to malfunction.

10. "Quick and dirty" patching of a program unit is almost never a good idea.

11. Testing can only show the presence of errors, not their absence. Testing is never finished; it is only stopped.

▲ ADT Tips

1. The most important attribute of each object is its *type*, which determines what values the object may have, what operations can be performed on it, and what these operations produce.

2. Simple data types are for data values that are single entities; structured data types are for collections of data values.

▣ Programming Problems

1. Write the following unstructured program segment in structured form (but different from those given in Problems 2 and 3):

```
int row = 0,
      col;
A: col = 0;
   if (col < n) goto B;
   goto A;
B: if (row < n) goto C;
   goto E;
C: if (mat[row][col] == item) goto D;
   col++;
   if (col < n) goto B;
   row++;
   goto A;
D: cout << "item found\n";
   goto F;
E: cout << "item not found\n";
F: ;
```

2. Although the following program segment is structured, it is not a correct solution to Problem 1:

```
/* Search the entries of the n X n matrix mat in
   rowwise order for an entry equal to item */

bool found;
for (int row = 0; row < n; row++)
   for (int col = 0; col < n; col++)
      if (mat[row][col] == item)
         found = true;
      else
         found = false;
if (found)
   cout << "item found\n";
else
   cout << "item not found\n";
```

   a. Write a program that incorporates this program segment and then perform black-box testing of it, beginning with the matrix $\text{mat} = \begin{bmatrix} 45 & 77 & 93 \\ 78 & 79 & 85 \\ 72 & 96 & 77 \end{bmatrix}$ and $\text{item} = 77$ as the first set of test data. Produce enough output to show that your testing has turned up an error.

b. Use program tracing to determine what is wrong with this program segment.

3. Why is the following correct program segment not a good solution to Problem 1? (Consider its efficiency.)

```
/* Search the entries of the n X n matrix mat in
   rowwise order for an entry equal to item */

bool found = false;
for (int row = 0; row < n; row++)
   for (int col = 0; col < n; col++)
      if (mat[row][col] == item)
         found = true;
if (found)
   cout << "item found\n";
else
   cout << "item not found\n";
```

4. The following function performs a linear search of a list 1 of length 11 for the item it, returning 0 or 1 depending on whether it is not found. Many principles of good programming are violated. Describe some of these and rewrite the function in an acceptable format.

```
int LS(int 1[], int 11, int it)
/* Search 1 for it */
{
int i=0,f=0;A:if (1[i]==it)
goto B; if (i==11) goto
C;/*ADD 1 TO i*/i++;goto A;
B:f=1;C:return f;
}
```

CHAPTER 2

Introduction to Abstract Data Types

CHAPTER CONTENTS

Chapter Objectives

- Distinguish between abstract data types (ADTs) and implementations of ADTs.
- Review C++'s simple data types, the ADTs they model, and how they are implemented.
- See examples (e.g., `int`, `double`, and `bool`) of how implementations of ADTs are sometimes not faithful representations of the ADTs and the implications of this for programming.
- Look at two simple mechanisms (`typedef` and enumerations) that programmers can use to define new data types.
- Take a first look at pointers and some of the simple operations on them.

The design phase of software development described in Chapter 1 included (among other things) deciding how to organize the data involved in a problem and how to design algorithms for the operations on the data. These two aspects—data and operations—make up what is called an *abstract data type* (*ADT*), which is one of the major themes of this text. ADTs, however, must be implemented by finding ways to store the data and to carry out the operations on the data.

The basic data types provided in programming languages consist of data values and operations on the data and thus can be thought of as ADTs. In this chapter we review the fundamental types of C++ as ADTs and also describe how they are implemented. We also show—albeit in a simple way—how new data types can be created and added to the language. This will culminate in Chapter 4, where we build new types by using classes.

2.1 A First Look at ADTs and Implementations

Solving a problem involves processing data, and an important part of the solution is the careful organization of the data. This requires that we identify

1. the *collection of data items* and
2. basic *operations* that must be performed on them.

Such a collection of data items together with the operations on the data is called an **abstract data type** (commonly abbreviated as **ADT**). The word *abstract* refers to the fact that the data and the basic operations defined on it are being studied independently of how they are implemented. We are thinking of *what* can be done with the data, not *how* it is done.

For example, one aspect of the financial aid problem considered in the preceding chapter was the collection of financial aid awards. We also identified several operations on this collection: retrieving the amount or the source of financial aid, displaying a financial aid award, and changing the amount or the source. This collection of financial aid awards together with these operations thus makes up an abstract data type that models financial aid. In the same way, the collection of student financial aid records is an ADT that models a student record maintained by the financial aid office. The collection of data consists of the student aid records and the operations are: retrieving the id, name, number of financial aid awards, or the awards; displaying a student aid record; changing the id, name, number of financial aid awards, or the awards.

An **implementation** of an ADT consists of **storage structures** to store the data items and **algorithms** for the basic operations. For the financial aid problem we developed a `FinancialAidAward` class. Its data members `amount` and `source` stored the financial aid information. The function members `getAmount()`, `getSource()`, `display()`, `setAmount()`, and `setSource()` implemented the basic operations on financial aid awards. We also described a `StudentAidRecord` class. Its data members `id`, `name`, `numAwards`, and `finAid` stored a student's id, name, number of financial aid awards, and an array of awards. The function members `getId()`, `getName()`, `getNumAwards()`, `getFinancialAid()`, `display()`, `setId()`, `setName()`, `setNumAwards()`, and `setFinancialAid()` implemented the basic operations on student financial aid records.

This idea of **data abstraction**, in which the definition of the data type is separated from its implementation, is an important concept in software design. It makes it possible to study and use the data type without being concerned about the details of its implementation. In fact, this is usually the approach used for predefined data types such as `int`, `double`, `char`, and `bool`. Most of the time, programmers use these data types without worrying about how they are implemented. Nevertheless, these types can be used more effectively and efficiently if the programmer has some understanding of the implementation used. For this reason, in this chapter we review some of the basic data types of C++ and examine their implementations.

2.2 C++'s Simple Data Types

As we indicated in the preceding section, problem solving invariably involves manipulating some kind of data. In its most basic form, data values (as well as instructions) are encoded in the memory of a computer as sequences of 0s and 1s. This is because the devices that make up a computer's memory are two-state devices and hence are ideally suited for storing information that is coded using only two symbols. If one of the states is interpreted as 0 and the other as 1, then a natural scheme for representing information is one that uses only the two binary digits, or **bits**, 0 and 1. The two-state devices used in computer memory are organized into groups called **bytes**, each of which consists of eight bits. These bytes are in turn organized into **words**. These memory units—bits, bytes, and words—are the basic storage structures for all simple data types and, indeed, for all data stored in a computer.

The fundamental data types such as int, float, double, char, and bool in C++ are called **simple data types** because a value of one of these types is atomic; that is, it consists of a single entity that cannot be subdivided. Nevertheless, they can be viewed as models of abstract data types because they describe a collection of values and provide implementations of the operations on those values. In turn, they are themselves implemented using memory locations as storage structures, and their basic operations are implemented by the hardware or software of the computer system. In this section we review these simple data types, note the ADTs they model, and how they are implemented.

Integer Data

Unsigned Integers The set of *nonnegative integers*, sometimes called *cardinal numbers* or *whole numbers*, is $\{0, 1, 2, 3, \dots\}$. We are all familiar with the basic arithmetic operations on these numbers such as + and × and relational operators such as < and >. The nonnegative integers with these operations, therefore, constitute an abstract data type.

This ADT is modeled in C++ by three data types: unsigned short, unsigned, and unsigned long (which are shorthands for unsigned short int, unsigned int, and unsigned long int, respectively). Values of these types are stored as bit strings in memory locations whose sizes must satisfy the following:

sizeof(short unsigned) ≤ sizeof(unsigned) ≤ sizeof(long unsigned)

Here, sizeof is the C++ operator that returns the size of a type (or an expression) in bytes. Typically, unsigned short values are stored in 2 bytes, unsigned values in 4 bytes, and unsigned long values in 4 or 8 bytes. For example, 58 can be represented as a 16-bit binary numeral[1]

$$58 = 0000000000111010_2$$

and stored in two bytes:

0	0	0	0	0	0	0	0	0	0	1	1	1	0	1	0

Signed Integers The set $\{\dots, -3, -2, -1, 0, 1, 2, 3, \dots\}$ of *integers* together with the familiar arithmetic operations also is an ADT. It is modeled in C++ by the data types short (or short int), int, and long (or long int). The memory requirements for these types are normally the same as those for short unsigned, unsigned, and long unsigned, respectively.

---

[1] See Appendix B for more information about binary representation.

The most common scheme for representing integers in binary is called **two's complement** notation. In this scheme, the leftmost bit is the sign bit (0 for nonnegative values, 1 for negative). The nonnegative integers are then represented in the same manner as was described for unsigned integers, with the sign bit set to 0.[2] But the representation of a negative integer $-n$ is obtained by first finding the base-two representation for n, complementing it (that is, changing each 0 to 1 and each 1 to 0), and then adding 1 to the result.[3] For example, the two's complement representation of -6 using a string of 16 bits is obtained as follows:

1. Represent 6 as a 16-bit base-two number   0000000000000110
2. Complement this bit string   1111111111111001
3. Add 1   1111111111111010

The integer -6 can thus be stored in two bytes as

1	1	1	1	1	1	1	1	1	1	1	1	1	0	1	0

Note that the leftmost bit, which is the sign bit, will always be 1 for a negative integer.

The algorithms to implement the usual arithmetic operations on integers are similar to the familiar algorithms for carrying out these operations using base-ten representation. The basic addition and multiplication tables are

+	0	1
0	0	1
1	1	10

×	0	1
0	0	0
1	0	1

Thus, the sum $5 + 7$ is calculated by adding, bit by bit, the base-two representations of these numbers, carrying when necessary:

```
              111← carry bits
    0000000000000101
  + 0000000000000111
    0000000000001100
```

The bottom bit string is the binary representation of the sum 12. Similarly, the sum $5 + (-6)$ is calculated as

```
    0000000000000101
  + 1111111111111010
    1111111111111111
```

which yields the two's complement representation of -1.

---

[2] Writing a positive integer such as 12345 as 12345U specifies that it is to be stored as an unsigned value; attaching the suffix L, 12345L, specifies that it is to be stored as a long value; and attaching both— 12345LU or 12345UL—specifies an unsigned long value.

[3] A simpler way to do this is to locate the rightmost 1 in step 1 and flip all the bits to its left.

Overflow As we will see repeated many times in the rest of this text, *the implementation of an abstract data type is usually not a completely faithful representation of the ADT.* Using C++'s int type to implement integers provides a good illustration. One difference between them is that the set $\{\ldots, -3, -2, -1, 0, 1, 2, 3, \ldots\}$ of integers is infinite, but int can represent only a finite range of these values. There are only 2^n different combinations of 0s and 1s in a string of n bits, so there are only 2^n different integers that can be represented using n bits. For example, the smallest integer that can be represented in two's complement notation using $n = 16$ bits is 1000000000000000, which represents $-2^{15} = -32768$; and the largest integer is 0111111111111111, which represents $2^{15} - 1 = 32767$. For $n = 32$ bits, only the range of integers from $-2^{31} = -2147483648$ through $2^{31} - 1 = 2147483647$ can be represented. Limitations such as these on the set of representable data values are inherent in all ADTs that have infinitely many data items, because only a finite amount of memory is available to store these items.

The integers that bound the range of int values in a given version of C++ are the values of the constants INT_MIN and INT_MAX defined in the library climits. Similar minimum and maximum values for the other integer types are also given in this library. Attempting to use a value outside this range is referred to as **overflow.** What effect it has on program execution is not specified in the C++ standard and is therefore implementation dependent. Typically, what results is unusual program behavior like that demonstrated in Figure 2.1, that will puzzle most beginning programmers (and anyone who is not familiar with two's complement notation). Before reading the discussion that follows the execution trace, see if you can figure out what caused the strange output. Why did the values suddenly stop increasing and become negative?

Figure 2.1 Overflow Demonstration—Version 1

```
//-- Program to demonstrate the effects of overflow

#include <iostream>
using namespace std;

int main()
{
   int number = 2;

   for (int i = 1; i <= 15; i++)
   {
      cout << number << endl;
      number *= 10;
   }
}
```

Figure 2.1 (continued)

Execution Trace (GNU C++ 3.1):
2
20
200
2000
20000
200000
2000000
20000000
200000000
2000000000
-1474836480
-1863462912
-1454759936
-1662697472
552894464

▲

Note that the output changed from positive to negative when the value of number was 2000000000, so the next value should be 20000000000. Also note that this is larger than 2147483647, the largest integer that can be represented in 32 bits. So we have overflow. The values produced after overflow may seem to be just random "garbage" values but, in fact, they are produced in a perfectly reasonable way. To see this, suppose we make some small changes in this program as shown in Figure 2.2.

Figure 2.2 Overflow Demonstration—Version 2

```
//-- Program to demonstrate the effects of overflow

#include <iostream>
#include <climits>
using namespace std;

int main()
{
   int number = INT_MAX - 3;

   for (int i = 1; i <= 7; i++)
   {
      cout << number << endl;
      number++;
   }
}
```

Figure 2.2 (continued)

Execution Trace:

2147483644

2147483645

2147483646

2147483647

-2147483648

-2147483647

-2147483646

▲

The two's complement representation of 2147483647, the value of number when the switch from positive to negative occurs, is

01111111111111111111111111111111

Now when number++ is executed, 1 is added to number:

11111111111111111111111111111111← carry bits

01111111111111111111111111111111

$$\underline{\qquad\qquad\qquad\qquad\qquad\qquad\qquad + \ 1}$$

10000000000000000000000000000000

The result is the two's complement representation of –2147483648. (The leftmost carry bit is lost.) On each subsequent pass through the loop, 1 is added to the previous value of number in the usual way.

We see, therefore, that for this version of C++ (and for most versions), overflow causes a **"wrap-around" behavior.** When a value in the range [INT_MIN, INT_MAX] reaches one end it simply begins again at the other end, as though the integers were arranged in a circle with INT_MIN next to INT_MAX. We could enlarge the range of representable integers that can be stored by using more bytes, but this does not resolve the problem of overflow.

If we examine our earlier example of overflow when 2000000000 was multiplied by 10 by adding 2000000000 ten times, we obtain the following binary representations of the values generated:

```
01110111001101011001010000000000    2000000000  (1*integer)
11101110011010110010100000000000    -294967296  (2*integer)
01100101101000001011110000000000    1705032704  (3*integer)
11011100110101100101000000000000    -589934592  (4*integer)
01010100000010111100100000000000    1410065408  (5*integer)
11001011010000010111100000000000    -884901888  (6*integer)
01000010011101110000110000000000    1115098112  (7*integer)
10111001101011001010000000000000   -1179869184  (8*integer)
00110000111000100011010000000000     820130816  (9*integer)
10101000000010111100100000000000   -1474836480  (10*integer)
```

Once again, the wrap-around effect along with two's complement representation provide an explanation of the values produced.

These examples show another reason why an implementation of an abstract data structure may not be a completely faithful representation of the ADT. *The operations in the implementation may not perform in exactly the same way as the corresponding operations of the ADT.*

Real Data

Real values, also called *floating-point* values, are modeled in C++ by the single-precision type `float`, the double-precision type `double`, and the extended-precision type `long double`. Type `double` is the default type used for processing real data. A suffix F can be attached to a real literal, as in `123.45F`, to specify that it is to be processed as a `float` value; attaching L specifies a `long double` value.

In a decimal numeral representing a real value, the digits to the right of the decimal point are also coefficients of powers of 10. In this case, however, the exponents are negative integers. For example, the numeral 0.317 can be written in expanded form as

$$3 \times 10^{-1} + 1 \times 10^{-2} + 7 \times 10^{-3}$$

The point in a base-two numeral representing a real value is called a **binary point**, and the positions to the right of the binary point represent negative powers of the base 2. For example, the expanded form of 110.101 is

$$(1 \times 2^2) + (1 \times 2^1) + (0 \times 2^0) + (1 \times 2^{-1}) + (0 \times 2^{-2}) + (1 \times 2^{-3})$$

and thus it has the decimal value

$$4 + 2 + 0 + \frac{1}{2} + \frac{0}{4} + \frac{1}{8} = 6.625$$

Before the binary representation of a real number is stored in memory, it is usually converted to **floating-point form**, which is like scientific notation except that the base is two rather than ten,

$$b_1.b_2b_3 \cdots \times 2^k$$

where each b_i is 0 or 1, and $b_1 = 1$ (unless the number is 0). $b_1.b_2b_3...$ is called the **mantissa** (or **fractional part** or **significand**) and k is the **exponent** (or **characteristic**). To illustrate, consider the real number 22.625, which can be represented in binary as

$$10110.101_2$$

Rewriting this in floating-point form

$$1.0110101_2 \times 2^4$$

is easy, since multiplying (dividing) a base-two number by 2 is the same as moving the binary point to the right (left). 1.0110101_2 is the mantissa and 4 is the exponent.

There is some variation in the schemes used to store such floating-point binary representations in computer memory, but typically they involve storing the sign of the number (0 for positive, 1 for negative) in one bit of a block of memory and dividing the rest of the block into two parts, one for the mantissa and the other for the exponent. For example, one representation uses 32 bits for single precision reals: the leftmost bit stores the sign, the next 8 bits store the exponent + 127, and the remaining 23 bits store the part of the mantissa that follows the binary point. For example, 6.625 would be stored as follows:

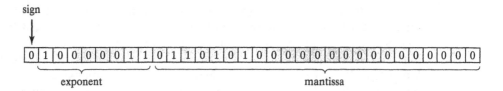

sign

exponent   mantissa

More information about this representation (known as the *IEEE Floating-Point Format*) can be found on the website for this text.

Because the binary representation of the exponent may require more than the available number of bits, we see that the **overflow** problem discussed in connection with integers also occurs in storing a real number whose exponent is too large. An 8-bit exponent restricts the range of real values to approximately -10^{38} to 10^{38}, and overflow occurs for values outside this range. A negative exponent that is too small to be stored causes an **underflow**. Real values represented using an 8-bit exponent must be greater than approximately 10^{-38} or less than -10^{-38}, and underflow occurs between these values:

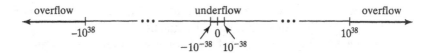

Also, there obviously are some real numbers whose mantissas have more than the allotted number of bits; consequently, some of these bits will be lost when such numbers are stored. In fact, most real numbers do not have finite binary representations and thus cannot be stored exactly in any computer. For example, the binary representation of the real number 0.7 is

$$(0.10110011001100110011001100110 \ldots)_2$$

where the block 0110 is repeated indefinitely. Because only a finite number of these bits can be stored, the stored representation of 0.7 will not be exact. For example, if only the first twenty-four bits are stored and all the remaining bits are truncated, the stored representation of 0.7 will be

$$0.101100110011001100110011$$

which has the decimal value 0.6999999284744263. If the binary representation is rounded to 24 bits, then the stored representation of 0.7 is

$$0.101100110011001100110010$$

which has the decimal value 0.7000000476837159. In either case, the stored value is not exactly 0.7. This error in the stored representation of a real value, called **roundoff error**, can be reduced, but not eliminated, by storing a larger number of bits. A 24-bit mantissa gives approximately 7 significant decimal digits for real values and a 48-bit mantissa gives approximately 14 significant digits.

The accumulation of roundoff errors in a chain of calculations may be so large that the result of the calculations is far from the correct value, which can lead to serious consequences. A real-world example of this is the Patriot missile failure described in Section 1.4. A Patriot missile battery in Dharan, Saudi Arabia, failed to intercept a Scud missile during the Gulf War in 1991 with the result that 28 American soldiers were killed and 98 were injured. The cause of the failure was identified as an inaccurate calculation of the elapsed time since start-up due to roundoff errors of the kind we just described. Specifically, the time measured by the system clock was multiplied by 0.1 to produce the time in tenths of seconds. Like most decimal fractions, the binary representation of 0.1 does not terminate:

$$(0.000110011001100110011001100110011 \ldots)_2$$

The 24-bit register in the Patriot stored only an approximation to this number,

$$(0.00011001100110011001100)_2$$

which is in error by approximately 0.000000095. The system had been running for 100 hours and during this time, the roundoff errors had accumulated to more than 0.34 seconds. During this time a Scud missile traveling approximately 5550 feet per second could travel about 1890 feet, which means that the calculated distance to the missile could be off by 1/3 mile.

 We must remember that roundoff errors do occur and be careful with the code we write so they do not cause a program to fail. For example, if we need to calculate and display some y coordinates given by function values at points on the x axis from 0 to 5 that are 0.1 units apart, we should *not* write a loop like the following:

```
for (double x = 0; x != 5.0; x += 0.1)
{
    y = f(x);
    cout << "x = " << x << "\t y = " << y << endl;
}
```

The roundoff error in the internal representation of 0.1 will accumulate in the computed values of x so that they will never be exactly equal to 5.0; the result is an infinite loop! Instead of this loop with x != 5.0 as the loop condition, we should write

```
for (double x = 0; x <= 5.0; x += 0.1)
{
    y = f(x);
    cout << "x = " << x << "\t y = " << y << endl;
}
```

 so that repetition will terminate as soon as the value of x exceeds 5.0. This example shows that *care must be taken when comparing two real values with the relational operators* == *and* !=.

Once again, an implementation—with C++'s real types (float, double, and long double)—is not a completely faithful representation of an ADT—the (mathematical) real numbers and operations on reals. As with integers, only a finite range of real numbers can be stored because of the limited number of bits allotted to the exponent. Unlike integers, however, not all real numbers within this range can be stored because of the limit on the number of bits in the mantissa. In fact, only a finite subset of these real numbers can be stored exactly, and this means that there are infinitely many real numbers that cannot be stored exactly.

Also, as we have seen, the operations for types `float`, `double`, and `long double` do not perform in exactly the same way as the corresponding operations on real numbers. In particular, many algebraic properties such as

Associative Property: $(a + b) + c = a + (b + c)$
Distributive Property: $a \cdot (b + c) = a \cdot b + a \cdot c$
Inverse Property: $a \cdot (1 / a) = 1$ for $a \neq 0$

although universally true for the operations in the real number system, will almost always fail for the C++ real types.

Character Data

A text document is written using a set of characters that is appropriate for that kind of document. This character set will obviously be different from one kind of text to another; for example, a report submitted to a scientific journal will probably use some symbols that are not used in a personal letter; and an English novel surely needs different characters than a Greek manuscript.

Two main character sets are used in programming languages. **ASCII** (American Standard Code for Information Interchange) is the most common, but some languages such as Java use **Unicode**.[4] Both of these are based on the assignment of a numeric code to each of the characters in the character set. In C++, characters are normally processed using the `char` type, which represents each character using a numeric code that can be stored in one byte. For example, the ASCII code of c is 99 = 01100011_2, which can be stored in a single byte:

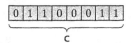

Unicode is a large international character set that includes most of the written languages of the world, mathematical symbols, and other symbols, and must therefore provide codes for many characters. Whereas a single byte can encode only 2^8 = 256 characters, Unicode can represent 2^{16} = 65,536 characters because it uses two-byte codes. For example, the code for c (99, the same as in ASCII) would be stored in two bytes:

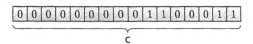

The code for the non-ASCII character π (Greek pi) is 960 = 0000001111000000_2 and can also be stored in two bytes:

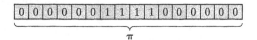

---

[4] Appendix A contains a table of ASCII codes. Information about Unicode is available at www.unicode.org.

C++ provides the *wide character type* wchar_t to store characters in larger character sets like Unicode.

One important operation involving character values is comparison to determine whether two characters are the same or whether one character is "less than" another in the sense that it precedes the other character in lexicographic order. This comparison is carried out in programming languages using the integer codes that represent the characters. Two characters are equal if their codes are equal, and one character is less than the other if the code of the first is less than the code of the second.

In C++, character values can be processed as integer values:

int(charValue) = the numeric code of charValue

In fact, values of type char can be combined with numeric values in arithmetic expressions; the numeric code of the char value will be used. For example, the value of 'c' + 1 (assuming ASCII representation) is $99 + 1 = 100$; using this expression to assign a value to a char variable ch as in ch = 'c' + 1; will assign ch the character 'd'.

Boolean Data

The set of *logical* values is much smaller than that of integers, real numbers, and character sets. It consists of only two values *false* and *true*. In computing, these are usually referred to as **boolean** values.[5] The key operations are *conjunction, disjunction*, and *negation*, which are better known as the *and, or,* and *not* operations, respectively. They are defined by the following **truth tables,** which display the values produced by these logical operations for all possible values of two logical values *p* and *q*:

p	not *p*
true	false
false	true

p	*q*	*p* and *q*	*p* or *q*
true	true	true	true
true	false	false	true
false	true	false	true
false	false	false	false

Boolean values and operations are modeled in C++ with the bool type. There are two bool literals: false and true. They are implemented with 0 representing false and 1 (or any nonzero value) representing true. Accordingly, when a numeric value is converted to type bool, 0 is converted to false and any nonzero value to true:

$$\text{bool}(numVal) = \begin{cases} \text{false if } numVal \text{ is } 0 \\ \text{true if } numVal \text{ is not } 0 \end{cases}$$

---

[5] George Boole (1815–1864) was a British mathematician who developed an algebra of logic in which expressions could be formed to process logical values.

Conversely, when a `bool` value in C++ is converted to an integer, `false` is converted to 0 and `true` to 1:

$$\text{int}(\textit{boolVal}) = \begin{cases} 0 \text{ if } \textit{boolVal} \text{ is false} \\ 1 \text{ if } \textit{boolVal} \text{ is true} \end{cases}$$

These conversions between numeric values and boolean values take place automatically in input and output of `bool` values. For example, in the following statements, the value `true` of okay will be displayed as 1:

```
bool okay = true;
cout << okay << endl;     // Outputs 1
```

If we insert the format manipulator `boolalpha` in the output statement,

```
cout << boolalpha << okay << endl;  // Outputs true
```

the value of okay and all subsequent `bool` values will be displayed in text format—i.e., as strings `"false"` and `"true"`—(unless a `noboolalpha` manipulator is encountered).

The same is also true for input: inputting 0 for a `bool` variable will result in `false` being assigned to that variable; inputting 1 will produce `true`. If the `boolalpha` manipulator is used in an input statement,

```
cin >> boolalpha >> okay; // Input text string for true, false
```

then the actual character strings `false` and `true` can be entered and the corresponding `bool` value will be assigned to okay.

This conversion of a numerical value to a boolean value is, in fact, done automatically whenever a number appears in a boolean expression. It will be interpreted as false if it is 0 and as true otherwise. For example, if `true` was entered for okay in the preceding input statement, the code segment

```
int x;
cin >> x;
if (x && okay)
    cout << "YES\n";
else
    cout << "NO\n";
```

will produce NO as output if we enter 0 for x, but it will produce YES if we enter any nonzero value. If we changed the boolean expression in the `if` statement to

```
if (x = 0)
```

the output would be NO regardless of what value was entered for x because x = 0 (which we probably intended to write as x == 0) is an assignment expression that produces the value 0, which is interpreted as false.

Three boolean operations are defined in C++: `&&` (and), `||` (or), and `!` (not).[6] They can be defined by truth tables that agree with those given earlier for the

---

[6] These must not be confused with the bitwise and (&) and or (|) operations. Other bitwise operations are complement (~), left-shift (<<), and right-shift (>>).

corresponding logical operations:

p	$\sim p$
true	false
false	true

p	q	p && q	$p \mid\mid q$
true	true	true	true
true	false	false	true
false	true	false	true
false	false	false	false

Here p and q are expressions of type bool.

✔ Quick Quiz 2.2

1. What is an abstract data type (ADT)?
2. What is an implementation of an ADT?
3. _____ refers to the separation of the definition of a data type from its implementation.
4. A(n) _____ is a binary digit; a(n) _____ is a group of eight binary digits.
5. An attempt to store an integer greater than the maximum allowed will result in _____.
6. The decimal value of 10111_2 is _____.
7. The decimal value of 101.11_2 is _____.
8. In the floating-point representation 1.011×2^5, 1.011 is called the _____.
9. In the floating-point representation of a real value, a negative exponent that is too small to be stored causes a(n) _____.
10. If a and b are integers that can be stored exactly, then all integers between a and b can also be stored exactly. (True or false)
11. If a and b are real values that can be stored exactly, then all real values between a and b can also be stored exactly. (True or false)

✈ Exercises 2.2

Find the 16-bit two's complement representation of the integers in Exercises 1–6.

1. 99   2. 5280   3. 255
4. –255   5. 1024   6. –1024

Show how each of the real numbers in Exercises 7–12 will be stored using IEEE floating-point representation if extra bits in the mantissa are (a) truncated or (b) rounded.

7. 0.625   8. 25.625   9. 14.78125
10. 0.015625   11. 0.1   12. 2.01

Indicate how the characters in the strings in Exercises 13–18 would be represented using ASCII (see Appendix A).

13. BE   14. be   15. ABLE

16. No Go!   17. 1234   18. 12.34

Find the integer (base-ten value) represented by the bit strings of length 16 in Exercises 19–24, assuming two's complement representation.

19. 0000000001000000   20. 0110111001101111

21. 1011111111111110   22. 1100000000000001

23. 1001100110011001   24. 1010101010101010

For Exercises 25–30, find the real value represented by the bit string, assuming IEEE floating-point representation.

25. 01000000010000000000000000000000   26. 01000000110000000000000000000000

27. 01000011111111100000000000000000   28. 00111111111000000000000000000000

29. 01010101010101010000000000000000   30. 11000000001011000000000000000000

31. Assuming ASCII representation (see Appendix A), find the pair of characters represented by the leftmost byte and the rightmost byte in the bit string in Exercise 19.

32. Repeat Exercise 31 but for the bit string in Exercise 20.

33. Find the pair of boolean values represented by the leftmost byte and the rightmost byte in the bit string in Exercise 19.

34. Repeat Exercise 33 but for the bit string in Exercise 20.

2.3 Programmer-Defined Data Types

As programmer languages developed, new features were incorporated into them that made it possible for a programmer to extend the language by adding new data types. In this section we describe some of the ways new types can be created and introduce others that will be described in detail in later chapters.

Typedefs

The **typedef** mechanism can be used to create a new type by giving a new name to an existing type. One form of it is

```
typedef OldType NewType;
```

which declares that *NewType* is a synonym for *OldType*. For example, following the declaration

```
typedef double real;
```

either of the type identifiers `double` or `real` may be used.

This will be useful in later chapters when we build *container types* that store collections of data values. We can use a generic name such as `ElementType` for the type of these values when developing the container. Later we can declare a specific type to be used with a **typedef** statement such as

```
typedef double ElementType;
```

If we want to use the container with a different type of data values such as int, we need only change this typedef statement:

```
typedef int ElementType;
```

The typedef mechanism is also very useful to associate a type name with an array. We will defer a demonstration of this to our study of arrays in the next chapter.

Enumerations

As we saw in the preceding section, the literals false and true in the bool type behave almost as though they were defined by constant declarations:

```
const int false = 0,
          true = 1;
```

The constants 0 and 1 (as well as any nonzero value) are converted to false and true, respectively, when they occur in boolean expressions and also when used as input values for bool variables. Conversely, the bool literals false and true become 0 and 1, respectively, when converted to integers and also when they are output (unless the boolalpha manipulator is used).

C++ provides a mechanism that can be used to create other types whose literals are identifiers, each of which is associated with a unique integer, and which behave essentially the same as these integers. For example, the statement

```
enum Color {RED, ORANGE, YELLOW, GREEN, BLUE, INDIGO, VIOLET};
```

creates a new type named Color whose values are the seven colors listed between the curly braces. Because the valid values are explicitly listed or *enumerated* in the declaration, this type is called an **enumeration** and the identifiers listed are called its **enumerators**. Thus, in this example, Color is the name of the enumeration, and its enumerators are the identifiers[7]

```
RED, ORANGE, YELLOW, GREEN, BLUE, INDIGO, VIOLET
```

When the compiler encounters a declaration of an enumerated type, it performs an object-to-integer mapping, associating the integer 0 with the first identifier in this list, the integer 1 with the second, and so on. Thus, for the preceding declaration, the compiler makes the following associations:

RED	ORANGE	YELLOW	GREEN	BLUE	INDIGO	VIOLET
$\updownarrow$	$\updownarrow$	$\updownarrow$	$\updownarrow$	$\updownarrow$	$\updownarrow$	$\updownarrow$
0	1	2	3	4	5	6

Similarly, the declaration

```
enum Gender {FEMALE, MALE};
```

declares a new type Gender whose values are the identifiers FEMALE and MALE; the compiler will associate the integer 0 with FEMALE and the integer 1 with MALE.

---

[7] Because the compiler essentially treats an enumeration as a series of constant integer declarations, we will use the same uppercase naming convention for enumerators that we use for named constants.

If we alter this slightly, we can create our own version of a boolean type:

```
enum boolean {FALSE, TRUE};
```

The declaration

```
enum HandTool {HAMMER, PLIERS, SAW, SCREWDRIVER};
```

constructs a new type HandTool whose values are HAMMER, PLIERS, SAW, and SCREW-DRIVER, and associates the integers 0, 1, 2, and 3 with these identifiers, respectively.

C++ also allows us to specify explicitly the values given to the enumerators. For example, the declaration

```
enum NumberBase {BINARY = 2,
                 OCTAL = 8,
                 DECIMAL = 10,
                 HEXADECIMAL = 16};
```

associates the identifiers BINARY, OCTAL, DECIMAL, and HEXADECIMAL with the values 2, 8, 10, and 16, respectively:

BINARY   OCTAL   DECIMAL   HEXADECIMAL

↕   ↕   ↕   ↕

2   8   10   16

Thus, if we wanted to have the values 1, 2, . . . , 7 associated with the seven colors given earlier (instead of 0 through 6), we could use the declaration

```
enum Color {RED = 1, ORANGE = 2, YELLOW = 3, GREEN = 4,
            BLUE = 5, INDIGO = 6, VIOLET = 7};
```

or, more compactly,

```
enum Color {RED = 1, ORANGE, YELLOW, GREEN,
            BLUE, INDIGO, VIOLET};
```

because the integer associated with an enumerator is, by default, one more than the integer associated with the preceding enumerator.

The association of specific integers with enumerators behaves in much the same manner as for type bool. In particular, if an enumerator is used in an arithmetic expression, it will be converted automatically to the integer associated with it. The same is true for output of enumerators. For example, suppose we have the original definition of enumeration type Color:

```
enum Color {RED, ORANGE, YELLOW, GREEN, BLUE, INDIGO, VIOLET};
```

Then, in the following statements, the value BLUE of shade will be displayed as 4:

```
Color shade = BLUE;
cout << shade << endl;      // Outputs 4
```

Classes

The most important way to add a new type to C++ is by building a class for that type. We saw an example of this in the preceding chapter, where we created a Financial-Aid type to model financial aid objects and a StudentAidRecord type to model student financial aid records. We will have much more to say about classes in Chapter 4.

✔ Quick Quiz 2.3

1. Write a typedef statement that makes logical a synonym for bool.

Questions 2–11 use the following definitions:
```
enum English {ZERO, ONE, TWO, THREE, FOUR};
enum German {EIN = 1, ZWEI, DREI, VIER};
enum PigLatin {EROZAY, EETHRAY = 3, IVEFAY = 5, IXSAY};
enum Nonsense {FEE, FI = 6, FO, FUM, FOO = 3, BAR};
```

2. What type is defined by the first definition?

3. In the first definition, ZERO is called a(n) _____.

4. What value is associated with THREE?

5. What value is associated with DREI?

6. What value is associated with IXSAY?

7. What value is associated with FEE?

8. What value is associated with FUM?

9. What value is associated with BAR?

10. EETHRAY < IVEFAY. (True or false)

11. FOO > BAR. (True or false)

12. Write an enumeration declaration for the names of the days of the week.

✑ Exercises 2.3

1. Write a typedef statement that makes byte a synonym for char.

2. Write typedef statements that make both Real and SinglePrecision synonyms for float.

3. Write an enumeration MonthAbbrev whose enumerators are abbreviations of the months of the year and consist of the first three letters of the months' names.

Exercises 4–9 assume the enumerated type MonthAbbrev of Exercise 3. For each, find the value of the given expression.

4. JAN < AUG	5. SEP <= SEP	6. SEP + 1
7. APR - 1	8. AUG + 2	9. AUG - 2

10. Write an enumeration `Digit` whose enumerators are the names of the integers 0, 1, ..., 9.

11. Write an enumeration `Currency` whose enumerators are the names of U. S. coins with values up to one dollar and in which the integer associated with an enumerator is the value of that coin; for example, one enumerator would be `DIME` associated with the integer 10.

2.4 Pointers

When the compiler encounters declarations such as

```
double doubleVar;
int intVar = 1234;
char charVar = 'A';
```

it creates the variables being declared (`intVar`, `doubleVar`, and `charVar`), which means that

1. memory is allocated for a value of the specified type,
2. the variable's name is associated with the address of that memory, and
3. that memory is initialized with values provided in the declaration (if any).

Thus, if the address of the next available memory location is 0x005208320 and if chars are allocated 1 byte, ints are allocated 4 bytes, and doubles are allocated 8 bytes, we might have memory allocated for the variables `intVar`, `doubleVar`, and `charVar` as shown by the **memory map** in Figure 2.3.[8]

Figure 2.3 Memory Map

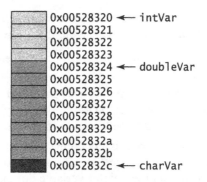

```
0x00528320  ←  intVar
0x00528321
0x00528322
0x00528323
0x00528324  ←  doubleVar
0x00528325
0x00528326
0x00528327
0x00528328
0x00528329
0x0052832a
0x0052832b
0x0052832c  ←  charVar
```

The address of a variable can be found by using the **address-of operator (&)**:

&*variable* is the address of *variable*

---

[8] Integer literals that begin with 0x are in *hexadecimal notation*. See Appendixes B and C.7 for information about hexadecimal representation.

Thus, for the preceding scenario, we have

&intVar is 0x005208320
&doubleVar is 0x005208324
&charVar is 0x00520832c

To make addresses more useful, C++ provides pointer variables. A **pointer variable** (or simply **pointer**) is a variable whose value is a memory address. In the next chapter, we will see how pointers are used in dynamic allocation of arrays—that is, allocating memory for an array during execution (as opposed to the static arrays considered in Section 3.2). In Chapter 6 and several later chapters, we will see how pointers are used in building linked structures whose storage can grow and shrink during execution. These are the most important uses of pointers in this text. In preparation for this, we look at some of the fundamental properties of pointers in this section.

Declaring and Initializing Pointers

Declarations of pointers have the following forms:

Declarations of Pointers

Forms:

```
Type * pointerVariable;
Type * pointerVariable = address;
```
where

Type is any type and *address* is an address of an object of the specified *Type*.[9]

Purpose:

Declares a variable named *pointerVariable* that can store the address of an object of the specified *Type*. Note the following:

- The asterisk operator * *must* precede each identifier that is to serve as a pointer.
- In the second form, the initializing address must be that of an object whose type is the same as the type to which the pointer points. The pointer is said to be **bound** to that type.
- 0 can be assigned to any pointer variable. In this context it is often called the **null address**, because 0 is not the address of any object, and serves to indicate that the pointer variable does not refer to an object. It can be thought of as a **zero pointer** literal.

---

[9] The spaces before and after the asterisk are not mandatory. Two common alternatives used by programmers are
- Attach the asterisk to the type identifier: `Type* pointerVariable;`
- Attach the asterisk to the variable: `Type *pointerVariable;`

The program in Figure 2.4 declares pointer variables iptr and jptr that can store addresses of memory locations for int values and pointer variables dptr and eptr that can store addresses of memory locations for double values. Pointers iptr and jptr are assigned the addresses of int variables i and j, respectively, and dptr and eptr the addresses of double variables d and e, respectively. These addresses are then displayed.[10]

Figure 2.4 Demonstration of Pointers and Addresses

```
//--- Demonstration of pointer variables and addresses

#include <iostream>
using namespace std;

int main()
{
  int i = 11,
      j = 22;
  double d = 3.3,
         e = 4.4;
                     // Declare pointer variables that:
  int * iPtr,        //    store addresses of ints
      * jPtr;
  double * dPtr,     //    store addresses of doubles
         * ePtr;
  iPtr = &i;         // value of iPtr is address of i
  jPtr = &j;         // value of jPtr is address of j
  dPtr = &d;         // value of dPtr is address of d
  ePtr = &e;         // value of ePtr is address of e
  cout << "&i = " << iPtr << endl
       << "&j = " << jPtr << endl
       << "&d = " << dPtr << endl
       << "&e = " << ePtr << endl;
}
```

Execution Trace:

```
&i = 0xbffffd20
&j = 0xbffffd24
&d = 0xbffffd28
&e = 0xbffffd30
```

▲

---

[10] For some versions of C++ it may be necessary to use (void*) *pointerVariable* in an output statement for addresses to display correctly.

From the output of this program we see that the address of variable i is the hexadecimal value 0xbffffd20, the address of j is 0xbffffd24, the address of d is 0xbffffd28, and the address of e is 0xbffffd30; and these addresses are stored in the pointer variables iptr, jptr, dptr, and eptr, respectively. We can visualize the layout of the program's data in memory as follows:

0xbffffd20	11	i
0xbffffd24	22	j
0xbffffd28	3.3	d
0xbffffd30	4.4	e
	0xbffffd20	iPtr
	0xbffffd24	jPtr
	0xbffffd28	dPtr
	0xbffffd30	ePtr

Note that (using hexadecimal arithmetic)

```
0xbffffd24 - 0xbffffd20 = 4
```

which indicates that the size of an int on this particular machine is 4 bytes (32 bits), and that

```
0xbffffd30 - 0xbffffd28 = 8
```

which indicates that the size of a double is 8 bytes (64 bits).

It is important to remember that *the asterisk operator * must precede each variable in a pointer declaration.* For example, the declarations of dPtr and ePtr

```
double * dPtr,
       * ePtr;
```

in Figure 2.4 correctly declare them to be pointers to doubles. However, if we wrote

```
double * dPtr,
         ePtr;
```

only dPtr would be a pointer variable; ePtr would be an ordinary double variable.

A typedef declaration can be used to make this repeated use of the asterisk in pointer declarations unnecessary by associating a type identifier with a pointer type. For example, we could first declare

```
typedef double * DoublePointer;
```

and then use DoublePointer to declare dPtr and ePtr:

```
DoublePointer dPtr,
              ePtr;
```

Such declarations also improve the readability of pointer declarations, especially when pointer parameters are being declared.

As we have noted, 0 can be assigned to any pointer variable to make it a *null pointer*. For example, the declaration

    int * iPtr = 0;

and the assignment statement

    dPtr = 0;

are both valid and use the null address to make iPtr and dPtr null pointers. These are sometimes pictured as a solid dot or with an engineering ground symbol or with the word "null" as pictured by the last three representations in the following diagram. But one of the most commonly used representations and the one we will use in this text is the first one shown where we simply draw a diagonal in the box used to represent the value of the pointer:

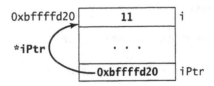

Basic Pointer Operations

C++ supports a variety of operations on pointers, including dereferencing, assignment, and comparison. We will briefly examine each of these in turn. In the next chapter we will consider some of the basic arithmetic operations on pointers.

Dereferencing and Indirection   A pointer variable stores only an address of a memory location. Accessing the contents of that memory location via the pointer requires using a special operator *, called the **dereferencing operator**, in an expression of the form

    *pointerVariable

This expression provides access to the memory location whose address is stored in *pointerVariable*; if this memory location already has a name, we can think of *pointerVariable* as an *alias* or *synonym* for this location to which *pointerVariable* points.

To illustrate, from the output in Figure 2.4, we see that the value of iPtr is 0xbffffd20, which is the address of a memory location where an integer is stored; it is, in fact, the address of the memory location containing 11 whose name is i. So *iPtr is an alias for this location, and the value of *iPtr is 11, because 11 is the value stored in this location. We can visualize this configuration as follows:

Thus, as shown in the program in Figure 2.5, the value of variable i can be accessed via the expression *iPtr, because *iPtr is an alias for i. Similarly *jPtr, *dPtr, and *ePtr are aliases for j, d, and e, respectively, and can thus be used to access their values.

In general, the value of a variable v can be *accessed indirectly* by applying the *
operator to a pointer variable vPtr whose value is the address of v. For this reason,
the * operator is called the **indirection operator.**

Figure 2.5 Dereferencing Pointers

```
//--- Demonstration of dereferencing pointers

#include <iostream>
using namespace std;

int main()
{
  int i = 11,
      j = 22;
  double d = 3.3,
         e = 4.4;
                            // Declare pointer variables that:
  int * iPtr,           //     store addresses of ints
      * jPtr;
  double * dPtr,        //     store addresses of doubles
           * ePtr;
  iPtr = &i;            // value of iPtr is address of i
  jPtr = &j;            // value of jPtr is address of j
  dPtr = &d;            // value of dPtr is address of d
  ePtr = &e;            // value of ePtr is address of e

  cout << "\nAt address " << iPtr
       << ", the value " << *iPtr << " is stored.\n"
       << "\nAt address " << jPtr
       << ", the value " << *jPtr << " is stored.\n"
       << "\nAt address " << dPtr
       << ", the value " << *dPtr << " is stored.\n"
       << "\nAt address " << ePtr
       << ", the value " << *ePtr << " is stored.\n";
}
```

Execution Trace:

```
At address 0xbffffd20, the value 11 is stored.

At address 0xbffffd24, the value 22 is stored.

At address 0xbffffd28, the value 3.3 is stored.

At address 0xbffffd30, the value 4.4 is stored.
```

▲

As this program demonstrates, *a dereferenced pointer is a variable* and can be used in the same way as all variables of the type to which the pointer is bound. For example, if the statement

```
i = *jPtr;
```

were added to the program in Figure 2.5, the value of i would be changed from 11 to 22, because *jptr is the memory location whose address is 0xeffff860, and the value 22 stored there would be assigned to i. The statement

```
*iPtr = j;
```

would produce the same result, because *iptr is an int variable and refers to the same memory location as i. This statement would copy the value of j into this location, which means that the value of i would be changed to 22.

The indirection operator can be applied more than once to produce additional levels of indirection. For example, the declarations

```
typedef int * IntPointer;    // or without using typedef:
IntPointer * ptr;            //     int * * ptr;
```

declare ptr to be a pointer to a memory location that contains a pointer to another memory location where an int can be stored.

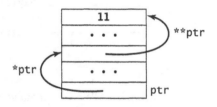

The value of **ptr would be 11.

Care should be taken before dereferencing a pointer to ensure that the pointer is not null and refers to a specific location in memory, because dereferencing a null or undefined pointer typically causes a fatal run-time error. In some versions of C++, however, it may access some "garbage" memory location and execution proceeds, possibly producing incorrect results. This is sometimes called the **dangling pointer problem**.

Assignment Pointer variables can be assigned the values of other pointer variables that are *bound to the same type*. For example, if we were to add the statement

```
jPtr = iPtr;
```

to the program in Figure 2.5, then the value of iPtr would be copied to jPtr so that they have the same memory address as their value; that is, both point to the same memory location, as the following diagrams illustrate:

Before the assignment

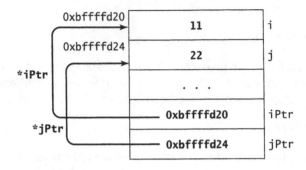

After the assignment jPtr = iPtr;

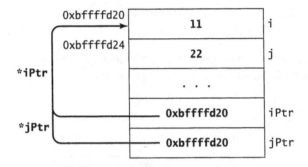

After the assignment statement is executed, jPtr no longer points to j, but now points to i. Thus, dereferencing jPtr will produce an alias for i. For example, an output statement

```
cout << *jPtr;
```

will display the value 11 instead of 22, and the statement

```
*jPtr = 44;
```

will change the value of the variable i from 11 to 44:

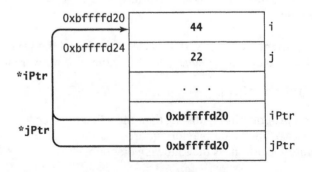

This example shows that pointer usage is a very powerful (and dangerous) feature of programming languages that requires special precautions. Statements such as

```
*jptr = 44;
```

which change the value of a variable (j) in a statement in which that variable is not named are generally considered to be poor programming practice, because they make programs more difficult to debug by hiding such changes. This is known as **the aliasing problem** in programming, because of variables such as *iptr and *jptr that are aliases for i.

Comparison Relational operators can be used to compare two pointers that are *bound to the same type.* The most common operation is to use == and != to determine if two pointer variables both point to the same memory location. For example, the boolean expression

```
iPtr == jPtr
```

is valid and returns true if and only if the address in iPtr is the same as the address in jPtr. However, if pointers nPtr and dPtr are declared by

```
int * nPtr;
double * dPtr;
```

the comparison

```
nPtr == dPtr    // ERROR!
```

is not valid, because nPtr and dPtr are bound to different types.

The *null address may be compared with any pointer variable.* For example, the conditions

```
nPtr == 0
```

and

```
dPtr == 0
```

are both valid boolean expressions.

Dynamic Memory Allocation—the new Operation

Memory can be requested from the operating system during program execution by using the new operation. A simple form of such a request is

```
new Type
```

where *Type* may be any type. This expression issues a run-time request for a block of memory that is large enough to store a value of the specified Type. If the request can be granted, new returns the starting address of the block of memory. If the request cannot be granted, a fatal error occurs and execution terminates (except as described in the next chapter).

Since the new operation returns an address and addresses can be stored in pointer variables, this operation is almost always used in conjunction with a pointer. For example, when the statements

```
int * intPtr;
intPtr = new int;
```

are executed, the expression new int issues a request to the operating system for a block of memory large enough to store an integer value (that is, for sizeof(int) bytes of memory). If the operating system is able to grant the request, intPtr will be assigned the address of this memory location.

For example, suppose that new returns the address 0x13eff860:

Because there is no name associated with this newly allocated memory, it is called an **anonymous variable**; it *cannot be accessed directly* in the same way other variables are accessed. However, its address is stored in intPtr, so this anonymous variable can be *accessed indirectly* by dereferencing intPtr, using the expression *intPtr:

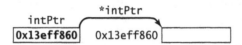

Statements such as the following can be used to operate on this anonymous variable:

```
cin >> *intPtr;      // store an input value in anon. variable

if (*intPtr < 100)  // apply relational op. to anon. variable
   (*intPtr)++;      // apply arithmetic op. to anon. variable
else
   *intPtr = 100;    // assign a value to anon. variable
```

In short, anything that can be done with an "ordinary" integer variable can be done with this anonymous integer variable by accessing it indirectly via intPtr.

A Note about Reference Parameters

Consider the following C++ function to exchange the values of two int variables:

```
void swap(int & first, int & second)
{
   int temp = first;
   first = second;
   second = temp;
}
```

The values of two int variables x and y can be exchanged with the call

```
swap(x, y);
```

The first C++ compilers were C preprocessors that read a C++ program, produced functionally equivalent C code, and ran it through the C compiler. However, C has no reference parameters, so how could such compilers deal with reference parameters? They used pointers and the dereferencing operator. For example, the preceding function swap() would be translated to

```
void swap(int * first, int * second)
{
  int temp = *first;
  *first = *second;
  *second = temp;
}
```

and the preceding function call to

```
swap(&x, &y);
```

From this example, we see how the call-by-reference parameter mechanism can be implemented. A reference parameter is translated into a pointer variable and the corresponding argument into the address of the argument. The pointer parameter is then automatically dereferenced wherever it is used in the function, producing aliases (i.e., references) for the arguments.

Pointers as Arguments and Parameters Pointers can also be passed as arguments to functions. The parameters corresponding to such arguments may be either value or reference parameters, but the pointer argument and the corresponding parameter must be bound to the same type. The return type of a function may also be a pointer.

One must realize, however, that even when a copy of a pointer argument's value is made and assigned to the corresponding parameter, both the argument and the parameter will still refer to the same memory location:

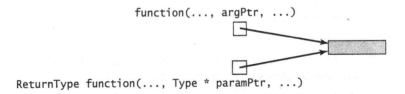

```
function(..., argPtr, ...)
```

```
ReturnType function(..., Type * paramPtr, ...)
```

This means that, in the preceding diagram, either argPtr or paramPtr can change the contents of the memory location to which they point. Thus, we have another example of the aliasing problem.

✔ Quick Quiz 2.4

1. A pointer variable stores a(n) _____.
2. _____ is the address-of operator.
3. _____ is the dereferencing operator.
4. _____ is the indirection operator.

Questions 5–14 assume the declarations

```
double * x,
        y = 1.1;
```

and that `double` values are stored in 8 bytes of memory. Answer each of Questions 5–10 with (a) address or (b) `double` value.

5. The value of x will be a(n) _____.

6. The value of y will be a(n) _____.

7. The value of &y will be a(n) _____.

8. The value of &x will be a(n) _____.

9. The value of *x will be a(n) _____.

10. The value of (*x) * y will be a(n) _____.

11. In the assignment x = 0;, 0 is called the _____ address.

12. The output produced by the statements x = &y; cout << *x; is _____.

13. The output produced by the statements x = &y; *x = 3.3; cout << y; is _____.

14. The _____ operator is used to request memory during program execution. If enough memory is available, it returns the _____ of a block of memory.

15. The newly allocated memory location in Question 14 is called a(n) _____ variable.

✦ Exercises 2.4

1. What three things must the compiler do when it encounters a variable declaration?

Exercises 2–8 assume the following declarations:

```
int i1 = 11,
    i2 = 22;
double d1 = 3.45,
       d2 = 6.78;
```

2. Write declarations for variables p1 and p2 whose values will be addresses of memory locations in which a `double` can be stored.

3. Write a statement to assign the addresses of d1 and d2 to the variables p1 and p2, respectively, in Exercise 2, or explain why this is not possible.

4. Write a statement to assign the address of i2 to the variable p2 in Exercise 2, or explain why this is not possible.

5. Write declarations that initialize variables ptr1 and ptr2 with the addresses of i1 and i2, respectively.

6. Write a statement that will make variables p1 and p2 of Exercise 2 point to the same memory location.

7. Write a statement that will copy the value stored in the memory location pointed to by ptr2 into the memory location pointed to by ptr1, for ptr1 and ptr2 as in Exercise 5.

8. Write statements that use the variables p1 and p2 of Exercise 3, but *not* the variables d1 and d2, to interchange the values of d1 and d2.

9. Using `typedef`, create an alias type `CharPointer` for pointers to type `char`.

For Exercises 10–15, use the `sizeof` operator to find how many bytes your version of C++ allocates for the given item.

10. an `int` value

11. a `float` value

12. a `double` value

13. a `short int` value

14. a value whose type is an enumeration defined by

```
enum WType {who, what, where, when, why};
```

15. Pointers to the items in Exercises 10–14.

16. Describe the output produced by the following statements:

```
int * foo, * goo;

foo = new int;
*foo = 1;
cout << (*foo) << endl;
goo = new int;
*goo = 3;
cout << (*foo) << (*goo) << endl;
*foo = *goo + 3;
cout << (*foo) << (*goo) << endl;
foo = goo;
*goo = 5;
cout << (*foo) << (*goo) << endl;
*foo = 7;
cout << (*foo) << (*goo) << endl;
goo = foo;
*foo = 9;
cout << (*foo) << (*goo) << endl;
```

SUMMARY

▨ Chapter Notes

- An *abstract data type* (*ADT*) is a collection of data items together with operations on the data. An *implementation* of an ADT consists of storage structures for the data items and algorithms for performing the operations.

- *Data abstraction* refers to the separation of the definition of a data type from its implementation; it is an important concept in software design.

- The implementation of an abstract data type is usually not a completely faithful representation of the ADT.

- Remember that roundoff errors caused by inexact representations of real values can accumulate and cause a program to fail.

☞ Programming Pointers

1. Generating an integer outside the range of representable integers is known as *overflow.* The typical result is "wrap-around" of the range of representable integers with the smallest negative integer following the largest positive integer.

2. For a floating-point value, generating an exponent that is too large to be stored causes an *overflow* ; generating a negative exponent that is too small to be stored causes an *underflow* .

3. *Roundoff* error, the error in the stored representation of a real value, may lead to annoying (or even serious) incorrect results when it accumulates in a sequence of calculations.

4. The asterisk operator * must precede each variable in a pointer declaration. Using the `typedef` mechanism and descriptive identifiers to declare pointer types reduces the chance of violating this. It also increases the readability of programs.

5. Each pointer variable is bound to a fixed type; a pointer is the address of a memory location in which only a value of that type can be stored.

6. Care must be used when operating on pointers because they have memory addresses as values. In particular:

   ■ A pointer `ptr` can be assigned a value in the following ways:

`ptr = &var;`	(where `var` is of the type to which `ptr` points)
`ptr = 0;`	(the null address)
`ptr = anotherPtr;`	(where `anotherPtr` is bound to the same type as `ptr`)
`ptr = new T;`	(where T is the type to which `ptr` points)

   ■ Relational operators can be used to compare pointers, but the two pointers must be bound to the same type or one or both may be the null address.

   ■ Pointers may be used as parameters, but corresponding parameters and arguments must be bound to the same type. A function may also return a pointer as its return value, but the type to which that pointer is bound must be the same as the type to which the function is declared to point.

7. Do not confuse memory locations with the contents of memory locations. If `ptr` is a pointer, its value is the address of a memory location; `*ptr` accesses this memory location so its value is what is stored at that location. Both `ptr++` and `(*ptr)++` are valid (if `ptr` is bound to an integer type), but the first increments the address in `ptr`, while the second increments the contents of the memory location at that address.

8. Having the null address as a value is not the same as being undefined. A pointer becomes defined when it is assigned the address of a memory location or the null address. Assigning a pointer the null address is analogous to initializing a numeric variable to zero.

9. Any attempt to dereference a null or an undefined pointer will normally generate a run-time error. In some versions of C++, however, execution proceeds using some "garbage" memory location, which may obviously produce incorrect results. This is known as the *dangling pointer problem.*

10. Changing the value of a variable in a statement in which that variable is not named is generally considered poor programming practice, because it produces a difficult-to-find logical error. This is known as the *aliasing problem.*

▲ ADT Tips

1. *Data abstraction*, in which the definition of the data type is separated from its implementation, is an important concept in software design.

2. ADTs are implemented by providing storage for the data items and algorithms to carry out the operations on the data.

3. The implementation of an abstract data type is usually not a completely faithful representation of the ADT.

4. Pointers will prove useful in later chapters in building data structures that can grow and shrink as needed.

⌨ Programming Problems

Section 2.2

1. Write and test a function printBinary() that displays int values in binary using the number of bits used in your version of C++ to store ints. (*Note*: sizeof(*T*) gives the amount of memory allocated for values of type *T*.) For example, if ints are allocated 32 bits, the function should display 00000000000000000000000000010001 for the value 17.

 One way to produce this output is with the help of C++ bitwise operators as outlined in the following algorithm (if these are not familiar to you, you can find information about them in Appendix C and on the text's website):

   1. Initialize an unsigned int variable *mask*, with a value whose binary representation has a 1 followed by all 0s; e.g., 10000000000000000000000000000000 for 32-bit representation. (*Helpful Hint*: 0x80000000 is the hexadecimal representation of an integer constant with this bit pattern.)

   2. For a counter running from 1 through the number of bits, do the following:
      a. If the bitwise-and (&) of the given integer and *mask* is nonzero

         Display '1'

      Else

         Display '0'

      b. Shift the bits in *mask* one position to the right (using >>).

   Suggestion: Work through an example by hand to ensure that you understand how the algorithm works before trying to convert it to code.

2. Use your program in Problem 1 to find binary representations of the integers in Exercises 1–6. Does your version of C++ use two's complement representation for integers?

3. Write a program that reads lines of input consisting of a bitwise operator (see Problem 1)— &, |, ~, ^, <<, or >>—followed by integer operand(s) and then outputs the integer operands, the bitwise operator, and the result obtained by applying the operator to the operands. Display all numbers both in decimal form and in their 32-bit binary representation, using the printBinary() function from Problem 1. For example, the input

   & 13 27

might produce the output

```
Applying the bitwise AND operator & to the following
          13 = 0000000000000000000000000001101
          27 = 0000000000000000000000000011011
produces
           9 = 0000000000000000000000000001001
```

and the input

```
~ 1
```

produce the output

```
Applying the bitwise NOT operator ~ to the following
           1 = 00000000000000000000000000000001
produces
          -2 = 11111111111111111111111111111110
```

4. Write a program to determine whether integer overflow in your version of C++ results in the "wrap-around" behavior described in the text.

5. Write a program that evaluates each of the following pairs of real-valued expressions, and experiment with it to see if you can find values of the variables a, b, and c for which the expressions are not equal:

   a. $a \cdot (b + c) = a \cdot b + a \cdot c$

   b. $(a + b) + c$ and $a + (b + c)$

   c. $a \cdot (1 / a)$ and 1 for $a \neq 0$

Section 2.3

6. Build a library for the enumeration type MonthAbbrev of Exercise 3. It should contain the definition of the enumeration MonthAbbrev and some basic operations on this type including at least the following:

   a. An output function that displays each enumerator as a string (rather than an integer)

   b. An input function that allows the user to enter a string representing a month abbreviation and assigns the corresponding enumerator to a MonthAbbrev variable

   c. A successor function that returns the enumerator that follows a specified enumerator; for example, the successor of MON is TUE.

   Then write a driver program that tests all of your operations. *Note:* If you know about operator overloading, you might use operator<<() for (a), operator>>() for (b), and operator++() for (c).

7. Proceed as in Problem 6, but for the enumeration type Digit of Exercise 10.

8. Proceed as in Problem 6, but for the enumeration type Currency of Exercise 11.

9. Use the library of Problem 8 in a change-making program that receives an amount purchased and payment received, with both amounts in cents, and which "speaks" the change received by displaying it using the enumerators of type Currency.

Section 2.4

10. Write a program to determine the addresses of memory locations allocated to various variables as follows:

    a. Declare two short int variables, two int variables, and two long int variable and then output the address of each variable.

    b. Draw a memory map similar to that in Figure 2.3 that shows the starting address of each variable.

    c. Calculate the size of the memory location allocated to each type by subtracting the address of the first variable from the address of the second variable of the same type.

    d. Add statements to your program that use the sizeof operator—see Problem 1—to find the size of the memory location allocated to each type.

11. Repeat Problem 10, but with two short int variables, two int variables, two long int variables, two bool variables, and two char variables.

12. Repeat Problem 10, but with two float variables, two double variables, and two long double variables.

13. Write a simple calculator program that repeatedly allows the user to select +, −, *, or / from a menu of operations on real values and then enter the two operands, and which then computes the result of applying the selected operation to those operands. However, the *only named variables you may use are pointer variables*; all others must be anonymous variables.

CHAPTER 3

Data Structures and Abstract Data Types

CHAPTER CONTENTS

Chapter Objectives

- Look at abstract data types (ADTs) and implementations of ADTs in more detail.
- Introduce arrays as ADTs.
- See how arrays are implemented by C++ static arrays.
- (Optional) Describe two- and higher-dimensional arrays.
- Extend the discussion of pointers from the preceding chapter by studying dynamic arrays.
- (Optional) Show how C++ structs can be used to model objects with multiple attributes.
- Describe the procedural programming paradigm by means of an example.

As we have noted, the two major aspects of software design are organizing the data involved in a problem and designing algorithms for the operations on the data. The data to be processed must be organized in a way that reflects the relationships among the data items and so that the data can be processed efficiently. As we also have noted, deciding how to store these data items and designing algorithms to perform the operations on the data cannot be separated; they must be done in parallel.

Because these structures for organizing data and algorithms must be implemented in some programming language, they must be designed to take advantage of the features of that language. This means that where possible, they should be based on the predefined data types, operations, and other features provided in the language.

In this chapter we review the data structures provided in C++, briefly describe how they are implemented, and also explain how they can be used to implement abstract data types.

3.1 Data Structures, Abstract Data Types, and Implementations

To illustrate the process of organizing and structuring data in a problem, let us consider an example. Suppose that Trans-Fryslan Airlines operates a single 10-passenger airplane. TFA would like to modernize its operations and, as a first step, needs a program that will determine for each flight, which seats have been assigned and which are still available.

In this problem, it is clear that the basic object is a collection of 10 seats and, for each seat, some indication of whether it has been assigned. We must be able to perform the following operations: (1) Examine the collection of seats to determine which of them are available; (2) reserve a seat; and (3) cancel a seat assignment. To perform these operations, it is convenient to think of the seats as organized in a list.

After organizing the data as a list of 10 seats and identifying the basic operations to be performed, we can consider ways to implement this structure. A variety of implementations are possible. For example, we might represent the list of seats by 10 simple variables of type char:

```
char seat1, seat2, . . . , seat10;
// ' ' indicates seat is available
// 'X' indicates seat has been assigned
```

Although this is a simple representation of the list of seats, the algorithms to perform the required operations are somewhat awkward. For example, the algorithm to scan the list of seats and to produce a listing of those seats that are available might be as follows:

Algorithm to List Available Seats

1. If seat1 is equal to ' '
      Display 1.
2. If seat2 is equal to ' '
      Display 2.
3. If seat3 is equal to ' '
      Display 3.
      .
      .
      .
10. If seat10 is equal to ' '
      Display 10.

An algorithm for reserving a seat is even more awkward:

Algorithm to Reserve a Seat

1. Set done to false.
2. If seat1 is equal to ' ' do the following:
   a. Display "Do you wish to assign Seat #1?".
   b. Get response from user.
   c. If response is 'y' then do the following:
      i. Set seat1 to 'X'.
      ii. Set done to true.
3. If not done and seat2 is equal to ' ' do the following:
   a. Display "Do you wish to assign Seat #2?".
   b. Get response from user.
   c. If response is 'y' then do the following:
      i. Set seat2 to 'X'.
      ii. Set done to true.

`// ...`
`//` and so on for 8 more seats

An algorithm for canceling a seat assignment would be equally inelegant.

C++ functions could be written to implement these algorithms, but they would be clumsy to say the least. They would be inflexible and difficult to modify and would become even more awkward if TFA replaced its 10-seat airliner with a larger aircraft having more seats.

These difficulties certainly suggest that it may be appropriate to consider other ways to represent the data of this problem. One alternative is to represent the list of seats as an array (see the next section)—or as a vector (see Section 9.4)—whose elements are of type char:

```
const int MAX_SEATS = 10; // upper limit on the number of seats
char seat[MAX_SEATS];
```

Because the elements of an array can easily be accessed by using the subscript operator, the algorithms to implement the required operations are much simpler:

Algorithm to List Available Seats

1. For number ranging from 0 to MAX_SEATS – 1 do the following:
   If seat[number] is equal to ' '
      Display number.

Algorithm to Reserve a Seat

1. Read number of seat to be reserved.
2. If `seat[number]` is equal to `' '`
   Set `seat[number]` to equal to `'X'`.
   Else
   Display a message that the seat having this number has already been assigned.

The algorithm for canceling a seat assignment is similar to that for reserving a seat.

To upgrade the program that incorporates these algorithms for a larger airplane with 25 seats we need only change the definition of the constant MAX_SEATS:

```
const int MAX_SEATS = 25; // upper limit on the number of seats
```

Unlike the earlier implementation, no changes would be required in the algorithms and functions for the operations!

Although this is a very simple example, it does illustrate the concept of an **abstract data type (ADT)** that we introduced in the preceding chapter. Recall that an ADT consists of

1. *a collection of data items* and

2. *operations* on the data items

In this example, the collection of data items is a list of seats or some representation of them (for example, a seating chart of the plane). The basic operations are (1) scan the list to determine which seats are assigned, and (2) change a seat's status from available to assigned or from assigned to available.

An **implementation** of an ADT such as this consists of *storage structures*, commonly called **data structures**, to store the data items and *algorithms* for the basic operations. In the preceding example, two implementations are given. In the first, the storage structure consists of 10 simple variables, and in the second implementation, it is an array. In both cases, algorithms for the basic operations are given, but those in the second implementation are considerably easier and more appealing than those in the first.

The terms *abstract data type* and *data structure* are often used interchangeably. However, we will use *abstract data type* when data is studied at a logical or conceptual level, independent of any programming language or machine considerations. The term *data structure* refers to a construct in some programming language that can be used to store data.

As Figure 3.1 demonstrates, C++ provides a large collection of data types and structures. In this chapter we will focus on the data structures provided in C and therefore also in C++. The fundamental types, arrays, structs, and unions are provided in both C and C++; the others—classes, `complex`, and those listed below them in the right branch of the diagram—are available only in C++.

The C-style data structures are emphasized in this chapter for two reasons:

- Using them as storage structures can sometimes provide "lean-and-mean" implementations of many ADTs. For example, we will use arrays to implement stacks in Chapter 7 and queues in Chapter 8. We could use vector, and although this simplifies the implementations considerably, it can add considerable overhead (e.g., operations that are never used).

- It is common that computer science students and graduates are expected to know the basic features of C in their places of employment, so it is important for them to study these features in their coursework.

Figure 3.1 C++ Data Types

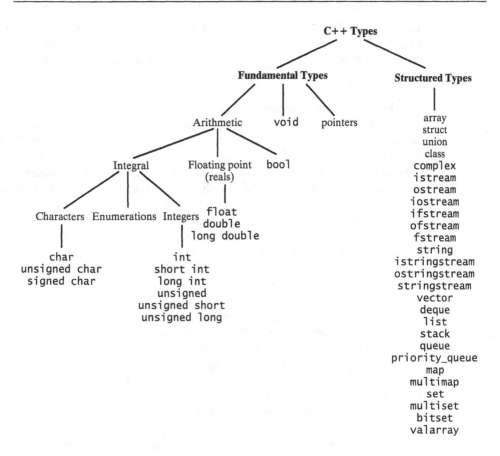

3.2 Static Arrays

In addition to simple data types to store individual data items, most high-level programming languages also provide data structures that can be used to build storage structures for *collections* of data items. As we will see many times in the chapters that follow, these data structures can then be used to implement abstract data types.

In this section we consider the most common of these data structures, the **array**. Although arrays are usually studied in the context of some programming language, they can be studied abstractly, that is, independently of how they are implemented in any particular language. As an abstract data type, an array may be defined as follows:

Array ADT
Collection of data elements: A fixed-size sequence of elements, all of the same type.
Basic operation: Direct access to each element in the array by specifying its position so that values can be retrieved from or stored in that position.

Thus, an array has a fixed number of elements and these are arranged in a sequence so there is a first element, a second element, and so on. Also, the data collection in an array is *homogeneous*; that is, all the array elements must be of the same type. For example, we might have an array of integers, an array of characters, or even an array of arrays.

Direct or **random access** means that each array element can be accessed simply by specifying its position in the array, so that the time required to access each element in the array is the same for all elements, regardless of their positions in the array. For example, in an array of 100 elements, the time required to access the seventy-fifth element is the same as that for the fifth. This is quite different from **sequential access**, in which one can access an element only by first accessing all those that precede it. Clearly, in this case, the time required to access the seventy-fifth element would be considerably greater than that needed for the fifth.

Instead of discussing arrays abstractly, we will focus in this text on arrays as *data structures*, because that is our main interest in them: to use them to build storage structures for the data elements of other ADTs. In most high-level languages, an array is declared by specifying a name for it, its size, and the type of its elements. A particular element of the array is then accessed by attaching to the array name one or more **indices** (also called **subscripts**) that specify the position of that element in the array. If only one index is used, the array is said to be **one-dimensional**; arrays involving more than one index are called **multidimensional** arrays.

For compatibility with the C programming language, C++ retains C-style arrays but has also provided an OOP approach to arrays by encapsulating them along with some very useful and powerful operations in classes valarray and vector.[1] We will defer discussion of these classes (see Chapter 9), however, and consider only C-style arrays for now.

There are two categories of arrays: **static arrays**, for which the compiler determines how memory will be allocated for the array, and **dynamic arrays** for which memory allocation takes place during execution. In this section we are focusing on static arrays; dynamic arrays are considered in Section 3.4. We will look first at one-dimensional arrays, which are used for storing sequences of data values; then we will

---

[1] Actually these are *class templates*, which are type-independent containers in which the actual type of the elements is passed in via a type parameter. Class templates are considered in detail in Chapter 9.

consider two-dimensional arrays, which are useful for storing tabular data; and finally, we will take a brief look at higher-dimensional arrays.

One-Dimensional Static Arrays

C++ declarations of one-dimensional static arrays have the following forms:

One-Dimensional Static Array Declaration

Forms:

```
ElementType arrayName[CAPACITY];
ElementType arrayName[CAPACITY] = {initializer_list};
```

where

ElementType is any type;

arrayName is the name of the array object being defined;

CAPACITY is a constant expression that specifies the number of elements in the array; it is optional in the second form; and

initializer_list is a list of comma-separated constants of type *Element-Type*.

Purpose:

Instructs the compiler that a block of consecutive memory locations[2] will be needed to hold *CAPACITY* objects of type *ElementType*, and associates the name *arrayName* with that storage. The array is **zero-based**; that is, the elements of the array are indexed $0, 1, 2, \ldots, CAPACITY - 1$.

In the second form, the array elements are initialized with the constants in *initializer_list*; if *CAPACITY* is omitted, the capacity of the array will be the number of constants in *initializer_list*. If the array's capacity is specified and there are fewer initial values than the capacity, the remaining elements are initialized with 0 (converted to *ElementType*). It is an error to list more initial values than the declared capacity.[3]

Note how the properties of a C++ array implement the definition of an array as an ADT:

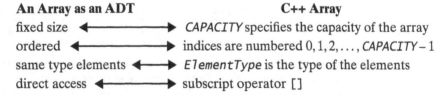

An Array as an ADT	C++ Array
fixed size	*CAPACITY* specifies the capacity of the array
ordered	indices are numbered $0, 1, 2, \ldots, CAPACITY - 1$
same type elements	*ElementType* is the type of the elements
direct access	subscript operator []

Notice also that the subscript operation is the only operation defined for C++ arrays.

---

[2] In Section 3.4 we will see how an array's capacity can be specified during execution rather than at compile time.

[3] How the compiler is to handle this error is not specified in the C++ standard. In some cases, the array will be filled with values from the list and any remaining values will be ignored.

To illustrate array declarations, consider arrays a, b, c, and d to store collections of 10 integers declared by

```
int a[10],
    b[10] = {0, 11, 22, 33, 44, 55, 66, 77, 88, 99},
    c[10] = {10, 20, 30},
    d[10] = {0};
```

or better, using a named constant to specify the array capacity,

```
const int CAPACITY = 10;

int a[CAPACITY],
    b[CAPACITY] = {0, 11, 22, 33, 44, 55, 66, 77, 88, 99},
    c[CAPACITY] = {10, 20, 30},
    d[CAPACITY] = {0};
```

The elements of the array a are named a[0], a[1], ..., a[9], and each of these is a variable of type int. The elements of the array b are named b[0], b[1], ..., b[9] and are initialized with the specified values: b[0] = 0, b[1] = 11, b[2] = 22, ..., b[9] = 99:

	b[0]	b[1]	b[2]	b[3]	b[4]	b[5]	b[6]	b[7]	b[8]	b[9]
b	0	11	22	33	44	55	66	77	88	99

Since the capacity specifier can be omitted when an initializer list is used, the definition of b could also be written

```
int b[] = {0, 11, 22, 33, 44, 55, 66, 77, 88, 99};
```

The first three elements of the array c are initialized with 10, 20, and 30, and the remaining elements with 0:

	c[0]	c[1]	c[2]	c[3]	c[4]	c[5]	c[6]	c[7]	c[8]	c[9]
c	10	20	30	0	0	0	0	0	0	0

 All the elements of d will be initialized to 0 since the initializer list sets the first element to 0 and all the remaining elements are automatically set to 0. Note that this is *an easy way to initialize an array to contain all zeros*:

	d[0]	d[1]	d[2]	d[3]	d[4]	d[5]	d[6]	d[7]	d[8]	d[9]
d	0	0	0	0	0	0	0	0	0	0

If several arrays of 10 integers are needed (especially as parameters of functions), it is better to associate a name with this array type using a variation of the **typedef mechanism** described in Section 2.3. The typedef statement for arrays has the form

```
typedef ElementType ArrayType[CAPACITY];
```

This statement declares that *ArrayType* is a synonym for an array with *CAPACITY* elements of type *ElementType*. For example, the statements

```
const int CAPACITY = 10;
typedef int IntegerArray[CAPACITY];
```

declare that `IntegerArray` is a synonym for an array with 10 elements of type `int`. We could then use `IntegerArray` to rewrite the earlier array declarations:

```
IntegerArray a,
             b = {0, 11, 22, 33, 44, 55, 66, 77, 88, 99},
             c = {10, 20, 30},
             d = {0};
```

Although arrays may be initialized in their definitions, *the assignment operator =* *is not defined for arrays*. Copying one array to another must be done elementwise. For example, the following statements can be used to copy the elements of b into the array a:

```
for (int i = 0; i < CAPACITY; i++)
    a[i] = b[i];
```

Character Arrays The elements of an array may be of any type and, in particular, they may be characters. Character arrays (also called *C strings*) can be initialized in the same manner as numeric arrays—for example,

```
const int NAME_CAPACITY = 10;
char name[NAME_CAPACITY] =
                {'J', 'o', 'h', 'n', ' ', 'D', 'o', 'e'};
```

but they may also be initialized with a string literal:

```
char name[NAME_CAPACITY] = "John Doe";
```

Both definitions construct name as an array whose capacity is 10 and whose first eight elements are the eight characters in `"John Doe"`.

When fewer values are supplied than the declared capacity of the array, as in these declarations, a zero used to fill uninitialized elements is interpreted as the **null character** `'\0'` whose ASCII code is 0, which is used here as an end-of-string mark:[4]

name	J	o	h	n		D	o	e	\0	\0
	[0]	[1]	[2]	[3]	[4]	[5]	[6]	[7]	[8]	[9]

String-processing functions can use this null character to find the end of the string. For example, the statement

```
cout << name;
```

outputs

```
John Doe
```

because it is equivalent to the following loop:

```
for (int i = 0; name[i] != '\0'; i++)
    cout << name[i];
```

---

[4] `\0` is the escape sequence for the null character. Since its octal numeric code is 000, it could also be written as `\000`. We will use the customary short version `\0` in this text.

The output operator and the string-processing functions in the `cstring` library (see Appendix C) cannot be expected to perform correctly on character arrays in which there is no terminating null character. To provide room for at least one null character, the capacity of a character array must always be at least one more than the size of the largest string to be stored in the array.

The Subscript Operation

An array declaration instructs the compiler that a block of consecutive memory locations must be reserved that is large enough to store the elements of the array. The address of the first element is called the **base address** of the array and the array variable is actually a **pointer** to this element; that is, its value is the base address of the array.

The addresses of other array elements are translated into offsets from this base address. This **address translation** is performed by the **subscript operator** []. For example, if b is the base address of a and `int`s are stored in four bytes, then the first integer a[0] will be stored in the four bytes beginning at address b, the second integer a[1] in the four bytes beginning at address $b + 4$, the next integer a[2] in the four bytes beginning at address $b + 8$, and in general, a[i] in four bytes beginning at address $b + 4i$. The diagram in Figure 3.2 illustrates this allocation of memory for the

Figure 3.2 Memory Allocation for an Array

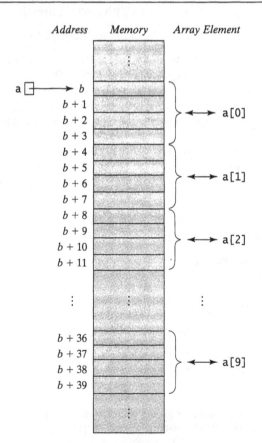

array a. In general, if each element of array a is of type ElementType, which requires *n* bytes for storage, the ith array element a[i] will be stored in the block of *n* bytes beginning at address $b + n \cdot i$.

Arrays as Parameters

Functions can be written that accept arrays via parameters and then operate on the arrays by operating on individual array elements. For example, we can output the elements of an int array with a function like that shown in Figure 3.3.

Figure 3.3 Array Output Function

```
void display(int theArray[], int numValues)
/*-------------------------------------------------------------------

   Display values in an array of integers.

   Precondition:  0 <= numValues < capacity of theArray.
   Postcondition: The first numValues integers stored in theArray have
      been output to cout.
  ----------------------------------------------------------------*/
{
  for (int i = 0; i < numValues; i++)
    cout << theArray[i] << "   ";
  cout << endl;
}
```

▲

As this example illustrates, placing a pair of brackets ([]) after the name of a parameter indicates that the parameter is an array, and that it is not necessary to specify the capacity of the array. In this case, *there is no restriction on the capacity of the array argument passed to the function.*

 This approach does not extend to multidimensional arrays, however, and it is therefore better to associate type identifiers with arrays (using typedef as described earlier) and then *use these type identifiers to declare the types of array parameters*; for example,

```
const int CAPACITY = 100;
typedef int IntArray[CAPACITY];
          .
          .
          .
void display(IntArray theArray, int numValues)
{
  for (int i = 0; i < numValues; i++)
    cout << theArray[i] << "   ";
  cout << endl;
}
```

It is also important to know that *an array is passed to a function by passing its base address; that is, arrays are always passed by reference, which means that modifying an array parameter will also modify the corresponding argument.* To illustrate this, consider the function `read()` in Figure 3.4 that is a counterpart to the preceding function `display()`.

Figure 3.4 Array Input Function

```
#include <cassert>

void read(IntArray theArray, int capacity, int numValues)
/*-------------------------------------------------------------------------
   Input values into an array of integers from the keyboard.

   Preconditions: 0 <= numValues <= capacity, which is the capacity of
         theArray.
   Postcondition: numValues integers entered from the keyboard have been
         stored in the first numValues positions of theArray.
   ---------------------------------------------------------------------*/
{
    assert (numValues >= 0 && numValues <= capacity);

    for (int i = 0; i < numValues; i++)
       cin >> theArray[i];
}
```

▲

Now consider the following statements in which `IntArray` and `CAPACITY` are as defined earlier:

```
    IntArray a;
    read(a, CAPACITY, 5);   // Read 5 integers into a
```

When the second statement is executed, the base address of a is passed to `theArray` so that in the function `read()`, `theArray` has the same base address as a. This means that any modification to `theArray` also modifies a.

Out-of-Range Errors

It is important to note that *most C++ compilers do not by default check whether indices are within the range determined by an array's declaration. Allowing an index to get out of bounds can produce some puzzling results.*

To illustrate this, consider the program in Figure 3.5.

Figure 3.5 Demonstrating the Effect of Out-of-Range Indices

```
/*------------------------------------------------------------------------
  Demonstration of what can happen when array indices get out of bounds.

   Input:   Three arrays of integers
   Output:  The three arrays before and after modification using
            out-of-range indices.
  ------------------------------------------------------------------------*/

#include <iostream>
using namespace std;

const int CAPACITY = 4;
typedef int IntArray[CAPACITY];

void read(IntArray theArray, int capacity, int numValues);
void display(IntArray theArray, int numValues);

int main()
{
   IntArray a, b, c;

   cout << "Enter " << CAPACITY << " integer values for:\n";
   cout << "Array a: ";
   read(a, CAPACITY, CAPACITY);
   cout << "Array b: ";
   read(b, CAPACITY, CAPACITY);
   cout << "Array c: ";
   read(c, CAPACITY, CAPACITY);

   cout << "\n------ Part I of the demonstration -----\n\n"
           "The arrays are:\n";
   cout << "a: ";
   display(a, CAPACITY);
   cout << "b: ";
   display(b, CAPACITY);
   cout << "c: ";
   display(c, CAPACITY);
```

Figure 3.5 (continued)

```
//--- Now change array elements in b, but using
//--- some out-of-range indices.
int below = -3,
    above = 6;
b[below] = -999;
b[above] = 999;

cout << "\n------ Part II of the demonstration -----\n\n"
        "The arrays after out-of-range errors are:\n";
cout << "a: ";
display(a, CAPACITY);
cout << "b: ";
display(b, CAPACITY);
cout << "c: ";
display(c, CAPACITY);
cout << endl;
}


//--- Insert here the definition of read() from Figure 3.4
//--- and the definition of display() from Figure 3.3
```

▲

The output produced by this program on one system is[5]

```
Enter 4 integer values for:
Array a: 0 1 2 3
Array b: 4 5 6 7
Array c: 8 9 10 11

------ Part I of the demonstration -----

The arrays are:
a: 0  1  2  3
b: 4  5  6  7
c: 8  9  10  11
```

---

[5] This output was produced using GNU C++. Some systems allocate memory from higher addresses to lower and the output in this case may be like the following (produced by CodeWarrior C++):

```
a = 0  1  2  3
b = 4  5  6  7
c = 8  9  10  11

a = 0  1  999  3
b = 4  5  6  7
c = 8  -999  10  11
```

```
------ Part II of the demonstration -----

The arrays after out-of-range errors are:
a = 0  -999  2  3
b = 4  5  6  7
c = 8  9  999  11
```

Even through there are no assignments of the form a[i] = *value* or c[i] = *value* to change values stored in a and c, the second element of a was changed to –999 and the third element of c was changed to 999. This happened because the address translation used to locate elements in array b simply counted forward or backward from the base address of b. The illegal array reference b[-3] was three memory locations before the base address of b, which, on this system, was the same as a[1], as pictured in Figure 3.6. Similarly, b[6] accessed the same memory location as that for c[2]. Thus, modifying b[-3] and b[6] changed a[1] and c[2], respectively.

Figure 3.6 Address Translation with Out-of-Range Addresses

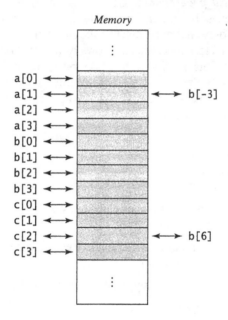

Problems with Arrays

There are other difficulties besides the out-of-range errors that can occur with array indices. One of these is that

■   The capacity of an array cannot change during program execution.

This means that an array's capacity must be set large enough to store the largest data set to be processed. This can result either in a considerable waste of memory—for example, storing 25 elements in an array of capacity 5000—or in array indices getting out of range with unfortunate results like those just described.

As we will see in Section 3.4, C++ does provide a mechanism for allocating arrays dynamically, which allows the user to enter an array's capacity during execution. It also provides the type `vector` (described in Section 9.4), which uses dynamically allocated arrays for storage.

Another deficiency is that

■ An array is not an object (in the OOP sense).

One of the principles of object-oriented programming is that *an object should be self-contained*, which means that it should carry within itself the information necessary to describe and operate on it. Arrays violate this principle. In particular, they carry inside themselves neither their capacity nor the number of values they currently are storing.

For this reason, array-processing functions usually require two and sometimes three parameters just to characterize the array being processed. This was demonstrated by the `display()` function in Figure 3.3 and the `read()` function in Figure 3.4. We must pass to `read()`, for example, not only the array to be input but also its capacity and the number of values it will store; and this is *not consistent with the aims of object-oriented programming*. If we wish to treat a sequence of values as a single object (which is the reason for storing the values in an array), then it should be necessary to pass only that one object to the function.

The C++ class mechanism allows different data members to be stored within a single object. This provides a solution to the second problem—by storing an array, its capacity and its size within a class structure, a single class object can encapsulate all three pieces of information. This is the approach used by the `vector` and `valarray` types described in Chapter 9.

✔ Quick Quiz 3.2

1. Define array as an ADT.

2. _____ access means that each array element can be accessed simply by specifying its location in the array.

3. An array is an appropriate data structure for organizing homogeneous data collections. (True or false)

4. List the elements (if any) that an array a will contain if it is declared by

        int a[5] = {1};

5. `'\0'` denotes the _____ character.

6. Elements of an array are accessed with the _____ operator.

7. The address of the first element is called the _____ of the array and the name of the array is actually a(n) _____ to this element.

8. Passing an array into a function is actually passing an address. (True or false)

9. Most compilers check whether array indices are out of range. (True or false)

10. What are two problems with arrays?

◆ Exercises 3.2

In the following exercises, assume that chars are stored in one byte, ints in 4 bytes, doubles in 8 bytes, values of type T in 10 bytes, and values of type Day in 4 bytes, where Day is the enumeration defined by

enum Day {SUN, MON, TUE, WED, THU, FRI, SAT, NUM_DAYS};

For Exercises 1–5, find how many bytes are required for an array a of the specified type.

1. char a[10]
2. double a[10]
3. T a[7]
4. int a[26]
5. Day a[NUM_DAYS]

For Exercises 6–10, assume that the base address of a is 1000.

6. For array a in Exercise 1, find where a[3] and a[9] are stored.
7. For array a in Exercise 2, find where a[3] and a[9] are stored.
8. For array a in Exercise 3, find where a[4] and a[6] are stored.
9. For array a in Exercise 4, find where a[1] and a[2] are stored.
10. For array a in Exercise 5, find where a[TUE] and a[SAT] are stored.
11–15. For the arrays in Exercises 1–5, indicate with diagrams like those in the text where each element of a is stored if the base address of a is b. Also, give the general address translation formula for a[i].

3.3 Multidimensional Arrays (optional)

Two-dimensional arrays are useful when processing data arranged in rows and columns. Similarly, a three-dimensional array is appropriate when the data can be arranged in rows, columns, and ranks. When several characteristics are associated with the data, still higher dimensions may be appropriate, with each dimension corresponding to one of these characteristics.

Two-Dimensional Arrays

To illustrate the use of two-dimensional arrays, suppose we wish to store and process a table of test scores for several different students on several different tests:

	Test 1	Test 2	Test 3	Test 4	Test 5
Student 1	99.0	93.5	89.0	91.0	97.5
Student 2	66.0	68.0	84.5	82.0	87.0
Student 3	88.5	78.5	70.0	65.0	66.5
⋮	⋮	⋮	⋮	⋮	⋮
Student 30	100.0	99.5	100.0	99.0	98.0

A **two-dimensional array** is an appropriate data structure to store these values. A simple form of a declaration for such an array in C++ is

```
ElementType arrayName[NUM_ROWS][NUM_COLUMNS];
```

For example, we could declare a two-dimensional array `scoresTable` to store this table of test scores by

```
const int NUM_STUDENTS = 30,
          NUM_TESTS = 5;
double scoresTable[NUM_STUDENTS][NUM_TESTS];
```

Alternatively, we could use a `typedef` to declare a general array type `TwoDimArray`,

```
const int NUM_ROWS = 30,
          NUM_COLUMNS = 5;
typedef double TwoDimArray[NUM_ROWS][NUM_COLUMNS];
```

and then use this type identifier to define a two-dimensional array variable such as `scoresTable`:

```
TwoDimArray scoresTable;
```

In either case, the notation

```
scoresTable[2][3]
```

refers to the score 65.0 in row 2 and column 3 of `scoresTable` (counting from 0 for both rows and columns). In general, the notation

```
scoresTable[r][c]
```

refers to the entry in row r and column c, that is, to the score for student r on test c.

This notation for a doubly-subscripted variable may seem unusual to people who have programmed in other languages where the preceding array reference would commonly be written `scoresTable[r, c]`. This does not cause a syntax error in C++ because the *comma is an operator that produces the second of its two operands*:

the value of `c, d` *is* `d`

This means that `scoresTable[r, c]` does not refer to the element in row r and column c but rather is the same as `scoresTable[c]`, which is the cth row of `scoresTable`.

The elements of a two-dimensional array are typically processed using nested loops to vary the two indices, most often in a rowwise manner. For example, the following statements might be used to input the scores for a class of students and store them in `scoresTable`:

```
int numStudents, numTests;

cout << "# students and # of tests? ";
cin >> numStudents >> numTests;

cout << "Enter " << numTests << " test scores for student\n";
```

```
for (int r = 0; r < numStudents; r++)
{
   cout << '#' << r + 1 << ':';
   for (int c = 0; c < numTests; c++)
      cin >> scoresTable[r][c];
}
```

Higher-Dimensional Arrays

The two-dimensional array scoresTable models one page of a gradebook. To model the entire gradebook, we can use a three-dimensional array:

```
const int NUM_RANKS = 10, NUM_ROWS = 30, NUM_COLUMNS = 5;
typedef double ThreeDimArray[NUM_RANKS][NUM_ROWS][NUM_COLUMNS];

ThreeDimArray gradeBook;
```

The array reference gradeBook[2][3][4] then refers to the score on page 2 of the gradebook (numbered from 0) for student 3 (numbered from 0) on test 4 (numbered from 0).

In some problems, arrays with even more dimensions may be useful. For example, consider an automobile dealership that characterizes the vehicles it sells with five attributes: year, model code, make, style, and color. We might maintain an inventory of these vehicles with a five-dimensional array inventory declared by[6]

```
const int MIN_YEAR = 1990,
          MAX_YEAR = 2004;
const int NUM_MODELS = 6;
enum Color {BLUE, GREEN, BROWN,
            RED, YELLOW, GRAY, NUM_COLORS};
enum Make  {FORD, LINCOLN, MERCURY, NUM_MAKES};
enum Style {SEDAN, CONVERTIBLE, VAN, MINI_VAN,
            SPORT_UTILITY, NUM_STYLES};

typedef int InventoryArray[MAX_YEAR - MIN_YEAR + 1,
                           NUM_MODELS, NUM_COLORS,
                           NUM_MAKES, NUM_STYLES];

InventoryArray inventory;
```

The statement

```
inventory[13][3][BLUE][FORD][MINI_VAN]--;
```

could then be used to record the sale of one 2003 model-3 blue Ford minivan. (Note that enumerators can be used as indices because of their association with integer values as described in Section 2.3.)

---

[6]   The extra identifier at the end of each enumeration listing provides a name for the number of "real" enumerators for that type. Thus, NUM_COLORS is the number (6) of Colors, NUM_MAKES is the number (3) of Make enumerators, and NUM_STYLES is the number (5) of Styles.

In general, n-dimensional arrays can be defined and subscript operators can be used to access the array elements. C++ places no limit on the number of dimensions of an array, but the number of values in each dimension must be specified. The general form of an array declaration is as follows:

General C++ Static Array Declaration

Forms:

```
ElementType arrayName[DIM₁][DIM₂]...[DIMₙ];
ElementType arrayName[DIM₁][DIM₂]...[DIMₙ]
                                = {initializer_list};
```

where

ElementType is any type;

arrayName is the name of the array object being defined;

each DIM_i must be a nonnegative constant expression; and

in the second form, the *initializer_list* is a list of values of type *ElementType*, possibly enclosed with internal braces { and }.

Purpose:

Defines an n-dimensional object whose elements are of type *ElementType*, in which $DIM_1, DIM_2, \ldots, DIM_n$ are the numbers of elements in each dimension. If the *initializer_list* is present, the values are placed in the array in a generalized rowwise order, that is, with the leftmost indices varying most slowly.

Array of Array Declarations

One way to view a multidimensional array is as an **array of arrays**—that is, an array whose elements are other arrays. For example, consider the table of test scores described earlier:

```
const int NUM_ROWS = 30,
          NUM_COLUMNS = 5;
double scoresTable[NUM_ROWS][NUM_COLUMNS];
```

Since NUM_ROWS is 30, this table can be thought of as a one-dimensional array, whose 30 elements are its rows:

scoresTable:

[0]
[1]
[2]
[3]

⋮

[29]

Of course, each of the rows in `scoresTable` is itself a one-dimensional array of five real values:

```
scoresTable:    [0]    [1]    [2]    [3]    [4]
        [0] ┌──────┬──────┬──────┬──────┬──────┐
            └──────┴──────┴──────┴──────┴──────┘
        [1] ┌──────┬──────┬──────┬──────┬──────┐
            └──────┴──────┴──────┴──────┴──────┘
        [2] ┌──────┬──────┬──────┬──────┬──────┐
            └──────┴──────┴──────┴──────┴──────┘
        [3] ┌──────┬──────┬──────┬──────┬──────┐
            └──────┴──────┴──────┴──────┴──────┘
                            ⋮
       [29] ┌──────┬──────┬──────┬──────┬──────┐
            └──────┴──────┴──────┴──────┴──────┘
```

A table can thus be viewed as a one-dimensional array whose components are also one-dimensional arrays.

C++ allows array declarations to be given in a form that reflects this perspective. If we first declare the type identifier `ScoreList` as a synonym for an array of test scores,

```
const int NUM_SCORES = 5;
typedef double ScoreList[NUM_SCORES];
```

then values of type `ScoreList` are one-dimensional arrays of `double` values. We can then use this new type to declare a second type `TwoDimScoreTable` as an array whose elements are `ScoreList` objects:

```
const int NUM_ROWS = 30;
typedef ScoreList TwoDimScoreTable[NUM_ROWS];
```

This declares the name `TwoDimScoreTable` as a new type, whose values are two-dimensional arrays of `double` values. The resulting type can then be used to declare a two-dimensional array `TwoDimScoreTable` variable as before:

```
TwoDimScoreTable scoresTable;
```

Regardless of which approach is used, the notation

```
scoresTable[2]
```

refers to row 2 in the table (counting from 0),

```
            [0]    [1]    [2]    [3]    [4]
        [2] ┌──────┬──────┬──────┬──────┬──────┐
            └──────┴──────┴──────┴──────┴──────┘
```

and the notation

```
scoresTable[2][4]
```

refers to the last entry in this row.

This idea can be extended to higher-dimensional arrays. For example, the three-dimensional array gradebook considered earlier can also be thought of as an array of arrays. In particular, since the gradebook is a sequence of pages, the entire three-dimensional array can be viewed as an array of pages of test scores, meaning a one-dimensional array whose components are two-dimensional arrays. If we adopt this point of view, we might declare the three-dimensional array gradeBook by adding the declarations

```
const int NUM_PAGES = 10;
typedef TwoDimScoreTable ThreeDimScoreArray[NUM_PAGES];
ThreeDimScoreArray score;
```

to the preceding declarations. The notation

```
score[2]
```

refers to the entire scores table recorded on the third page (counting from 0), which might be the following two-dimensional array of test scores:

	[0]	[1]	[2]	[3]	[4]
[0]	99.0	93.5	89.0	91.0	97.5
[1]	66.0	68.0	84.5	82.0	87.0
[2]	88.5	78.5	70.0	65.0	66.5
⋮	⋮	⋮	⋮	⋮	⋮
[29]	100.0	99.5	100.0	99.0	98.0

As in the previous example, each row in a scores table can be viewed as a one-dimensional array of test scores, and each table can therefore be viewed as a one-dimensional array of the test-score arrays. The doubly indexed expression

```
score[2][0]
```

refers to the first row in the table of scores on page 2,

99.0	93.5	89.0	91.0	97.5

and the triply-indexed expression

```
score[2][0][4]
```

accesses the last score in this row:

97.5

The implementation of multidimensional arrays is somewhat more complicated than that for one-dimensional arrays. Memory is organized as a sequence of memory locations, and each multiply-indexed array reference must be translated into an address of the form

base-address + offset

The array-of-arrays representation is what makes this possible. To illustrate, consider the two-dimensional 30 × 5 array scoresTable we described earlier and suppose that we want to access the element scoresTable[29][3]:

	[0]	[1]	[2]	[3]	[4]
[0]	99.0	93.5	89.0	91.0	97.5
[1]	66.0	68.0	84.5	82.0	87.0
[2]	88.5	78.5	70.0	65.0	66.5
⋮	⋮	⋮	⋮	⋮	⋮
[29]	100.0	99.5	100.0	99.0	98.0

If a double requires 8 bytes of storage, this array declaration informs the compiler that space will be needed for $30 \times 5 = 150$ doubles, which means that $150 \times 8 = 1200$ consecutive bytes will be needed to store the array elements. In C++, these elements are stored in **rowwise** order (also called *row major* order), with the first $5 \times 8 = 40$ bytes beginning at the base address of scoresTable used to store the elements in the first row of scoresTable, the next 40 bytes for the second row, and so on, as pictured in Figure 3.7. From this diagram, we see that the address of scoresTable[29][3] is $b + 1184$, where b is the base address of the array.

Figure 3.7 Memory Allocation for a Two-Dimensional Array

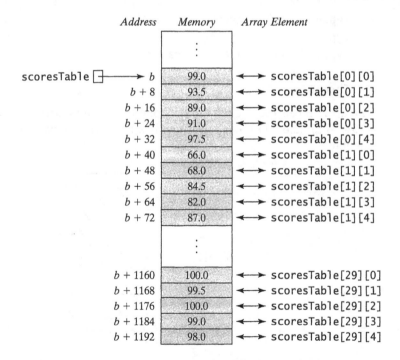

The formulas for this address translation can be derived from those given earlier for one-dimensional arrays if a two-dimensional array is viewed as a one-dimensional array whose elements are also one-dimensional arrays. To see this, we will assume rowwise storage and view scoresTable as a one-dimensional array having

30 elements (the rows of scoresTable), each of which requires $5 \times 8 = 40$ bytes for storage. Thus, by the address translation formula for one-dimensional arrays, storage for the ith row of scoresTable, scoresTable[i], begins with the byte whose address is

base(scoresTable[i]) = base(scoresTable) + 40i

Since this ith row of scoresTable is itself a one-dimensional array with base address base(scoresTable[i]), storage for the jth element in this row, scoresTable[i][j], begins at the byte with address

base(scoresTable[i]) + 8j

that is, scoresTable[i][j] begins at the byte whose address is

base(scoresTable) + 40i + 8j

Similarly, the address translation formulas for one- and two-dimensional arrays can be used to derive formulas for three-dimensional arrays if they are viewed as one-dimensional arrays whose elements are two-dimensional arrays (or as two-dimensional arrays whose elements are one-dimensional arrays). For example, consider the three-dimensional array b declared by

double b[3][4][3];

or equivalently,

```
typedef double Across[3];
typedef Across Slice[4];
typedef Slice ThreeDimArray[3];

ThreeDimArray b;
```

The array b can thus be viewed as a one-dimensional array having three elements, b[0], b[1], and b[2], each of which is a two-dimensional array with 4 rows and 3 columns:

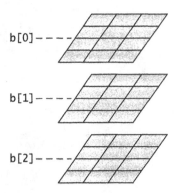

If each double requires 8 bytes of storage, then 96 bytes will be needed to store each of the tables b[0], b[1], and b[2]. Thus, b[i] is stored beginning at the byte with address

base(b[i]) = base(b) + 96i

Since each b[i] is a two-dimensional array, the address translation formulas for two-dimensional arrays give as the beginning address for b[i][j][k]

$$\text{base}(\text{b[i]}) + 24\text{j} + 8\text{k}$$
$$= \text{base}(\text{b}) + 96\text{i} + 24\text{j} + 8\text{k}$$

The general address formula is left is an exercise.

Address translation formulas for arrays having more than three dimensions can be derived similarly, but their complexity increases as the number of dimensions increases (see Exercise 11).

Multidimensional Arrays as Parameters

We noted earlier that for one-dimensional arrays, placing a pair of brackets ([]) after the name of a parameter indicates that the parameter is an array, and that it is not necessary to specify the capacity of the array. For example,

```
void display(int theArray[], int numValues);
```

was the prototype of our first version of a function to display the values stored in a one-dimensional array of integers. One might think that the obvious modification for a two-dimensional array would be to use two pairs of brackets ([][]) after the parameter's name:

```
void display(int the2DArray[][],
             int rowsUsed, int columnsUsed);
// --- Incorrect
```

But this does not work. As we've seen, two-dimensional arrays are treated as one-dimensional arrays of arrays. For address translations to work within a function for an array parameter, the function must know the base address (which is passed to it from the corresponding array argument) and the number of columns. Thus, although the first pair of brackets may be empty, the others must contain a constant specifying the number of columns. For example, we could write

```
const int NUM_STUDENTS = 30,
          NUM_TESTS = 5;

void display(int the2DArray[][NUM_TESTS],
             int rowsUsed, int columnsUsed);

int main()
{
   double scoresTable[NUM_STUDENTS][NUM_TESTS];

   //-- Statements to input scoresTable

   display(scoresTable, numStudents, numTests);
}
```

The same thing is true for arrays of higher dimensions.

The problem with this approach is the inflexibility of the function. All of the dimensions except the first for a multi-dimensional array parameter are constants that will need to be changed whenever we use the function with an array argument that has different dimensions. This is the reason we stated earlier that it is better to define a type identifier for arrays and then use it to declare the types of all arrays being used; for example,

```
const int NUM_ROWS = 30,
          NUM_COLUMNS = 5;
typedef double TwoDimArray[NUM_ROWS][NUM_COLUMNS];

void display(TwoDimArray the2DArray,
             int rowsUsed, int columnsUsed);

int main()
{
   TwoDimArray scoresTable;

   //-- Statements to input scores into scoresTable

   display(scoresTable, numStudents, numTests)
}
```

✔ Quick Quiz 3.3

1. t[3][5] is a value in column 3 of two-dimensional array t. (True or false).
2. t[3,5] is a value in row 3 of two-dimensional array t. (True or false)
3. Three-dimensional arrays can be viewed as one-dimensional arrays whose elements are two-dimensional arrays. (True or false)
4. Describe the array defined by int m[2][4] = {{1, 2, 3, 4}, {5, 6, 7, 8}};.
5. Describe the array defined by int m[4][2] = {1, 2, 3, 4, 5, 6, 7, 8};.
6. Describe the array defined by the following declarations:
   ```
   typedef int TypeA[2];
   typedef TypeA TypeB[2];
   typedef TypeB TypeC[3];
   TypeC array = {1, 2, 3, 4, 5, 6, 7, 8, 9, 10, 11, 12};
   ```

⬥ Exercises 3.3

Exercises 1–7 assume that chars are stored in one byte, ints in 4 bytes, doubles in 8 bytes, values of type T in 10 bytes, and values of type Day in 4 bytes, where Day is the enumeration defined by

```
enum Day {SUN, MON, TUE, WED, THU, FRI, SAT, NUM_DAYS};
```

In Exercises 1–4, find where the indicated elements of a two-dimensional array t of the specified type are stored, if the base address of t is 100 and storage is rowwise.

1. `char t[5][5];` `t[1][3]` and `t[2][2]`
2. `double t[4][10];` `t[0][8]` and `t[3][2]`
3. `int t[8][7];` `t[3][2]` and `t[1][6]`
4. `T t[7][6];` `t[TUE][3]` and `t[FRI][2]`

5–8. Proceed as in Exercises 1–4, but for columnwise storage.

9. Derive a general address translation formula for `t[i][j]`, where t is a two-dimensional array whose elements require w bytes of memory for storage. Assume that memory is allocated in a (a) rowwise manner; (b) columnwise manner.

10. Derive a general address translation formula for `b[i][j][k]` for a three-dimensional array b whose elements require w bytes of memory for storage, by viewing b as a one-dimensional array whose elements are two-dimensional arrays.

11. Derive the address translation formula for `f[i][j][k][l]`, where f is a four-dimensional array defined by

    `double f[N1][N2][N3][N4];`

by viewing f as a one-dimensional array with N1 elements, each of which is a three-dimensional $N2 \times N3 \times N4$ array of `double`s. Assume that three-dimensional arrays are allocated storage as described in Exercise 10.

3.4 Dynamic Arrays

In Section 3.2, we saw that the array declaration

```
const int CAPACITY = 10;
double arrayName[CAPACITY];
```

informs the compiler that a block of memory must be allocated that is large enough to hold ten `double` values and that the variable `arrayName` is to store the starting address of this block. Such fixed-size arrays have two drawbacks:

- If the size of the array exceeds the number of values to be stored in it, then memory is wasted by the unused elements.
- If the size of the array is smaller than the number of values to be stored in it, then the problem of array overflow may occur.

At the root of these problems is the fact that the array's capacity is fixed when the program is *compiled*. In our example, the size of the block of memory allocated for `arrayName` cannot be changed, except by editing the declaration of `CAPACITY` and then recompiling the program.

What is needed are arrays whose capacities are specified during execution. Such *dynamic arrays* can be constructed using the mechanism C++ provides for dynamic memory allocation. At its simplest, such a mechanism requires two operations:

1. Acquire additional memory locations as they are needed
2. Release memory locations when they are no longer needed

C++ provides the predefined operators new and delete to perform these two operations of memory allocation and deallocation during program execution.

The new Operation—Dynamic Arrays

As we saw in Section 2.4, memory can be requested from the operating system during program execution by using the new operation. The general form of such a request is as follows:

The new Operator

Forms:

```
new Type
new(nothrow) Type
new Type[capacity]
new(nothrow) Type[capacity]
```

where

Type may be any type, and nothrow is a constant defined in the standard library <new>.

Purpose:

Issue a run-time request for a block of memory that is large enough to store:
- a value of the specified Type for the first two forms
- an array with capacity elements of the specified Type for the last two forms

If the request can be granted, new returns the starting address of the block of memory. If the request cannot be granted, then:
- in the first and third forms, new throws a bad_alloc exception (defined in <new>), which causes execution to terminate if this exception is not caught
- in the second and fourth forms, new returns the null address 0.

In practice, new is rarely used to allocate space for single values of a simple type such as int. Instead, it is used to allocate space for arrays or for class objects. To illustrate the former, consider an integer array anArray declared by

```
int anArray[6];
```

As we saw in Section 3.2, the value associated with the name anArray is the base address of the array, that is, the address of the first element of the array. The type of object anArray is int[6].

A type such as int[6] can be used with new to allocate memory for an array during execution. For example, the statements

```
int * arrayPtr;
arrayPtr = new int[6];
```

allocate space for an array of six integers. Until the second statement is executed, arrayPtr is simply a pointer variable bound to type int whose value is undefined.

After it is executed (assuming that sufficient memory is available), `arrayPtr` contains the base address of the newly allocated array. If that address is 0x1101abc0, we might picture the situation as follows:

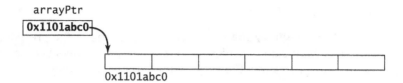

However, we have seen previously that the value associated with the name of a static array is its base address. This means that *if the base address of a dynamically-allocated array is stored in a pointer variable, then the elements of that array can be accessed via the pointer in exactly the same way that the elements of a statically-allocated array are accessed via its name, by using the subscript operator* (`[]`). That is, the first element of the new array can be accessed with `arrayPtr[0]`, the second element with `arrayPtr[1]`, the third element with `arrayPtr[2]`, and so on:

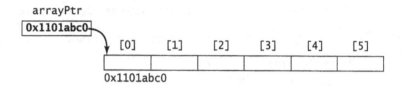

Note that this is consistent with our description of the array-address mapping described in Section 3.2. The value of the pointer variable `arrayPtr` is the base address of the array, and for a given index i, the subscript operator

```
arrayPtr[i]
```

simply accesses the memory location whose address is `arrayPtr + i * sizeof(int)`.

The advantage of dynamic allocation is that it is not necessary to know the size of the array at compile time. For example, we can write

```
cout << "How many entries? ";       // find how big the
cin >> numEntries;                   //   array should be
double * dPtr =                      // allocate an array
      new double[numEntries];        //   with that capacity

cout << "Enter your values.\n";      // fill it with values
for (int i = 0; i < numEntries; i++)
   cin >> dPtr[i];
```

Unlike arrays whose memory is allocated at compile time, arrays whose memory is allocated during execution can be tailored to the exact size of the collection of values to be stored in them. The wasted memory problem is solved because an array will not be too large. The overflow problem is solved because the array will not be too small.

In summary, the new operator can be used to allocate anonymous array variables at run time, and the capacities of these arrays can be tailored to the number of values to be stored in the arrays. By storing the base address of an array in a pointer variable, most things that can be done with a static array can be done with the dynamic array using the pointer.

Pointer Arithmetic   The introduction to pointers in the preceding chapter did not include a discussion of arithmetic operations on pointers because they are most useful in array processing. These operations are the following:

increment (++), decrement (--)

pointer + an integer, pointer - an integer

pointer += an integer, pointer -= an integer

To explain these operations, it is helpful to make use of the **sizeof operator** described in Section 2.4. It can be applied to any type T or to any expression and returns

- the number of bytes required to store a value of type T, or
- the number of bytes required to store the value of the expression.

The sizeof operator can thus be applied to either objects or types:

sizeof(*type-specifier*)

sizeof *expression*

Note that in the first case, the type specifier must be enclosed within parentheses. To illustrate, the expression

sizeof(char)

evaluates to 1, because char values are allocated one byte. Similarly, if longVar is of type long int and long int objects are stored in four bytes, the expression

sizeof longVar

will evaluate to 4.

Now we can explain the arithmetic operators for pointers. Suppose that a pointer variable ptr is declared by

Type * ptr;

Then the expressions

ptr++ and ++ptr

add the value sizeof(*Type*) to the address in ptr. Similarly,

ptr-- and --ptr

subtract the value sizeof(Type) from the address in ptr. If *intExp* is an integer expression, the value of the expression

ptr + intExp

is the value of *ptr + intExp* * `sizeof(Type)`, and the shortcut assignment

```
ptr += intExp;
```

assigns this value to `ptr`. Similarly, the value of the expression

```
ptr - intExp
```

is the value *ptr - intExp* * `sizeof(Type)`, and the shortcut assignment

```
ptr -= intExp;
```

assigns it to `ptr`.

To illustrate how these operations are used, suppose that `ptr` is a pointer whose value is the address of the first element of an array of `double` elements,

```
double dArray[10];          // array of 10 doubles
double * ptr = dArray;      // pointer to array's first element
```

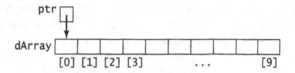

Now consider the following loop:

```
for (int i = 0; i < 10; i++)
{
    *ptr = 0;
    ptr++;
}
```

On the first pass through the loop, `ptr` is dereferenced and the value 0 is assigned to the memory location at that address. `ptr` is then incremented, making it point to the second element of the array:

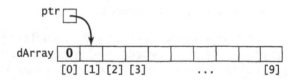

The next pass again dereferences `ptr`, sets that memory location to zero, and increments `ptr`:

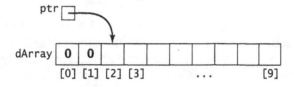

This continues with each subsequent iteration. On the final pass, the last element of the array is set to zero and `ptr` is again incremented, so that it points to the first address past the end of the array:

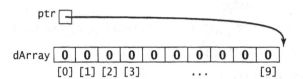

A pointer can thus be used to iterate through consecutive blocks of memory, accessing them in whatever way a particular problem requires. (As we will see in Chapter 9, this is precisely how **iterators** move through sequential containers such as `vector` in C++'s Standard Template Library.)

We can also write a version of the `for` loop in the preceding example that doesn't introduce the extra pointer `ptr`. As we have seen, `dArray` is itself a pointer variable whose value is the base address of the array. From the properties of pointer arithmetic, therefore, `dArray`, `dArray + 1`, `dArray + 2`, . . ., point to the individual elements of this array, so that dereferencing these pointers, `*dArray`, `*(dArray + 1)`, `*(dArray + 2)`, . . ., gives the actual array elements. Thus, the loop could also be written

```
for (int i = 0; i < 10; i++)
   *(dArray + i) = 0;    // or dArray[i] = 0;
```

As the comment suggests,

`dArray[i]` *is equivalent to* `*(dArray + i)`

Failures of new When execution of a program begins, the program has available to it a "storage pool" of unallocated memory locations, called the **heap** or **free store**. The effect of the new operation is to request the operating system to

1. Remove a block of memory from the heap

2. Allocate that block to the executing program

The block can be used by the executing program if it stores the address of that block (the value produced by the new operation) in a pointer variable.

The size of the heap is limited, however, and each execution of new causes the pool of available memory to shrink. This means that eventually new may request more memory than is available in the heap, so the operating system will not be able to fill the request. There are several different results of such failures.

If new is used in the form

new *Type*   or   new *Type*[*capacity*]

and there is not enough memory to satisfy the request, new **throws a bad_alloc exception**. If no action is taken in the program unit in which this new expression appears, execution will be terminated and an error message will usually be displayed. The program in Figure 3.8 illustrates this kind of failure.

Figure 3.8 Failure of new—Version 1

```
//-- Demonstration #1 of new failure -- Uncaught bad_alloc exception

#include <iostream>
#include <new>        // new, bad_alloc
using namespace std;

int main()
{
   const int NUM_ARRAYS = 10;
   cout << "How large should the arrays of doubles be? ";
   int capacity;
   cin >> capacity;

   double * arrayPtr[NUM_ARRAYS];
   int i;
   for (i = 0; i < NUM_ARRAYS; i++)
   {
      arrayPtr[i] = new double [capacity];
      cout << "Allocated " << capacity
           << " doubles for i = " << i << endl;
   }
   cout << "All " << NUM_ARRAYS << " arrays of "
        << capacity << " doubles were allocated successfully." << endl;
}
```

Execution Trace #1 (CodeWarrior):
```
How large should the arrays of doubles be? 1000
Allocated 1000 doubles for i = 0
Allocated 1000 doubles for i = 1
Allocated 1000 doubles for i = 2
Allocated 1000 doubles for i = 3
Allocated 1000 doubles for i = 4
Allocated 1000 doubles for i = 5
Allocated 1000 doubles for i = 6
Allocated 1000 doubles for i = 7
Allocated 1000 doubles for i = 8
Allocated 1000 doubles for i = 9
All 10 arrays of 1000 doubles were allocated successfully.
```

Figure 3.8 (continued)

Execution Trace #2 (CodeWarrior):
```
How large should the arrays of doubles be? 10000
Allocated 10000 doubles for i = 0
Allocated 10000 doubles for i = 1
Allocated 10000 doubles for i = 2
Allocated 10000 doubles for i = 3
Allocated 10000 doubles for i = 4
Allocated 10000 doubles for i = 5
Allocated 10000 doubles for i = 6
Allocation failed for i = 7
```

Execution Trace #3 (GNU C++ 3.1):
```
How large should the arrays of doubles be? 100000000
Allocated 100000000 doubles for i = 0
Allocated 100000000 doubles for i = 1
Allocated 100000000 doubles for i = 2
Allocated 100000000 doubles for i = 3
*** malloc: vm_allocate(size=800002048) failed with 3
*** malloc[460]: error: Can't allocate region
Abort
```

▲

As the first execution trace of this program shows, 10 arrays of one thousand doubles were allocated successfully. But in the second trace, after memory for 6 arrays of ten thousand doubles had been allocated, not enough memory remained for a 7th array. The third trace shows the rather cryptic error message in GNU C++ when memory could not be allocated.

For operations like new that can throw exceptions, we can (and should) use the **try-catch mechanism** to take appropriate action when an exception is thrown. Exceptions are described in more detail in Appendix D. Here we simply give one example (see Figure 3.9).

Figure 3.9 Failure of new—Version 2

```
//-- Demonstration #2 of new failure -- Use try-catch mechanism
//-- to handle bad_alloc exception.

#include <iostream>
#include <new>        // new, bad_alloc
using namespace std;
```

Figure 3.9 (continued)

```cpp
int main()
{
   const int NUM_ARRAYS = 10;
   cout << "How large should the arrays of doubles be? ";
   int capacity;
   cin >> capacity;

   double * arrayPtr[NUM_ARRAYS];
   int i;

   try
   {
      for (i = 0; i < NUM_ARRAYS; i++)
      {
         arrayPtr[i] = new double [capacity];
         cout << "Allocated " << capacity
              << " doubles for i = " << i << endl;
      }
   }
   catch (bad_alloc ex)
   {
      cout << "Exception: " << ex.what() <<
           << "for i = " << i << endl;
      exit(1);
   }

   cout << "All " << NUM_ARRAYS << " arrays of "
        << capacity << " doubles were allocated successfully." << endl;

}
```

Execution Trace #1 (CodeWarrior):
```
How large should the arrays of doubles be? 1000
Allocated 1000 doubles for i = 0
Allocated 1000 doubles for i = 1
Allocated 1000 doubles for i = 2
Allocated 1000 doubles for i = 3
Allocated 1000 doubles for i = 4
Allocated 1000 doubles for i = 5
Allocated 1000 doubles for i = 6
Allocated 1000 doubles for i = 7
```

Figure 3.9 (continued)

```
Allocated 1000 doubles for i = 8
Allocated 1000 doubles for i = 9
All 10 arrays of 1000 doubles were allocated successfully.
```

Execution Trace #2 (CodeWarrior):
```
How large should the arrays of doubles be? 10000
Allocated 10000 doubles for i = 0
Allocated 10000 doubles for i = 1
Allocated 10000 doubles for i = 2
Allocated 10000 doubles for i = 3
Allocated 10000 doubles for i = 4
Allocated 10000 doubles for i = 5
Allocated 10000 doubles for i = 6
Exception: bad_alloc for i = 7
```

Execution Trace #3 (GNU C++ 3.1):
```
How large should the arrays of doubles be? 100000000
Allocated 100000000 doubles for i = 0
Allocated 100000000 doubles for i = 1
Allocated 100000000 doubles for i = 2
Allocated 100000000 doubles for i = 3
*** malloc: vm_allocate(size=800002048) failed with 3
*** malloc[691]: error: Can't allocate region

Exception: St9bad_alloc -- for i = 4
```

▲

In Figure 3.9, the requests to new (or any operation that may throw an exception) for memory are made in a **try block**. If the statements inside this try block execute successfully with no exceptions thrown, all **catch blocks** that follow it are bypassed and execution continues with the statements that follow them. This is illustrated by the first execution trace.

In the second execution trace, we see that execution was not aborted but rather proceeded to the catch block for a bad_alloc exception and executed the statements in it. We see that this also happened with the third execution trace, although the cryptic error message still appeared.

Another approach is to use the versions of new with the constant nothrow defined in <new>:

new(nothrow) *Type*   and   new(nothrow) *Type*[*capacity*]

These use a version of new that does not throw an exception but rather returns a null address if memory cannot be allocated. The program in Figure 3.10 is a modification of the two preceding programs that uses this form to allocate the arrays of doubles.

Figure 3.10 Failure of new—Version 3

```
//-- Demonstration #3 of new failure -- Use nothrow version of new
//-- and check whether it returns a null address.

#include <iostream>
#include <new>        // new, nothrow
using namespace std;

int main()
{
    const int NUM_ARRAYS = 10;
    cout << "How large should the arrays of doubles be? ";
    int capacity;
    cin >> capacity;

    double * arrayPtr[NUM_ARRAYS];
    int i;
    for (i = 0; i < NUM_ARRAYS; i++)
    {
        arrayPtr[i] = new(nothrow) double [capacity];
        if (arrayPtr[i] == 0)        // null address
        {
            cout << "Allocation failed for i = " << i << endl;
            exit(1);
        }
        cout << "Allocated " << capacity
            << " doubles for i = " << i << endl;
    }
    cout << "All " << NUM_ARRAYS << " arrays of "
        << capacity << " doubles were allocated successfully." << endl;
}
```

Execution Trace #1 (CodeWarrior):
```
How large should the arrays of doubles be? 1000
Allocated 1000 doubles for i = 0
Allocated 1000 doubles for i = 1
Allocated 1000 doubles for i = 2
Allocated 1000 doubles for i = 3
Allocated 1000 doubles for i = 4
Allocated 1000 doubles for i = 5
```

Figure 3.10 (continued)

```
Allocated 1000 doubles for i = 6
Allocated 1000 doubles for i = 7
Allocated 1000 doubles for i = 8
Allocated 1000 doubles for i = 9
All 10 arrays of 1000 doubles were allocated successfully.
```

Execution Trace #2 (CodeWarrior):
```
How large should the arrays of doubles be? 10000
Allocated 10000 doubles for i = 0
Allocated 10000 doubles for i = 1
Allocated 10000 doubles for i = 2
Allocated 10000 doubles for i = 3
Allocated 10000 doubles for i = 4
Allocated 10000 doubles for i = 5
Allocated 10000 doubles for i = 6
Allocation failed for i = 7
```

Execution Trace #3 (GNU C++ 3.1):
```
How large should the arrays of doubles be? 100000000
Allocated 100000000 doubles for i = 0
Allocated 100000000 doubles for i = 1
Allocated 100000000 doubles for i = 2
Allocated 100000000 doubles for i = 3
*** malloc: vm_allocate(size=800002048) failed with 3
*** malloc[526]: error: Can't allocate region
Allocation failed for i = 4
```

▲

Here we see in the second execution trace that when memory allocation failed, new did return the null address, the if statement caused our own error message to be displayed, and the program terminated. In the third execution trace we see the same behavior, although the cryptic error message still appeared when memory allocation failed.

As the programs in Figures 3.8–3.10 illustrate, versions of C++ vary in how they implement the new operation. For example, some return a null address for failures even when new is used without the nothrow option; others return a null address whenever <new> isn't included. In this text we will generally use the nothrow version of new in programs that require dynamic allocation of memory.

The delete Operation We have described in some detail how memory can be allocated dynamically using the new operator. Now we look at an analogous method to reclaim memory allocated by new. In C++, this can be accomplished by using the **delete operation**. Just as new is a request by the executing program for memory from the heap, the delete operation is a request to return memory to the heap where it can be reused in later allocations. The new and delete operations are thus complementary.

The general form of the delete operation is as follows:

The delete Operation

Forms:

```
delete pointerVariable
delete [] arrayPointerVariable
```

Purpose:

The first form frees the dynamically allocated memory whose address is stored in *pointerVariable*. The second form frees the block of memory dynamically allocated to an array whose address is stored in *arrayPointerVariable*.

For example, if intPtr has been allocated memory from the heap with

```
int * intPtr = new int;
```

then the statement

```
delete intPtr;
```

will release the memory location pointed to by intPtr, making it available for allocation at a later time. Following the operation, the value of intPtr will be undefined, and so the result of any attempt to dereference it

```
*intPtr
```

is unpredictable, possibly producing a run-time error. To avoid such problems, some programmers always set the value of such pointers to the null address,

```
delete intPtr;
intPtr = 0;
```

so that a statement of the form

```
if (intPtr != 0)
    // ... ok - intPtr can be safely dereferenced
else
    // ... not ok - intPtr's memory has been deallocated
```

can be used to guard access to the memory pointed to by intPtr.

Similarly, if dPtr is a pointer to the first element of an array allocated at run time, as in

```
cin >> numValues;
double * dPtr = new(nothrow) double[numValues];
```

then that array's memory can be returned to the heap by using the array version of the delete operation:

```
delete [] dPtr;
```

Memory Leaks It is important for programs that allocate memory using new to deallocate that memory using delete. To see why, consider the following innocent-looking code:

```
do
{
    int * intPtr = new(nothrow) int[10];
    assert(intPtr != 0);
    // ... use the array via intPtr to solve a problem

    cout << "\nDo another (y or n)? ";
    cin >> answer;
}
while (answer != 'n');
```

The first time the loop executes, an array of 10 integers will be allocated:

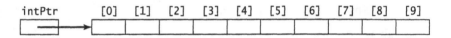

The second time the loop executes, a second array will be allocated and its address will be stored in intPtr. However, delete was not used to return the first array to the heap, and so it is still allocated to the program:

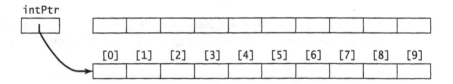

Since intPtr was the only means of accessing the first anonymous array and we overwrote its address in intPtr, that array is now "lost" or "marooned" memory—it can neither be accessed by the program nor returned to the heap.

The third time the loop executes, a third array is allocated and its address is stored in intPtr, marooning the second anonymous array:

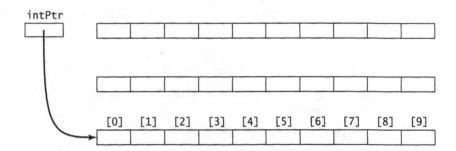

With each repetition of the loop, 10 more memory locations will be lost. If the loop executes enough times, so much memory may be lost that the assertion (intPtr != 0) will become false and terminate the program. Because such code loses memory over time, this situation is called a **memory leak**.

 To avoid memory leaks, the memory to which a pointer points should always be deallocated before the pointer is assigned a new address:

```
do
{
    int * intPtr = new(nothrow) int[10];
    assert(intPtr != 0);

    // ... use the array via intPtr to solve a problem
    delete [] intPtr;

    cout << "\nDo another (y or n)? ";
    cin >> answer;
}
while (answer != 'n');
```

This will ensure that the memory pointed to by a pointer is released to the heap and will thus avoid a memory leak.

A memory leak can also occur if we use the wrong form of the delete operation for an array—that is, if we use

```
delete arrayPtr;      // Wrong form of delete
```

instead of

```
delete [] arrayPtr;      // Correct form of delete
```

Since arrayPtr stores the address of the first element of the array, the first form may deallocate only this memory location, without releasing the remaining locations allocated to the array back to the heap.

Other Uses of Pointers

Command-Line Arguments   Command-line arguments are used with many of the system commands in command-line environments such as Unix. For example, the command

```
emacs textfile
```

is used to execute a program named emacs, search for the file named textfile, and (assuming that it is found) open it for editing. The name of the file textfile is an example of a **command-line argument**. Just as entering the name of the program (emacs) is like calling the main function of a program, entering the name of the program followed by textfile is like calling the main function of a program and passing it textfile as an argument.

Command-line arguments can be passed to the main function `main()` via two parameters, usually named `argc` and `argv`:

- `argc` (the argument count): an `int` whose value is the number of strings on the command line when the command to execute the binary executable of the program is given
- `argv` (the argument vector): an array of pointers to `chars`; `argv[i]` is the address of the `i`th character string on the command line

See Appendix D for examples of how these parameters can be used.

Functions as Arguments   Sometimes it is useful to *pass a function* as an argument to another function. For example, many functions that implement numerical methods for finding roots of functions, solving equations, approximating integrals, and so on can be written most generally if the functions are passed to them as arguments.

To permit one function to be passed to another function as an argument, C++ stipulates that

The value of a function is the starting address of that function.

That is, a function is a pointer. Just as an array variable is a pointer whose value is the base address of that array, a function `f` is a pointer whose value is the starting address of that function. A `typedef` declaration of the form

```
typedef ReturnType (*functionPtr)(ParameterTypeList);
```

declares the name `functionPtr` as a type whose objects are pointers to functions whose return type is *ReturnType* and whose parameters match those in *ParameterTypeList*. See Appendix D for examples of how this can be used to declare function parameters in other functions and to pass functions as arguments to these parameters.

✔ Quick Quiz 3.4

1. The _____ operator is used to request memory during program execution. If enough memory is available, it returns the _____ of a block of memory.
2. The newly allocated memory location in Question 1 is called a(n) _____ variable.
3. If there is not enough memory available for a value of type T, the expression

   new T

   will _____.
4. If there is not enough memory available for a value of type T, the expression

   new(nothrow) T

   will _____.
5. The _____ operation is used to release memory during program execution.
6. Given the declarations

   ```
   int a[] = {44, 22, 66, 11, 77, 33};
   int * p = a;
   ```

   what is the value of `p[2]`?

7. In Question 6, a is a dynamic array. (True or false)

8. Write a statement to deallocate the memory that was allocated to the array dubArray with the statement

```
double * dubArray = new double[100];
```

9. Command-line arguments are passed to a main function main() via two parameters usually named _____ and _____.

10. (True or false) A function is a pointer.

✦ Exercises 3.4

For Exercises 1–5, write C++ statements to do what is asked.

1. Allow the user to enter *n*, the number of values to be processed; then allocate an anonymous array of *n* double values, storing its address in doublePtr.

2. Fill the anonymous array of Exercise 1 with *n* input values, entered from the keyboard.

3. Compute and display the average of the values in the anonymous array of Exercise 1.

4. Deallocate the storage of the anonymous array of Exercise 1.

5. In Exercise 1, if the value of doublePtr is 1000 and double values are stored in 8 bytes, draw a memory map showing the addresses of the first few elements of the anonymous array.

6. Assuming that addresses are stored in 4 bytes and double values in 8 bytes, tell what output will be produced by the following statements:

```
double dubValues[] = {1.1, 2.2, 3.3, 4.4, 5.5};
double * dubPtr = dubValues;
for (int i = 0; i < 5; i++)
  cout << sizeof(dubPtr + i) << "  "
       << sizeof(*(dubPtr + i)) << "  "
       << *(dubPtr + i) << endl;
```

3.5 C-Style Structs (optional)

In the preceding sections we described C-style arrays, both static and dynamic. As we will see in later chapters, they play an important role in C++ by providing a data structure that can be used in implementing some abstract data types in which the collection of data elements is homogeneous (i.e., all the data elements are the same type).

More frequently, however, the objects in a problem that need to be modeled have *multiple attributes*. For example, a temperature such as 32°F has two attributes: number of degrees and a scale (Fahrenheit, Celsius, Kelvin). We might thus picture a temperature object as follows:

| 32.0 | F |

degrees   scale

Similarly, a date object representing the last day of the 20th century,

December	31	1999
month	*day*	*year*

has three attributes: a *month*, a *day*, and a *year*.

Because such objects cannot be represented easily using simple types, programming languages such as C and Pascal provide **aggregate types** for data items that have multiple attributes—*structs* in C and *records* in Pascal.[7]

Declarations of structs in C and in their simplest form in C++ have the following forms:

C++ Struct Declarations

Declaration of a struct (simplified):

```
struct TypeName
{
    declarations of members  // of any types
};
```

Forms of declarations of struct objects:

```
TypeName structName;

TypeName structName = {initializer_list};
```
where

the members may be of any type; and

in the second form, the types of the values in `initializer_list` match the types of the corresponding members in the struct declaration.

Purpose:

Instructs the compiler that a block of memory locations must be reserved to store values of the specified types and that the name `structName` is to be associated with that storage. In the second form, the struct's members are initialized with the values in `initializer_list`.

To illustrate, we might declare a type `Temperature` by

```
struct Temperature
{
    double degrees;   // number of degrees
    char scale;       // temp. scale (F, C, K, ...)
};
```

---

[7] C (and thus C++) also provides **unions**, an aggregate type similar to structs, but differing from them in that the members of a struct are allocated different memory locations, whereas the members of a union share memory. Unions are seldom used in C++, however, because they are not needed. The inheritance property of classes can be used to accomplish in an object-oriented way the structuring of data made possible with unions and structs. See the text's website for more information about structs and unions.

3.5 C-Style Structs (optional)

The declarations

```
Temperature temp;
const Temperature FREEZING = {32, 'F'};
```

can then be used to declare temp to be a Temperature variable with its members uninitialized and FREEZING to be a constant with its degrees member initialized to 32 and its scale member initialized to F:

```
FREEZING   32.0    F
         degrees scale
```

A type Date for processing dates might be declared by

```
struct Date
{
   char month[10];   // name of month
   int day,          // day number
       year;         // year number
};
```

and a Date variable endOf20thCentury declared by

```
Date endOf20thCentury = {"December", 31, 1999};
```

which initializes endOf20thCentury's month member to December, its day member to 31, and its year member to 1999:

```
endOf20thCentury   December   31   1999
                    month     day  year
```

As another example, records maintained for users of a computer system might contain a user identification number, a password, a resource limit, and the resources used to date, as in this example:

```
unsigned  char[12]    double       double
  12345   UR2MUCH      100.00       37.45
idNumber password   resourceLimit resourcesUsed
```

A data type for these records can be declared by

```
struct ComputerUsageInfo
{                          // user's
  unsigned idNumber;       //  id number
  char password[12];       //  password
  double resourceLimit,    //  limit on computer resources
         resourcesUsed;    //  resources used to date
};
```

A `ComputerUsageInfo` variable `userRecord` can then be declared by

```
ComputerUsageInfo userRecord;
```

The data members of a struct may be of any type. They need not be simple types as in the preceding examples, but they may be structured data types such as arrays or other structs. For example, for a student in a computer science class, we might wish to store the student's name, birth date, computer-usage information, and a list of four test scores. For this we can use the preceding structured types `Date` and `ComputerUsageInfo` to specify the types of two of the data members of a struct `StudentClassRecord`:

```
const int MAX_SCORES = 4;
struct StudentClassRecord
{                                     // student's
   char name[20];                     //   complete name
   Date birth;                        //   birthdate
   ComputerUsageInfo usage;           //   user info
   int score[MAX_SCORES];             //   test scores
};
```

The statement

```
StudentClassRecord aStudent;
```

then declares a `StudentClassRecord` variable `aStudent` and

```
CONST int COURSE_LIMIT = 50;
StudentClassRecord cpsc186[COURSE_LIMIT];
```

declares an array of 50 `StudentClassRecord` values. Each array element contains four data members in which the first is a string, the second is a struct with three members (`month`, `day`, `year`), the third is a struct with four members (`idNumber`, `password`, `resourceLimit`, `resourcesUsed`), and the fourth is an array of four doubles.

Structs such as `aStudent` that contain other structures are sometimes called **nested structures** to indicate that some structures are "nested" inside other structures. They are also frequently referred to as **hierarchical structures**, as suggested by the following diagram:

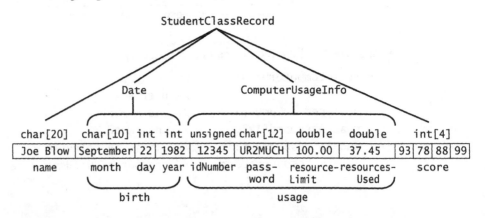

Struct Operations   Just as the subscript operator [] provides direct access to the elements of an array, *member access operators* provide direct access to the members of a struct (or class). One of these is the **dot operator (.)** used in expressions of the form

```
struct_object.member_name
```

The following are some examples:

```
// Calculate the Celsius equivalent of temp
Temperature tempCels;
tempCels.degrees = (temp.degrees - 32.0) / 1.8;
tempCels.scale = 'C';


// Input values into the members of currentDate
cin >> currentDate.month >> currentDate.day
    >> currentDate.year;


// Sum the scores in aStudent
int sum = 0;
for (int i = 0; i < 4; i++)
   sum += aStudent.score[i];


// Output the birth month and id number of aStudent
cout << "Birth month: " << aStudent.birth.month << endl
     << "Id Number:   " << aStudent.usage.idNumber << endl;
```

A sequence of similar assignment statements could be used to copy one struct to another by copying one member at a time. However, this can be accomplished more simply with an assignment statement of the form

```
struct_variable = struct_object;
```

where the struct variable and the struct object have the same type.

Pointers to Structs

Pointers can be bound to any type, in particular, to a struct. For example, a pointer to a Date object defined by

```
Date * datePtr = &endOf20thCentury;
```

stores the address of the Date object endOf20thCentury in datePtr, which we can picture as follows:

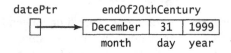

The members of endOf20thCentury can be accessed (indirectly) via datePtr in two ways. One way is to combine the indirection operator with the dot operator. For example, the value (31) of the day data member can be accessed by using

```
(*datePtr).day
```

In this expression, the pointer `datePtr` is first dereferenced to access the object to which it points and the dot operator is then used to access the day data member.

This notation is rather cumbersome, however, because it involves two operators and the indirection operation must be parenthesized because it has lower priority than the dot operator. For this reason, C++ provides an operator that accomplishes the same thing in one operation:

```
datePtr->day
```

Here, the left operand of the **arrow operator** `->` is a *pointer* to a struct (or class) object and the right operand is a *member* of that object. An expression of the form

```
ptr->member
```

is equivalent to the expression

```
(*ptr).member
```

This operator provides a convenient way to access an object's members, and the "arrow" notation clearly indicates that the member is being accessed through a pointer.

✔ Quick Quiz 3.5

1. (True or false) C-style structs are used for data items that have a single attribute.
2. The elements of a struct in C++ are accessed with the _____ operator.

For Questions 3 and 4, assume that type T is a struct in which two of the members are of type `int` and are named m and n, that x is of type T, and that p is a pointer to an object of type T.

3. Write a statement that can be used to store the value 100 in the member m of x.
4. Write a statement that can be used to input values into the data members m and n of x.
5. Write a statement that can be used to output the values of the data members m and n of x.
6. Write two different expressions that can be used to access the data member m of a struct pointed to by p.
7. Write a statement that can be used to input values into the data members m and n of the data members of the object pointed to by p.
8. Write a statement that can be used to output the values of the data members m and n of the data members of the object pointed to by p.

3.6 Procedural Programming

In the **procedural-programming paradigm** engendered by many *procedural* languages such as C, Fortran, and Pascal, programmers concentrate on writing subprograms (procedures/functions/subroutines) to perform various tasks. This is because the basic approach in this problem-solving methodology is as follows:

1. Identify the basic tasks to be performed in solving a problem, which may involve dividing the problem into simpler subproblems and identifying subtasks for these subproblems.

2. Implement the actions required to do these tasks and subtasks as subprograms, passing the data items being processed from one subprogram to another.

3. Group these subprograms together to form a program or perhaps a collection of programs/modules/libraries, which together make up a complete system for solving the problem.

This procedural approach to programming might thus be said to be *action oriented*. Someone once described it as concentrating on the *verbs* of a problem's specification in designing a solution. This is in contrast to the **object-oriented-programming paradigm** where a programmer determines what objects are needed for a problem and how they should work together to solve the problem. The focus of OOP is thus on objects rather than on subprograms, on the *nouns* in the specification of the problem rather than on the *verbs*. To illustrate the procedural approach, we will show how C-style structs can be used to create a data type. In Section 4.3 we will redo this problem using the OOP approach.

Example of Procedural Programming

Problem   To create a type Time for processing times in standard hh:mm AM/PM form and in military-time form.

Data Attributes   Time objects will have the following four attributes:

Hours (an integer in the range 1 through 12)
Minutes (an integer in the range 0 through 59)
AM or PM indicator (the character 'A' or 'P')
Military time (a nonnegative integer)

Each Time value will therefore consist of four values corresponding to these four attributes.

Some Operations   Many operations would be necessary to provide a complete model of time. For simplicity, we will consider only the following:

Set the time
Display the time
Advance the time
Determine whether one time is less than another time

Implementation   We need storage structures for the four values that make up a Time object. Because these are not all of the same type, we will use a struct. We will write functions to perform the operations on Time objects. We can then package the declarations together in a header file Time.h and the definitions of the functions in an implementation file Time.cpp. Figure 3.11 shows these files.[8] It also shows a test-driver program. (See the next chapter for more information about header and implementation files and how to translate a program that involves them.)

---

[8] See Appendix C.9 if you are not familiar with C++'s *conditional operator* ?: used in the definitions of the set() and toMilitary() functions.

Figure 3.11 A Time Data Type—Procedural Approach

```
/*== Time.h =====================================================

   This header file defines the data type Time for processing time.
   Basic operations are:
      set:      To set the time
      display:  To display the time
      advance:  To advance the time by a certain amount
      lessThan: To determine if one time is less than another
================================================================*/


#include <iostream>

struct Time
{
   unsigned hour,
            minute;
   char AMorPM;          // 'A' or 'P'
   unsigned milTime;     // military time equivalent
};

void set(Time & t, unsigned hours, unsigned minutes, char AMPM);
/*-------------------------------------------------------------
   Set the time to a specified value.

   Receive:    Time object t
               hours, the number of hours in standard time
               minutes, the number of minutes in standard time
               AMPM ('A' if AM, 'P' if PM)
   Pass back: The modified Time t with data members set to the
                 specified values
-----------------------------------------------------------*/


void display(const Time & t, ostream & out);
/*-------------------------------------------------------------
   Display time t in standard and military format using output stream out.

   Receive:    Time t and ostream out
   Output:     The time t to out
```

Figure 3.11 (continued)

```
        Pass back: The modified ostream out with a representation of t
                   inserted into it
      ----------------------------------------------------------------------*/

void advance(Time & t, unsigned hours, unsigned minutes);
/*-------------------------------------------------------------------
   Increment a time by a specified value.

   Receive:   Time object t
              hours, the number of hours to add
              minutes, the number of minutes to add
   Pass back: The modified Time t with data members incremented by the
              specified values
   ---------------------------------------------------------------------*/


bool lessThan(const Time & t1, const Time & t2);
/*-------------------------------------------------------------------
/* Determines if one time is less than another time.

   Receive:   Times t1 and t2
   Return:    True if t1 < t2, false otherwise.
   ---------------------------------------------------------------------*/
```

```
/*== Time.cpp =================================================================

    Definitions of the functions that implement Time operations whose
    prototypes are in Time.h.
   =============================================================================*/

#include <iostream>
using namespace std;
#include "Time.h"

/** Utility functions **/

int toMilitary(unsigned hours, unsigned minutes, char AMPM);
void toStandard(unsigned military,
                unsigned & hours, unsigned & minutes, char & AMPM);
```

Figure 3.11 (continued)

```
//--- Definition of set() -------------------------------------------
void set(Time & t, unsigned hours, unsigned minutes, char AMPM)
{
   if (hours >= 1 && hours <= 12 &&
       minutes >= 0 && minutes <= 59 &&
       (AMPM == 'A' || AMPM == 'P'))
   {
      t.hour = hours;
      t.minute = minutes;
      t.AMorPM = AMPM;
      t.milTime = toMilitary(hours, minutes, AMPM);
   }
   else
      cerr << "*** Can't set time with these values ***\n";
      // t remains unchanged
}


//--- Definition of display() -------------------------------------
void display(const Time & t, ostream & out)
{
   out << t.hour << ':'
       << (t.minute < 10 ? "0" : "") << t.minute
       << ' ' << t.AMorPM << ".M.  ("
       << t.milTime << " mil. time)";
}


//--- Definition of advance() -------------------------------------
void advance(Time & t, unsigned hours, unsigned minutes)
{
   // Advance using military time
   t.milTime += 100 * hours + minutes;
   unsigned milHours = t.milTime / 100,
            milMins = t.milTime % 100;

   // Adjust to proper format
   milHours +=  milMins / 60;
   milMins %= 60;
   milHours %= 24;
   t.milTime = 100 * milHours + milMins;
```

Figure 3.11 (continued)

```
    // Now set standard time
    toStandard(t.milTime, t.hour, t.minute, t.AMorPM);
}

//--- Definition of lessThan() ------------------------------------------
bool lessThan(const Time & t1, const Time & t2)
{
    return (t1.milTime < t2.milTime);
}


//----- DEFINITIONS OF UTILITY FUNCTIONS -------

int toMilitary (unsigned hours, unsigned minutes, char AMPM)
/*------------------------------------------------------------------------
    Convert standard time to military time.

    Receive: hours, minutes, AMPM
    Return:  The military time equivalent
------------------------------------------------------------------------*/
{
    if (hours == 12)
      hours = 0;
    return hours * 100 + minutes + (AMPM == 'P' ? 1200 : 0);
}

void toStandard(unsigned military,
                unsigned & hours, unsigned & minutes, char & AMPM)
/*------------------------------------------------------------------------
    Convert military time to standard time.

    Receive:   military, a time in military format
    Pass back: hours, minutes, AMPM -- equivalent standard time
------------------------------------------------------------------------*/
{
    hours = (military / 100) % 12;
    if (hours == 0)
      hours = 12;
```

Figure 3.11 (continued)

```
    minutes = military % 100;
    AMPM = (military / 100) < 12 ? 'A' : 'P';
}
```

```
/*== Driver =============================================================
                Driver program to test Time library.
    ==========================================================================*/


#include <iostream>
using namespace std;
#include "Time.h"

int main()
{
    Time mealTime,
         goToWorkTime;
    set(mealTime, 5, 30, 'P');
    cout << "We'll be eating at ";
    display(mealTime, cout);
    cout << endl;
    set(goToWorkTime, 5, 30, 'P');  // Try other values also: 'A' -> 'P'
    cout << "You leave for work at ";
    display(goToWorkTime, cout);
    cout << endl;
    if (lessThan(mealTime, goToWorkTime))
       cout << "If you hurry, you can eat first.\n";
    else
       cout << "Sorry you can't eat with us.\n";
    advance(goToWorkTime, 0, 30);    // Try other values also: 0 -> 12)
    cout << "Your boss called.  You go in later at ";
    display(goToWorkTime, cout);
    cout << endl;
    if (lessThan(mealTime, goToWorkTime))
       cout << "If you hurry, you can eat first.\n";
    else
       cout << "Sorry you can't eat with us.\n";
    cout << endl;
}
```

Figure 3.11 (continued)

Execution Trace:

```
We'll be eating at 5:30 P.M.  (1730 mil. time)
You leave for work at 5:30 P.M. (1730 mil. time)
Sorry you can't eat with us.
Your boss called.  You go in later at 6:00 P.M. (1800 mil. time)
If you hurry, you can eat first.
```

▲

SUMMARY

▓▌ Chapter Notes

- An *abstract data type* (*ADT*) is a collection of data items together with operations on the data. An *implementation of an ADT* consists of storage structures for the data items and algorithms for performing the operations.

- The main properties of an *array* are: (1) it has a fixed-size; (2) it is a sequence; and (3) its elements must all be of the same type. Its basic operation is the *subscript operator*, which provides direct access to each element in the array by specifying its position.

- Direct access is achieved by an address translation that produces the offset from the base address of the array to the element's position. An array variable is actually a pointer to this element; that is, its value is the base address of the array.

- An array is passed to a function by passing its base address. This means that arrays are always passed by reference, so that modifying an array parameter will also modify the corresponding argument.

- Most C++ compilers do not check whether indices are within the range determined by an array's declaration. Allowing an index to get out of bounds can produce some puzzling results.

- The capacity of an array cannot change during program execution.

- An array is not an object (in the OOP sense) because it has no built-in operations.

- An *n*-dimensional array can be viewed as a one-dimensional array whose elements are $n-1$ dimensional arrays.

- An array reference array[i] is equivalent to the pointer dereference *(array + i).

- Elements of a dynamic array can be accessed by using the subscript operator in the same manner as for static arrays.

- Pointer arithmetic operations are the following:
  - increment (++), decrement (––)
  - pointer + an integer, pointer – an integer
  - pointer += an integer, pointer –= an integer

- By default, the new operator throws an exception when a memory request cannot be satisfied. If it is used in the form new(nothrow), no exception will be thrown but the null address 0 will be returned.

■ To avoid *memory leaks,* dynamically-allocated memory should always be deallocated by means of the `delete` operation when it is no longer needed.

■ The `->` operator can be used in an expression of the form `ptr->member` to access a member of a struct (or class). This is equivalent to the expression `(*ptr).member`.

■ *Procedural programming* focuses on writing subprograms (procedures/functions/subroutines) to perform various tasks required in a problem. *Object-oriented programming* focuses on the objects in the problem.

☞ Programming Pointers

1. In C++

   ■ Arrays are zero-based.

   ■ Supplying more initial values in an array declaration than the array's capacity is an error. If too few initial values are supplied, 0 is used to initialize the remaining elements.

   ■ The capacity of `char` arrays should be large enough to store the terminating null character.

   ■ It is good practice to associate type identifiers with arrays (using `typedef`) and then use these type identifiers to declare the types of array objects.

   ■ Modifying an array parameter in a function modifies the corresponding array argument.

2. Arithmetic operations on pointers are restricted. For example, pointer values (memory addresses) cannot be added, subtracted, multiplied, or divided. However, we can increment a pointer with `++`, decrement it with `--`, add an integer value `i` to it, or subtract `i` from it. These operations change the address in the pointer by adding/subtracting `sizeof(Type)` for the first two operations and `i * sizeof(Type)` for the last two, where Type is the type to which the pointer is bound.

3. Use `#include <new>` to enable the standard `new` and `delete` operations in a program.

4. When memory is allocated using the `nothrow` version of `new`, the value returned can be tested to check whether the operation failed by checking if the null address 0 was returned. For the non-nothrow version of `new`, a `bad_alloc` exception is thrown if the operation fails and execution will terminate automatically unless the `try-catch` mechanism is used to catch and handle the exception.

5. Memory locations that were once associated with a pointer variable and that are no longer needed should be returned to the heap by using the `delete` function. Special care is required to avoid memory leaks. For example, if p and q are pointer variables bound to the same type, the assignment statement `p = q;` causes p to point to the same memory location as that pointed to by q. Any memory location previously pointed to by p becomes inaccessible and cannot be disposed of properly unless it is pointed to by some other pointer. Temporary pointers should be used to maintain access, as the following statements demonstrate:

   ```
   tempPtr = p;
   p = q;
   delete tempPtr;
   ```

6. Any attempt to dereference a null or an undefined pointer will normally generate a runtime error. In some versions of C++, however, execution proceeds using some "garbage" memory location, which may obviously produce incorrect results. This is known as the *dangling pointer problem.*

7. Changing the value of a variable in a statement in which that variable is not named is generally considered poor programming practice, because it produces a difficult-to-find logical error. This is known as the *aliasing problem*.

▲ ADT Tips

1. *Data abstraction*, in which the definition of the data type is separated from its implementation, is an important concept in software design.

2. As an ADT, an *array* is a fixed-size sequence of elements, all of the same type, each of which can be accessed by specifying its position. Its basic operation is direct access to each element in the array by specifying its position so that values can be retrieved from or stored in that position.

3. Arrays are appropriate for organizing *homogeneous* data collections.

4. Arrays have the following weaknesses:
   - Their capacity cannot change during execution.
   - They are not self-contained.

5. Dynamically-allocated arrays can have their capacities set during execution.

6. Pointers along with dynamic memory allocation and deallocation will prove useful in later chapters in building data structures that can grow and shrink as needed.

7. C-style structs are compatible with procedural programming, but not with object-oriented programming, because they do not provide for built-in operations for objects (although C++ structs do).

▣ Programming Problems

Section 3.2

1. Letter grades are sometimes assigned to numeric scores by using the grading scheme commonly known as *grading on the curve*. In this scheme, a letter grade is assigned to a numeric score according to the following table:

x = Numeric Score	Letter Grade
$x < m - \frac{3}{2}\sigma$	F
$m - \frac{3}{2}\sigma \leq x < m - \frac{1}{2}\sigma$	D
$m - \frac{1}{2}\sigma \leq x < m + \frac{1}{2}\sigma$	C
$m + \frac{1}{2}\sigma \leq x < m + \frac{3}{2}\sigma$	B
$m + \frac{3}{2}\sigma \leq x$	A

Here, m is the mean score and σ is the standard deviation; for a set of n numbers $x_1, x_2, \ldots,$ x_n, these are defined as follows (where $\sum\limits_{i=1}^{n}$ denotes the sum as i ranges from a to b):

$$m = \frac{1}{n}\sum_{i=1}^{n} x_i \qquad \sigma = \sqrt{\frac{1}{n}\sum_{i=1}^{n}(x_i - m)^2}$$

Write a program to read a list of real numbers representing numeric scores, call functions to calculate their mean and standard deviation, and then call a function to determine and display the letter grade corresponding to each numeric score.

2. Peter the postman became bored one night and, to break the monotony of the night shift, he carried out the following experiment with a row of mailboxes in the post office. These mailboxes were numbered 1 through 150, and beginning with mailbox 2, he opened the doors of all the even-numbered mailboxes, leaving the others closed. Next, beginning with mailbox 3, he went to every third mail box, opening its door if it were closed, and closing it if it were open. Then he repeated this procedure with every fourth mailbox, then every fifth mailbox, and so on. When he finished, he was surprised at the distribution of closed mailboxes. Write a program to determine which mailboxes these were.

3. A prime number is an integer greater than 1 whose only positive divisors are 1 and the integer itself. The Greek mathematician Eratosthenes developed an algorithm, known as the *Sieve of Eratosthenes*, for finding all prime numbers less than or equal to a given number n—that is, all primes in the range 2 through n. Consider the list of numbers from 2 through n. Two is the first prime number, but the multiples of 2 (4, 6, 8, . . .) are not, and so they are crossed out in the list. The first number after 2 that was not crossed out is 3, the next prime. We then cross out from the list all higher multiples of 3 (6, 9, 12, . . .). The next number not crossed out is 5, the next prime, and so we cross out all higher multiples of 5 (10, 15, 20, . . .). We repeat this procedure until we reach the first number in the list that has not been crossed out and whose square is greater than n. All the numbers that remain in the list are the primes from 2 through n. Write a program that uses this sieve method and an array to find all the prime numbers from 2 through n. Execute the program for $n = 550$ and for $n = 5500$.

4. Write a program to add two large integers with up to 300 digits. One approach is to treat each number as a list, each of whose elements is a block of digits of that number. For example, the integer 179,534,672,198 might be stored with *block*[0] = 198, *block*[1] = 672, *block*[2] = 534, *block*[3] = 179. Then add two integers (lists), element by element, carrying from one element to the next when necessary.

5. Proceeding as in Problem 4, write a program to multiply two large integers with up to 300 digits.

Section 3.3

6. A demographic study of the metropolitan area around Dogpatch divided it into three regions—urban, suburban, and exurban—and published the following table showing the annual migration from one region to another (the numbers represent percentages):

	Urban	Suburban	Exurban
Urban	1.1	0.3	0.7
Suburban	0.1	1.2	0.3
Exurban	0.2	0.6	1.3

For example, 0.3 percent of the urbanites (0.003 times the current population) move to the suburbs each year. The diagonal entries represent internal growth rates. Using a two-dimensional array with an enumerated type for the indices to store this table, write a program to determine the population of each region after 10, 20, 30, 40, and 50 years. Assume that the initial populations of the urban, suburban, and exurban regions are 2.1 million, 1.4 million, and 0.9 million, respectively.

7. If A and B are two $m \times n$ matrices, their *sum* is defined as follows: If A_{ij} and B_{ij} are the entries in the ith row and jth column of A and B, respectively, then $A_{ij} + B_{ij}$ is the entry in the ith row and jth column of their sum, which will also be an $m \times n$ matrix. Write a program to read two $m \times n$ matrices, display them, and calculate and display their sum.

8. The product of an $m \times n$ matrix A with an $n \times p$ matrix B is the $m \times p$ matrix $C = A * B$ whose entry C_{ij} in the ith row and jth column is given by

$$C_{ij} = \text{the sum of the products of the entries of row } i \text{ of } A \text{ with column } j \text{ of } B$$
$$= A_{i1} * B_{1j} + A_{i2} * B_{2j} + \ldots + A_{in} * B_{nj}$$

Write a program that will read two matrices A and B, display them, and calculate and display their product (or a message indicating that it is not defined).

9. A *magic square* is an $n \times n$ matrix in which each of the integers $1, 2, 3, \ldots, n^2$ appears exactly once and all column sums, row sums, and diagonal sums are equal. For example, the following is a 5×5 magic square in which all the rows, columns, and diagonals add up to 65:

17	24	1	8	15
23	5	7	14	16
4	6	13	20	22
10	12	19	21	3
11	18	25	2	9

The following is a procedure for constructing an $n \times n$ magic square for any odd integer n. Place 1 in the middle of the top row. Then, after integer k has been placed, move up one row and one column to the right to place the next integer $k + 1$, unless one of the following occurs:

■ If a move takes you above the top row in the jth column, move to the bottom of the jth column and place $k + 1$ there.

- If a move takes you outside to the right of the square in the ith row, place $k + 1$ in the ith row at the left side.

- If a move takes you to an already filled square or if you move out of the square at the upper right-hand corner, place $k + 1$ immediately below k.

Write a program to construct an $n \times n$ magic square for any odd value of n.

10. Suppose that each of the four edges of a thin square metal plate is maintained at a constant temperature and that we wish to determine the steady-state temperature at each interior point of the plate. To do this, we divide the plate into squares (the corners of which are called *nodes*) and find the temperature at each interior node by averaging the four neighboring temperatures; that is, if T_{ij} denotes the old temperature at the node in row i and column j, then

$$\frac{T_{i-1j} + T_{ij-1} + T_{ij+1} + T_{i+1,j}}{4}$$

will be the new temperature.

To model the plate, we can use a two-dimensional array, with each array element representing the temperature at one of the nodes. Write a program that first reads the four constant temperatures (possibly different) along the edges of the plate, and some guess of the temperature at the interior points, and uses these values to initialize the elements of the array. Then determine the steady-state temperature at each interior node by repeatedly averaging the temperatures at its four neighbors, as just described. Repeat this procedure until the new temperature at each interior node differs from the old temperature at that node by no more than some specified small amount. Then print the array and the number of iterations used to produce the final result. (It may also be of interest to print the array at each stage of the iteration.)

11. The game of *Life*, invented by the mathematician John H. Conway, is intended to model life in a society of organisms. Consider a rectangular array of cells, each of which may contain an organism. If the array is viewed as extending indefinitely in both directions, then each cell has eight neighbors, the eight cells surrounding it. In each generation, births and deaths occur according to the following rules:

- An organism is born in any empty cell having exactly three neighbors.

- An organism dies from isolation if it has fewer than two neighbors.

- An organism dies from overcrowding if it has more than three neighbors.

- All other organisms survive.

To illustrate, the following shows the first five generations of a particular configuration of organisms:

Write a program to play the game of *Life* and investigate the patterns produced by various initial configurations. Some configurations die off rather rapidly; others repeat after a certain number of generations; others change shape and size and may move across the array; and still others may produce "gliders" that detach themselves from the society and sail off into space.

Section 3.4

12. Write a program for the grading-on-the-curve problem in Problem 2, but use a dynamically-allocated array.

13. Write a program for the Peter-the-postman problem in Problem 3, but use a dynamically-allocated array.

14. Write a program for the prime-number-finder problem in Problem 4, but use a dynamically-allocated array.

4

More about OOP and ADTs—Classes

CHAPTER CONTENTS

Chapter Objectives

- Contrast object-oriented programming with procedural programming.
- Review classes in C++.
- Study in detail a specific example of how a class is built.
- Show how operators can be overloaded for new types.
- Show how conditional compilation directives are used to avoid redundant declarations.
- Discuss pointers to class objects—the this pointer, in particular.

In Chapter 1 we described the software development process and noted that this text would focus on the design phase and, in particular, on data structures and abstract data types. These were described in some detail in the preceding two chapters and illustrated with examples with which you are perhaps already familiar.

Chapter 1 also mentioned that our primary design approach in this text would be object-oriented. We briefly introduced OOP there, and in this chapter we will begin studying it in earnest. We will first compare and contrast it with *procedural programming*, which has been the major programming paradigm for many years.

The rest of the chapter will be a study of C++ classes. Classes are precisely what is needed to implement most ADTs and are at the core of object-oriented programming. We will show how the data type Time described in the preceding chapter in the context of procedural programming can be redesigned as a class that is consistent with the object-oriented paradigm. Because your study of classes may have focused on *using* classes with little (if any) practice in *building* classes, we will be much more detailed in our study of classes than we were for the data types in the preceding chapter. If your experience with classes is more extensive, you may choose to skim or skip over some of these extended presentations.

4.1 Procedural vs. Object-Oriented Programming

In Section 3.6 we described the *procedural-programming* paradigm and illustrated it by developing a Time data type for modeling time objects. As we noted there, this approach to programming is *action oriented* because it focuses on the tasks that must be done to solve a problem. Functions, procedures, or subroutines are developed to carry out these tasks. For example, the Time library (see Figure 3.11) included set(), display(), advance(), and lessThan() functions that set a Time value to a specified time, output a Time value, advance a Time value by a specified amount, and compare two Time values, respectively. One thing to note about these functions is that they all process Time values that are sent to them via parameters. This is characteristic of procedural programming (PP). The data is stored in some data structure and shipped around between various functions/procedures/subroutines for processing. Note that the documentation for the functions in Figure 3.11 uses "receive" and "pass back" specifications that reflect this behavior.

This is in contrast to the **object-oriented-programming paradigm** where a programmer determines what objects are needed for a problem and how they should work together to solve the problem. The focus of OOP is thus on objects rather than on subprograms, on the *nouns* in the specification of the problem rather than on the *verbs*.

In the object-oriented-programming paradigm, programmers concentrate on creating types called *classes*, which contain *data members* and *function members* that operate on the data. The functions are actually part of the structure, and we "send a message" to an object telling it to "operate on itself" using one of these functions. The specifications of these functions are usually expressed as *preconditions* that describe the state of an object before it is operated upon and *postconditions* that describe its state afterward.

If we think of the Time data type as modeling a digital watch, then the procedural approach is analogous to wrapping up your digital watch whenever it needs to be set, displayed, advanced, or compared with another one and sending it somewhere to have that operation performed. The service facility performs the required task and then returns the watch to you. Although this is appropriate for some operations such as repairing a watch, it is not appropriate for the time operations we are considering. For example, having to ship our watch somewhere every time we need to set it would be very inconvenient to say the least. And how ludicrous it would be if, whenever we want to know what time it is, we have to send the watch someplace where they put it in display mode (perhaps by turning on the backlight) and then send it back to us.

In the next section we will develop a Time data type using the OOP approach. To set a digital watch in OOP, we push a button sending a message to the watch to put itself in set mode and accept new values for hours and minutes; to display the time, we push a button that sends a message to the watch to turn on its backlight; and so on. This approach obviously models a digital watch more realistically than the procedural approach.

✔ **Quick Quiz 4.1**

Answer Questions 1–5 with "procedural programming" or "object-oriented programming."

1. The focus of _____ is on developing subprograms to perform certain tasks.
2. The focus of _____ is on identifying objects and how they should work together to solve a problem.
3. _____ focuses on the verbs of a problem's specification whereas _____ focuses on its nouns.
4. In _____, data items being processed are passed from one subprogram to another.
5. In _____, messages are sent to an object instructing it to operate on itself in some way.

4.2 Classes

In Section 3.5 *structs* were described as they are used in the C programming language. C++ retains structs from its parent language, but it also provides *classes*. Structs and classes have similarities:

- Both can be used to model objects with different attributes (characteristics) represented as *data members*. They can thus be used to organize nonhomogeneous data sets.
- They have essentially the same syntax.

The basic difference is the following:

- *Members of a class by default are private* (cannot be accessed from outside an object), whereas *members of a struct by default are public* (can be accessed from outside an object). In C++, the access privileges—private or public—can be specified explicitly for both structs and classes.

Thus, choosing whether to use a struct or a class in C++ is not based on their capabilities. In C++, a struct is simply a class in which all members are public by default.

Differences between "Traditional" (C) Structs and OOP (C++) Structs and Classes

Structs and classes in C++ are extensions of C's structs. Like C-style structs, they may contain **data members** (also called **data fields** or **attribute members**) to represent *attributes* (*characteristics*) of objects being modeled. But the main difference between structs and classes in C++ and structs in C is that they may also contain **function members** (also called **member functions** or **methods**[1]) to represent *operations* (*behaviors*) of those objects. This is an important difference for the following reasons:

- It provides a way to implement ADTs because the storage for the data items and the functions for the basic operations can be **encapsulated** in a single structure.

---

[1] It is common to call the two parts of a class *data members* and *member functions*. ("Data members" and "function members" are really more correct.) We will use the terms *function members* and *member functions* interchangeably.

- It leads to a new style of programming—*object-oriented* rather than *procedural*. Objects can now be **self-contained**, carrying their own operations around with them—sometimes called the **I-can-do-it-myself principle**—instead of having to be shipped off to external functions that operate on them and send them back.

In this text we will follow the practice that many programmers use: *Structs will be used only in the C-sense—that is, to encapsulate only data; classes will be used whenever both data and operations are to be encapsulated.*

Class Declarations

The general form of a class declaration that we will use in this text is as follows:

Class Declaration

Form:
```
class ClassName
{
 public:
   Declarations of public members
 private:
   Declarations of private members
};
```

Notes:

1. Declarations of the data members are normally placed in the private section and declarations (prototypes) of the function members are placed in the public section.
2. Public members can be accessed by both member and nonmember functions.
3. Private members can be accessed only by member functions (and by friend functions described later).
4. Some programmers prefer to put the private section first. In this text we will put the public section first to emphasize the operations that make up the public user interface.
5. Although not commonly done, a class may have several private and public sections; the keyword `private` followed by a colon (`:`) marks the beginning of each private section and the keyword `public` followed by a colon (`:`) marks the beginning of each public section.
6. *Warning: A semicolon (;) must appear after the closing brace of a class declaration. Omitting it is a common error that can be difficult to find.*

Class Libraries   Class declarations are usually placed in a file called a **header file** (or **interface file**) whose name is the class name followed by a ".h" extension: `ClassName.h`. To see an example, refer back to Section 1.3. Figure 1.11 shows the header file `FinancialAidAward.h` for a class named `FinancialAidAward`.

The following is the class declaration in this header file, but with the documentation of the function members omitted here to save space:

```
class FinancialAidAward
{
 public: // Function members

    //-- Constructors
    FinancialAidAward();
    FinancialAidAward(string src, double amt);

    //-- Accessors
    double getAmount() const;
    string getSource() const;

    //-- Output
    void display() const;

    //-- Mutators
    void setAmount(double newAmount);
    void setSource(string newSource);

  private: // Data members
    string source;      // source of financial aid
    double amount;      // amount of financial aid

}; // end of class declaration
```

Except in special cases that we will describe later, only the prototypes of function members are placed inside the class declaration. Their definitions are usually placed in a separate file called an **implementation file** whose name matches that of the corresponding header file, but with the .h extension replaced by .cpp: *Class-Name*.cpp.[2] Figure 1.12 in Section 1.3 shows the implementation file FinancialAid-Award.cpp for the FinancialAidAward class.

These two files make up a library called a **class library**, and programs that wish to use the class defined in this library are called **client programs**. Such a program must include the library's header with a compiler directive of the form

```
#include "ClassName.h"
```

For example, the program in Figure 1.10 for testing a financial aid update function uses

```
#include "FinancialAidAward.h"     // FinancialAidAward class
```

to include the header file for the FinancialAidAward class. Note the difference between the notation

```
#include "FinancialAidAward.h"
```

---

[2] Or with some other compiler-dependent suffix such as .cp or .cc.

used for the `FinancialAidAward` library's header file and the notation

```
#include <iostream>
```

used for the `iostream` library. The *angle brackets* (< and >) in the second case inform the C++ compiler that this is one of the standard libraries. By contrast, enclosing the name of a library's header file in *double quotes* indicates to the C++ compiler that this is a programmer-defined library.

Translating a Library   Translation of a program consists of two separate steps:

1. **Compilation,** in which a source program is translated to an equivalent machine-language program, called an *object program*, which is stored in an *object file,* and
2. **Linking,** in which any calls to functions that are defined in a library are linked to their definitions, creating an *executable program*, which is stored in an *executable file*.

Since a programmer-defined library must also be compiled (if it hasn't been already), translation of a program that uses a library may require three separate actions:

1. separate compilation of the program's source file, creating an object file;
2. separate compilation of the library's implementation file, creating a different object file (unless the library's implementation file has already been compiled);
3. linking function calls in the program's object file to the function definitions in the library's object file, creating an executable program.

The diagram in Figure 4.1 illustrates this process. The dashed arrows from the library header file to the program source file and the library implementation indicate that this header file gets compiled also, by virtue of its being included in these files.

Figure 4.1 Program Translation

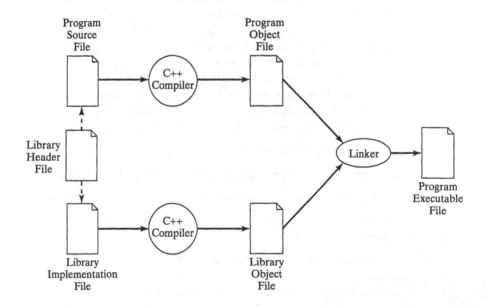

Exactly how this multi-file translation is carried out will depend on the system being used. In a command-line environment such as GNU C++, separate commands can be used to compile the program and each library that hasn't already been compiled and another command can be used to link the resulting object files together; for example,

```
g++ -c client.cpp
g++ -c ClassName.cpp
g++ client.o ClassName.o -o client
```

The first command compiles the program client.cpp (including the header file ClassName.h of the class library) and produces an object file client.o. In a similar manner, the second command compiles the implementation file ClassName.cpp and produces an object file ClassName.o. The last command links these two object files together and produces the binary executable client. (The single command g++ client.cpp ClassName.cpp -o client will cause all three commands to be executed.)

In integrated environments such as *Metrowerks CodeWarrior* and *Visual C++*, a multi-file translation is coordinated by a special file called a *project*. Using appropriate menu choices, one creates a project and adds source files such as client.cpp and ClassName.cpp. Once this has been done, another menu choice can be used to automatically compile each file in the project, link the resulting object files into a binary executable, and then run the resulting executable.

Objects   A particular instance of a class is called an **object**; that is, the type of an object is a class:

```
ClassName objectName;
```

(This is the "object" in *object-oriented programming*.) For example, the program in Figure 1.10 used the statements

```
const int NUMBER_OF_RECORDS = 3;
StudentAidRecord arr[NUMBER_OF_RECORDS];
```

to declare an array arr of StudentAidRecord objects.

An object can access its public members by using the **dot operator**:

```
objectName.memberName
```

For example, in the for loop

```
for (int i = 0; i < NUMBER_OF_RECORDS; i++)
{
    arr[i].display();
    cout << endl;
}
```

in Figure 1.10, the statement

```
arr[i].display();
```

sends a message to the StudentAidRecord object arr[i] to display itself using its display() function member.

This concludes our quick overview of class declarations, class libraries, client programs, and objects. We next take a very detailed look at how to build a class, namely, a Time class.

✔ **Quick Quiz 4.2**

1. What is the basic difference between structs and classes?
2. Unlike C's structs, C++ structs and classes can contain both _____ members and _____ members.
3. What is the I-can-do-it-myself principle?
4. A class declaration is usually put in a(n) _____ file whose name has the form *ClassName*.h.
5. Definitions of the function members of class are usually put in a(n) _____ file whose name has the form *ClassName*.cpp.
6. What two steps are involved in translating a program?
7. Compiling a program creates a(n) _____ program that is stored in a(n) _____ file.
8. To create an executable program, each function call in a program must be _____ to the definition of that function, which may be in a library.
9. A particular instance of a class is called a(n) _____.

4.3 Example: A First Version of a User-Defined Time Class

In the Time data type developed in the preceding chapter, Time values were structs with four data members—hour, minute, AMorPM, and milTime—and they were processed by passing them around among various functions—set(), display(), advance(), and lessThan(). As we noted in Section 4.1, we might think of the approach as follows. Whenever it is necessary to set the time, display it, advance it, or compare it with another time, we wrap up our digital watch and send it off to the manufacturer or some service company who will process it and then send it back to us, perhaps changing the watch as requested—set or advanced—or sending back some value—the time displayed on the watch or in the case of lessThan(), a value of true or false to indicate the outcome of the comparison of two watches that were sent to it.

We will now use an OOP approach that models a digital watch more realistically. In this approach we can think of sending messages to the watch, perhaps by pushing buttons, and asking it to perform various operations on itself. To emphasize this *I-can-do-it-myself principle*, we will use names of the form *myThis* and *myThat* for the data members as a reminder that a Time object is operating on itself.

We will proceed quite slowly and methodically in our study of classes and how they are used to define new data types, because this may be your first look at how such classes are designed and built. Accordingly, the first version of a class Time in Figure 4.2 is deliberately kept simple by focusing on only two of the operations, set and display.

Figure 4.2 Interface for Time Data Type—OOP Approach

```
/*-- Time.h ---------------------------------------------------------

   This header file defines the data type Time for processing time.
   Basic operations are:
      set:     To set the time
      display: To display the time
-------------------------------------------------------------------*/


#include <iostream>

class Time
{
 public:
/******** Function Members ********/
  void set(unsigned hours, unsigned minutes, char am_pm);
  /*-----------------------------------------------------------------

     Set the data members of a Time object to specified values.

     Preconditions: 1 <= hours <= 12, 0 <= minutes <= 59,
         and am_pm is either 'A' or 'P'.
     Postcondition: Data members myHours, myMinutes, and myAMorPM
         are set to hours, minutes, and am_pm, respectively, and
         myMilTime to the equivalent military time.
     -------------------------------------------------------------*/


  void display(ostream & out) const;
  /*-----------------------------------------------------------------

     Display time in standard and military format using output stream out.

     Precondition:  The ostream out is open.
     Postcondition: The time represented by this Time object has been
         inserted into ostream out.
     -------------------------------------------------------------*/


 private:
/********** Data Members **********/
  unsigned myHours,
          myMinutes;
  char myAMorPM;        // 'A' or 'P'
  unsigned myMilTime;   // military time equivalent

}; // end of class declaration
```

▲

Note the keyword `const` at the end of the heading for function member `display()`. This makes `display()` a **const function**, which means that it cannot modify any of the data members in the class. Any attempt to do so or any action that has the potential of modifying a data member (such as sending it to some other function that might) will produce a compile-time error. Whenever a function member should not modify any of the class's data members, it is good practice to prototype and define it as a const function.

Notice also that, unlike the `display()` function in our procedural-programming example in Section 3.6, the `display()` function member for our `Time` class has a reference parameter declared by `ostream & out`. This allows us to use `display()` with various `ostream` objects, as in

```
mealTime.display(cout);
```

and

```
mealTime.display(cerr);
```

and because class `ofstream` is derived from `ostream` (see Section 5.1), we can also use `display()` with `ofstream` objects to produce output to a file:

```
mealTime.display(outStream);
```

The `ostream` *parameter* `out` *must be a reference parameter* so that it is an alias for the corresponding `ostream` argument. When we call `display()` with `cout`, for example, as in

```
mealTime.display(cout);
```

and `display()` inserts output into `out`, we want it to actually be going into `cout` so that it will appear on the screen. If `out` were a value parameter instead, it would be a copy of `cout` rather than an alias for it.

 ### Why not make all class members public?

The main reason for making a class's data members private is to make them inaccessible to users of the class. This is known as **information hiding**. Allowing client programs to access the data members of an object directly could result in invalid values being stored in the data members—for example, 123 in `myHours`, 99 in `myMinutes` and 'X' in `myAMorPM`, making a `Time` object represent the invalid time 123:99 X.M.

Another reason for information hiding is that, over time, as a class is used, it sometimes becomes apparent that it needs to be updated by modifying some of the data members, perhaps adding some new ones and possibly removing others. Possible reasons for making these changes include the following:

- The class will better model some real-world object.
- Operations can be performed more efficiently.
- Operations can be implemented more easily.

If client programs are allowed access to the data members directly, then these programs depend directly on those data members. They must all be modified if the class's data members are modified, which results in the following:

- Increased upgrade time
- Increased programmer cost

- Decreased programmer productivity
- Reduced profits due to:
  - Software late getting to market with the possible result of losing out to competitors
  - Loss of customer confidence in software reliability

Keeping the data members "hidden" forces programs to interact with an object through its public function members, which provide the **interface** between programs and the class. If this interface does not change, then programs that use an object will not require change.

> **THE CARDINAL RULE OF INFORMATION HIDING**
> *Hide the data members of a class by making them private.*

Implementation of a Class

As we noted in the preceding section, the declaration of a class is usually placed in a header file `ClassName.h`, where `ClassName` is the name of the class, and the definitions of the class's function members are usually placed in the corresponding implementation file `ClassName.cpp`. Because these function definitions are outside the class declaration where their prototypes are located and because other classes may have function members with the same names, the compiler must be told to which class these definitions belong. This is done by using the **scope operator** `::` to prepend the class name to the function name:

```
ReturnType ClassName::functionName(param_declaration_list)
{
    . . .
}
```

The resulting name of the form `ClassName::functionName` is called the **qualified name** or the **full name** of the function.

Figure 4.3 shows an implementation file for the Time class.[3] Note that the corresponding header file Time.h must be included in this file. Also note that a class's implementation file may contain definitions of other functions that are not member functions. In this example, there is a utility function for converting from standard to military time. (Another to convert from military time to standard time will be added later.) Whether to make such functions class members is a design decision. They could always be added later.

---

[3] Two of the function definitions contain a **conditional expression** of the form

```
(condition ? expression₁ : expression₂)
```

The value of this expression will be the value of *expression₁* if *condition* is true and will be the value of *expression₂* if it is false.

Figure 4.3 Implementation of Time Data Type—OOP Approach

```cpp
/*-- Time.cpp-------------------------------------------------------

    Definitions of the function members of the Time class declared
    in Time.h and definitions of utility functions that convert
    between military and standard time.

    -----------------------------------------------------------------*/

#include <iostream>
using namespace std;

#include "Time.h"

/*** Utility Functions -- Prototypes ***/

int toMilitary(unsigned hours, unsigned minutes, char am_pm);

//----- Definition of set function -----

void Time::set(unsigned hours, unsigned minutes, char am_pm)
{
   // Check class invariant
   if (hours >= 1 && hours <= 12 &&
       minutes >= 0 && minutes <= 59 &&
       (am_pm == 'A' || am_pm == 'P'))
   {
      myHours = hours;
      myMinutes = minutes;
      myAMorPM = am_pm;
      myMilTime = toMilitary(hours, minutes, am_pm);
   }
   else
     cerr << "*** Can't set time with these values ***\n";
   // Object's data members remain unchanged
}


//----- Definition of display function -----
```

Figure 4.3 (continued)

```cpp
void Time::display(ostream & out) const
{
   out << myHours << ':'
       << (myMinutes < 10 ? "0" : "") << myMinutes
       << ' ' << myAMorPM << ".M.  ("
       << myMilTime << " mil. time)";
}


/*** Utility Functions -- Definitions ***/
int toMilitary(unsigned hours, unsigned minutes, char am_pm)
/*-------------------------------------------------------------------
   Convert standard time to military time.

   Precondition:  hours, minutes, am_pm satisfy the class invariant.
   Postcondition: Military time equivalent is returned.
----------------------------------------------------------------*/
{
   if (hours == 12)
      hours = 0;

   return hours * 100 + minutes + (am_pm == 'P' ? 1200 : 0);
}
```

▲

To test this first version of class Time, we might use a test-driver program like that in Figure 4.4.

Figure 4.4 Test Driver for Time Data Type

```cpp
//--- Test driver for class Time

#include <iostream>
using namespace std;
#include "Time.h"

int main()
{
   Time mealTime;

   mealTime.set(5, 30, 'P');
```

Figure 4.4 (continued)

```
    cout << "We'll be eating at ";
    mealTime.display(cout);
    cout << endl;

    cout << "\nNow trying to set time with illegal hours (13)" << endl;
    mealTime.set(13, 0, 'A');
    cout << "Now trying to set time with illegal minutes (60)" << endl;
    mealTime.set(5, 60, 'A');
    cout << "Now trying to set time with illegal AM/PM ('X')" << endl;
    mealTime.set(5, 30, 'X');
}
```

Execution Trace:

```
We'll be eating at 5:30 P.M.   (1730 mil. time)

Now trying to set time with illegal hours (13)
*** Can't set time with these values ***
Now trying to set time with illegal minutes (60)
*** Can't set time with these values ***
Now trying to set time with illegal AM/PM ('X')
*** Can't set time with these values ***
```

▲

Again, note the difference from the procedural approach. Rather than ship the object mealTime off to various functions for processing, *we send messages to the object to operate on itself.* For example, to set my digital watch to 5:30 P.M., I don't wrap it up and mail it off somewhere to have it set; rather, I push a button. Similarly, to display the time, I don't wrap up my watch and mail if off somewhere and have them tell me what time it is. I have it display the time to me itself, perhaps pushing a button to turn on the backlight so that I can see it.

Some Observations

■ Because member functions are members of a class object, they can operate on that object without having it passed to them via a parameter. Another way to view this is as follows:

● *A member function receives the class object to be operated on implicitly, rather than explicitly via a parameter.*

This is not the case for nonmember functions, however; thus,

● *If a nonmember function needs to operate on an object, it must receive it via a parameter.*

- We usually put the prototypes of function members inside the class declaration and their definitions in the implementation file; the function names in these definitions must be qualified with the scope operator (::).

- If a function member is simple (e.g., fewer than 5 or 6 operations), some programmers will put its definition (instead of its prototype) inside the class declaration. In this case, the compiler will treat it as an **inline** function, which means that it may replace each call to this function with the actual code of the function, replacing each parameter with the corresponding argument.[4] This saves the usual overhead of a function call (see Section 7.4), but it does clutter the class's interface and may result in "code bloat."

In our early examples, we will not emphasize function inlining and will put all function definitions in a class's implementation file.

- A **class invariant** should be formulated that can be tested to ensure that the data members always contain valid values. Whenever an operation modifies any of the data members, it should always establish that the class invariant still holds. This means that other member functions are guaranteed of each data member's validity and need not check it themselves. For example, for class Time, the class invariant is

$(1 \le$ myHours $\le 12)$ and $(0 \le$ myMinutes $\le 59)$ and
(myAMorPM has the value 'A' or 'P')

In set(), we tested the arguments to ensure that this invariant would be true after the function is executed:

```
if (hours >= 1 && hours <= 12 &&
    minutes >= 0 && minutes <= 59 &&
    (am_pm == 'A' || am_pm == 'P'))
{
  myMinutes = minutes;
  myAMorPM = am_pm;
  myMilTime = toMilitary(hours, minutes, am_pm);
}
else
  cerr << "*** Can't set time with these values ***\n";
```

An alternative way to test this is to use the **assert() mechanism** (from <cassert>):

```
#include <cassert>

//----- Function to implement the set operation -----
void Time::set(unsigned hours, unsigned minutes,
               char am_pm)
{
  assert(hours >= 1 && hours <= 12 &&
         minutes >= 0 && minutes <= 59 &&
         (am_pm == 'A' || am_pm == 'P'));
```

---

[4] An alternative way to inline a function member is to put it's definition below the class declaration in the header file, qualifying its name as usual, but precede its heading with the specifier inline.

```
        myMinutes = minutes;
        myAMorPM = am_pm;
        myMilTime = toMilitary(hours, minutes, am_pm);
    }
```

The error messages generated by `assert()` may not be very clear to a user, however. Thus, although this is convenient to use while debugging, it is good practice to switch to an `if-else` statement as described earlier once the correctness of the definition has been verified.

- Function members that ought not modify any of the class's data members should be prototyped and defined as const functions. Attempts to change data members or putting them in danger of being modified (e.g., by sending them to some other function that might modify them) will result in compiler errors.

4.4 Class Constructors

Constructing an object consists of

1. *allocating memory* for the object, and
2. *initializing* the object.

In our example, for the declaration

```
Time mealTime;
```

memory will be allocated for `mealTime`'s data members, but because default value are not specified for these data members, we can only assume that they contain "garbage" values. For example, `myHours` might have the value –17834, `myMinutes` the value –99, `myAMorPM` the value '#', and `myMilTime` the value 91903.

```
                mealTime
        myHours    | -17834 |
        myMinutes  |  -99   |
        myAMorPM   |   #    |
        myMilTime  | 91903  |
```

Lack of initialization is a common source of errors. For example, if we forgot to use the `set()` operation to initialize the `Time` object `mealTime`, we might later be using an invalid `Time` object with garbage values like the preceding in the data members.

It would be better if the programmer knew the values with which every `Time` object will be initialized. These could be either

- initial values specified in the `Time` object's declaration, or
- specific default values if no initial values are specified

This can be accomplished by using function members called **constructors**, which have the following properties:

1. *Their primary role (for now) is to initialize the data members of objects (either with default values or with values provided as arguments).*

2. *Their names are always the same as the class name.*

3. *They are public function members.*

4. *They do not return a value; they have no return type (not even* void*). Often they are quite simple and can be inlined.*

5. *A constructor gets called whenever an object is declared.*

6. *If no constructor is given in a class, memory will still be allocated for each data member of an object.*

 Because of the importance of initialization, *constructors should be the first function members that are written when building a class.* Although we deviated from this policy in our Time class in order to demonstrate what happens in a class with no constructors, we will follow this guideline from here on.

We will have two constructors for our Time class: a **default constructor** that has no arguments and that initializes a Time object to a default value of our choosing (12:00 midnight) and an **explicit-value constructor** that has arguments whose values are used to initialize the data members. Figure 4.5 shows these constructors. (See the source files—*Chap4/Figures4.5-10*—on the text's website for complete versions of Time.h and Time.cpp and a test driver.)

Figure 4.5 Class Constructors for Time Data Type

```
/*-- Time.h -------------------------------------------------------

   This header file defines the data type Time for processing time.
   Basic operations are:
      Default constructor -- Initializes object to 12:00 AM
      Explicit-value constructor
      set:     To set the time
      display: To display the time
-----------------------------------------------------------------*/

#include <iostream>

class Time
{
 public:
 /******** Function Members ********/

   /***** Class constructors *****/
   Time();
   /*-------------------------------------------------------------
      Construct a class object (default).
```

Figure 4.5 (continued)

```
    Precondition:  None.
    Postcondition: The Time object is initialized to 12:00 A.M.;
        that is, myHours, myMinutes, and myAMorPM are initialized
        to 12, 0, 'A', respectively, and myMilTime to 0.
    ------------------------------------------------------------------*/


Time(unsigned initHours, unsigned initMinutes, char initAMPM);
/*-----------------------------------------------------------------
    Construct a class object (explicit values).

    Precondition: initHours, initMinutes, and initAMPM are initial
        values for the data members; they must preserve the class
        invariant.
    Postcondition: Data members myHours, myMinutes, and myAMorPM
        have been initialized to initHours, initMinutes, and initAMPM,
        respectively, and myMilTime to the corresponding military time.
    ------------------------------------------------------------------*/


  /***** Other Function Members *****/
  //----- Prototypes of set(), display()

 private:
 /********** Data Members **********/
    unsigned myHours,
            myMinutes;
    char myAMorPM;          // 'A' or 'P'
    unsigned myMilTime;     // military time equivalent

}; // end of class declaration
```

```
/*-- Time.cpp----------------------------------------------------

    This file implements the Time function members.

    ------------------------------------------------------------------*/


#include "Time.h"
```

Figure 4.5 (continued)

```
/*** Utility Functions -- Prototypes ***/
int toMilitary(unsigned hours, unsigned minutes, char am_pm);

//----- Definition of default constructor
Time::Time()
: myHours(12), myMinutes(0), myAMorPM('A'), myMilTime(0)
{
}


//----- Definition of explicit-value  constructor -----

Time::Time(unsigned initHours, unsigned initMinutes, char initAMPM)
{
   // Check class invariant
   if (initHours >= 1 && initHours <= 12 &&
       initMinutes >= 0 && initMinutes <= 59 &&
       (initAMPM == 'A' || initAMPM == 'P'))
   {
      myHours = initHours;
      myMinutes = initMinutes;
      myAMorPM = initAMPM;
      myMilTime = toMilitary(initHours, initMinutes, initAMPM);
   }
   else
      cerr << "*** Invalid initial values ***\n";
}


//----- Definitions of set(), display(), toMilitary()
```

▲

Defining Constructors   The definition of a class constructor has the following form:

Constructor Definition

Form:

```
ClassName::ClassName(parameter_list)
: member_initalizer_list
{
    // body of constructor definition
}
```

where

the *member_initializer_list* is a list (possibly empty) preceded by a colon and consisting of **member initializers** of the form

dataMember(argument_list)

separated by commas; it may be on the same line as the function heading.

Result:

When the class constructor is called, each member initializer is used to initialize the named data member with the values in *argument_list*, invoking their own constructors for data members that are objects. These initializers are called in the order in which they are declared in the class, not according to their order in the initializer list; to avoid confusion, these should be the same. After the member initializers are finished, the body of the constructor is executed.

We will look first at the default constructor for our Time class. When it is called, the arguments 12, 0, 'A', and 0 are used to initialize the data members myHours, myMinutes, myAMorPM, and myMilTime, respectively. Since there is nothing else for the constructor to do, the function body is empty.

We could have omitted some or all of the member initializers (including the colon if all are omitted) and used assignment statements in the function body instead. For example, we could have written this definition for the default constructor in the following form:

```
Time::Time()
{
    myHours = 12;
    myMinutes = 0;
    myAMorPM = 'A';
    myMilTime = 0;
}
```

The form used in Figure 4.5 is preferred, however, because it is more efficient and because, in some cases, member initializers provide the only way to initialize a data member.[5] We did not use a member-initializer list in the definition of the explicit-value constructor for our Time class because we needed to check the values being sent to it to ensure that they did not violate the class invariant before using them to initialize the data members.

To test our constructors, we might use the following declarations in a driver program:

```
Time mealTime,
     bedTime(11,30,'P');
```

---

[5]   See, for example, Section 10.4.6.1 of *The C++ Programming Language*, Third Edition by Bjarne Stroustrup (Boston, MA: Addison Wesley, 1997).

The first declaration constructs mealTime using the default constructor, since there are no arguments passed to the constructor. Memory is allocated for mealTime and the data members are initialized to 12, 0, 'A', and 0, respectively. The second declaration constructs bedTime using the explicit-value constructor. Memory is allocated for bedTime and the arguments 11, 30, and 'P' are used to initialize the data members myHours, myMinutes, myHours, and myMilTime to 11, 30, 'P', and 2330, respectively.

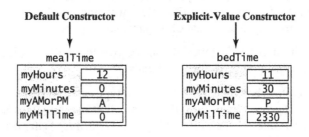

Execution of the statements

```
mealTime.display(cout);
cout << endl;
bedTime.display(cout);
cout << endl;
```

will produce

```
12:00 A.M. (0 mil. time)
11:30 P.M. (2330 mil. time)
```

If we do not provide a constructor for a class, the compiler will generate a default constructor that will simply allocate memory for the data members (and will invoke the default constructors of those that are objects). *If we provide a constructor for a class, we should also provide a default constructor because the compiler will not generate one.* Without a default constructor, declarations of the form

```
ClassName object_name;
```

will not be allowed.

Constructors can also be invoked directly by using construction notation:

```
ClassName(arguments)
```

For example, the statements

```
Time().display(cout);
cout << endl;
Time(1, 2, 'A').display(cout);
cout << endl;
```

will produce

```
12:00 A.M.  (0 mil. time)
1:02 A.M.   (103 mil. time))
```

Even though they are not classes, the C++ fundamental types (int, double, char, bool, etc.) do have default constructors. If *T* denotes any of these types, the value of *T*() is 0 converted to that type. For example, the value of int() is 0 and the value of char() is the null character '\0'.

Overloading Functions   Notice that in our class Time, there are two functions with the same name Time. This is allowed in C++ for ordinary functions as well as function members of a class, provided that the parameter lists of the functions differ in the number and/or types of parameters. Such a function name is said to be **overloaded**. Another way to express the rule governing overloading is in terms of a function's **signature**, which is the list of its parameter types:

The name of a function can be overloaded, provided *no two definitions of the function have the same signature.*

Remember, however, that the return type or void specifier in a function's heading is not part of its signature, which means that *two functions with the same name and the same parameter types but with different return types are not allowed.*

When an overloaded function such as Time() is called, it is the compiler's responsibility to determine which of the collection of overloaded functions is to be used. It does this by comparing the types of the arguments with the signatures in the collection until it finds a match. For example, the function call Time(1, 2, 'A') has the signature int, int, char, so the compiler associates this call with the explicit-value constructor; the function call Time() has an empty signature, so the compiler associates this call with the default constructor;

Default Arguments   C++ allows the use of **default arguments** for functions to supply values for parameters for which there is no corresponding argument. These default values for parameters are specified by using the assignment operator:

```
( . . ., parameter = default_value, . . .)
```

Two important things to remember about default arguments are that

- Parameters with default arguments must be the last parameters in a parameter list; that is, they must appear after all parameters without default arguments.

- Default values cannot be specified in both the prototype and the definition of a function. Usually they are given in function prototypes.

However, one must also be careful when using them, because a program bug can easily result. If you accidentally leave out an argument in a function call, the program may compile and execute but produce incorrect results.

The default-argument mechanism provides an alternative to having two different constructors in our Time class: we can replace them with a single constructor that uses default arguments. We will specify the default values in the constructor's prototype so that any client program that includes Time.h can use them:

```
Time(unsigned initHours = 12, unsigned initMinutes = 0,
     char initAMPM = 'A');
/*-------------------------------------------------------------
   Construct a class object.
```

Precondition: initHours, initMinutes, and initAMPM are initial
    values for the data members; they must preserve the class
    invariant. They have default values 12, 0, and 'A',
    respectively.
Postcondition: Data members myHours, myMinutes, and myAMorPM
    have been initialized to initHours, initMinutes, and
    initAMPM, respectively, or to their default values, and
    myMilTime to the corresponding military time.
--*/

This version of the Time constructor does, in fact, provide the equivalent of four different constructors that correspond to the different combinations of default arguments that are used. For example, the declarations

```
Time t1, t2(5), t3(5, 30), t4(5, 30, 'P');
```

will create four Time objects: t1 is initialized using all three of the default arguments (12, 0, and 'A') to initialize the data members myHours, myMinutes, and myHours; t2 is initialized using the supplied value (5) for myHours and the last two default arguments (0 and 'A') for my-Minutes and myAMorPM; for t3, the supplied values (5 and 30) are used for myHours and myMinutes and the last default argument ('A') is used for myAMorPM; and t4 uses only the supplied arguments (5, 30, and 'P') to initialize myHours, myMinutes, and myHours. The following diagrams summarize:

t1		t2		t3		t4	
myHours	12	myHours	5	myHours	5	myHours	5
myMinutes	0	myMinutes	0	myMinutes	30	myMinutes	30
myAMorPM	A	myAMorPM	A	myAMorPM	A	myAMorPM	P
myMilTime	0	myMilTime	500	myMilTime	530	myMilTime	1730

4.5 Other Class Operations

In addition to the operations for Time objects that we have described in the two preceding sections, there are several other operations that are commonly added to a class. They include the following:

- Copy operations: initialization and assignment
- Accessors and mutators
- Input and output operations
- Relational operations such as <, ==, and >

And there typically are additional operations that are peculiar to the particular class being built. In this section we will illustrate these operations for our Time class.

Copy Operations—Initialization and Assignment

Two default copy operations are provided for all classes:

1. Copy during initialization
2. Copy during assignment

Each makes a copy of an object in a *member-by-member* manner—that is, by copying each member. (For cases in which this is not appropriate, we can define a *copy constructor* for the first kind of copy and overload the assignment operator for the second kind. Copy constructors and the assignment operator are described in more detail in Section 6.3.)

To illustrate these copy operations, suppose that midnight and bedTime are the Time objects declared by the following:

```
Time midnight,
     bedTime(11,30,'P');
```

As we saw there, the default constructor will create an object bedTime that represents 12:00 A.M. and the explicit-value constructor will create bedTime to represent 11:30 P.M.:

```
            midnight                          bedTime
      myHours     12                    myHours      11
      myMinutes    0                    myMinutes    30
      myAMorPM     A                    myAMorPM     P
      myMilTime    0                    myMilTime   2330
```

Then

```
Time t = bedTime;
```

is a legal definition of a Time object t as is

```
Time t(bedTime);
```

Both allocate memory for t and then copy the members of bedTime into these memory locations, thus initializing t to be a copy of bedTime:

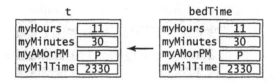

```
                t                              bedTime
      myHours     11                    myHours      11
      myMinutes   30                    myMinutes    30
      myAMorPM     P                    myAMorPM     P
      myMilTime  2330                   myMilTime   2330
```

The same initialization results from

```
Time t = Time(11, 30, 'P');
```

which uses the explicit-value constructor to construct a (temporary) Time object and then copies it into t.

Although the preceding copy operations may look like assignments, they are not—a default copy constructor is called to do the initialization. However, C++ does provide a default member-by-member copy operation for assignment. For example, the assignment statement

```
t = midnight;
```

will copy the members of midnight into t, replacing any previous values stored in the members of t:

Accessors and Mutators

Because the data members of a class are (usually) private, they can be accessed only by member (and friend) functions. It is often necessary, however, to make the values stored in some or all of these members more widely accessible. For this, **accessor** methods (also called **extractors** or **retrievers**) can be provided. They are used only to retrieve the values stored in data members; but they may not change them. Only **mutators** (also called **modifiers**) such as Time's set() operation described in Section 4.3 are allowed to modify data members.

To illustrate, suppose we wish to allow clients to retrieve the value stored in a data member of a Time object. We will do this only for the myMilTime member; the others are essentially the same. Because it does not modify any of the class's data members, it should be a const function. Figure 4.6 shows this accessor getMilitary-Time(). (See the source files—*Chap4/Figures4.5-10*—on the text's website for complete versions of Time.h and Time.cpp and a test driver.)

Figure 4.6 Accessors for Time Data Type

```
/*-- Time.h --------------------------------------------------------------

    . . .
-------------------------------------------------------------------------*/

#include <iostream>

class Time
{
 public:
/********* Function Members *********/
```

Figure 4.6 (continued)

```
   /***** Class constructors *****/
   //----- Prototypes of constructor(s) here


   /***** Accessors *****/
   unsigned getMilitaryTime() const;
   /*-------------------------------------------------------------------

       Retrieve the value stored in the myMilTime data member.

       Precondition:  None.
       Postcondition: Value stored in myMilTime is returned.
   ----------------------------------------------------------------*/


   //---- Prototypes for some/none/all of the other accessors
   //---- getHours, getMinutes(), getAMPM()


   /***** Other Function Members *****/
   //----- Prototypes of set(), display()

 private:
 /********** Data Members **********/
    unsigned myHours,
             myMinutes;
    char myAMorPM;          // 'A' or 'P'
    unsigned myMilTime;     // military time equivalent


}; // end of class declaration
```

```
/*-- Time.cpp ------------------------------------------------------
    . . .
 ----------------------------------------------------------------*/


#include "Time.h"

/*** Utility Functions -- Prototypes ***/
int toMilitary(unsigned hours, unsigned minutes, char am_pm);


//----- Definition of default constructor
//----- Definition of explicit-value constructor
```

Figure 4.6 (continued)

```
//----- Definition of getHours()
unsigned Time::getMilitaryTime() const
{
    return myMilTime;
}


//----- Definitions of other accessors
//----- Definitions of set(), display(), toMilitary
```

▲

Overloading Operators

One C++ feature that is very useful in building classes is **operator overloading**, which means, as it does for functions, that the same operator symbol can be used in more than one way. We have already seen and used this feature several times; for example, a + b will use integer addition if a and b are ints; a + b will use real addition if a and b are doubles; a + b will use complex-number addition if a and b are of complex type; a + b will use string concatenation if a and b are of string type. The operator + has obviously been overloaded for these various C++ types.

With only a couple of exceptions, we can overload a C++ operator Δ for programmer-defined types by defining a function with the name operatorΔ() but whose signature is distinct from any existing definition of operatorΔ():[6]

Operator	Function
Δ	operatorΔ()

If this function *is a function member* of a class C, the compiler will treat an expression of the form

$$a \ \Delta \ b$$

where a is of type C, as a call to this function member with the second operand (b) as its only (explicit) argument:

$$a.operatorΔ(b)$$

If, however, an operator function of the form operatorΔ() is *not a function member*, then an expression of the form

$$a \ \Delta \ b$$

will be treated by the compiler as the function call

$$operatorΔ(a, b)$$

---

[6] Only the operators ::, ., and .* cannot be overloaded. Also, the *arity* of an operator may not be changed; for example, binary operators such as / and = cannot be made into unary operators.

Overloading Input/Output Operators

Output   One of the early functions to add to a class is an output function so that it can be used in debugging the class while it is being built. In our first version of class Time, we have used a function member display() to output Time objects. For example, to output the Time object mealTime to the screen, we sent a message to it instructing it to display itself using cout:

```
mealTime.display(cout);
```

It would be more convenient, however, to overload the output operator << for a Time object so that statements such as

```
cout << "We'll be eating at " << mealTime << endl;
```

can be used instead of having to interrupt the chain of << operators to send a display() message:

```
cout << "We'll be eating at ";
mealTime.display(cout);
cout << endl;
```

We can do this by overloading the function operator<<() for our Time class.

We must decide, however, whether it should be a class member or an ordinary (nonmember) function. If operator<<() were a member function, then, as we have seen, an output statement such as

```
cout << mealTime;
```

would be treated by the compiler as sending a message to cout,

```
cout.operator<<(mealTime);
```

which would mean that operator<<() must be a member of class ostream, not a member of class Time. However, even if we could add this new function member to the standard class ostream, we wouldn't want to tamper with the standard <iostream> library.

So operator<<() must be an ordinary function, which means that an output statement such as

```
cout << mealTime;
```

will be treated by the compiler as the function call

```
operator<<(cout, mealTime);
```

Thus, operator<<() must have two parameters, the first of type ostream and the second of type Time.

To overload the output operator << for our Time class, therefore, we need to define a function of the form

```
ReturnType operator<<(ostream_parameter, Time_parameter)
{
}
```

As we described earlier in this section for the display() function member, the ostream parameter must be a *reference parameter* so that it is an alias for the corresponding `ostream` argument; and, as is common for class objects, we will use a *const reference parameter* for the second parameter. This avoids the overhead of making a copy of the object, and making it a const parameter protects the corresponding argument. Thus, our function becomes

```
ReturnType operator<<(ostream & out, const Time & t)
{
}
```

The next question we must address is what the function's return type should be. We could simply make this a `void` function as in

```
void operator<<(ostream & out, const Time & t)
{
    t.display(out);
}
```

The only problem with this is that an output statement can output only one `Time` object and it must be the last one; for example,

```
cout << "We eat at " << mealTime;
```

is okay, but

```
cout << "We eat at " << mealTime << endl;
```

is not.

To see why this is the case, consider a generic chained output expression of the form

```
cout << x << y
```

Because `<<` is *left associative* (i.e., it is applied from left to right in a chained expression), this is equivalent to

```
(cout << x) << y
```

The subexpression `cout << x` is thus evaluated first and, as we have seen, this can be accomplished with a call to function `operator<<()`:

```
(operator<<(cout, x)) << y
```

After this function call is completed, we want the chained output expression to become

```
cout << y
```

This means that the first function call must return an `ostream` and it must be `cout`; that is, it must return the `ostream` argument (`cout`) that is associated with the first parameter (`out`). We can accomplish this as follows:[7]

- Make the function's return type `ostream &`
- Have the function return its first parameter (`out`)

---

[7] If a function's return type is T and it returns a value v of type T, it actually returns a *copy* of v. Making the return type T & returns a reference to v—that is, an alias for v—so that both refer to the same T value.

An alias for out will be returned, and since out is an alias for cout (because it is a reference parameter), the function operator() will actually produce output to cout and will return this modified ostream.

The output function for our new type Time thus becomes

```
ostream & operator<<(ostream & out, const Time & t)
{
    t.display(out);
    return out;
}
```

Input   To add an input operator to our Time class, we can proceed in much the same way as we did for output:

1. Add a function member read() that reads values, checks them against the class invariant, and if they are valid, stores them in the data members of a Time object.

2. Call read() from a nonmember function operator>>() that is similar to operator<<():

```
istream & operator>>(istream & in, Time & t)
{
    t.read(in);
    return in;
}
```

Note that t is a reference parameter, making it an alias for the corresponding argument—a variable—so that reading values into t actually stores them in this variable. But it obviously cannot be a constant reference parameter because it will be changed when values are input for it.

Figure 4.7 shows the overloaded operator<<() and operator>>() functions. Note that their prototypes in Time.h are outside the class declaration since these are not function members. Also, for this same reason, the function names in their definitions in Time.cpp are not qualified with Time::. (See the source files—*Chap4/Figures4.5-10*—on the text's website for complete versions of Time.h and Time.cpp and a test driver.)

Figure 4.7 Input and Output Operators for Time Data Type

```
/*-- Time.h ------------------------------------------------------------

    . . .

--------------------------------------------------------------------*/

#include <iostream>

class Time
{
 public:
 /******** Function Members ********/
```

Figure 4.7 (continued)

```
   /***** Class constructors *****/
   //----- Prototypes of constructor(s) here

   /***** Accessors *****/
   //----- Prototypes of accessors here

   /***** Input/Output *****/
   void display(ostream & out) const;
   /*-----------------------------------------------------------------
     Display time in standard and military format using output stream out.

     Precondition:  The ostream out is open.
     Postcondition: The time represented by this Time object has been
         inserted into ostream out.
   -----------------------------------------------------------------*/

   void read(istream & in);
   /*-----------------------------------------------------------------
     Read a time value from input stream in.

     Precondition:  The istream in is open; input from in has the form
         hh:mm xM; values hh, mm, and X satisfy the class invariant.
     Postcondition: Input values have been removed from in and stored
         in the data members.
   -----------------------------------------------------------------*/

   /***** Other Function Members *****/
   //----- Prototype of set()

private:
/********** Data Members **********/
   unsigned myHours,
            myMinutes;
   char myAMorPM;          // 'A' or 'P'
   unsigned myMilTime;     // military time equivalent

}; // end of class declaration
```

Figure 4.7 (continued)

```
/***** Operators << and >> *****/
ostream & operator<<(ostream & out, const Time & t);
/*------------------------------------------------------------------

   Overloaded output operator

   Precondition:  The ostream out is open.
   Postcondition: The time represented by this Time object has been
       inserted into ostream out (via display()); reference to out
       is returned.
   ------------------------------------------------------------------*/


istream & operator>>(istream & in, Time & t);
/*------------------------------------------------------------------

   Overloaded input operator

   Precondition:  The istream in is open; input from in has the form
       hh:mm xM; values hh, mm, and X satisfy the class invariant.
   Postcondition: Values have been extracted from in (via read()) and
       stored in this Time object's data members; reference to in is
       returned.
   ------------------------------------------------------------------*/
```

```
/*-- Time.cpp--------------------------------------------------------

   This file implements the Time function members.

   ------------------------------------------------------------------*/

#include "Time.h"

/*** Utility Functions -- Prototypes ***/
int toMilitary(unsigned hours, unsigned minutes, char am_pm);

//----- Definition of default constructor
//----- Definition of explicit-value constructor
//----- Definitions of accessors and set()
```

Figure 4.7 (continued)

```
//----- Definition of display function -----

void Time::display(ostream & out) const
{
   out << myHours << ':'
       << (myMinutes < 10 ? "0" : "") << myMinutes
       << ' ' << myAMorPM << ".M.  ("
       << myMilTime << " mil. time)";
}


//----- Definition of read function -----

void Time::read(istream & in)
{
   unsigned hours,     // Local variables to hold input values from in so
            minutes;   //   they can be checked against the class invariant
   char     am_pm,     //   before putting them in the data members
            ch;        // To gobble up : and the 'M' in input

   in >> hours >> ch >> minutes >> ampm >> ch;

   // Check the class invariant
   if (hours >= 1 && hours <= 12 &&
       minutes >= 0 && minutes <= 59 &&
       (am_pm == 'A' || am_pm == 'P'))
   {
      myHours = hours;
      myMinutes = minutes;
      myAMorPM = am_pm;
      myMilTime = toMilitary(hours, minutes, am_pm);
   }
   else
      cerr << "*** Invalid input for Time object ***\n";
}


//----- Definition of operator<<()
```

Figure 4.7 (continued)

```
ostream & operator<<(ostream & out, const Time & t)
{
   t.display(out);
   return out;
}


//----- Definition of operator>>()

istream & operator>>(istream & in, Time & t)
{
   t.read(in);
   return in;
}


//----- Definition of toMilitary()
```

▲

Friend Functions The input and output of Time objects by the input and output operators for our Time class are actually carried out by auxiliary member functions such as read() and display(); operator<<() simply sends a message to the Time object to use display() to output itself on a specified ostream, and operator>>() sends a message to the Time object to use read() to input a value for itself from a specified istream. *Even though it requires two functions—a member function and a nonmember function to call it—this method is used by most programmers and is the method you are encouraged to use.*

Some programmers use a different approach, however, that eliminates the member functions (read() and display()) and uses only operator>>() and operator<<(). A description of this method is included here so that you can understand it when you see examples of it in code, but *it is not recommended because it violates the information-hiding tenet of object-oriented programming.*

As we have seen, operator>>() and operator<<() cannot be member functions for the Time class, which means that they cannot access the data members of a Time object without receiving special permission. C++ provides a mechanism that makes it possible for nonmember functions to break through the wall of privacy that surrounds and protects a class's data members:

Placing the prototype of a nonmember function within a class declaration but preceding it with the keyword friend *declares that function to be a **friend function** that has permission to access members in the class's private section(s).*

We will illustrate this with the output operator. Suppose we put the declaration

```
friend ostream & operator<<(ostream & out, const Time & t);
```

inside the declaration of our Time class. Then we give a new definition like the following for operator<<() that is an easy modification of that for display():

```
ostream & operator<<(ostream & out, const Time & t)
{
  out << t.myHours << ':'
      << (t.myMinutes < 10 ? "0" : "") << t.myMinutes
      << ' ' << t.myAMorPM << ".M.  ("
      << t.myMilTime << " mil. time)";

  return out;
}
```

Note that because *a friend function is not a member function*, it has the following properties:

- Its definition is not qualified using the class name and the scope operator (::).
- It receives the class object on which it operates as a parameter.
- It uses the dot operator to access the data members.

Other Operations: Advance and the Relational Operators

There are two other operations that must be carried out by our Time class: advancing a Time object by a given number of hours and minutes and comparing two Time objects to determine if one is less than another. We will now consider how this can be done.

The Advance Operation The advance operation increments a time by a specified number of hours and minutes. Now we must decide whether a function advance() for this operation should be a member function. To help with this decision, it is useful to consider the question from two different perspectives:

From an internal perspective: I receive a number of hours and a number of minutes and I advance myself by adding the number of hours to myHours and the number of minutes to myMinutes.

From an external perspective: A Time object, a number of hours, and a number of minutes are sent to a function that advances the time represented by the Time object by adding the number of hours to the Time object's hours and adding the number of minutes to the Time object's minutes.

The internal perspective seems most natural because this operation must actually modify some of the object's data members. The function member `advance()` described in Figure 4.8 implements this operation. (See the source files—*Chap4/Figures4.5-10*—on the text's website for complete versions of `Time.h` and `Time.cpp` and a test driver.)

Figure 4.8 Advance Operation for `Time` Data Type

Add the following in the public section of the class declaration in *Time.h*:

```
/***** Increment operation *****/
void advance(unsigned hours, unsigned minutes);
/*----------------------------------------------------------------------

    Increment a Time object by a specified value.

    Precondition:  hours is the number of hours to add and minutes
        is the number of minutes to add.
    Postcondition: The time represented by this Time object had been
        incremented by this number of hours and minutes.
-----------------------------------------------------------------------*/
```

Add the prototype and definition of the utility function `toStandard()` in Figure 4.2 and the following definition of `advance()` to *Time.cpp*:

```
//----- Definition of advance function -----
void Time::advance(unsigned hours, unsigned minutes)
{
    // Increment the myMilTime member
    myMilTime += 100 * hours + minutes;

    // Adjust to proper format
    unsigned  milHours = myMilTime / 100,
    milMins = myMilTime % 100;
    milHours += milMins / 60;
    milMins %= 60;
    milHours %= 24;
    myMilTime = 100 * milHours + milMins;

    // Now set the standard time data members
    toStandard(myMilTime, myHours, myMinutes, myAMorPM);
}
```

Relational Operators C++ has six relational operators: <, >, ==, <=, >=, and !=. Each of these operators can be overloaded for our Time class. We will describe only how to add the less-than (<) operator by overloading the operator<() function; the other relational operators are similar.

As with the advance operation, we must decide whether the function operator<() for this operation should be a member function. Once again, we will look at the question from two different perspectives:

From an internal perspective: I compare myself with another Time object and determine if I am less than that other object

From an external perspective: Two Time objects are compared to determine if the first is less than the second

Either point of view is reasonable, and some programmers will make the overloaded function a member function whenever possible. In this case, its prototype would be

```
bool operator<(const Time & t);
```

and its definition as follows:

```
bool Time::operator<(const Time & t)
{
    return myMilTime < t.getMilTime();
}
```

The boolean expression

```
mealTime < bedTime
```

would then be evaluated by sending mealTime a < message with bedtime as argument:

```
mealTime.operator<(bedTime)
```

We will opt for the external perspective, however. It seems more natural to think of an external observer looking at two digital watches to see which one has the earlier time than to think of sending the second watch to the first (perhaps using a cable to transfer information) and having the first watch determine whether its time is earlier than that of the other. This approach is also consistent with the following guideline used by many programmers:

When overloading an operator for a class, use a member function if the operator modifies its first operand; use a nonmember function if the operator simply produces a new value based on its two operands.

Figure 4.9 shows how the < operation can be incorporated our into Time class using this approach. (See the source files—*Chap4/Figures4.5-10*—on the text's website for complete versions of Time.h and Time.cpp and a test driver.)

Figure 4.9 Less-than Operation for `Time` Data Type

Add the following to Time.h after the class declaration:

```
/***** Relational operators *****/

bool operator<(const Time & t1, const Time & t2);
/*---------------------------------------------------------------------
    Determine if one Time object is less than (i.e., earlier than)
    another Time object.

    Precondition:  None.
    Postcondition: true is returned if t1 is less than t2 and
        false otherwise.
-----------------------------------------------------------------*/


//--- Prototypes of other relational operators
```

Add the following to Time.cpp:

```
/***** Relational operators *****/
//----- Definition of operator<() -----
bool operator<(const Time & t1, const Time & t2)
{
    return t1.getMilTime() < t2.getMilTime();
}


//--- Definitions of other relational operators
```

▲

Summary and a Few Other Items

When an object needed to solve a problem cannot conveniently be represented with the predefined C++ data types, the class mechanism can be used to create a new data type *NewTypeName* to represent the object, which is then usually stored in a class library with

- The class declaration stored in the header file (*NewTypeName*.h)
- The definitions of class operations stored in an implementation file (*NewTypeName*.cpp)
- The implementation file compiled separately

The usual procedure for a program to use this new data type is as follows:

- Insert the class declaration into the program using

    ```
    #include "NewTypeName.h"
    ```

- Compile the program and *NewTypeName*.cpp separately.
- Link the program's object file and the library's object file.

General Form of a Class Declaration   A common form for a class declaration is

```
class ClassName
{
 public:
  declarations/prototypes of public members
 private:
  declarations of private members
};
```

- Class members can be either *data members or function members.*
- Public members of an object can be accessed by sending the object a message using the *dot operator*:

  objectName.publicMemberName

- Private members can be accessed only by function members and by friends of the class.
- A function member has full access to all private members of a class; its full name begins with the name of its class and the *scope operator*:

  ReturnType NewTypeName::functionName(parameter_list)
  { . . . }

- The name of a *constructor* function is the name of the class. A constructor is invoked each time execution encounters an object's declaration, making it an ideal way to initialize an object's data members.
- Every class should have a default constructor (with no parameters). If no constructors are defined for a class, the compiler will generate a default constructor; otherwise, the programmer must provide one.
- Any function that a class names as a *friend* is not a function member but still has access to the private members of the class.

The Problem of Redundant Declarations   A class such as Time might be used in a program, in libraries, or in other class libraries, and thus it could easily happen that it gets included several times in the same file; for example:

A program needs the Time class, so it #includes "Time.h"

The program also needs library Lib, so it #includes "Lib.h"

but Lib.h also #includes "Time.h"

The library Time.h thus gets included in the program more than once. This will cause "redeclaration" errors during compiling because, in particular, the class Time is declared more than once.

A common way to prevent the declarations in a library such as Time.h from being included more than once in a file is to use **conditional compilation**. The declarations in

Time.h are wrapped inside preprocessor directives as shown in Figure 4.10, which gives an outline of the contents of the Time library.[8] Complete versions of Time.h and Time.cpp, including all documentation and code and also a test driver, can be found in the source files—*Chap4/Figures4.5-10*—on the text's website.

The first directive #ifndef TIME tests to see whether the identifier TIME has been defined. (It is common practice to use the name of the class in uppercase for this identifier.) If it has not, processing proceeds to the second directive #define TIME, which defines TIME (to be 1), and then continues on through what follows and on to the #endif and beyond. If it has been defined, the preprocessor removes all code that follows until a #elif, #else, or #endif directive is encountered.

Thus, the first time the preprocessor encounters the declaration of class Time, it defines the name TIME. If it encounters the class declaration again, since TIME has been defined, all code between #ifndef TIME and #endif is stripped, thus removing the redeclaration.

Figure 4.10 Conditional Compilation Directives to Prevent Redundant Declarations

```
/*-- Time.h -----------------------------------------------------------

   This header file defines the data type Time for processing time.
   Basic operations are:
      Default constructor -- Initializes object to 12:00 AM
      Explicit-value constructor
      read:      To read a time
      display:   To display the time
      >>, <<:    Input and Output operators
      accessors: getHours, getMinutes, getAMPM, getMilTime
      set:       To set the time
      advance:   To advance the time by a certain amount
      relops:    <, >, ==, <=, >=, !=
   ------------------------------------------------------------------*/


#include <iostream>

#ifndef TIME
#define TIME
```

---

[8] The preprocessor scans through a file removing comments, including files, and processing other directives (which begin with #) before the file is passed to the compiler.

Figure 4.10 (continued)

```
class Time
{
 public:
 /******** Function Members ********/
 //--- Class constructors --- see Figure 4.5
  Time();
  Time(unsigned initHours, unsigned initMinutes, char initAMPM);

  //--- Accessors  --- see Figure 4.6
   unsigned getHours() const;
   unsigned getMinutes() const;
   unsigned getAMPM() const;
   unsigned getMilTime() const;

  //--- Input/Output  --- see Figure 4.7
  void display(ostream & out) const;
  void read(istream & in);

  //--- Set operation  --- see Figure 4.2
  void set(unsigned hours, unsigned minutes, char am_pm);

  //--- Increment operation  --- see Figure 4.8
  void advance(unsigned hours, unsigned minutes);

 private:
 /********** Data Members **********/
   unsigned myHours,
            myMinutes;
   char myAMorPM;        // 'A' or 'P'
   unsigned myMilTime;   // military time equivalent

}; // end of class declaration

/********** Nonmember Functions **********/

//--- Operators << and >> --- see Figure 4.7
ostream & operator<<(ostream & out, const Time & t);
istream & operator>>(istream & in, Time & t);
```

Figure 4.10 (continued)

```
//--- Relational operators --- see Figure 4.9
bool operator<(const Time & t1, const Time & t2);
bool operator>(const Time & t1, const Time & t2);
bool operator==(const Time & t1, const Time & t2);
bool operator<=(const Time & t1, const Time & t2);
bool operator>=(const Time & t1, const Time & t2);
bool operator!=(const Time & t1, const Time & t2);

#endif
```

```
/*-- Time.cpp--------------------------------------------------------

   This file implements the Time function members.

   ------------------------------------------------------------------*/

#include "Time.h"

//--- Prototypes of utility functions --- see Figure 3.11
int toMilitary(unsigned hours, unsigned minutes, char AMPM);
void toStandard(unsigned military,
                unsigned & hours, unsigned & minutes, char & AMPM);

//--- Definitions of constructors --- see Figure 4.5
//--- Definitions of accessors:  getMinutes(), getHours(),
//--- getAMPM(), getMilTime() --- see Figure 4.6

//--- Definitions of I/O functions:  display(), read(),
//--- operator<<(), operator>>() --- see Figure 4.7

//--- Definition of set function --- see Figure 4.3

//--- Definition of advance function --- see Figure 4.8

//--- Definitions of relational operators:  operator<(), operator>(),
//--- operator==(), operator<=(), operator>=, operator!= --- see Figure 4.9

//--- Definitions of utility functions:  toMilitary(), toStandard()
//--- see Figure 3.11
```

Pointers to Class Objects

In Section 3.5 we described pointers to structs and the operations that can be used with such pointers. Pointers can also be bound to classes and the same operations can be used. For example, if we declare a `Time` object `t`,

```
Time t;
```

we can declare a pointer to that `Time` object and use it to store the address of that object,

```
Time * timePtr = &t;
```

which can be pictured as follows:

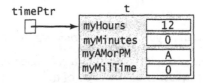

The public members of `t` can be accessed (indirectly) via `timePtr`. For example, a `getMilTime()` message can be sent to this time object via `timePtr` to retrieve the value (0) of its `myMilTime` data member in two different ways. The first and simplest method is to use the *arrow operator*:

```
timePtr->getMilTime()
```

The second method, which is equivalent to the preceding, is to combine the indirection operator with the dot operator:

```
(*timePtr).getMilTime()
```

In this expression, the pointer `timePtr` is first dereferenced to access the object to which it points (i.e., `t`), and the dot operator is then used to send that object the `get-MilTime()` message. At noted before, the first set of parentheses is necessary here because the indirection operation has lower priority than the dot operator.

The `this` Pointer

One important pointer that is made available to every function member in a class is named `this`, a keyword that names a pointer whose value is the address of the object that contains that function:

> *In every class,* `this` *is a pointer whose value is the address of the object. The value of the dereferenced pointer* `*this` *is the object itself.*

We might picture this as follows:

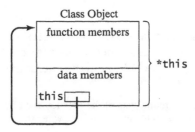

Dereferencing this provides a way to (indirectly) access that object. One time that this is useful is when an object needs to return itself in a function member. Two different actions must be taken in order for this to occur correctly:

1. We can use

```
return *this;
```

to dereference this pointer to the object and return the object.

2. Normally, a return statement in a function,

```
return object;
```

first constructs a copy of *object* and then returns this copy. We can force it to return *object* itself by *making the function's return type a reference:*

```
ReturnType & functionName(parameter_list);
```

The function will then return a reference to *this, which is simply an alias for the object, rather than a copy of it.[9]

To illustrate, suppose we modify the set() function member in class Time as follows:

```
Time & Time::set(unsigned hours, unsigned minutes, char am_pm)
{

    // same as before (See Figure 4.3)

    return *this;
}
```

If t is a Time object, then the function call t.set(11, 59, 'P'); sets the data members to the specified values, but it also returns a reference to *this, which is thus simply another name for t. This means that we can *chain* this function call with another; for example

```
t.set(11, 59, 'P').display(cout);
```

is evaluated as

```
( t.set(11, 59, 'P') ).display(cout);
```

because the dot operator is left associative. The call to set() is done first and sets the data members in t as just described; since it returns a reference to t, the display() function will be applied to this same object and thus displays the newly set values in t.

More That Could be Done This completes our development of the class Time. There obviously are other operations that could (and should) be added or modified. For example, we could add the increment operations ++ and += in place of

---

[9] It follows that, if the return type of the function is a reference, the object being returned cannot be a local variable, because its lifetime would end when the function terminates.

advance() and perhaps the decrement operations -- and -= as well. And there are other changes and modifications we could make, but we must move on to other topics.

✔ Quick Quiz 4.5

1. What is information hiding?
2. Why should data members of a class be private?
3. In definitions of function members of a class, their names are qualified with the class name using the _____ operator.
4. Declaring a function to be _____ suggests to the compiler that it replace a function call with the actual code of the function.
5. A(n) _____ should be formulated and tested to ensure that a class's data members always contain valid values.
6. What are two aspects of constructing an object?
7. A(n) _____ constructor is used when an object declaration does not supply initial values for the data members of the object; a(n) _____ constructor initializes them to specific values supplied in the object's declaration.
8. Functions can be overloaded provided they have different _____.
9. Two default copy operations provided for all classes are copy during _____ and copy during _____.
10. An operator Δ can be overloaded by overloading a function with the name _____.
11. Using a const reference parameter avoids making a copy of the corresponding argument but yet protects that argument from being changed. (True or false)
12. A _____ function is a nonmember function that can access a class's data members.
13. _____ compilation can be used to prevent a file from being included more than once.

⟐ Exercises 4.5

For Exercises 1–6, define the private portion of a class to model the given item.

1. A class Date for dates consisting of a month, day, and year
2. A class PhoneNumber for telephone numbers consisting of area code, local exchange, and number
3. A class Checker for the position of a checker on a board
4. A class CartesianPoint for a point (x, y) in a Cartesian coordinate system
5. A class PolarPoint for a point (r, θ) in a polar coordinate system
6. A class Card for cards in a deck of playing cards

7–12. Add appropriate operations to the classes in Exercises 1–6 and implement them with functions. To test these classes, you should write driver programs as instructed in Programming Problems 1–6 at the end of this chapter.

For Exercises 13–15, develop a class for the given information, selecting operations that are appropriate for an object of that type. To test these classes, you should write driver programs as instructed in Programming Problems 7–9 at the end of this chapter.

13. Information about a person: name, birthday, age, gender, social security number, height, weight, hair color, eye color, and marital status

14. Statistics about a baseball player: name, age, birthdate, position (pitcher, catcher, infielder, outfielder)

15. Weather statistics: date; city and state, province, or country; time of day; temperature; barometric pressure; weather conditions (clear skies, partly cloudy, cloudy, stormy)

For Exercises 16–18, write appropriate class declarations to describe the information in the specified file. See the descriptions of these files at the end of this chapter.

16. `InventoryFile`

17. `UserIdFile`

18. `StudentFile`

SUMMARY

▓ Chapter Notes

- *Procedural programming* focuses on tasks to be performed to solve a problem. *Object-oriented programming* focuses on the objects in a problem and how they work together to solve it.

- Both structs and classes in C++ can contain function members and data members. The default access to these members is public for structs and private for classes.

- An *object* is a particular instance of a class.

- Const function members of a class cannot modify any data members of that class or put them in danger of being modified by some other function.

- *Information hiding* refers to data members of a class being declared private in order to protect them from being accessed (and perhaps modified incorrectly) by client programs.

- The *qualified* (or *full*) *name* of a member of a class has the form `ClassName::item` and is used to specify the name of the class to which the item belongs.

- *Inlining* a function suggests to the compiler that it replace a function call with the actual code of the function.

- A *class invariant* expresses the conditions that must be true of the values in the data members.

- A *default constructor* of a class is invoked for object declarations that do not specify initial values for the data members; an *explicit-value constructor* is invoked for object declarations that do specify initial values for data members.

- *Overloading* a function name is allowed provided that no two definitions of the function have the same *signature* (list of parameter types). A C++ operator Δ can be overloaded by defining the function `operatorΔ()`.

■ C++ functions may have default arguments.

■ *Accessors* are function members that retrieve values of data members; *mutators* can modify these values.

■ Every object has a pointer data member named `this` whose value is the address of that object; the dereferenced pointer `*this` refers to the object itself.

☞ Programming Pointers

1. Members of a class are private by default unless explicitly declared to be public. Members of a struct are public by default unless explicitly declared to be private.

2. Data members of a class should be made private to protect them from being accessed by nonmember (and nonfriend) functions. Use function members to provide access to data members that you wish to be accessible. Public members can be accessed from nonmember functions by using the dot operator.

3. Member functions can be thought of as receiving a class object implicitly; nonmember functions must receive class objects explicitly via parameters.

4. Definitions of member functions outside a class declaration must be qualified with the class name using the `::` operator: `ClassName::functionName()`. Nonmember functions are not qualified.

5. Simple function members can be inlined by preceding their definitions with the keyword `inline` and putting the definitions in the class's header file after the class declaration or by replacing their prototypes in the class declaration with their definitions.

6. Function members that do not modify any of the class's data members should be prototyped and defined as const functions.

7. A class's function members can access private data members of class objects they receive as parameters.

8. Class invariants should be formulated to ensure that the data members always contain valid values. Whenever an operation modifies data members, it should always establish that the class invariant still holds.

9. A class constructor has the following properties:

    ■ Has the same name as the class

    ■ Must be a member function and is usually prototyped or defined in the public section

    ■ Does not return a value and has no return type (not even `void`)

    ■ Is often quite simple and can be inlined

    ■ Is called whenever an object of that class is declared

10. If you do not provide a constructor for a class, the compiler will generate a *default* constructor. If you do provide a constructor for a class, you should also provide a default constructor, because the compiler will not supply one, and uninitialized declarations of instances of that class will not be allowed.

11. A nonmember function cannot directly access private members of a class unless the class grants it permission by declaring it to be a *friend* function. This is done by putting the function's prototype inside the class declaration and preceding it (but not its definition) by the keyword `friend`.

12. Overloaded functions must have different signatures; simply having different return types is not enough.

13. Parameters with default arguments must appear at the end of the parameter list.

14. An operator Δ is overloaded by overloading the function operatorΔ(). For a binary operator, an expression of the form a Δ b will be evaluated by the function call a.operatorΔ(b) if operatorΔ() is a member function of the class of which a is an instance, and by the function call operatorΔ(a, b) if it is not.

15. The input and output functions operator>>() and operator<<() cannot be member functions of programmer-defined classes.

16. Use conditional compilation directives to prevent the contents of a class library from being included more than once:

```
#ifndef CLASS_NAME
#define CLASS_NAME
//-- The declaration of ClassName
#endif
```

▲ ADT Tips

1. Making the data members of a class private to prevent access to them from outside the class is known as *information hiding*. Its purpose is to protect these data members from being modified from outside in unacceptable ways.

2. When implementing an ADT with a class, using function members to implement operations is generally preferred over using friend functions. The friend mechanism is not consistent with the principle of information hiding, which protects the data members from outside access. If it is necessary to implement an operation with a function that is external to the class, it is better to provide access to the private data members by means of public accessor and mutator function members.

▣ Programming Problems

Section 4.5

1. Write a driver program to test the class Date of Exercise 7.

2. Write a driver program to test the class PhoneNumber of Exercise 8.

3. Write a driver program to test the class Checker of Exercise 9.

4. Write a driver program to test the class CartesianPoint of Exercise 10.

5. Write a driver program to test the class PolarPoint of Exercise 11.

6. Write a driver program to test the class Card of Exercise 12.

7. Write a driver program to test the personal information class of Exercise 13.

8. Write a driver program to test the baseball statistics class of Exercise 14.

9. Write a driver program to test the weather statistics class of Exercise 15.

Problems 10–12 deal with lines in the Cartesian plane. The *point–slope equation* of a line with slope m and passing through point P with coordinates (x_1, y_1) is

$$y - y_1 = m(x - x_1)$$

The *slope-intercept equation* of a line with slope m and y-intercept b is

$$y = mx + b$$

10. Write and test a `LineSegment` class, described by two `CartesianPoint` endpoints (see Exercises 4 and 10). In addition to the usual operations (such as constructors, input, and output), this class should provide operations to compute
    a. The midpoint of the line segment joining two points
    b. The equation of the perpendicular bisector of this line segment

11. Write and test a class for a `Line`, described by its slope and a point on the line, with functions that
    a. Find the point–slope equation of the line
    b. Find the slope–intercept equation of the line

12. Write a program to read the point and slope information for two lines and to determine whether they intersect or are parallel. If they intersect, find the point of intersection and also determine whether they are perpendicular. Use the classes `CartesianPoint` from Exercises 4 and 10 and `Line` from Problem 11 to represent points and lines, respectively.

13. A *complex number* has the form $a + bi$, where a and b are real numbers and $i^2 = -1$. The standard C++ library includes a class `complex` for processing complex numbers. Examine the structure of this class to find the operations it provides and what data members it uses. Write a program to read two complex numbers and a symbol for an operation and that then performs the indicated operation.

14. A *rational number* is of the form a/b, where a and b are integers with $b \neq 0$. Develop and test a class for processing rational numbers. The class should have a numerator data member and a denominator data member. It should read and display all rational numbers in the format a/b; for output, just display a if the denominator is 1. The following examples illustrate the operations that should be provided.

Input	Output	Comments
3/8 + 1/6	13/24	$a/b + c/d = (ad + bc)/bd$ reduced to lowest terms
3/8 – 1/6	5/24	$a/b - c/d = (ad - bc)/bd$ reduced to lowest terms
3/8 * 1/6	1/16	$a/b * c/d = ac/bd$ reduced to lowest terms
3/8 / 1/6	9/4	$a/b / c/d = ad/bc$ reduced to lowest terms
3/8 I	8/3	Invert a/b
8/3 M	2 + 2/3	Write a/b as a mixed fraction
6/8 R	3/4	Reduce a/b to lowest terms
6/8 G	2	Greatest common divisor of numerator and denominator
1/6 L 3/8	24	Lowest common denominator of a/b and c/d
1/6 < 3/8	true	$a/b < c/d$?
1/6 <= 3/8	true	$a/b \leq c/d$?
1/6 > 3/8	false	$a/b > c/d$?
1/6 >= 3/8	false	$a/b \geq c/d$?
3/8 = 9/24	true	$a/b = c/d$?
2/3 X + 2 = 4/5	X = – 9/5	Solution of linear equation $(a/b)X + c/d = e/f$

Descriptions of Data Files

The following describe the contents of data files used in exercises in the text. Listings of them are available on the text's website (see *DataFiles* in the source files).

InventoryFile:

Item number: an integer
Number currently in stock: an integer (in the range 0 through 999)
Unit price: a real value
Minimum inventory level: an integer (in the range 0 through 999)
Item name: a character string

The file is sorted so that item numbers are in increasing order.

StudentFile:

This is a file of student records organized as follows. They are arranged so that student numbers are in increasing order.

Student number: an integer
Student's name: two character strings (last, first) and a character (middle initial)
Hometown: two character strings of the form city, state
Phone number: a character string
Gender: a character (M or F)
Year: a 1-digit integer (1, 2, 3, 4, or 5 for special)
Major: a character string
Total credits earned to date: an integer
Cumulative GPA: a real value

StudentUpdateFile:

This is a file of student grade records organized as follows. They are sorted so that student numbers are in increasing order. There is one update record for each student in the file *StudentFile*.

Student number: an integer (same as those used in the file *StudentFile*)
For each of five courses:
      Course name: a seven-character string (e. g., CPSC185)
      Letter grade: a two-character string (e. g., A–, B+, C , where the last string is a C followed by a blank)
      Course credit: an integer

UserIdFile:

This is a file of computer system records organized as follows. They are arranged so that identification numbers are in increasing order.

Identification number: an integer
User's name: two strings of the form last name, first name
Password: a string
Resource limit (in dollars):   an integer with up to four digits
Resources used to date: a real value

LeastSquaresFile:

This is a text file in which each line contains a pair of real numbers representing the *x* coordinate and the *y* coordinate of a point.

CHAPTER 5

Standard C++ Input/Output and String Classes

CHAPTER CONTENTS

Chapter Objectives

- Study in detail the C++ classes for input and output.
- Look at the C++ hierarchy of I/O classes and note in particular how C++ classes for file I/O are derived from the classes for interactive I/O.
- Study in detail the C++ string class.
- Show how string streams can be used for in-memory I/O.
- Illustrate with an example how string operations are used in text editors.
- (Optional) Introduce some of the basic ideas of pattern matching in strings.
- (Optional) Introduce the basic methods of data encryption.

In the preceding chapter, we took a first look at the class (and struct) mechanism in C++ and saw that it can be used to build a new type to model real-world objects. We introduced and illustrated the basic features of classes with a Time class:

- Classes can encapsulate data items that have different attributes.
- Classes can encapsulate data and operations on that data.
- A variable or constant whose type is a class is called an *object*.
- Declaring an object automatically invokes a constructor to initialize the data members of that object.
- A class's data members should be private so they cannot be accessed from outside the class except by using accessor or mutator function members provided in the class (or via the friend mechanism). This is known as *information hiding*.

- Usually, only the prototypes of function members are inside the class declaration and are public. The definitions of these functions are in a separate implementation file (unless they are simple, in which case they can be inlined in the header file).

- Operators such as <<, >>, and the relational operators (<, >, ==, <=, >=, !=) can be overloaded.

We will have much more to say about how to build classes, including more examples.

In this chapter we look at two of the standard classes that C++ provides. We look first at how C++ uses classes for interactive I/O and file I/O and then take a detailed look at the C++ string class.

5.1 The C++ Standard I/O Classes

The challenge in creating an I/O system is to hide the complexity of how input and output are actually carried out. Input may be entered from a keyboard or from an input file and may be coming from a workstation, a microcomputer, or a computer terminal connected to a server. Output from the program may be directed to the screen of a text-only computer terminal or to an appropriate window for a computer running a windowing system (e.g., X-windows, Macintosh, or Windows). Or output may be sent to an output file. Complicating things even more is the fact that a program may be running *locally* on a machine or *remotely* (i.e., on a different machine across a network).

What is needed is an *abstraction* that programmers can use without having to concern themselves with the messy details of how data actually gets from an input source to a program or from a program to an output destination. And the abstraction used in C++ to hide the low-level I/O details is the idea of a **stream** from Unix. Input is viewed as a stream of characters flowing from the keyboard or other input source into a program, like a stream of water flowing from one place to another:

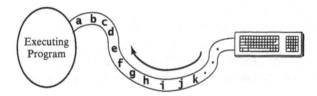

And output is viewed as a stream of characters flowing from a program to the screen or other output destination:

The first versions of C++ developed in 1980 by Bjarne Stroustrup relied upon the I/O system of its parent language C. Although it is still usable in C++ via the

<cstdio> library, we will focus instead on the I/O system based on streams developed for C++ by Jerry Schwarz, one of its early users. After considerable work, feedback from users, and revision, the resulting set of classes is today's <iostream> library. The most important classes in <iostream> are istream for input streams and ostream for output streams:[1]

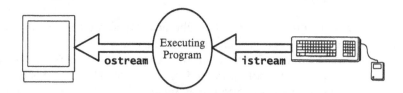

A more recent addition is the iostream class that supports both stream input and stream output.

In this section we will be describing these standard I/O classes along with the corresponding classes for file I/O.

The istream Class

The istream class models a flow of characters from an arbitrary input device to an executing program. When characters are entered from the input device, they enter an istream object that transmits the characters from the input device to the program. One standard istream object associated with the keyboard is defined in the standard <iostream> library so that any C++ program that includes <iostream> will automatically have an input stream flowing from the keyboard to the program. This object is named **cin**.

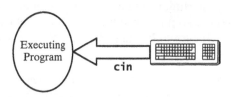

The >> Operator   The **input operator >>** is defined in the <iostream> library so that when it is applied to an istream object and a variable,

>   *istreamObject* >> *variable*

the operator tries to extract a sequence of characters corresponding to a value of the type of *variable* from *istreamObject*. For this reason, >> is also known as the **extraction operator**. If there are no characters in the istream, it *blocks execution* from proceeding until characters are entered. Like most binary operations, it can be used repeatedly to obtain values for several variables:

>   *istreamObject* >> *variable*$_1$ >> *variable*$_2$ >> $\cdots$ >> *variable*$_n$

---

[1]   The classes istream and ostream are obtained from *class templates* (see Chapter 9) basic_istream and basic_ostream, which you can think of as patterns for classes in which the type of the characters in the stream is unspecified. Using char for this type gives the classes istream and ostream; using wchar_t produces wide-character streams wistream and wostream.

To illustrate, suppose that `age` and `idNumber` are `int` variables and the following statement is executed:

```
cin >> age >> idNumber;
```

If the user enters

18 12345↵

where ↵ denotes an end-of-line character generated by the Return/Enter key, the characters 1, 8, a space, 1, 2, 3, 4, 5, and an end-of-line character are entered into the `istream` object `cin`. The `>>` operator extracts characters from `cin` until it encounters a character that cannot be in an `int` value—the space in this case. These extracted characters are then converted to an integer value 18 and stored in `>>`'s right operand `age`. The space and the characters following it are left in `cin` and will be used in the next input operation.

 By default, the `>>` operator extracts and discards leading **white space**—spaces, tabs, and end-of-line characters. In our example, this means that the next `>>` will extract and throw away the space left in `cin` earlier and then extract the characters 1, 2, 3, 4, and 5, stopping at the end-of-line character, which will be left in `cin`. The extracted digits will be converted to the integer value 12345 and stored in `idNumber`.

If the user enters

18.0 12345↵

however, the first `>>` extracts only the characters 1 and 8 and converts them to the integer 18, which is assigned to `age`. The . and 0 and the characters following them remain in `cin`. When the next `>>` attempts to read another integer for `idNumber`, it encounters the period, which cannot begin an integer. The result is that no characters are extracted so no new value is read for `idNumber`, and all of these characters remain in `cin`. It should be clear that this kind of error can easily lead to an infinite loop.

Stream States Every stream can be in various *states*, depending on its condition. If all is well with the stream, its state is said to be *good*. If the stream has been corrupted in some way (usually with the loss of some data), its state is *bad*. If the last I/O operation on the stream did not succeed but no data was lost, the stream's state is *fail*. An input stream is in an *end-of-file* state when an input operation encountered an end-of-file mark before finding any data.

A collection of **flags**—*goodbit*, *badbit*, *failbit*, and *eofbit*—is associated with a stream to represent its state. The C++ I/O classes provide the boolean-valued functions shown in Table 5.1 that report on the values of the various flags. They are most useful for input streams to check whether input operations were successful.

To illustrate how these are used, consider again the preceding example when the stream `cin` contains

.0 12345↵

When the `>>` operator encounters the period while trying to read an integer, it will set `cin`'s *good* flag to false and its *fail* flag to true. Thus, the value of

```
cin.good()
```

TABLE 5.1: Stream State Methods

Message	Returns True if and only if
st.good()	all is well for stream object st
st.bad()	an unrecoverable error occurred in stream object st
st.fail()	a recoverable error occurred in stream object st
inst.eof()	end-of-file mark encountered in *istream* object *inst* before finding any data

will be false and the value of

```
cin.fail()
```

will be true.

The end-of-file function eof() returns true when >> encounters a special end-of-file mark before finding any data. Different operating systems use different control characters for this end-of-file mark. Unix systems use Control-d and DOS-based systems use Control-z.

The assert() mechanism along with the first three status methods provide a simple way to check for data-entry errors. For example, we can send cin the good() message to check whether an input operation has succeeded,

```
assert( cin.good() );
```

or we could use one of the other status messages such as

```
assert( !cin.fail() );
```

The eof() message can be used to check for end-of-input as in

```
int number;
for (;;)
{
    cout << "Enter an integer (Ctrl-D to stop): ";
    cin >> number;
    if (cin.eof()) break;
    // process number
}
```

Once an input operation fails, no data remaining in the istream object can be extracted from that stream until its *good*, *bad*, and *fail* states are reset to their initial values. This is accomplished by sending a clear() message to the object,

```
istreamObject.clear();
```

which will reset the status flags. However, it does not actually remove the offending input from the stream. For this, the istream class provides the ignore() method to extract and discard one or more characters in the stream:

```
istreamObject.ignore();
```

will skip the next character in cin. More generally, a message of the form

```
istreamObject.ignore(num_chars_to_skip, stop_char);
```

where *num_chars_to_skip* is an integer expression and *stop_char* is a character, will remove *num_chars_to_skip* characters or until *stop_char* is removed, whichever occurs first. The default value of *num_chars_to_skip* is 1 and the default value of *stop_char* is the end-of-file mark. For example, the message

```
cin.ignore(20, ' ');
```

might be used to skip all characters up to the next blank (assuming that it is within the next 20 characters), and

```
cin.ignore(80, '\n');
```

might be used to skip all characters remaining on a given line of input (assuming that the end of the line is within 80 characters). Combined with clear(), ignore() is useful for detecting bad input characters and removing them from the input stream:

```
cin >> variable;
if (cin.fail())      // e.g., invalid input character
{
  cin.ignore(80, '\n');
  cin.clear();
}
```

Other istream Features   As we have noted, by default, the >> operator skips leading white space. Suppose, however, that we want to read all characters, including white-space characters. For example, a word-processing program may need to count the lines of input by reading each input character and incrementing a counter each time that character is a return character. One way to read white-space characters is to use an **input manipulator**—an identifier that changes some property of the istream when it is used in an input statement. If we use the **noskipws manipulator** in an input statement, say,

```
istreamObject >> ... >> noskipws >> ...
```

then, in all subsequent input, white-space characters will not be skipped. The **skipws manipulator** can be used to reactivate white-space skipping.

Alternatively, the istream class provides a method named **get()** that reads a single character without skipping white space. For example, the message

```
cin.get(ch);
```

where ch is of type char, will read the next character from cin into ch, even if it is a white-space character.

Table 5.2 lists some of the most commonly used operations on input streams. In the descriptions given here, *inst* is an istream (or ifstream); *var* is a variable for which >> is defined; *ch* is a char variable, *stop* is a char literal, variable, or constant; *chArray* is a char array; *n* and *offset* are integers. Expanded descriptions of these and other stream operations are given in Appendix D.

TABLE 5.2: Input Stream Operations and Methods

Operation	Description
`inst >> var`	Input (extraction) operator; leading white-space characters are skipped and terminating white-space characters are left in *inst*

`inst.get(ch)`
or
`ch = inst.get()`
	Input a single character—any character, even white space—from *inst* into *ch*

`inst.get(chArray, n, stop)`	Input characters from *inst* into *chArray* until $n-1$ characters have been read or the character *stop* (default value `'\n'`) is encountered (but not extracted), or the end-of-file occurs; a terminating null character is added to *chArray*
`inst.getline(chArray, n, stop)`	Same as get(), except that it removes the terminating character *stop* from *inst*
`inst.read(chArray, n)`	Input characters from *inst* into *chArray* until *n* characters have been read or the end-of-file occurs
`inst.readsome(chArray, n)`	Same as read(), but return the number of characters extracted
`inst.peek()`	Return the next character to be read from *inst*, but leave it in the stream
`inst.ignore(n, stop)`	Extract and discard the next *n* (default $n = 1$) characters in *inst* or until the character *stop* (default end-of-file) is encountered and removed, whichever occurs first
`inst.width(n)`	Set the maximum number of characters to be read from *inst* by the next >> to $n-1$
`inst.putback(ch)`	Put *ch* back into *inst*
`inst.unget()`	Put the most recent character read back into *inst*
`inst.seekg(offset, base)`	Move the read position *offset* bytes from *base*, which is one of ios::beg, ios::cur, or ios::end, denoting the beginning, current, and end positions, respectively, in *inst*
`inst.tellg()`	Return an integer that is the current read position (offset from the beginning) in *inst*

The ostream Class

Just as the istream class models a flow of characters from an arbitrary input device to an executing program, the ostream class models a flow of characters from an executing program to an arbitrary output device. When characters are output by a program, they enter an ostream object that transmits the characters to whatever device the user is using for output—a window, a terminal, etc. Here, we will simply refer to the output device as the screen.

The << Operator   The output operator << is defined in the <iostream> library so that when it is applied to an ostream object and an expression,

```
ostreamObject << expression
```

it will evaluate the expression, convert its value into the corresponding sequence of characters, and insert those characters into the ostream object. For example, if the constant PI is defined by

```
const double PI = 3.14159;
```

then, in the output statement

```
cout << PI;
```

the << function converts the double value 3.14159 into the corresponding characters 3, ., 1, 4, 1, 5, and 9, and inserts each character into cout.

For this reason, << is also known as the **stream insertion** operator. When used repeatedly to output several expressions,

$$ostreamObject << expression_1 << expression_2 << \cdots << expression_n$$

it simply inserts the characters that result from converting the expression values into the ostream object, one after the other. Other output operations are listed in Table 5.3; expanded descriptions of these and other stream operations are given in Appendix D. In the descriptions given here, *ost* is an ostream (or ofstream); *exp* is an expression for which << is defined; *ch* is of type char; *chArray* is a char array; *n*, *offset*, and *base* are integers.

TABLE 5.3: Output Stream Operations and Methods

Operation	Description
ost << exp	Output (insertion) operator; the value of the expression *exp* is converted to characters, which are inserted into *ost*
ost.put(ch)	Output the single character *ch* to *ost*
ost.write(chArray, n)	Output *n* characters of *chArray* to *ost*
ost.flush()	Empty *ost*'s output buffer
ost.seekp(offset, base)	Move the write position *offset* bytes from *base*, which is one of ios::beg, ios::cur, or ios::end, denoting the beginning, current, and end positions, respectively, in *ost*
ost.tellp()	Return an integer that is the current write position (offset from the beginning) in *ost*

The Standard ostream Objects   Three standard ostream objects associated with the screen are defined in the standard <iostream> library: cout, cerr, and clog. Any C++ program that includes <iostream> will automatically have these output streams flowing to the screen:

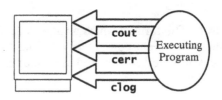

These three standard ostream objects can be described as follows:

cout: the standard buffered output stream for displaying normal output

cerr and clog: standard output streams for displaying error or diagnostic messages (clog is buffered; cerr is not); assert() typically writes its diagnostic messages to cerr.

 To say that cout *is buffered* (as is clog) means that characters inserted into it actually are held in a section of memory called a **buffer**. They remain there until the ostream object is flushed, which, as its name suggests, empties the buffer onto the screen. Since cerr is *unbuffered*, it causes its output to appear on the screen immediately.

 This buffering of output can sometimes cause confusion. One example of this is when temporary output statements are inserted in source code to help with debugging a program as described in Section 1.4. If we insert the debug statement

```
cout << "DEBUG:  Ready to calculate amount\n";
```

in a section of code and the program crashes without the debug information

```
DEBUG:  Ready to calculate amount
```

appearing on the screen, we might conclude that the source of the error we are seeking comes before this output statement. But this may not be true; the statement may have been executed and the output didn't make it to the screen because it is in the output buffer. We should instead use

```
cerr << "DEBUG:  Ready to calculate amount\n";
```

because cerr sends its output directly to the screen, which means that if we don't see it, this statement was not reached.

There are several ways that the output buffer used for cout (and clog) can be flushed:

- It is flushed automatically when it becomes full.
- It is flushed automatically whenever cin is used.
- The **output manipulator endl** causes output to go a new line and flushes the buffer.
- The output manipulator **flush** flushes the buffer.

Thus, using end1 (instead of \n) in our original debug statement,

```
cout << "DEBUG:  Ready to calculate amount" << endl;
```

would also ensure that the debug information would appear on the screen when this statement is executed.

Format Control The form in which a value is displayed is called its *format*, and **format manipulators** can be used to specify various format features. Table 5.4 lists these manipulators. When they are inserted into an ostream object with the output operator <<,

```
ostreamObject << . . . << format_manipulator << . . .
```

 they produce the specified effect. *Except for the last one (setw()), the format is in effect for all subsequent output until changed by some other manipulator.* Although most of them are used to format output, note that some of them are used with istreams or with both istreams and ostreams.

Here are some examples to illustrate the use of these manipulators. The statements

```
int i = 17;
cout << showbase           // show base indicator
     << oct << i << endl    // switch to octal output
     << dec << i << endl    // back to decimal output
     << hex << i << endl;   // switch to hex output
```

will produce the output

```
021
17
0x11
```

because $21_8 = 17_{10} = 11_{16}$. Note that because of the persistence of a format manipulator's effect, all subsequent output would be in hexadecimal unless changed with another manipulator.

The following output statement uses the fixed, showpoint, and setprecision() manipulators to display monetary values with two decimal places:

```
cout << "\nThe total equipment cost is $"
     << fixed << showpoint
     << setprecision(2)
     << equipmentCost << endl;
```

Note that the <iomanip> library must be included to use setprecision().

The width of an output *field*—the space used to display a value—is 0 by default, and automatically grows to accommodate the value. The setw(*n*) manipulator can be used to set the width of the *next* field to *n*. However, every insertion automatically resets the field width to zero, and so setw(*n*) *must be used immediately prior to the insertion of each value whose field width is to be n.* The following statements illustrate

TABLE 5.4: Format Manipulators

Format Manipulator	Description
fixed	Use fixed-point notation for output of real values
scientific	Use scientific notation for output of real values
showpoint	Show decimal point in output of real numbers
noshowpoint	Stop using showpoint
dec	Use base-10 representation for integer input or output
hex	Use base-16 (hexadecimal) representation for integer input or output
oct	Use base-8 (octal) representation for integer input or output
showbase	Display integer values indicating their base (e.g., 0x for hex)
noshowbase	Stop using showbase
showpos	Display + sign for nonnegative values
noshowpos	Stop using showpos
boolalpha	Read or display bool values as true or false
noboolalpha	Stop using boolalpha
uppercase	In scientific, use E for exponent; in hexadecimal, use symbols A–F
nouppercase	Stop using uppercase
unitbuf	Flush the output stream after each output operation
flush	Flush the output stream
endl	Insert newline character into output stream and flush the stream
left	Left-justify output
right	Right-justify output
internal	Add fill character between sign or base and value
From <iomanip>:	
setprecision(n)	Set the precision (number of places after the decimal point) in output of reals to n
setfill(ch)	Use character ch to fill extra spaces in output fields
setw(n)	Set the width of the next output field to n

the use of `setw()` to format output in two columns, the first of width 3 and the second of width 10:

```
cout << fixed << showpoint << setprecision(2)
    << "MONTH    BALANCE\n"
       "=====    =======" << endl;
for (int month = 0; i < numMonths; i++)
{
    cout << setw(3) << month + 1 << "    "
         << setw(10) << amount[month] << endl;
}
```

File I/O: `ifstream` and `ofstream` Classes

With interactive I/O, the <iostream> library automatically establishes connections between programs executing in main memory and the keyboard and between the program and the screen. This is not the case for file I/O, however. If a program is to perform input from or output to a file, it must construct a stream for this purpose. This operation is called **opening** a stream to the file. A program that is to read from a file must open an **ifstream** to that file and a program that is to write to a file must open an **ofstream** to that file. An **fstream** object can be used both for input from and output to a file. These classes are declared in the <fstream> library so that any program wishing to use them must contain the #include <fstream> directive.

Declaring, Opening, and Closing File Streams   Before a program can read values from a text file, it must construct an `ifstream` object to act as a connection from the file to the program. It must first be declared to be of type `ifstream`:

```
ifstream inStream;
```

Similarly, a program that writes values to a file must first construct an `ofstream` object to act as a connection from the program to the file. This can be accomplished with

```
ofstream outStream;
```

These statements declare the objects `inStream` and `outStream` as uninitialized file streams—as *potential* connections between the program and files. They become *actual* connections by sending them the open() message:

```
inStream.open(name_of_input_text_file);
outStream.open(name_of_output_text_file);
```

These two steps—declare and open—can be combined by using initializing declarations:

```
ifstream inStream(name_of_input_text_file);
ofstream outStream(name_of_output_text_file);
```

In either case, the name of the file to be used for input or output can be "hard-wired" into the program as in

```
ifstream inStream("CompanyInfo");
```

or it can be entered during execution and stored in a `string` variable from which it can be retrieved and used to open a stream to the file:

```
string inputFileName;
cout << "Enter name of input file: ";
cin >> inputFileName;

ifstream inStream(inputFileName.data());²
```

 The first method is generally considered bad practice. File-processing programs must be tested with files containing test data for which the output can be verified, and inputting the names of these files is clearly preferred over changing the name of the file in the program each time and recompiling. Perhaps one might consider hardwiring a file name into a program that has been tested in cases where the name of the file being used is always the same.

 By default, opening an `ofstream` to a file is *destructive*; that is, if the file exists, its contents will be destroyed. For situations in which this destruction is undesirable, the `open()` message can be sent with a second **mode argument**, which can be any of those shown in Table 5.5. For example, to open an `ofstream` to a file whose name is stored in the `string` variable `outFileName` and to which data is to be added at the end of the file, we can use `ios::app` as a second argument, as follows:

```
outStream.open(outFileName.data(), ios::app);
```

This second argument makes the `open()` message *nondestructive* so that the old contents of the output file are preserved, and any additional values written to the file

TABLE 5.5: File-Opening Modes

Mode	Description
`ios::in`	The default mode for `ifstream` objects. Open a file for input, nondestructively, with the read position at the file's beginning.
`ios::trunc`	Open a file and delete any contents it contains (i.e., *truncate* it).
`ios::out`	The default mode for `ofstream` objects. Open a file for output, using `ios::trunc`.
`ios::app`	Open a file for output, but nondestructively, with the write position at the file's end (i.e., for *appending*).
`ios::ate`	Open an existing file with the read position (for `ifstream` objects) or write position (for `ofstream` objects) *at the end* of the file.
`ios::binary`	Open a file for which I/O will be done in binary mode rather than text mode. Bytes are read from the file into `char` arrays using `read()` and written from `char` arrays to the file using `write()`.

---

² `inputFileName.c_str()` may also be used. As described in the next section, `data()` and `c_str()` are methods that retrieve the actual character string stored in a `string` object.

will be *appended* to it. File modes can also be combined using the bitwise-or (|) operator. For example, to open a stream to a file whose name is stored in the `string` variable `ioFileName` so that it can be used for both input and output, we could use

```
fstream inoutStream;
inoutStream.open(ioFileName.data(), ios::in | ios::out);
```

There are a number of errors that can foil an attempt to open a stream to a file; for example, an input file may not exist or it cannot be found. Obviously, if this happens, any subsequent attempts to read from that file will also fail. Testing whether an attempted opening of a stream was successful is easily done using the `is_open()` method. A message of the form[3]

```
fstreamName.is_open();
```

will return `true` if *fstream_name* was successfully opened and `false` if the open operation failed.

We have seen that opening a file stream establishes that object as a connection between a program and a file. This stream is disconnected when execution leaves the scope of that file stream object, just as a local variable's value is lost when execution leaves the scope of that variable. In particular, a file stream declared within a function will be disconnected when execution leaves that function (if not before).

A file stream can also be disconnected from a file by sending it the `close()` message:

```
fstreamName.close();
```

This will sever the connection between the program and the file, leaving *fstream-Name* undefined.

The I/O Class Hierarchy

In the introduction to *object-oriented programing* in Chapter 1, we listed the three characteristics of OOP:

- Encapsulation
- Inheritance
- Polymorphism

The relationships between the C++ I/O classes provide an excellent example of the second property.

The I/O classes form a *class hierarchy* (see Chapter 14) in which `iostream` is a *subclass* of both `istream` and `ostream`, which are, in turn, subclasses of a basic `ios` class that handles the low-level details of formatting, buffers, and so on. The file I/O classes `ifstream`, `ofstream`, and `fstream` provided in the `<fstream>` library (and the string stream classes `istringstream`, `ostringstream`, and `stringstream` provided in the `<sstream>` library described in the next section) are subclasses of

---

[3] The success or failure of the open operation can also be tested using the `good()` or `fail()` functions; for example, `assert(inStream.good());` or `assert(!inStream.fail());`.

istream, ostream, and iostream, respectively. The following diagram pictures this class hierarchy (an arrow from one class to another indicates that the first class is a subclass of the second):

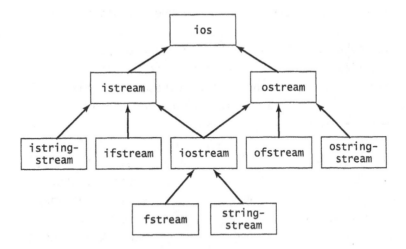

Subclasses of a class *inherit* all the members of this *parent class*, which means that all of the parent class operations can be performed on subclass objects. In particular, the ifstream, ofstream, and fstream classes inherit all the members of istream, ostream, and iostream, respectively. And this means that all of the operations on istream, ostream, and iostream objects can also be performed on ifstream, ofstream and fstream objects, respectively, along with several new operations that are limited to file streams.

Until you write your first few file-processing programs, you won't realize how remarkable this really is! *All of the operations for interactive I/O can be used for file I/O.* For example, once an ifstream object fin has been declared and connected to a text file, we can read a value from it in exactly the same way that we did for interactive I/O:

```
fin >> variable;
```

Rather than repeat and adapt our descriptions of interactive-I/O operations for file I/O, it seems much more enjoyable and helpful to look instead at an example like that in Figure 5.1.[4] The main file I/O features are shown in color. Note how after the file streams are opened, the rest of the operations are used in almost exactly the same way as for interactive I/O.

---

[4] This program has been adapted from the prequel to this text: *C++: An Introduction to Programming,* 3rd edition, by Joel Adams and Larry Nyhoff (Upper Saddle River, NJ: Prentice Hall, Inc. 2003),

Figure 5.1 Example Demonstration of File I/O

```
/*-------------------------------------------------------------------
    Read numeric data stored in a file, compute the minimum, maximum, and
    average of the numbers, and write these statistics to an output file.

    Input(keyboard): names of the input and output files
    Input(file):     a sequence of numeric values
    Output(file):    a count of the values, the minimum value,
                     the maximum value, and the average value
-------------------------------------------------------------------*/

#include <iostream>              // cin, cout
#include <fstream>               // ifstream, ofstream
#include <string>                // string, getline()
#include <cassert>               // assert()
#include <cfloat>                // DBL_MIN and DBL_MAX
using namespace std;

int main()
{
    cout << "This program computes the number, maximum, minimum, and\n"
            "average of an input list of numbers in one file,\n"
            "and places its results in another file.\n\n";

    // ----------- Input Section ----------------------------------

    cout << "Enter the name of the input file: ";
    string inputFileName;
    getline(cin, inputFileName);            // get name of input file
                                            // open an input stream
    ifstream fin;                           //  to the input file,
    fin.open(inputFileName.data());         //  establish a connection,
    assert( fin.is_open() );                //  and check for success

    int count = 0;                          // number of values
    double reading,                         // value being processed
           maximum = DBL_MIN,               // largest seen so far
           minimum = DBL_MAX,               // smallest seen so far
           sum = 0.0;                       // running total
```

Figure 5.1 (continued)

```
for (;;)                              // loop:
{
   fin >> reading;                    //   read a value from file

   if ( fin.eof() ) break;            //   if eof, quit

   count++;                           //   update: count,
   sum += reading;                    //           sum,
   if (reading < minimum)
      minimum = reading;              //           minimum,
   if (reading > maximum)
      maximum = reading;              //           maximum
}                                     // end loop

fin.close();                          // close the connection


// ------------ Output Section ---------------------------------

cout << "Enter the name of the output file: ";
string outputFileName;
getline(cin, outputFileName);
                                       // open an output stream
ofstream fout(outputFileName.data());  //  to the output file,
                                       //  establish a connection,
assert( fout.is_open() );              //  and check for success
                                       // write results to file
fout << "\n--> There were " << count << " values";

if (count > 0)
   fout << "\n    ranging from " << minimum
            << " to " << maximum
            << "\n    and their average is " << sum / count
            << endl;

fout.close();                         // close the stream

cout << "Processing complete.\n";
}
```

Figure 5.1 (continued)

Execution Trace:

```
This program computes the number, maximum, minimum, and
average of an input list of numbers in one file,
and places its results in another file.

Enter the name of the input file: data5-1.txt
Enter the name of the output file: output5-1.txt
Processing complete.
```

Listing of input file *data5-1.txt*:
```
88 66 99 100
77 66 44 55
95 85
```

Listing of output file *output5-1.txt*:

```
--> There were 10 values
    ranging from 44 to 100
    and their average is 77.5
```

▲

✔ Quick Quiz 5.1

1. What are two of the main classes in the <iostream> library?

2. _____ is a class for inputting characters from an arbitrary input device to an executing program.

3. _____ is a class for outputting characters from an executing program to an arbitrary output device.

4. The <iostream> library establishes a(n) _____ object named _____ that connects a program and the keyboard.

5. The <iostream> library establishes a(n) _____ object named _____ that connects a program and the screen.

6. Three states of an istream are _____, _____, and _____.

7. The statement assert(cin.____); will stop program execution if there is a data-entry error.

8. The method _____ in the istream class is used to reset the states of an input stream.

9. The method _____ in the istream class is used to skip characters in an input stream.

10. (True or false) By default, >> skips white space in an input stream.

11. (True or false) The method get() skips white space in an input stream.

12. _____ is a manipulator that can be used to insert a newline character in an output stream and then flush the stream.

13. (True or false) When the statement

    ```
    cout << setw(10) << 1.234 << 5.678 << endl;
    ```

    is executed, the real numbers 1.234 and 5.678 will be displayed in 10-space fields.

14. Before a program can read data from a file, a(n) _____ object must connect the program to that file.

15. Before a program can write output to a file, a(n) _____ object must connect the program to that file.

16. (True or false) Almost none of the operations on interactive-IO streams can be performed on file streams.

17. Write a statement to declare a file stream named inputStream that will be used for input from a file and another statement that uses the open() function to connect this stream to a file whose name is stored in the string variable empFileName.

18. Repeat Question 17 but use the initialization-at-declaration mechanism.

19. Repeat Question 17 but for a file stream named outputStream that will be used for output to a file whose name is stored in the string variable reportFileName.

20. Repeat Question 19 but use the initialization-at-declaration mechanism.

21. (True or false) The declaration ifstream inStream("Info"); will destroy the contents of the file named Info.

22. (True or false) The declaration ofstream outStream("Info"); will destroy the contents of the file named Info.

23. Write a statement that will stop program execution if an attempt to open the ifstream inputStream fails.

24. Write a statement to disconnect the ifstream in Question 23.

5.2 The C++ String Types

String processing is an important part of many problems. For example, in processing employee information it might be necessary to store the name of each employee along with other information. A program for maintaining an inventory might require processing product names, names of manufacturers, their addresses, and so on. Many problems involve sequences of characters such as words and sentences in text-editing and word-processing, files and messages that must be encrypted for security and/or reliability, searches for words, phrases, and patterns in text files, and so on. As computers have evolved from number crunchers to general-purpose machines, the number of problems in which strings must be input, stored, processed, and output has increased. A string data type is needed to store character strings and operate on them in various ways.

The operations needed to process strings vary from one problem to the next. However, in most text-editing and word-processing applications, they include those listed in the following description of strings as an abstract data type (and usually more):

String ADT

Collection of Data Elements
A finite sequence of characters drawn from some given character set

Basic Operations

• Input & Output	Read and display strings
• Length	Find the number of characters in a string
• Compare	Determine if two strings are the same, or if one string precedes another in lexicographic order
• Concatenate	Join two strings together
• Copy	Copy a string or a substring of a given string to another string
• Find	Locate one string or a character within another string
• Insert	Insert one string into another string
• Delete	Delete part of a string
• Replace	Replace part of a string with another string

To illustrate these basic operations, suppose that *str1* is the string "en", *str2* is "list", and *str3* is "light". The length of *str1* is 2, the length of *str2* is 4, and the length of *str3* is 5. Because 'e' < 'l', *str1* < *str2*. In comparing *str2* with *str3*, we search from the left for the first nonmatching characters and find 'g' < 's', which means that *str3* < *str2*. The concatenation of *str1* with *str2* is

"enlist"

the concatenation of *str2* with *str1* is

"listen"

and the concatenation of *str1* with *str3* with *str1* gives

"enlighten"

Copying the substring of *str2* of length 2 beginning at the second character gives the string

"is"

and replacing this substring with "aria" gives

"lariat"

C-Style Strings

Although the C programming language does not have a predefined string data type, it does provide some string-processing capabilities, which are thus also part of C++. Because you may see some of these features in C++ programs or use them yourself in a program where the full-blown C++ standard `string` type isn't needed, we will take a quick look at C-style strings.

As we saw in Section 3.2, C uses `char` arrays to store strings, but appends a null character \0 at the end of the string. For example, the definitions

```
char animal[10] = "elephant",
     bird[] = "robin";
```

construct the `char` array `animal` with 10 elements initialized with the characters in the string `elephant` followed by two null characters,

```
animal | e | l | e | p | h | a | n | t | \0 | \0 |
         [0] [1] [2] [3] [4] [5] [6] [7] [8] [9]
```

and the `char` array `bird` with 6 elements initialized with the characters in the string `robin` followed by a null character:

```
bird | r | o | b | i | n | \0 |
       [0] [1] [2] [3] [4] [5]
```

String-processing functions can use this null character to find the end of the string. For example, the statements

```
for (int i = 0; animal[i] != '\0'; i++)
  cout << animal[i];
```

can be used to display only the characters of the string used to initialize `animal`. Functions to implement the other basic string operations such as find, insert, delete, and replace are similar in their use of the subscript operator [] to access individual positions in the array and the null character to detect the end of the string stored in the array.

Character arrays such as `animal` and `bird` can be output in C++ using the output operator. For example, the statement

```
cout << animal;
```

produces the same output as the preceding `for` loop. They can be input using the input operator. To illustrate, suppose the statement

```
cin >> animal;
```

is used to input a string into `animal`. The input operator first skips leading white space (unless the format manipulator `noskipws` has been used). It then extracts characters from `cin` storing them in the `char` array `animal` until the end of the file is reached or a white-space character is encountered, which will not be removed from the `istream`. After this, it terminates the string with a null character. Thus, if we input

```
tom cat
```

the value read for `animal` will be

   tom

If the input statement is encountered again, the space preceding `cat` will be skipped and the string `cat` will be read and assigned to `animal`. The `istream` class has many other member functions such as `get()`, `getline()`, `read()`, `readsome()`, and `width()` that can be used for inputting strings.

Table 5.6 lists several functions for processing C-style strings provided in various C libraries.[5] In their descriptions, *s*, *s1*, and *s2* are `char` arrays with a null character in the last array position(s), and *ch* is a character. Other string-processing functions are described in Appendix C.

TABLE 5.6: Functions for Processing C-Style Strings

Operation	Description
From `<cstring>`:	
`strcat(s1, s2)`	Modify *s1* by concatenating *s2* onto the end of it
`strcpy(s1, s2)`	Modify *s1* by replacing its characters with copies of those in *s2*
`strcmp(s1, s2)`	Compare *s1* and *s2*, returning a negative integer, 0, or a positive integer according as *s1* is less than, equal to, or greater than *s2*
`strlen(s)`	Return the length (number of non-null characters) of s
`strstr(s1, s2)`	Search in *s1* for the first occurrence of *s2*, returning a pointer to the first character of this occurrence or null if *s2* is not found in *s1*
From `<cstdlib>`:	
`atof(s)`	Convert *s* to a `double` (if possible) and return this value
`atoi(s)`	Convert.*s* to an `int` (if possible) and return this value
`atol(s)`	Convert *s* to a `long int` (if possible) and return this value
From `<cctype>`:	
`islower(ch)`	Return true if *ch* is lowercase and false otherwise
`isupper(ch)`	Return true if *ch* is uppercase and false otherwise
`tolower(ch)`	Return the lowercase equivalent of *ch* if *ch* is uppercase
`toupper(ch)`	Return the uppercase equivalent of *ch* if *ch* is lowercase

---

[5] Libraries provided in C with a name of the form `<lib.h>` have been renamed in C++ as `<clib>`, in which the prefix `c` is attached and the extension `.h` is dropped. In particular, C's string library `<string.h>` is renamed `<cstring>`. Early versions of C++ libraries also were named with the `.h` extension; for example, `<iostream.h>`, which has the new name `<iostream>`. Many versions of C++ support both names and some programmers still use the older names. One must be careful, however; including `<string.h>` in a program will include the C string library and *not* the C++ string library.

The last four character-processing functions are included in Table 5.6 because they can be used to process strings character by character. For example, to change a string stored in a char array str to all uppercase, we can use

```
for (int i = 0; i < strlen(str); i++)
  if (islower(str[i])
    str[i] = toupper(str[i]);
```

A String Class To design an OOP string type we could design a class StringType that has as one of its data members a char array myStorage to store the string's characters. We would probably make myStorage a dynamic array as described in Section 3.4 and have a class constructor allocate memory for it with the new operation, using a capacity specified in a declaration of a StringType object. We would then add various string-processing member functions to operate internally on these data members. For example, to implement the length operation, we could have a member function length() that would search myStorage for a terminating null character, which we would ensure is placed at the end of each string by all constructors and other operations that modify a StringType object:

```
unsigned StringType::length()
{
    int i = 0;
    while (myStorage[i] != '\0')
        i++;
    return i;
}
```

Alternatively, we could simply have length() call the function strlen() from <cstring>, as in

```
#include <cstring>
unsigned StringType::length()
{
    return strlen(myStorage);
}
```

which would perform a similar search for the null character. For efficiency, we might add a myLength data member that gets updated whenever the string gets modified. The length() member function would then be a simple accessor function.

Developing a complete class for strings is instructive, but we leave this as an exercise (see Programming Problem 27). We will instead focus on the C++ standard string class in the <string> library. Because it provides a very large collection of string operations, we will use it in this text for most of the examples that require string processing. The rest of this section is devoted to a careful study of this string class. If you have studied and used it in an earlier course, this can provide a quick review.

The C++ string Class

To use the C++ string class, one must remember to include the <string> library:[6]

```
#include <string>
```

This makes available a very large collection of operations for processing strings. In this section we will describe the main operations provided by this string class.[7]

Definitions and Constructors   There are several different ways that a string object can be defined. In addition to the default constructor, there are constructors that initialize an object with another string object, with a char array or part of it, or with copies of a character. In their descriptions in Table 5.7 (and also in Appendix D), *str* is a string; *ca* is a char array; *str_ca* is a string or a *char* array; *ch* is a char; and *n* is an integer.

For example, the declarations

```
string name1,
       name2(""),
       name3 = "";
```

construct name1, name2, and name3 as string objects and initialize them with the **empty string,** which contains no characters. A literal for the empty string can be written as two consecutive double quotes (""). The declarations

```
char vowels[] = "aeiou";
string s("abcdefghijklmn"),
       s1(vowels, 3),
       s2(s), s3(s, 2), s4(s, 2, 5),
       snore(10, 'z');
```

TABLE 5.7: String Constructors

Operation	Description
string *s*;	Constructs *s* as an empty string
string *s*(*str_ca*);	Constructs *s* to contain a copy of string or char array *str_ca*
string *s*(*ca*, *n*);	Constructs *s* to contain a copy of the first *n* characters in char array *ca*
string *s*(*str*, *pos*, *n*);	Constructs *s* to contain a copy of the first *n* characters in string *str*, starting at position *pos* (default 0); if *n* is too large or is omitted, characters are copied only to the end of *str*
string *s*(*n*, *ch*);	Constructs *s* to contain *n* copies of the character *ch*

---

[6]   See the warning in Footnote 5 about the difference between <string> and <string.h>.

[7]   In the same way that the classes istream and ostream are obtained from class templates basic_istream and basic_ostream by using char for the unspecified element type (see Footnote 1), the class string is obtained by using char for the unspecified type in the class template basic_string. Using wchar_t produces the wide-character string class wstring. Class templates are described in Chapter 9.

construct `string` objects `s`, `s1`, `s2`, `s3`, `s4`, and `snore` and initialize them to contain the following strings:

```
s:     abcdefghijklmn
s1:    aei
s2:    abcdefghijklmn
s3:    cdefghijklmn
s4:    cdefg
snore: zzzzzzzzzz
```

Storage A `string` object must store the individual characters that make up the string value it represents. Some implementations use `char` arrays for short strings and dynamic storage structures for longer strings that grow and shrink because of frequent insertions and deletions. Exactly what the storage structure for strings is and how it is managed is implementation dependent. There are, however, `string` member functions that provide some information about it. Some of these are described in Table 5.8 and others are described in Appendix D. In the descriptions of these methods, *s* is of type `string`.

TABLE 5.8: String Storage Information Methods

Operation	Description
`s.capacity()`	Returns the capacity of the storage allocated in *s*
`s.size()` and `s.length()`	Return the length of *s*
`s.empty()`	Returns `true` if *s* contains no characters, `false` otherwise
`s.max_size()`	Returns the largest possible capacity of *s*

Input/Output String input and output are quite similar to input and output for other types of objects. The output operator `<<` can be used to display `string` literals and expressions. Input can be accomplished by using the input operator `>>` or the nonmember function `getline()`. In the descriptions of these operations in Table 5.9, *ostr* is an `ostream` or `ofstream`, *istr* is an `istream` or `ifstream`, and *s* is a `string`.

To illustrate, consider the statements

```
cin >> name1;
cout << "name1: " << name1 << endl;
```

If we input the string `A1-Ley-Cat`, the output produced will be

```
name1: A1-Ley-Cat
```

If we replace the dashes with spaces, however, and input the string `A1 Ley Cat`, the output produced will be

```
name1: A1
```

TABLE 5.9: String I/O Operations

Operation	Description
`ostr << s`	Inserts characters of *s* into *ostr*; returns *ostr*
`istr >> s`	Extracts and discards leading white-space characters from *istr* and then extracts and stores characters in *s* until *s*.max_size() characters have been extracted, the end of file occurs, or a white-space character is encountered, in which case the *white-space character is not removed* from *istr*; returns *istr*
`getline(istr, s, term)`	Extracts characters from *istr* and stores them in *s* until *s*.max_size() characters have been extracted, the end of file occurs, or character *term* is encountered, in which case *term is removed from* `istr` *but is not stored in s*. If *term* is omitted, `'\n'` is used.

because the input operator >> stops reading characters when the blank is encountered; the rest of the input (" Ley Cat") is left in the input stream cin and will be read in subsequent input statements.

By contrast, if we use the same inputs for the statements

```
getline(cin, name2)
cout << "name2: " << name2 << endl;
```

the output produced in the first case will be

```
name2: Al-Ley-Cat
```

and in the second case, will be

```
name2: Al Ley Cat
```

because getline() reads an entire line of input.

Care must be taken when using both >> and getline(). Input stops when >> encounters a a white-space character but it *does not remove it from the input stream* cin. If this character is the end-of-line character and the next input operation uses getline() to read a value for a string variable, it encounters the end of line immediately and an empty string is assigned to the variable.

To illustrate, consider the statements

```
cin >> name1;
cout << "name1: " << name1 << endl;
getline(cin, name2)
cout << "name2: " << name2 << endl;
getline(cin, name3);
cout << "name3: " << name3 << endl;
```

If we input

```
Al Ley Cat
Road Runner
```

the output produced will be

```
name1: A1
name2:  Ley Cat
name3: Road Runner
```

However, if we input

```
A1
Ley Cat
Road Runner
```

the output produced will be

```
name1: A1
name2:
name3: Ley Cat
```

Input stops when >> encounters the end-of-line character following A1, but it does not remove it from the input stream cin. Consequently, when getline() attempts to read a line for name2, it encounters the end of line immediately, and assigns an empty string to name2. To remove the end-of-line character, we could use

```
char ch = cin.get();
```

or

```
cin.ignore(80, '\n');
```

which would also remove characters preceding the end-of-line character.

Editing Operations In our description of a string as an ADT, we listed concatenation, insertion, deletion, and replacement as basic string operations that combine or modify strings. The concatenation operation is provided in string by the (overloaded) + operator, and the others by member functions. In the common forms given in Table 5.10 (see Appendix D for others), s and *str* are strings; *ca* is a char array; *str_ca* is a string or a char array; *str_ca_ch* is a string, a char array, or a character; *ch* is a character; and *n*, *n1*, *n2*, *pos*, *pos1*, and *pos2* are integers.

TABLE 5.10: String Editing Operations

Operation	Description
s + *str_ca_ch*	Returns the result of concatenating s and *str_ca_ch*
s.append(*str_ca*)	Appends *str_ca* at the end of s; returns s
s.append(*ca*, *n*)	Appends the first *n* characters in *ca* at the end of s; returns s
s.append(*n*, *ch*)	Appends *n* copies of *ch* at the end of s; returns s

TABLE 5.10: String Editing Operations (continued)

Operation	Description
s.insert(*pos*, *str*)	Inserts a copy of *str* into *s* at position *pos*; returns *s*
s.insert(*pos1*, *str*, *pos2*, *n*)	Inserts a copy of *n* characters of *str*, starting at position *pos2*, into *s* at position *pos1*; if *n* is too large, characters are copied only until the end of *str* is reached; returns *s*
s.insert(*pos*, *ca*, *n*)	Inserts a copy of the first *n* characters of *ca* into *s* at position *pos*; inserts all of its characters if *n* is omitted; returns *s*
s.insert(*pos*, *n*, *ch*)	Inserts *n* copies of the character *ch* into *s* at position *pos*; returns *s*
s.erase(*pos*, *n*)	Removes *n* characters from *s*, beginning at position *pos* (default value 0); returns *s*
s.replace(*pos1*, *n1*, *str*)	Replaces the substring of *s* of length *n1* beginning at position *pos1* with *str*; if *n1* is too large, all characters to the end of *s* are replaced; returns *s*
s.replace(*pos1*, *n1*, *ca*, *n2*)	Replaces a substring of *s* as before, but with the first *n2* characters in *ca*; returns *s*
s.swap(*str*)	Swaps the contents of *s* and *str*; return type is void
swap(*s*, *str*)	Swaps the contents of *s* and *str*; return type is void

Here are a few examples that illustrate these functions:

```
string name = "Michigan",
       greatLake;
cout << "\tname: " << name << endl;

//-- Concatenate "Lake " and name's value
//-- and assign the result to greatLake
greatLake = "Lake " + name;
cout << "(concatenate)\n\tgreatLake: "
     << greatLake << endl;

//-- Append "der" to value of name
name.append("der");
cout << "(append)\n\tname: " << name << endl;
```

```
//-- Erase first 6 characters of name and then erase
//-- 2 characters from the result, starting at position 3
name.erase(0, 6).erase(3, 2);
cout << "(erase)\n\t" << "name: " << name << endl;

//-- Insert "Gr" at position 0 of name
name.insert(0, "Gr");
cout << "(insert)\n\t" << name + " " + greatLake << endl;

//-- Swap name and greatLake
name.swap(greatLake);
cout << "(swap)\n\t" << name +" " + greatLake << endl;
```

They produce the following output:

```
        name: Michigan
(concatenate)
        greatLake: Lake Michigan
(append)
        name: Michigander
(erase)
        name: and
(insert)
        Grand Lake Michigan
(swap)
        Lake Michigan Grand
```

Copiers There are several operations that make copies of a string or a part of a string. Some of these, such as the assignment operator, assign this copy to another *string* object. In the descriptions in Table 5.11 (see Appendix D for other forms of these operations), *s*, *ca*, `str_ca`, `str_ca_ch`, *pos*, *n*, and *ch* are as before.

Operation	Description
`s = str_ca_ch`	Assigns a copy of `str_ca_ch` to *s*
`s += str_ca_ch`	Appends a copy of `str_ca_ch` to *s*
`s.assign(str_ca)`	Assigns a copy of `str_ca` to *s*; returns *s*
`s.assign(ca, n)`	Assigns to *s* a string consisting of the first *n* characters in *ca*; returns *s*
`s.assign(n, ch)`	Assigns to *s* a string consisting of *n* copies of *ch*; returns *s*
`s.substr(pos, n)`	Returns a copy of the substring consisting of *n* characters from *s*, beginning at position *pos* (default value 0)

Accessing Individual Characters The (overloaded) subscript operator`[]` and the member function `at()` described in Table 5.11 can be used to access the character at

TABLE 5.11: String Element Accessors

Operation	Description
s[i]	Returns a reference to the character at position *i* in *s*. No exception is raised if *i* is out of range.
s.at(i)	Returns a reference to the character at position *i* in string *s*. An out-of-range exception is raised if *i* is out of range.

a specified position in a string (counting from 0). In the descriptions, s is a string and *i* is an integer.

The subscript operator does not check for out-of-range indices, but at() does. For example, the out-of-range error in the following example will be caught:

```
string s = "ABCDE";
int i = 5;
try
{
   cout << s.at(i) << endl;
}
catch (exception rangeExc)  // #include <exception> needed
{
   cout << "Error in s.at(i) for i = 5\n"
        << rangeExc.what() << endl;
}
cout << "Done checking\n";
```

The error message will not be displayed, however, if s.at(i) is replaced by s[i].

Search Operations The string class provides a plethora of operations for locating strings and individual characters in a string. Table 5.12 gives some of the forms of these search operations (see Appendix D for others); *str_ca_ch* is a string, char array, or a *char*; *s*, *pos*, *n*, and *ch* are as before. In the descriptions, npos is a special public class constant (UINT_MAX in some versions of C++) defined within the string class. Because it is a class constant, it must be referenced outside the class by **string::npos**.

Here are a few examples that illustrate these functions:

```
string s = "abcdeabcdeabcdeABCDE";
cout << "s: " << s << endl;

cout << "s.find(\"cde\"): "
     << s.find("cde") << endl;

cout << "s.rfind(\"cde\"): "
     << s.rfind("cde") << endl;
```

```
cout << "s.find_first_of(\"udu\"): "
     << s.find_first_of("udu")
     << "\ns.find_first_of(\"udu\", 5): "
     << s.find_first_of("udu", 5) << endl;

cout << "s.find_last_of(\"udu\"): "
     << s.find_last_of("udu")
     << "\ns.find_last_of(\"udu\", 10): "
     << s.find_last_of("udu", 10) << endl;

cout << "s.find_first_of(\"usrp\"): "
     << s.find_first_of("usurp")
     << "\n*** NOTE:  string::npos = "
     << string::npos << endl;

cout << "s.find_first_not_of(\"udead\"): "
     << s.find_first_not_of("udead") << endl;

cout << "s.find_last_not_of(\"udead\"): "
     << s.find_last_not_of("udead") << endl;
```

TABLE 5.12: String Element Accessors

Operation	Description
s.find(*str_ca_ch*, *pos*)	Returns the first position $\geq$ *pos* such that the next characters of *s* match those in *str_ca_ch*; returns npos if there is no such position; 0 is the default value for *pos*
s.find_first_of(*str_ca_ch*, *pos*)	Returns the first position $\geq$ *pos* of a character in *s* that matches any character in *str_ca_ch*; returns npos if there is no such position; 0 is the default value for *pos*
s.find_first_not_of(*str_ca_ch*, *pos*)	Returns the first position $\geq$ *pos* of a character in *s* that does *not* match any of the characters in *str_ca_ch*; returns npos if there is no such position; 0 is the default value for *pos*
s.find_last_of(*str_ca_ch*, *pos*)	Returns the highest position $\leq$ *pos* of a character in *s* that matches any character in *str_ca_ch*; returns npos if there is no such position; npos is the default value for *pos*
s.find_last_not_of(*str_ca_ch*, *pos*)	Returns the highest position $\leq$ *pos* of a character in *s* that does not match any character in *str_ca_ch*; returns npos if there is no such position; npos is the default value for pos
s.rfind(*str_ca_ch*, *pos*)	Returns the highest position $\leq$ *pos* such that the next *str_ca_ch*.size() characters of s match those in *str_ca_ch*; returns npos if there is no such position; npos is the default value for *pos*

They produce the following output:

```
s: abcdeabcdeabcdeABCDE
s.find("cde"): 2
s.rfind("cde"): 12
s.find_first_of("udu"): 3
s.find_first_of("udu", 5): 8
s.find_last_of("udu"): 13
s.find_last_of("udu", 10): 8
s.find_first_of("usurp"): 4294967295
*** NOTE: string::npos = 4294967295
s.find_first_not_of("udead"): 1
s.find_last_not_of("udead"): 19
```

Comparisons All of the usual relational operators are overloaded in the string class; strings may be compared with other strings or with C-style strings (i.e., char arrays.) Also, a compare() function is provided that is similar to the C function strcmp(), but which may also be used to compare parts of strings. Some common forms of these operations are given in Table 5.13 (see Appendix D for others); s is a string object; str_ca, str_ca_1 and str_ca_2 are string objects or char arrays.

TABLE 5.13: String Comparisons

Operation	Description
$str\_ca_1 < str\_ca_2$ $str\_ca_1 <= str\_ca_2$ $str\_ca_1 > str\_ca_2$ $str\_ca_1 >= str\_ca_2$ $str\_ca_1 == str\_ca_2$ $str\_ca_1 != str\_ca_2$	Return true or false as determined by the relational operator
s.compare(str_ca)	Returns a negative value, 0, or a positive value according as s is less than, equal to, or greater than str_ca

string and C-Style Strings Some problems require a C-style string instead of a string object. For example, as we noted in Section 5.1, the name supplied to the open() operation for the file streams ifstream, ofstream, and fstream must be a string literal or a string stored in a char array. The C++ string class provides the three member functions in Table 5.14 to convert a string object s into a C-style string.

Either data() or c_str() can be used to extract from a file name the char array required by the open operation:

```
fStream.open(fileName.data())
```

or

```
fStream.open(fileName.c_str())
```

TABLE 5.14: String Converters

Operation	Description
s.c_str()	Returns a constant char array containing the characters stored in s, terminated by a null character
s.data()	Returns a constant char array containing the characters stored in s, but not terminated by a null character
s.copy(charArray, pos, n)	Replaces charArray with n characters from s, starting at position pos or at position 0, if pos is omitted; if n is too large, characters are copied only until the end of s is reached; returns the number of characters copied

String Streams

The streams we have considered up to now have been connected to input and output devices or to files. It is also possible to connect a stream to a string in memory and to read input from the string or to write output to it. This is sometimes called **in-memory I/O** and is made possible by means of **string streams** defined in the <sstream> library:[8]

istringstream	For input from a string
ostringstream	For output to a string
stringstream	For input from and output to a string

As we noted in the preceding section, these string stream classes are derived from their interactive-I/O counterparts istream, ostream, and iostream, respectively, and thus inherit the I/O operations from these parent classes. For example, we can use the input operator to read values from an istringstream object insstr,

insstr >> $variable_1$ >> $variable_2$ >> . . . >> $variable_n$;

and the output operator to output values to an ostringstream object outsstr:

outsstr << $expression_1$ << $expression_2$ << . . . << $expression_n$;

The various I/O manipulators and the other I/O features described in the preceding section can also be used with string streams.

In addition, the string stream classes have member functions that are unique to them: default constructors; explicit-value constructors that create string streams and initialize them with a specified string value; and a member function str() that retrieves the string stored in a string stream or replaces it with a new one. These are described in Table 5.15; insstr is an istringstream object, outsstr is an ostringstream object, and s is any of the three kinds of string stream objects.

---

[8] The corresponding types for wide characters (of type wchar_t) are wistringstream, wostringstream, and wstringstream.

TABLE 5.15: String Stream Operations

Operation	Description

Default constructors:
`istringstream insstr;`
`ostringstream outsstr;`
`stringstream sstr;`
	Construct empty string streams

Explicit-value constructors:
`istringstream insstr(stringVal);`
`ostringstream outsstr(stringVal);`
`stringstream sstr(stringVal);`
	Construct a string stream and initialize it with the characters in *stringVal*. (These constructors may also have a second argument that is a mode specifier as described in Section 5.1)

`outsstr << value`	Convert *value* to a string of characters and insert these into `outsstr`
`insstr >> variable`	Extracts and discards leading white-space characters from `insstr` and then extracts characters corresponding to a value of the type of *variable*, converts them to such a value, and assigns it to *variable* (in the same way the `>>` is used to input values from `istreams`).
`s.str()`	Returns the `string` object that contains a copy of the contents of the string stream *s*
`s.str(stringVal)`	Replaces the contents of the string stream *s* with the string in *stringVal*

String streams are a very useful in programs such as **graphical user interfaces** (**GUIs**), in which all input and output is done via strings. To do numeric processing of input values, the text string that is input must be broken up into pieces called **tokens** using some string-tokenizer mechanism (e.g., `strtok()` in the `<cstring>` library). String-to-number converters (e.g., `atoi()` and `atof()` in `<cstring>`) are then needed to convert these tokens to an appropriate numeric type. For output, number-to-string converters are needed to convert numeric values to strings.

The program in Figure 5.2 is a simple demonstration of how this can be done using string streams. It constructs an `istringstream` from the `string` date, uses the input operator `>>` to break it up into individual tokens, some of which are words and others are integers, and displays these on separate lines. This indicates how an `istringstream` object can be used do both string tokenizing and string-to-number conversions. The program then produces some formatted output to the `ostringstream` ostr and then uses `str()` to make a copy of the string in an `ostream` and in an `ofstream`. This illustrates how we can do some rather elaborate formatting one time, outputting it to a string, from where it can be output anywhere we might want.

Figure 5.2 String Stream Demo

```cpp
#include <iostream>
#include <fstream>
#include <iomanip>
#include <cassert>
#include <sstream>
using namespace std;

int main()
{
    string date = "U.S. independence:  July 4, 1776";

    istringstream istr(date);

    string word1, word2, month;
    int day, year;
    char comma;

    istr >> word1 >> word2 >> month >> day >> comma >> year;
    cout << "Contents of string stream istr, one word per line:\n"
         << word1 << '\n' << word2 << '\n' << month << '\n'
         << day << comma << '\n' << year << '\n' << endl;

    const int Y2K = 1999;
    ofstream outfile("file5-2.out");
    assert(outfile.is_open());

    ostringstream ostr;

    ostr << word1 << "bicentennial: " << month
         << setw(2) << day << ", " << year + 200 << endl;

    cout << "Contents of string stream ostr:\n" << ostr.str();
    outfile << ostr.str();
}
```

Figure 5.2 (continued)

Execution Trace:

```
Contents of string stream istr, one word per line:
U.S.
independence:
July
4,
1776


Contents of string stream ostr:
U.S. bicentennial: July 4, 1976
```

Contents of *file5-2.out***:**

```
U.S. bicentennial: July 4, 1976
```

▲

✔ Quick Quiz 5.2

1. To store strings, C uses a(n) _____ array with a(n) _____ appended at the end.
2. "" is a(n) _____ string.
3. A(n) _____ can be used to associate a stream with a **string** and to read input from the string or to write output to it.

Questions 4–17 assume the declarations

```
string s1,
       s2 = "neu",
       s3 = "roses are red";
```

and that the data entered for input operations is

```
The cat in the hat
```

4. `s1.size()` = _____, `s2.size()` = _____, `s3.size()` = _____
5. `cin >> s1;` will assign _____ to s1
6. `getline(cin, s1);` will assign _____ to s1
7. After `s1 = s2 + s3;` is executed, s1 will have the value _____.
8. `s2[1]` = _____
9. `s2.append("tron")` = _____
10. After `s3.insert(10, "colo")` is executed, s3 will have the value _____
11. `s3.erase(4, s3.length()-4)` = _____
12. `s3.replace(0, 1, s2.substr(0,1))` = _____
13. `s3.find("re")` = _____.

14. s3.find_first_of(s2) = _____
15. s2 < s3. (True or false)
16. s3.compare(s2) = _____

◆ Exercises 5.2

The following exercises ask you to write functions to do various kinds of string processing. To test these functions you should write driver programs as instructed in Programming Problems 13–23 at the end of this chapter.

1. Write a function to count occurrences of a string in another string.

2. Write a function that accepts the number of a month and returns the name of the month.

3. Write a function that accepts the name of a month and returns the number of the month.

4. Write a function that, given a string of lowercase and uppercase letters, returns a copy of the string in all lowercase letters; and another function that, given a string of lowercase and uppercase letters, returns a copy of the string in all uppercase letters. (*Hint:* Use the functions provided in <cctype>.)

5. Write a function replace_all(), such that a call

      newString = replace_all(*str*, *substring*, *newSubstring*);

   will return a copy of string *str* with each occurrence of *substring* replaced by *newSubstring*.

6. Write a function that, given the three components of a name (the first name, middle name or initial, and last name), returns a single string consisting of the last name, followed by a comma, and then the first name and middle initial. For example, given "John", "Quincy", and "Doe", the function should return the string "Doe, John Q.".

7. Proceed as in Exercise 6, but design the function to accept a single string object consisting of a first name, a middle name or initial, and a last name. As before, the function should return a single string consisting of the last name, followed by a comma, and then the first name and middle initial. For example, given "John Quincy Doe", the function should return the string "Doe, John Q.".

8. Write a function that reads a string of digits, possibly preceded by + or −, and converts this string to the integer value it represents. Be sure that your function checks that the string is well formed, that is, that it represents a valid integer. (*Hint:* Use the functions provided in <cctype> and <cstdlib>.)

9. Proceed as in Exercise 8, but for strings representing real numbers in either decimal or scientific form.

10. A string is said to be a ***palindrome*** if it does not change when the order of its characters is reversed. For example,

    madam
    463364
    ABLE WAS I ERE I SAW ELBA

are palindromes. Write a function that, given a string, returns true if that string is a palindrome and returns false otherwise.

11. Write a function that accepts two strings and determines whether one string is an **anagram** of the other, that is, whether one string is a permutation of the characters in the other string. For example, "dear" and "dare" are anagrams of "read."

5.3 Case Study: Text Editing

The preparation of textual material such as letters, books, and computer programs often involves the insertion, deletion, and replacement of parts of the text. The software of most computer systems includes an **editor** or **word processor** that makes it easy to carry out these operations. The problem here is to write a simple text-editor program that uses string operations to implement a few basic text-editing operations. Since C++ does not have a standard graphics library, our text editor will not have a *GUI* (*graphical user interface*) in which the various editing commands can be selected from pull-down menus. Instead the user will use "hot keys" from a menu of editing options.

More specifically, the program will allow the user to select from a menu of text-editing operations: insert, delete, replace, get a new line of text, and quit. The text to be edited will be read from a text file, one line at a time. Each line will be displayed on the screen, and the user can edit it using the operations provided. After editing is complete, that line will be written to an output file and the next line will be read and processed in a similar manner.

In designing a solution to this problem, there is one main object: a text editor. It will provide the following operations:

- Construct a text editor, given the name of the input file to be edited and the name of the output file to contain the edited text
- Run the editor, accepting and carrying out user-specified commands
- Display a menu of editing commands (insert, delete, replace, get a new line of text, quit)
- Insert a string into the current line of text
- Delete a string from the current line of text
- Replace a string in the current line of text with another string
- Get the next line of text
- Wrap up the editing process

The file-processing operations from Section 5.1 provide what we need to handle the file opening, I/O, and closing. And the `string` operations from the previous section make it easy to implement the basic editing operations.

Figure 5.3 shows the files *TextEditor.h* and *TextEditor.cpp* that implement the `TextEditor` class. Its function members implement the operations just listed and its data members are the following:

- `myInstream`: an `ifstream` from the file to be edited opened by the constructor
- `myOutstream`: an `ofstream` to the file of edited text opened by the constructor

- myLine: a string that stores the current text being edited

The driver program simply gets the name of the input file from the user, attaches the string ".out" to produce the name of the output file, constructs a TextEditor object editor for these files, and sends it a run() message.

Figure 5.3 Text Editor

```
/*-- TextEditor.h ---------------------------------------------------------

   This header file defines the data type TextEditor for editing text files.
   Basic operations are:
      Constructor:  Construct a TextEditor object for given files
      run()         Run the editor
      showMenu():   Display the menu of editing "hot keys"
      insert():     Insert a string in a line of text
      erase():      Remove a string from a line of text
      replace():    Replace a string by another string in a line of text
      next():       Output edited line and get next line to edit
      quit():       Wrap up editing
   -----------------------------------------------------------------------*/


#include <iostream>
#include <string>
#include <fstream>

class TextEditor
{
 public:
  /******** Function Members ********/
  TextEditor(string inputFile, string outputFile);
  /*-----------------------------------------------------------------------
     Construct a text editor for files named inputFile and outputFile.

     Precondition:  inputFile is the file to be edited.
     Postcondition: outputFile contains the edited text.
     ---------------------------------------------------------------------*/


  void run();
  /*-----------------------------------------------------------------------
     Run the editor.
```

Figure 5.3 (continued)

```
   Precondition:  None.
   Postcondition: Text from inputFile has been edited and output to
       outputFile.
   --------------------------------------------------------------*/


void showMenu();
/*------------------------------------------------------------------

   Display menu of editing commands.

   Precondition:  None.
   Postcondition: Menu has been output to cout.
   --------------------------------------------------------------*/


void insert(string str1, string str2);
/*------------------------------------------------------------------

   Insert a string into a line of text.

   Precondition:  None.
   Postcondition: str1 has been inserted before str2 in myLine if
       str2 is found in myLine; otherwise, myLine is unchanged.
   --------------------------------------------------------------*/


void erase(string str);
/*------------------------------------------------------------------

   Remove a string from a line of text.

   Preconditions: None.
   Postcondition: str has been removed from myLine if str is found
       in myLine; otherwise, myLine is unchanged.
   --------------------------------------------------------------*/


void replace(string str1, string str2);
/*------------------------------------------------------------------

   Replace one string with another in a line of text.

   Precondition:  None.
   Postcondition: str1 has been replaced with str2 in myLine if str1
       is found in myLine; otherwise, myLine is unchanged.
   --------------------------------------------------------------*/
```

Figure 5.3 (continued)

```
  void next();
  /*-----------------------------------------------------------------
    Move on to next line of text to edit.

    Precondition:  None.
    Postcondition: String that was in myLine has been output to
        myOutstream and a new line read from myInstream into myLine.
    ---------------------------------------------------------------*/

  void quit();
  /*-----------------------------------------------------------------
    Quit editing.

    Precondition:  None.
    Postcondition: String that was in myLine has been output to
        outputFile and any lines remaining in inputFile have been
        copied to outputFile.
    ---------------------------------------------------------------*/

 private:
  /******** Data Members ********/
  ifstream myInstream;
  ofstream myOutstream;
  string myLine;
};
```

```
/*-- TextEditor.cpp -------------------------------------------------

   Contains definitions of the function members of class TextEditor.
   ---------------------------------------------------------------*/

#include <iostream>
#include <string>
#include <cctype>
using namespace std;

#include "TextEditor.h"
```

Figure 5.3 (continued)

```
//--- Utility function to eat spaces from cin
void eatBlanks()
{
  char blank;
  while (cin.peek() == ' ')
    cin.get(blank);
}


//--- Definition of constructor
TextEditor::TextEditor(string inputFile, string outputFile)
{
  myInstream.open(inputFile.data());
  myOutstream.open(outputFile.data());
  if (!myInstream.is_open() || !myOutstream.is_open())
  {
    cerr << "Error in opening files.";
    exit(-1);
  }
}


//--- Definition of run()
void TextEditor::run()
{
  showMenu();
  cout << "Enter an editing command following each prompt >\n\n";
  getline(myInstream, myLine);
  cout << "TEXT: "   << myLine << endl;
  char command;
  string str1, str2;
  for (;;)
  {
    if (myInstream.eof()) break;
    cout << '>';
    cin >> command;
    cin.ignore(1, '\n');
    switch(toupper(command))
    {
```

Figure 5.3 (continued)

```
            case 'I' : eatBlanks();
                       getline(cin, str1);
                       cout << "Insert before what string? ";
                       getline(cin, str2);
                       insert(str1, str2);
                       break;
            case 'D' : eatBlanks();
                       getline(cin, str1);
                       erase(str1);
                       break;
            case 'R' : eatBlanks();
                       getline(cin, str1);
                       cout << "With what? ";
                       getline(cin, str2);
                       replace(str1, str2);
                       break;
            case 'N' : next();
                       break;
            case 'Q' : quit();
                       break;
            default :  cout << "\n*** Illegal command ***\n";
                       showMenu();
                       cout << "TEXT:" << myLine << endl;
      }// end of switch

      if (!myInstream.eof())
        cout << "TEXT: " << myLine << endl;
   }
   cout << "\n*** Editing complete ***\n";
}


//--- Definition of showMenu
void TextEditor::showMenu()
{
  cout << "Editing commands are:\n"
          "  I str: Insert string str before another string\n"
          "  D str:   Delete string str\n"
```

Figure 5.3 (continued)

```
               "  R str:    Replace string str with another string\n"
               "  N :       Get next line of text\n"
               "  Q :       Quit editing\n";
}


//--- Definition of insert()
void TextEditor::insert(string str1, string str2)
{
  int position = myLine.find(str2);
  if (position != string::npos)
    myLine.insert(position, str1);
  else
    cout << str2 << " not found\n";
}


//--- Definition of erase()
void TextEditor::erase(string str)
{
  int position = myLine.find(str);
  if (position != string::npos)
    myLine.erase(position, str.length());
  else
    cout << str << " not found\n";
}


//--- Definition of replace()
void TextEditor::replace(string str1, string str2)
{
  int position = myLine.find(str1);
  if (position != string::npos)
    myLine.replace(position, str1.length(), str2);
  else
    cout << str1 << " not found\n";
}
```

Figure 5.3 (continued)

```
//--- Definition of next()
void TextEditor::next()
{
  myOutstream << myLine << endl;
  getline(myInstream, myLine);
  cout << "\nNext line:\n";
}

//--- Definition of quit()
void TextEditor::quit()
{
  myOutstream << myLine << endl;
  for (;;)
  {
    getline(myInstream, myLine);
    if (myInstream.eof()) break;
    myOutstream << myLine << endl;
  }
}
```

```
/*-- driver.cpp -------------------------------------------------------
   Driver program for TextEditor class.  It gets the name of a file to
   be edited from the user, appends ".out" for the output file, builds
   a TextEditor object editor for these files, and sends it the run()
   message.
   ----------------------------------------------------------------------*/

#include <iostream>
#include <string>
using namespace std;
```

Figure 5.3 (continued)

```
#include "TextEditor.h"
int main()
{
  string inFileName,
         outFileName;
  cout << "Enter the name of the input file: ";
  getline(cin, inFileName);
  outFileName = inFileName +".out";
  cout << "The output file is " << outFileName << "\n\n";
  TextEditor editor(inFileName, outFileName);
  editor.run();
}
```

Listing of text file *file5-3* used in sample run:

```
Foursscore and five years ago, our mothers
brought forth on continent
a new nation conceived in liberty and and dedicated
to the preposition that all men
are created equal.
```

Execution Trace:
```
Enter the name of the input file: file5-3
The output file is file5-3.out

Editing commands are:
  I str: Insert string str before another string
  D str:   Delete string str
  R str:   Replace string str with another string
  N :      Get next line of text
  Q :      Quit editing
Enter an editing command following each prompt >

TEXT: Foursscore and five years ago, our mothers
>D s
TEXT: Fourscore and five years ago, our mothers
>R five
With what? seven
TEXT: Fourscore and seven years ago, our mothers
```

Figure 5.3   (continued)

```
>R moth
With what? fath
TEXT: Fourscore and seven years ago, our fathers
>N

Next line:
TEXT: brought forth on continent
>I this
Insert before what string? con
TEXT: brought forth on this continent
>N

Next line:
TEXT: a new nation conceived in liberty and and dedicated
>D and
TEXT: a new nation conceived in liberty and dedicated
>N

Next line:
TEXT: to the preposition that all men
>R pre
With what? pro
TEXT: to the proposition that all men
>q

*** Editing complete ***
```

Listing of edited file (*file5-3.out*) produced:

```
Fourscore and seven years ago, our fathers
brought forth on this continent
a new nation conceived in liberty and dedicated
to the proposition that all men
are created equal.
```

▲

5.4 Introduction to Pattern Matching (optional)

In Section 5.2, we described several of the string operations provided in the C++ string class. In particular, we considered several search functions for finding one string in another string. Each of them is an instance of the general *pattern-matching problem* of searching for some *pattern* in a piece of *text*. It occurs in a variety of applications, such as text editing, searching a file with Unix's grep command, and bioinformatic algorithms for searching genomes. It must be implemented efficiently, therefore. In this section we look at some possible implementations.

One way to proceed is with a straightforward "brute force" approach. To illustrate it, suppose we wish to find the string *pattern* = 'abcabd' in *text* = "abcabcabdabba". The search begins at the first position of each. The first five characters match but a mismatch occurs when the next characters are compared:

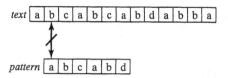

So we backtrack to the beginning of *pattern*, shift one position to the right in *text*, and start the search over again:

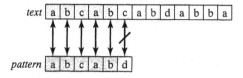

This time a mismatch occurs immediately, so we backtrack once more to the beginning of *pattern*, shift another position to the right in *text*, and try again:

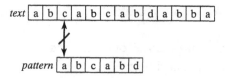

Another mismatch of the first characters occurs, so we backtrack and shift once again:

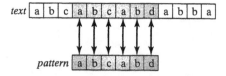

On the next search, all of the characters in *pattern* match the corresponding characters in *text*, and thus *pattern* has been located in *text*.

In this example, only three backtracks were required, and two of these required backing up only one character. The situation may be much worse, however. To illustrate, suppose that the text to be searched consists of one hundred characters, each of which is the same, and the pattern consists of 49 of these same characters followed by a different character, for example,

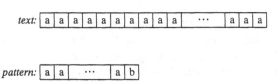

In beginning the search for *pattern* in *text*, we find that the first 49 characters match, but that the last character in *pattern* does not match the corresponding character in *text*:

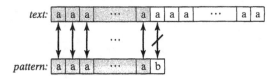

We must therefore backtrack to the beginning of *pattern*, shift one position to the right in *text*, and repeat the search. As before, we make 49 successful comparisons of characters in *pattern* with characters in *text* before a mismatch occurs:

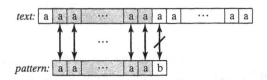

This same thing happens again and again until eventually we reach the end of *text* and are able to determine that *pattern* is not found in *text*. After each unsuccessful scan, we must backtrack from the last character of *pattern* way back to the first character and restart the search one position to the right in *text*.

The source of inefficiency in this algorithm is the backtracking required whenever a mismatch occurs. To illustrate how it can be avoided, consider again the first example in which *pattern* = "abcabd" and *text* = "abcabcabdabba":

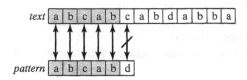

In the first scan, we find that *pattern*[0] = *text*[0], *pattern*[1] = *text*[1], *pattern*[2] = *text*[2], *pattern*[3] = *text*[3], and *pattern*[4] = *text*[4], *but pattern*[5] ≠ *text*[5]:

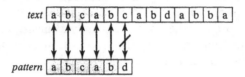

Examining *pattern*, we see that *pattern*[0] ≠ *pattern*[1]; thus *pattern*[0] cannot possibly match *text*[1] because *pattern*[1] did. Similarly, since *pattern*[0] is different from *pattern*[2], which matched *text*[2], neither can *pattern*[0] match *text*[2]. Consequently, we can immediately "slide" *pattern* three positions to the right, eliminating the backtracks to positions 1 and 2 in *text*. Moreover, examining the part of *pattern* that has matched a substring of *text*,

abcab

we see that we need not check *pattern*[0] and *pattern*[1] again, since they are the same as *pattern*[3] and *pattern*[4], respectively, which have already matched characters in *text*:

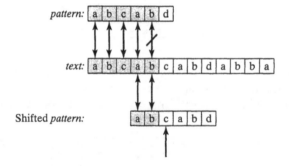

This partial match means that we can continue our search at position 5 in *text* and position 2 in *pattern*; no backtracking to examine characters before that in the position where a mismatch occurred is necessary at all!

The non-backtracking phenomenon in this example is what characterizes the better pattern-matching algorithms such as the *Knuth–Morris–Pratt algorithm*. Details about it and examples illustrating it can be found on the text's website. Another efficient approach is the Boyer–Moore method described in most algorithms texts.

The Knuth–Morris–Pratt solution to the pattern-matching problem has an interesting history. A theorem proved by Cook in 1970 states that any problem that can be solved using an abstract model of a computer called a *pushdown automaton* can be solved in time proportional to the size of the problem using an actual computer (more precisely, using a random access machine). In particular, this theorem implies the existence of an algorithm for solving the pattern-matching problem in time proportional to $m + n$, where m and n are the sizes of the pattern and text, respectively.

Knuth and Pratt painstakingly reconstructed the proof of Cook's theorem and so constructed the pattern-matching algorithm described in this section. At approximately the same time, Morris constructed essentially the same algorithm while considering the practical problem of designing a text editor. Thus, we see that not all algorithms are discovered by a "flash of insight" and that theoretical computer science does indeed sometimes lead to practical applications.

5.5 Introduction to Data Encryption (optional)

The basic string operations such as length, position, concatenate, copy, insert, and delete that we considered in the Section 5.2 are the operations most useful in text-editing applications. There are, however, some important kinds of string processing that require other basic operations. In this section we consider one such application, data encryption, and the basic operations of *substitution* and *permutation* that are important in this application.

Encryption refers to the coding of information to keep it secret. It is accomplished by transforming the string of characters containing the information to produce a new string that is a coded form of the information. This is called a **cryptogram** or **ciphertext** and may be safely stored or transmitted. At a later time it can be deciphered by reversing the encrypting process to recover the original information, which is called **plaintext**.

Data encryption has been used to send secret military and political messages since the days of Julius Caesar. Recent applications include the Washington-Moscow hotline, electronic funds transfer, electronic mail, database security, and many other situations in which the transmission of secret data is crucial. Less profound applications have included Captain Midnight secret decoder rings that could be obtained in the 1950s for twenty-five cents and two Ovaltine labels, puzzles appearing in the daily newspaper, and many other frivolous applications. In this section we describe some encryption schemes ranging from the Caesar cipher scheme of the 1st century B.C. to the Data Encryption Standard and the public key encryption schemes of the 20th century.

The simplest encryption schemes are based on the string operation of **substitution**, in which the plaintext string is traversed and each character is replaced by some other character, according to a fixed rule. For example, the **Caesar cipher** scheme consists of replacing each letter by the letter that appears k positions later in the alphabet for some integer k. (The alphabet is thought of as being arranged in a circle, with A following Z.) In the original Caesar cipher, k was 3, so that each occurrence of A in the plaintext was replaced by D, each B by E, ..., each Y by B, and each Z by C. For example, using the character set

$$A B C D E F G H I J K L M N O P Q R S T U V W X Y Z$$

we would encrypt the string "IDESOFMARCH" as follows:

To decode the message, the receiver uses the same **key** *k* and recovers the plaintext by applying the inverse transformation, that is, by traversing the ciphertext string and replacing each character by the character *k* positions earlier in the alphabet. This is obviously not a very secure scheme, since it is possible to "break the code" by simply trying the 26 possible values for the key *k*.

An improved substitution operation is to use a **keyword** to specify several different displacements of letters rather than the single offset *k* of the Caesar cipher. In this **Vignère cipher** scheme, the same keyword is added character by character to the plaintext string, where each character is represented by its position in the character set and addition is carried out modulo 26. For example, suppose the character set and positions of characters are given by

Position	0	1	2	3	4	5	6	7	8	9	10	11	12
Character	A	B	C	D	E	F	G	H	I	J	K	L	M

	13	14	15	16	17	18	19	20	21	22	23	24	25
	N	O	P	Q	R	S	T	U	V	W	X	Y	Z

and that the keyword is DAGGER. The plaintext IDESOFMARCH is then encrypted as follows:

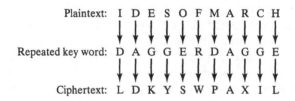

```
        Plaintext:  I D E S O F M A R C H
                    ↓ ↓ ↓ ↓ ↓ ↓ ↓ ↓ ↓ ↓ ↓
Repeated key word:  D A G G E R D A G G E
                    ↓ ↓ ↓ ↓ ↓ ↓ ↓ ↓ ↓ ↓ ↓
       Ciphertext:  L D K Y S W P A X I L
```

Again, the receiver must know the key and recovers the plaintext by subtracting the characters in this keyword from those in the ciphertext.

A different substitution operation is to use a *substitution table*, for example:

Original character:	A	B	C	D	E	F	G	H	I	J	K	L	M
Substitute character:	Q	W	E	R	T	Y	U	I	O	P	A	S	D

	N	O	P	Q	R	S	T	U	V	W	X	Y	Z
	F	G	H	J	K	L	Z	X	C	V	B	N	M

The string IDESOFMARCH would then be encoded as follows:

```
 Plaintext:  I D E S O F M A R C H
             ↓ ↓ ↓ ↓ ↓ ↓ ↓ ↓ ↓ ↓ ↓
Ciphertext:  O R T L G Y D Q K E I
```

To decode the ciphertext string, the receiver must again know the key, that is, the substitution table.

Since there are 26! (approximately 10^{28}) possible substitution tables, this scheme is considerably more secure than the simple Caesar cipher scheme. Experienced cryptographers can easily break the code, however, by analyzing frequency counts of certain letters and combinations of letters.

Another basic string operation in some encryption schemes is **permutation**, in which the characters in the plaintext or in blocks of the plaintext are rearranged. For example, we might divide the plaintext string into blocks (substrings) of size 3 and permute the characters in each block as follows:

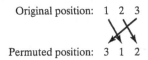

Original position: 1 2 3

Permuted position: 3 1 2

Thus, the message IDESOFMARCH is encrypted as follows (after the addition of a randomly selected character X so that the string length is a multiple of the block length):

Plaintext: I DE S O F M A R C H X

Ciphertext: D E I O F S A R M H X C

To decode the ciphertext string, the receiver must know the key permutation and its inverse:

Original position: 1 2 3
Permuted position: 2 3 1

Data Encryption Standard

Most modern encryption schemes use both of these techniques, by combining several substitution and permutation operations. One of the best known is the **Data Encryption Standard (DES)** developed in the early 1970s by the federal government and the IBM corporation.

In DES, the input is a bit string of length 64 representing a block of characters in the plaintext string (for example, the concatenation of the ASCII codes of eight characters), and the output is a 64-bit string that is the ciphertext. The encryption is carried out as a complicated series of permutations and substitutions. The substitution operations used are similar to those in earlier examples. Some are obtained by the addition of keywords and others use a substitution table.

Because it was thought to be almost impossible to break, DES was adopted by the National Institute of Standards and Technology (formerly the National Bureau of Standards) as the standard encryption scheme for sensitive federal documents. It soon became one of the most widely used methods of data encryption.

Questions about whether the 48-bit keys used in the substitutions were long enough and the substitution keys sophisticated enough to provide the necessary security were soon raised, however. And in 1998, DES was broken by the Electronic Frontier Foundation (EFF) using custom-designed chips and a personal computer running for 56 hours. Although it was reaffirmed in 1999 by the federal government as the encryption scheme of choice, it has since been replaced with a new standard for encryption known as the Advanced Encryption Standard (AES).

Public-Key Encryption

Each of the encryption schemes considered thus far requires that both the sender and the receiver know the key or keys used in encrypting the plaintext. This means that although the cryptogram may be transmitted through some public channel such as a telephone line that is not secure, the keys must be transmitted in some secure manner, for example, by a courier. This problem of maintaining secrecy of the key is compounded when it must be shared by several people.

Another popular type of encryption scheme eliminates this problem by using two keys, one for encryption and one for decryption. These schemes are called **public-key encryption schemes** because the encryption key is not kept secret. The keys used in these systems have the following properties:

1. For each encryption key there is exactly one corresponding decryption key, and it is distinct from the encryption key.
2. There are many such pairs of keys, and they are relatively easy to compute.
3. It is almost impossible to determine the decryption key if one knows only the encryption key.
4. The encryption key is made public by the receiver to all those who will transmit messages to him or her, but only the receiver knows the decryption key.

In 1978, Rivest, Shamir, and Adelman proposed a method for implementing a public-key encryption scheme.[9] The public key is a pair (e, n) of integers, and a message string M is encrypted by (1) dividing M into blocks $M_1, M_2, \ldots, M_k$; (2) converting each block M_i of characters to an integer P_i in the range 0 through $n - 1$ (for example, by concatenating the ASCII codes of the characters); and (3) raising each block to the power e and reducing modulo n:

$$\text{Plaintext:} \quad M = M_1 M_2 \cdots M_k \rightarrow P_1 P_2 \cdots P_k$$

$$\text{Ciphertext:} \quad C = C_1 C_2 \ldots C_k, \quad C_i = P_i^e \ \% \ n$$

(Here % is the mod operator in C++.) The cipher text C is decrypted by raising each block C_i to the power d and reducing modulo n, where d is a secret decryption key.

To illustrate, suppose that $(17, 2773)$ is the public encryption code and that we use $0, 1, 2, \ldots, 25$ as the numeric codes for the letters 'A', 'B', 'C', \ldots, 'Z', respectively. To encrypt a string such as $M = $ "IDESOFMARCH" using the RSA algorithm, we divide M into 2-character blocks $M_1, M_2, \ldots, M_6$ (after appending the randomly

---

[9] R. L. Rivest, A. Shamir, and L. Adelman, "A method for obtaining digital signatures and public-key cryptosystems," *Communications of the ACM* 21, 2 (February 1978): 120–126.

selected character X) and represent each block M_i as an integer P_i by concatenating the numeric codes of the characters that make up the block:

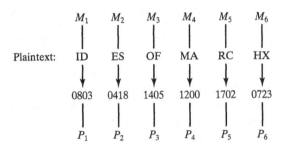

	M_1	M_2	M_3	M_4	M_5	M_6
Plaintext:	ID	ES	OF	MA	RC	HX
	0803	0418	1405	1200	1702	0723
	P_1	P_2	P_3	P_4	P_5	P_6

Each of these blocks P_i is then encrypted by calculating $C_i = P_i \% 2773$:

Ciphertext:	0779	1983	2641	1444	0052	0802
	C_1	C_2	C_3	C_4	C_5	C_6

For this encryption key, the corresponding decrypting key is $d = 157$. Thus, we decrypt the ciphertext by calculating $C_i^{157} \% 2773$ for each block C_i. For the preceding ciphertext, this gives

Decrypted ciphertext: 0803 0418 1405 1200 1702 0723

which is the numeric form of the original message.

In the preceding example, we chose the number n to be the product of the two primes 47 and 59. Rivest, Shamir, and Adelman, however, suggested that n should be the product of two large "random" primes p and q, $n = p \cdot q$, each having several hundreds of digits. The security of the RSA scheme depends on the difficulty of finding the prime factors of large numbers.

 We have only scratched the surface of the important area of cryptography and security. Much more information about it can be found on the Internet. The website for this text contains more information about the DES and RSA schemes.

SUMMARY

📖 Chapter Notes

- The C++ model for input and output is a *stream*, `istream`s for input from the keyboard and `ostream`s for output to the screen.

- The *state* of an `istream`—good, bad, fail—can be checked by sending a message—`good()`, `bad()`, `fail()`—to the `istream` object (e.g., `cin`). The `clear()` message can be used to reset states, and the `ignore()` message can be used to skip characters in the stream.

- The *input operator* `>>` skips leading white space (space, tab, or newline). The `noskipws` and `skipws` manipulators can be used to turn this feature off or on. The `get()` method provides a useful alternative for reading any character, whether white space or not.

■   The `endl` manipulator inserts a newline character (`'\n'`) into an `ostream` to end a line of output and then flushes it. The `ostream` `cout` is flushed automatically whenever the `istream` `cin` is used.

■   The format of output is controlled by inserting *format manipulators* into output lists. Except for `setw()`, which affects only the next output value, these manipulators control the format of all subsequent output in the program unless changed by some other manipulator.

■   The file stream classes `ifstream` and `ofstream` are subclasses of `istream` and `ostream`, respectively, and thus inherit the operations of these classes.

■   When the input operator `>>` is applied to a `string` object, it extracts non-white-space characters from an `istream` and transfers them into a `string` object until a whitespace character is encountered.

■   The `getline()` function stops extracting and transferring characters when a newline character is encountered. It can thus be used to read an entire line of input. To read characters only up to the next white-space character, the input operator `>>` should be used.

■   The `string` class provides many useful methods for text processing (e.g., searching a string; extracting, inserting, deleting, and replacing substrings; accessing individual characters; concatenation).

■   *String streams* make in-memory I/O possible by connecting streams to a string in memory and reading input from the string or writing output to it.

☞ Programming Pointers

1.   The input operator `>>` will skip leading white space when inputting a string value, but will stop reading characters when a white-space character is encountered (or the end of the file is reached); this white-space character will not be removed from the input stream. The string function `getline()` will not skip leading white space and will read characters until the end-of-line character (or other specified delimiter) is encountered, and it will remove it from the input stream.

2.   Care must be taken when mixing calls to `>>` and `getline()`. If a call to `>>` precedes a call to `getline()` and the values being read are separated by a newline character, then an additional call to `get()` should be inserted between `>>` and `getline()` to consume the newline character. Otherwise, `getline()` will stop reading immediately when it encounters that newline and no value will be read.

3.   If no character in an input stream is found—including the end-of-file mark—that can belong to a value of the type of the variable, the input operation is said to fail. Because no characters are removed from the stream, an infinite loop can easily result. Including a statement such as

```
if (cin.fail()) break;
```

after the input statement can be used to detect this condition and terminate repetition. The `ignore()` function member can be used to remove offending characters from the stream.

4.   Once the eof, bad, or fail state bits have been set in a stream, no subsequent operations can be performed on that stream until those bits have been cleared (using the `clear()` member)—but see the preceding programming pointer.

5.   Parameters to hold stream arguments must be reference parameters, because an input or output operation changes the stream's read or write position, respectively.

6. If a program is to read data from a file, an `ifstream` must be declared and initialized as a connection between the program and the file. If it is to write data to a file, an `ofstream` must be declared and initialized as a connection between the program and the file.

7. A file stream should be closed using the member `close()` once use of that stream has been completed.

8. String streams are useful for parsing input strings. They also make it possible to do some rather elaborate formatting one time and then output it to a string from where it can be output to various destinations.

9. Use the string operation `data()` or `c_str()` to extract the char array containing a string stored in a `string` object. For example, use `streamName.open(fileName.data());` to open a stream to a file whose name is stored in the `string` object `fileName`.

▲ ADT Tips

1. The C++ I/O classes illustrate the importance of *abstraction* in designing and implementing data types. Programmers can use `istream` and `ostream` objects without having to concern themselves with the messy implementation details of how input and output actually occur.

2. The C++ I/O class hierarchy illustrates how one class can be reused in building another class and how all of the members of the first class are automatically inherited by the new class. We will see how to reuse classes in this way and the importance of inheritance in later chapters.

3. C++ provides many standard structured data types that are implemented very efficiently. Thus, there is often no reason to "reinvent the wheel" by creating a data type when the language already provides one. For example, the many powerful string operations provided in the C++ `string` class make it unnecessary to create a new string class (except perhaps in special applications).

▦ Programming Problems

Section 5.1

1. Write a program to concatenate two files; that is, to append one file to the end of the other.

2. Write a program that reads a text file and counts the vowels in the file.

3. Write a program that reads a text file and counts the occurrences in the file of a specified string entered during execution of the program.

4. Write a program that reads a text file and counts the characters in each line. The program should display the line number and the length of the shortest and longest lines in the file, as well as the average number of characters per line.

5. Write a program to copy one text file into another text file in which the lines are numbered 1, 2, 3, . . . with a number at the left of each line.

6. Write a program that reads a text file and writes it to another text file, but with leading blanks and blank lines removed.

7. Write a program that reads a file containing a C++ program and produces a file with all comments stripped from the program.

8. Write a simple text-formatting program that reads a text file and produces another text file in which blank lines are removed, multiple blanks are replaced with a single blank, and no lines are longer than some given length. Put as many words as possible on the same line. You will have to break some lines of the given file, but do not break any words or put punctuation marks at the beginning of a new line.

9. Extend the *text-formatting* program of the preceding problem to right-justify each line except the last in the new text file by adding evenly distributed blanks in lines where necessary.

10. Write a program to search the file UserIdFile (see file descriptions at the end of Chapter 4) to find and display the resources used to date for specified users whose identification numbers are entered during execution of the program.

11. Write a program to search the file InventoryFile (see file descriptions at the end of Chapter 4) to find an item with a specified item number. If a match is found, display the item number and the number currently in stock; otherwise, display a message indicating that it was not found.

12. At the end of each month, a report is produced that shows the status of each user's account in UserIdFile (see file descriptions at the end of Chapter 4). Write a program to accept the current date and produce a report of the following form:

```
                       USER ACCOUNTS--mm/dd/yy
                          RESOURCE              RESOURCES
         USER-ID            LIMIT                  USED
         -------------------------------------------------
         10101             $750                   $381
         10102             $650                   $599***
            .                .                      .
            .                .                      .
            .                .                      .
```

Here, mm/dd/yy is the current date, and the three asterisks (***) indicate that the user has already used 90 percent or more of the resources available to him or her.

Section 5.2

13. Write a program to test the string-counting function of Exercise 1.

14. Write a program to test the month-name function of Exercise 2.

15. Write a program to test the month-number function of Exercise 3.

16. Write a program to test the case-conversion functions of Exercise 4.

17. Write a program to test the function replace_all() of Exercise 5.

18. Write a program to test the name-formatting function of Exercise 6.

19. Write a program to test the name-formatting function of Exercise 7.

20. Write a program to test the string-to-integer function of Exercise 8.

21. Write a program to test the string-to-real function of Exercise 9.

22. Write a program to test the palindrome-checking function of Exercise 10.

23. Write a program to test the anagram-checking function of Exercise 11.

24. Write a program that analyzes text contained in a file by finding the number of nonblank characters, number of nonblank lines, number of words, and number of sentences and that calculates the average number of characters per word and the average number of words per sentence.

25. Write a program to input a string and then input several lines of text. Determine whether the first string occurs in each line, and if so, print asterisks (*) under each occurrence.

26. The game of Hangman is played by two persons. One person selects a word and the other tries to guess the word by guessing individual letters. Design and implement a program to play Hangman.

27. (Project) Build a `StringType` class to implement a string ADT as described at the beginning of this section. Use a dynamic `char` array to store the string's characters; one of the class constructors should create this array using a capacity specified in the declaration of a `StringType` object; use some default capacity for the default constructor. Implement the operations listed in the ADT description of strings. *Note*: When a `StringType` object's lifetime is over, memory allocated for the data members will be reclaimed automatically but the array allocated dynamically by the constructor will not and a memory leak will result. To avoid this, add a **destructor** to your class whose name is `~StringType()`, has no return type nor parameters, and that uses the `delete` operation to deallocate the array data member. This destructor will be called automatically whenever a `StringType` object's lifetime is over. (See Section 6.3 for more information about class destructors.)

Section 5.4 (optional)

28. Write a program to implement the Caesar cipher scheme.

29. Write a program to implement the Vignère cipher scheme.

30. Write a program to encrypt and decrypt a message by using a substitution table.

31. Write a program to encrypt and decrypt a message by using a permutation scheme.

Lists

CHAPTER CONTENTS

Chapter Objectives

- To study list as an ADT.
- Build a static-array-based implementation of lists and note its strengths and weaknesses.
- Build a dynamic-array-based implementation of lists, note its strengths and weaknesses, and see the need for adding a destructor, a copy constructor, and assignment to the class methods.
- Take a first look at linked lists and note their strengths and weaknesses.
- Study a pointer-based implementation of linked lists.
- (Optional) Study an array-based implementation of linked lists.

Lists of various kinds are common in everyday life:

- Lists of groceries we need to buy at the supermarket
- A list of jobs that we need to do
- A list of appointments we have to keep
- Class lists that inform an instructor who is enrolled in that class
- The list of assignments for a course

- A reading list for that course
- The dean's list of all students who have achieved a certain GPA
- Mailing lists of names and addresses where some printed matter is to be sent
- Voter lists, which are of special interest to persons running for office

Some lists have only one element:

- The list of vowels in the word "list"
- The list of even prime numbers (2)

And some lists are empty:

- The list of even prime numbers greater than 3
- Your grocery list after you check out (hopefully)

There are even lists of lists:

- The lists of lists described so far in this chapter introduction

Lists are everywhere! They are even provided in some programming languages:

- The main data structure provided in Lisp (*List* processing) is the list

Every list involves a collection of things and there certainly are operations that we perform on lists—add "milk" to the grocery list; scratch off "ice cream"; read through the list and check things off to make sure we have everything; and so on. A list, therefore, can be viewed as an abstract data type. It is this ADT and some ways of implementing it that are the topics of study in this chapter.

6.1 List as an ADT

As we just noted, a list is a collection of things. Abstracting from the preceding examples, we recognize that there are certain common properties of the collection in each list:

- It is *homogeneous*—the elements are all of the same type.
- It has a *finite length* (the number of elements).
- The elements are *arranged sequentially*:
  - There is a first element and a last element.
  - Every element except the last has a unique successor and every element except the first has a unique predecessor.

The operations performed on lists will vary considerably from one situation to the next; some of them will be tied quite closely to the type of the elements and the particular way that the list is being used. But they will usually include those listed in the following description of a list as an ADT:

List ADT
Collection of Data Elements A sequence with a finite number of data items, all of the same type.
Basic Operations • *Construction:* Create an empty list. • *Empty:* Check if the list is empty. • *Insert:* Insert an item into the list. • *Delete:* Remove an item from the list. • *Traverse:* Go through the list or a part of it, accessing and processing the elements in order. This operation is also referred to as *iterating* through the list.[1]

In a given application of lists, there would almost certainly be more operations than the five listed here. For example, in addition to the default constructor that creates an empty list, there may be an explicit-value constructor that initializes the list with the contents of an array. There may be a *sort* operation that arranges the list elements so they are in ascending order, or in descending order, or so that some key fields in the elements are in ascending order, and so on.

Also, we have deliberately given rather imprecise descriptions of the last three operations to allow for various possibilities. For a particular kind of list, some additional specifications would make these more precise, perhaps imposing some restrictions on these operations. For example, in the next chapter we will study *stacks*, for which insertion and deletion can be performed at only one end of the list. Then, in Chapter 8, we will consider *queues*, for which insertions can be done only at one end of the list and deletions at the other end.

For the traversal operation, additional specifications are needed to spell out what is involved in *accessing* and *processing* list elements and how many of them are to be examined. We are using the generic term *traversal*, because we want it to encompass several commonly used list operations that have this general behavior such as the following:

■ *Search a list:* Traverse the list, examining list elements (or some key field in them) for a particular item, stopping when it has been found or the entire list has been checked

■ *Output a list:* Traverse the entire list, displaying each list element

■ *Copy a list:* Traverse the entire list, copying the list elements into another list

■ *Save a list:* Traverse the entire list, writing each list element to a file

---

[1] As we will see in Chapter 9, *iterators* play a key role in how the sequential containers in C++'s Standard Template Library are processed.

- *Rearrange a list:* Traverse the entire list (perhaps partially), rearranging the list elements according to some rule. Many sorting methods use repeated traversals of this kind.

Parts of the algorithms that we give to implement the traversal operation will similarly be somewhat generic, containing instructions such as "process the element at this location." In functions that implement these algorithms we will usually process list elements by outputting them. Modifying these algorithms and functions for other kinds of traversals is usually quite straightforward.

Designing and Building a List Class

In our study of ADTs, we wear two hats in this book—a user hat and a builder hat:

Up to now we have primarily been *users* of data types. As we turn our attention to **containers**–objects that store collections of data items—we will also *build* classes to implement many of them. This will help us to do two things:

- Gain more practice in building classes to implement ADTs—*container* classes in particular
- Understand how and why several of these containers are implemented in the C++ Standard Template Library

Building a class consists of two steps:

1. *Design the class*
2. *Implement the class*

We begin, therefore, by looking at the design of a list class.

Designing a List Class   Designing a class to implement an ADT consists of identifying those function members (also called methods) that are needed to carry out the ADT's operations. Time invested in this design phase will pay off in the end when it results in a well-planned class that is easy to use. It is important that we *describe the function members independently of how the class will be implemented.* At this point, we have no idea what data members will be available, so the *function members must be described in some manner that does not depend on any particular representation of the objects. What* a method does and not *how* it does it is what is important. The resulting specification then constitutes the *blueprint* for building the class.

In our definition of a list as an ADT, we identified five basic operations: construct, empty, insert, remove, and traverse. In our initial version of traversal, we will process the list elements by displaying them; this will, therefore, be an output operation for the list class. Our class must, therefore, have (at least) the following function members:

- *Constructor:* Constructs an empty list
- *empty():* Examines a list and produces false or true depending on whether the list contains any values

- *insert()*:   Modifies a list by adding a value at a specified position in the list
- *delete()*:   Modifies a list by removing the element at a specified position in the list
- *display()*:   Traverse the list, displaying the elements

Implementing a List Class   Once a class has been designed, it must be implemented, which involves two steps:

1. Defining data members to store the data values
2. Defining the function members identified in the design phase

For a container class such as a list, the data members provide the storage structures for the container's elements together with any other items that will prove useful or necessary in implementing the operations. We will first use an array to store the list elements and then, in Section 6.4, we will consider a linked-list implementation.

6.2 An Array-Based Implementation of Lists

A list must store a collection of values, so we begin by considering what kind of storage structure(s) to use. In our first implementation, we will use an array to store the list elements. This can be either a static array or a dynamic array. In this section we will use the simpler approach with a static array. As we will see in the next section, using a dynamic array requires some additional operations to deal with dynamic memory allocation.

Selecting a Storage Structure

Lists are often implemented using an array to store the list elements for the following reasons:

- The elements of a list are arranged sequentially as are the elements of an array.
- Most programming languages provide an array data type.
- Developing algorithms for the basic list operations is quite easy.

An array thus seems to be a natural storage structure for implementing a list.

The most common method for storing the list elements in the array is to have the sequential orderings match—that is, store successive list elements in consecutive array locations: the first list element in location 0, the second list element in location 1, and so on.

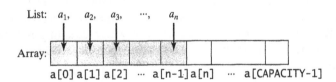

In general, the ith list element is stored in array position i – 1.

Of course, the array must be large enough to hold all of the list elements. This means that we need to choose an array capacity that is large enough to store the largest list that will be used. If we make it too small, we run the risk of array overflow, and if we make it too large, we waste memory.

To guard against array overflow, we need to keep track of how many list elements the array currently stores. Since arrays do not have this information built in, we should have an integer variable to keep a count of the list elements that occupy array positions.

Implementing the Operations

Implementing the basic list operations is straightforward. In the following algorithms, *array* refers to the array that will store the list elements, *capacity* is its capacity, and *size* is the number of list elements that are stored in the array.

Constructor   Because we are using a static array, we can let the compiler handle the memory allocation for it and our constructor need only set *size* to 0.

Empty   For this, we need only check whether *size* is 0.

Traverse   Lists are easily traversed using a loop in which the array index varies over the elements of the array that stores list elements.

 ### Algorithm for Traverse

For index *i* ranging from 0 to *size* – 1:
    Process *array*[*i*].

Insert   Implementing the insertion operation is somewhat more complicated. For example, suppose we wish to insert the new value 56 after the element 48 in the list of integers

$$23, 25, 34, 48, 61, 79, 82, 89, 91, 99$$

to produce the new list

$$23, 25, 34, 48, 56, 61, 79, 82, 89, 91, 99$$

The array used as the basic storage has a fixed capacity, which limits the number of list elements it can store. Thus, it may not be possible to insert a new item into a list because there is no room in the array for it.

Another complication arises from the fact that list elements are stored in consecutive positions of the array. Consequently, to insert a new item, it usually is necessary to move array elements to make room for it. For example, for the insertion operation just described, the array elements in positions 4 through 9 must first be shifted into positions 5 through 10 before the new element can be inserted at position 4:

| 23 | 25 | 34 | 48 | 61 | 79 | 82 | 89 | 91 | 99 | ? | ⋯ | ? |

| 23 | 25 | 34 | 48 | 56 | 61 | 79 | 82 | 89 | 91 | 99 | ⋯ | ? |

The insert algorithm must, therefore, contain instructions to do this shifting of array elements:

Algorithm for Insert

//--- Insert *item* at position *pos* in a list.

// First check if there's room in the array
1. If *size* is equal to *capacity*
    Issue an error message and terminate this operation.

// Next check if the position is legal.
2. If *pos* < 0 or *pos* > *size*
    Signal an illegal insert position and terminate this operation.
    Otherwise:
    // Shift array elements right to make room for *item*
    a. For *i* ranging from *size* down to *pos* + 1:
        array[*i*] = *array*[*i* – 1]
    // Now insert *item* at position *pos* and increase the list size
    b. *array*[*pos*] = *item*
    c. *size*++

The efficiency of this insert algorithm obviously depends on the number of array elements that must be shifted to make room for the new item—that is, on the number of times that the instructions in the loop are executed. In the worst case, the new item must be inserted at the beginning of the list, which requires shifting all of the array elements. When items may be inserted at any positions in the list, on the average, one-half of the array elements must be shifted to make room for a new item. Thus, we can say that, in both the worst case and on average, the computing times for this insert algorithm *grows* linearly with the size of the list. Using the big-O notation introduced in Section 1.2, we can express the computing time as $O(n)$, where n is the list size.

The best case occurs when the new item is inserted at the end of the list. Because no array elements need to be shifted in this case, the computing time does not depend on the size of the list. Insertions can be carried out in constant time; therefore, the best-case computing time is $O(1)$. Two important special kinds of lists for which this is true are *stacks* and *queues*, which we will study in detail in Chapters 7 and 8, respectively.

Delete Implementing the delete operation also requires shifting array elements. For example, to delete the second item in the list

$$23, 25, 34, 48, 56, 61, 79, 82, 89, 91, 99$$

we must shift the elements in positions 2 through 10 into locations 1 through 9 to "close the gap" in the array:

| 23 | 25 | 34 | 48 | 56 | 61 | 79 | 82 | 89 | 91 | 99 | ··· | ? |

| 23 | 34 | 48 | 56 | 61 | 79 | 82 | 89 | 91 | 99 | 99 | ··· | ? |

An algorithm for deleting the element in the array data member at location *pos* must therefore contain instructions to do this shifting of elements:

Algorithm for Delete

//--- Delete the element at position *pos* in a list.

// First check that list isn't empty
1. If *size* is 0
     Issue an error message and terminate this operation.

// Next check that *index* is legal
2. If *pos* < 0 or *pos* ≥ *size*
     Issue an error message and terminate this operation.
   Otherwise:
     // Shift array elements left to close the gap
     a. For index *i* ranging from *pos* to *size* − 2:
          array[*i*] = *array*[*i* + 1]
     // Decrease the list size
     b. *size*− −

The computing time of such a function is easily seen to be the same as that of an insert function—O(*n*) in the worst and average cases and O(1) in the best case.

Because insertion and deletion in this implementation may require shifting many array elements, these operations may be quite slow. Thus, although this implementation is suitable for lists whose contents are fairly constant, it may not be acceptable for those in which a large number of insertions and deletions are performed. In applications in which it is necessary to insert or delete items at any position in the list, better implementations are obtained by using linked lists, which are described later in this chapter.

A List Class With Static Array Storage

The first problem to be addressed in using an array data member to store the list elements has to do with the type of the array's elements and its capacity. In Section 3.2, we saw that a declaration of a static array has the form

```
ElementType array[CAPACITY];
```

Thus, we must decide what to use for *ElementType* and for the constant *CAPACITY* in the declaration of this array.

For *ElementType*, we will use (for now) a **typedef declaration** of the form

```
typedef Some_Specific_Type ElementType;
```

to make *ElementType* a synonym for *Some_Specific_Type*, which its the actual type of the list elements. For example, the declaration

```
typedef int ElementType;
```

makes `ElementType` a synonym for `int`. We will use `ElementType` throughout the class declaration and its implementation so that in the future, if we want a list of doubles, we need only change the `typedef` declaration to

```
typedef double ElementType;
```

For a list of characters, we need only change it to

```
typedef char ElementType;
```

and so on. When the class library is recompiled, the type of the array's elements will be `double` or `char` or whatever other type we put in this `typedef` declaration.

But now the question is where to put this declaration. If we put it inside the class declaration, then each reference to the type identifier `ElementType` outside the class will need to be qualified by writing `List::ElementType`. Because this is somewhat inconvenient (and easy to forget), we will instead put this `typedef` declaration ahead of the class declaration. This will make the type identifier `ElementType` easier to access throughout the class and in any files that `#include List.h`. It will also be easy to find when it needs to be changed for some other type of list elements.

Another reason for putting the `typedef` declaration outside the class declaration is that in later versions of the class, we can do away with it completely by using the more modern alternative—the **template** mechanism—to build a pattern for a `List` class whose element type is left unspecified. The element *type is then passed as a special kind of parameter* at compile time. This is the approach used for the C++ standard containers (which originated in STL, the Standard Template Library). Class templates will be described in Chapter 9.

To set the array capacity, we will use a constant definition of the form

```
const int CAPACITY = SOME_CONSTANT_VALUE;
```

Once again, we face the question of where to put this declaration. To be inside the class declaration, it must be preceded by the keyword `static`,

```
static const int CAPACITY = SOME_CONSTANT_VALUE;
```

to make it a **static data member.**[2] *Class objects have their own copies of ordinary (nonstatic) data members, but there is only one copy of a static data member, which the objects share.* Like type identifiers, constant members declared inside a class must be qualified when they are used outside the class—e.g., `List::CAPACITY`.

Because of this inconvenience (along with that described in the footnote), we will put this constant definition before the class declaration along with the `typedef` declaration to make it easy to access throughout the list class and in files that

---

[2] Although simply putting such declarations of static constant members inside a class declaration works in some versions of C++, the C++ standard states that static constant members must also be defined somewhere, but without the initializer value. For example, we could put

```
const int List::CAPACITY;
```

in `List.cpp`. Because of this unfortunate property, a simpler alternative that is commonly used is to declare integer constant members in a class with an anonymous enumeration—for example,

```
enum {CAPACITY = SOME_CONSTANT_VALUE};
```

The standard also states that only static *integer* constant data members are allowed.

#include the class's header file. Also, it will be easy to find and modify if it is necessary to change the array's capacity.

Figure 6.1 shows a List class produced by coding the array-based implementation just described. Also shown is a test driver and a trace of its execution. The traverse operation is implemented as the display() method. Also, the instruction "terminate this operation" in the insert algorithm is implemented as a termination of execution if there is no room in the array for a new item. It is implemented as a simple return for an invalid insert position and for the erase operation. Other possibilities are to throw an exception that a client program could catch and handle or to return a boolean value to the client program: true if the operation was successful and false if it failed.

Figure 6.1 A List Class—Implementation Using a Static Array

```
/*-- List.h -----------------------------------------------------------


   This header file defines the data type List for processing lists.
   Basic operations are:
      Constructor
      empty:    Check if list is empty
      insert:   Insert an item
      erase:    Remove an item
      display:  Output the list
      <<:       Output operator
----------------------------------------------------------------------*/

#include <iostream>

#ifndef LIST
#define LIST

const int CAPACITY = 1024;
typedef int ElementType;

class List
{
 public:
 /******** Function Members ********/
   /***** Class constructor *****/
   List();
   /*-------------------------------------------------------------------

      Construct a List object.
```

Figure 6.1 (continued)

```
   Precondition:  None
   Postcondition: An empty List object has been constructed; mySize is 0.
   -------------------------------------------------------------------*/


/***** empty operation *****/
bool empty() const;
/*-------------------------------------------------------------------

   Check if a list is empty.

   Precondition:  None
   Postcondition: true is returned if the list is empty, false if not.
   -------------------------------------------------------------------*/


/***** insert and erase *****/
void insert(ElementType item, int pos);
/*-------------------------------------------------------------------

   Insert a value into the list at a given position.

   Precondition:  item is the value to be inserted; there is room in
      the array (mySize < CAPACITY); and the position satisfies
      0 <= pos <= mySize.
   Postcondition: item has been inserted into the list at the position
      determined by pos (provided there is room and pos is a legal
      position).
   -------------------------------------------------------------------*/


void erase(int pos);
/*-------------------------------------------------------------------

   Remove a value from the list at a given position.

   Precondition:  The list is not empty and the position satisfies
      0 <= pos < mySize.
   Postcondition: element at the position determined by pos has been
      removed (provided pos is a legal position).
   -------------------------------------------------------------------*/


/***** output *****/
void display(ostream & out) const;
/*-------------------------------------------------------------------

   Display a list.
```

Figure 6.1 (continued)

      Precondition: The ostream out is open.
      Postcondition: The list represented by this List object has been
          inserted into out.
      --*/

```cpp
 private:
 /******** Data Members ********/
   int mySize;                        // current size of list stored in myArray
   ElementType myArray[CAPACITY];   // array to store list elements

}; //--- end of List class

//------ Prototype of output operator
ostream & operator<< (ostream & out, const List & aList);

#endif
```

━━

```cpp
/*-- List.cpp------------------------------------------------------

   This file implements List member functions.
   ------------------------------------------------------------------*/

#include <cassert>
using namespace std;

#include "List.h"

//--- Definition of class constructor
List::List()
: mySize(0)
{}

//--- Definition of empty()
bool List::empty() const
{
   return mySize == 0;
}
```

Figure 6.1 (continued)

```cpp
//--- Definition of display()
void List::display(ostream & out) const
{
   for (int i = 0; i < mySize; i++)
     out << myArray[i] << "  ";
}


//--- Definition of output operator
ostream & operator<< (ostream & out, const List & aList)
{
   aList.display(out);
   return out;
}


//--- Definition of insert()
void List::insert(ElementType item, int pos)
{
   if (mySize == CAPACITY)
   {
      cerr << "*** No space for list element -- terminating "
              "execution ***\n";
      exit(1);
   }
   if (pos < 0 || pos > mySize)
   {
      cerr << "*** Illegal location to insert -- " << pos
           << ".  List unchanged. ***\n";
      return;
   }

   // First shift array elements right to make room for item

   for(int i = mySize; i > pos; i--)
      myArray[i] = myArray[i - 1];

   // Now insert item at position pos and increase list size
   myArray[pos] = item;
   mySize++;
}
```

Figure 6.1 (continued)

```cpp
//--- Definition of erase()
void List::erase(int pos)
{
   if (mySize == 0)
   {
      cerr << "*** List is empty ***\n";
      return;
   }
   if (pos < 0 || pos >= mySize)
   {
      cerr << "Illegal location to delete -- " << pos
           << ".  List unchanged. ***\n";
      return;
   }

   // Shift array elements left to close the gap
   for(int i = pos; i < mySize; i++)
       myArray[i] = myArray[i + 1];

   // Decrease list size
    mySize--;
}
```

```cpp
//--- Program to test List class.

#include <iostream>
using namespace std;

#include "List.h"

int main()
{
   // Test the class constructor
   List intList;
   cout << "Constructing intList\n";
```

Figure 6.1 (continued)

```
// Test empty() and output of empty list
if (intList.empty())
   cout << "Empty List: \n"
        << intList << endl;       // Test output of empty list

// Test insert()
for (int i = 0; i < 9; i++)
{
   cout << "Inserting " << i << " at position " << i/2 << endl;
   intList.insert(i, i/2);        //  -- Insert i at position i/2
   //Test output
   cout << intList << endl;
}
cout << "List empty? " << (intList.empty() ? "Yes" : "No") << endl;

cout << "\nTry to insert at position -1" << endl;
intList.insert(0, -1);
cout << "\nTry to insert at position 10" << endl;
intList.insert(0, 10);

// Test erase()
int index;
cout << endl;
while (!intList.empty())
{
   cout << "Give an index of a list element to remove: ";
   cin >> index;
   intList.erase(index);
   cout << intList << endl;
}
cout << "List is empty" << endl;

cout << "\nInserting " << CAPACITY<< " integers\n";
for (int i = 0; i < CAPACITY; i++)
  intList.insert(i, i);
cout << "Attempting to insert one more integer:\n";
intList.insert(-1, 0);
}
```

Figure 6.1 (continued)

Execution Trace:
```
Constructing intList
Empty List:

Inserting 0 at position 0
0
Inserting 1 at position 0
1  0
Inserting 2 at position 1
1  2  0
Inserting 3 at position 1
1  3  2  0
Inserting 4 at position 2
1  3  4  2  0
Inserting 5 at position 2
1  3  5  4  2  0
Inserting 6 at position 3
1  3  5  6  4  2  0
Inserting 7 at position 3
1  3  5  7  6  4  2  0
Inserting 8 at position 4
1  3  5  7  8  6  4  2  0
List empty? No

Try to insert at position -1
*** Illegal location to insert -- -1.  List unchanged. ***

Try to insert at position 10
*** Illegal location to insert -- 10.  List unchanged. ***

Give an index of a list element to remove: 9
Illegal location to delete -- 9.  List unchanged. ***
1  3  5  7  8  6  4  2  0
Give an index of a list element to remove: 8
1  3  5  7  8  6  4  2
Give an index of a list element to remove: 5
1  3  5  7  8  4  2
Give an index of a list element to remove: 3
1  3  5  8  4  2
```

Figure 6.1 (continued)

```
Give an index of a list element to remove: 0
3  5  8  4  2
Give an index of a list element to remove: 4
3  5  8  4
Give an index of a list element to remove: 3
3  5  8
Give an index of a list element to remove: 0
5  8
Give an index of a list element to remove: 0
8
Give an index of a list element to remove: 0

List is empty

Inserting 1024 integers
Attempting to insert one more integer:
*** No space for list element -- terminating execution ***
```

▲

6.3 An Array-Based Implementation of Lists with Dynamic Allocation

The List class in the preceding section was fairly easy to build because we used a static array to store the list elements. As we noted there, the major deficiency of this approach is its "one size fits all" basis. One capacity is specified for the arrays that store list elements in *every* List object. If it is too small, we limit the size of lists that can be stored; but if we declare it too large, we waste memory. It would be better if each List object could specify what this capacity should be. And this is what the implementation using a dynamic array makes possible.

Switching to a dynamically-allocated array entails only a few changes in the data members of the List class:

1. Eliminate the constant declaration that specifies the array's capacity and add a variable data member to store the capacity specified by the user in an object's declaration.
2. Change the array data member to a pointer that will store the address of the memory allocated during execution for the array.

We will thus change the declarations of the data members to

```
private:
/******** Data Members ********/
   int mySize;                    // current size of list stored
```

```
      int myCapacity;            // capacity of array
      ElementType * myArray;   // pointer to dynamic array
```

The empty(), display(), and erase() member functions require no change, and in insert(), we need only change CAPACITY to myCapacity. It is the constructor that requires significant changes. Because we are using a dynamic array, the constructor must actually construct something (and not simply initialize data members as our constructors have done up to now). It will have to take care of allocating memory for the array.

Figure 6.2 shows how the modified constructor does this:

```
      myArray = new(nothrow) ElementType[maxSize];
      assert(myArray != 0);
```

Here we are using the nothrow version of the new operator described in Section 3.4, which returns a null pointer if there is not enough memory available to allocate for the array. The assert statement will terminate execution and display an error message if this happens. Also highlighted in Figure 6.2 are some other new function members that we will discuss next.

Figure 6.2 A List Class—Array-Based Implementation with Dynamic Allocation

```
/*-- DList.h ------------------------------------------------------------

  This header file defines the data type List for processing lists.
  Basic operations are:
     Constructor
     Destructor
     Copy constructor
     Assignment operator
     empty:    Check if list is empty
     insert:   Insert an item
     erase:    Remove an item
     display:  Output the list
     << :      Output operator
-------------------------------------------------------------------*/


#include <iostream>

#ifndef DLIST
#define DLIST

typedef int ElementType;
```

Figure 6.2 (continued)

```
class List
{
 public:
 /******** Function Members ********/
   /***** Class constructor *****/
   List(int maxSize = 1024);
   /*------------------------------------------------------------
     Construct a List object.

     Precondition:  maxSize is a positive integer with default value 1024.
     Postcondition: An empty List object is constructed; myCapacity ==
         maxSize (default value 1024); myArray points to a dynamic
         array with myCapacity as its capacity; and mySize is 0.
     ----------------------------------------------------------------*/


   /***** Class destructor *****/
   ~List();
   /*------------------------------------------------------------
     Destroys a List object.

     Precondition:  The life of a List object is over.
     Postcondition: The memory dynamically allocated by the constructor
         for the array pointed to by myArray has been returned to the heap.
     ----------------------------------------------------------------*/


   /***** Copy constructor *****/
   List(const List & origList);
   /*------------------------------------------------------------
     Construct a copy of a List object.

     Precondition:  A copy of origList is needed; origList is a const
         reference parameter.
     Postcondition: A copy of origList has been constructed.
     ----------------------------------------------------------------*/


   /***** Assignment operator *****/
   const List & operator=(const List & rightHandSide);
   /*------------------------------------------------------------
     Assign a copy of a List object to the current object.
```

Figure 6.2 (continued)

```
      Precondition: none
      Postcondition: A copy of rightHandSide has been assigned to this
          object. A const reference to this list is returned.
      --------------------------------------------------------------------*/


    /***** empty operation *****/
    bool empty() const;
    //--- See Figure 6.1 for documentation


    /***** insert and erase *****/
    void insert(ElementType item, int pos);
    //--- See Figure 6.1 for documentation (replace CAPACITY with myCapacity)


    void erase(int pos);
    //--- See Figure 6.1 for documentation


    /***** output *****/
    void display(ostream & out) const;
    //--- See Figure 6.1 for documentation

 private:
 /******** Data Members ********/
    int mySize;                 // current size of list
    int myCapacity;             // capacity of array
    ElementType * myArray;      // pointer to dynamic array

}; //--- end of List class

//------ Prototype of output operator
ostream & operator<< (ostream & out, const List & aList);

#endif
```

```
/*-- DList.cpp-------------------------------------------------------

   This file implements List member functions.
   ---------------------------------------------------------------------*/
```

Figure 6.2 (continued)

```cpp
#include <cassert>
#include <new>
using namespace std;

#include "DList.h"

//--- Definition of class constructor
List::List(int maxSize)
: mySize(0), myCapacity(maxSize)
{
   myArray = new(nothrow) ElementType[maxSize];
   assert(myArray != 0);
}


//--- Definition of class destructor
List::~List()
{
   delete [] myArray;
}


//--- Definition of copy constructor
List::List(const List & origList)
: mySize(origList.mySize), myCapacity(origList.myCapacity)
{
  //--- Get new array for copy
   myArray = new(nothrow) ElementType[myCapacity];

   if (myArray != 0)                      // check if memory available
     //--- Copy origList's elements into this new array
     for(int i = 0; i < mySize; i++)
        myArray[i] = origList.myArray[i];
   else
   {
     cerr << "*** Inadequate memory to allocate storage for list ***\n";
     exit(1);
   }
}
```

Figure 6.2 (continued)

```
//--- Definition of assignment operator
const List & List::operator=(const List & rightHandSide)
{
   if (this != &rightHandSide)  // check that not self-assignment
   {
      //-- Allocate a new array if necessary
      if (myCapacity != rightHandSide.myCapacity)
      {
         delete[] myArray;
         myCapacity = rightHandSide.myCapacity;
         myArray = new(nothrow) ElementType[myCapacity];

         if (myArray == 0)       // check if memory available
         {
            cerr << "*Inadequate memory to allocate stack ***\n";
            exit(1);
         }
      }
      //--- Copy rightHandSide's list elements into this new array
      mySize = rightHandSide.mySize;
      for(int i = 0; i < mySize; i++)
         myArray[i] = rightHandSide.myArray[i];
   }
   return *this;
}


//--- Insert definition of empty() from Figure 6.1

//--- Insert definition of display() from Figure 6.1

//--- Insert definition of output operator from Figure 6.1

//--- Insert definition of insert() from Figure 6.1 and replace
//--- CAPACITY with myCapacity

//--- Insert definition of erase() from Figure 6.1
```

▲

A program that includes List.h can then declare List objects with statements such as

```
cout << "What is the maximum size of lists you will need? ";
int maxListSize;
cin >> maxListSize;
List aList1, aList2(maxListSize);
```

When these statements are executed, aList1 will be constructed as an empty list stored in an array with capacity 1024; and if 500 is entered as the value for maxList-Size, aList2 will be constructed as an empty list stored in an array with capacity 500. We might picture this as follows:

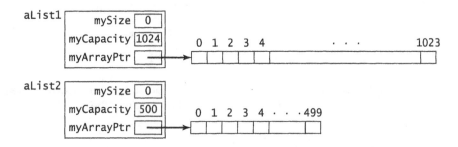

Dynamic Allocation in Classes—Destructors, Copy Constructors, and Assignment

As you can see in Figure 6.2, using dynamically-allocated storage in a class such as List requires the addition of some new members to the class:

1. *Destructor:*	To deallocate dynamically-allocated memory within an object
2. *Copy constructor:*	To make copies of objects—for instance, for value parameters and when initializing a new object with an existing object
3. *Assignment operator:*	To assign one object to another

We will consider each of these in turn and show why they are needed and how they carry out their tasks.

Class Destructor For the classes that were used in earlier chapters, when an object obj is declared using one of these classes, the constructor is called to initialize obj. When the lifetime of obj is over, the memory allocated to obj's members is reclaimed automatically because it is handled by the compiler.

For objects with some data members allocated memory dynamically, however, a new problem arises. To illustrate, consider the `List` object `aList` declared in the following block:

```
{
    //--- Some preliminary processing
    List aList;
    //--- Statements to process aList
}
```

When the declaration of `aList` is encountered, its data members `mySize`, `myCapacity`, and `myArray` are allocated memory automatically:

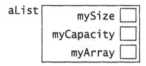

The `List` constructor is then called to allocate memory for the array used to store the list elements and to initialize the other data members:

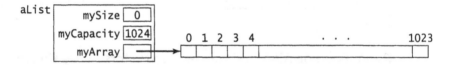

When the end of the block is reached, the lifetime of `aList` ends and the memory allocated for `mySize`, `myCapacity`, and the pointer `myArray` is automatically reclaimed. But this is not true for the dynamically allocated array pointed to by `myArray` and a large memory leak like those described in Section 3.4 occurs:

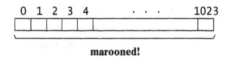

This block of memory cannot be accessed by the program that created the `List` object nor is it returned to the heap.

To remedy this situation, a **destructor** function member must be provided in the class.

- The *destructor's role is to reclaim any dynamically-allocated memory contained in an object.*

- At any point in a program *where an object goes out of scope, the compiler will automatically insert a call to this destructor.*

By providing a destructor for any class that uses dynamically-allocated memory, a class object will automatically release that memory at the end of its lifetime, avoiding a memory leak. This makes class objects self-contained, which is another characteristic of good design.

The name of a destructor is always the name of the class preceded by a tilde (~) character:

The Class Destructor

Forms:

~*ClassName*()

Purpose:

This function is called automatically to reclaim any memory allocated dynamically in an object of type *ClassName* whenever such an object should no longer exist. It will be called first, before deallocation of memory for other items in that object. Note that like a constructor, a destructor has no return type. However, unlike a constructor, a destructor cannot have parameters; thus a class can have only one destructor.

Common situations in which an object's destructor is called include the following:

- At the end of each block in which that object is declared (provided it is not static)[3]
- When execution of a program terminates for a static object
- At the end of a function definition in which that object is a value parameter
- If that object is created by a copy constructor and is no longer needed
- If that object was created using new and is destroyed using delete
- When some object containing that object as a data member is destroyed

---

For our List class in Figure 6.2, the destructor is named ~List. It uses the delete [] operation to deallocate the memory dynamically allocated by new for the array pointed to by myArray. For example, suppose that aList is declared by

List aList(10);

and that the integers 11, 22, 33 have been inserted into aList in this order:

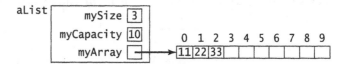

---

[3]   Like static data members described earlier, local variables and constants in functions can be declared to be static. Unlike *automatic* (nonstatic) variables that are destroyed when execution reaches the closing curly brace (}) of the block containing the declaration of that variable, a static variable exists until program execution is finished.

When aList's lifetime is over, its destructor will be called first, which reclaims its dynamically-allocated array:

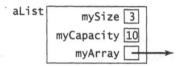

And since the allocation of memory to mySize, myCapacity, and myArray was handled by the compiler, it will also take care of its deallocation in the usual manner.

Copy Constructor   There are times when a copy of an object must be made.

- When an argument is passed as a value parameter, the parameter must be constructed as a copy of the argument.

- When a function returns a local object, the function terminates, ending the lifetime of that object, so an (anonymous) copy of the object called a *temporary* must be constructed to transmit the return value back to the caller.

- Whenever temporary storage of an object is needed, a copy of that object must be made.

- Whenever an object is initialized in a declaration of the form

    Type obj = initial_value;

    or

    Type obj(initial_value);

    obj must be constructed as a copy of *initial_value*.

If a class does not provide a **copy constructor** for making copies of an object, then a default one that does simple member-by-member copying will be used. Although this has been adequate for classes considered up to now, it does not accomplish what is needed for a class having a data member that is a pointer to dynamically-allocated memory. To see why, suppose aList is the List object given earlier. If there is no copy constructor in List class, the default copy constructor will do a member-wise copy of the data members mySize, myCapacity, and myArray of aList. Although this is correct for mySize and myCapacity, it is not what we want for myArray; the *address* stored in myArray is copied but not the dynamically allocated array at that address. The result of this copy operation, known as a **shallow copy**, is that the myArray data members in both aList and its copy point to the same array:

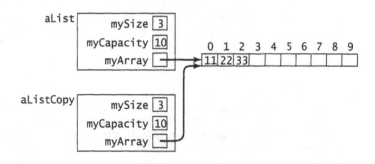

This gives rise to an example of the **aliasing problem** in which there are two names (myArray in aList and myArray in aListCopy) for the same thing (the array).

We see, therefore, that when a class has no copy constructor but does have a data member that is a pointer, the *default copy constructor does not make a distinct copy* of the object pointed to by that pointer. This can be a problem. For example, if aListCopy is a value parameter in a function that modifies aListCopy's dynamic array, these modifications will simultaneously change the array in aList. This should not happen with a value parameter! What is needed is a **deep copy** that creates a *distinct copy* of aList, in which the array in aListCopy is a distinct copy of the array in aList:

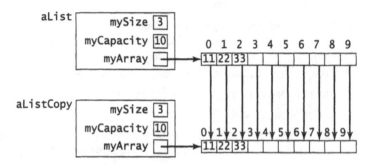

To make this possible, C++ allows a class to have its own copy constructor defined as follows:

Class Copy Constructor

Forms:

   ClassName(const *ClassName* & *original*);

where

   ClassName is the name of the class containing this function;

   original must be a reference to the object being copied; and,

   because it is *a constructor*, it must be a function member, its name is the class name, and it has no return type.

Purpose:

This is a function used by the compiler to construct a copy of the argument corresponding to *original*. It is called whenever such a copy is needed, including when

- an object of type *ClassName* is passed as a value parameter;
- the return value of a function is a value of type *ClassName*;
- an object of type *ClassName* is initialized when it is declared; or
- the evaluation of an expression produces an intermediate (or temporary) value of type *ClassName*.

Note that the parameter of a copy constructor *must be* a reference parameter (and should be a const reference parameter, as well) because, if it were defined as a value parameter, then a call to the function would proceed as follows:

1. Pass *original* as a value parameter, which means that a copy of *original* must be made.
2. To make a copy of *original* as a value parameter, the copy constructor is called again (with *original* as its argument).
3. To pass *original* as a value parameter to that copy constructor, a copy of *original* is needed.
4. To make a copy of *original*, the copy constructor is called again (with *original* as its argument).

and so on, resulting in an infinite chain of function calls! Defining *original* as a reference parameter avoids this infinite recursion because the reference (address) of *original* is passed, instead of a copy of *original*.

For our List class in Figure 6.2, the copy constructor is declared by

```
List(const List & origList);
```

In its definition it does the following:

■ Copies the values in the data members mySize and myCapacity from origList into the data members mySize and myCapacity of the list being constructed.

■ Uses new to allocate a new array pointed to by myArray that has the same capacity as the array in origList.

■ Uses a loop to do an element-by-element copy of the elements of the array in origList to this newly-allocated array in the copy.

Assignment Like constructors and destructors, the compiler also provides for each class a default definition for the assignment operator (=) that, like the default copy constructor, simply does a member-by-member copy of the object being assigned. As with the copy constructor, this works fine unless the class allocates memory dynamically. The problem is similar to the copy constructor problem. For example, an assignment statement

```
aListCopy = aList;
```

would produce the same situation as that pictured earlier. The default assignment operator makes a shallow copy so that the myArray data members of aList and aListCopy both point to the same anonymous array. Moreover, a memory leak occurs because the old array in aListCopy is not deallocated:

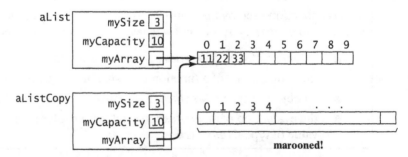

This means that the class designer must overload the assignment operator (opera-tor=()) so that it deallocates the old array in an object and then does a deep copy of the array being assigned.

The general form of the assignment operation can be described as follows:

Assignment operation

Forms:

Prototype:

```
const ClassName & operator=(const ClassName & rightHandSide);
```

Definition:

```
const ClassName & ClassName::operator=(const ClassName &
                                         rightHandSide)
{
    // ... make a copy of rightHandSide

    return *this;
}
```

where

ClassName is the name of the class containing this function; and
rightHandSide is a reference to the object being copied.

Purpose:

For classes with dynamically-allocated memory, overload operator=() to avoid a memory leak and make the object receiving this message a distinct copy of *rightHandSide*.
Note: operator=() *must be defined as a member function.*

In our discussion of operator overloading in Section 4.5, we noted that, if some operator Δ is implemented as a function member of a class, then an expression of the form

$$a \; \Delta \; b$$

is interpreted as sending a Δ message to a, passing it b as an argument:

```
a.operatorΔ(b)
```

This means that, because the assignment operator must be a member function, an assignment

```
listLeft = listRight;
```

will be interpreted as

```
listLeft.operator=(listRight);
```

The behavior of the assignment operator is similar to that of the copy constructor, with three main differences:

■ Whereas the copy constructor only constructs a *new* object that is a copy of a
given object, the assignment operator must build a copy and then assign it to
an *existing* object that already has a value. Usually, it must destroy the old
value, deallocating its memory to avoid a memory leak, and then replace it
with the new value.

■ The copy constructor need not deal with *self-initializations*, such as

```
ClassName object = object;   // not allowed
```

but the assignment operator must be concerned with *self-assignments*:

```
object = object;   // self-assignment is okay
```

If it were not, destroying the old value of *object* on the left-hand side would
also destroy the value of the *object* on the right-hand side, leaving nothing to
assign.

■ The copy constructor returns no value and thus has no return type, but the
assignment operation should return the object on the left-hand side of the
assignment to support chained assignments. That is, an assignment like

```
list3 = list2 = list1;
```

must first assign `list1` to `list2` and then assign `list2` to `list3`. Since such
a call will be processed as

```
list3.operator=( list2.operator=(list1) );
```

the expression `list2.operator=(list1)` must return `list2`. This means
that, when an object receives the `operator=` message, it must return *itself* as
a value that can be assigned to another object. This can be accomplished by
making the return type of `operator=()` a const reference to type `List` and
having it return `*this`.

The definition of `operator=()` is given in Figure 6.2. The condition

```
this != &rightHandSide
```

in the opening `if` statement checks that this is not self-assignment by checking
whether the object being assigned a value and the value being assigned have the
same address. If they don't, then a check is made to see whether the array capacities
of the two objects are different:

```
myCapacity != rightHandSide.myCapacity
```

If so, the array in the object being assigned a value is deleted and a new one is allocated. In either case, the elements of `rightHandSide` are copied into the object
being assigned, element by element as in the copy constructor.

A Final Note

The following is a general rule of thumb to remember in designing a class:
If a class allocates memory at run time using new, then it should provide

- a *destructor* that releases dynamically allocated memory to the heap,
- a *copy constructor* that the compiler can use to make distinct copies, and
- an *assignment operator* that a programmer can use to make distinct copies.

Remembering this rule will help you to build classes whose objects are self-contained, that are free of memory leaks, and that behave in the way a user expects.

The number of times the class constructors, destructor, and copy constructor get called automatically when a class is used will surprise most people. The simple program in Figure 6.3 demonstrates this. It is a driver program for the List class template developed in this section but which was modified by adding output statements to the constructor, destructor, copy constructor, and assignment operator to trace when they are called.

Figure 6.3 Calls to Constructors and Destructor

```
/*------------------------------------------------------------------
    This program demonstrates how often a class's constructor,
    destructor, and copy constructor can get called automatically
    by the compiler. It uses the List class from Fig. 6.2 but with
    output statements inserted into the constructor, destructor,
    and copy constructor to trace when they are called.
------------------------------------------------------------------*/

#include <iostream>
using namespace std;

#include "DList.h"

void print (List aList)
/*------------------------------------------------------------------
    Function to print a list.

    Precondition:  aList is a value parameter
    Postcondition: Contents of aList have been displayed
------------------------------------------------------------------*/
{
    cout << aList << endl;
}
```

Figure 6.3 (continued)

```cpp
int main()
{
   int listLimit;
   cout << "Enter maximum number of list elements: ";
   cin >> listLimit;

   cout << "\n*** Next Statement:  List list1(listLimit);\n";
   List list1(listLimit);
   for (int i = 0; i <= 4; i++)
   {
      cout << "*** Next Statement:  list1.insert(i, i);\n";
      list1.insert(i, i);
   }
   cout << "\n*** Next Statement:  List list2 = list1;\n";
   List list2 = list1;
   cout << "\n*** Next Statement:  print(list2);\n";
   print(list2);
   cout << "\n*** Next Statement:  List list3;\n";
   List list3;
   cout << "\n*** Next Statement:  list3 = list2;\n";
   list3 = list2;
   cout << "\n*** Next Statement:  print(list3);\n";
   print(list3);

   cout << "\n*** Next Statement:  return 0;\n";
   return 0;
}
```

Execution Trace:

```
Enter maximum number of list elements: 5

*** Next Statement:  List list1(listLimit);
CONSTRUCTOR
*** Next Statement:  list1.insert(i, i);
*** Next Statement:  list1.insert(i, i);
*** Next Statement:  list1.insert(i, i);
*** Next Statement:  list1.insert(i, i);
*** Next Statement:  list1.insert(i, i);
```

Figure 6.3 (continued)

```
*** Next Statement:  List list2 = list1;
COPY CONSTRUCTOR


*** Next Statement:  print(list2);
COPY CONSTRUCTOR
0  1  2  3  4
DESTRUCTOR


*** Next Statement:  List list3;
CONSTRUCTOR


*** Next Statement:  list3 = list2;
ASSIGNMENT OP


*** Next Statement:  print(list3);
COPY CONSTRUCTOR
0  1  2  3  4
DESTRUCTOR


*** Next Statement:  return 0;
DESTRUCTOR
DESTRUCTOR
DESTRUCTOR
```

▲

Future Improvements   Our List class has some deficiencies that restrict its usefulness:

Deficiency #1:   The array used to store list elements has a fixed capacity and may, therefore, not be able to store some of the lists needed in a program. The user may not know in advance the upper limit on list sizes to use in the List declarations. It would be helpful if the array could grow when it becomes full.

Solutions: One approach is to allocate a new larger array when this happens, copy the elements from the array pointed to by myArray into it, set myArray to point to this new array, and then delete the old array. This is the approach used with vectors described in Chapter 9, so we will defer discussion of it until then.

   Another approach is to use a *linked-list* implementation; we will study this in detail in the next section. As we will see, it will also eliminate the inefficient element shifting that goes or in the insert and delete operations.

Deficiency #2: The List class is bound to a particular type for the elements. If, for example, someone wants to use a list of doubles, he or she must change the typedef declaration in List.h:

```
typedef double ElementType;
```

Since this changes List.h, all programs that include it must be recompiled and linked together.

A more serious problem is that we can't use two different types of lists in the same program—for example, a List of ints and a List of doubles—because we can't use two different typedef declarations in the same file to associate two different types with the generic type ElementType.

Solutions: One way to proceed would be to create two different List classes with different names such as ListInt and ListDouble. A better and more modern solution is to change our List class to a *class template* so that it becomes a generic container that can process any type of list elements. We will study templates in Chapter 9.

✔ Quick Quiz 6.3

1. Define list as an ADT.
2. What are the two steps in building a class?
3. What two steps are involved in implementing a class?
4. In the array-based implementations of a list, insertion in the worst case and on the average has computing time O(_____).
5. In the array-based implementations of a list, deletion in the worst case and on the average has computing time O(_____).
6. The array-based implementation of a list works well for lists with many insertions and deletions. (True or false)
7. Write a prototype for the copy constructor of a class named C.
8. Write a prototype for the destructor of a class named C.
9. The parameter of a copy constructor should always be a value parameter to ensure that a distinct copy is made. (True or false)
10. The assignment operator for a class must be a function member. (True or false)
11. The compiler supplies a _____ copy constructor that simply copies an object member by member.
12. When is it essential that a class have its own copy constructor and why?
13. The problem of dynamically-allocated memory getting marooned is called a(n) _____.
14. When an object's lifetime is over, the object's _____ is called automatically.
15. When is it essential that a class have its own destructor and why?
16. When is it essential that a class have its own assignment operator and why?

✥ Exercises 6.3

A *polynomial of degree n* has the form

$$a_0 + a_1x + a_2x^2 + \cdots + a_nx^n$$

where $a_0, a_1, \ldots, a_n$ are numeric constants called the *coefficients* of the polynomial and $a_n \neq 0$. For example,

$$1 + 3x - 7x^3 + 5x^4$$

is a polynomial of degree 4 with integer coefficients 1, 3, 0, –7, and 5. One common implementation of a polynomial stores the degree of the polynomial and the list of coefficients. This is the implementation to be used in the exercises that follow. As you add the various operations to the Polynomial class you are building, you should also write a program to test your class, as instructed in Programming Problem 1 at the end of this chapter.

1. Write a declaration for a Polynomial class whose data members are an integer for the degree and an array for the list of coefficients and with basic operations of input and output.

2. Implement the input operation in Exercise 1.

3. Implement the output operation in Exercise 1. Display the polynomial in the usual mathematical format with x^n displayed as x^n.

4. Add an evaluate operation to your Polynomial class that allows the user to enter a value for *x* and that calculates the value of the polynomial for that value.

5. Add an addition operation to your Polynomial class.

6. Add a multiplication operation to your Polynomial class.

6.4 Introduction to Linked Lists

The arrangement of the elements of a list in a sequence means that there is a first element, a second element, and so on. Thus, any implementation of lists must incorporate a method for specifying this arrangement. In the array-based implementations considered in the preceding sections, this sequential arrangement of list elements is modeled *implicitly* by the natural ordering of the array elements, since the first list element is stored in the first position of the array, the second list element in the second position, and so on. It is this implicit specification of how the list elements are arranged that necessitates shifting them in the array when items are inserted or deleted, causing the inefficiency for dynamic lists (those that change frequently due to insertions and deletions). In this section we look at an alternative way to implement lists in which this inefficiency is eliminated by specifying *explicitly* the arrangement of the list elements.

What Are They?

In any structure used to store the elements of a list, it must be possible to perform at least the following operations if the sequential arrangement of the list elements is to be preserved:

- Locate the first element

- Given the location of any list element, find its successor
- Locate the end of the list

For the array-based implementations of the preceding sections, it is the strict manner in which the second requirement is satisfied that causes the inefficiency: For the list element stored in array location i, its successor must be stored in the next array location $i + 1$. Relaxing this requirement is what leads to linked lists.

A **linked list** is a sequence of elements called **nodes**, each of which has two parts:

1. A *data part* that stores an element of the list
2. A *next part* that stores a *link* (or *pointer*) that indicates the location of the node containing the next list element. If there is no next element, then a special **null value** is used.

Also, the location of the node storing the first list element must be maintained. This will be the null value, if the list is empty.

To illustrate, a linked list storing the integers 9, 17, 22, 26, 34 might be pictured as follows:

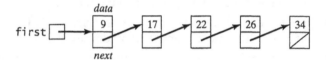

In this diagram, `first` points to the first node in the list. The *data* part of each node stores one of the integers in the list and the arrow in the *next* part represents a link to the next node. The diagonal line in the *next* part of the last node represents a null link and indicates that this list element has no successor.

Implementing the Basic List Operations

We now consider how the basic list operations given in the preceding section can be implemented in this setting.

Construction To construct an empty list, we simply make `first` a null link to indicate that it does not refer to any node:

`first = null_value;`

first⬚

Empty We can then perform the second list operation, determining whether a list is empty, simply by checking whether `first` is null:

`first == null_value`

Traverse The third basic list operation is list traversal. To traverse a linked list such as the preceding list of integers, we begin by initializing an auxiliary variable `ptr` to point to the first node:

Initialize `ptr` to `first`.

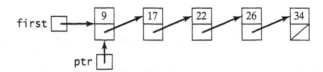

We process the list element 9 stored in this node and then move to the next node by following the link from the current node—analogous to incrementing an index by 1 in a sequential storage implementation:

Process the data part of the node referred to by `ptr`.
`ptr` = next part of the node currently referred to by `ptr`.

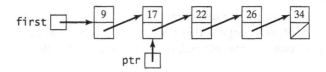

We continue in this way until we reach the node containing 34:

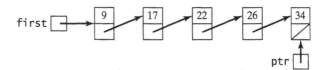

If we now attempt to move to the next node, `ptr` becomes null, signaling the end of the list:

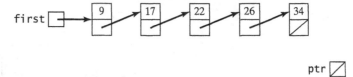

In summary, a linked list can be traversed as follows:

```
ptr = first;
while (ptr != null_value)
{
    Process data part of node referred to by ptr
    ptr = next part of node referred to by ptr
}
```

Note that this algorithm is correct even for an empty list, since in this case `first` is the null value and the `while` loop is bypassed.

To display the list elements, the processing step in this algorithm is simply to output the data part of the node. To search the list for a given item, it might be

if (item == *data part of node referred to by* ptr)
    Terminate the loop. // ptr gives the location of a node containing item

If we change == to <=, this will locate where to insert item to maintain an **ordered** linked list in which the list elements are in ascending order.

Insertion   To insert a new data value into a linked list, we must first obtain a new node and store the value in its data part. We assume that there is a storage pool of available nodes and some mechanism for obtaining a new node from it whenever one is needed. The second step is to connect this new node to the existing list, and for this, there are two cases to consider: (1) insertion after some element in the list and (2) insertion at the beginning of the list.

To illustrate the first case, suppose we wish to insert 20 after 17 in the preceding linked list, and suppose that predptr refers to the node containing 17. We first obtain a new node temporarily pointed to by newptr and store 20 in its data part:

1. Get a new node pointed to by newptr.
    Set the data part of this node equal to 20.

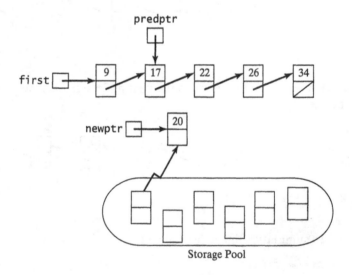

Storage Pool

We insert it into the list by first setting its next part equal to the link in the node referred to by predptr so that it points to its successor:

2. Set the next part of the node pointed to by newptr equal to the next part of the node referred to by predptr.

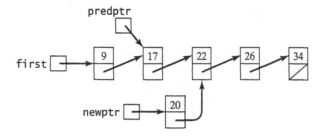

Now reset the link in the predecessor node to point to this new node:

3. Set the next part of the node referred to by predptr equal to newptr.

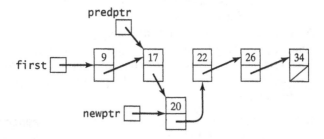

Note that this insert procedure also works at the end of the list. For example, suppose we want to insert a node containing 55 at the end of the list:

1. Same as before, but put 55 in the new node.

2. Same as before. This makes the link in the new node a null link.

3. Same as before.

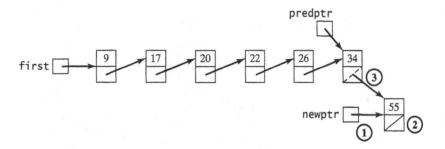

To illustrate the second case, suppose we wish to insert a node containing 5 at the beginning of the list. The first two steps are the same as before, but we need to modify steps 2 and 3:

1. Same as before, but put 5 in the new node.

2. Set the next part of the new node equal to first, which makes it point to the first node in the list.

3. Set first to point to the new node.

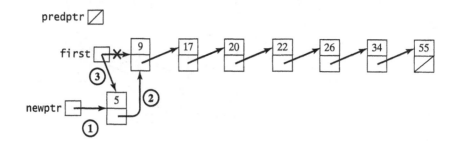

Deletion   For deletion, there are also two cases to consider: (1) deleting an element that has a predecessor and (2) deleting the first element in the list. We will assume that there is some operation that can be used to return a node pointed to by a specified pointer to the storage pool.

As an illustration of the first case, suppose we wish to delete the node containing 22 from the preceding linked list; that `ptr` points to the node to be deleted; and that `predptr` refers to its predecessor (the node containing 20). We can do this with a bypass operation that sets the link in the predecessor to point to the successor of the node to be deleted:

1. Set the next part of the node referred to by `predptr` equal to the next part of the node pointed to by `ptr`.

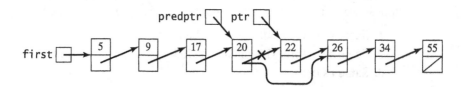

2. Return the node pointed to by `ptr` to the storage pool.

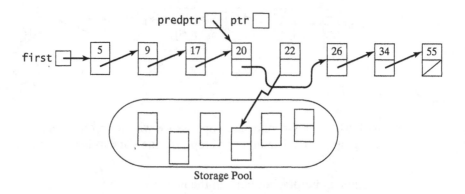

Storage Pool

Note that this also works at the end of the list:

1. Same as before. This makes the link in the predecessor a null link.
2. Same as before.

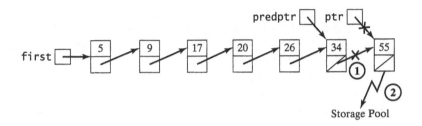

The second case is easy and consists of simply resetting first to point to the second node in the list and then returning the deleted node to the storage pool of available nodes:

1. Set first equal to the next part of the node pointed to by ptr.
2. Same as before.

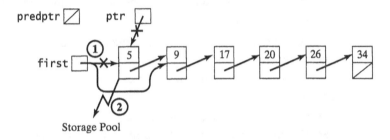

Summary

As this discussion demonstrates, it is possible to insert an item into a linked list at a given position or to delete an element at a given position *without shifting list elements.* This means that, unlike the array-based implementation, these operations can be performed *in constant time.*

At this stage, however, we have described linked lists only abstractly, at a logical level, and have not considered how to implement them. For this, we will need at least the following capabilities:

1. Some means of dividing memory into nodes, each having a data part and a link part, and some implementation of pointers.
2. Operations to access the values stored in each node, that is, operations to access the data part and the next part of the node pointed to by some pointer.
3. Some means of keeping track of the nodes in use as well as the available free nodes and of transferring nodes between those in use and the pool of free nodes.

Only a few programming languages (such as LISP, an acronym for LISt Processing) provide linked lists as predefined data structures. The Standard Template Library in C++ provides a linked list container list. In most languages, however, it is necessary to implement linked lists using other predefined data structures. In the next sections we describe two different implementations, and in Section 11.3 we show how to use the standard C++ list type.

We've seen what is gained in a linked implementation; what is lost? In moving from the array-based implementation of a list to a linked-list storage structure, we pay a price: *We no longer have direct access to each element of the list; we have direct access only to the first element.*

This means that it is not as easy and is less efficient to carry out some kinds of list-processing activities in the linked implementation. To access any particular position in a list in the array-based implementation, we can use the direct access property of the array that stores the list elements, and go directly to that position. But for a linked-list implementation, we have to begin at the first node and traverse the list, bypassing nodes we don't want, until we reach the one we need. Here is one example. To add a value at the end of a list implemented using the sequential-storage method, we can use, for example,

```
myArray[mySize] = value;
mySize++;
```

To add a value at the end of a linked list, however, we must traverse the list to locate the last node:

Get a new node; set its data part to value and make its next part a null link.

If the list is empty

Set first to point to the new node.

Else:

Traverse the list to find the last node.

Set the link in the last node to point to the new node.

Other examples are sorting and searching algorithms that require direct access to each element in the list; they cannot be used (efficiently) with linked lists.

✔ Quick Quiz 6.4

1. The elements of a linked list are called _____.
2. Each element in a linked list has two parts: a(n) _____ part and a(n) _____ part.
3. If a node has no successor, its link is set to a special _____ value.
4. In a linked list, insertion at a specified place in the list is an O(_____) operation.
5. In a linked list, deletion at a specified place in the list is an O(_____) operation.
6. One of the strengths of linked lists is direct access to each node. (True or false)

⬦ Exercises 6.4

In the following exercises, you may assume that operations as described in the text can be used to obtain a new node from the storage pool and to return nodes to the storage pool and that there is a special null value.

1. Write an algorithm to count the nodes in a linked list with first node pointed to by first.
2. Write an algorithm to determine the average of a linked list of real numbers with first node pointed to by first.

3. Write an algorithm to insert a node before the last node of a linked list with first node pointed to by `first`.

4. Write an algorithm to determine whether the data items in a linked list with first node pointed to by `first` are in ascending order.

5. Determine the computing times of the algorithms in Exercises 1 through 4.

6. Write an algorithm to search a linked list with first node pointed to by `first` for a given item and, if the item is found, return a pointer to the predecessor of the node containing that item.

7. Write an algorithm to insert a new node into a linked list with first node pointed to by `first` after the nth node in this list for a given integer n.

8. Write an algorithm to delete the nth node in a linked list with first node pointed to by `first`, where n is a given integer.

9. The *shuffle-merge* of two lists $x_1, x_2, \ldots, x_n$ and $y_1, y_2, \ldots, y_m$ is the list

$$z = x_1, y_1, x_2, y_2, \ldots, x_n, y_n, y_{n+1}, \ldots, y_m \text{ if } n < m,$$
$$z = x_1, y_1, x_2, y_2, \ldots, x_m, y_m, x_{m+1}, \ldots, x_n \text{ if } n > m,$$

or

$$z = x_1, y_1, x_2, y_2, \ldots, x_n, y_n \text{ if } n = m$$

Write an algorithm to shuffle-merge two linked lists with first nodes pointed to by `first1` and `first2`, respectively. The items in these two lists should be copied to produce the new list; the original lists should not be destroyed.

10. Proceed as in Exercise 9 but do not copy the items. Just change links in the two lists (thus destroying the original lists) to produce the merged list.

11. Suppose the items stored in two linked lists are in ascending order. Write an algorithm to merge these two lists to yield a list with the items in ascending order.

12. Write an algorithm to reverse a linked list with first node pointed to by `first`. Do not copy the list elements; rather, reset links and pointers so that `first` points to the last node and all links between nodes are reversed.

6.5   A Pointer-Based Implementation of Linked Lists in C++

As we will see in Chapter 11, C++ has a `list` class that stores list elements in a linked list (but with a more complex structure than we have been considering). Like most of the other standard containers, it provides many list operations, because it is intended for use in a wide variety of list-processing problems. But there are times when one doesn't need or want all of the operations, and a "lean and mean" linked-list class that contains the basic list operations would be more suitable. In this section we will show how C++ pointers and dynamic allocation and deallocation mechanisms described in Chapter 3 can be used to implement such a class.

Node Structure

Before we can build a linked list class, we must first consider how to implement the nodes that make up a linked list. Since each node has two different parts—a data part and a next part—it is natural to have a `Node` class with two data members, `data` and `next`. In this class, `data` will be of a type that is appropriate for storing a list element, and the `next` member will be a pointer to the node that stores the successor of this element:

```
class Node
{
 public:
  ElementType data;
  Node * next;
  // Some function members
};
```

Note that this definition of a Node is a *recursive* (or *self-referential*) *definition*, because it uses the name Node in its definition; the `next` member is defined as a pointer to a Node.

One might wonder why we have made the data members of Node public. This is because the declaration of class Node will be inside the List class. Making the data members of Node public makes them accessible to all of the member and friend functions of List.[4] However, the declaration of Node will be inside the private section of the List class, and these data members will not be accessible outside the class:

```
#ifndef LIST
#define LIST

typedef int ElementType;
class List
{
 /*** Node class ***/
 private:
  class Node
  {
   public:
    ElementType data;
    Node * next;
    // Some Node function members
  };
  typedef Node * NodePointer;

 public:
 /*** List's function members ***/

 private:
 /*** List's data members ***/
 };
#endif
```

---

[4] We could accomplish this also by making Node a struct, whose members are public by default. However, in this text, we use struct for C-style structs that contain no function members and class when there are.

The properties of C++ pointers along with C++'s new and `delete` operations can be used to declare pointers to nodes and to allocate and deallocate nodes.

- To declare a pointer to nodes:

  ```
  Node * ptr;
  ```

  or

  ```
  typedef Node * NodePointer;
  NodePointer ptr;
  ```

- To allocate a new node pointed to by `ptr`:

  ```
  ptr = new Node;
  // uses default Node constructor

  ptr = new Node(dataVal);
  // uses Node constructor to set data part
  // to dataVal and next part to null

  ptr = new Node(dataVal, linkVal);
  // uses Node constructor to set data part
  // to dataVal and next part to linkVal
  ```

- To deallocate a node pointed to by `ptr`:

  ```
  delete ptr;
  ```

- To access the data and next part of node pointed to by `ptr`:

  ```
  ptr->data and ptr->next
  ```

Data Members for Linked-List Implementation

The linked lists we have considered in the preceding section are characterized by the following properties:

1. There is a pointer to the first node in the list.
2. Each node contains a pointer to the next node in the list.
3. The last node contains a null pointer.

As we will see in Chapter 11, there are many other variations—circular, doubly linked, and lists with head nodes, to name but a few. We will call the kind of linked lists we've been considering **simple linked lists**.

For a list implementation that uses simple linked lists, only one data member is needed: a pointer to the first node. But, for convenience, another data member that keeps a count of the elements in the list is usually added. Thus, we would put the following declarations in the class:

```
/*** List's data members ***/
NodePointer first;    // points to first node
int mySize;           // number of nodes
```

A typical List object aList might then be pictured as follows:

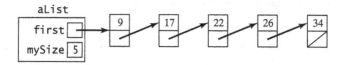

If we used only one data member, then each time we needed to know the length of the list, we would have to traverse the list and count the elements:

1. Set count to 0.
2. Make ptr point to the first node.
3. While ptr is not null:
      a. Increment count.
      b. Make ptr point at the next node.
   End while
4. Return count.

Function Members for Linked-List Implementation

As we will see in Chapter 11, where we look at different kinds of lists, there are many different operations on linked lists. Here we will describe only some of the basic ones. To save space, we will leave most of the details of implementing these as exercises.

Constructor   The constructor creates an empty list. It need only make first a null pointer and initialize mySize to 0:

```
//--- Constructor
LinkedList::LinkedList()
: first(0), mySize(0)
{
}
```

Basic List Operations   The member functions that carry out the basic list operations are straightforward implementations of the algorithms given in the preceding section. For example, a list is traversed as previously described by initializing a pointer ptr to the first node and then advancing it through the list by following the next fields and processing the data stored in each node:

```
// List traversal
ptr = first;
while (ptr != 0)
{
  /* Appropriate statements to process ptr-> data */
  ptr = ptr->next;
}
```

Replacing the comment inside the loop with an output statement would produce an output operation for List.

The descriptions we gave earlier for the insert and delete operations lend themselves easily to algorithms and then to definitions of methods for these operations. Recall that they both require having a pointer positioned at the node that precedes the point of insertion or deletion. Positioning this pointer is done with an appropriate version of list traversal.

Assuming that predptr has been positioned, we can insert a node with code like the following. It assumes that the class Node has an explicit-value constructor that creates a node containing a specified data value and sets its next pointer to 0.

```
newptr = new Node(dataVal);    // newptr of type NodePointer
if (predptr != 0)              // Not inserting at front
{
   newptr->next = predptr->next;
   predptr->next = newptr;
}
else                           // Inserting at front
{
   newptr->next = first;
   first = newptr;             // reset first
}
```

And we can delete the specified node with code like the following:

```
if (predptr != 0)              // Not deleting first node
{
   ptr = predptr->next;
   predptr->next = ptr->next;  // bypass
}
else                           // Deleting first node
{
   ptr = first;
   first = ptr->next;          // reset first
}
delete ptr;                    // return node to heap
```

Destructor   A destructor is needed for the same reason as for dynamically-allocated arrays. If we don't provide one, the default destructor used by the compiler for a linked list will cause memory leaks. The memory allocated to the data members first and mySize is reclaimed automatically, but the nodes in the linked list are marooned:

marooned!

The destructor will traverse the list, deallocating each node along the way.

Copy Constructor and Assignment A copy constructor and an assignment operator also are needed for the same reasons as for dynamically allocated arrays. If we don't provide them, the default copy constructor and assignment operator (which just do memberwise copying) used by the compiler for a linked list will produce

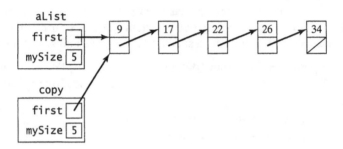

A copy constructor and an assignment operator must be provided that traverse the list, allocate a new node corresponding to each node in the list, and link them together:

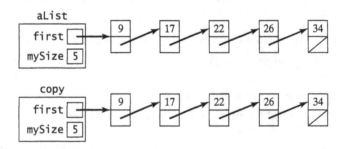

 We might note in this connection that there are times when we want to *prevent copying and/or assignments*; for example, streams are not allowed to be copied. We can accomplish this by putting a copy constructor and/or assignment operator—neither of which needs to do anything—in a private section of the class.

We have described in considerable detail what one must know to develop a List class and we leave the actual building of this class as an exercise (see Exercise 19). This class would have many similarities to the simpler linked stack and queue classes for which code is given in Chapters 7 and 8.

◆ Exercises 6.5

Exercises 1–7 assume the following declarations (which are used to process singly-linked lists as described in this section):

```
class Node
{
 public:
   int data;
   Node * next;
};

Node * p1, * p2, * p3;
```

Assume also that the following statements have been executed:

```
p1 = new(nothrow) Node;
p2 = new(nothrow) Node;
p3 = new(nothrow) Node;
```

Tell what will be displayed by each of the code segments or explain why an error occurs.

1. ```
   p1->data = 123;
   p2->data = 456;
   p1->next = p2;
   p2->next = 0;
   cout << p1->data << "   " << p1->next->data << endl;
   ```
2. ```
   p1->data = 12;
   p2->data = 34;
   p1 = p2;
   cout << p1->data << "   " << p2->data << endl;
   ```
3. ```
   p1->data = 12;
   p2->data = 34;
   *p1 = *p2;
   cout << p1->data << "   " << p2->data << endl;
   ```
4. ```
   p1->data = 123;
   p2->data = 456;
   p1->next = p2;
   p2->next = 0;
   cout << p2->data << "   " << p2->next->data << endl;
   ```
5. ```
   p1->data = 12;
   p2->data = 34;
   p3->data = 34;
   ```
   ```

```
        p1->next = p2;
        p2->next = p3;
        p3->next = 0;
        cout << p1->data << "   " << p1->next->data << endl;
        cout << p2->data << "   " << p2->next->data << endl;
        cout << p1->next->next->data << endl;
        cout << p3->data << endl;
```
6.
```
    p1->data = 111;
    p2->data = 222;
    p1->next = p2;
    p2->next = p1;
    cout << p1->data << "   " << p2->data << endl;
    cout << p1->next->data << endl;
    cout << p1->next->next->data << endl;
```
7.
```
    p1->data = 12;
    p2->data = 34;
    p1 = p2;
    p2->next = p1;
    cout << p1->data << "   " << p2->data << endl;
    cout << p1->next->data << "   " << p2->next->data << endl;
```

Exercises 8–17 use the following linked list and node pointers p1, p2, p3, and p4:

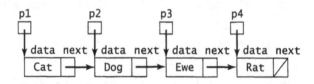

Draw a similar diagram to show how this configuration changes when the given program segment is executed, or explain why an error occurs.

8. `p1 = p2->next;`

9. `p4 = p1;`

10. `p4->data = p1->data;`

11. `p4->next->data = p1->data;`

12. `p2->next = p3->next;`

13. `p4->next = p1;`

14. `p1->next = p3->next;`
    `p1 = p3;`

15. `p1 = p3;`
    `p1->next = p3->next;`

16. ```
p4->next = p3->next;
p3->next = p2->next;
p2->next = p1->next;
```

17. ```
p4->next = p3;
p4->next->next = p2;
p4->next->next->next = p1;
p1 = 0;
```

Exercises 18–23 ask you to write various functions and classes. You should test them with driver programs as instructed in Programming Problems 7–12 at the end of this chapter.

18. Write a function that counts the nodes in a linked list.

19. Build a complete List class, using a linked-list implementation as described in this section. For basic operations it should have a constructor, destructor, copy constructor, assignment, and the basic list operations: empty, traverse, insert, and delete. Also, include a linear search operation to search the linked list for a given item, returning a pointer to a node containing the item in its data part, or a null pointer if it is not found.

20. For the List class in Exercise 19, add a member function to reverse the linked list; that is, the last node becomes the first node, and all links between nodes are reversed.

21. For the List class in Exercise 19, add a boolean-valued function that determines whether the data items in the linked list are arranged in ascending order.

6.6 An Array-Based Implementation of Linked Lists (optional)

In the preceding section we described how C++ pointers and dynamic allocation and deallocation operations can be used in implementing linked lists. In this section we show how arrays—and, in particular, arrays of structs (or classes)—can be used to implement linked lists. This provides a way to implement linked lists without using pointers and dynamic allocation and deallocation. It also sheds light on how the C++ standard list class template considered in Chapter 11 implements linked lists.

Node Structure

Nodes in a linked list contain two parts: a data part that stores an element of the list; and a next part that points to a node containing the successor of this list element or that is null if this is the last element in the list. This suggests that each node can be represented as a struct and that the linked list can be represented as an array of structs.[5] Each struct will contain two members: a data member that stores a list element and a next member that will point to its successor by storing its index in the

---

[5] We will use a struct for nodes rather than a class, because it is a C-style struct that has no function members. We could, of course, use a class whose members are declared to be public.

array. Thus, appropriate declarations for the array-based storage structure for linked lists are as follows:

```
/*** Node Declarations ***/

struct NodeType
{
  ElementType data;
  int next;
};
const int NULL_VALUE = -1; // a nonexistent location

/*** The Storage Pool ***/
const int NUMNODES = 2048;
NodeType node[NUMNODES];
int free;                      // points to a free node
```

To illustrate, consider a linked list containing the names Brown, Jones, and Smith in this order:

Here first is a variable of type int and points to the first node by storing its location in the storage pool node. Suppose for simplicity that NUMNODES is 10, so that the array node constructed by the preceding declarations consists of 10 structs, each of which has a data member for storing a name and a next member for storing the location of its successor.[6] The nodes of the linked list can be stored in any three of these array locations, provided that the links are appropriately set and first is maintained as a pointer to the first node. For example, the first node might be stored in location 7 in this array, the second node in location 1, and the third in location 3. Thus, first would have the value 7, node[7].data would store the string "Brown", and node[7].next would have the value 1. Similarly, we would have node[1].data = "Jones" and node[1].next = 3. The last node would be stored in location 3 so that node[3].data would have the value "Smith". Since there is no successor for this node, the next field must store a null pointer to indicate this fact; that is, node[3].next must have a value that is not the index of any array location, and for this, the value –1 is a natural choice for the null value.

The following diagram displays the contents of the array node and indicates how the next members connect these nodes. The question marks in some array locations indicate undetermined values because these nodes are not used to store this linked list.

---

[6] In languages that do not provide structs, node can be replaced by *parallel* arrays data and next, so that data[i] and next[i] correspond to the data members node[i].data and node[i].next.

```
            node     data        next
            [0]  │    ?    │      ?    │
            [1]  │  Jones  │      3    │◄──────┐
            [2]  │    ?    │      ?    │ ┐     │
            [3]  │  Smith  │     -1    │◄┘     │
            [4]  │    ?    │      ?    │       │
            [5]  │    ?    │      ?    │       │
   first    [6]  │    ?    │      ?    │       │
   ┌─┐          
   │7├──────► [7]  │  Brown  │      1    │──────┘
   └─┘      [8]  │    ?    │      ?    │
            [9]  │    ?    │      ?    │
```

To traverse this list, displaying the names in order, we begin by finding the location of the first node by using the pointer `first`. Since `first` has the value 7, the first name displayed is "Brown", stored in `node[7].data`. Following the next member leads us to array location `node[7].next = 1`, where the name "Jones" is stored in `node[1].data`, and then to location `node[1].next = 3`, where "Smith" is stored. The null value –1 for `node[3].next` signals that this is the last node in the list.

In general, to traverse any linked list, we use the method given in the traversal algorithm of Section 6.4:

1. Initialize `ptr` to `first`.
2. While `ptr` ≠ NULL_VALUE do the following:
    a. Process the data part of the node pointed to by `ptr`.
    b. Set `ptr` equal to the next part of the node pointed to by `ptr`.
   End while

In the current array-based implementation of linked lists, these instructions are implemented by the following code, where `ptr` is of type `int`:

```
ptr = first;
while (ptr != NULL_VALUE)
{
   /* Appropriate statements to process
      node[ptr].data are added here */
   ptr = node[ptr].next;
}
```

Now suppose we wish to insert a new name into this list, for example, to insert "Grant" after "Brown". We must first obtain a new node in which to store this name. Seven locations are available, namely, positions 0, 2, 4, 5, 6, 8, and 9 in the array. Let us assume for now that this storage pool of available nodes has been organized in such a way that a call to a function `newNode()` returns the index 9 as the location of an available node. The new name is then inserted into the list using the method described in the preceding section: `node[9].data` is set equal to "Grant"; `node[9].next` is set equal to 2 so that it points to the successor of "Brown"; and the link field `node[7].next` of the predecessor is set equal to 9.

node	data	next
[0]	?	?
[1]	Jones	3
[2]	?	?
[3]	Smith	-1
[4]	?	?
[5]	?	?
[6]	?	?
[7]	Brown	9
[8]	?	?
[9]	Grant	1

first 7

Organizing the Storage Pool

This example illustrates that the elements of the array **node** are of two kinds. Some of the array locations—namely 1, 3, 7, and 9—are used to store nodes of the linked list. The others represent unused "free" nodes that are available for storing new items as they are inserted into the list. We have described in detail how the nodes used to store list elements are organized, and we must now consider how to structure the storage pool of available nodes.

One simple way is to begin by linking all the nodes together to form the storage pool by letting the first node point to the second, the second to the third, and so on. The link field of the last node will be null, and a pointer **free** is set equal to 0 to provide access to the first node in this storage pool:[7]

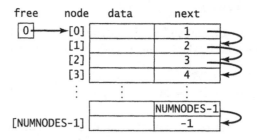

A function call `ptr = newNode()` returns the location of a free node by assigning to `ptr` the value `free` and removing that node from the free list by setting `free` equal to `node[free].next`. Thus, if "Mills" is the first name to be inserted into a linked list, it will be stored in the first position of the array `node`, because `free` has the value 0; `first` will be set to 0; and `free` will become 1:

---

[7] In the terminology of the next chapter, the storage is maintained as a *linked stack*.

node	data	next
first [0] → [0]	Mills	-1
free [1] → [1]	?	2
[2]	?	3
[3]	?	4
[4]	?	5
[5]	?	6
[6]	?	7
[7]	?	8
[8]	?	9
[9]	?	-1

If "Baker" is the next name to be inserted, it will be stored in location 1 because this is the value of free, and free will be set equal to 2. If the list is to be maintained in alphabetical order, first will be set equal to 1; node[1].next will be set equal to 0; and node[0].next will be set equal to –1:

node	data	next
[0]	Mills	-1
first [1] → [1]	Baker	0
free [2] → [2]	?	3
[3]	?	4
[4]	?	5
[5]	?	6
[6]	?	7
[7]	?	8
[8]	?	9
[9]	?	-1

If "Wells" is the next name inserted into the list, the following configuration will result:

node	data	next
[0]	Mills	2
first [1] → [1]	Baker	0
[2]	Wells	-1
free [3] → [3]	?	4
[4]	?	5
[5]	?	6
[6]	?	7
[7]	?	8
[8]	?	9
[9]	?	-1

When a node is deleted from a linked list, it should be returned to the storage pool of free nodes so that it can be reused later to store some other list element. A function call deleteNode(ptr) simply inserts the node pointed to by ptr at the beginning of the free list by first setting node[ptr].next equal to free and then setting free equal to ptr. For example, deleting the name "Mills" from the preceding linked list produces the following configuration:

	node	data	next
free 0 →	[0]	Mills	3
first 1 →	[1]	Baker	0
	[2]	Wells	-1
	[3]	?	4
	[4]	?	5
	[5]	?	6
	[6]	?	7
	[7]	?	8
	[8]	?	9
	[9]	?	-1

Note that it is not necessary to actually remove the string "Mills" from the data part of this node because changing the link of its predecessor has *logically* removed it from the linked list. This string "Mills" will be overwritten when this node is used to store a new name.

Using these ideas, we could develop a library that manages the array Node and the list of free nodes along with functions to get a new node or to return one to the free list. It could then be used to build a List class. We will leave the details as exercises.

◆ Exercises 6.6

1. An ordered linked list of characters has been constructed using the array-based implementation described in this section. The following diagram shows the current contents of the array that stores the elements of the linked list and the storage pool:

node	data	next
[0]	J	3
[1]	Z	6
[2]	C	0
[3]	P	-1
[4]	B	2
[5]	M	1
[6]	K	7
[7]	Q	8
[8]	?	9
[9]	?	-1

first = 4
free = 5

   a. List the elements of this list.
   b. List the nodes in the storage pool in the order in which they are linked together.

2. Assuming the contents of the array node pictured in Exercise 1, show the contents of node and the values of first and free after the letter F is inserted into the list so that the resulting list is still in alphabetical order.

3. Proceed as in Exercise 2 but for the operation Delete J.

4. Proceed as in Exercise 2 but for the following sequence of operations:

 Delete J, Delete P, Delete C, Delete B.

5. Proceed as in Exercise 2 but for the following sequence of operations:

 Insert A, Delete P, Insert K, Delete C.

6. Assuming the array-based implementation in this section, write a function to count the nodes in a linked list.

7. Assuming the array-based implementation in this section, write a boolean-valued function that determines whether the data items in the list are arranged in ascending order.

8. Assuming the array-based implementation in this section, write a function that returns a pointer to the last node in a linked list.

9. Assuming the array-based implementation in this section, write a function to reverse a linked list in the manner described in Exercise 12 of Section 6.4.

SUMMARY

▣! Chapter Notes

- Building a class consists of two steps: (1) *design the class and* (2) *implement the class.*
- An array-based implementation of a list may involve much shifting of array elements for lists that change frequently due to insertion and deletion of elements.
- Implementing containers with classes that use dynamic allocation should provide the following methods: a destructor, a copy constructor, and an assignment operator.
- Wherever an object goes out of scope, the compiler will insert a call to its destructor to reclaim dynamically-allocated memory within the object.
- An object's *copy constructor* is invoked whenever a copy of that object must be made (e.g., for a value parameter). In classes that allocate memory dynamically, they are needed to make distinct copies of objects (*deep copies*).
- In classes that allocate memory dynamically, an *assignment operator* is needed to provide deep copying and to avoid memory leaks in assignments.
- A *linked list* is a sequence of elements called *nodes*, each of which has a data part that stores an element of the list and a next part that stores a link (or pointer) that indicates the location of the node containing the next list element.
- Insertion and deletion at a specified point in a linked list are O(1) operations, which means they can be done in constant time.

☞ Programming Pointers

1. Make certain that the pointer members of a class are initialized by its constructors. Many errors can be avoided simply by ensuring that, when an object is created, its pointer members are initialized by default to null.

2. Never rely upon the default copy constructor or assignment operator for a class that uses dynamic memory allocation because for such classes, these default operations will not

make distinct copies of an object. This is another example of the *aliasing problem*, since changes to a copy of an object can inadvertently change the original object.

3. Do not rely upon the default destructor for a class containing a data member that points to some container because for such classes, this default operation will destroy only the pointer and leave stranded the memory allocated to the container.

4. If an object contains pointer members, test its operations exhaustively. It is quite easy for execution to miss the run-time and logical errors in sections of code that manipulate pointers, unless tests are performed that explicitly check those sections of code. Better yet, have others test your operations, since they will try to do things you might not have anticipated.

▲ ADT Tips

1. Building a class consists of two steps: (1) Design the class and (2) implement the class.

2. In designing a class, describe the operations independently of how the class will be implemented, that is, in a way that does not depend on any particular representation of the class objects.

3. Implementing a class involves two steps: (1) Define data members to represent the object(s) being modeled and (2) define the operations identified in the design phase.

4. If a problem solution involves a dynamic list, then a linked list may be a more time-efficient way to store and process that list. In a sequential-storage implementation, the values are stored in adjacent locations in an array. This means that when values are inserted into (or deleted from) an array-based list of *n* values, an average of *n*/2 of the values will have to be shifted to make room for the new value. The time required to shift these values makes insertion (and deletion) a time-expensive operation. By contrast, the values in a linked list are stored in (nonadjacent) nodes, which are attached to one another using links. Inserting (and deleting) a value at a given point in the list simply involves setting the values of (at most) two of these links.

5. If a problem solution involves many accesses to the interior values of a list, then an array-based list may be a more time-efficient way to store and process that list. In a linked list, all values except the first must be accessed sequentially; that is, to access a specific node, we must access all those that precede it, beginning with the first node in the list. An average of *n*/2 accesses are thus required to access a node in a linked list of length *n*. By contrast, all values of an array-based list can be accessed directly, permitting such lists to be processed more quickly.

6. In programming languages that do not provide a run-time heap and dynamic allocation and deallocation, a storage pool of free nodes can be simulated using an array of structures (or parallel arrays). It is usually managed as a linked stack (see the next chapter) and allocate and deallocate operations are simply the push and pop operations for a stack.

7. Pay attention to special cases in processing linked lists and be careful not to lose access to nodes. In particular, remember the following "programming proverbs":

   ■ *Don't take a long walk off a short linked list.* It is an error to attempt to process elements beyond the end of the list. As an example, consider the following incorrect attempts to search a linked list with first node pointed to by first for some itemSought:

   Attempt 1:
   ```
   ptr = first;
   while (ptr->data != itemSought)
     ptr = ptr->next;
   ```

If the item is not present in any node of the linked list, ptr will eventually reach the last node in the list; ptr then becomes null, and an attempt to examine its data member produces an error.

Attempt 2:

```
/* This time I'll make sure I don't fall off the end of the
   list by stopping if I find itemSought or reach a node whose
   link member is null. */

bool found = false;
ptr = first;
while ((! found) && (ptr->next != 0))
  if (ptr->data == itemSought)
    found = true;
  else
    ptr = ptr->next;
```

Although this avoids the problem of moving beyond the end of the list, it will fail to locate the desired item (that is, set found to true) if the item sought is the last one in the list. When ptr reaches the last node, ptr->next is null, and repetition is terminated without examining the data member of this last node. Another problem is that if the item is found in the list, the remaining nodes (except the last) will also be examined.

Attempt 3:

```
// Another attempt to avoid running past the end of the list.

ptr = first;
while ((ptr->data != itemSought) && (ptr != 0))
  ptr = ptr->next;
```

This solution is almost correct, but like the first attempted solution, it results in an error if the item is not in the list. The reason is that boolean expressions are evaluated from left to right. Thus, when the end of the list is reached and ptr becomes null, the first part of the boolean expression controlling repetition is evaluated, and the result of dereferencing a null pointer is usually an error.

Attempt 4:

```
// Okay, so I'll just reverse the two parts of the condition

ptr = first;
while ((ptr != 0) && (ptr->data != itemSought))
  ptr = ptr->next;
```

This is a correct solution, thanks to the short-circuit evaluation of boolean expression in C++; that is, if ptr is null, then the first part of the condition ptr != 0 evaluates to false, and so the condition "short-circuits," leaving the second condition unevaluated. Note that if short-circuit evaluation were not utilized, this second condition would be evaluated, and the attempt to dereference the null pointer ptr would result in an error.

- *You can't get water from an empty well.* Don't try to access elements in an empty list; this case usually requires special consideration. For example, if first is null, then initializing ptr to first and attempting to access ptr->data or ptr->next is an error. To avoid such errors, such operations should be guarded as in

```
if (first != 0)
   // do the required processing
else
// the list is empty
```

- *Don't burn bridges before you cross them.* Be careful to change links in the correct order, or you may lose access to a node or to many nodes! For example, in the following attempt to insert a new node at the beginning of a linked list

```
first = newNodePtr;
newNodePtr->next = first;
```

the statements are not in correct order. As soon as the first statement is executed, first points to the new node, and access to the remaining nodes in the list (those formerly pointed to by first) is lost. The second statement then simply sets the link member of the new node to point to itself:

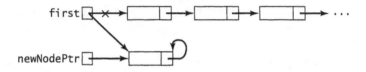

The correct sequence is to first connect the new node to the list and then reset first:

```
newNodePtr->next = first;
first = newNodePtr;
```

Programming Problems

Section 6.3

1. Write a driver program to test the Polynomial class developed in the exercises.

2. Use the Polynomial class developed in the exercises in a menu-driven program for processing polynomials. Options on the menu should include polynomial addition, polynomial multiplication, printing a polynomial, and evaluating a polynomial for a given value of the variable.

Section 6.5

3. Write a driver program to test your node-counter function in Exercise 18.

4. Write a driver program to test your List class in Exercise 19.

5. Write a driver program to test your modified List class in Exercise 20.

6. Write a driver program to test your modified List class in Exercise 21.

7. A limited number of tickets for the Hoops championship basketball game go on sale tomorrow, and ticket orders are to be filled in the order in which they are received. Write

a program that a box-office cashier can use to enter the names and addresses of the persons ordering tickets together with the number of tickets requested, and store this information in a list. The program should then produce a sequence of mailing labels (names, addresses, and number of tickets) for orders that can be filled.

8. Modify the program in Problem 7 to check that no one receives more than four tickets and that multiple requests from the same person are disallowed.

Section 6.6

9. Write a memory management library as described in this section. Then build and test a List class that stores the list elements in a linked list as described in this section.

Stacks

CHAPTER CONTENTS

Chapter Objectives

- To study a stack as an ADT.
- Build a static-array-based implementation of stacks.
- Build a dynamic-array-based implementation of stacks.
- Build a linked implementation of stacks.
- Show how a run-time stack is used to store information during function calls.
- (Optional) Study postfix notation and see how stacks are used to convert expressions from infix to postfix and how to evaluate postfix expressions.

An implementation of an abstract data type consists of storage structures to store the data items and algorithms for the basic operations and relations, and as we saw in the preceding chapter with the list ADT, there may be several different implementations. Some of these may perform better in some applications than others, and knowledge of the strengths and weaknesses of the various implementations helps with choosing one that is most appropriate for a particular problem.

In addition to lists, there are several other important container ADTs, and in this chapter we consider one of these—the *stack*—and some of its applications. Stacks are often implemented using an array because most programming languages provide an array data structure and using it to implement a stack is quite easy. Also, as we will see, the shifting of array elements that is necessary when a new element is inserted into a list or when a list element is removed can be eliminated for stacks, producing a very efficient implementation.

We will begin the chapter by building a Stack class implemented in this way, first using a static array and then using a dynamic array. We will also build a Stack class that uses a linked list to store the stack elements. In Chapter 9 we will show how these implementations can be improved and will consider some alternative implementations:

- Make it a class template so it becomes a generic container type that can process any type of stack elements.

- Use a vector for the storage container so that the stack's capacity can increase as necessary.

- Look at the stack container provided in *STL*, the *Standard Template Library*, which is a part of standard C++.

7.1 Introduction to Stacks

Consider the following problems:

Problem 1

A program is to be written to simulate a certain card game. One aspect of this simulation is to maintain a discard pile. On any turn, a player may discard a single card from her hand to the top of this pile, or she may retrieve the top card from this discard pile. Is there an appropriate data type to model this discard pile?

Problem 2

A program is to be written to model a railroad switching yard. One part of the switching network consists of a main track and a siding onto which cars may be shunted and removed at any time. Is there a data type we can use to model the operation of this siding?

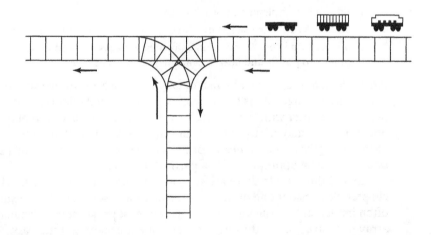

Problem 3

One task that must be performed during execution of a function f() is to keep track of enough information about f()—parameter values, local variables, and so on[1]—that, when execution of f() is interrupted by a call to another function g(), execution of f() can resume when g() terminates. Obviously, g() might call another function h() so that information about g() must be stored so it can resume execution later. And h() might call another function, and so on. Complicating the situation is the possibility that one of these functions might also call itself—a phenomenon known as *recursion* (which we will study in Chapter 10). How should this function information be stored?

Problem 4

Data items are stored in computer memory using a binary representation. In particular, positive integers are commonly stored using the base-two representation described in Section 2.2. This means that the base-ten representation of an integer that appears in a program or in a data file must be converted to a base-two representation. One algorithm for carrying out this conversion uses repeated division by 2, with the successive remainders giving the binary digits in the base-two representation from right to left. For example, the base-two representation of 26 is 11010, as the following computation shows. What data type can be used to keep track of these remainders?

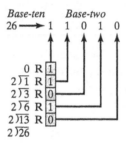

Each of these problems involves a collection of related data items: a pile of cards in Problem 1, a set of railroad cars in Problem 2, a collection of function information in Problem 3, and a sequence of remainders in Problem 4. In Problem 1, the basic operations are adding a card to and removing a card from the top of the discard pile. In Problem 2, the basic operations are pushing a car onto the siding and removing the last car previously placed on the siding. In Problem 3, when a function terminates, a return is made to the last function that was interrupted. Function information must therefore be stored in such a way that the last information stored will be the first removed from storage. From the diagram in Problem 4, we note that the bits that comprise the base-two representation of 26 have been generated in reverse order, from right to left, and that the remainders must therefore be stored in some structure so they can later be displayed in the usual left-to-right order.

In each case we need a "last-discarded-first-removed," "last-pushed-onto-first-removed," "last-stored-first-removed," "last-generated-first-displayed" container. To illustrate this behavior, we focus on Problem 4. To display the base-two representation of an integer like 26 in the usual left-to-right sequence, we must "stack up" the remainders generated during the repeated division by 2, as illustrated in the diagram

---

[1] This is called an *activation record* and is described in more detail in Section 7.4.

in Problem 4. When the division process terminates, we can retrieve the bits from this stack of remainders in the required "last-in-first-out" order.

Assuming that a stack data type is available, we could use an algorithm like the following to convert from base-ten to base-two and display the result:

Base-Conversion Algorithm

/*   Algorithm to display the base-two representation of a base-ten number.   */

1. Declare an empty stack to hold the remainders.
2. While *number* ≠ 0:
   a. Calculate the *remainder* that results when *number* is divided by 2.
   b. Put the *remainder* on the top of the stack of remainders.
   c. Replace *number* by the integer quotient of *number* divided by 2.
   End while.
3. While the stack of remainders is not empty,
   a. Retrieve and remove the *remainder* from the top of the stack of remainders.
   b. Append *remainder* to the output already produced.
   End while.

The diagram in Figure 7.1 traces this algorithm for the integer 26.

This type of last-in-first-out processing occurs in a wide variety of applications; consequently, a data type that embodies this idea is very useful. This **last-in-first-out (LIFO)** data structure is called a **stack**.

Adding an item to a stack is referred to as *pushing* that item onto the stack, and removing an item from the stack is referred to as *popping* the stack. One common explanation for this terminology is the operation of a spring-loaded stack of plates in a cafeteria:

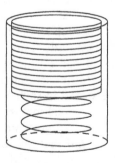

This stack functions in the following way:

- If a plate is added to the stack, those below it are pushed down and cannot be accessed.
- If a plate is removed from the stack, those below it pop up one position.
- The stack becomes empty when there are no plates in it.
- The stack is full if there is no room in it for more plates.

Figure 7.1 Using a Stack to Convert a Number from Base Ten to Base Two

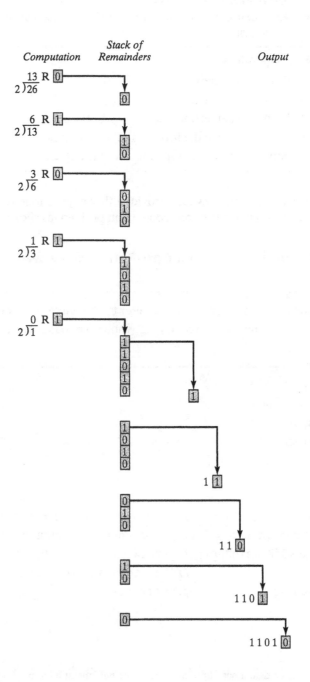

This leads to the following definition of a stack as an abstract data type:

Stack ADT

Collection of Data Elements

A sequence of data items that can be accessed at only one end, called the *top* of the stack.

Basic Operations

- Construct a stack (usually empty)
- Check if the stack is empty
- Push: Add an element at the top of the stack
- Top: Retrieve the top element of the stack
- Pop: Remove the top element of the stack[2]

If we had a stack class that provided these operations, it would be easy to develop a short program for the base-conversion problem as shown in Figure 7.2.

Figure 7.2 Conversion from Base Ten to Base Two

```
/*-------------------------------------------------------------------
   This program uses a stack to convert the base-ten representation
   of a positive integer entered as input to base two, which is
   then output.
   -------------------------------------------------------------------*/

#include <iostream>
using namespace std;
#include "Stack.h"            // our own -- <stack> for STL version

int main()
{
   unsigned number,          // the number to be converted
            remainder;        // remainder when number is divided by 2
   Stack stackOfRemainders;  // stack of remainders
                             // Change Stack to stack<int> for STL version
   char response;            // user response
```

---

[2] In some definitions of the stack ADT, the pop operation also returns the element removed from the stack. The approach in this text is consistent with the pop operation in C++'s standard (STL) stack container.

Figure 7.2 (continued)

```
do
{
   cout << "Enter positive integer to convert: ";
   cin >> number;
   while (number != 0)
   {
      remainder = number % 2;
      stackOfRemainders.push(remainder);
      number /= 2;
   }
   cout << "Base-two representation: ";

   while ( !stackOfRemainders.empty() )
   {
      remainder = stackOfRemainders.top();
      stackOfRemainders.pop();
      cout << remainder;
   }
   cout << endl;
   cout << "\nMore (Y or N)? ";
   cin >> response;
}
while (response == 'Y' || response == 'y');
}
```

▲

7.2 Designing and Building a **Stack** Class—Array-Based

As we noted in the preceding chapter, building a class consists of two steps:

1. *Design the class*
2. *Implement the class*

We begin, therefore, by looking at the design of a stack class.

As with the List classes developed in Chapter 6, we begin by describing the function members that will be needed to carry out the operations listed in the stack ADT description. And we do this independently of implementation details, such as what data members will be used.

In our definition of a stack as an ADT, we identified five basic operations: constructor, empty, push, top, and pop. Our class must, therefore, have function members for (at least) these operations:

■ *constructor*: Constructs an empty stack

- *empty():*   Examines a stack and returns false or true depending on whether the stack contains any values
- *push():*   Modifies a stack by adding a value at the top of the stack
- *top():*   Retrieves the value at the top of the stack
- *pop():*   Modifies a stack by removing the value at the top of the stack

To help with debugging, an output operation is usually added to display snapshots of the stack contents while the other operations are being tested:

- *display():*   Displays all the elements stored in the stack

Now that our stack class has been designed, it must be implemented by

1. defining data members to store the stack's elements and
2. defining the operations identified in the design phase.

Selecting Storage Structures

A stack must store a collection of values, so we begin by considering what kind of storage structure(s) to use. Because a stack is a sequence of data items, we will use an array to store these items, with each stack element occupying one position in the array. This also will provide an implementation that can be realized in almost any programming language. In the next section we will develop a linked-list implementation.

A First (Inefficient) Attempt   If we think of modeling a spring-loaded stack of plates described earlier, then it seems natural to use an array for the stack elements with position 0 serving as the top of the stack. For example, suppose we have a stack with an array of capacity 8, and suppose the stack contains the 6 integers 77, 121, 64, 234, 51, and 29, with 77 at the top and the other integers in the given order below it. We might picture this as follows, where ? denotes a "garbage" value in the array:·

```
[0]    77
[1]   121
[2]    64
[3]   234
[4]    51
[5]    29
[6]     ?
[7]     ?
```

Consider, however, what happens if we now perform the three operations push 95, push 80, and pop, in this order:

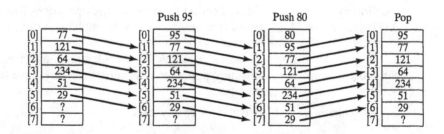

Notice that each time a new value is pushed onto the stack, all the items in the stack must be moved down one slot in the array to make room for it at the top. Similarly, each time a value is removed from the stack, all of the items in the array from position 1 on must be moved up so that the top value is in location 0. Although this may be a good model of a spring-loaded stack of plates, when one wants to study the dynamics of how the device performs, it is grossly inefficient for many other kinds of stacks.

A Better Approach The shifting of array elements in the preceding implementation is time consuming and unnecessary and can easily be avoided. Rather than thinking of a spring-loaded stack of plates, we think of a stack of books on a table (or a discard pile in a card game, or a stack of pancakes, or if your prefer, the stack-of-plates container but with the spring removed or broken). We can add and remove books at the top of this stack without ever moving any of the other books in the stack!

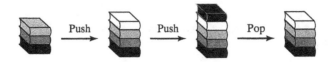

For a spring-loaded stack of plates, the top of the stack is fixed, and so the bottom plate (and therefore all of the other plates) move when we add or remove a plate at the top of the stack. For a stack of books, however, only the top moves when we add or remove a book; the bottom of the stack stays fixed (as do all of the other books).

To model this view of a stack, we need only "flip the array over," fixing position 0 at the bottom of the stack, and let the stack grow toward the end of the array, using a variable *myTop* to keep track of the top of the stack, and then push and pop at this location:

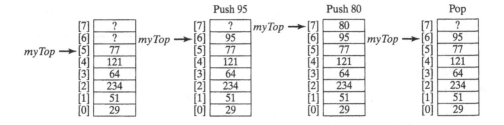

Note that no shifting of array elements is necessary.

So, we can begin building our stack class by selecting data members:

- An *array* to hold the stack elements
- An *integer* to indicate the top of the stack

For the array data member, we can use either of our approaches for the List class in the preceding chapter: use a static array or use a dynamic array. We begin with the static approach and, after building this version of the Stack class, look at a dynamic array implementation.

The array capacity and type of the stack elements are set in the same way that we did for the first implementation of the List class in Section 6.2. We put their declarations

```
const int STACK_CAPACITY = . . .;
typedef int StackElement;
```

ahead of the class declaration, so that they will be easy to change when we need a new stack element type or when we need to change the capacity.

Now we can write our class declaration as shown in Figure 7.3.

Figure 7.3 **Class Declaration for a Stack Data Type**

```
/*-- Stack.h -------------------------------------------------------

  This header file defines a Stack data type.
  Basic operations:
    constructor:  Constructs an empty stack
    empty:        Checks if a stack is empty
    push:         Modifies a stack by adding a value at the top
    top:          Retrieves the top stack value; leaves stack unchanged
    pop:          Modifies stack by removing the value at the top
    display:      Displays all the stack elements

  Class Invariant:
    1. The stack elements (if any) are stored in positions
       0, 1, . . ., myTop of myArray.
    2. -1 <= myTop < STACK_CAPACITY
--------------------------------------------------------------------*/

#ifndef STACK
#define STACK

const int STACK_CAPACITY = 128;
typedef int StackElement;

class Stack
{
 public:
  /***** Function Members *****/
 private:
  /***** Data Members *****/
```

Figure 7.3   (continued)

```
StackElement myArray[STACK_CAPACITY];
   int myTop;
};
```

`#endif`

▲

Implementing the Operations

To complete this implementation of a stack, functions must be written to perform the basic stack operations. We will first develop algorithms for each of them individually and then give the code that implements them.

Constructor   The compiler will handle the allocation of memory for the data members myArray and myTop, so the Stack constructor need only do the initialization necessary to create an empty stack. Because myTop always points at the array element containing the top element, it seems natural to assign myTop the value –1 to signal an empty stack:

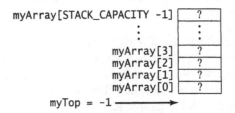

Empty   The operation to check if a stack is empty is now trivial since it need only check the myTop data member to see whether it is –1 and return true if it is and false otherwise.

Push   The push operation is the insert operation for a stack. It will receive a value of type StackElement and add it to the top of the stack.

However, like the array-based implementation of lists in the preceding chapter, the array data member may become full, in which case the value cannot be added to the stack. Thus, our algorithm for the push operation must first check whether there is room in the array for the new value.

 Algorithm for the Push Operation

If myArray is not full (i.e., myTop < STACK_CAPACITY – 1)

1. Increment myTop by 1.
2. Store the value in myArray[myTop].

Otherwise
   Signal that there is no storage space for the value and terminate this operation.

There are several ways to handle the array-full condition:

- Display an error message and terminate execution
- Display an error message, but allow execution to proceed
- Throw an exception
- Return a boolean value that signals whether the operation was successful (true) or it failed (false)

In the Stack class in Figure 7.4, the first method is used.

Top   The top operation is to retrieve the value at the top of the stack. It is thus a simple accessor function that returns the element myArray[myTop]. However, if the stack is empty, myTop has the value –1, which produces an invalid array reference, so some appropriate action must be taken.

 ### Algorithm for the Top Operation

If the stack is not empty
    Return the value in myArray[myTop].
Otherwise
    Indicate that the stack is empty and return a "garbage value."

To implement this algorithm, we must find or construct a garbage value of type StackElement to return in the case that the stack is empty. Since StackElement can be any type, we can't use a specific literal as a return value. The implementation of the top operation in the Stack class in Figure 7.4 returns the value stored in an uninitialized local variable garbage.

Pop   The last stack operation is a pop operation to remove the top stack element. This is accomplished simply by decrementing myTop by 1. However, if the stack is empty, some other action is required, because decrementing myTop would give it the value –2, which violates the class invariant. The following algorithm handles this stack-full condition with the second approach described earlier for a stack-full condition; that is, a stack-empty message is displayed but execution is allowed to continue.

 ### Algorithm for the Pop Operation

If the stack is not empty
    Decrement myTop by 1.
Otherwise
    Indicate that the stack is empty.

Output   An output operation is not one of the basic operations listed in our definition of a stack as an ADT. However, as operations are implemented, they need to be tested, so an output operation is usually added early in the implementation process. For our Stack class this can be a function member display() that simply displays the values stored in myArray[myTop] down through myArray[0]. Figure 7.4 shows a prototype and definition for display() and Figure 7.5 shows how we might use it in a test driver.

The Complete Stack Class

Figure 7.4 shows the complete Stack class. The class declaration is in the header file Stack.h and the definitions of the function members are in the implementation file Stack.cpp.[3]

Figure 7.4 The Stack Class—Version 1 with Static Array

```
/*-- Stack.h ------------------------------------------------------------

   This header file defines a Stack data type.
   Basic operations:
     constructor:  Constructs an empty stack
     empty:        Checks if a stack is empty
     push:         Modifies a stack by adding a value at the top
     top:          Retrieves the top stack value; leaves stack unchanged
     pop:          Modifies stack by removing the value at the top
     display:      Displays all the stack elements

   Class Invariant:
     1. The stack elements (if any) are stored in positions
        0, 1, . . ., myTop of myArray.
     2. -1 <= myTop < STACK_CAPACITY
------------------------------------------------------------------------*/


#include <iostream>

#ifndef STACK
#define STACK

const int STACK_CAPACITY = 128;
typedef int StackElement;

class Stack
{
 public:
  /***** Function Members *****/
```

---

[3] As noted in Chapter 3, some programmers would inline simple functions such as the constructor, empty(), and display() by putting their definitions in Stack.h, after the class declaration, and preceding the function headings with the keyword inline.

Figure 7.4 (continued)

```
/***** Constructor *****/
Stack();
/*-------------------------------------------------------------------
  Construct a Stack object.

  Precondition: None.
  Postcondition: An empty Stack object has been constructed (myTop is
      initialized to -1 and myArray is an array with STACK_CAPACITY
      elements of type StackElement).
  -----------------------------------------------------------------*/

bool empty() const;
/*-------------------------------------------------------------------
  Check if stack is empty.
  Precondition: None
  Postcondition: Returns true if stack is empty and false otherwise.
  -----------------------------------------------------------------*/

void push(const StackElement & value);
/*-------------------------------------------------------------------
  Add a value to a stack.

  Precondition:  value is to be added to this stack
  Postcondition: value is added at top of stack provided there is space;
      otherwise, a stack-full message is displayed and execution is
      terminated.
  -----------------------------------------------------------------*/

void display(ostream & out) const;
/*-------------------------------------------------------------------
  Display values stored in the stack.

  Precondition:  ostream out is open.
  Postcondition: Stack's contents, from top down, have been output to out.
  -----------------------------------------------------------------*/

StackElement top() const;
/*-------------------------------------------------------------------
  Retrieve value at top of stack (if any).
```

Figure 7.4 (continued)

```
    Precondition:  Stack is nonempty
    Postcondition: Value at top of stack is returned, unless the stack is
        empty; in that case, an error message is displayed and a "garbage
        value" is returned.
    ----------------------------------------------------------------*/

  void pop();
  /*----------------------------------------------------------------
    Remove value at top of stack (if any).

    Precondition:  Stack is nonempty.
    Postcondition: Value at top of stack has been removed, unless the
        stack is empty; in that case, an error message is displayed and
        execution allowed to proceed.
    ----------------------------------------------------------------*/

 private:
  /***** Data Members *****/
  StackElement myArray[STACK_CAPACITY];
  int myTop;
}; // end of class declaration

#endif
```

```
/*-- Stack.cpp-----------------------------------------------------
            This file implements Stack member functions.
   ----------------------------------------------------------------*/

#include <iostream>
using namespace std;

#include "Stack.h"

//--- Definition of Stack constructor
Stack::Stack()
: myTop(-1)
{}
```

Figure 7.4 (continued)

```
//--- Definition of empty()
bool Stack::empty() const
{
   return (myTop == -1);
}


//--- Definition of push()
void Stack::push(const StackElement & value)
{
   if (myTop < STACK_CAPACITY - 1) //Preserve stack invariant
   {
      ++myTop;
      myArray[myTop] = value;
   }
   else
   {
      cerr << "*** Stack full -- can't add new value ***\n"
              "Must increase value of STACK_CAPACITY in Stack.h\n";
      exit(1);
   }
}


//--- Definition of display()
void Stack::display(ostream & out) const
{
   for (int i = myTop; i >= 0; i--)
      out << myArray[i] << endl;
}


//--- Definition of top()
StackElement Stack::top() const
{
   if ( !empty() )
      return (myArray[myTop]);
   else
   {
      cerr << "*** Stack is empty -- returning garbage value ***\n";
      StackElement garbage; return garbage;
   }
}
```

Figure 7.4 (continued)

```
//--- Definition of pop()
void Stack::pop()
{
   if ( !empty() )
      myTop--;
   else
      cerr << "*** Stack is empty -- can't remove a value ***\n";
}
```

▲

Figure 7.5 shows a driver program to test the stack class. The first execution trace creates a stack with 4 elements and indicates that the basic operations are working correctly. The second execution trace demonstrates the effects of attempting to create a stack with more elements than allowed with the array capacity set in Stack.h.

Figure 7.5 Driver Program to Test Stack Class

```
/*-------------------------------------------------------------------
                Driver program to test the Stack class.
   ---------------------------------------------------------------*/

#include <iostream>
using namespace std;

#include "Stack.h"

int main()
{
   Stack s;
   cout << "Stack created.  Empty? " << boolalpha << s.empty() << endl;

   cout << "How many elements to add to the stack? ";
   int numItems;
   cin >> numItems;
   for (int i = 1; i <= numItems; i++)
      s.push(i);

   cout << "Stack contents:\n";
   s.display(cout);
```

Figure 7.5 (continued)

```
    cout << "Stack empty? " << s.empty() << endl;

    cout << "Top value: " << s.top() << endl;

    while (!s.empty())
    {
      cout << "Popping " << s.top() << endl;
      s.pop();
    }
    cout << "Stack empty? " << s.empty() << endl;
    cout << "Top value: " << s.top() << endl;
    cout << "Trying to pop: " << endl;
    s.pop();
}
```

Execution Trace #1:

```
Stack created.  Empty? true
How many elements to add to the stack? 4
Stack contents:
4
3
2
1
Stack empty? false
Top value: 4
Popping 4
Popping 3
Popping 2
Popping 1
Stack empty? true
*** Stack is empty -- returning garbage value ***
Top value: 0
Trying to pop:
*** Stack is empty -- can't remove a value ***
```

Execution Trace #2:

```
Stack created.  Empty? true
How many elements to add to the stack? 129
*** Stack full -- can't add new value ***
Must increase value of STACK_CAPACITY in Stack.h
```

▲

The declaration

```
Stack s;
```

in the program in Figure 7.5 constructs the stack s as follows:

```
s
   myTop  -1
           0  1  2  3  4           . . .           127
   myArray | ? | ? | ? | ? | ? |      . . .       | ? |
```

The array data member myArray contains 128 uninitialized elements, and the constructor sets myArray to –1 to indicate an empty stack.

In the first execution trace, the four integers 1, 2, 3, and 4 are pushed onto s producing

```
s
   myTop   3
           0  1  2  3  4           . . .           127
   myArray | 1 | 2 | 3 | 4 | ? |      . . .       | ? |
```

The output produced by sending the message display(cout) to s verifies this. Finally, the pop operation is applied repeatedly until s is empty. An attempt to pop another element from s then fails, producing the stack-empty message.

Using a Dynamic Array to Store the Stack Elements

The preceding implementation of a stack uses the same capacity for the arrays that store the stack elements in every Stack object. Setting this capacity large enough to handle all stack(s) that will be used can obviously result in considerable wasted space. Setting it too small, however, is troublesome because it is inconvenient and annoying to enter a collection of data and then have the program crash or start producing incorrect or unreliable results because the container cannot hold all of the data values. Also, changing this capacity requires modifying the definition of STACK_CAPACITY in Stack.h, which means that all programs and libraries that include Stack.h must be recompiled.

An alternative is to follow the example of the list implementation in the preceding chapter and use a dynamic array. This will allow the user to specify the capacity of the stack in its declaration. As we saw, however, in classes that use dynamically allocated storage, the constructor does more than just initialization, and some new function members are required:

1. *Constructor:*   Handles allocation of memory to dynamic data members and initializations of all data members

2. *Destructor*: To deallocate dynamically-allocated memory in an object

3. *Copy constructor*: To make copies of objects—for example, for value parameters and to initialize a new object with an existing object

4. *Assignment operator*: To assign one object to another

We begin by changing STACK_CAPACITY to a variable data member and the declaration of myArray to a pointer:

```
typedef int StackElement
class Stack
{
 public:
 /***** Function Members *****/
  // --- SAME AS BEFORE ---
 private:
 /***** Data Members*****/
  int myTop,              // top of stack
      myCapacity;         // capacity of stack
  StackElement * myArray; // dynamic array to store elements
};
```

Now we must look at what changes are required in the function members and implement the new function members.

Constructor In our earlier stack implementation, the compiler handled the allocation of the array data member and the only thing the constructor had to do was set myTop to –1 to denote an empty stack. Now, however, the constructor must really construct something, namely, the array that will store the stack elements.

We want to permit declarations such as

```
Stack s1;
Stack s2(cap);
```

to construct s1 as a stack with some default capacity and s2 as a stack with integer capacity cap. For this, we can use a constructor with a default argument:

```
Stack(int numElements = 128);
```

The following is an algorithm for this constructor:

Algorithm for the Constructor

1. Check that the specified stack capacity numElements is positive. Terminate execution if it isn't.

2. Set myCapacity to numElements.

3. Allocate an array pointed to by myArray and with capacity myCapacity.

4. If memory is allocated for this array
      Set myTop to –1.
   Otherwise
      Display an error message and terminate execution.

 Code implementing this algorithm is shown in Figure 7.6. (See the source files—
Chap7/Figures7.6–10—on the text's website for complete versions of Stack.h and
Stack.cpp and a test driver.)

Figure 7.6 The Stack Class Constructor

```
/*-- DStack.h --------------------------------------------------------

  This header file defines a Stack data type.
  Basic operations:
    constructor:  Constructs an empty stack
    empty:        Checks if a stack is empty
    push:         Modifies a stack by adding a value at the top
    top:          Accesses the top stack value; leaves stack unchanged
    pop:          Modifies stack by removing the value at the top
    display:      Displays all the stack elements

  Class Invariant:
    1. The stack elements (if any) are stored in positions
       0, 1, . . ., myTop of myArray.
    2. -1 <= myTop < myCapacity
-----------------------------------------------------------------*/

#include <iostream>

#ifndef DSTACK
#define DSTACK

typedef int StackElement;

class Stack
{
 public:
 /***** Function Members *****/
```

Figure 7.6 (continued)

```
/***** Constructors *****/

  Stack(int numElements = 128);
  /*---------------------------------------------------------------------
    Construct a Stack object.

    Precondition:  None.
    Postcondition: An empty Stack object has been constructed (myTop is
        initialized to -1 and myArray is an array with numElements
        (default 128) elements of type StackElement).
  ---------------------------------------------------------------------*/
  bool empty() const;
  //-- Same documentation as in Figure 7.5

  void push(const StackElement & value);
  //-- Same documentation as in Figure 7.5

  void display(ostream & out) const;
  //-- Same documentation as in Figure 7.5

  StackElement top() const;
  //-- Same documentation as in Figure 7.5

  void pop();
  //-- Same documentation as in Figure 7.5

 private:
 /***** Data Members *****/
  int myCapacity,              // capacity of stack
      myTop;                   // top of stack
  StackElement * myArray;      // dynamic array to store elements

}; // end of class declaration


#endif
```

Figure 7.6 (continued)

```cpp
//--- DStack.cpp -----------------------------------------------

#include <iostream>
#include <cassert>
#include <new>
using namespace std;

#include "DStack.h"

//--- Definition of Stack constructor
Stack::Stack(int numElements)
{
   assert (numElements > 0);   // check precondition
   myCapacity = numElements;   // set stack capacity
                               // allocate array of this capacity
   myArray = new(nothrow) StackElement[myCapacity];
   if (myArray != 0)           // memory available
      myTop = -1;
   else
   {
      cerr << "Inadequate memory to allocate stack \n"
              " -- terminating execution\n";
      exit(1);
   }                           // or assert(myArray != 0);
}

//--- Definition of empty()
//--- Same as in Figure 7.5

//--- Definition of push()
//--- Replace STACK_CAPACITY with myCapacity in definition in Figure 7.5

//--- Definition of display()
//--- Same as in Figure 7.5

//--- Definition of top()
//--- Same as in Figure 7.5

//--- Definition of pop()
//--- Same as in Figure 7.5
```

▲

A program that includes the header file can use

```
Stack s1;
cout << "Enter second stack's capacity: ";
int cap;
cin >> cap;
Stack s2(cap);
```

s1 will be constructed as a stack with capacity 128 and s2 will be constructed as a stack with capacity cap.

Empty, Push, Top, Pop, and Output Operations As indicated in Figure 7.6, the prototypes of empty(), push(), top(), pop(), and display() are the same as in the static array implementation. Their definitions require accessing the elements of the array data members, but as we saw in Section 3.4, the subscript operator [] can be used in the same manner for dynamically allocated arrays as for static arrays. Nothing needs to be changed in the definitions of these functions in the earlier implementation except to replace STACK_CAPACITY with myCapacity in the definition of push().

 Class Destructor A destructor is needed in our Stack class for the same reason it was needed for our List class in Section 6.3: to avoid a memory leak by deallocating the array allocated by the constructor. For example, if st is the stack

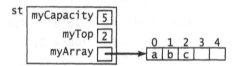

and st's lifetime is over, its destructor ~Stack() will be called to deallocate the dynamic array pointed to by myArray:

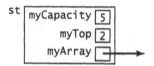

The memory allocated for st's data members myCapacity, myTop, and myArray will then be reclaimed in the usual manner.

The definition of the Stack destructor in Figure 7.7 deallocates the memory allocated for the array pointed to by myArray in the same manner as the List destructor (see Section 6.3):

```
delete [] myArray;
```

 (See the source files—*Chap7/Figures7.6–10*—on the text's website for complete versions of Stack.h and Stack.cpp and a test driver.)

Figure 7.7 The Stack Class Destructor

Add the following in the public section of the Stack class declaration in *Stack.h*:

```
/***** Destructor *****/
  ~Stack();
  /*-----------------------------------------------------------------
    Class destructor

    Precondition:  None
    Postcondition: The dynamic array in the stack has been deallocated.
  -----------------------------------------------------------------*/
```

Add the following to *Stack.cpp*:

```
//--- Definition of Stack destructor
Stack::~Stack()
{
   delete [] myArray;
}
```

▲

Copy Constructor   The copy constructor in a class is invoked whenever a copy of an object of that type is needed. This occurs, for example,

- in initializations
- when an object is passed to a value parameter
- when the value returned by a function is an object
- when temporary storage for an object is needed

If a class has no copy constructor, the compiler uses a default copy constructor that does a member-by-member copy.

As we saw in the preceding chapter, this is adequate for classes without dynamically-allocated data, but not for classes containing pointers to dynamically-allocated arrays (or other structures). To illustrate this for our Stack class, suppose that st is the stack considered earlier,

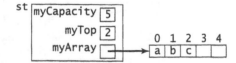

and that a copy stCopy of st is needed. The default copy constructor will copy the value in the myCapacity member of st into the myCapacity member of stCopy and the value in the myTop member of st into the myTop member of stCopy:

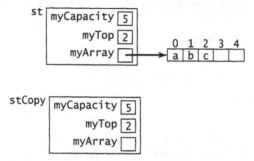

It will also copy the value in the myArray member of st into the myArray member of stCopy. However, this value is the address of the array pointed to by the myArray member of stCopy, which means that in stCopy, myArray points to this same array:

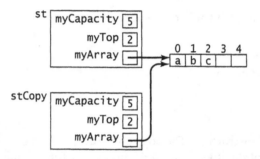

This is another example of the *aliasing problem* in which the same thing is referred by two different names. The *shallow copy* made by the default copy constructor is not a completely distinct copy, so that modifying the copy will also modify the original object.

The copy constructor in the Stack class does a *deep copy*, producing a distinct copy of the original stack:

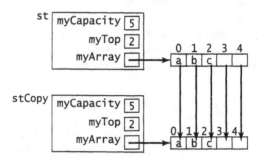

Its definition in Figure 7.8 is similar to that of the copy constructor for the List class in Section 6.3; it allocates a new array in the Stack object being constructed that has the same capacity as that in the Stack object being copied and then uses a for loop to copy the elements of the original stack into this new array. (See the source files— *Chap7/Figures7.6–10*—on the text's website for complete versions of Stack.h and Stack.cpp and a test driver.)

Figure 7.8 The Stack Copy Constructor

Add the following in the public section of the Stack class declaration in *Stack.h*:

```
Stack(const Stack & original);
/*-------------------------------------------------------------------

  Copy Constructor
  Precondition:  original is the stack to be copied and is received as
     a const reference parameter.
  Postcondition: A copy of original has been constructed.
  ----------------------------------------------------------------*/
```

Add the following to *Stack.cpp*:

```
//--- Definition of Stack copy constructor
Stack::Stack(const Stack & original)
: myCapacity(original.myCapacity), myTop(original.myTop)
{
   //--- Get new array for copy
   myArray = new(nothrow) StackElement[myCapacity];
   if (myArray != 0)                     // check if memory available
      // copy original's array member into this new array
      for (int pos = 0; pos <= myTop; pos++)
         myArray[pos] = original.myArray[pos];
   else
   {
      cerr << "*Inadequate memory to allocate stack ***\n";
      exit(1);
   }
}
```

▲

Assignment Operator   As we saw in the preceding chapter, the default definition of the assignment operator (=) supplied by the compiler also does a member-by-member copy of the object being assigned. This gives rise to the same aliasing problem as with the copy constructor. It also causes a memory leak, because the old array in the stack being assigned a value is not deallocated.

The definition of the assignment operator for the Stack class is shown in Figure 7.9. It implements the following algorithm:

Algorithm for Assignment Operator

/* Assume a Stack assignment of the form *st = rightHandSide*. */

1. First check for a self-assignment of the form *st = st*. (This can be done by checking whether the address of the current Stack object (which is stored in the pointer variable this of an object) is the same as the address of the Stack object being assigned (&*rightHandSide*).
   If it is not, then proceed as follows:
   a. Check whether the capacities of the arrays in the two stacks are the same.
      If they are not:
         i. Delete the array in the current object
        ii. Allocate a new array with the same capacity as that in *rightHand-Side*.
   b. Copy the values of myCapacity and myTop in *rightHandSide* into the corresponding data members myCapacity and myTop of the current object.
   c. Copy the array elements in *rightHandSide* into the array of the current object.
2. Return the current Stack object (*this).

(See the source files—*Chap7/Figures7.6–10*—on the text's website for complete versions of Stack.h and Stack.cpp and a test driver.)

Figure 7.9 The Stack Assignment Operator

Add the following in the public section of the Stack class declaration in *Stack.h*:

```
/***** Assignment *****/
 const Stack & operator=(const Stack & rightHandSide);
 /*-------------------------------------------------------------------
    Assignment Operator
    Precondition:  rightHandSide is the stack to be assigned and is
       received as a const reference parameter.
    Postcondition: The current stack becomes a copy of rightHandSide
       and a const reference to it is returned.
  -------------------------------------------------------------------*/
```

Figure 7.9 (continued)

Add the following to *Stack.cpp*:

```
//--- Definition of assignment operator
const Stack & Stack::operator=(const Stack & rightHandSide)
{
   if (this != &rightHandSide)                  // check that not st = st
   {
      //-- Allocate a new array if necessary
      if (myCapacity != rightHandSide.myCapacity)
      {
         delete[] myArray;                      // destroy previous array

         myCapacity = rightHandSide.myCapacity;  // copy myCapacity
         myArray = new StackElement[myCapacity];
         if (myArray == 0)                      // check if memory available
         {
            cerr << "*** Inadequate memory ***\n";
            exit(1);
         }
      }

      myTop = rightHandSide.myTop;              // copy myTop member
      for (int pos = 0; pos <= myTop; pos++)   // copy stack elements
         myArray[pos] = rightHandSide.myArray[pos];

   }
   return *this;
}
```

▲

The Complete Stack Class Figure 7.10 shows the content of the complete Stack class that uses a dynamic array to store the stack element. Also shown is a short driver program that tests the stack operations. Note that the copy constructor is tested by passing stack s to the value parameter st of function print(). From the execution trace, we see that, not only is st a correct copy of s, but s was not changed by the copy constructor. Also, note that a chained assignment is used to test the assignment operator. Complete versions of Stack.h and Stack.cpp, including documentation, and the test driver can be found on the text's website—see *Chap7/ Figures7.6–10* in the source files.)

Figure 7.10 The Stack Class—Version 2 with Dynamic Array

```
/*-- DStack.h ---------------------------------------------------

   This header file defines a Stack data type.
       . . .
   Class Invariant:
     1. The stack elements (if any) are stored in positions
        0, 1, . . ., myTop of myArray.
     2. -1 <= myTop < myCapacity
--------------------------------------------------------------*/


#include <iostream>

#ifndef DSTACK
#define DSTACK

typedef int StackElement;

class Stack
{
 public:
 /***** Function Members *****/

   Stack(int numElements = 128);
   // Constructor's documentation is in Figure 7.6

   Stack(const Stack & original);
   // Copy constructor's documentation is in Figure 7.8

   ~Stack();
   // Destructor's documentation is in Figure 7.7

   Stack & operator= (const Stack & original);
   // Assignment operator's documentation is in Figure 7.9

   bool empty() const;
   // See documentation in Figure 7.4

   void push(const StackElement & value);
   // See documentation in Figure 7.4
```

Figure 7.10 (continued)

```cpp
   void display(ostream & out) const;
   // See documentation in Figure 7.4

   StackElement top() const;
   // See documentation in Figure 7.4

   void pop();
   // See documentation in Figure 7.4

 private:
 /***** Data Members *****/
   int myCapacity,          // capacity of stack
       myTop;               // top of stack
   StackElement * myArray;  // dynamic array to store elements

}; // end of class declaration

#endif
```

```cpp
//--- DStack.cpp --------------------------------------------------

#include <new>
using namespace std;

#include "DStack.h"

//--- Insert definition of Stack constructor from Figure 7.6

//--- Insert definition of Stack copy constructor from Figure 7.8

//--- Insert definition of Stack destructor from Figure 7.7

//--- Insert definition of assignment operator from Figure 7.9

//--- Insert definition of empty() from Figure 7.5

//--- Insert definition of push() from Figure 7.5
```

Figure 7.10 (continued)

```
//--- Insert definition of display() from Figure 7.5

//--- Insert definition of top() from Figure 7.5

//--- Insert definition of pop() from Figure 7.5
```

```
/*-------------------------------------------------------------------
                   Driver program to test the Stack class.
   ----------------------------------------------------------------*/

#include <iostream>
using namespace std;

#include "DStack.h"

void print(Stack st)
{ st.display(cout); }

int main()
{
   int cap;
   cout << "Enter stack capacity: ";
   cin >> cap;

   Stack s(cap);
    cout << "Stack created.  Empty? " << boolalpha << s.empty() << endl;

   cout << "How many elements to add to the stack? ";
   int numItems;
   cin >> numItems;
   for (int i = 1; i <= numItems; i++)
      s.push(100*i);
   cout << "Stack empty? " << s.empty() << endl;

   cout << "Contents of stack s (via  print):\n";
   print(s); cout << endl;
```

Figure 7.10 (continued)

```
      cout << "Check that the stack wasn't modified by print:\n";
      s.display(cout); cout << endl;

      Stack t, u;
      t = u = s;
      cout << "Contents of stacks t and u after t = u = s (via  print):\n";
      cout << "u:\n"; print(u); cout << endl;
      cout << "t:\n"; print(t); cout << endl;

      cout << "Top value in t: " << t.top() << endl;

      while (!t.empty())
      {
        cout << "Popping t:  " << t.top() << endl;
        t.pop();
      }
      cout << "Stack t empty? " << t.empty() << endl;
      cout << "\nNow try to retrieve top value from t." << endl;
      cout << "Top value in t: " << t.top() << endl;
      cout << "\nTrying to pop t: " << endl;
      t.pop();
}
```

Execution Trace #1:

```
Enter stack capacity: 5
Stack created.  Empty? true
How many elements to add to the stack? 3
Stack empty? false
Contents of stack s (via  print):
300
200
100

Check that the stack wasn't modified by print:
300
200
100
```

Figure 7.10 (continued)

```
Contents of stacks t and u after t = u = s (via  print):
u:
300
200
100


t:
300
200
100


Top value in t: 300
Popping t:  300
Popping t:  200
Popping t:  100
Stack t empty? true

Now try to retrieve top value from t.
*** Stack is empty  -- returning garbage value ***
Top value in t: 0

Trying to pop t:
*** Stack is empty -- can't remove a value ***
```

Execution Trace #2:
```
Enter stack capacity: 3
Stack created.  Empty? true
How many elements to add to the stack? 5
*** Stack full -- can't add new value ***
Must increase the capacity of t.
```

▲

A Look Ahead

The array-based implementations of a stack in this section impose an upper limit on the size of the stack, because an array has a fixed size. This means that users of one of these stack classes must know in advance what capacity to specify for the stacks they are using. This may not be possible to determine, however, and a user can only estimate what the largest stack needed will be. Estimating too high can result in considerable wasted space, but estimating too low can result in a stack overflow.

There is a solution to this problem in our second stack implementation. Instead of terminating execution when there is no space left in the array referred to by myArray, replace it with a larger array:[4]

If myArray is full:

1. Allocate a larger array pointed to by some pointer temp—for example, an array that has 10 more elements:

```
temp = new(nothrow) StackElement[myCapacity + 10];
```

2. Use a for loop to copy the elements of myArray into the first part of this new array:

```
for (int i = 0; i < myCapacity; i++)
   temp[i] = myArray[i];
```

3. Deallocate myArray:

```
delete [] myArray;
```

4. Set myArray to point to this new array:

```
myArray = temp;
```

We will leave as an exercise the details of modifying the Stack class in this way.

Another weakness with our implementations of stacks (and of lists in the preceding chapter) is that the type of the elements must be set with a typedef statement in the class's header file. Changing this statement requires recompilations of libraries and programs that include this header file. But a more serious problem is that we can use only one element type at a time. If we need a stack of ints and a stack of strings, for example, we must create two different stack classes, say,

■ IntStack, obtained by setting StackElement to int in the typedef statement and replacing all occurrences of the word Stack with IntStack in the header and implementation files; and

■ StringStack, obtained by setting StackElement to string in the typedef statement and replacing all occurrences of the word Stack with String-Stack in the header and implementation files.

Obviously, this is extremely cumbersome and inconvenient. In Chapter 9 we will consider class templates and show how we can have the compiler take care of this for us.

✔ Quick Quiz 7.2

1. The last element added to a stack is the _____ one removed. This behavior is known as maintaining the elements in _____ order.

2. Define stack as an ADT.

Questions 3–5 assume that Stack is the class described in this section with Stack-Element set to int and STACK_CAPACITY or myCapacity set to 5. Give the value of myTop and the contents of the array referred to by myArray in the stack s after the code segment is executed, or indicate why an error occurs.

---

[4] This is the approach used by array-based containers such as vector in the Standard Template Library described in Section 9.4.

3. Stack s;
```
s.push(123);
s.push(456);
s.pop();
s.push(789);
s.pop();
```

4. Stack s;
```
s.push(111);
i = s.top();
s.push(222);
s.pop();
s.push(i);
```

5. Stack s;
```
for (int i = 0; i < 5; i++)
    s.push(2*i);
s.pop();
s.pop();
```

◆ Exercises 7.2

For Exercises 1–4, assume that Stack is the class described in this section with StackType set to int and STACK_CAPACITY or myCapacity set to 5. Give the value of myTop and the contents of the array referred to by myArray in the stack s after the code segment is executed, or indicate why an error occurs.

1. Stack s;
```
s.push(10);
s.push(22);
s.push(37);
s.pop();
s.pop();
```

2. Stack s;
```
s.push(10);
s.push(9);
s.push(8);
while (!s.empty())
    s.pop();
```

3. Stack s;
```
for (int i = 1; i <= 6; i++)
    s.push(10*i);
```

4. ```
   Stack s;
   s.push(11);
   i = s.top();
   s.pop();
   ```

Exercises 5–9 ask you to add some function members to one of the Stack classes in this section. You may use either of the array-based implementations—the static array version or the dynamic array version.

5. The array-based implementations of stacks in this section impose an upper limit on the maximum size that a stack may have. Write a member function full() for the Stack class that returns true or false according to whether or not the array used to store the stack elements is full.

6. Write documentation, a prototype, and a definition for a member function bottom() for the Stack class that returns the bottom element of the stack.

7. Repeat Exercise 6, but for a function bottom() that is neither a member function nor a friend function of the Stack class.

8. Proceed as in Exercise 6, but design a function nthElement() to retrieve the nth stack element (counting from the top), leaving the stack without its top n elements.

9. Proceed as in Exercise 8, but leave the stack contents unchanged.

10. Consider the following railroad switching network:

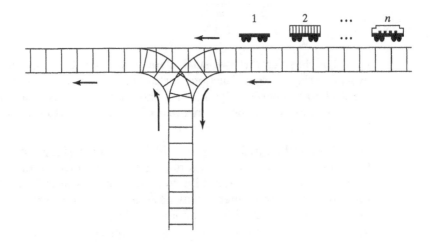

Railroad cars numbered 1, 2, . . ., n on the right track are to be permuted and moved along on the left track. As described in Problem 2 of Section 7.1, a car may be moved directly onto the left track, or it may be shunted onto the siding to be removed at a later time and placed on the left track. The siding thus operates like a stack, a push operation moving a car from the right track onto the siding and a pop operation moving the "top" car from the siding onto the left track.
   ```

    a. For $n = 3$, find all possible permutations of cars that can be obtained (on the left track) by a sequence of these operations. For example, push 1, push 2, move 3, pop 2, pop 1 arranges them in the order 3, 2, 1. Are any permutations not possible?

    b. Find all possible permutations for $n = 4$. What permutations (if any) are not possible?

    c. Repeat (b) for $n = 5$.

    d. *Challenge:* In general, what permutations of the sequence $1, 2, \ldots, n$ can be obtained when a stack is used in this manner?

11. Suppose that some application requires using two stacks whose elements are of the same type. A natural storage structure of such a two-stack data type would consist of two arrays and two top pointers. Explain why this may not be a space-wise efficient implementation.

12. A better storage structure for a two-stack data type than that described in Exercise 11 would be to use a single array for the storage structure and let the stacks grow toward each other.

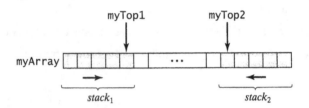

Design a class for this two-stack data type using this implementation and a dynamic array. In your functions for the basic stack operations, the number of the stack to be operated upon, 1 or 2, should be passed as a parameter. Also, the push operation should not fail because of a stack-full condition until *all* locations in the storage array have been used.

13. Storing more than two stacks in a single one-dimensional array in such a way that no stack-full condition occurs for any of the stacks until all the array elements have been used cannot be done as efficiently as in Exercise 12, because some of the array elements will have to be shifted. Nevertheless, design a dynamic-array-based class for an n-stack data type using this implementation, $n > 2$. In the functions for the basic stack operations, the stack number being operated upon, $1, 2, \ldots, n$, should be passed as a parameter. (*Hint:* You might partition the storage array into n equal subarrays, one for each stack, and use two arrays of "pointers," myBottom and myTop, to keep track of where the bottoms and the tops of the stacks are located in the storage array. When one of these stacks becomes full, search to find the nearest empty location(s) in the array, and then move stacks as necessary to enlarge the storage space for this stack.)

7.3 Linked Stacks

Another alternative to using an array to store elements of a stack is to use a linked list (see Sections 6.4 and 6.5). This will allow the stack to grow without limit (except for available memory) and to shrink without wasting unused storage. Also, it seems natural to implement a stack using a linked list because only the first node of a linked list is directly accessible and the elements of a stack can be accessed only at its top.

Selecting a Storage Structure

A Stack class that uses a linked list to store the stack elements needs only one data member, a pointer myTop to the node at the top of the stack as shown in the declaration in Figure 7.11.

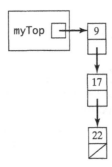

Note that the Node constructor sets the data part of the new node equal to item and the next part equal to a specified link as described in Section 6.5 for linked lists in general.

Figure 7.11 Linked-List-Based Declaration for a Stack Class

```
class Stack
{
 public:
  /***** Function Members *****/
  //-- Prototypes are the same as in the preceding section

 private:
   /*** Node class ***/
   class Node
   {
    public:
      StackElement data;
      Node * next;
```

Figure 7.11 (continued)

```
    //--- Node constructor
    Node(StackElement value, Node * link = 0)
    /*-------------------------------------------------------------
      Precondition:  None.
      Postcondition: A Node has been constructed with value in its data
          part and its next part set to link (default 0).
      -------------------------------------------------------------*/
    : data(value), next(link)
    {}
  };


  typedef Node * NodePointer;


  /***** Data Members *****/
  NodePointer myTop;        // pointer to top of stack
}; // end of class declaration
```

                                                                    ▲

Implementing the Operations

Constructor and Empty Operation To construct an empty list, we simply make myTop a null link to indicate that it does not refer to any node:

```
    myTop = 0;
```

Checking whether a stack is empty is simply checking whether myTop is null:

```
    return myTop == 0;
```

Code for the constructor and the empty() function is given in Figure 7.12.

Push, Top, Pop, and Output Operations The push operation is simple insertion at the beginning of a linked list. We get a new node containing the item to be added to the stack and have it point to the top node in the stack:

```
    myTop = new Stack::Node(value, myTop);
```

The Node constructor sets the data part of the new node equal to value and the next part equal to myTop. The following diagram illustrates pushing the integer 5 onto the stack given earlier:

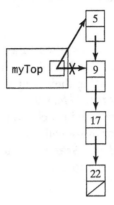

Retrieving the top element is trivial:

```
return myTop->data;
```

And the pop operation is simple deletion of the first node in a linked list:

```
ptr = myTop;
myTop = myTop->next;
delete ptr;
```

The following diagram illustrates popping the three-element stack given earlier:

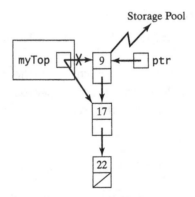

Output of the stack elements is accomplished by a simple traversal of the linked list that stores the stack elements. Starting with the node pointed to by myTop, we output the value stored in that node and then move to the next node, stopping when we reach the end of the list:

```
for (ptr = myTop; ptr != 0; ptr = ptr->next)
    out << ptr->data << endl;
```

Prototypes and definitions of the push(), top(), pop(), and display() functions are given in Figure 7.12, which presents the complete code for this linked implementation of a stack.

Destructor, Copy Constructor, Assignment Operator   Like the output operation, the destructor traverses the linked list that stores the stack elements, but deallocating nodes instead of displaying their contents. We must take care, however, to pay heed to the *Don't burn bridges before you cross them* programming proverb in the ADT Tips at the end of the previous chapter. Before deallocating a node, we must set a pointer to its successor or we will lose access to the rest of the list.

The definition of the Stack destructor in Figure 7.12 does this by using two pointers: currPtr points to the node being deallocated and nextPtr points to its successor:

```
Stack::NodePointer currPtr = myTop,
                   nextPtr;
while (currPtr != 0)
{
   nextPtr = currPtr->next;
   delete currPtr;
   currPtr = nextPtr;
}
```

The copy constructor also traverses the linked list that stores the stack elements, copying each item into a new node, and attaching this node to the linked list of the stack copy. We first make a copy of the first node and set a pointer lastPtr to this node:

```
// Copy first node
myTop = new Stack::Node(original.top());

// Set pointers to run through the stacks' linked lists
Stack::NodePointer lastPtr = myTop,
                   origPtr = original.myTop->next;
```

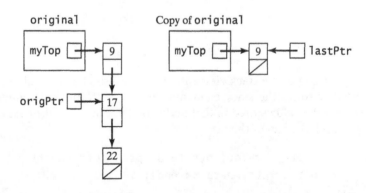

Then we attach a new node containing the next stack element in the node pointed to by origPtr to the linked list in the copy and move both origPtr and lastPtr to the next nodes in their respective lists:

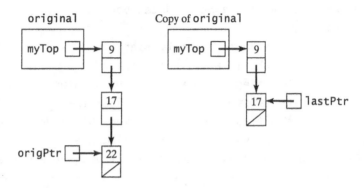

This is repeated until origPtr becomes null, indicating that the copy is complete:

```
while (origPtr != 0)
{
    lastPtr->next = new Stack::Node(origPtr->data);
    lastPtr = lastPtr->next;
    origPtr = origPtr->next;
}
```

The complete definition of the copy constructor is shown in Figure 7.12.

The assignment operator is very similar to the copy constructor, except that it must first check that this is not a self-assignment:

```
this != &rightHandSide
```

Then, to avoid the memory leak, it must destroy the linked list in the stack being assigned a new value. In the code in Figure 7.12, this is accomplished by an explicit call to the destructor:

```
this->~Stack();
```

The code in the copy constructor is then used to make a copy of the stack being assigned, and a reference to this object is returned.

The Complete Stack Class: Linked List Version

Complete source code for the linked-list version of a Stack class we have been developing is given in Figure 7.12. This is also available on the book's website—see *Chap7/ Figure7.12* in the source files—along with a driver program like that in Figure 7.10 to test the class.

Figure 7.12 The Stack Class—Version 3 with Linked List

```
/*-- LStack.h ------------------------------------------------------------

   This header file defines a Stack data type.
   Basic operations:
     constructor:  Constructs an empty stack
     empty:        Checks if a stack is empty
     push:         Modifies a stack by adding a value at the top
     top:          Accesses the top stack value; leaves stack unchanged
     pop:          Modifies stack by removing the value at the top
     display:      Displays all the stack elements
   Note: Execution terminates if memory isn't available for a stack element.
   ---------------------------------------------------------------------*/


#include <iostream>
using namespace std;
#ifndef LSTACK
#define LSTACK

typedef int StackElement;

class Stack
{
 public:
 /***** Function Members *****/
 /***** Constructors *****/
   /*------------------------------------------------------------------
     Construct a Stack object.

     Precondition:  None.
     Postcondition: An empty Stack object has been constructed
         (myTop is initialized to a null pointer).
     ---------------------------------------------------------------*/

   Stack(const Stack & original);
   //-- Same documentation as in Figure 7.8

 /***** Destructor *****/
   ~Stack();
   /*------------------------------------------------------------------
     Class destructor
```

Figure 7.12 (continued)

```
      Precondition:   None
      Postcondition: The linked list in the stack has been deallocated.
      --------------------------------------------------------------------*/

 /***** Assignment *****/
  const Stack & operator= (const Stack & rightHandSide);
  //-- Same documentation as in Figure 7.9

  bool empty() const;
  //-- Same documentation as in Figure 7.5

  void push(const StackElement & value);
  //-- Same documentation as in Figure 7.5

  void display(ostream & out) const;
  //-- Same documentation as in Figure 7.5

  StackElement top() const;
  //-- Same documentation as in Figure 7.5

  void pop();
  //-- Same documentation as in Figure 7.5

private:
  /*** Node class ***/
  class Node
  {
   public:
     StackElement data;
     Node * next;
     //--- Node constructor
     Node(StackElement value, Node * link = 0)
     /*-------------------------------------------------------------------
        Precondition:   value is received
        Postcondition: A Node has been constructed with value in its data
            part and its next part set to link (default 0).
        -------------------------------------------------------------------*/
     : data(value), next(link)
     {}
  };
```

Figure 7.12 (continued)

```
    typedef Node * NodePointer;

    /***** Data Members *****/
    NodePointer myTop;        // pointer to top of stack

}; // end of class declaration

#endif
```

```
//--- LStack.cpp -----------------------------------------------

#include <new>
using namespace std;

#include "LStack.h"

//--- Definition of Stack constructor
Stack::Stack()
: myTop(0)
{}

//--- Definition of Stack copy constructor
Stack::Stack(const Stack & original)
{
   myTop = 0;
   if (!original.empty())
   {
      // Copy first node
      myTop = new Stack::Node(original.top());

      // Set pointers to run through the stacks' linked lists
      Stack::NodePointer lastPtr = myTop,
                         origPtr = original.myTop->next;
```

Figure 7.12 (continued)

```
      while (origPtr != 0)
      {
         lastPtr->next = new Stack::Node(origPtr->data);
         lastPtr = lastPtr->next;
         origPtr = origPtr->next;
      }
   }
}


//--- Definition of Stack destructor
Stack::~Stack()
{
   // Set pointers to run through the stack
   Stack::NodePointer currPtr = myTop,   // node to be deallocated
                      nextPtr;           // its successor
   while (currPtr != 0)
   {
      nextPtr = currPtr->next;
      delete currPtr;
      currPtr = nextPtr;
   }
}


//--- Definition of assignment operator
const Stack & Stack::operator=(const Stack & rightHandSide)
{
   if (this != &rightHandSide)            // check that not st = st
   {
      this->~Stack();                     // destroy current linked list
      if (rightHandSide.empty())          // empty stack
         myTop = 0;
      else
      {                                   // copy rightHandSide's list
         // Copy first node
         myTop = new Stack::Node(rightHandSide.top());
```

Figure 7.12 (continued)

```
            // Set pointers to run through the stacks' linked lists
            Stack::NodePointer lastPtr = myTop,
                               rhsPtr = rightHandSide.myTop->next;

            while (rhsPtr != 0)
            {
                lastPtr->next = new Stack::Node(rhsPtr->data);
                lastPtr = lastPtr->next;
                rhsPtr = rhsPtr->next;
            }
        }
    }
    return *this;
}


//--- Definition of empty()
bool Stack::empty() const
{
    return (myTop == 0);
}


//--- Definition of push()
void Stack::push(const StackElement & value)
{
    myTop = new Stack::Node(value, myTop);
}


//--- Definition of display()
void Stack::display(ostream & out) const
{
    Stack::NodePointer ptr;
    for (ptr = myTop; ptr != 0; ptr = ptr->next)
        out << ptr->data << endl;
}


//--- Definition of top()
StackElement Stack::top() const
{
    if (!empty())
        return (myTop->data);
```

Figure 7.12 (continued)

```
   else
   {
      cerr << "*** Stack is empty "
              " -- returning garbage ***\n";
      StackElement * temp = new(StackElement);
      StackElement garbage = *temp;       // "Garbage" value
      delete temp;
      return garbage;
   }
}


//--- Definition of pop()
void Stack::pop()
{
   if (!empty())
   {
      Stack::NodePointer ptr = myTop;
      myTop = myTop->next;
      delete ptr;
   }
   else
      cerr << "*** Stack is empty -- can't remove a value ***\n";
}
```

```
/*-------------------------------------------------------------------
                  Driver program to test the Stack class.
   -----------------------------------------------------------------*/

#include <iostream>
using namespace std;

#include "LStack.h"

void print(Stack st)
{ st.display(cout); }

int main()
{
   Stack s;
   cout << "Stack created.  Empty? " << boolalpha << s.empty() << endl;
```

Figure 7.12 (continued)

```
cout << "How many elements to add to the stack? ";
int numItems;
cin >> numItems;
for (int i = 1; i <= numItems; i++)
    s.push(100*i);
cout << "Stack empty? " << s.empty() << endl;

cout << "Contents of stack s (via  print):\n";
print(s); cout << endl;
cout << "Check that the stack wasn't modified by print:\n";
s.display(cout); cout << endl;

Stack t, u;
t = u = s;
cout << "Contents of stacks t and u after t = u = s (via  print):\n";
cout << "u:\n"; print(u); cout << endl;
cout << "t:\n"; print(t); cout << endl;

cout << "Top value in t: " << t.top() << endl;

while (!t.empty())
{
  cout << "Popping t:  " << t.top() << endl;
  t.pop();
}
cout << "Stack t empty? " << t.empty() << endl;
cout << "Top value in t: " << t.top() << endl;
cout << "Trying to pop t: " << endl;
t.pop();
}
```

Execution Trace:
```
Stack created.  Empty? true
How many elements to add to the stack? 3
Stack empty? false
Contents of stack s (via  print):
300
200
100
```

Figure 7.12 (continued)

```
Check that the stack wasn't modified by print:
300
200
100

Contents of stacks t and u after t = u = s (via  print):
u:
300
200
100

t:
300
200
100

Top value in t: 300
Popping t:   300
Popping t:   200
Popping t:   100
Stack t empty? true

Now try to retrieve top value from t.
*** Stack is empty  -- returning garbage ***
Top value in t: 13691

Trying to pop t:
*** Stack is empty -- can't remove a value ***
```

▲

🖝 Exercises 7.3

In the exercises that follow, assume that Stack is the class described in this section with StackElement set to int. Draw a diagram like those in this section that pictures the stack s after the code segment is executed, or indicate why an error occurs.

1. Stack s;
   s.push(50);
   s.push(66);

```
    s.push(25);
    s.pop();
    s.pop();
2.  Stack s;
    s.push(22);
    s.push(33);
    s.push(44);
    while (!s.empty())
        s.pop();
3.  Stack s;
    for (int i = 1; i <= 5; i++)
        s.push(100*i);
4.  Stack s;
    s.push(11);
    i = s.top();
    s.pop();
```

5. Write documentation, a prototype, and a definition for a member function bottom() for the Stack class that returns the bottom element of the stack.

6. Proceed as in Exercise 5, but design a function nthElement() to retrieve the nth stack element (counting from the top).

7.4 Use of Stacks in Function Calls

Once a stack class like those in the preceding section has been thoroughly tested, it can be used as a new data type in programs simply by including the header file for that class. For example, the program in Figure 7.1 contains the compiler directive

```
#include "Stack.h"
```

which inserts the header file for the first Stack type of Section 7.1 to solve the base-ten to base-two conversion problem. In this section we show how stacks are used for function calls—see Problem 3 at the beginning of Section 7.1—and in the next section we will look at how they are used to construct and evaluate postfix expressions.

Whenever a function begins execution (i.e., is activated), an **activation record** (or **stack frame**) is created to store the **current environment** for that function, which includes such things as the values of its parameters, contents of registers, the function's return value, local variables, and the address of the instruction to which execution is to return when the function finishes execution. If execution is interrupted by a call to another (or the same) function, this activation record must be saved so that it can be used when execution of this function resumes to restore these items to what they were before the interruption.

Because functions may call other functions and thus interrupt their own execution, some data structure must be used to store these activation records so they can be recovered and the system can be reset when a function resumes execution. Suppose, for example, that the main function in a program calls function f, which, in turn, calls function g. When the main function is initiated, its activation record is created. When it calls f, so that f becomes active, its activation record is also created. Similarly, when f calls g, g becomes the active function, and its activation record is created. When execution of g terminates and control is passed back to f so that it resumes execution, the values that were recorded in its activation record at the time f was interrupted are the ones needed to resume execution of f. Likewise, when f terminates and the main function is reactivated, its activation record is needed to restore the values being used before its interruption. In each case, the fact that the last function interrupted is the first one reactivated suggests that a stack can be used to store these activation records so that they can be retrieved in a last-in-first-out order. A stack is, therefore, the appropriate structure, and since it is manipulated during *execution*, it is called the **run-time stack**.

To illustrate, consider the following program segment:

```
//--- #includes and prototypes of f1, f2, f3 here

int main()
{
   int a = 3;
   f1(a);
   cout << endl;        // A: Return here after f1 finishes
}

//--- Function f1()
void f1(int x)
{
   cout << f2(x + 1);   // B: Return here after f2 finishes
}

//--- Function f2()
int f2(int p)
{
   int q = f3(p/2);     // C: Return here after f3 finishes
   return 2*q;
}

//--- Function f3()
int f3(int n)
{
  return n*n + 1;
}
```

When main() begins executing, an activation record for it is created and is pushed onto the (empty) run-time stack:

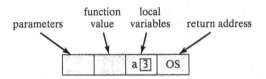

(Here, "OS" denotes that when execution of main() is completed, it returns to the operating system.)

When execution of the main program is interrupted by the function call f1(a), an activation record for f1() is created that stores the parameter 3 and the return address A (plus other items of information) and is pushed onto the run-time stack:

Function call f1(a)

top →	x 3		A	AR for f1()
		a 3	OS	AR for main()

Execution of f1() is interrupted by the function call f2(x + 1), so f2() becomes active, which means that an activation record for it is created and stored on the run-time stack:

Function call f2(x + 1)

top →	p 4	q ☐	B	AR for f2()
	x 3		A	AR for f1()
		a 3	OS	AR for main()

Similarly, execution of f2() is interrupted by a function call to f3(), so an activation record for f3() is created and pushed onto the run-time stack:

Function call f3(p/2)

top →	n 2		C	AR for f3()
	p 4	q ☐	B	AR for f2()
	x 3		A	AR for f1()
		a 3	OS	AR for main()

When a function terminates, the value to be returned and the address of the instruction at which execution is to resume are retrieved from the function's activation record, which is popped from the run-time stack. This "exposes" the activation record of the function that was previously executing and was interrupted, which can be used to restore the environment of the interrupted function so it can resume execution.

To illustrate, when the `return` statement in function `f3()` is encountered, the return value 5 and the return address C are retrieved from its activation record, which is popped from the run-time stack, exposing the activation record for `f2()`:

Return from `f3()`

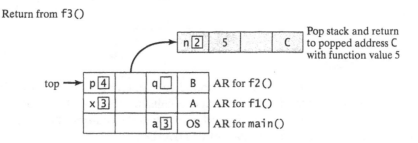

Pop stack and return to popped address C with function value 5

Function `f2()` can then resume execution at the statement labeled C, using its activation record to restore key items and the value 5 returned by `f3()` to assign a value to the local variable q. When `f2()`'s `return` statement is encountered, its activation record is popped from the run-time stack, and the return value 10 and return address B can be retrieved:

Return from `f2()`

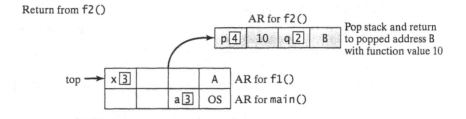

Pop stack and return to popped address B with function value 10

Execution of `f1()` can now resume at the statement labeled B. Its activation record, which is on the top of the run-time stack, is used to restore the environment that existed when execution was interrupted by the function call `f2(x + 1)`. The value 10 returned by `f2()` is then output and execution of `f1()` is complete, so its activation record is popped from the run-time stack:

Return from `f1()`

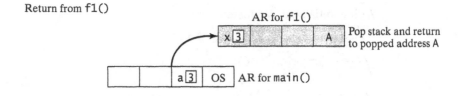

Pop stack and return to popped address A

Execution of `main()` can now resume at the statement labeled A. After this output statement is encountered, `main()`'s activation record is popped from the run-time stack, and execution terminates with a return to the operating system:

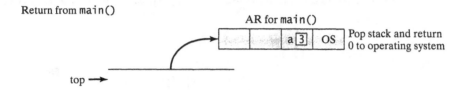

Return from main()

AR for main()

top ⟶

a 3   OS

Pop stack and return
0 to operating system

In Section 4.3 we mentioned that simple functions can be **inlined** to avoid the overhead associated with function calls by replacing them with the actual code of the function. It is the pushing and popping of the run-time stack we've just described that constitutes the major part of this overhead.

Understanding how a stack is used in function calls is also the key to understanding *recursion*, in which a function calls itself. Recursion is discussed in Chapter 10, and in Section 10.3 you will see diagrams like the preceding that illustrate pushing and popping the run-time stack for a recursive function.

✔ Quick Quiz 7.4

1. Whenever a function begins execution, a(n) _____ is created to store the current environment for that function.
2. A(n) _____ stack stores the activation records during a program execution.
3. When a function is activated, its activation record is _____ the run-time stack.
4. When execution of a function is completed, its activation record is _____ the run-time stack.
5. When execution of an interrupted function is resumed, its _____ is used to restore its environment to what it was before interruption.

⬥ Exercises 7.4

For each of the following, use a sequence of diagrams like those in the text to trace the action of the run-time stack for the example in this section, but with the specified changes:

1. With a initialized to 5 instead of 3.

2. With a initialized to 5 instead of 3 and f2() replaced by

```
//--- Function f2()
int f2(int p)
{
    int q = f3(p/3);      // C
    return 3*q + 1;
}
```

3. With a initialized to 5 instead of 3 and f2() replaced by

```
//--- Function f2()
int f2(int p)
{
   return 2*p + 1;
}
```

4. With a initialized to 5 instead of 3 and f3() replaced by

```
//--- Function f3()
int f3(int n)
{
   return n*f4(n) + 1;    // D
}

//--- Function f4()
int f4(int k)
{
   return k*k*k;
}
```

5. With a initialized to 5 instead of 3 and f1() replaced by

```
void f1(int x)
{
   cout << f3(x) + f2(x + 1);    // B
}
```

6. With a initialized to 5 instead of 3 and f1() replaced by

```
void f1(int x)
{
   cout << f2( f3(x) );    // B
}
```

7. As in Exercise 6, but use the version of f3() in Exercise 4.

7.5 Case Study: Postfix (RPN) Notation

The task of a compiler is to generate the machine instructions required to carry out the statements of a source program written in a high-level language. One part of this task is to generate machine instructions for evaluating arithmetic expressions like that in the assignment statement

```
x = a * b + c;
```

The compiler must generate machine instructions like the following:

1. LOAD a   Retrieve the value of a from the memory location where it is stored and load it into the accumulator register

2. MULT b   Multiply the value in the accumulator register by the value retrieved from the memory location associated with b

3. ADD c   Add the value retrieved from the memory location associated with c to the value in the accumulator register

4. STORE x   Store the value in the accumulator register in the memory location associated with x

In most programming languages, arithmetic expressions are written in **infix** notation (e.g., a * b + c), in which the symbol for each binary operation is placed between the operands. Many compilers first transform these infix expressions into **postfix** notation (or *prefix* notation, described in the exercises), in which the operator follows the operands, and then generates machine instructions to evaluate these postfix expressions. This two-step process is used because the transformation from infix to postfix is straightforward, and postfix expressions are, in general, easier to evaluate than infix expressions.

When infix notation is used for arithmetic expressions, parentheses are often needed to indicate the order of the operations. For example, parentheses are placed in the expression

$$2 * (3 + 4)$$

to indicate that the addition is to be performed before the multiplication. If the parentheses were omitted, giving 2 * 3 + 4, the standard precedence rules dictate that the multiplication be performed before the addition.

In the early 1950s, the Polish logician Jan Lukasiewicz observed that parentheses are not necessary in postfix notation, also called **Reverse Polish Notation** (**RPN**). For example, the infix expression 2 * (3 + 4) can be written in postfix notation as

$$2 \quad 3 \quad 4 \quad + \quad *$$

Evaluating Postfix Expressions

As an illustration of how postfix expressions are evaluated, consider the expression

$$1 \quad 5 \quad + \quad 8 \quad 4 \quad 1 \quad - \quad - \quad *$$

which corresponds to the infix expression (1 + 5) * (8 – (4 – 1)). This expression is scanned from left to right until an operator is found. At that point, the last two preceding operands are combined using this operator. For our example, the first operator encountered is +, and its operands are 1 and 5:

$$\underline{1 \quad 5 \quad +} \quad 8 \quad 4 \quad 1 \quad - \quad - \quad *$$

Replacing this subexpression with its value 6 yields the reduced postfix expression

$$6 \quad 8 \quad 4 \quad 1 \quad - \quad - \quad *$$

Resuming the left-to-right scan, we next encounter the – and determine its two operands:

$$6 \quad 8 \quad \underline{4 \quad 1 \quad -} \quad - \quad *$$

Applying this operator then yields

$$6 \quad 8 \quad 3 \quad - \quad *$$

The next operator encountered is another –, and its operands are 8 and 3:

$$6 \ \underline{8 \ 3 \ -} \ *$$

Evaluating this difference gives

$$6 \ 5 \ *$$

The final operator is *, and operating on the expression

$$\underline{6 \ 5 \ *}$$

yields the value 30.

This method of evaluating a postfix expression requires that the operands be stored until an operator is encountered in the left-to-right scan. At this point, the last two operands must be retrieved and combined using this operation. This suggests that a last-in-first-out structure—that is, a stack—should be used to store the operands. Each time an operand is encountered, it is pushed onto the stack. Then, when an operator is encountered, the top two values are popped from the stack; the operation is applied to them, and the result is pushed back onto the stack. The following algorithm summarizes this procedure:

 ### Algorithm to Evaluate Postfix Expressions

/* A postfix expression is received and its value is returned (unless an error occurred). A stack is used to store operands. */

1. Initialize an empty stack.

2. Repeat the following until the end of the expression is encountered:
   a. Get the next token (constant, variable, arithmetic operator) in the postfix expression.
   b. If the token is an operand, push it onto the stack. If it is an operator, then do the following:
      i. Pop the top two values from the stack. (If the stack does not contain two items, an error due to a malformed postfix expression has occurred and evaluation is terminated.)
      ii. Apply the operator to these two values.
      iii. Push the resulting value back onto the stack.

3. When the end of the expression is encountered, its value is on top of the stack. In fact, it must be the only value in the stack and if it is not, an error due to a malformed postfix expression has occurred.

Figure 7.13 illustrates the application of this algorithm to the postfix expression

$$2 \ 4 \ * \ 9 \ 5 \ + \ -$$

The up arrow (↑) indicates the current token.

Figure 7.13 Evaluation of Postfix Expression 2 4 * 9 5 + −

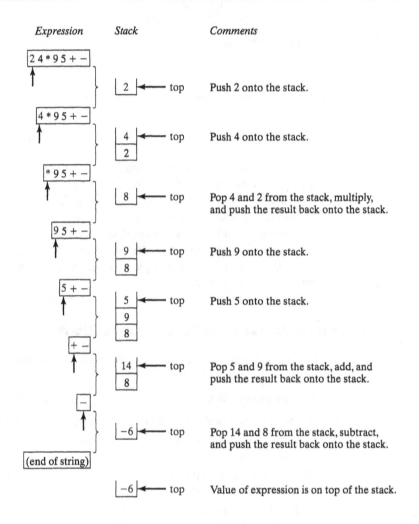

Expression	Stack	Comments
2 4 * 9 5 + −	2 ← top	Push 2 onto the stack.
4 * 9 5 + −	4 2 ← top	Push 4 onto the stack.
* 9 5 + −	8 ← top	Pop 4 and 2 from the stack, multiply, and push the result back onto the stack.
9 5 + −	9 8 ← top	Push 9 onto the stack.
5 + −	5 9 8 ← top	Push 5 onto the stack.
+ −	14 8 ← top	Pop 5 and 9 from the stack, add, and push the result back onto the stack.
−	−6 ← top	Pop 14 and 8 from the stack, subtract, and push the result back onto the stack.
(end of string)	−6 ← top	Value of expression is on top of the stack.

Converting Infix Expressions to Postfix

There are several methods for converting infix expressions to other forms. We begin with one that uses a graphical parenthesis-free representation of an expression known as an **expression tree**. As we will see in more detail in Chapter 12, trees are pictured using circles to represent **nodes** that store data, and these are connected by line segments called **edges**. In an expression tree, each node contains either an operator or an operand. Each node that contains a binary operator is connected to two nodes called **children**, and the node containing the operator is called their **parent**. The left child contains the operator's first operand and is drawn below and to the left of its parent; the right child contains the operator's second operand and is drawn below and to the right of its parent. For example, the following diagram shows an expression tree that represents the expression a * b:

For more complicated expressions, an operand may be an expression **subtree** representing a subexpression. For example, the following expression trees represent a * b + c, a * (b + c), and (a + b) * (c / (d - e)):

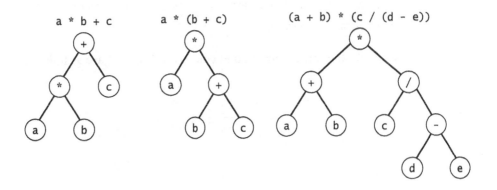

These examples demonstrate how infix expressions can be represented graphically without using parentheses.

To obtain the postfix expression corresponding to an expression tree, we must traverse (i.e., walk through) the tree in a Left-Right-Parent order.[5] This means that for each node, before we can "visit" it, we must first visit its left child and then its right child. For the infix expression a * b + c, this traversal produces

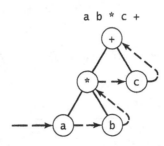

---

[5] Traversing the tree in a Left-Parent-Right order gives the *infix* expression, but parentheses must be inserted around each subexpression; for example, ((a * b) + c). Traversing the tree in a Parent-Left-Right order gives a *prefix* expression in which operators are written before their operands; for example, + * a b c. See the exercises later in this chapter for more about prefix notation.

Similar Left-Right-Parent traversal of the expression tree for **a * (b + c)** produces the postfix expression

a b c + *

and for **(a + b) * (c / (d – e))**,

a b + c d e – / *

Another method for converting infix expressions to postfix that is good for conversions "by hand" might be called the *fully parenthesize-move-erase method*:

1. Fully parenthesize the expression.

2. Replace each right parenthesis by the corresponding operator.

3. Erase all left parentheses.

For example, the three steps used to convert **a * b + c** are as follows:

1. ((a * b) + c)

2. ((a * b) + c) ⟶ ((a b * c +

3. a b * c +

The three steps for converting **a * (b + c)** are

1. (a * (b + c))

2. (a * (b + c)) ⟶ ((a b c + *

3. a b c + *

and the steps for converting **(a + b) * (c / (d – e))** are

1. ((a + b) * (c / (d – e)))

2. ((a + b) * (c / (d – e))) ⟶ ((a b + (c (d e – / *

3. a b + c d e – / *

Neither of the two preceding methods of converting infix to postfix lends itself to easy implementation with a C++ function. Instead, a method that uses a stack to store the operators is preferred. As an illustration of how a stack can be used in this conversion, consider the infix expression

$$7 + 2 * 3$$

In a left-to-right scan of this expression, 7 is encountered and may be displayed immediately. Next, the operator + is encountered, but because its right operand has not yet been displayed, it must be stored and thus is pushed onto a stack of operators:

Output	Stack
7	+

Next, the operand 2 is encountered and displayed. At this point, it must be determined whether 2 is the right operand for the preceding operator + or is the left operand for the next operator. We determine this by comparing the operator + on the top of the stack with the next operator *. Since * has higher priority than +, the preceding operand 2 that was displayed is the left operand for *; thus, we push * onto the stack and search for its right operand:

Output	Stack
7 2	* +

The operand 3 is encountered next and displayed. Since the end of the expression has now been reached, the right operand for the operator * on the top of the stack has been found, and so * can now be popped and displayed:

Output	Stack
7 2 3 *	+

The end of the expression also signals that the right operand for the remaining operator + in the stack has been found, and so it, too, can be popped and displayed, yielding the postfix expression

$$7 \quad 2 \quad 3 \quad * \quad +$$

Parentheses within infix expressions present no real difficulties. A left parenthesis indicates the beginning of a subexpression, and when encountered, it is pushed onto the stack. When a right parenthesis is encountered, operators are popped from the stack until the matching left parenthesis rises to the top. At this point, the subexpression originally enclosed by the parentheses has been converted to postfix, so the parentheses may be discarded and the conversion continues. All of this is contained in the following algorithm:

 Algorithm to Convert an Infix Expression to Postfix

/* An infix expression is received and the corresponding postfix expression is output. A stack is used to store operators. */

1. Initialize an empty stack of operators.
2. While no error has occurred and the end of the infix expression has not been reached, do the following:
    a. Get the next input *token* (constant, variable, arithmetic operator, left parenthesis, right parenthesis) in the infix expression.
    b. If *token* is
        i.   a left parenthesis: Push it onto the stack.
        ii. a right parenthesis: Pop and display stack elements until a left parenthesis is encountered, but do not display it. (It is an error if the stack becomes empty with no left parenthesis found.)
        iii. an operator: If the stack is empty or *token* has a higher priority than the top stack element, push *token* onto the stack.
             Otherwise, pop and display the top stack element; then repeat the comparison of *token* with the new top stack item.
             Note: A left parenthesis in the stack is assumed to have a lower priority than that of operators.
        iv. an operand: Display it.
3. When the end of the infix expression is reached, pop and display stack items until the stack is empty.

Figure 7.14 illustrates this algorithm for the infix expression

$$7 * 8 - (2 + 3)$$

An up arrow ($\uparrow$) has been used to indicate the current input symbol and the symbol displayed by the algorithm.

The program in Figure 7.15 implements this algorithm for converting an infix expression to postfix using the Stack data type developed in this chapter. A stack with StackElement set to char is used to store the operators. The program assumes that the input is a valid infix expression and does very little checking to determine if it is a well-formed arithmetic expression. (See Section 10.3 for a description of how simple arithmetic expressions can be checked to determine whether they are well formed.)

Figure 7.14 Converting Infix Expression 7 * 8 – (2 + 3) to Postfix

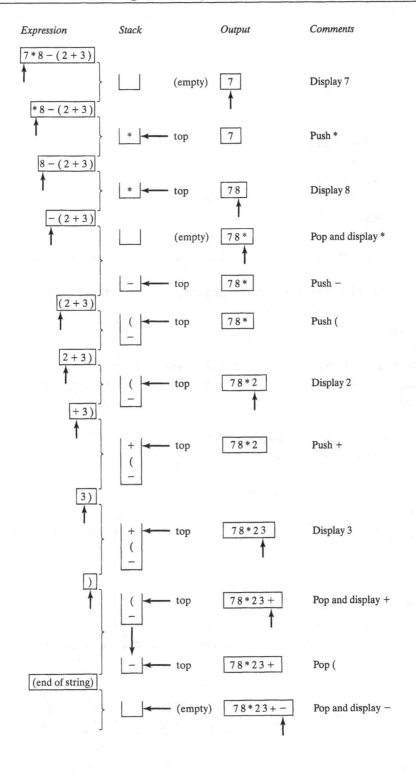

Figure 7.15 Converting Infix Expressions to Postfix

```
/*-----------------------------------------------------------------
    Convert infix expressions to postfix.

    Input:  An infix expression and user responses
    Output: The postfix expression
 ----------------------------------------------------------------*/

#include <iostream>          // <<, >>, cout, cin
#include <string>            // string, ==, find, npos
#include <cassert>           // assert()
#include <cctype>            // alnum()
using namespace std;

#include "DStack.h"          // Stack class with StackElement = char

string postfix(string exp); // prototype of postfix() function

int main()
{
   string infixExp;          // infix expression
   cout << "NOTE: Enter # for infix expression to stop.\n";
   for (;;)
   {
      cout << "\nInfix expression? ";
      getline(cin, infixExp);

      if (infixExp == "#") break;

      cout << "Postfix expression is " << postfix(infixExp) << endl;
   }
}

string postfix(string exp)
/*-----------------------------------------------------------------
    Function to convert an infix expression exp to postfix.
```

Figure 7.15 (continued)

```
Precondition:   None
Postcondition: Postfix expression corresponding to exp is returned
    or an error message displayed if exp is not well-formed.
-------------------------------------------------------------------------*/
{
   char token,                    // character in exp
        topToken;                 // token on top of opStack
   Stack opStack;                 // stack of operators
   string postfixExp;             // postfix expression
   const string BLANK = " ";
   for (int i = 0; i < exp.length(); i++)
   {
      token = exp[i];
      switch(token)
      {
         case ' ' : break;        // do nothing -- skip blanks
         case '(' : opStack.push(token);
                    break;
         case ')' : for (;;)
                    {
                       assert (!opStack.empty());
                       topToken = opStack.top();
                       opStack.pop();
                       if (topToken == '(') break;
                       postfixExp.append(BLANK + topToken);
                    }
                    break;
         case '+' : case '-' :
         case '*' : case '/': case'%':
                    for (;;)
                    {
                       if (opStack.empty() ||
                           opStack.top() == '(' ||
                           (token == '*' || token == '/' || token == '%') &&
                           (opStack.top() == '+' || opStack.top() == '-'))
```

Figure 7.15 (continued)

```
                            {
                                opStack.push(token);
                                break;
                            }
                            else
                            {
                                topToken = opStack.top();
                                opStack.pop();
                                postfixExp.append(BLANK + topToken);
                            }
                        }
                        break;
        default :   // operand
                    postfixExp.append(BLANK + token);
                    for(;;)
                    {
                        if ( !isalnum(exp[i+1]) ) break; // end of identifier
                        i++;
                        token = exp[i];
                        postfixExp.append(1, token);
                    }
        }
    }
    // Pop remaining operators on the stack
    for (;;)
    {
        if (opStack.empty()) break;
        topToken = opStack.top();
        opStack.pop();
        if (topToken != '(')
        {
            postfixExp.append(BLANK + topToken);
        }
        else
        {
            cout << " *** Error in infix expression ***\n";
            break;
        }
    }
    return postfixExp;
}
```

Figure 7.15 (continued)

Execution Trace:

```
NOTE: Enter # for infix expression to stop.

Infix expression? alpha + beta
Postfix expression is  alpha beta +

Infix expression? alpha * beta + 123
Postfix expression is  alpha beta * 123 +

Infix expression? alpha * (beta + 123)
Postfix expression is  alpha beta 123 + *

Infix expression? (a + b) * (c / (d - e))
Postfix expression is  a b + c d e - / *

Infix expression? a - (b - (c - (d - (e - f))))
Postfix expression is  a b c d e f - - - - -

Infix expression? a - b - c - d - e - f
Postfix expression is  a b - c - d - e - f -

Infix expression? (a * (b - c)
Postfix expression is  *** Error in infix expression ***
 a b c - *

Infix expression? #
```

▲

✔ Quick Quiz 7.5

For Questions 1–4, use infix, prefix, and postfix as answers.

1. a b + is written in _____ notation.
2. a + b is written in _____ notation.
3. + a b is written in _____ notation.
4. RPN is another name for _____ notation.
5. The value of 5 4 - 3 2 + * is _____
6. Convert (a - (b - c)) * d to postfix notation.
7. Convert the postfix expression a b - c - d * to infix notation.

◆ Exercises 7.5

In Exercises 1–11, assume that a = 7.0, b = 4.0, c = 3.0, and d = –2.0. Evaluate the postfix expression.

1. a b + c / d *

2. a b c + / d *

3. a b c d + / *

4. a b + c + d +

5. a b + c d + +

6. a b c + + d +

7. a b c d + + +

8. a b - c - d -

9. a b - c d - -

10. a b c - - d -

11. a b c d - - -

For the postfix expressions in Exercises 12–14, trace the algorithm for evaluating postfix expressions by showing the contents of the stack immediately before each of the tokens marked with a caret is read. Also, give the value of the postfix expression.

12. 32 5 3 + / 5 *
          ∧   ∧

13. 2 17 - 5 / 3 *
         ∧   ∧

14. 19 7 15 5 - - -
             ∧ ∧ ∧

Convert the infix expressions in Exercises 15–22 to postfix.

15. a * b + c - d

16. a + b / c + d

17. (a + b) / c + d

18. a + b / (c + d)

19. (a + b) / (c + d)

20. (a - b) * (c - (d + e))

21. (((a - b) - c) - d) - e

22. a - (b - (c - (d - e)))

For the infix expressions in Exercises 23–27, trace the algorithm for converting infix to postfix by showing both the stack and the accumulated output immediately before each of the tokens marked with a caret is read. Also, show the postfix expression.

23. a + b / c - d
        ∧ ∧ ∧

24. (a + b) / c - d + e
            ∧   ∧

25. a + b / (c - d) - e
          ∧   ∧ ∧

26. a + b / (c - d) * e
          ∧   ∧ ∧

27. a + b / ((c - d) * e) - f
        ∧   ∧   ∧ ∧

Convert the postfix expressions in Exercises 28–35 to infix notation:

28. a b c + - d *

29. a b + c d - *

30. a b c d + - *

31. a b + c - d e * /

32. a b / c / d /

33. a b / c d / /

34. a b c / d / /   35. a b c d / / /

The symbol – cannot be used for the unary minus operation in postfix notation because ambiguous expressions result. For example, 5 3 - - could be interpreted as either 5 - (-3) = 8 or -(5 - 3) = -2. In Exercises 36–45, suppose instead that ~ is used for unary minus.

Evaluate the postfix expressions in Exercises 36–41 if a = 7, b = 5, and c = 3:

36. a ~ b c + -   37. a b ~ c + -

38. a b c ~ + -   39. a b c + ~ -

40. a b c + - ~   41. a b c - - ~ ~ ~

Convert the infix expressions in Exercises 42–45 to postfix:

42. a * (b + ~c)

43. ~(a + b / (c - d))

44. (~a) * (~b)

45. ~(a - (~b * (c + ~d)))

Convert the logical expressions in Exercises 46–52 to postfix:

46. a && b || c

47. a && (b || !c)

48. !(a && b)

49. (a || b) && (c || (d && !e))

50. (a == b) || (c == d)

51. ((a > 3) && (a < 9)) || !(a > 0)

52. ((b * b - 4 * a * c) >= 0) && ((a > 0) || (a < 0))

53–60. An alternative to postfix notation is *prefix* notation, in which the symbol for each operation precedes the operands. For example, the infix expression 2 * 3 + 4 would be written in prefix notation as + * 2 3 4, and 2 * (3 + 4) would be written as * 2 + 3 4. Convert each of the infix expressions in Exercise 15–22 to prefix notation.

In Exercises 61–68, assume that a = 7.0, b = 4.0, c = 3.0, and d = –2.0. Evaluate each of the prefix expressions (see Exercises 53–60):

61. * a / + b c d   62. * / + a b c d

63. - a - b - c d   64. - - a b - c d

65. - a - - b c d   66. - - - a b c d

67. * + a b - c d   68. + * a b - c d

Convert the prefix expressions in Exercises 69–76 to infix notation (see Exercises 53–60):

69. * + a b - c d   70. + * a b - c d

71. - - a b - c d   72. - - a - b c d

73. - - - a b c d   74. / + * a b - c d e

75. / + * a b c - d e   76. / + a * b c - d e

SUMMARY

Chapter Notes

- Because elements of a stack may be inserted and removed only at one end (the top), no shifting of elements in an array storing the stack elements is required.

- A run-time stack is used to store activation records of functions during program execution. The records store the current environment when function execution is suspended because of a call to some other function, making it possible to resume execution of the function later.

- Stacks are useful in converting infix expressions to postfix and for evaluating postfix expressions.

Programming Pointers

1. An activation record for a function is pushed onto a runtime stack whenever that function is called. It is popped from the runtime stack when execution of that function is completed. This is the overhead that is avoided when functions are inlined.

2. Understanding how a stack is used in function calls is the key to understanding recursive functions.

ADT Tips

1. A stack has *last-in-first-out* (*LIFO*) behavior.

2. Focusing too much on a real-world object that is being modeled can sometimes lead to an implementation that is not efficient for other objects of the same or similar kinds. For example, an array-based implementation of a stack that imitates closely the performance of a spring-loaded stack of plates leads to excessive data movement, which is inefficient for most other kinds of stacks.

Programming Problems

Section 7.2 & 7.3

1. Empirical evidence suggests that *any program that comes close to using all available space will eventually run out of space.* Consequently, shifting stacks around in an array as described in Exercise 13 of Section 7.2 so that all possible array locations are used seems rather futile. Redesign the implementation so that no push operations are attempted if there are fewer than LOWER_LIMIT unused locations left in the array.

2. Use one of the Stack classes in a program that reads a string, one character at a time, and determines whether the string contains balanced parentheses, that is, for each left parenthesis (if there are any) there is exactly one matching right parenthesis later in the string.

3. Problem 2 can be solved without using a stack; in fact, a simple integer variable can be used. Describe how, and write a program that uses your method to solve the problem.

4. For a given integer $n > 1$, the smallest integer $d > 1$ that divides n is a prime factor. We can find the *prime factorization* of n if we find d and then replace n by the quotient of n divided by d, repeating this until n becomes 1. Write a program that determines the prime factorization of n in this manner, but that displays the prime factors in descending order. For example, for $n = 3960$, your program should produce

$$11 * 5 * 3 * 3 * 2 * 2 * 2$$

5. A program is to be written to find a path from one point in a maze to another.

　　a. Describe how a two-dimensional array could be used to model the maze.

　　b. Describe how a stack could be used in an algorithm for finding a path.

　　c. Write the program.

Section 7.5

6. Modify the infix-to-postfix program in Figure 7.15 so that it provides tracing information similar to that in Figure 7.14. To make the output more manageable, you may simplify it to something like the following trace for the expression 7 * 8 - (2 + 3):

```
Token     Output     Stack (bottom to top)
-----     ------     ---------------------
  7          7       empty
  *                    *
  8          8       *
  -          *       -
  (                  - (
  2          2       - (
  +                  - ( +
  3          3       - ( +
  )          +       -
             -       empty
```

7. Modify the infix-to-postfix program in Figure 7.15 to detect and report infix expressions that are improperly formed.

8. The algorithm given in the text for converting from infix to postfix assumes *left associativity*; that is, when two or more consecutive operators of the same priority occur, they are to be evaluated from left to right; for example, 6 - 3 - 1 is evaluated as (6 - 3) - 1 and not as 6 - (3 - 1). *Right associativity*, however, is usually used for exponentiation; for example, in Fortran, exponentiation is denoted by ** and the expression 2 ** 3 ** 4 is evaluated as 2 ** (3 ** 4) = $2^{(3^4)}$ = 2^{81}, not as (2 ** 3) ** 4 = $(2^3)^4$ = 8^4. Extend the algorithm in the text to allow ** as an additional binary operator with highest priority. *Hint:* One approach is to use two different priorities for each operator—one for when it is in the infix expression and the other for when it is in a stack.

9. Extend the infix-to-postfix program in Figure 7.15 so that it can also convert infix expressions that contain the binary operators << and >> in addition to +, -, *, /, and %.

10. Proceed as in Exercise 9, but also allow the exponent operator ** (see Problem 8).

11. Proceed as in Exercise 9 or 10, but also allow the unary operator ~ (see the note preceding Exercise 36).

12. Write a program to implement the algorithm for evaluating postfix expressions that involve only single-digit integers and the integer operations +, -, *, and /. To trace the action of postfix evaluation, display each token as it is encountered, and display the action of each stack operation. For example, the output of your program might resemble the following for the postfix expression 9 2 1 + / 4 *:

```
Token = 9      Push 9
Token = 2      Push 2
Token = 1      Push 1
Token = +      Pop  1      Pop  2      Push 3
Token = /      Pop  3      Pop  9      Push 3
Token = 4      Push 4
Token = *      Pop  4      Pop  3      Push 12
Token =        Pop 12
```

13. Modify the postfix evaluation program of Problem 12 to detect and report postfix expressions that are not well formed.

14. Modify the postfix evaluation program of Problem 12 to

   a. Process postfix expressions that contain the integer operators +, -, *, /, and %.

   b. Also allow postfix expressions that contain the unary operator ~ (see the note preceding Exercise 36).

   c. Allow integers with more than one digit.

15. Modify the postfix evaluation program of Problem 12 so that it generates machine instructions in assembly code for evaluating the expression using one accumulator register and the following instructions:

   LOAD x   Place the value of x in the accumulator register
   STORE x   Store the contents of the accumulator register into variable x
   ADD x   Add the value of x to the contents of the accumulator register
   SUB x   Subtract the value of x from the contents of the accumulator register
   MULT x   Multiply the contents of the accumulator register by the value of x
   DIV x   Divide the contents of the accumulator register by the value of x

   For example, the postfix expression a b c + * d e * - should give the following sequence of instructions:

```
LOAD b
ADD c
STORE temp1
LOAD a
MULT temp1
STORE temp2
LOAD d
MULT e
STORE temp3
LOAD temp2
SUB temp3
STORE temp4
```

   where each tempi is a temporary variable.

16. Write a program to convert a postfix expression to the corresponding fully-parenthesized infix expression. For example, a b + and a b + c d - * should produce (a + b) and ((a + b) * (c - d)), respectively.

Queues

CHAPTER CONTENTS

Chapter Objectives

- To study a queue as an ADT.
- Build a static-array-based implementation of queues.
- Build a dynamic-array-based implementation of queues.
- Build a linked implementation of queues.
- Show how queues are used in I/O buffers and scheduling in a computer system.
- (Optional) See how queues are used in simulations of phenomena that involve waiting lines.

In the preceding chapter, we defined stacks, considered array-based and linked implementations of stacks in some detail, and looked at several of their applications. In this chapter we consider queues, which are similar to stacks and have at least as many applications as stacks. Queues can also be implemented using arrays as the basic storage structures, but as we will discover, a bit more effort is required to construct an efficient array-based implementation of a queue than for a stack. We will also look at linked-list implementations of queues. The chapter closes with a simulation of an information/reservations center in which an "on-hold" queue is used to store incoming telephone calls.

8.1 Introduction to Queues

According to Webster, a **queue** is a "waiting line," and as such, they abound in everyday life. Familiar examples include the following:

- a line of persons waiting to check out at a supermarket
- a line of persons waiting to purchase a ticket for a film

- a line of planes waiting to take off at an airport
- a line of vehicles at a toll booth

Arriving customers, planes, vehicles, and the like enter the line at the rear, and are removed from the line and served when they reach the front, so that the first to enter the queue is the first served. Because the first thing to enter the queue has been waiting the longest, it seems *fair* that it should be the first one served. (People get irritated when others "jump ahead" of them in a line, because this *fairness principle* is violated.) Stated differently, whereas a stack exhibits last-in-first-out (LIFO) behavior; a queue exhibits **first-in-first-out (FIFO)** behavior.

As an abstract data type, a queue is a special kind of list in which the basic insert and delete operations are restricted to the ends of the list. Unlike stacks in which elements are popped and pushed only at one end of the list, items are removed from a queue at one end, called the **front** (or **head**) of the queue, and elements are added only at the other end called the **back** (or **rear** or **tail**). Other basic operations are constructing an empty queue and determining if a queue is empty. More formally, the abstract data type queue can be specified as follows:

Queue ADT

Collection of Data Elements

A sequence of data items with the property that items can be removed only at one end, called the *front* of the queue, and items can be added only at the other end, called the *back* of the queue.

Basic Operations[1]

- Construct a queue (usually empty)
- Check if queue is empty
- enqueue: Add an element at the back of the queue
- front: Retrieve the element at the front of the queue
- dequeue: Remove the element at the front of the queue

---

[1] The basic insertion and deletion operations for queues have traditionally been called *enqueue* for "enter the queue" and *dequeue* for "delete from the queue", respectively. The standard queue container in the Standard Template Library (see Chapter 9) uses "push" and "pop."

Example: Drill and Practice Problems

Problem Suppose that a program is to be designed to provide drill-and-practice exercises in elementary arithmetic. More precisely, suppose that these exercises are problems involving the addition of randomly generated integers. If a student answers correctly, another problem is generated; but if he or she answers incorrectly, the problem is stored so that it can be asked again at the end of the session.

Objects and Operations One of the objects in this problem is an addition problem, and we will assume for now that an AdditionProblem class to model such problems is available. The addends in an AdditionProblem object will be randomly generated positive integers in some range specified by the user in the object's declaration. A display() operation is provided to output a problem along with an answer() that returns the problem's answer. Source code for this class is given at the end of this section.

  We also need a container to store the problems answered incorrectly. Because it seems natural to ask these problems on later rounds in the same order in which they were presented initially, a queue is an appropriate container for storing these problems. We will assume that a class Queue is available that we can use for such a queue that we will name *problemQueue*. We will then show how the basic queue operations can be used in this drill-and-practice program. Building a queue class is the focus of the next two sections.

Algorithm The following algorithm outlines the basic approach of the drill-and-practice program:

 Algorithm for Drill and Practice

1. Read *numProblems* and maximum addend to use in the problems.
2. Generate *numProblems* problems and add them to *problemQueue*.
3. // Conduct the practice rounds
   For *round* = 1 to *MAX_ROUNDS* do the following:
     a. Initialize *numberMissed* = 0.
     b. For *count* = 1 to *numProblems*, do the following:
         i. Display a *problem* and read *userAnswer*.
         ii. If *userAnswer* == *problem*'s answer
             Display a "correct" message.
           Else
             Display a "sorry" message, add *problem* to *problemQueue*, and increment *numberMissed*.
       // End for loop

     c. If *numberMissed* == 0
         Display a congratulatory message and exit the loop.
       Else
         i. Display an appropriate message about another round.
         ii. Set *numProblems* = *numberMissed*.
     // End for loop

// Wrapup

4. If *numberMissed* == 0

    Display an appropriate quiz-complete message.

    Otherwise do the following

        a. Display an appropriate too-many-tries message.

        b. While *problemQueue* is not empty

            i. Retrieve and remove *problem* at front of *problemQueue*.

            ii. Display it along with its answer.

        // End while loop

        c. Display an appropriate need-for-practice message.

Code Figure 8.1 implements the preceding objects, operations, and algorithm. The program assumes the availability of a `Queue` class that can store addition problems—for example, the `Queue` class in Figure 8.2 with `AdditionProblem` declared to be a synonym for `QueueElement` in the `typedef` statement. The declaration

```
Queue problemQueue;
```

constructs an empty queue of `AdditionProblem` objects. (An alternative is to use the standard `queue` class template described in the next chapter; see the opening documentation of the program for instructions on how to use it here.) The statements in which queue operations are used are highlighted in color.

An execution trace is also given and following it are listings of the header and implementation files for the class `AdditionProblem`. The declaration

```
AdditionProblem problem(maxAddend);
```

in the program constructs an `AdditionProblem` object with random integer addends ≤ `maxAddend`. `AdditionProblem` provides the following operations:

    `answer()`: Retrieve the answer to the problem

    `<<`:   Output operator

Figure 8.1 Drill-and-Practice Arithmetic Problems

```
/*------------------------------------------------------------------
  Drill-and-Practice Program that generates random drill-and-practice
  addition problems. Problems that are answered incorrectly are
  queued and asked again until all are answered correctly or maximum
  number of tries is reached.

  Input:   Number of problems to generate, student's answers to
           problems
  Output:  Messages, problems, correct answers, number of problems
           answered correctly
```

Figure 8.1 (continued)

```
Note:    Program assumes that Queue.h contains a declaration of a
         class Queue like that described in Sections 8.2 and 8.3
         whose elements are of type AdditionProblem. An alternative
         is to use the C++ standard queue class template by making
         the following changes:
             #include "Queue.h" --> #include <queue>
             Queue wrongQueue --> queue<AdditionProblem> wrongQueue
             enqueue --> push
             dequeue --> pop
    ------------------------------------------------------------------*/


#include <iostream>                // cin, cout, >>, <<
using namespace std;

#include "AdditionProblem.h"       // AdditionProblem, initialize()
#include "Queue.h"                 // A queue class for AdditionProblems

int main()
{
   int numProblems,               // number of problems asked
       maxAddend;                 // maximum addend in a problem
   const int MAX_ROUNDS = 3;      // maximum number of rounds in
                                  //   which to try the problems
   initialize();                  // initialize random number generator

   cout << "*** Let's practice our addition skills! *** \n\n"
           "How many problems would you like? ";
   cin >> numProblems;
   cout << "What's the largest addend you would like? ";
   cin >> maxAddend;

   // Generate numProblems problems and store them in a queue.
   Queue problemQueue;            // queue of problems
   for (int i = 1; i <= numProblems; i++)
   {
      AdditionProblem problem(maxAddend);
      problemQueue.enqueue(problem);
   }
```

Figure 8.1 (continued)

```
// Conduct the practice rounds
AdditionProblem problem;      // next addition problem
int userAnswer,               // user's answer to a problem
    numberMissed;             // number of problems missed
for (int round = 1; round <= MAX_ROUNDS; round++)
{

    // One round of problems

    numberMissed = 0;

    for (int count = 1; count <= numProblems; count++)
    {
        problem = problemQueue.front();
        problemQueue.dequeue();
        cout << problem;
        cin >> userAnswer;
        if (userAnswer == problem.answer())
            cout << "Correct!\n\n";
        else
        {
            cout << "Sorry -- Try again later\n\n";
            problemQueue.enqueue(problem);
            numberMissed++;
        }
    }

    if (numberMissed == 0)
    {
        cout << "Congratulations! You correctly answered all the"
                " problems in Round #" << round << endl;
        break;
    }
    else
    {
        cout << "\nYou missed " << numberMissed << " problems in Round #"
                << round << ".\n";
```

Figure 8.1 (continued)

```
        if (round < MAX_ROUNDS)
            cout << "You may now try them again.  Good luck!\n";
        numProblems = numberMissed;
    }
}


// Wrapup
if (numberMissed == 0)
    cout << "You have finished the quiz and have successfully.\n"
            "answered all the problems.  Good job!" << endl;
else
{
    cout << "\nYou have reached the limit on the number of tries "
            "allowed.\nHere are the problems you missed:\n\n";
    while (!problemQueue.empty())
    {
        problem = problemQueue.front();
        problemQueue.dequeue();
        cout << problem << " Answer: " << problem.answer() << "\n\n";
    }
    cout << "Perhaps it would be a good idea to practice some more.\n";
}
}
```

Execution Trace:

```
*** Let's practice our addition skills! ***

How many problems would you like? 4
What's the largest addend you would like? 100
30 + 18 = ? 48
Correct!

16 + 58 = ? 66
Sorry -- Try again later

37 + 70 = ? 97
Sorry -- Try again later
```

Figure 8.1 (continued)

```
59 + 74 = ? 143
Sorry -- Try again later


You missed 3 problems in Round #1.
You may now try them again.  Good luck!
69 + 74 = ? 133
Sorry -- Try again later

16 + 58 = ? 73
Sorry -- Try again later

37 + 70 = ? 107
Correct!


You missed 2 problems in Round #2.
You may now try them again.  Good luck!
59 + 74 = ? 123
Sorry -- Try again later

69 + 74 = ? 143
Correct!


You missed 1 problems in Round #3.

You have reached the limit on the number of tries allowed.
Here are the problems you missed:

16 + 58 = ?  Answer: 74

Perhaps it would be a good idea to practice some more.
```

Figure 8.1 (continued)

```
/*-- AdditionProblem.h ------------------------------------------------

   This header file contains the declaration of class AdditionProblem.

   Basic operations:
     constructor: Generates problem with random addends -- uses random
                  number generator rand() from cstdlib
     display():   Displays the problem
     answer():    Returns answer to problem
-----------------------------------------------------------------------*/


#include <iostream>

#ifndef ADDITION_PROBLEM
#define ADDITION_PROBLEM

class AdditionProblem
{
 public:
  /***** Function Members *****/

  AdditionProblem(int maxAddend = 100);
  /*-------------------------------------------------------------------

     Construct an addition problem.

     Precondition:  Receives maxAddend, the largest integer to use in a
         problem.
     Postcondition: An addition problem has been constructed with addends
         that are random integers in the range 0 through maxAddend and
         myTries initialized to 1.
  -------------------------------------------------------------------*/
```

Figure 8.1 (continued)

```
   void display(ostream & out) const;
  /*------------------------------------------------------------------
    Display the addition problem.

    Precondition:  ostream out is open.
    Postcondition: Problem has been output to out.
    ----------------------------------------------------------------*/

   int answer() const;
  /*------------------------------------------------------------------
    Get answer to addition problem.

    Precondition:  None.
    Postcondition: Answer to this addition problem is retrieved.
    ----------------------------------------------------------------*/

 private:
  /***** Data Members *****/
   int myAddend1,
       myAddend2,
       myAnswer;
};



//--- Initialize random number generator
void initialize();

//--- Output operator
ostream & operator<<(ostream & out, const AdditionProblem & problem);

#endif
```

```
/*-- AdditionProblem.cpp -----------------------------------------
     This file implements operations for AdditionProblem objects.
   ----------------------------------------------------------------*/
```

Figure 8.1 (continued)

```cpp
#include <cstdlib>
#include <ctime>
using namespace std;

#include "AdditionProblem.h"

//--- Definition of AdditionProblem constructor
AdditionProblem::AdditionProblem(int maxAddend = 10)
{
   myAddend1 = rand() % (maxAddend + 1);
   myAddend2 = rand() % (maxAddend + 1);
   myAnswer = myAddend1 + myAddend2;
}

//--- Definition of display()
void AdditionProblem::display(ostream & out) const
{
   out << myAddend1 << " + " << myAddend2 << " = ? ";
}

//--- Definition of answer()
int AdditionProblem::answer() const
{
   return (myAddend1 + myAddend2);
}

//--- Definition of output operator
ostream & operator<<(ostream & out, const AdditionProblem & problem)
{
   problem.display(out);
   return out;
}

//--- Definition of initialize()
void initialize()
{
  long seed = long(time(0));     // seed for random number generator
  srand(seed);
}
```

▲

8.2 Designing and Building a Queue Class—Array-Based

Because a queue resembles a stack in many ways, we might imitate the array-based implementation of a stack considered in Chapter 7 to construct an array-based implementation of a queue. Thus, we might use

- myArray to store the elements of the queue:

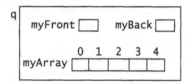

- two integer variables:

myFront   The position in the array of the element that can be removed—the position of the front queue element

myBack   The position in the array at which an element can be added—the position *following* the last queue element

Thus, we might picture a Queue object q as follows:

An item is added to the queue by storing it at position myBack of the array, provided that myBack does not exceed some maximum size specified for the array, and then incrementing myBack by 1.

The difficulty with this implementation is that elements "walk off the end" of the array, so that eventually all the array elements may have to be shifted back to the beginning positions. (One reviewer of this text has used the very descriptive phrase "queue creep" for this behavior.) For example, consider a queue in which the capacity of the array data member is 5 and whose elements are integers. The sequence of operations add 70, add 80, add 50 produces the following configuration:

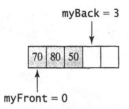

Now suppose that two elements are removed,

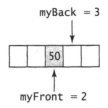

myBack = 3

50

myFront = 2

and that 90 and 60 are then added:

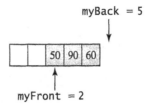

myBack = 5

50 90 60

myFront = 2

Before another item can be inserted into the queue, the elements in the array must be shifted back to the beginning of the array:

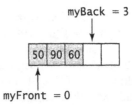

myBack = 3

50 90 60

myFront = 0

This shifting of array elements is very inefficient, especially when the elements are large objects. A better alternative is to simply let myBack start over at the beginning of the array when it goes off the end. What we are doing, therefore, is thinking of the array as *circular*, with the first element following the last. This can be done by incrementing myFront and myBack using addition modulo the array's capacity. For the sequence of operations just considered, this implementation yields the following configurations:

myFront = 0

enqueue 70
enqueue 80
enqueue 50

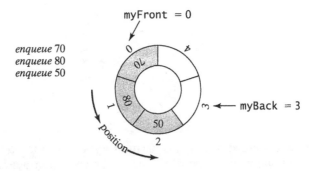

myBack = 3

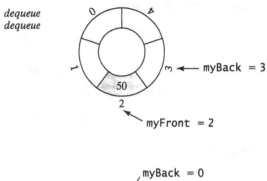

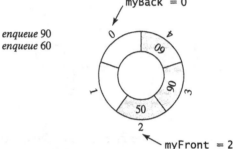

Another insertion is now possible without our having to move any array elements; we simply store the item in position myBack = 0.

Now consider the basic operation to determine if a queue is empty. If the queue contains a single element, it is in position myFront of the array, and myBack is the vacant position following it. If this element is deleted, myFront is incremented by 1 so that myFront and myBack have the same value. Thus, to determine if a queue is empty, we need only check the condition myFront == myBack. The queue constructor will initialize myFront and myBack both to 0.

Just as the array implementation for a stack introduced the possibility of a stack-full condition, the implementation of a queue raises the possibility of a queue-full condition. To see how this condition can be detected, suppose that the array is almost full, with only one empty location remaining:

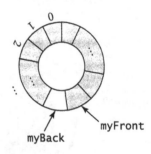

If an item were stored in this location, myBack would be incremented by 1, giving it the same value as myFront. However, the condition myFront == myBack indicates that the queue is empty. Thus, we *cannot distinguish between an empty queue and a full queue* if this location is used to store an element. But we can avoid this difficulty if we maintain one empty position in the array so that myFront will never equal myBack except when the queue is empty.

There are several alternatives to keeping an empty slot in the array. One commonly used is to add an integer data member count to the class, which stores the number of elements currently in the queue. Another is to use a boolean data member full instead of the integer member count, which is set to true when the queue becomes full and is false otherwise. Queue classes developed using these approaches are left as exercises.

Using a Static Array to Store the Queue Elements

Figure 8.2 shows a Queue class that uses a circular static array myArray with capacity QUEUE_CAPACITY to store the queue elements. An empty slot is maintained between the front and back elements so that queue-full and queue-empty conditions can be distinguished. The data members myFront and myBack record the position of the front element and the position following the last element, respectively.

The constructor simply initializes both of the members myFront and myBack to 0 (or to any other value in $0, 1, \ldots,$ QUEUE_CAPACITY $- 1$); and a queue will be empty when the boolean expression myFront == myBack is true.

An algorithm for the *enqueue* operation is as follows:

Algorithm for Enqueue

/*   Add a *value* at the back of the queue   */

1. Set *newBack* equal to (myBack + 1) % QUEUE_CAPACITY.
2. If *newBack* is equal to myFront
   Signal that a queue error (queue full) occurred.
   Otherwise
   a.   Set myArray[myBack] equal to *value.*
   b.   Set myBack equal to *newBack.*

The front operation need only retrieve myArray[myFront] provided that the queue is not empty, and the following is an algorithm for the *dequeue* operation:

Algorithm for Dequeue

/*   Remove the element at the front of the queue. */
   If the queue is empty
   Signal that a queue error (queue empty) occurred.
   Otherwise
   Set myFront equal to (myFront + 1) % QUEUE_CAPACITY.

Figure 8.2 A Queue Class with Implementation Using a Static Array

```
/* Queue.h contains the declaration of class Queue.
   Basic operations:
     Constructor: Constructs an empty queue
     empty:       Checks if a queue is empty
     enqueue:     Modifies a queue by adding a value at the back
     front:       Accesses the front queue value; leaves queue unchanged
     dequeue:     Modifies a queue by removing the value at the front
     display:     Displays the queue elements from front to back
   Class Invariant:
     1. The queue elements (if any) are stored in consecutive positions
        in myArray, beginning at position myFront.
     2. 0 <= myFront, myBack < QUEUE_CAPACITY
     3. Queue's size < QUEUE_CAPACITY
------------------------------------------------------------------------*/


#include <iostream>

#ifndef QUEUE
#define QUEUE

const int QUEUE_CAPACITY = 128;
typedef int QueueElement;

class Queue
{
 public:
  /***** Function Members *****/
  /***** Constructor *****/
  Queue();
  /*------------------------------------------------------------------

    Construct a Queue object.

    Precondition:  None.
    Postcondition: An empty Queue object has been constructed; myFront
        and myBack are initialized to -1 and myArray is an array with
        QUEUE_CAPACITY elements of type QueueElement.
    ------------------------------------------------------------------*/
```

Figure 8.2 (continued)

```
bool empty() const;
/*-------------------------------------------------------------------
  Check if queue is empty.
  Precondition: None.
  Postcondition: True is returned if the queue is empty and false is
      returned otherwise.
  -----------------------------------------------------------------*/


void enqueue(const QueueElement & value);
/*-------------------------------------------------------------------
  Add a value to a queue.

  Precondition:  value is to be added to this queue.
  Postcondition: value is added to back of queue provided there is space;
      otherwise, a queue-full message is displayed and execution
      terminated.
  -----------------------------------------------------------------*/


void display(ostream & out) const;
/*-------------------------------------------------------------------
  Output the values stored in the queue.

  Precondition:  ostream out is open.
  Postcondition: Queue's contents, from front to back, have been output
      to out.
  -----------------------------------------------------------------*/


QueueElement front() const;
/*-------------------------------------------------------------------
  Retrieve value at front of queue (if any).

  Precondition:  Queue is nonempty.
  Postcondition: Value at front of queue is returned, unless queue is
      empty; in that case, an error message is displayed and a "garbage
      value" is returned.
  -----------------------------------------------------------------*/
```

Figure 8.2 (continued)

```
  void dequeue();
  /*-------------------------------------------------------------------
     Remove value at front of queue (if any).

     Precondition:  Queue is nonempty.
     Postcondition: Value at front of queue has been removed, unless queue
        is empty; in that case, an error message is displayed.
     -------------------------------------------------------------------*/

 private:
  /***** Data Members *****/
  int myFront,
      myBack;
  QueueElement myArray[QUEUE_CAPACITY];
}; // end of class declaration

#endif
```

```
/*-- Queue.cpp-------------------------------------------------------
             This file implements Queue member functions.
   -------------------------------------------------------------------*/

#include <iostream>
using namespace std;

#include "Queue.h"

//--- Definition of Queue constructor
Queue::Queue()
: myFront(0), myBack(0)
{}

//--- Definition of empty()
bool Queue::empty() const
{
    return (myFront == myBack);
}
```

Figure 8.2 (continued)

```cpp
//--- Definition of enqueue()
void Queue::enqueue(const QueueElement & value)
{
   int newBack = (myBack + 1) % QUEUE_CAPACITY;
   if (newBack != myFront)      // queue isn't full
   {
      myArray[myBack] = value;
      myBack = newBack;
   }
   else
   {
      cerr << "*** Queue full -- can't add new value ***\n"
              "Must increase value of QUEUE_CAPACITY in Queue.h\n";
      exit(1)
   }
}


//--- Definition of display()
void Queue::display(ostream & out) const
{
   for (int i = myFront; i != myBack; i = (i + 1) % QUEUE_CAPACITY)
      out << myArray[i] << "  ";
   cout << endl;
}


//--- Definition of front()
QueueElement Queue::front() const
{
   if ( !empty() )
      return (myArray[myFront]);
   else
   {
      cerr << "*** Queue is empty -- returning garbage value ***\n"
      QueueElement garbage;
      return garbage;
   }
}


//--- Definition of dequeue()
void Queue::dequeue()
```

Figure 8.2 (continued)

```
{
   if ( !empty() )
      myFront = (myFront + 1) % QUEUE_CAPACITY;
   else
      cerr << "*** Queue is empty -- "
              "can't remove a value ***\n";
}
```

▲

Using a Dynamic Array to Store the Queue Elements

Using a single capacity for the arrays that store the elements in every Queue object
suffers from the same weaknesses as described in the preceding chapter for stacks.
Setting it too large can waste considerable memory; but setting it too small can cause
a program to crash or to produce incorrect results because the container cannot hold
all of the data. Also, changing the definition of QUEUE_CAPACITY in Queue.h to
change the capacity of a queue requires recompilation of all programs and libraries
that include Queue.h.

Changing the implementation to use a dynamic array requires essentially the
same changes as we described for stacks. In the class declaration, we simply change
the declaration of the myArray member to a pointer and QUEUE_CAPACITY to a variable data member:

```
typedef int QueueElement;
class Queue
{
 public:
 /***** Function Members *****/
   // --- Changes are similar to those for stacks

 private:
 /***** Data Members*****/
   int myFront,              // front
       myBack;               //    and back of queue
   int myCapacity;           // capacity of queue
   QueueElement * myArray;   // dynamic array to store elements
 };
```

The changes in the constructor are much the same as for stacks, as are the destructor,
copy constructor, and assignment operator that should be added to the class. We
leave the details as exercises.

Once these changes are made, a program can use declarations such as

```
cout << "Enter the queue's capacity: ";
int cap;
cin >> cap;
Queue q(cap);
```

If the user enters 5 as the value for cap, q will be constructed as an empty queue with capacity 5:

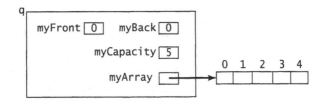

✔ Quick Quiz 8.2

1. The last element added to a queue is the _____ one removed. This behavior is known as maintaining the elements in _____ order.

2. Define queue as an ADT.

Questions 3–5 assume that Queue is the class described in this section with QueueElement set to int and QUEUE_CAPACITY or myCapacity set to 5. Give the value of myFront, myBack, and the contents of the array referred to by myArray in the queue q after the code segment is executed, or indicate why an error occurs.

3. Queue q;

   ```
   q.enqueue(123);
   q.enqueue(456);
   q.dequeue();
   q.enqueue(789);
   q.dequeue();
   ```

4. Queue q;

   ```
   q.enqueue(111);
   i = q.front();
   q.enqueue(222);
   q.dequeue();
   q.enqueue(i);
   ```

5. Queue q;

   ```
   for (int i = 0; i < 5; i++)
       q.enqueue(2*i);
   q.dequeue();
   q.dequeue();
   ```

◆ Exercises 8.2

For Exercises 1–4, assume that q is a queue implemented as described in this section (using a circular array), with QueueElement = char and capacity 5, and that ch is of type char. Using a diagram like

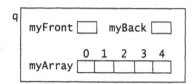

show the values of myFront and myBack and the contents of myArray for the Queue object q after the program segment has been executed; also indicate any errors that occur.

1. ```
   q.enqueue('A');
   q.enqueue('B');
   q.enqueue('C');
   ch = q.front();
   q.dequeue();
   q.enqueue(ch);
   ```

2. ```
   q.enqueue('X');
   q.enqueue('Y');
   q.enqueue('Z');
   while (!q.empty())
   {
      ch = q.front();
      q.dequeue();
   }
   ```

3. ```
   ch = 'q';
   for (int i = 1; i <= 3; i++)
   {
      q.enqueue(ch);
      ch++;
      q.enqueue(ch);
      ch = q.front();
      q.dequeue();
   }
   ```
   ```

```
4. ch = 'A';
   for (int i = 1; i <= 4; i++)
   {
     q.enqueue(ch);
     ch++;
     q.enqueue(ch);
     ch = q.front();
     q.dequeue();
   }
```

Several of the following exercises ask you to write functions or classes. You should also write driver programs to test them as instructed in the Programming Problems 1–12 at the end of this chapter.

5. Complete the development of the class Queue that uses a dynamic array by writing definitions for the constructor, empty(), enqueue(), front(), display(), and dequeue() function members. Also, add a destructor, a copy constructor, and an assignment operator.

6. Although a queue, like a stack, cannot (in theory) become full, the array-based implementation of queues described in this section requires that an upper limit be placed on the maximum size that a queue may have. Write a member function full() for

   a. the Queue class in Figure 8.2
   b. a Queue class that uses a dynamic array

   that returns true or false according to whether or not the array used to store the queue elements is full.

7. Write documentation, a prototype, and a definition for a member function size() for a Queue class like those described in this section that returns the number of elements in the queue.

8. Repeat Exercise 7, but for a function size() that is neither a member function nor a friend function of the Queue class.

9. Proceed as in Exercise 7, but design a function back() that returns the element at the back of a queue.

10. Repeat Exercise 9, but for a function back() that is neither a member function nor a friend function of the Queue class.

11. Proceed as in Exercise 7, but design a function nthElement() to retrieve the nth queue element, leaving the queue without its first n elements.

12. Proceed as in Exercise 11, but leave the queue contents unchanged.

13. Using the basic queue and stack operations, write an algorithm to reverse the elements in a queue.

14. In Problem 2 of Section 7.1 and in Exercise 10 of Section 7.2, we considered a railroad-switching network that could be modeled with a stack. Now consider

the following network:

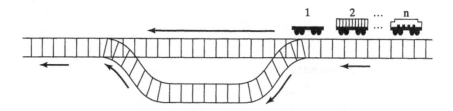

Again, railroad cars numbered 1, 2, . . ., *n* on the right track are to be permuted and moved along on the left track. As the diagram suggests, a car may be moved directly onto the left track, or it may be shunted onto the siding (which acts like a queue) to be removed at a later time and placed on the left track.

  a. For *n* = 3, find all possible permutations of cars that can be obtained (on the left track) by a sequence of these operations. For example, add 1, add 2, move 3, remove, remove arranges them in the order 3, 1, 2. Are any permutations not possible?

  b. Find all possible permutations for *n* = 4. What permutations (if any) are not possible?

  c. Repeat (b) for *n* = 5.

  d. *Challenge*: In general, what permutations of the sequence 1, 2, . . ., *n* can be obtained by using a queue in this manner?

15. Build a Queue class like that Figure 8.2, but use an integer data member count that stores the number of elements currently in the queue, as described in the text, to distinguish between a queue-full and a queue-empty condition instead of keeping an empty slot between the front and the back elements.

16. An implementation using a count data member as in Exercise 15 can dispense with the myBack data member. Build a Queue class like that in Exercise 15 with a count data member but no myBack data member.

17. Proceed as in Exercise 15, but use a boolean data member full instead of the integer member count, as described in the text.

18. In Exercise 12 of Exercises 7.2 we described an efficient implementation of a two-stack data structure that uses a single array for the storage structure. Describe a similar implementation of a two-queue data structure.

8.3 Linked Queues

As we noted for stacks in Chapter 7, array-based implementations of a container place an upper limit on the size of the container, because an array has a fixed size. This means, in particular, that to use one of the array-based queue classes of the preceding section, one must know in advance what capacity to specify for the queues that will be needed and then either set the value of QUEUE_CAPACITY in Queue.h (for our first queue class) or specify the capacity of the stack in its declaration (for our second queue class). However, for some problems involving queues, it may be difficult or impossible to determine beforehand the capacity of the queues that will be needed. In this case, if we are using a dynamic array for the queue elements, we could allocate a larger array, copy the queue elements into it, and replace the old array with this one. See Section 7.2 for more details about this approach.

A Natural Linked-List Implementation

Another alternative to an array-based implementation of queues is to proceed as we did for stacks in Section 7.3 and use a linked list to store the queue elements. Because a linked list can grow by adding new nodes, a linked queue can grow as large as necessary (or until available memory is exhausted); there is no need to set some upper bound on the capacity in advance. Also, a linked queue can shrink as elements are removed by returning deleted nodes to the memory heap.

The linked lists considered up to now have provided access to only the first node in the list by maintaining a pointer to this node. If we make this first node the front of the queue, as seems natural, then the operations to retrieve the front element and to remove the front element are implemented in the same way as the top and pop operations for a linked stack. However, adding values at the back of the queue would require traversing the entire list each time to find the back of the queue.

This list traversal can be avoided if we adopt the approach of the array-based implementations in the preceding section and maintain two pointers, myFront, which points to the node at the front of the queue, and myBack, which points to the node at the back. For example, a linked queue containing the integers 9, 17, 22, 26, and 34 in this order, might be pictured as

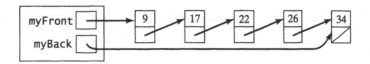

In this implementation, the constructor can simply initialize myFront and myBack to be null pointers, which represents an empty queue:

The empty operation need only check whether myFront (or myBack) is null. The copy constructor and assignment operator must traverse the linked list storing the queue elements to make a copy, as described for linked stacks in Section 7.3. And in the same manner as described there, the destructor must traverse the linked list and return each node to the heap. Code for these function members is given in Figure 8.3.

Retrieving the element at the front of the queue is trivial,

```
return myFront->data;
```

provided that the queue is not empty. Removing the front element of a nonempty queue is simple deletion of the first node in a linked list, but care must be taken if the queue becomes empty to reset myBack to null:

```
ptr = myFront;
myFront = myFront->next;
delete ptr;
if (myFront == 0)    // queue is now empty
   myBack = 0;
```

Adding a value at the back of the queue is insertion after the last node of a linked list:

```
newptr = new Node(value);
if (empty())
  myFront = myBack = newptr;
else
{
  myBack->next = newptr;
  myBack = newptr;
}
```

Here, the Node constructor sets the data part of the new node equal to item and the next part equal to the null pointer.

Figure 8.3 gives the complete code for this linked implementation of a queue.

Figure 8.3 The Queue Class—Linked-List Implementation

```
/*-- LQueue.h -----------------------------------------------------

  This header file defines a Queue data type.
  Basic operations:
    constructor:  Constructs an empty queue
    empty:        Checks if a queue is empty
    enqueue:      Modifies a queue by adding a value at the back
    front:        Accesses the top queue value; leaves queue unchanged
    dequeue:      Modifies queue by removing the value at the front
    display:      Displays all the queue elements
  Note: Execution terminates if memory isn't available for a queue element.
 ------------------------------------------------------------------*/


#include <iostream>
#ifndef LQUEUE
#define LQUEUE
```

Figure 8.3 (continued)

```cpp
typedef int QueueElement;

class Queue
{
 public:
/***** Function Members *****/
/***** Constructors *****/

  Queue();
  /*------------------------------------------------------------------

    Construct a Queue object.

    Precondition:  None.
    Postcondition: An empty Queue object has been constructed.
        (myFront and myBack are initialized to null pointers).
  -------------------------------------------------------------------*/


  Queue(const Queue & original);
  /*------------------------------------------------------------------

    Copy Constructor

    Precondition:  original is the queue to be copied and is received
        as a const reference parameter.
    Postcondition: A copy of original has been constructed.
  -------------------------------------------------------------------*/

/***** Destructor *****/
  ~Queue();
  /*------------------------------------------------------------------

    Class destructor

    Precondition:  None.
    Postcondition: The linked list in the queue has been deallocated.
  -------------------------------------------------------------------*/

/***** Assignment *****/
const Queue & operator= (const Queue & rightHandSide);
  /*------------------------------------------------------------------

    Assignment Operator
```

Figure 8.3 (continued)

Precondition: rightHandSide is the queue to be assigned and is
    received as a const reference parameter.
Postcondition: The current queue becomes a copy of rightHandSide
    and a reference to it is returned.
--*/


```
bool empty() const;
```
```
/*----------------------------------------------------------------
  Check if queue is empty.

  Precondition:   None.
  Postcondition: Returns true if queue is empty and false otherwise.
----------------------------------------------------------------*/
```

```
void enqueue(const QueueElement & value);
```
```
/*----------------------------------------------------------------
  Add a value to a queue.

  Precondition:   value is to be added to this queue.
  Postcondition: value is added at back of queue.
----------------------------------------------------------------*/
```

```
void display(ostream & out) const;
```
```
/*----------------------------------------------------------------
  Display values stored in the queue.

  Precondition:   ostream out is open.
  Postcondition: Queue's contents, from front to back, have been
      output to out.
----------------------------------------------------------------*/
```

```
QueueElement front() const;
```
```
/*----------------------------------------------------------------
  Retrieve value at front of queue (if any).

  Precondition:   Queue is nonempty.
  Postcondition: Value at front of queue is returned, unless the queue
      is empty; in that case, an error message is displayed and a
      "garbage value" is returned.
----------------------------------------------------------------*/
```

Figure 8.3 (continued)

```cpp
  void dequeue();
  /*------------------------------------------------------------------
    Remove value at front of queue (if any).

    Precondition:  Queue is nonempty.
    Postcondition: Value at front of queue has been removed, unless
        queue is empty; in that case, an error message is displayed
        and execution allowed to proceed.
  ------------------------------------------------------------------*/


private:
  /*** Node class ***/
  class Node
  {
   public:
     QueueElement data;
     Node * next;
     //--- Node constructor
     Node(QueueElement value, Node * link = 0)
     /*------------------------------------------------------------------
        Precondition:  value and link are received
        Postcondition: A Node has been constructed with value in its
            data part and its next part set to link (default 0).
     ------------------------------------------------------------------*/
        : data(value), next(link)
        {}
  };

  typedef Node * NodePointer;

  /***** Data Members *****/
  NodePointer myFront,        // pointer to front of queue
              myBack;         // pointer to back of queue

}; // end of class declaration

#endif
```

Figure 8.3 (continued)

```
/*--- LQueue.cpp --------------------------------------------------------
             This file implements LQueue member functions.
-----------------------------------------------------------------------*/


#include <new>
using namespace std;

#include "LQueue.h"

//--- Definition of Queue constructor
Queue::Queue()
: myFront(0), myBack(0)
{}

//--- Definition of Queue copy constructor
Queue::Queue(const Queue & original)
{
   myFront = myBack = 0;
   if (!original.empty())
   {
      // Copy first node
      myFront = myBack = new Queue::Node(original.front());

      // Set pointer to run through original's linked list
      Queue::NodePointer origPtr = original.myFront->next;
      while (origPtr != 0)
      {
         myBack->next = new Queue::Node(origPtr->data);
         myBack = myBack->next;
         origPtr = origPtr->next;
      }
   }
}

//--- Definition of Queue destructor
Queue::~Queue()
{
  // Set pointer to run through the queue
  Queue::NodePointer prev = myFront,
                     ptr;
```

Figure 8.3 (continued)

```
  while (prev != 0)
    {
      ptr = prev->next;
      delete prev;
      prev = ptr;
    }
}


//--- Definition of assignment operator
const Queue & Queue::operator=(const Queue & rightHandSide)
{
    if (this != &rightHandSide)          // check that not q = q
    {
        this->~Queue();                  // destroy current linked list
        if (rightHandSide.empty())       // empty queue
          myFront = myBack = 0;
        else
        {                                // copy rightHandSide's list
          // Copy first node
          myFront = myBack = new Queue::Node(rightHandSide.front());

          // Set pointer to run through rightHandSide's linked list
          Queue::NodePointer rhsPtr = rightHandSide.myFront->next;
          while (rhsPtr != 0)
          {
              myBack->next = new Queue::Node(rhsPtr->data);
              myBack = myBack->next;
              rhsPtr = rhsPtr->next;
          }
        }
    }
    return *this;
}


//--- Definition of empty()
bool Queue::empty() const
{
    return (myFront == 0);
}
```

Figure 8.3 (continued)

```
//--- Definition of enqueue()
void Queue::enqueue(const QueueElement & value)
{
   Queue::NodePointer newptr = new Queue::Node(value);
   if (empty())
      myFront = myBack = newptr;
   else
   {
      myBack->next = newptr;
      myBack = newptr;
   }
}


//--- Definition of display()
void Queue::display(ostream & out) const
{
   Queue::NodePointer ptr;
   for (ptr = myFront; ptr != 0; ptr = ptr->next)
      out << ptr->data << " ";
   out << end;
}


//--- Definition of front()
QueueElement Queue::front() const
{
   if (!empty())
      return (myFront->data);
   else
   {
      cerr << "*** Queue is empty "
              " -- returning garbage ***\n";
      QueueElement * temp = new(QueueElement);
      QueueElement garbage = *temp;      // "Garbage" value
      delete temp;
      return garbage;
   }
}
```

Figure 8.3 (continued)

```cpp
//--- Definition of dequeue()
void Queue::dequeue()
{
   if (!empty())
   {
      Queue::NodePointer ptr = myFront;
      myFront = myFront->next;
      delete ptr;
      if (myFront == 0)      // queue is now empty
         myBack = 0;
   }
   else
      cerr << "*** Queue is empty -- can't remove a value ***\n";
}
```

```cpp
/*-------------------------------------------------------------------
                  Driver program to test the Queue class.
   ----------------------------------------------------------------*/

#include <iostream>
using namespace std;

#include "LQueue.h"

void print(Queue q)
{ q.display(cout); }

int main()
{
    Queue q1;
    cout << "Queue created.  Empty? " << boolalpha << q1.empty() << endl;

    cout << "How many elements to add to the queue? ";
    int numItems;
    cin >> numItems;
    for (int i = 1; i <= numItems; i++)
       q1.enqueue(100*i);
```

Figure 8.3 (continued)

```
   cout << "Contents of queue q1 (via print):\n";
   print(q1); cout << endl;

   Queue q2;
   q2 = q1;
   cout << "Contents of queue q2 after q2 = q1 (via print):\n";
   print(q2); cout << endl;

   cout << "Queue q2 empty? " << q2.empty() << endl;

   cout << "Front value in q2: " << q2.front() << endl;

   while (!q2.empty())
   {
      cout << "Remove front -- Queue contents: ";
      q2.dequeue();
      q2.display(cout);
   }
   cout << "Queue q2 empty? " << q2.empty() << endl;
   cout << "Front value in q2?" << endl << q2.front() << endl;
   cout << "Trying to remove front of q2: " << endl;
   q2.dequeue();
}
```

Execution Trace:

```
Queue created.  Empty? true
How many elements to add to the queue? 5
Contents of queue q1 (via print):
100  200  300  400  500

Contents of queue q2 after q2 = q1 (via print):
100  200  300  400  500

Queue q2 empty? false
Front value in q2: 100
Remove front -- Queue contents: 200  300  400  500
Remove front -- Queue contents: 300  400  500
Remove front -- Queue contents: 400  500
```

Figure 8.3 (continued)

```
Remove front -- Queue contents: 500
Remove front -- Queue contents:
Queue q2 empty? true
Front value in q2?
*** Queue is empty  -- returning garbage ***
13691
Trying to remove front of q2:
*** Queue is empty -- can't remove a value ***
```

▲

Using a Circular Linked List

In the preceding section we described an implementation of queues in which the array that stored the elements was thought of as a circular array with the first element following the last. This suggests that it might be useful to consider an analogous **circular linked list** obtained by setting the link of the last node in a linked list of the kind we've been considering, sometimes called a **linear linked list,** to point to the first node. For example, for the linear linked list

the corresponding circular linked list would be pictured as follows:

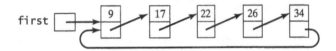

For some applications of circular linked lists, it is advantageous to maintain a pointer to the last node rather than the first; for example,

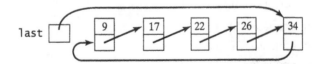

In this case, we have direct access to the last node and almost direct access to the first node, since last->next points to the first node in the list. This variation is thus especially useful when it is necessary to access repeatedly the elements at the ends of the list. In particular, it is well suited for linked queues. Developing a queue class that uses a circular linked list in this manner is left as an exercise.

✔ **Quick Quiz 8.3**

1. How does a circular linked list differ from a linear linked list?
2. Why is it sometimes convenient to maintain a pointer to the last node in a circular linked list rather than to the first node?

In Questions 3–5, assume that the type of q is the class Queue described in this section with QueueElement set to char. Assume also that q uses a linear linked list to store the queue elements. Draw a diagram like that in this section that pictures the queue q after the code segment is executed, or indicate why an error occurs.

3. ```
   Queue q;
   q.enqueue(123);
   q.enqueue(456);
   q.dequeue();
   q.enqueue(789);
   q.dequeue();
   ```

4. ```
   Queue s;
   q.enqueue(111);
   i = q.front();
   q.enqueue(222);
   q.dequeue();
   q.enqueue(i);
   ```

5. ```
   Queue q;
   for (int i = 0; i < 5; i++)
       q.enqueue(2*i);
   q.dequeue();
   q.dequeue();
   ```

◆ **Exercises 8.3**

For Exercises 1–4, assume that q is a queue implemented as described in this section (using a linear linked list), with QueueElement = char. Draw a diagram like that in this section that pictures the queue q after the code segment is executed, or indicate why an error occurs.

1. ```
   q.enqueue('A');
   q.enqueue('B');
   q.enqueue('C');
   ch = q.front();
   q.dequeue();
   q.enqueue(ch);
   ```

2. ```
   q.enqueue('X');
   q.enqueue('Y');
   ```
   ```

```
        q.enqueue('Z');
        while (!q.empty())
        {
          ch = q.front();
          q.dequeue();
        }
```

3.  ```
    ch = 'q';
    for (int i = 1; i <= 3; i++)
    {
      q.enqueue(ch);
      ch++;
      q.enqueue(ch);
      ch = q.front();
      q.dequeue();
    }
    ```

4.  ```
    ch = 'A';
    for (int i = 1; i <= 4; i++)
    {
      q.enqueue(ch);
      ch++;
      q.enqueue(ch);
      ch = q.front();
      q.dequeue();
    }
    ```

The following exercises ask you to write functions or classes. You should also write driver programs to test them as instructed in the programming problems at the end of this chapter.

5. Write documentation, a prototype, and a definition for a member function back() that returns the element at the back of a queue for a Queue class like that described in this section that uses a linear linked list to store the queue elements.

6. Proceed as in Exercise 5, but design a function nthElement() to retrieve the nth queue element, leaving the queue without its first n elements.

7. Proceed as in Exercise 6, but leave the queue contents unchanged.

8. Complete the development of the class Queue that uses a circular linked list with a single pointer myBack to the last node. Give definitions for the constructor, empty(), enqueue(), front(), display(), and dequeue() function members. Also, add a destructor, a copy constructor, and an assignment operator.

8.4 Application of Queues: Buffers and Scheduling

One important use of queues in computing systems is for **input/output buffering**. The transfer of information from an input device or to an output device is a relatively slow operation, and if the processing of a program must be suspended while data is transferred, program execution is slowed dramatically. One common solution to this problem uses sections of main memory known as **buffers** and transfers data between the program and these buffers rather than between the program and the input/output device directly.

In particular, consider the problem in which data processed by a program must be read from a disk file. This information is transferred from the disk file to an input buffer in main memory while the central processing unit (CPU) is performing some other task:

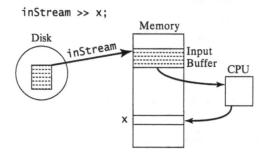

When input for a variable is required by the program, the next value stored in this buffer is retrieved. While this value is being processed, additional data values can be transferred from the disk file to the buffer. Clearly, the buffer must be organized as a first-in-first-out structure, that is, as a queue. A queue-empty condition indicates that the input buffer is empty and program execution is suspended while the operating system loads more data into the buffer. Of course, such a buffer has a limited size, and thus a queue-full condition must also be used to signal when it is full and no more data is to be transferred from the disk file to the buffer.

The insert and delete operations for a queue are restricted so that insertions are performed at only one end and deletions at the other. In some applications, however, insertions and deletions must be made at both ends. For example, in scrolling a window up and down on the screen, lines are added and removed at the top and also at the bottom:

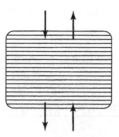

To model these situations, a double-ended queue, abbreviated to **deque** (pronounced "deck"), is the data structure that should be used (but it could as well be called a "dack" for "double-ended stack"). Deques are described in more detail in Section 9.7.

Another example of this behavior is interactive input, where the user can insert data into the input buffer by entering it from the keyboard, but the user may also be able to delete information by depressing a delete or backspace key. For example, the following diagram illustrates the user entering 1234 by pressing 1, 2, 3, 5 and these four keystrokes are recorded in an input buffer; the backspace key is then used to remove the character 5 and the correct digit 4 is entered and recorded:

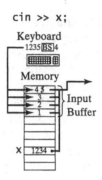

A deque could be used to model the action of this buffer. However, because data values are only removed and not inserted at the one end, a better model might be a queue–stack hybrid, sometimes called a **scroll** (although more colorful names might be "queue-and-a-half," "heque," or "quack").

Queues are also commonly used to model waiting lines that arise in the operation of computer systems. These queues are formed whenever more than one process requires a particular resource, such as a printer, a disk drive, or the central processing unit. As processes request a particular resource, they are placed in a queue to wait for service by that resource. For example, several personal computers may be sharing the same printer, and a **spool**[2] **queue** is used to schedule output requests in a first-come-first-served manner. If some process requests the printer to perform some output, that output is copied to disk, and the process is added to a spool queue of processes waiting for the printer. When the output from the current process terminates, the printer is released from that process and is assigned to the next one in the spool queue.

Queues may also be used to schedule tasks as they move through the computer. To illustrate, consider the following diagram in which some binary executable created by compiling and linking a program has been saved in a disk file F, and the user now wishes to execute it:

---

[2] "Spool" is an acronym for **S**imultaneous **P**eripheral **O**peration **O**n-**L**ine.

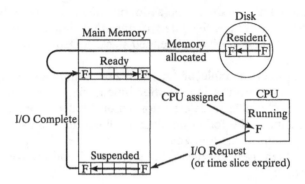

The file F resides on disk and needs to be loaded into memory and processed with the CPU. There may be many such files waiting to be loaded into memory. A queue, called the **resident queue**, might be used to organize these files that are on disk, waiting for memory. When file F reaches the front of the queue, memory gets allocated for it, and when it has all the other system resources it needs except the CPU, it enters the **ready queue**. Eventually, when F reaches the front of this queue, the CPU gets assigned to it and begins processing it. If F contains an I/O request (or it keeps the CPU until some preassigned *time slice* expires), it gives up the CPU and enters a **suspended queue**, where it is waiting for the operating system to do the I/O transfer. When this happens, F reenters the ready queue and waits for the CPU.

In most modern systems, the ready queue is probably not really a queue, because something more sophisticated than first-come-first-served CPU scheduling is used. One alternative is to use a **priority queue**. In this variation of a queue, a certain priority is associated with each item, and they are stored in such a way that those with higher priority are near the front of the queue so that they will be removed from the queue and assigned the CPU before those of lower priority:

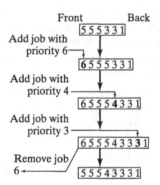

Along with stacks and queues, deques and priority queues are containers provided in the C++ standard library, which we will look at in Chapter 9. Implementations of deques and scrolls as classes are left to the exercises.

✔ Quick Quiz 8.4

1. A(n) _____ queue stores processes waiting for a printer.
2. A(n) _____ is a section of main memory used to transfer data between a program and an input/output device.
3. A(n) _____ is a double-ended queue.
4. A(n) _____ allows items to be inserted and removed at one end and only removed at the other.
5. In a(n) _____ , items are stored in such a way that those having the highest priority are removed first.

Answer Questions 6–8 using: resident, ready, suspended.

6. Jobs that have everything they need to run except the CPU are kept in a(n) _____ queue.
7. A(n) _____ queue organizes files on disk that are waiting for memory.
8. Jobs that surrender the CPU because of an I/O request are placed in a(n) _____ queue.

⬥ Exercises 8.4

1. Imitating the implementation of a queue using a circular array, construct an implementation of a deque. Select appropriate data members and write functions to implement the basic operations (constructor, check if the deque is empty, add at the front, add at the back, remove at the front, remove at the back, and an output operation).
2. Construct an implementation of a scroll, selecting appropriate data members and writing functions to implement the basic operations

8.5 Case Study: Information Center Simulation

As we noted in the preceding section, queues may be used to model waiting lines. In fact, *queueing theory* is such an important area of computer science, operations research, and other areas of applied mathematics and computing that many books are devoted to it and many universities offer courses in it.

Almost all waiting lines are dynamic; that is, their lengths change over time, growing as new items arrive and are added to the queues, shrinking as items are removed from the queues and serviced. The term **simulation** refers to modeling such a dynamic process and using this model to study the behavior of the process. The behavior of some **deterministic** processes can be modeled with an equation or a set of equations. For example, processes that involve exponential growth or decay are commonly modeled with an equation of the form $A(t) = A_0 e^{kt}$, where $A(t)$ is the amount of some substance A present at time t, A_0 is the initial amount of the substance, and k is a rate constant.

In many problems, however, the process under study involves **randomness**—for example, Brownian motion, the arrival of airplanes at an airport, the number of defective parts manufactured by a machine, the addition problems in the drill-and-practice problem in Section 8.1, and so on. Computer programs that simulate such processes use a **random number generator** to introduce randomness into the values produced during execution. This is a subprogram that produces a number selected *at random* from some fixed range in such a way that a sequence of these numbers tends to be uniformly distributed over the given range. Although true random numbers are generated by random physical processes, such as radioactive decay, some mathematical formulas produce sequences of **pseudorandom numbers** that are adequate for most purposes.

The behavior of a queue also often involves randomness, because it is usually not known in advance exactly when there will be a new arrival or exactly how much time will be required to service a specified item. As an illustration, we consider the operation of an information/reservation center that services calls made by customers to a toll-free number, such as one provided by an airline or a rental car company. When a call arrives at this center, it is placed in a queue of incoming calls. When an agent is available, he or she services the call at the front of the queue.

Problem Analysis and Specification

The overall simulation should proceed as follows: A simulated countdown timer is set to the number of minutes that calls will be accepted and then is repeatedly decremented by 1 (minute) until it reaches 0. On each "tick" of the timer, a check is made to determine if service has been completed for the current call, and if so, it is removed from the queue of incoming calls and simulated service begins on the next call in the queue (if any). A check is also made to determine if a new call has arrived. If it has, its arrival time is recorded, a random service time for it is generated and recorded, and the call is placed in the queue for processing in a first-come-first-served manner when an agent becomes available. When the timer reaches zero, no new calls are accepted, but service continues until all the calls in the queue have been processed.

As we noted earlier, the simulation is to run for a specified period of time, and thus one input item must be a time limit. Since it is necessary to simulate the arrival and service of calls, information about arrival rates and service times is also needed. Thus, the input will be

Input: Time limit
          Arrival rate of calls
          Distribution of service times

When the simulation is complete, statistics that measure the performance of the information center must be reported. Here, we will report only two of these:

Output: Number of calls processed
           Average waiting time per call

Other performance measures such as the average queue length and the average turnaround time are described in the exercises.

Building a Simulation Class

Data Members   The three input items and the two output items are the basic data values involved in the simulation. An object of type Simulation will store these five values in its data members.

The first data member, `myLengthOfSimulation`, stores the time limit for the simulation. The value of the second data member, `myArrivalRate`, is the probability that a call will arrive in a given minute. For example, if the average time between calls is five minutes, then the arrival rate is 1/5 = 0.2 calls per minute. The third data member is an array `myServicePercent`. It records information regarding the time required to service a call:

`myServicePercent[0]` = percent of calls serviced in 1 minute or less
`myServicePercent[1]` = percent of calls serviced in 2 minutes or less
`myServicePercent[2]` = percent of calls serviced in 3 minutes or less

   . . .

For our `Simulation` class, we will use `NUM_CATEGORIES` = 5 categories of times needed to service an incoming call. The user enters the percentages of calls that require 1, 2, 3, 4, or 5 minutes, and these are accumulated to give the values in `myServicePercent`. For example, if the user enters 50, 25, 15, 7, 3, the values stored in the array `myServicePercent` are 50, 75 (= 50 + 25), 90 (= 50 + 25 + 15), 97 (= 50 + 25 + 15 + 7), and 100 (the sum of all the percentages):

	[0]	[1]	[2]	[3]	[4]
myServicePercent	50	75	90	97	100

   Other data members that will be needed are a countdown timer `myTimer` of type `Timer`, a class that is described later in this section, and a queue `myIncomingCalls` of incoming calls. The `Queue` class we will use is the linked queue class described in the preceding section. Its element type will be `Call`, a class we will describe later in this section to model incoming calls.
   Figure 8.4 shows the structure of the class `Simulation` that has these data members. As indicated, it will have the basic operations needed to conduct the simulation: run the simulation, which will involve checking if new calls arrive and servicing incoming calls, and then display the results when the simulation is finished.

Figure 8.4 The Simulation Class—Data Members

```
/*-- Simulation.h ------------------------------------------------------

Header file to define a Simulation data type for simulating the operation
of an information/reservation center that services telephone calls.

Basic operations:
  constructor:        constructs a Simulation object
  run():              carry out the simulation
  display():          output results of the simulation
```

Figure 8.4 (continued)

```
        service():           service an incoming call
        checkForNewCall(): check if a new call has come in


    Note:   Assumes availability of a queue class with elements of type Call.
    ---------------------------------------------------------------------*/


#include <iostream>        // istream, ostream, >>, <<
#include <ctime>          // time()


#ifndef SIMULATION
#define SIMULATION


#include "Timer.h"
#include "Call.h"
#include "LQueue.h"        // Queue with elements of type Call

const int NUM_CATEGORIES = 5;
class Simulation
{
 public:
  /***** Function Members *****/

 private:
  /***** Data Members *****/
  //-- Inputs
  int     myLengthOfSimulation;
  double myArrivalRate;
  int     myServicePercent[NUM_CATEGORIES];

  //-- Outputs
  int     myCallsReceived;
  double myTotalWaitingTime;

  //-- Countdown Timer
  Timer myTimer;
```

Figure 8.4 (continued)

```
   //-- Queue of calls waiting for service
   Queue myIncomingCalls;


}; // end of class declaration


#endif
```

▲

Constructor The constructor in the class Simulation initializes the data members needed to conduct the simulation and report the results. The three input data members are initialized by the constructor using values entered during execution. The two output data members, myCallsReceived and myTotalWaitingTime, record the values needed when outputting the results and are initialized to 0. The other two data members myTimer and myIncomingCalls are objects of type Timer and Queue, respectively, and are initialized by their constructors.

The constructor also initializes the random number generator rand() provided in the <cstdlib> library, using srand() from this same library and the clock time obtained from <ctime>. Source code for the constructor is given in Figure 8.5.

The run() Method The run() method in the Simulation class (see Figure 8.5) is the operation that actually starts and manages the simulation. It implements the following algorithm:

Algorithm for Running the Simulation

1. Initialize busyTimeRemaining to 0, thus making service available to the first incoming call. (This variable indicates at each time during the simulation, how long it will be before a new call can be serviced.)

2. While myTimer has not run out:
   a. Continue service of a previous call or begin service on the next call in the queue myIncomingCalls (if there are any).
   b. Check to see if a new call has arrived, and if so, add it to the queue myIncomingCalls.
   c. Have myTimer tick off 1 time unit.

3. While calls remain in the incoming queue,
   a. Service the call at the front of the queue.
   b. Have myTimer tick off 1 time unit.

4. Display the results.

Steps 2a and 3a are performed by the `service()` method; step 2b by `checkForNew-Call()`; steps 2c and 3b by sending a message to `myTimer` to use its `tick()` method; and step 4 by `display()`.

The service() Method The `service()` method in the `Simulation` class (see Figure 8.5) services each call as it gets to the front of the queue `myIncomingCalls`. It implements the following algorithm:

Algorithm for Servicing a Call

Check if `busyTimeRemaining > 0`. If it is, this means that a call is currently being serviced, so simply decrement `busyTimeRemaining` by 1 to indicate another minute of servicing that call.
Otherwise do the following:
If the queue `myIncomingCalls` is not empty:
    a. Retrieve and remove *nextCall* from the front of `myIncomingCalls`.
    b. Set `busyTimeRemaining` = the service time in *nextCall* to indicate that service will begin on this call
    c. Update `myTotalWaitingTime`, the total waiting time for all calls in the queue `myIncomingCalls` by adding (*nextCall*'s arrival time) – (`myTimer`'s remaining time) to it.

The checkForNewCall() Method The following is an algorithm for this method:

Algorithm to Check for Arrival of a New Call

1. Generate a random integer x in the range 0 to 100.
2. If $x < 100 *$ `myArrivalRate`
    // This is interpreted as the arrival of a new call:

Call arrives	No call arrives

0   20   100

    a. Generate a new random number r in the range 0 to 100. This will be used to determine a service time for the call.
    b. Determine the corresponding service category by finding the smallest index i for which $r <=$ `myServicePercent[i]`
    c. Construct a new `Call` object with its arrival time set to the remaining time on `myTimer` and its service time initialized to $i + 1$.
    d. Add this new `Call` object to the `incomingCalls` queue.
    e. Update the total number of calls received by incrementing `myCallsReceived` by 1.

The numbers produced by the random number generator are assumed to be uniformly distributed over the interval from 0 to 100. Consequently, if many such numbers are generated, we expect approximately 20 percent of them to be in the subinterval (0, 20). In terms of our simulation, this means that the probability that a call arrives in a given minute should be approximately 0.2, as desired.

When a new call arrives, its arrival time is recorded but its service time is random. It is determined by using the array myServicePercent. For example, suppose this array contains the values 50, 75, 90, 97, and 100—50 percent of the calls are serviced in less than 1 minute, 75 percent in less than 2 minutes, and so on. We generate a random integer in the interval (0, 100); the subinterval in which it falls—(0, 50], (50, 75], (75, 90], (90, 97], or (97, 100)—determines the service time for the call:

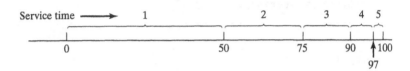

Source code for the function member checkForNewCall() that implements this algorithm is given in Figure 8.5.

The display() Method   At the end of the simulation, the total number of calls processed and the average waiting time per call are displayed. The number of calls is stored in the data member myCallsReceived, and the average waiting can be calculated by divided myTotalWaitingTime by myCallsReceived.

Source code for the function member display() and for all of the other function members is given in Figure 8.5. Also shown is a small driver program and an execution trace. The driver program simply creates a Simulation object and sends it a run() message.

Figure 8.5 The Simulation Class—Function Members

Insert the following prototypes in the public section of the class Simulation in Figure 8.4.

```
/***** Function Members *****/
/***** Constructor *****/
Simulation();
/*------------------------------------------------------------
  Construct a Simulation object.

  Precondition:  None
  Postcondition: Input data members have been initialized with values
     entered by the user; output data members have been initialized
     to 0; and random number generator has been initialized.
------------------------------------------------------------*/
```

Figure 8.5 (continued)

```
/***** Running the simulation *****/
void run();
/*-------------------------------------------------------------------
   Run the simulation.

   Precondition:  None.
   Postcondition: Simulation of phone service has been completed and
       performance statistics output.
   -----------------------------------------------------------------*/


/***** Output *****/
void display(ostream & out);
/*-------------------------------------------------------------------
   Display results of the simulation.

   Precondition:  ostream out is open.
   Postcondition: Total number of calls and the average waiting time
       for calls have been output to out.
   -----------------------------------------------------------------*/


/***** Call processing *****/
void service(int & busyTimeRemaining);
/*-------------------------------------------------------------------
   Service the current call (if any).

   Precondition:  None
   Postcondition: busyTimeRemaining has been decremented by one if a call
       was being serviced; otherwise, if there were incoming calls, a
       call has been removed from myIncomingCalls, its service time
       assigned to busyTimeRemaining, and its waiting time in the queue
       added to myTotalWaitingTime.
   -----------------------------------------------------------------*/


void checkForNewCall();
/*-------------------------------------------------------------------
   Check if a new call has arrived and if so, add it to the
   queue of incoming calls.
```

Figure 8.5 (continued)

```
   Precondition:  None.
   Postcondition: myIncomingCalls has been updated.
   ----------------------------------------------------------------------*/
```

▬▬▬▬▬▬▬▬▬▬▬▬▬▬▬▬▬▬▬▬▬▬▬▬▬▬▬▬▬▬▬▬▬▬

```cpp
/*-- Simulation.cpp --------------------------------------------------
     Definitions of function members of class Simulation.
   ----------------------------------------------------------------------*/


#include <iostream>        // istream, ostream, >>, <<
#include <cstdlib>         // rand(), srand()
#include <ctime>           // time()
using namespace std;

#include "Simulation.h"

//--- Definition of constructor
Simulation::Simulation()
{
   //-- Initialize output statistics
   myCallsReceived = 0;
   myTotalWaitingTime = 0;
   //-- Get simulation parameters
   cout << "Enter arrival rate (calls per hour): ";
   int callsPerHour;
   cin >> callsPerHour;
   myArrivalRate = callsPerHour / 60.0;   // convert to calls per minute

   cout << "Enter percent of calls serviced in\n";
   int percent,
       sum = 0;
   for (int i = 0; i < NUM_CATEGORIES - 1; i++)
   {
      cout << "  <= " << i + 1 << " min. ";        cin >> percent;
      sum += percent;
      myServicePercent[i] = sum;
   }
   myServicePercent[NUM_CATEGORIES - 1] = 100;
```

Figure 8.5 (continued)

```cpp
    cout << "Enter # of minutes to run simulation: ";
    cin >> myLengthOfSimulation;

  // Set the countdown timer
  myTimer.set(myLengthOfSimulation);

  //-- Initialize random number generator
  long seed = long(time(0));     // seed for random number generator
  srand(seed);
}

//--- Definition of run()
void Simulation::run()
{
  // Begin the simulation
  int busyTimeRemaining = 0;
  while (myTimer.timeRemaining() > 0)
  {
    service(busyTimeRemaining);
    checkForNewCall();
    myTimer.tick();
  }
  cout << "\nNot accepting more calls -- service those waiting\n";

  // Service any remaining calls in incomingCalls queue
  while (!myIncomingCalls.empty())
  {
    service(busyTimeRemaining);
    myTimer.tick();
  }

  // Output the results
  display(cout);
}
```

Figure 8.5 (continued)

```cpp
//--- Definition of display()
void Simulation::display(ostream & out)
{
   out << "\nNumber of calls processed:   " << myCallsReceived
       << "\nAve. waiting time per call:  "
       <<        myTotalWaitingTime / myCallsReceived
       << " minutes" << endl;
}


//--- Definition of service()
void Simulation::service(int & busyTimeRemaining)
{
   if (busyTimeRemaining > 0)          // servicing a call
      busyTimeRemaining--;             // service it for another minute
   else
      if (!myIncomingCalls.empty())  // calls are waiting -- get one
      {
         Call nextCall = myIncomingCalls.front();
         myIncomingCalls.dequeue();
         busyTimeRemaining = nextCall.getServiceTime();

         // Update total waiting time
         myTotalWaitingTime +=
               nextCall.getArrivalTime() - myTimer.timeRemaining();
      }
}


//--- Definition of checkForNewCall()
void Simulation::checkForNewCall()
{
   int x = rand() % 100;

   if (x < 100 * myArrivalRate)
   {
      // A new call has arrived.  Generate a random service time for it
      int r = rand() % 100;
```

Figure 8.5 (continued)

```
        int serviceTime = 0;
        while (r > myServicePercent[serviceTime])
            serviceTime++;

        // Construct a new call and add it to queue of incoming calls
        Call newCall(myTimer, serviceTime + 1);
        myIncomingCalls.enqueue(newCall);
        myCallsReceived++;
    }
}
```

```
/*-------------------------------------------------------------------------
    Driver program for simulation of information/reservation center that
    services telephone calls
    -------------------------------------------------------------------------*/

using namespace std;

#include "Simulation.h"

int main()
{
  Simulation sim;
  sim.run();
}
```

Execution Trace:
```
Enter arrival rate (calls per hour): 15
Enter percent of calls serviced in
  <= 1 min. 50
  <= 2 min. 25
  <= 3 min. 15
  <= 4 min. 7
Enter # of minutes to run simulation: 500
```

Figure 8.5 (continued)

```
Not accepting more calls -- service those waiting

Number of calls processed:   112
Ave. waiting time per call:   2.57143 minutes
```

▲

The Timer and Call Classes

Another object in the simulation is the countdown timer, modeled by a class Timer whose basic operations are as follows:

constructor:	constructs a Timer object with a specific initial time (default 0 minutes)
set():	mutator to set/reset the timer
tick():	decrease timer by 1 time unit (minute)
timeRemaining():	determines how much time remains

It has only one data member (myMinutes).

Another object is a call to the information center, modeled by a class Call with the following basic operation:

constructors:	construct a Call object initialized with randomly determined arrival time and service times (default 0)
getArrivalTime():	accessor to get time the call arrived
getServiceTime():	get time needed to service the call
display():	display information about the call
<<:	output operator for a Call object

Such calls are characterized by the time they arrive and the amount of time required to service the call, so these are the data members.

The source code for the Timer and Call classes can be found on the text's website (see the source files—*Chap8/Figures8.4–5*).

SUMMARY

Chapter Notes

■ A queue has FIFO (first-in-first-out) behavior. Items are inserted at one end (the back) and removed at the other (the front).

■ An efficient array-based implementation of a queue can be obtained by thinking of the array as circular.

■ Queues (or some variation such as deques or priority queues) are used to schedule resources in a computer system. Examples are input/output buffers; a spool queue for items waiting to be printed; a resident queue of jobs waiting to be loaded from disk into memory; a ready queue of jobs waiting for the CPU; a suspended queue of jobs whose execution has been suspended, for example, while waiting for input or output.

■ Queuing theory is an important area of study in computer science, operations research, and other areas of applied mathematics and computing.

☞ Programming Pointers

1. Random number generators are used to produce (pseudo-) random numbers in programs that simulate random behavior.

2. Event-driven simulations like the information-center application in Section 8.5 often make use of queues to model waiting lines.

▲ ADT Tips

1. A *queue has first-in-first-out* (*FIFO*) or *first-come-first-served* (*FCFS*) behavior.

2. Sometimes changing the usual way in which a data structure is viewed leads to a modification that yields an efficient implementation of an ADT. For example, using an array naively in implementing a queue suffers from having to shift elements in the array to avoid "falling off the end"; but viewing the array as a circular array leads to a very efficient implementation.

3. In using a circular array to implement a queue, it must be possible to distinguish between queue-empty and queue-full condition. Common approaches are to leave one array location empty, keep a count of the number of elements, or use a boolean variable that records whether the queue is full.

4. A *deque* allows items to be inserted and removed at *both* ends.

5. A *scroll* allows items to be inserted and removed at one end and only removed at the other.

🔲 Programming Problems

Section 8.2

1. Write a driver program to test the class Queue from Exercise 5.

2. Write a driver program to test the function full() from Exercise 6.

3. Write a driver program to test the function size() from Exercise 7.

4. Repeat Problem 3, but for the function size() from Exercise 8.

5. Write a driver program to test the function back() from Exercise 9.

6. Repeat Problem 5, but for the function back() from Exercise 10.

7. Write a driver program to test the function nthElement() from Exercise 11.

8. Repeat Problem 7, but for the function nthElement() from Exercise 12.

9. Write a driver program to test the Queue class from Exercise 15.

10. Write a driver program to test the Queue class from Exercise 16.

11. Write a driver program to test the Queue class from Exercise 17.

12. Write and test a class for the two-queue structure in Exercise 18.

13. Write a program that generates a random sequence of letters and/or digits, displays them to the user one at a time for a second or so, and then asks the user to reproduce the sequence. Use a queue to store the sequence of characters.

14. Write a program that reads a string of characters, pushing each character onto a stack as it is read and simultaneously adding it to a queue. When the end of the string is encountered, the program should use the basic stack and queue operations to determine if the string is a palindrome (see Exercise 10 of Section 5.2).

15. In text-editing and word-processing applications, one formatting convention sometimes used to indicate that a piece of text is a footnote or an endnote is to mark it with some special delimiters such as { and }. When the text is formatted for output, these notes are not printed as normal text but are stored in a queue for later output. Write a program that reads a document containing endnotes indicated in this manner, collects them in a queue, and prints them at the end of the document.

Section 8.3

16. Write a driver program to test the function back() from Exercise 5.

17. Write a driver program to test the function nthElement() from Exercise 6.

18. Repeat Problem 17, but for the function nthElement() from Exercise 7.

19. Write a driver program to test the class Queue from Exercise 8 that uses a circular linked list to store the queue elements.

Section 8.4

20. Write a driver program to test your deque class from Exercise 1.

21. Write a driver program to test your scroll class from Exercise 2.

Section 8.5

22. Modify the simulation system in this section so that the average turnaround time is also calculated and displayed. The turnaround time for a given call is the difference between the time when service for that call is completed and the time the call arrived.

23. Modify the simulation system in this section so that the average queue length is also calculated and displayed. If n minutes are simulated and $L_1, L_2, \ldots, L_n$ are the lengths of the incoming-calls queue at times $1, 2, \ldots, n$, respectively, then the average queue length is $(L_1 + L_2 + \cdots + L_n)/n$.

24. Modify the simulation system in this section so that several agents are available to service calls. Investigate the behavior of various queue statistics as the number of agents varies.

25. Suppose that in addition to the simulation parameters given in the example in this section, another is the number of calls rejected because the number of calls in the incoming-calls queue has exceeded some upper limit. Add this feature to the simulation system.

26. Suppose that another useful simulation parameter is the percentage of calls that cannot be serviced by an agent but must be transferred to a manager. In addition to the other random information generated for each call, also generate randomly an indicator of

whether or not it can be serviced by an agent. If it cannot, it should be added to a managerQueue, and a new service time should be generated for it. Modify the system of classes in this section to simulate this information center, and calculate various statistics such as those in the text and in Exercises 1 and 2 for each call, for each queue, and so on.

27. (Project) Suppose that a certain airport has one runway, that each airplane takes landingTime minutes to land and takeOffTime minutes to take off, and that on the average, takeOffRate planes take off and landingRate planes land each hour. Assume that the planes arrive at random instants of time. (Delays make the assumption of randomness quite reasonable.) There are two types of queues: a queue of airplanes waiting to land and a queue of airplanes waiting to take off. Because it is more expensive to keep a plane airborne than to have one waiting on the ground, we assume that the airplanes in the landing queue have priority over those in the takeoff queue.

Write a program to simulate this airport's operation. You might assume a simulated clock that advances in one-minute intervals. For each minute, generate two random numbers: If the first is less than landingRate / 60, a "landing arrival" has occurred and is added to the landing queue; and if the second is less than takeOffRate / 60, a "takeoff arrival" has occurred and is added to the takeoff queue. Next, check whether the runway is free. If it is, first check whether the landing queue is nonempty, and if so, allow the first airplane to land; otherwise, consider the takeoff queue. Have the program calculate the average queue length and the average time that an airplane spends in a queue. You might also investigate the effect of varying arrival and departure rates to simulate the prime and slack times of day, or what happens if the amount of time to land or take off is increased or decreased.

CHAPTER 9

ADT Implementations: Templates and Standard Containers

CHAPTER CONTENTS

Chapter Objectives

■ Survey how reusability and genericity themes have evolved in programming languages.
■ Study function templates.
■ Study class templates.
■ Look at vector in detail as an example of a container class template.
■ (Optional) Study multidimensional vectors.
■ Look at some of the other C++ standard containers (deque, stack, and queue)
■ (Optional) Introduce valarrays and bitsets as array-based class templates.

In the preceding chapters we have looked at lists, stacks, and queues as abstract data types and implemented them with classes. In this chapter we focus on the *data* component of an ADT, especially for *container ADTs* such as lists, stacks, and queues that store collections of data, but our approach will also impact the functions that implement the basic operations.

Our goal is to achieve greater reusability of functions and container ADTs by making them more *generic*, so that they can be applied to various types of data. The classes that we built for container ADTs have had some reusability. We set the type of a container's elements using a typedef statement such as

```
typedef double StackElement;
```

and we used the generic name StackElement throughout the rest of the class declaration and implementation. To change to another element type, we need only change this statement. For example, to have a stack of integers, we could simply replace double with int:

```
typedef int StackElement;
```

We also put this declaration near the beginning of the class's header file so that it would be easy to change. However, as we will see, the fact that *this declaration binds the container's elements to one particular type* severely limits reusability.

In this chapter we look at a more recent development in programming languages that makes it possible to achieve greater genericity in ADTs, namely *templates*. We first describe the template mechanism for functions and show how it makes it possible to write generic function templates, and then we show how the template mechanism for classes can be used to develop generic container class templates. We also look at some of the standard container class templates provided in C++.

9.1 Introduction: The Evolution of Reusability and Genericity

Since their beginnings with Fortran and COBOL in the mid-1950s, high-level programming languages have evolved from rather simple tools—sometimes crude and difficult to use and intended for writing programs for specific problems—into powerful sophisticated general-purpose tools for solving a wide variety of problems. A major theme in this development has been to modify some language features and add others to make it easier to *reuse code and thus avoid reinventing the wheel*. One of the trends that has contributed to this reusability has been increased use of *generic code* that can be used with different types of data.

In Chapter 1 we mentioned the text *Algorithms + Data Structures = Programs*, written by Niklaus Wirth, inventor of the Pascal language, which stressed that data and algorithms cannot be separated. It is interesting to see how this has played out in the development of programming languages. Features that have fostered reusability of algorithms and their implementations in code have been paralleled by corresponding features that have made container data types more generic and therefore more reusable with different kinds of data.

The diagram in Figure 9.1 displays this parallelism. The right side of the diagram summarizes the evolution of *algorithmic* features of programming languages and the left side summarizes the evolution of *data* features.

From Algorithms to Algorithms

The right track of the diagram in Figure 9.1 begins with inline code, which is how many of the earliest algorithms were implemented. Gradually, however, as programmers tired of writing duplicate code, features were added to programming languages that made it possible to write sections of code called *subprograms* to perform specific tasks and have them executed at various places in the program—an early manifestation of avoiding wheel reinvention. Commands like JMP 100 in an early assembly language and GOSUB 100 in BASIC made it possible to transfer execution to a subprogram beginning at statement 100 that did a specific task such as displaying a menu

Figure 9.1 The Evolution of Reusability/Genericity

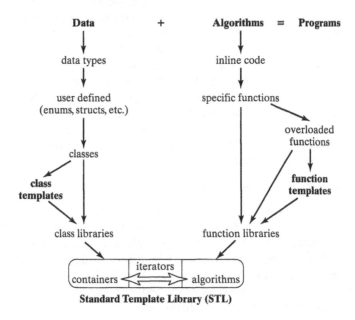

Standard Template Library (STL)

of options and then resume execution back in the (main) program. In some languages, the subprograms were named and could be called by this name; for example, CALL MENU in Fortran and PERFORM MENU in COBOL.[1] These subprograms came to be known as *subroutines, functions, or procedures* and it became possible to pass values to them and return values from them, providing still more ways to *reuse code* and simplify the programming task. For example, if a program needs to calculate square roots at several different places, it is surely easier to send each number to a square root function, which computes and returns the number's square root, than to write the code for the square-root algorithm every place it is needed.

This led to the development of large libraries of functions (and other subprograms), such as those in C and Fortran, for solving many different kinds of specific problems. Each library might contain several different functions for solving the same problem but with different types of data. For example, early versions of Fortran contained at least four different absolute value functions: ABS() for single-precision REAL values, DABS() for DOUBLE PRECISION values, IABS() for INTEGER values, and CABS() for COMPLEX values. Later versions of Fortran provided *generic functions*, which could be called with any of the four data types REAL, DOUBLE PRECISION, INTEGER, or COMPLEX. The multitude of specific functions were still there, but the programmer could usually avoid using them. If, for example, a program contained the generic function call ABS(X), the compiler would automatically replace it with an

---

[1] Somewhere in computer lore is a suggestion that use of the term "calling" as in "calling a function" originated with a member of a Fortran programming team *calling* across the room to another programmer asking to borrow his code for computing some mathematical function—e.g., a sine function. As the distraction caused by such calls increased, someone suggested putting these commonly used routines in the company's *library*.

appropriate specific function call ABS(X), DABS(X), IABS(X), or CABS(X) as determined by the type of X. Today, using the same name for different functions is referred to as **overloading** that name. Function overloading in C++ was described in Section 4.5 and will be reviewed in the next section.

Although overloading made it easier to use functions in a program, it still was necessary to develop large libraries of functions for the different data types. The recent addition of *function templates* in C++ has greatly simplified this task by allowing the programmer to write a template (i.e., pattern) for a function and have the *compiler* generate the function definition for a particular data type from the template. In the next section, we will study function templates and in Chapter 10, look at a few of the function templates that make up the *algorithms* component of the Standard Template Library.

From Data to Containers

The left track of the diagram in Figure 9.1 begins with simple data types to store and process a few kinds of data, mostly numeric and later alphanumeric. An early structured data type provided in programming languages was the array. Later it became possible to *extend a language* by defining new data types; for example, an enumeration in Pascal or C++ is a new, albeit simple, data type. Group data items in COBOL, records in Pascal, and structs in C made it possible to define new data types for processing nonhomogeneous collections of data.

For years, however, the emphasis was on finding better and more powerful ways to develop procedures for processing the data. As we described in Chapter 3, in this *procedural* style of programming, data was simply something that got shipped off to different subprograms for processing. As programming languages evolved, it became possible to define data types that not only stored data but also contained operations for processing this data. The Smalltalk programming language was developed, units were added to some versions of Pascal, classes from Simula were added to C giving C++, and similar constructs appeared in other languages. *Object-oriented programming* had made its appearance on the programming stage.

The most recent development in this data track has been the counterpart to function templates, namely, *class templates*. They make it possible to define data types into which other data types can be passed—for example, a Stack class template into which the type of the stack elements can be passed. The standard C++ istream, ostream, and string classes are, in fact, formed by passing the type char into the class templates basic_istream, basic_ostream, and basic_string, respectively. The container types in the Standard Template Library are also class templates. We will study class templates later in this chapter.

9.2 Function Genericity—Overloading and Templates

We have seen that we can make pieces of code reusable by encapsulating them within functions. For example, consider the problem of interchanging the values of two int variables x and y. Instead of using inline code

```
int temp = x;
x = y;
y = temp;
```

to exchange the values of x and y, we make this code reusable by writing it as a function:

```
void swap(int & first, int & second)
/*------------------------------------
   Precondition:  None.
   Postcondition: The values of first
       and second have been interchanged.
   ------------------------------------*/
{
   int temp = first;
   first = second;
   second = temp;

}
```

This code can then be used wherever it is needed simply by calling the function and passing as arguments the int variables whose values are to be exchanged:

```
int x = 11,
    y = 22;
swap(x, y);

   .

   .

   .

int w = 333,
    z = 444;
swap(w, z);

   .

   .

   .

int a = 5005,
    b = 6006;
swap(a, b);
```

Overloading

What about swapping the values of two non-integer variables? For example, suppose we want to interchange the values of two double variables. We cannot use the preceding function. One option is to use a function that encapsulates the same code with int replaced by double, but give the function a different name:

```
void dubSwap(double & first, double & second)
/*------------------------------------
   Precondition:  None.
   Postcondition: The values of first
       and second have been interchanged.
   ------------------------------------*/
```

```
{
  double temp = first;
  first = second;
  second = temp;
}
```

We saw in Section 4.4, however, that a function name may be **overloaded**—that is, it may be used for two different functions—provided that *no two definitions of the function have the same signature*, which is the list of its parameter types. This means that we could give the preceding function the same name swap as the earlier version:

```
void swap(double & first, double & second)
/*---------------------------------------
  Precondition:  None.
  Postcondition: The values of first
      and second have been interchanged.
  ---------------------------------------*/
{
  double temp = first;
  first = second;
  second = temp;
}
```

The signature of the first version of swap() is

```
(int &, int &)
```

and the signature of the second version is

```
(double &, double &)
```

so the condition in the overloading rule is satisfied. Remember, however, that the return type or void specifier in a function's heading is not part of its signature, which means that *two functions with the same parameter types but with different return types cannot be overloaded.*

Now, what if we needed a function to interchange the values of two char variables? Again, we can overload function swap():

```
void swap(char & first, char & second)
/*---------------------------------------
  Precondition:  None.
  Postcondition: The values of first
      and second have been interchanged.
  ---------------------------------------*/
{
  char temp = first;
  first = second;
  second = temp;
}
```

And we could go on in this manner for other types of variables, creating an entire library of overloaded swap() functions for every data type for which we might ever want to interchange two values.

When an overloaded function like swap() is called, it is the compiler's responsibility to determine which of the collection of overloaded functions is to be used. It does this by comparing the types of the arguments with the signatures in the collection until it finds a match. For example, if we call swap() with

```
int i1 = 11,
    i2 = 22;
swap(i1, i2);
```

the call has two int arguments, and so the compiler associates this call with the first definition of swap(), whose signature is (int &, int &). However, if we write

```
double d1 = 33.3,
       d2 = 44.4;
swap(d1, d2);
```

the function call has two double arguments, and so the compiler associates this call with the second definition of swap(), whose signature is (double &, double &). If there is no function in the collection with the required signature, compilation is terminated with an error message. For example, the statements

```
string s1 = "Hi",
       s2 = "Ho";
swap(s1, s2);
```

will produce a compiler error unless we add a version of swap() whose signature is (string &, string &).

Function Templates

Note that in the preceding example, each definition of swap() is doing exactly the same thing (on a different type of data). This should suggest that there is a better way to accomplish the same thing without so much duplication. The better way here is to recognize that the only differences in these definitions are the three places where a type is specified. If only we could define the function and leave these types blank, to be filled in later,

```
inline void swap(_____ & first, _____ & second)
{
    _____ temp = first;
  first = second;
  second = temp;
}
```

and somehow *pass the type* to the function when we call it, then we could replace all of the earlier definitions with one! *Templates* make it possible to do this.

The template mechanism is important and powerful and, as we noted, it is used throughout C++'s Standard Template Library (STL). *Templates make it possible for classes and functions to receive not only data values to be stored or operated on via*

parameters but also to receive the type of data via a parameter. They provide, therefore, a means of writing code that is generic and easier to reuse, since one template definition can be used to create multiple instances of a class or function, each storing and/or operating on a different type of data. We will describe function templates in this section and class templates in the next.

Templates work by declaring *type parameters* and using these in the function prototype and definition instead of specific types. This is done using a different kind of parameter list. To illustrate, the following is a function template for our swap problem:

```
template <typename DataType>           // <- the type parameter
void swap(DataType & first, DataType & second)
/*-----------------------------------------------------------

    A swap template for exchanging the values of any two
    variables of the same type DataType, for which the
    assignment operation is defined.

    Precondition:  None.
    Postcondition: The values of first and second
        have been interchanged.
    -----------------------------------------------------*/
{
   DataType temp = first;
   first = second;
   second = temp;
}
```

Rather than specify that the function is to exchange two values of a particular type such as char, int, and so on, this definition uses the *generic type identifier* DataType as a "placeholder" for the type of the values to be exchanged. More precisely, the line

```
template <typename DataType>
```

tells the compiler two things:

1. This is a function **template:** *a pattern from which a function can be created.*
2. The identifier DataType is the name of a **type parameter** for this function template that will be given a value when the function is called.

The rest of the definition simply specifies the behavior of the function, using the type parameter DataType in place of any specific type. In and of itself, the function template does nothing. When the compiler encounters a template like that for swap(), it simply stores it but doesn't generate any machine instructions. It uses the pattern given by our template to generate actual function definitions on an as-needed basis.

To illustrate, suppose that we replace the contents of our earlier library of swap functions with this single function template, and include it in the following program:

```
#include "SwapLibrary"
int main()
{
    int i1 = 11,
        i2 = 22;
    swap(i1, i2);
            .
            .
            .

    double d1 = 33.3,
           d2 = 44.4;
    swap(d1, d2);
            .
            .
            .

    string s1 = "Hi",
           s2 = "Ho";
    swap(s1, s2);
            .
            .
            .

}
```

When the compiler encounters the first call to swap(),

```
    swap(i1, i2);
```

in which the two arguments i1 and i2 are of type int, it uses the pattern given by our template to generate a *new* definition of swap() in which the type parameter DataType is replaced by int:

```
    void swap(int & first, int & second)
    {
        int temp = first;
        first = second;
        second = temp;
    }
```

When it reaches the second call,

```
    swap(d1, d2);
```

where the two arguments d1 and d2 are of type double, the compiler will use the same pattern to generate a second definition of swap() in which the type parameter DataType is replaced by double:

```
    void swap(double & first, double & second)
    {
        double temp = first;
        first = second;
        second = temp;
    }
```

When the compiler reaches the final call,

```
swap(s1, s2);
```

in which the two arguments s1 and s2 are of type string, it will use the pattern to generate a third definition of swap() in which the type parameter DataType is replaced by string:

```
void swap(string & first, string & second)
{
  string temp = first;
  first = second;
  second = temp;
}
```

We are spared from all of the redundant coding of the earlier approach because the compiler is providing multiple versions of the swap operation as they are needed. This single function template definition is sufficient, therefore, to interchange the values of any two variables, provided the assignment operator is defined for their type.

The general forms of function templates are as follows:

Function Template

Forms:

```
template <typename TypeParam>
function
```

or

```
template <class TypeParam>
function
```

More General Form:

```
template <specifier TypeParam₁,..., specifier TypeParamₙ>
function
```

In these forms, *TypeParam, TypeParam₁,* ... are generic type parameters representing the types of value(s) on which the function operates; each *specifier* is the keyword typename or class; and *function* is the prototype or definition of the function.

Notes:

- The word template is a C++ keyword specifying that what follows is a pattern for a function, *not an actual function prototype or definition.*
- The keywords typename and class may be used interchangeably in a type-parameter list.
- Whereas "normal" parameters (and arguments) appear within parentheses, *type parameters (and arguments for class templates) appear within angle brackets (< >).*
- Unlike regular functions, *function templates cannot be split into a header file containing their prototypes and a separately compiled file containing*

> *their definitions.* The definitions must get compiled along with the proto-types in any client program that #includes them. Thus, a common approach is to have a single file, but an alternative is to #include a sepa-rate file of definitions at the end of a file of prototypes.
>
> ■ A function template is only a *pattern* that describes how individual func-tions can be constructed from given actual types. This process of con-structing a function is called **instantiation.** In each instantiation, the type parameter is said to be **bound** to the actual type passed to it.
>
> ■ In the general form, each of the type parameters *must* appear at least once in the parameter list of the function if the compiler is to use only the types of the arguments in a function call to determine what types to bind to the type parameters. (See also Appendix D.)

In the preceding example, swap() was instantiated three times—once with type int, once with type double, and once with type string—and it could have been instantiated with any other type for which assignment (=) is defined. A function tem-plate can thus serve as a pattern for the definition of an unlimited number of instances.

For the compiler to be able to generate "real live" function definitions from a func-tion template such as swap(), it must "see" the actual definition of swap(), not just its prototype. This is the reason why function template prototypes cannot be kept in a header file *file.h* and the definitions in another file *file.cpp* that is to be compiled separately from client programs that #include "*file.h*". A common practice, and one that we will adopt in this text, is simply to put everything in the same file. An alter-native is to keep the prototypes in *file.h* and the definitions in another file named perhaps *file.template* and #include "*file.template*" at the end of *file.h*.

Another Example: Displaying an Array

Instantiation of a function template is carried out using the following algorithm:

1. Find the type parameters in the parameter list of the function template.
2. For each type parameter, determine the type of the corresponding argument.
3. Bind these two types together.

To illustrate this, consider the program in Figure 9.2

Figure 9.2 Using a Function Template to Display an Array

```
/*-------------------------------------------------------------------
    Program to illustrate the use of a function template to display
    an array with elements of any type for which << is defined.

    Output:  An array of ints and an array of doubles using display()
    --------------------------------------------------------------*/

#include <iostream>
using namespace std;
```

Figure 9.2 (continued)

```
template <typename ElementType>
void display(ElementType array[], int numElements)
/*-------------------------------------------------------------------
  Display elements of any type (for which the output operator is defined)
  stored in an array.

  Precondition:  ElementType is a type parameter.
  Postcondition: First numElements of array have been output to cout.
  --------------------------------------------------------------------*/
{
   for (int i = 0; i < numElements; i++)
      cout << array[i] << "  ";
   cout << endl;
}

int main()
{
   double x[] = {1.1, 2.2, 3.3, 4.4, 5.5};
   display(x, 5);
   int num[] = {1, 2, 3, 4};
   display(num, 4);
}
```

Execution Trace:
```
1.1  2.2  3.3  4.4  5.5
1  2  3  4
```

▲

When display(x, 5) is encountered, the compiler searches the parameter list of the function template display() and finds the type parameter ElementType. From the function call in main(), the compiler can determine that the type double (of x) should be bound to ElementType; the second parameter numElements does not involve a type parameter. Thus, the binding is complete and the compiler can generate the following instance of display():

```
void display(double array[], int numElements)
{
   for (int i = 0; i < numElements; i++)
      cout << array[i] << "  ";
   cout << endl;
}
```

In a similar manner, when it later encounters display(num, 4), the compiler generates an int version of display():

```
void display(int array[], int numElements)
{
  for (int i = 0; i < numElements; i++)
    cout << array[i] << "   ";
  cout << endl;
}
```

9.3 Class Genericity—Templates

In the preceding section we saw how it is possible to pass a type into a function template by using a type parameter. As we have noted before, it would surely improve
genericity of ADTs if we could do a similar thing with classes, especially for container
classes, where it would be convenient to be able to pass the type of the elements into
the container. In this section we show how class templates can be used in much the
same way as function templates to accomplish this. So that we can focus our attention
on how to convert a class into a class template, we will use the simplest container—a
stack—and the second class (using a dynamic array) that we developed for it in
Chapter 7. Conversions of our other versions of the Stack class, as well as classes for
other containers, follow the same procedure and are left as exercises.

What's Wrong with typedef?

For each of the *container classes* developed thus far, we used a generic name for the
container's elements and set it with the typedef mechanism. For example, for the
Stack classes, we use the generic element type StackElement and put the typedef
declaration that set it to a specific type before the class declaration (where it can easily be changed):

```
/*-- DStack.h --------------------------------------

    This header file defines a Stack data type.
    Basic operations:
       . . .
    -------------------------------------------------*/


typedef int StackElement;
class Stack
{
 public:
  /***** Function Members *****/
     . . .
  private:
  /***** Data Members *****/
     . . .
};
```

We need only change the type identifier following the keyword `typedef` to change the meaning of `StackElement` throughout the class.

There are, however, some problems with using `typedef` to gain this genericity:

- Problem 1: Since changing the `typedef` is a change to the header file, any program or library that uses the class must be recompiled.
- Problem 2 (*more serious*): Suppose we need two containers with different types of values; for example, a `Stack` of reals and a `Stack` of characters. A name declared using `typedef` can have only one meaning at a time. We would need to create two different container classes with two different names.

What we need is a way to make the container truly *type independent*. As we now show, this can be done using class templates.

Class Templates

In a **class template**, the *class is parameterized* so that it *receives the type of data stored in the class via a parameter* in much the same way that function templates parameterize functions. To convert the `Stack` class into a class template, we simply replace the `typedef` declaration preceding the class declaration with a `template` declaration like that for function templates; for example,

```
/*-- DStackT.h ------------------------------------

   This file contains a template for a Stack data type.
   StackElement is a type parameter received from a
   client program.
   Basic operations:
      . . .
   ----------------------------------------------------*/

template <typename StackElement>
class Stack
{
 public:
  /***** Function Members *****/
      . . .
 private:
  /***** Data Members *****/
      int myCapacity,
          myTop;
      StackElement * myArray;
};
```

Here, as with function templates, we can think of the type parameter StackElement as a blank type that will be filled in later:

```
template <typename _____>
class Stack
{
 public:
  /***** Function Members *****/

     . . .
 private:
  /***** Data Members *****/
 int myCapacity,
    myTop;
    _____ myArray[STACK_CAPACITY];
};
```

In general, the declaration of a class template has the following forms:

Class Template Declaration

Usual Form:

```
template <typename TypeParam>
class SomeClass
{
   // ... members of SomeClass ...
};
```

More General Form:

```
template <typename TypeParam₁,..., typename TypeParamₙ>
class SomeClass
{
   // ... members of SomeClass ...
};
```

In these forms, *TypeParam, TypeParam₁,...* are generic type parameters naming types of data to be stored in the container class *SomeClass*; and the keyword typename may be replaced with class.

Notes:

- The keyword template specifies that what follows is a *pattern* for a class, *not an actual class declaration*.

- The keywords typename and class may be used interchangeably in a type-parameter list.

- Unlike function members of regular classes, definitions of function members of a class template must be available to the compiler wherever the

---

> class template is used. A common way to accomplish this is to move all function definitions from the implementation file *ClassName*.cpp into the header file *ClassName*.h after the class declaration. An alternative is to keep them in a separate file (e.g., *ClassName*.template) and then #include that file at the end of *ClassName*.h.

A class template is only a *pattern* that describes how individual classes can be constructed from given actual types. This process of creating a class is called **instantiation**. This is accomplished by attaching the actual type to the class name in the declaration of an object:

```
SomeClass<Actual_Type> object;
```

For example, we could instantiate our Stack class template with the definitions

```
Stack<char> charStack;
Stack<double> dubStack;
```

When the compiler processes these declarations, it will generate two distinct Stack classes—two *instances*—one with StackElement replaced by char and the other with StackElement replaced by double. The constructor in the first class will construct charStack as an empty stack of characters and the constructor in the second class will construct dubStack as an empty stack of doubles.

There are three important rules that govern building class templates:

> - *All operations defined outside of the class declaration must be template functions.*
> - *Any use of the name of a template class as a type must be parameterized.*
> - *Definitions of operations for a template class must be available to the compiler wherever the class template is used.*

We will illustrate these three rules in our conversion of the dynamic-array-based Stack class from Section 7.2 into a class template.

Rule 1: *Definitions of functions outside the* Stack *class declaration must be defined as function templates.*

We defined all of the functions for our Stack *class* outside of the class declaration, and so each of these definitions must be preceded by a template declaration:

```
template <typename StackElement>
// ... definition of constructor

template <typename StackElement>
// ... definition of copy constructor

template <typename StackElement>
// ... definition of destructor

// And so on for the other function member definitions
```

Rule 2: *Wherever the class name* Stack *is used as the name of a type, it must be parameterized by appending* <StackElement> *to it.*

First of all, this rule applies to all of the functions—both prototypes and definitions—for which some parameter is of type Stack or the return type is Stack. In our class, these are the copy constructor and the assignment operator (and the output operator added in Figure 9.3):

```
template <typename StackElement>
class Stack
{
  ...
  // Copy constructor
  Stack(const Stack<StackElement> & original);
  ...
  // Assignment operator
  const Stack<StackElement> & operator=(
                        const Stack<StackElement> & original);
  ...
};
```

Rule 2 also applies to all uses of the class name preceding the scope operator (::) in function definitions:

```
template <typename StackElement>
Stack<StackElement>::Stack()
{ // ... definition of constructor }

template <typename StackElement>
Stack<StackElement>::Stack(const Stack<StackElement> & original)
{ // ... definition of copy constructor }

template <typename StackElement>
Stack<StackElement>::~Stack
{ // ... definition of destructor }

// And so on for the other function member definitions
```

Rule 3: *The preceding function template definitions must be available to the compiler wherever the class template is used.*

Figure 9.3 shows one way of satisfying this rule: put the template functions definitions below the class declaration in the file StackT.h. This ensures that, wherever StackT.h is included, the definitions also will be. Note that some of the simple functions have been inlined to avoid the overhead of function calls as described in Section 7.4.

It should be noted that

 Non-member functions are also governed by the three rules.

For example, in Figure 9.3, the output operator has been added as a non-member function:

```
//--- Definition of operator<<()
template <typename StackElement>
inline ostream & operator<<(ostream & out,
                            const Stack<StackElement> & st)
{
   st.display(out);
   return out;
}
```

It has been converted to a function template and the use of Stack as the type of its argument st has been parameterized.

Figure 9.3 A Stack Class Template

```
/*-- DStackT.h ---------------------------------------------------------
   This header file defines a template for a Stack data type.
   StackElement is a type parameter received from a client program.
   Basic operations:
      constructor:       Constructs an empty stack
      copy constructor:  Makes a copy of a stack
      destructor:        Deallocates memory allocated by constructor
      = :                Assignment operator
      empty:             Checks if a stack is empty
      push:              Modifies a stack by adding a value at the top
      top:               Accesses the top stack value; leaves stack unchanged
      pop:               Modifies stack by removing the value at the top
      << and display:    Displays all the stack elements

   Class Invariant:
      1. The stack elements (if any) are stored in positions
         0, 1, . . ., myTop of myArray.
      2. -1 <= myTop < myCapacity
--------------------------------------------------------------------*/


#include <iostream>
#include <cassert>

#ifndef DSTACKT
#define DSTACKT
```

Figure 9.3 (continued)

```
template <typename StackElement>
class Stack
{
 public:
/***** Function Members *****/
/***** Constructors *****/

  Stack(int numElements = 128);
  /*----------------------------------------------------------------
    Construct a Stack object.

    Precondition:  None.
    Postcondition: An empty Stack object has been constructed (myTop is
        initialized to -1 and myArray is an array with numElements
        (default 128) elements of type StackElement).
    ---------------------------------------------------------------*/


  Stack(const Stack<StackElement> & original);
  /*----------------------------------------------------------------
    Copy Constructor

    Precondition:  original is the stack to be copied and is received as
        a const reference parameter.
    Postcondition: A copy of original has been constructed.
    ---------------------------------------------------------------*/


/***** Destructor *****/
  ~Stack();
  /*----------------------------------------------------------------
    Class destructor

    Precondition:  None
    Postcondition: The dynamic array in the stack has been deallocated.
    ---------------------------------------------------------------*/


/***** Assignment *****/
  const Stack<StackElement> & operator=(
                        const Stack<StackElement> & rightHandSide);
  /*----------------------------------------------------------------
    Assignment Operator
```

Figure 9.3 (continued)

Precondition: rightHandSide is the stack to be assigned and is received as
    a const reference parameter.
Postcondition: The current stack becomes a copy of rightHandSide and a
    const reference to it is returned.
```
------------------------------------------------------------------------*/
```

```cpp
bool empty() const;
```
```
/*--------------------------------------------------------------------
```
Check if stack is empty.

Precondition: None
Postcondition: Returns true if stack is empty and false otherwise.
```
------------------------------------------------------------------------*/
```

```cpp
void push(const StackElement & value);
```
```
/*--------------------------------------------------------------------
```
Add a value to a stack.

Precondition: value is to be added to this stack
Postcondition: value is added at top of stack provided there is space;
    otherwise, a stack-full message is displayed and execution is
    terminated.
```
------------------------------------------------------------------------*/
```

```cpp
void display(ostream & out) const;
```
```
/*--------------------------------------------------------------------
```
Display values stored in the stack.

Precondition: ostream out is open.
Postcondition: Stack's contents, from top down, have been output to out.
```
------------------------------------------------------------------------*/
```

```cpp
StackElement top() const;
```
```
/*--------------------------------------------------------------------
```
Retrieve value at top of stack (if any).

Precondition: Stack is nonempty
Postcondition: Value at top of stack is returned, unless the stack is
    empty; in that case, an error message is displayed and a "garbage
    value" is returned.
```
------------------------------------------------------------------------*/
```

Figure 9.3 (continued)

```
  void pop();
  /*-----------------------------------------------------------------------
    Remove value at top of stack (if any).

    Precondition:  Stack is nonempty.
    Postcondition: Value at top of stack has been removed, unless the
        stack is empty; in that case, error message is displayed and
        execution allowed to proceed.
    --------------------------------------------------------------------*/


 private:
 /***** Data Members *****/
  int myCapacity,           // capacity of stack
      myTop;                // top of stack
  StackElement * myArray;   // dynamic array to store elements


}; // end of class declaration


//====== FUNCTION DEFINITIONS ======
#include <new>

//--- Definition of Stack constructor
template <typename StackElement>
Stack<StackElement>::Stack(int numElements)
{
   assert (numElements > 0);  // check precondition
   myCapacity = numElements;  // set stack capacity
                              // allocate array with this capacity
   myArray = new(nothrow) StackElement[myCapacity];
   if (myArray != 0)          // memory available
      myTop = -1;
   else
   {
      cerr << "Inadequate memory to allocate stack \n"
              " -- terminating execution\n";
      exit(1);
   }                          // or assert(myArray != 0);
}
```

Figure 9.3 (continued)

```
//--- Definition of Stack copy constructor
template <typename StackElement>
Stack<StackElement>::Stack(const Stack<StackElement> & original)
: myCapacity(original.myCapacity), myTop(original.myTop)
{
   //--- Get new array for copy
   myArray = new(nothrow) StackElement[myCapacity];
   if (myArray != 0)                       // check if memory available
      // copy original's array member into this new array
      for (int pos = 0; pos <= myTop; pos++)
         myArray[pos] = original.myArray[pos];
   else
   {
      cerr << "*Inadequate memory to allocate stack ***\n";
      exit(1);
   }
}


//--- Definition of Stack destructor
template <typename StackElement>
inline Stack<StackElement>::~Stack()
{
   delete[] myArray;
}


//--- Definition of assignment operator
template <typename StackElement>
const Stack<StackElement> & Stack<StackElement>::
                     operator=(const Stack<StackElement> & rightHandSide)
{
   if (this != &rightHandSide)                        // check that not st = st
   {
      //-- Allocate a new array if necessary
      if (myCapacity != rightHandSide.myCapacity)
      {
         delete[] myArray;                            // destroy previous array

         myCapacity = rightHandSide.myCapacity;   // copy myCapacity
```

Figure 9.3 (continued)

```cpp
         myArray = new StackElement[myCapacity];
         if (myArray == 0)                      // check if memory available
         {
            cerr << "*** Inadequate memory ***\n";
            exit(1);
         }
       }

     myTop = rightHandSide.myTop;              // copy myTop member
     for (int pos = 0; pos <= myTop; pos++)   // copy stack elements
        myArray[pos] = rightHandSide.myArray[pos];

  }
  return *this;
}


//--- Definition of empty()
template <typename StackElement>
inline bool Stack<StackElement>::empty() const
{
   return (myTop == -1);
}


//--- Definition of push()
template <typename StackElement>
inline void Stack<StackElement>::push(const StackElement & value)
{
   if (myTop < myCapacity - 1)        //Preserve stack invariant
   {
      ++myTop;
      myArray[myTop] = value;
   }
   else
   {
      cerr << "*** Stack full -- can't add new value ***\n"
              "Must increase Stack's capacity\n";
      exit(1);
   }
}
```

Figure 9.3 (continued)

```
//--- Definition of display()
template <typename StackElement>
inline void Stack<StackElement>::display(ostream & out) const
{
  for (int i = myTop; i >= 0; i--)
    out << myArray[i] << endl;
}


//--- Definition of operator<<()
template <typename StackElement>
inline ostream & operator<<(ostream & out,
                            const Stack<StackElement> & st)
{
   st.display(out);
   return out;
}


//--- Definition of top()
template <typename StackElement>
inline StackElement Stack<StackElement>::top() const
{
   if ( !empty() )
      return (myArray[myTop]);
   else
   {
      cerr << "*** Stack is empty -- returning garbage value ***\n";
      StackElement garbage;
      return garbage;
   }
}


//--- Definition of pop()
template <typename StackElement>
inline void Stack<StackElement>::pop()
{
  if (myTop >= 0)     // Preserve stack invariant
    myTop--;
```

Figure 9.3 (continued)

```
  else
    cerr << "*** Stack is empty -- can't remove a value ***\n";
}


#endif
```

▲

Figure 9.4 shows a test driver program for our Stack class template. It uses the class template to instantiate a stack of ints and a stack of chars.

Figure 9.4 Test Driver for the Stack Class Template

```
/*---------------------------------------------------------------------
                    Driver program to test the Stack class.
  ---------------------------------------------------------------------*/

#include <iostream>
#include <iomanip>
using namespace std;

#include "DStackT.h"

template <typename T>
void print(Stack<T> st)
{ st.display(cout); }

int main()
{
   int cap;
   cout << "Enter stack capacity: ";
   cin >> cap;

   Stack<int> intSt;    // stack of ints
   Stack<char> charSt;  // stack of chars
   for (int i = 1; i <= 4; i++)
     intSt.push(100*i);
   cout << intSt << endl;
```

Figure 9.4 (continued)

```
for (char ch = 'A'; ch <= 'D'; ch++)
   charSt.push(ch);
cout << charSt << endl;

cout << "Contents of stack intSt (via print):\n";
print(intSt); cout << endl;

Stack<int> t;
t = intSt;
cout << "Contents of stack t after t = stInt (via print):\n";
print(t); cout << endl;

cout << "Stack t empty? " << boolalpha << t.empty() << endl;

cout << "Top value in t: " << t.top() << endl;

while (!t.empty())
{
  cout << "Popping t:  " << t.top() << endl;
  t.pop();
}
cout << "Stack t empty? " << t.empty() << endl;
cout << "Top value in t: " << t.top() << endl;
cout << "Trying to pop t: " << endl;
t.pop();
}
```

Execution Trace:

```
Enter stack capacity: 5
400
300
200
100
```

Figure 9.4 (continued)

```
D
C
B
A

Contents of stack intSt (via print):
400
300
200
100

Contents of stack t after t = stInt (via print):
400
300
200
100


Stack t empty? false
Top value in t: 400
Popping t:   400
Popping t:   300
Popping t:   200
Popping t:   100
Stack t empty? true
*** Stack is empty -- returning garbage value ***
Top value in t: 0
Trying to pop t:
*** Stack is empty -- can't remove a value ***
```

▲

 In our discussion of the three rules for building class templates, it is important to understand the differences between the name of a class template, parameterizing that name, and instantiating it. The following example may help:

`Stack`	This is the name of a class template, a pattern for a class. It *is never* the name of a type (a class).
`Stack<StackElement>`	This is a parameterized name of a class template; it *becomes* a type (a class) when a specific type replaces the type parameter `StackElement`.

Stack<double>   This *is* a type (a class) and can be used to declare
stacks whose elements are doubles.

An Alternative Version of the Stack Class Template

Our examples of function templates in the preceding section and of class templates in this section each had only one type parameter in the template declaration. However, as we noted in the general forms of template declarations, *templates may have more than one type parameter; they may also have ordinary value parameters.*

This property makes it possible to convert the first version of a Stack class in Chapter 7 that uses a static array into a class template for which the user can specify the capacity of a stack in its declaration and pass this into the Stack class template as an int parameter along with the stack element type:

```
/*-- StackT.h ---------------------------------------------------
    Defines a template for a Stack data type.
    Receives type parameter StackElement and constant int
        STACK_CAPACITY.
       . . .
    ---------------------------------------------------------------*/

//  #includes

    template <typename StackElement, const int STACK_CAPACITY>
    class Stack
    {
     public:
      /***** Function Members *****/
      //... Prototypes of function members ...

     private:
      /***** Data Members *****/
       StackElement myArray[STACK_CAPACITY];
       int myTop;
    }; // end of class declaration

    /*
      Definitions of function templates, each preceded by
      template <typename StackElement, const int STACK_CAPACITY>
      and all occurrences of Stack as a type parameterized with
      Stack<StackElement, STACK_CAPACITY>
    */
```

This will allow definitions of stacks such as the following in client programs:

```
    const int CAP = 10;
    Stack<int, CAP> intSt;     // stack of at most 10 ints
    Stack<string, 3> strSt;    // stack of at most 3 strings
```

A Quick Peek at the Standard C++ Container Class Templates

As we have seen, class templates are type-independent patterns from which actual classes can be defined, and this is especially useful for defining *generic container classes*—classes whose objects store (i.e., contain) other objects. In the early 1990s, Alex Stepanov and Meng Lee of Hewlett Packard Laboratories extended C++ with a library of class and function templates, which has come to be known as the **Standard Template Library (STL).** In 1994, the ANSI/ISO standards committee adopted STL as part of standard C++.

The Standard Template Library has three different kinds of components:

- **Container class templates:** A group of class templates that provide standardized, generic, off-the-shelf structures for storing data
- **Iterators:** Generalized pointers that provide a generic way to access container elements and move from one element to another
- **Algorithm templates:** A group of function templates that provide standardized, generic, off-the-shelf functions for performing many of the most common operations on container objects

For the algorithms in STL to be truly generic, they must be able to operate on any container. To make this possible, each container provides iterators for the algorithms to use. Iterators thus provide the interface that is needed for STL algorithms to operate on STL containers.

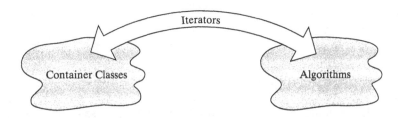

The Standard Template Library provides a rich variety of containers. Table 9.1 gives a brief description of these containers and indicates how they differ from one another. Each container has properties and operations that make it particularly useful for a large category of problems. In subsequent sections we will look at vector, deque, stack, and queue, including a brief first look at iterators. The list container is described in Chapter 11, maps are described briefly in Chapter 15, and the other containers are left for more advanced courses in data structures and algorithms. We will look at some of the STL's algorithms in Section 10.5.

The C++ standard also includes bitset and valarray as containers, but these are not a part of STL. Arrays, strings, valarrays, and bitsets have been termed by Bjarne Stroustrup, the creator of C++, as *almost containers*, and by others as *near containers*, because although they do contain elements, they do not share all of features of the interfaces of the STL containers. For example, the type of the elements of a string object is limited and string is most efficient for processing strings of characters. We have already considered arrays and strings in an earlier chapter and will briefly describe valarrays and bitsets in Section 9.8.

TABLE 9.1: STL's Containers

Containers	Description
vector	A dynamic-array-based class template that can grow when necessary; fast inserts and deletes only at the end
deque	Provides most of the same operations as vector, but does not use continguous memory allocation; fast inserts and deletes at both the beginning and the end
list	Stores list elements in a linked list; fast inserts and deletes anywhere
set	A set of objects, fast associative lookup, with no duplicates allowed
multiset	Same as set, but duplicates are allowed
map	Maps objects of one type into objects of another type in a 1-to-1 manner (a no-duplicate associative array)
multimap	Maps objects of one type into objects of another type in a 1-to-many manner (associative array with duplicates)
stack	A stack
queue	A queue
priority_queue	A priority queue

✔ Quick Quiz 9.3

1. A name that is used for different functions is said to be _____.
2. The following function prototypes may be in the same library. (True or false)

   char f(int x, int y);   char f(int x, char y);

3. The following function prototypes may be in the same library. (True or false)

   int f(int x, int y);   char f(int x, int y);

4. _____ make it possible for classes and functions to receive not only data values to be stored or operated on via parameters but also to receive the type of data via a parameter.
5. template <_____ T> is an example of a template declaration.
6. The process of constructing a function from a function template or a class from a class template is called _____.
7. Describe two problems with using the typedef mechanism to set the element type for a container class.
8. List the three rules that govern class templates.
9. STL is an acronym for _____.

10. STL was developed by Alex Stepanov and Meng Lee. (True or false)

11. What are the three components of STL?

12. _____ provide the interface between STL algorithms and STL containers.

◆ Exercises 9.3

Exercises 1–9 ask you to write templates. To test them you should write driver programs as instructed in Programming Problems 1–9 at the end of this chapter.

1. Write a function template to find the average of two values. (The average of a and b is $(a + b) / 2$.)

2. Write a function template to find the maximum of two values.

3. The *median* of three numbers is the middle number after the three numbers have been arranged in increasing order. Write a function template that finds the median of three values.

4. Write a function template `arraySum()` that accepts an array and the number of values stored in it and returns the sum of those values.

5. Write a function template `arrayMaxMin()` that accepts an array and the number of values stored in it and passes back the maximum and minimum of those values.

6. Write a function template `arraySearch()` that accepts an array, the number of values stored in it, and an item of the same type as the array elements, and then searches the values in the array for that item. It should return true if the item is found and false otherwise.

7. Convert one of the list classes from Chapter 6 to a class template.

8. Convert one of the queue classes from Chapter 8 to a class template.

9. Modify the class `CartesianPoint` from Exercise 4 of Section 4.5 to make it a class template in which the type parameter represents the type of the coordinates of points.

9.4 The vector Container[2]

The vector container can be thought of as an array class template that has an expandable capacity and a large set of built-in operations. Because many of these operations are powerful and useful to a C++ programmer, we will describe this container in considerable detail. If you have already studied vector in an earlier programming course, you can use this section for review and reference.

A much simplified form of vector's declaration as a class template in the standard library might look something like the following:

```
template <typename T>
class vector
{
  public:
    //===== Large collection of function members
```

---

[2] Parts of this section are reproduced from Joel Adams and Larry Nyhoff, *C++: An Introduction to Programming*, 3d ed., Prentice Hall, Inc., Upper Saddle River, NJ, 2003.

```
    private:
     //===== Data members, one of which is a dynamic array
     T * myArray;
    };
```

Here, T is a parameter for the type of values to be stored in the container.

The vector class template is declared in the standard <vector> library, which must be included in any program that uses vectors:

```
    #include <vector>
```

This allows us to make declarations like the following:

```
    vector<double> vec1;
    vector<string> vec2;
```

When the compiler processes the first declaration, it will create an instance of class vector with each occurrence of T replaced by double and will then use this class to construct an object vec1 whose elements will be doubles. Similarly, from the second declaration, the compiler will create another instance of class vector with each occurrence of T replaced by string and will then use this class to construct the object vec2 whose elements will be strings.

Declaring vector Objects

There are several constructors in vector, which make it possible to define vector objects in several different ways. In the following descriptions, *ElementType* is any data type; *initCap* is an integer expression; *initVal* is of type *ElementType*; *firstPtr* and *lastPtr* are pointers bound to type *ElementType*.

TABLE 9.2: vector **Constructors**

Declaration	Description
vector<*ElementType*> *objectName*;	Construct an empty vector
vector<*ElementType*> *objectName*(*initCap*);	Construct a vector with capacity = *initCap* and elements initialized by the default constructor for *ElementType*
vector<*ElementType*> *objectName*(*initCap*, *initVal*);	Like the preceding but initializes each element with *initVal*
vector<*ElementType*> *objectName*(*firstPtr*, *lastPtr*);	Construct a vector initialized with the contents of the memory location pointed to by *firstPtr* up to (but not including) that pointed to by *lastPtr*.

For example, the definition

```
    vector<double> dubVector;
```

constructs an empty vector<double> object dubVector. This means that its capacity is initially 0. However, its capacity can increase when necessary (as we will describe later) to store double elements.

Now consider a definition of the second kind:

```
int n;
cin >> n;
vector<double> dubVector(n);
```

Here, dubVector is constructed as a vector that contains n zeroes, since the default constructor for type double, double(), gives 0. Its initial capacity and size (number of values it stores) are thus both equal to n. For example, if the value 4 is entered for n, we can picture dubVector as follows:

```
dubVector  | 0 | 0 | 0 | 0 |
            [0] [1] [2] [3]
```

If we change the definition of dubVector to

```
int n;
double dubValue;
cin >> n >> dubValue;
vector<double> dubVector(n, dubValue);
```

dubVector will be filled with the value entered for dubValue. For example, if we enter 4 for n and 1.1 for dubValue, dubVector will contain four copies of 1.1:

```
dubVector |1.1|1.1|1.1|1.1|
           [0] [1] [2] [3]
```

The last kind of definition constructs a vector object that is initialized with the contents of the memory locations specified by the range of addresses pointed to by *first_ptr* up to *but not including* *last_ptr*. For example, consider the following definition of an array a of doubles and the definition of vector<double> object dubVector:

```
double a[] = {1.1, 2.2, 4.4, 8.8};
vector<double> dubVector(a, a+4);
```

Here, dubVector is constructed as a vector of doubles that contains copies of the double values in the range [a, a+4), that is, copies of a[0], a[1], a[2], a[3]. We might picture this construction as follows:

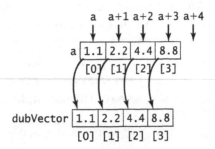

Some vector Operations

Built into vector is a rich set of operations. As we shall see, these operations allow a vector object to be treated much like an array, but without the limitations of arrays described in Chapter 3. Table 9.3 lists some of these operations; in the descriptions, *v*, *v1*, and *v2* are vectors with some specified type *T*; value is of type *T*; *i* and *n* are non-negative integers.

TABLE 9.3: Selected vector Operations

Operation	Description
v.capacity()	Return the number of locations *v* currently has
v.size()	Return the number of values currently stored in *v*
v.max_size()	Return the maximum number of locations *v* can ever have
v.empty()	Return true if and only if *v* contains no values (i.e., *v*'s size is 0)
v.reserve(*n*);	Grow *v* so that its capacity is *n* (does not affect *v*'s size)
v.push_back(*value*);	Append value at *v*'s end
v.pop_back();	Erase *v*'s last element
v.front()	Return a reference to *v*'s first element
v.back()	Return a reference to *v*'s last element
v[*i*]	Access the element of *v* whose index is *i*—no bounds checking of index is done
v.at(*i*)	Access the element of *v* whose index is *i*—bounds checking is done—throws out-of-range exception if index is out of range
v1 = v2	Assign a copy of *v2* to *v1*
v1.swap(*v2*)	Swap *v1*'s contents with *v2*'s
v1 == v2	Return true if and only if *v1* has the same values as *v2*, in the same order
v1 < v2	Return true if and only if *v1* is lexicographically less than *v2*

Information About a vector's Contents The first group of operations illustrates that, in contrast to C-style arrays, vectors are self-contained objects that can provide information about themselves:

- v.size() returns the number of values stored in *v*. As with C-style arrays, *the index of the first value of a* vector *is always 0*; but unlike a C-style array, which provides no way to identify its final value, *the index of the final value in a* vector *object v is always* v.size()-1.

- v.empty() is a simple alternative to the boolean expression v.size() == 0.

- `v.capacity()` returns the current capacity of `v`.
- `v.reserve()` can be used to set or increase (but not decrease) the capacity of `v`.

The following examples illustrate some of these operations:

```
vector<double> v;
cout << v.capacity() << ' ' << v.size() << ' '
    << v.max_size();
```

OUTPUT:
0 0 536870911

```
vector<double> v(3);
cout << v.capacity() << ' ' << v.size() << endl;
```

OUTPUT:
3 3

```
vector<double> v(3, 4.0);
cout << v.capacity() << ' ' << v.size() << endl
    << v.reserve(6)
    << v.capacity() << ' ' << v.size() << endl
```

OUTPUT:
3 3
6 3

Adding, Removing, and Accessing Elements   The second group of operations shows how values can be added to and removed from the end of a `vector` and how the first and last elements can be accessed:

- `v.push_back(value);` appends a copy of `value` to the end of `v`, increasing its size by 1. If necessary, the capacity of `v` is increased to accommodate the new value. As we will explain later, the amount of increase depends on the current capacity.
- `v.pop_back();` removes the last value in `v` by decreasing the size of `v` by 1 (and calling the value's destructor if it is an object). The capacity of `v` does not change.
- `v.front()` and `v.back()` access the first and last values in a `v`, respectively. These function members actually return references to the first and last values and not copies of these values. This means that the first and last elements of `v` can be modified by changing the values of `v.front()` and `v.back()`.

The following examples illustrate the use of these functions:

```
vector<double> v;
v.push_back(1.1); v.push_back(2.2); v.push_back(3.3);
cout << v.front() << ' ' << v.back() << endl;
v.pop_back();
cout << v.front() << ' ' << v.back() << endl;
```

```
v.front() = 4.4;   v.back() = 5.5;
cout << v.front() << ' ' << v.back() << endl;
```

OUTPUT:

```
1.1 3.3
1.1 2.2
4.4 5.5
```

The subscript operator is used in much the same manner as for arrays and string objects. For example, the following loop for displaying the values stored in a vector object v is almost the same as for arrays:

```
for (int i = 0; i < v.size(); i++)
   cout << v[i] << endl;
```

Also, as with C-style arrays, no check is made of the index to determine whether vector indices are in bounds—that is, in the range 0 through v.size() - 1. The effect of using an out-of-range index is system dependent. An alternative is to use the at() method, which throws an out_of_range exception if the index is out of bounds; for example,

```
try
{
   for (int i = a; i < b; i++)
      v.at(i) = v.at(i + 1);
}
// . . .
catch(out_of_range ex)
{
   cerr << "Index out of range\n";
}
```

If either of the indices i or i + 1 goes out of bounds, the out_of_range exception that is thrown causes execution of the try block to terminate and the catch block to be executed. (Exceptions and try and catch blocks were described in Section 3.4.)

It is important to remember that *using the subscript operator to append values to a* vector *will not update the* vector's *size nor will it cause its capacity to increase when the vector is full. Whenever possible, use* push_back() *(or* insert()) *to add values to a* vector because they update the vector's size and will trigger an increase in its capacity when necessary.[3] The following function template for inputting values into a vector shows how this is done:

```
template <typename T>
void read(istream & in, vector<T> & aVector)
/*-------------------------------------------------
   Read values from an istream into a vector.
```

---

[3] These methods also correctly update the iterator returned by end(), but the subscript operator does not. STL algorithms will thus not work properly if subscript is used to add values to a vector.

```
      Precondition:  T is a type parameter; << is
          defined for type T; istream in is open.
      Postcondition: Values are extracted from in
          and added to aVector.
    ----------------------------------------------*/
{
   T inputValue;

   for (;;)
   {
      in >> inputValue;
      if (in.eof()) break;

      aVector.push_back(inputValue);
   }
}
```

Only after a `vector` contains values should the subscript operator be used to access (or change) those values, for example, in an output function template such as the following:

```
template <typename T>
void display(ostream & out, const vector<T> & aVector)
/*------------------------------------------------
   Output values stored in a vector to an ostream.

   Precondition:  T is a type parameter T; << is
      defined for type T; ostream out is open.
   Postcondition: Values stored in aVector have
      been output to out.
    ----------------------------------------------*/
{
   for (int i = 0; i < aVector.size(); i++)
      out << aVector[i] << ' ';
}
```

Assignment and Swapping The assignment operator (=) behaves as one would expect:

```
      v1 = v2;
```

will change v1 to a copy of v2 after first destroying any previous value assigned to v1.

v1	0	1	2	3	
	[0]	[1]	[2]	[3]	

v1 = v2; →

v1	1	3	5	7	9
	[0]	[1]	[2]	[3]	[4]

v2	1	3	5	7	9
	[0]	[1]	[2]	[3]	[4]

v2	1	3	5	7	9
	[0]	[1]	[2]	[3]	[4]

To interchange the values of two `vector` variables `v1` and `v2` we could use code like that in the `swap()` functions we wrote in Section 9.2:

```
vector<T> temp = v1;
v1 = v2;
v2 = temp;
```

But it is simpler to use the `swap()` method:

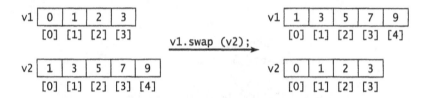

Relational Operators The equality operator (`==`) compares two `vectors` element by element and returns true if and only if they are identical—that is, only if their sizes match and their values match. It assumes that `==` is defined for the element type of the `vectors`. The less-than operator (`<`) also assumes that `<` is defined for the element type. It behaves much like the `string` less-than operation, performing an element-by-element comparison until a mismatch (if any) occurs. If the mismatched element in the first operand is less than the corresponding element in the second operand, the operation returns true; otherwise, it returns false. If all the elements of both `vectors` are compared and no mismatch is found, the operation returns false. For example, a comparison using the less-than operator as in

```
if (v2 < v1)
// ... do something appropriate
```

returns true for the following `vector<int>` objects `v1` and `v2` because at the first index (2) where the elements of `v1` and `v2` differ, the value (3) in `v2` is less than the value (4) in `v1`. The comparison `v1 < v2` would return false.

```
v1  | 1 | 2 | 4 | 8 |
     [0] [1] [2] [3]

v2  | 1 | 2 | 3 | 4 | 5 |
     [0] [1] [2] [3] [4]
```

A First Look Under the Hood—Increasing the Capacity

As we have noted, when a `vector` v becomes full—that is, `v.size()` `==` `v.capacity()` —and a new object is added by means of a `push_back()` (or `insert()`) operation, the capacity of the `vector` is increased automatically to accommodate the new elements. The algorithm used for this is as follows:

 ## Algorithm for Increasing the Capacity of a vector<T>

1. Allocate a new array to store the vector's elements.
2. Copy all existing elements (using the T copy constructor) to the new array.
3. Store the item being added in the new array.
4. Destroy the old array in the vector<T>.
5. Make the new array the vector<T>'s storage array.

We will now explore each of these five steps in more detail.

Step 1: Allocate a New Array to Store the vector's Elements How large should the array be? The simplest and most spacewise-efficient scheme would be to allocate just enough for the new object(s); that is, request space for v.size() + 1 elements. However, this would be a serious mistake if it happens often, because the next step is expensive. Thus, more memory is usually requested than is actually needed.

We consider first the following example, in which the vector v is empty:

```cpp
vector<double> v;
cout << v.capacity() << ' ' << v.size() << endl;
for (int i = 1; i <= 20; i++)
{
   v.push_back(i + 0.5);
   cout << v.capacity() << ' ' << v.size() << endl;
}
```

When these statements were executed (in GNU C++, CodeWarrior C++, and Visual C++), the output produced was

```
0  0
1  1  ← space for 1 double allocated
2  2  ← space for 2 doubles allocated
4  3  ← space for 4 doubles allocated
4  4
8  5  ← space for 8 doubles allocated
8  6
8  7
8  8
16  9  ← space for 16 doubles allocated
16  10
16  11
16  12
16  13
16  14
16  15
```

```
16 16
32 17 ← space for 32 doubles allocated
32 18
32 19
32 20
```

The first increase in the capacity was from 0 to 1, the second from 1 to 2, the third from 2 to 4, the fourth from 4 to 8, and so on. After the first increase, each time the capacity needed to be increased, it was doubled.

Now consider the case in which the vector is not empty. If we change the definition of v to vector<double> v(3, 0); then the output changes as follows:

```
3 3
6 4 ← capacity doubles
6 5
6 6
12 7 ← capacity doubles
12 8
   .
   .
   .
12 12
24 13 ← capacity doubles
   .
   .
   .
```

We see that in each case, the *capacity doubles when more space is needed*. This is a compromise between allocating small blocks of memory (which wastes time) and allocating large blocks of memory (which wastes space if only a few elements are needed). This also makes it possible to control somewhat the amount by which the capacity grows, by defining the vector object with a preallocated capacity or by using reserve() to set the capacity. For example, preallocating a capacity of 3 for vector<double> v forces the first new allocation to be a block of capacity 6:

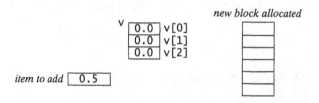

Step 2: Copy all Existing Elements (Using the T Copy Constructor) to the New Array If the insertion point is not at the end of the vector, all elements up to, but not including, the insertion point are copied into the new storage space; then all elements from the insertion point to the end of the vector (if any) are copied, with one

element skipped in the new vector, so there is room for the new object. The following diagram illustrates adding an element using push_back();

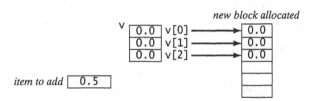

Step 3: Store the Item Being Added in the New Array   The item is copied to this location (using T's copy constructor). The following diagram illustrates appending the new item to v:

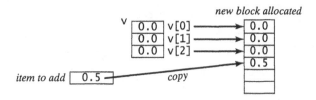

Step 4: Destroy the Old Array in the vector   Each element stored in the old array inside v is destroyed (using the T destructor), and the memory allocated for the array is reclaimed.

Step 5: Make the New Array the vector's Storage Array   Update the data members of v so that the new array becomes the array data member used to store the elements of v:

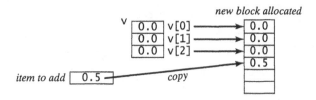

A First Look at Iterators

Although the subscript operator can be used to access the elements of a vector, this is not a generic way to access elements in containers (e.g., it cannot be used for a list). If an STL algorithm is to work on *any* STL container, some truly generic means of accessing the elements in a container is required. For this purpose, STL provides objects called **iterators** that can point at an element in a container, access the value within that element, and move from one element to another. The C++ standard defines them this way:

> *Iterators are a generalization of pointers that allow a C++ program to work with different data structures (containers) in a uniform manner.*

Each STL container provides an `iterator` type and (at least) two methods that return iterators:

- `begin()`: returns an iterator positioned at the first element in the container
- `end()`: returns an iterator positioned past the last element in the container

To illustrate, after the statements

```
vector<int> v;          // empty vector
v.push_back(9);         // append 9
v.push_back(8);         // append 8
v.push_back(7);         // append 7
```

are executed, `v.begin()` and `v.end()` produce iterators that we might picture as follows:

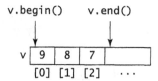

Since the type `iterator` is defined inside a container class, it must be preceded by the name of the class and the scope operator (`::`) when it is used outside the container class declaration. For example, the statement

```
vector<int>::iterator vecIter = v.begin();
```

defines `vecIter` as an iterator positioned at the first element of v:

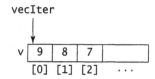

The basic operators that can be applied to iterators are described in Table 9.4.

TABLE 9.4: Iterator Operators

Operator	Description
For iterators in general:	
Increment (++)	Moves the iterator from its current position to the next element of the container; may be applied either as a prefix or postfix operator.
Decrement (--)	Moves the iterator from its current position to the preceding element of the container; may be applied either as a prefix or postfix operator.

TABLE 9.4: Iterator Operators (continued)

Operator	Description
Dereferencing (*)	Accesses the value stored at the position to which the iterator points; applied as a prefix operator.
For *random-access iterators* such as those in vector:	
Assignment (=)	For iterators of the same type, it1 = it2 sets it1's position to the same as it2's position.
Equality comparisons (== and !=)	For iterators of the same type, it1 == it2 is true if it1 and it2 are both positioned at the same element.
Addition (+), subtraction (-), corresponding assignment operators (+=, -=)	For iterator it and integer n (may be negative), it + n returns an iterator positioned n elements from it's current position.
Subscript operator ([])	For iterator it and integer n (may be negative), it[n] returns a reference to the nth element from it's current position.

The following statements illustrate several of these operators:

```
vector<double> v;
for (int i = 2; i <= 5; i++)
   v.push_back(2.2 * i);

vector<double>::iterator it, it1, it2;

for (it = v.begin(); it != v.end(); it++)
   cout << *it << ' ';
cout << " <--- original vector\n";

it1 = v.begin(), it2 = v.end();
*it1 = 1.1;
*(it2 - 1) = 9.9;
for (it = v.begin(); it != v.end(); it++)
   cout << *it << ' ';
cout << " <--- modify first & last via iterators\n";

it1 += 3;
it2 -= 3;
cout << *it1 << ' ' << *it2 << " <--- jump\n";
it1--;
++it2;
cout << *it1 << ' ' << *it2 << " <--- inc & dec\n";;
cout << it1[1] << ' ' << it1[-1] << " <--- subscript\n";
```

OUTPUT:
```
4.4 6.6 8.8 11  <--- original vector
1.1 6.6 8.8 9.9  <--- modify first & last via iterators
9.9 6.6 <--- jump
8.8 8.8 <--- inc & dec
9.9 6.6 <--- subscript
```

Now suppose we want to use output statements like those in the preceding code segment in an alternative version of the function template display() given earlier in this section, using iterators instead of indices. That version of display() began as follows:

```
template <typename T>
void display(ostream & out, const vector<T> & aVector)
```

Here, aVector is a constant reference parameter and thus cannot be modified by display(). However, as the earlier code demonstrates, iterators can modify a vector's elements. What are needed are **const iterators**, which are iterators that may not change the container in any way. And STL containers do provide a type **const_iterator** for this purpose. The following version of display() uses the const iterators provided by vector to iterate through the elements of aVector:

```
template <typename T>
void display(ostream & out, const vector<T> & aVector)
/*-----------------------------------------------------------
   Output values stored in a vector to an ostream.
   A const iterator is used to move through the vector.

   Precondition:  T is a type parameter T; << is
       defined for type T; ostream out is open.
   Postcondition: Values stored in aVector have been
       output to out.
   -----------------------------------------------------------*/
{
  for (vector<T>::const_iterator it = aVector.begin();
                     it != aVector.end(); it++)
    out << *it << ' ';
}
```

Unlike the earlier version of display() (which requires the subscript operator), this function template can be made into a generic display() *algorithm template* that allows the values in almost *any* STL container to be output to an ostream:

```
template <typename Container>
void display(ostream & out, const Container & cont)
/*-----------------------------------------------------------
   Output values stored in Container cont to an ostream.
   A const iterator is used to move through cont.
```

```
    Precondition:  Container is a type parameter; it
        provides a const_iterator and << is defined
        for it's element type; ostream out is open;
    Postcondition: Values stored in cont have been
        output to out.
    ----------------------------------------------------*/
 {
    for (Container::const_iterator it = cont.begin();
                            it != cont.end(); it++)
       out << *it << ' ';
 }
```

There is another kind of iterator called a **reverse iterator** that should be mentioned. Its purpose is to reverse the action of ++ to facilitate iterating through the container from the last element to the first. To illustrate its use, the following code outputs the elements of a vector<double> object in reverse order:

```
    for (vector<double>::reverse_iterator it = v.rbegin();
                            it != v.rend(); it++)
       cout << *it << ' ';
    cout << endl;
```

Here, v.rbegin() is a reverse iterator positioned at the last element of v and v.rend() is a reverse iterator positioned just before v's first element.

Some vector Methods Involving Iterators

Now that we have been introduced to STL's iterators, we have the background needed to understand a group of vector methods shown in Table 9.5 that utilize iterators. We conclude our study of the vector class template with brief descriptions and illustrations of these operators; in the descriptions, v is a vector with some specified type T; *value* is of type T; n is an integer; *iter*, *iter1*, and *iter2* are iterators.

TABLE 9.5: Some vector Operations that Use Iterators

Function Member	Description
v.begin()	Return an iterator positioned at v's first element
v.end()	Return an iterator positioned past v's last element
v.rbegin()	Return a reverse iterator positioned at v's last element
v.rend()	Return a reverse iterator positioned before v's first element
v.insert(*iter*, *value*)	Insert *value* into v at the location specified by *iter*

TABLE 9.5: Some vector Operations that Use Iterators (continued)

Function Member	Description
v.insert(*iter*, *n*, *value*)	Insert *n* copies of *value* into *v* at the location specified by *iter*
v.erase(*iter*)	Erase the value in *v* at the location specified by *iter*
v.erase(*iter1*, *iter2*)	Erase values in *v* from the location specified by *iter1* to that specified by *iter2*

The last two groups show that it is possible to insert and remove elements at any location in a vector, but iterators must be used to specify these locations. Also, these operations are as inefficient as for arrays—they must shift elements to make room for new ones and close gaps when items are removed.

To illustrate, consider the following vector<double> object v:

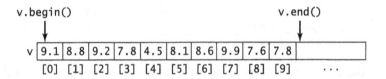

To remove the second element 8.8, we can use

```
v.erase(v.begin() + 1);
```

This removes 8.8 from v, shifting the remaining values to the left to fill its space, and updating v.size() and v.end() appropriately:

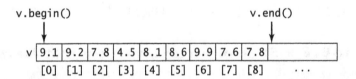

Wrap-up: vectors versus Arrays

The C-style array is a legacy of programming from the early 1970s. The C++ vector was designed in the 1990s and thus incorporates over 20 years of additional programming wisdom. The design of vectors (along with the other class templates in STL) gives it some definite advantages over arrays:

- The capacity of a vector can increase during execution; the capacity of an array is fixed and cannot be changed during execution.
- A vector is a self-contained object; an array is not. If the same operation can be implemented with either container, the array version will require more parameters.

- A `vector` is a class template and is thus not bound to a specific type for the elements; the compiler will generate whatever instances are needed. An array declaration, however, binds the elements to a specific type.

- `vector`'s function members (augmented with the STL algorithms) provide ready-to-use implementations of many common operations. Arrays require us to reinvent the wheel for most operations.

But both have their limitations. For an array or a `vector` of size *n*, inserting or erasing an element at the end can be done in *constant time*, that is, the time does not depend on *n*. However, to insert or erase at other positions in the array or `vector`, in the worst case we must move *n* elements; on the average, *n* / 2 elements must be moved.

In summary, arrays and `vector` objects work well for storing sequences in which direct access to the elements is necessary and insertions and deletions are infrequent or are restricted to the end of the list. Sequences whose sizes may vary greatly during processing, as well as those in which items are frequently inserted or deleted anywhere in the sequence and where sequential access is adequate, are better stored in *linked lists*, which were described in Chapter 6. As we will see in Chapter 11, STL's `list` container uses a variation of the linked lists we studied.

✔ Quick Quiz 9.4

Questions 1–15 assume that the following statements have been executed:

```
vector<int> a, b(5), c(5, 1), d(5);
d.push_back(77);
d.push_back(88);
```

1. The type of values stored in a is _____.
2. The capacity of a is _____ and its size is _____.
3. The capacity of b is _____ and its size is _____.
4. The capacity of c is _____ and its size is _____.
5. The capacity of d is _____ and its size is _____.
6. Describe the output produced by
   ```
   cout << c.front() << ' ' << c.back() << endl;
   ```
7. Describe the output produced by
   ```
   cout << d.front() << ' ' << d.back() << endl;
   ```
8. `a.empty()` (True or false).
9. `c < d` (True or false).
10. `c[1] == 1` (True or false).
11. Describe the output produced by
    ```
    for (int i = 0; i < c.size(); i++)
       cout << c[i] << ' ';
    ```
12. Describe the output produced by
    ```
    d.pop_back();
    for (int i = 0; i < d.size(); i++)
       cout << d[i] << ' ';
    ```

13. d.begin() returns an iterator positioned at _____ in d.
14. d.end() returns an iterator positioned _____ in d.
15. If d's capacity must increase, it will become _____.
16. vector objects are self-contained. (True or false).

For questions 17–20, assume the declarations

```
vector<double> xValue;
vector<int> number(5, 1);
```

Describe the contents of the vector after the statements are executed.

17.
```
for (int i = 0; i <= 4; i++)
    xValue.push_back(double(i) / 2.0);
```

18.
```
for (int i = 0; i < 5; i++)
    if (i % 2 == 0)
        number.push_back(2 * i);
    else
        number.push_back(2 * i + 1);
```

19.
```
for (int i = 1; i < 5; i++)
    number.push_back(2 * number[i - 1]);
```

20.
```
for (int i = 1; i <= 3; i++)
    number.pop_back();
for (int i = 1; i <= 3; i++)
    number.push_back(2);
```

◆ Exercises 9.4

For Exercises 1–11, assume that the following declarations have been made:

```
vector<int> number,
            v(10, 20),
            w(10);
        int num;
```

Assume also that, for exercises that involve input, the following values are entered:

```
99 33 44 88 22 11 55 66 77 -1
```

Describe the contents of the given vector after the statements are executed.

1.
```
for (int i = 0; i < 10; i++)
    number.push_back(i / 2);
```

2.
```
for (int i = 0; i < 6; i++)
    w.push_back(i / 2);
```

3.
```
for (;;)
{
    cin >> num;
    if (num < 0) break;
```

```
        number.push_back(num);
    }
```

4.
```
for (int i = 0; i <= 5; i++)
    number.push_back(i);
for (int i = 0; i < 2; i++)
    number.pop_back();
for (int i = 0; i <= 5; i++)
    number.push_back(i);
```

For Exercises 5–11, assume that the loop in Exercise 3 has been executed.

5.
```
for (int i = 0; i < number.size() - 1; i += 2)
    number[i] = number[i + 1];
```

6.
```
number.pop_back();
number.push_back(number.front());
```

7.
```
int temp = number.front();
number.front() = number.back();
number.back() = temp;
```

8.
```
for (int i = 0; i < number.size(); i++)
    w.pushback(number[i] + v[i]);
```

9.
```
while (v < number)
{
    v.erase(v.begin());
    number.erase(number.begin());
}
```

10.
```
vector<int>::iterator iter = number.begin();
while (*iter > 25)
{
    number.erase(iter);
    iter++;
}
```

11.
```
for (vector<int>::iterator iter = number.begin();
                            iter != number.end(); iter++)
    w.push_back(*iter + 1);
```

For Exercises 12–14, write definitions and statements to construct a vector with the required properties.

12. Stores the sequence of integers from 0 through 99.

13. Stores the sequence of integers from 0 through 99 in reverse order.

14. Has capacity 50 and the value stored in an element is true if the corresponding index is even and is false otherwise.

Exercises 15–16 ask you to write function templates. You should also write driver programs to test them as instructed in Programming Problems 10–11 at the end of this chapter.

15. Write a function template that returns `true` if the values stored in a `vector` are in ascending order and `false` otherwise, where operator `<` is assumed to be defined for type T.

16. Write a function template that returns the range of values stored in a `vector`, that is, the difference between the largest value and the smallest value, where operator `<` is assumed to be defined for type T.

9.5 Case Study: Counting Computer Logins

Problem When users logged in to a particular computer system during a given period of time, their login information was automatically recorded in a file. Because the same user may log in many times, this file may contain many entries for the same user. We wish to compile a log of information for distinct users.

Design The primary object in the problem is the log of users' login information. The operations on this log that will be needed are as follows:

Build the log of user information, which involves the following:

- Read the login information for a user from the file
- Search the log for a user's login information
- Add the information if it isn't already in the log

Display the log

Implementation We will build a `LoginLog` class template that provides the preceding operations. We will use a type parameter `Info` that represents the login information recorded for a user; the properties that are assumed for `Info` are described in the documentation. To store the user information, we will use a `vector<Info>` data member `myUserLog`.

The first suboperation in building the log is to read a user's login information from a file; this will be `Info`'s responsibility. For the search suboperation, we will use a *linear search* of `myUserLog`. (As we will see in the next chapter, STL provides a search algorithm that does this.)

Linear Search Algorithm

/* Perform a linear search of values stored in a `vector` v for `item` of the same type as the elements of v. Return its position if found and the size of v otherwise. */

1. Set index i = 0.
2. Repeat the following:
   If i ≥ size of v or `item` is equal to v[i]
   Return i.

> Otherwise
> >Increment i by 1.
> End repeat.

Since we need not maintain elements of myUserLog in any particular order, we can use the push_back() method for the third suboperation. For the output operation, we can adapt one of the display() function templates of the preceding section.

Coding Figure 9.5 shows a class LoginLog that models the log of the user information.

Figure 9.5 LoginLog Class Template

```
/*-- LoginLog.h -----------------------------------------------------------
  This header file defines a LoginLog class template for modeling a
  computer log of user information recorded during logins over some
  period of time.  The type parameter Info represents the login
  information recorded for a user.

  Basic operations:
    build:   Builds the log of information for distinct users
    search:  Searches the computer log for a particular user
    display: Displays the contents of the log

  Note:  >>, <<, and == must be defined for type Info.
-------------------------------------------------------------------------*/

#include <iostream>
#include <fstream>
#include <vector>
#include <cassert>

#ifndef LOGIN_LOG
#define LOGIN_LOG

template <typename Info>
class LoginLog
{
 public:
 /***** Function Members *****/
 /***** Constructor *****/
  //-- Let vector's constructor do the work
```

Figure 9.5   (continued)

```
  void build(string fileName);
  /*-----------------------------------------------------------------
     Build the log.

     Precondition:  None.
     Postcondition: Log has been built using input via a stream connected
         to fileName.
     -----------------------------------------------------------------*/


  int search(Info item) const;
  /*-----------------------------------------------------------------
     Search user log for a given Info object.

     Precondition:  None.
     Postcondition: The index in myUserLog where item is found is returned,
         myUserLog.size() if not found.
     -----------------------------------------------------------------*/


   void display(ostream & out) const;
  /*-----------------------------------------------------------------
     Output the log.

     Precondition:  ostream out is open.
     Postcondition: Log has been output to out.
     -----------------------------------------------------------------*/


 private:
    vector<Info> myUserLog;
};


//--- Definition of build()
template <typename Info>
void LoginLog<Info>::build(string fileName)
{
    ifstream fin(fileName.data());      // open input stream to file
    assert (fin.is_open());             // check if successful

    Info userInfo;
```

Figure 9.5 (continued)

```
   for(;;)
   {
      fin >> userInfo;
      if ( fin.eof() ) break;

      int pos = search(userInfo);
      if (pos == myUserLog.size())     // new user
         myUserLog.push_back(userInfo);
   }
}


//--- Definition of search
template <typename Info>
int LoginLog<Info>::search(Info item) const
{
   int i;
   for (i = 0; i < myUserLog.size(); i++)
      if (item == myUserLog[i])
         break;
   return i;
}


//--- Definition of display()
template <typename Info>
inline void LoginLog<Info>::display(ostream & out) const
{
   for (int i = 0; i < myUserLog.size(); i++)
      out << myUserLog[i] << endl;
}

#endif
```

▲

Figure 9.6 shows a program that uses LoginLog with login information that consists only of user-ids. Thus, a LoginLog<string> instantiation is used to process these user-ids. Also shown is an execution trace with a short file of user-ids and the output produced from this file.

Figure 9.6 **Program to Process User-Ids**

```
/*------------------------------------------------------------------
   Program to determine which users were logged into a computer
   system for a given period of time.

   Input (keyboard): Name of the user-id file
   Input (file):     User-ids
   Output (screen):  A list of distinct user-ids
   ------------------------------------------------------------------*/

#include <iostream>
#include <string>
using namespace std;

#include "LoginLog.h"

int main()
{
   // Get name of log file
   string userInfoFile;        // log file of user-ids
   cout << "Enter name of login-info file: ";
   getline(cin, userInfoFile);

   // Read the log from the file
   LoginLog<string> userIdLog;
   userIdLog.build(userInfoFile);

   // Display the log
   cout << "\nList of distinct user-ids who logged in:\n";
   userIdLog.display(cout);
}
```

Listing of UserIdFile:
S31416PI
S12345SL
S31416PI
S31313LN
S12345SL
S31416PI
S21718EX
S13331RC

Figure 9.6 (continued)

```
S77777UP
S12345SL
S31416PI
S21718EX
S99099RR
S12345SL
S77777UP
S31313LN
S31416PI
```

Execution Trace:
```
Enter name of login-info file: UserIdFile

List of distinct user-ids who logged in:
S31416PI
S12345SL
S31313LN
S21718EX
S13331RC
S77777UP
S99099RR
```

▲

9.6 Multidimensional vectors (Optional)

Multidimensional arrays described in Section 3.3 suffer the same deficiencies as one-dimensional arrays, the most serious of which is that they are not consistent with object-oriented programming because they are not self-contained. The vector class template of the preceding section is an obvious OOP alternative to one-dimensional arrays; a vector object does carry along inside itself its capacity, its size, and a large number of operations. In this section we outline a method for building multidimensional vector objects.

Two-Dimensional vector Objects

In Section 3.3 we saw that multidimensional arrays are treated as arrays of arrays. In particular, a two-dimensional array can be viewed as a one-dimensional array whose elements are themselves one-dimensional arrays. We can use the same approach to build a two-dimensional vector class template. A vector is a one-dimensional object, and a vector of vectors is, therefore, a two-dimensional object.

To illustrate, consider the following definition of a two-dimensional `vector` object `table`:

```
const int ROWS = 3,
             COLUMNS = 4;
vector< vector<double> > table(ROWS,
                          vector<double>(COLUMNS, 0.0));
```

 It is important to remember the space between the angle brackets (> >), because if we write

```
vector< vector<double>> table ...
```

the compiler will mistake >> for the input operator (or the right-shift bit operator).

The compiler uses a `vector` constructor twice to construct `table`. The inner call to the constructor

```
vector< vector<double> > table(ROWS,
                      vector<double>(COLUMNS, 0.0));
```

builds an anonymous `vector<double>` object containing four zeros:

[0]	[1]	[2]	[3]
0.0	0.0	0.0	0.0

This vector of `double`s is then passed as the initial value to the outer call to the constructor:

```
vector< vector<double> > table(ROWS,
                      vector<double>(COLUMNS, 0.0));
```

which uses it to initialize each of its three `vector` elements. The result is the following 3×4 `vector` of `vector`s of `double` values:

table:	[0]	[1]	[2]	[3]
[0]	0.0	0.0	0.0	0.0
[1]	0.0	0.0	0.0	0.0
[2]	0.0	0.0	0.0	0.0

The declaration

```
vector< vector<double> > aTable;
```

will construct `aTable` as an empty two-dimensional `vector`.

Two-Dimensional vector Operations

Subscript A single-subscript expression such as `table[0]` refers to one row of `table`,

table:	[0]	[1]	[2]	[3]
[0]	0.0	0.0	0.0	0.0

and a double-subscript expression such as table[0][2] refers to an element within the specified row of table:

```
table:  [0]    [1]    [2]    [3]
   [0]| 0.0  | 0.0  | 0.0  | 0.0 |
```

In general, the expression

```
table[r][c]
```

can be used to access the value stored in column c of row r.

The size() Method   Suppose that we want to determine the number of rows in a two-dimensional vector. If table is the 3 × 4 two-dimensional vector described earlier, then the expression

```
table.size()
```

returns the number of rows (3) in table. The expression

```
table[r].size()
```

can be used to find the number of columns in row r, because table[r] returns the vector of double values in table whose index is r, and applying size() to that vector returns the number of values in it. If table is rectangular, then each row will have the same size allowing us to apply size() to any row. If table is not rectangular, then the size of each row may be different, and so size() must be applied to each row separately.

We can use the size() function and the subscript (and other) vector operations to build many useful operations on two-dimensional vectors. For example, the following statements can be used to display a two-dimensional vector object table:

```
for (int row = 0; row < table.size(); row++)
{
  for (int col = 0; col < aTable[row].size(); col++)
    cout << setw(8) << table[row][col];
  cout << endl;
}
```

In the outer loop, the expression

```
table.size()
```

returns the number of rows in the argument corresponding to parameter table and the inner loop expression

```
table[row].size()
```

returns the number of columns in table[row].

The push_back() Method   Suppose that we need to add a new (fourth) row to table. This can be done by using the vector method push_back():

```
table.push_back( vector<double>(COLUMNS, 0.0) );
```

The expression

```
vector<double>(COLUMNS, 0.0)
```

is a call to the `vector` constructor to build an anonymous `vector` of zeros. The `push_back()` function then appends this vector to the existing rows in `table`:

table:	[0]	[1]	[2]	[3]
[0]	0.0	0.0	0.0	0.0
[1]	0.0	0.0	0.0	0.0
[2]	0.0	0.0	0.0	0.0
[3]	0.0	0.0	0.0	0.0

To add a column to `table`, `push_back()` can be used to append a `double` value to each row of `table`, because each row in `table` is itself a `vector` of `double` values:

```
for (int row = 0; row < table.size(); row++)
  table[row].push_back(0.0);
```

Execution of this loop will add a fifth column to `table`:

table:	[0]	[1]	[2]	[3]	[4]
[0]	0.0	0.0	0.0	0.0	0.0
[1]	0.0	0.0	0.0	0.0	0.0
[2]	0.0	0.0	0.0	0.0	0.0
[3]	0.0	0.0	0.0	0.0	0.0

Note that `push_back()` makes it easy to build nonrectangular tables. For example, consider the following code segment:

```
vector< vector<double> > aTable;

for (int col = 1; col <= 3; col++)
  aTable.push_back(vector<double>(col, 0.0));
```

Initially, `aTable` is constructed as an empty vector. The first pass through the `for` loop constructs an anonymous vector containing one zero and appends it to `aTable`:

aTable:	[0]
[0]	0.0

The second pass through the `for` loop constructs and appends another anonymous vector containing two zeros:

aTable:	[0]	[1]
[0]	0.0	
[1]	0.0	0.0

The third pass through the for loop constructs and appends a third anonymous vector of three zeros:

```
aTable:  [0]   [1]   [2]
    [0] | 0.0 |
    [1] | 0.0 | 0.0 |
    [2] | 0.0 | 0.0 | 0.0 |
```

Two-dimensional vectors thus need not be square, nor even rectangular. Such nonrectangular two-dimensional tables are sometimes called **jagged tables.**

◆ Exercises 9.6

For Exercises 1–6, write a function for a two-dimensional vector of doubles that returns the value asked for. You should write driver programs to test these functions as instructed in Programming Problems 12–17 at the end of this chapter.

1. The sum of the values in a given row
2. The sum of the values in a given column
3. The average of the values in a given row
4. The standard deviation of the values in a given row (see Programming Problem 1 in Chapter 3)
5. The average of the values in a column
6. The standard deviation of the values in a given column (see Programming Problem 1 in Chapter 3)
7. Construct a Matrix class that contains (at least) matrix addition and multiplication operations (see Programming Problems 7 and 8 at the end of Chapter 3) and I/O operations. Test your class with a driver program as instructed in Programming Problem 26 at the end of this chapter.

9.7 Other Standard Containers—deque, stack, and queue

We considered stacks in Chapter 7 and queues in Chapter 8, where we also briefly described deques. In this section we revisit these ADTs and describe their implementations in the standard library.

STL's deque Class Template

As an ADT, a **deque,** which is an abbreviation for *double-ended queue*, is a sequential container that functions like a queue (or a stack) at both ends. More precisely, we have:

Deque ADT

Collection of Data Elements
   A sequence of data items with the property that items can be added and removed only at the ends.

Basic Operations
- Construct a deque (usually empty)
- Check if the deque is empty

- Push_front: Add an element at the front of the deque
- Push_back: Add an element at the back of the deque
- Front: Retrieve the element at the front of the deque
- Back: Retrieve the element at the back of the deque
- Pop_front: Remove the element at the front of the deque
- Pop_back: Remove the element at the back of the deque

One of the basic containers in STL is the **deque class template**. It has

- the same operations as `vector` except that there is no `capacity()` and no `reserve()`
- two new operations:
  - `d.push_front(value);`   Push a copy of *value* at the front of *d*
  - `d.pop_front();`   Remove the element at the front of *d*

where *d* is a deque. We see, therefore, that deque can implement the deque ADT. The program in Figure 9.6 illustrates several of deque's operations.

Figure 9.7 Demonstration of STL's deque

```
/*-------------------------------------------------------------------------
            Program to demonstrate use of STL's deque container.
   -------------------------------------------------------------------------*/

#include <deque>
#include <iostream>;
using namespace std;

int main()
{
   deque<int> d;

   // Output number of values stored in d
   cout << d.size() << " elements in an empty deque\n";

   // Add first 6 integers alternately to front and back
   for (int i = 1; i <= 6; i += 2)
   {
      d.push_front(i);
      d.push_back(i+1);
   }
```

Figure 9.7 (continued)

```
    cout << "Contents after alternating adds at front and back:\n";
    for (int i = 0; i < d.size(); i++)
       cout << d[i] << " ";
    cout << endl;

    // Change back value to 999, remove front value;
       d.back() = 999;
    d.pop_front();

    // Display contents of d again, but use an iterator
    cout << "Contents (via iterators) after changing back "
          "and popping front:\n";
    for (deque<int>::iterator it = d.begin();
                         it != d.end(); it++)
       cout << *it << " ";
    cout << endl;

    // Dump contents of d from back to front
    cout << "Dumping the deque from the back:\n";
    while (!d.empty())
    {
       cout << d.back() << " ";
          d.pop_back();
    }
    cout << endl;
}
```

Execution Trace:
```
0 elements in an empty deque
Contents after alternating adds at front and back:
5 3 1 2 4 6
Contents (via iterators) after changing back and popping front:
3 1 2 4 999
Dumping the deque from the back:
999 4 2 1 3
```

Note that *STL's* **deque** *is not really a faithful implementation of a deque as an ADT; it has many extra operations.* For example, like **vector**, **deque** allows direct access to any of its elements via the subscript operator [], which is not a property of a deque as an ADT. It also has other operations similar to vector such as insertion and deletion at any point in the list, and its iterators have the same operations as for vector. Insertion and deletion at points other than the ends of the list are very inefficient, however, and in fact take longer than for vector.

One bad feature of the vector container is that, when its capacity must be increased, it must copy all the objects from its old internal array into the new larger one. Then it must destroy each object in the old array. This is a lot of overhead! With deque, this copying, creating, and destroying is avoided. Once an object is constructed, it can stay in the same memory locations as long as it exists, provided insertions and deletions take place at the ends of the deque.

The reason for this, is that unlike vectors, a deque is not stored in a single varying-sized block of memory, but rather in a collection of fixed-size blocks (typically, 4K bytes). One of its data members is essentially an array map whose elements point to the locations of these blocks. For example, suppose, for the sake of illustration, that each block consists of only five memory locations and that a deque<int> object d is formed by inserting elements as follows, beginning with an empty deque:

Push_front: 555
Push_back: 1, 2, 3, 4
Push_front: 666, 777, 888
Push_back: 99, 100

We might picture d as shown in Figure 9.8. When a data block gets full, a new one is allocated and its address is added to map. When map gets full, a new one is allocated and the current values are copied into the middle of it.

Figure 9.8 Storage of a deque<int> object d

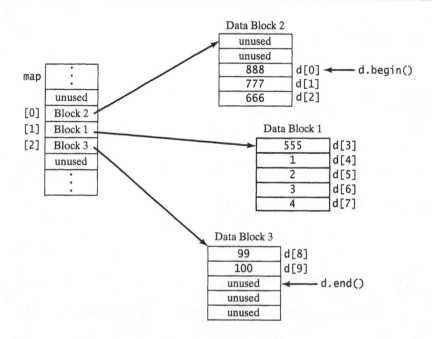

As we noted, insertion at points within the list for a deque takes longer than for a vector. To insert an item in the middle of a vector, elements from that location on need only be shifted one position to the right to make room. Insertion into the middle of a deque, however, may cause shifting across noncontiguous blocks, which obviously can be more time consuming. When a deque is used as prescribed in the ADT definition of a deque—that is, inserting and deleting elements only at the ends—the operation of deque is very efficient.

A New (But Unnecessary) Version of Our Stack Class Template

In Section 9.3 we improved our Stack type by making it a class template so that it can be used for any type of stack elements. It still has one serious deficiency, namely, that the stack can become full. It is not dynamic in that it cannot grow when necessary. As we noted in Section 7.3, one solution is to use a *dynamic array* and then let the stack capacity increase when necessary as follows:

1. Allocate a larger array temp.
2. Copy the elements of myArray into the first myCapacity locations in temp.
3. Deallocate myArray (with delete[]).
4. Set myArray = temp.

Instead, we developed a linked-list implementation of stacks that allows the stack to grow as large as needed and avoids the copying.

An alternative is to use a deque or a vector as a container for the stack elements; these work well because they can increase their capacity automatically as needed. Figure 9.9 shows how easy it is to implement stacks using a deque to store the stack elements.

Figure 9.9 A deque-Based Stack Template

```
//***** For documentation, see Fig. 9.3. *****//

#ifndef STACK_DEQUE
#define STACK_DEQUE

#include <iostream>
#include <deque>

template<typename StackElement>
class Stack
{
 public:
  /***** Function Members *****/
  // Constructor:  Let deque's constructor handle it.
  bool empty() const;
```

Figure 9.9 (continued)

```
    void push(const StackElement & value);
    void display(ostream & out) const;
    StackElement top() const;
    void pop();

 private:
  /***** Data Members *****/
   deque<StackElement> myDeque;    // deque to store elements
}; // end of class declaration

//--- Definition of empty operation
template <typename StackElement>
inline bool Stack<StackElement>::empty() const
{ return myDeque.empty(); }

//--- Definition of push operation
template <typename StackElement>
inline void Stack<StackElement>::push(const StackElement & value)
{ myDeque.push_back(value); }

//--- Definition of display operation
template <typename StackElement>
inline void Stack<StackElement>::display(ostream & out) const
{
    for (int pos = myDeque.size() - 1; pos >= 0; pos--)
        out << myDeque[pos] << endl;
}

//--- Definition of top operation
template <typename StackElement>
inline StackElement Stack<StackElement>:: top() const
{
    if (!myDeque.empty())
        return myDeque.back();
    //else
    cerr << "*** Stack is empty ***\n";
}
```

Figure 9.9 (continued)

```
//--- Definition of pop operation
template <typename StackElement>
inline void Stack<StackElement>:: pop()
{
   if (!myDeque.empty())
      myDeque.pop_back();
   else
      cerr << "*** Stack is empty -- can't remove a value ***\n";
}


#endif
```

▲

Basically, all we have done in Figure 9.9 is wrap a deque inside a class template and let it do all the work. Our function members are essentially just renamings of deque function members. And there is really no need to do this, because STL has done it for us!

STL's stack Adapter

The standard library includes a stack container. Actually, it is an **adapter** (as indicated by the fact that it is a class template that has *a container type as one of its type parameters*), which means basically that it acts as a "wrapper" around another class, giving it a *new user interface*. A *container adapter* such as stack uses the members of the encapsulated container to implement what looks like a new container.

A stack can be created with a declaration of the form

```
stack<T, C<T> > aStack;
```

where C may be any container that supports push_back() and pop_back() in a LIFO manner. In particular, C may be a vector, a deque, or a list (see Section 11.3). If no container is specified, deque *is the default container*; that is, a declaration of the form

```
stack<T> aStack;
```

is equivalent to

```
stack< T, deque<T> > aStack;
```

For the other containers, we must specify them explicitly:

```
stack< T, vector<T> > aStack1;
stack< T, list<T> > aStack2;
```

The following are basic operations for the standard stack container:

- Constructor: stack<T, C<T> > st; creates an empty stack st; it uses a container C to store the elements (default container is deque)
- empty()

- `top()`
- `push()`
- `pop()`
- `size()`
- Relational operators: `==, !=, <, <=, >, >=` (as defined for the container C)

From this list, we see that STL's `stack` is a faithful implementation of a stack as an ADT. It provides the five basic stack operations and adds the `size()` operation as well as the relational operators. It does, however, use a large amount of memory, because as we saw earlier, the capacity of its internal `deque` container starts with and grows by adding a large (typically 4K) block of memory. Also, there is quite a lot of unused "horsepower" in the large collection of built-in `deque` operations that gets masked by the `stack` wrapper.

STL's queue Adapter

The standard library also includes a `queue` container, which, like `stack`, is a container adapter. A queue can be created with a declaration of the form

```
queue<T, C<T> > aQueue;
```

where C may be any container that supports `push_back()` and `pop_front()`. In particular, C may be a `deque` or a `list` (see Section 11.3); if no container is specified, `deque` *is the default container*; that is, a declaration of the form

```
queue<T> aQueue;
```

is equivalent to

```
queue<T, deque<T> > aQueue;
```

To use a `list` as the container, we would write

```
queue<T, list<T> > aQueue;
```

The basic operations for `queue` are the same as for `stack`, except for the following:

- `front()` (instead of `top()`) retrieves the front item in the queue
- `pop()` implements the dequeue operation
- `push()` implements the enqueue operation
- `back()` retrieves the item at the back of the queue

✔ Quick Quiz 9.7

1. The word *deque* is an abbreviation for _____.
2. Define deque as an ADT.
3. STL's deque container has the same operations as specified in a definition of a deque as an ADT. (True or false)
4. Insertion at points within the list for a deque can take longer than for a `vector`. (True or false)
5. A deque is stored in a single contiguous block of memory. (True or false)

6. A class that acts as a wrapper around another class is called a(n) _____.
7. An adapter encapsulates a container to give it a new user _____.
8. What if anything is wrong with the declaration `stack< vector<double>> st;`?
9. Name two of STL's containers that are adapters.

9.8 Bitsets and Valarrays (optional)

As we noted at the end of Section 9.3, there are four types that could be classified as containers because they contain elements: arrays, `strings`, `valarrays`, and `bitsets`. However, each of them lacks some features of the interface that the STL containers have in common. We have considered arrays in detail in Chapter 3 and the `string` type in Chapter 5. This section gives a very brief overview of the other two. Expanded treatments of these containers can be found at the book's website.

Bitsets

A **bitset** object contains an array whose elements are bits. Thus, it is much like an array whose elements are of type `bool`, but unlike arrays, it provides operations for manipulating the bits it stores.

The `bitset` class template is declared in the standard `<bitset>` library, which must be included in any program that uses `bitsets`:

```
#include <bitset>
```

A `bitset` object *b* can then be constructed using one of the following declarations:

```
                             // Initialize b with N bits:
bitset<N> b;                 //   all 0
bitset<N> b(num);            //   of num
                             //      (zero fill to the left)
bitset<N> b(str, pos, n);    //   n bits of str, starting at pos
                             //      (zero fill to the left)
```

Here, *N* is a constant specifying the number of bits in *b*; *num* is a nonnegative integer; *str* is a `string` of zeros and ones; *pos* is a nonnegative integer with default value 0; and *n* is a nonnegative integer with default value *str*.`length()` - *pos*. To illustrate, consider the following examples:

```
#include <bitset>
using namespace std;

bitset<5> b0;
bitset<10> b1(49);
string bitstring = "101100111000";
bitset<16> b2(bitstring),
           b3(bitstring, 3),
           b4(bitstring, 0, 4);
```

The first declaration creates b0 as a `bitset` containing 5 zeros and the second creates b1 as a `bitset` containing 10 bits, the 6 bits 110001 in the binary representation of

49 and 4 zeros to the left:

b0 00000
b1 0000110001

Note that the bit positions are numbered in the same way that they usually are for memory words—from right to left:

```
9 8 7 6 5 4 3 2 1 0
```
b1 0 0 0 0 1 1 0 0 0 1

This means that one can think of a bitset<N> object as an N-bit binary number.

The last three declarations create bitsets containing 16 bits: b2 contains the 12 bits in bitstring padded with 4 zeros; b3 contains the last 9 bits in bitstring padded with 7 zeros; and b4 contains the first 4 bits in bitstring padded with 12 zeros:

b2 0000101100111000
b3 0000000100111000
b4 0000000000001011

Several operations are provided for manipulating individual bits or all of the bits of a bitset b:

■ & (bitwise and), | (bitwise or), ∧ (bitwise exclusive or),
   << (bitwise left shift), >> (bitwise right shift)
   For example, b3 & b4 produces 0000000000001000 and b4 << 2 gives
   0000000000101100

■ corresponding assignment operators: &=, |=, ~=, <<=, >>=

■ relational operators: ==, !=

■ the subscript operator []: b[i] is the i-th bit in b from the right

■ assignment of same-size bitsets

There also are several function members to change or check bits:

■ b.set()   set all bits of b to 1
■ b.reset()   set all bits of b to 0
■ b.set(i, bv)   set b[i] to bv; default value of bv is 1
■ b.reset(i)   set b[i] to 0
■ b.flip()   change all bits (0s to 1s and 1s to 0s)
■ b.flip(i)   change b[i]
■ b.size()   total number of bits
■ b.count()   number of bits that are 1
■ b.any()   true if any bit is 1 and false otherwise

- ■ `b.none()`   true if no bits are 1 and false otherwise
- ■ `b.test(`*i*`)`   true if `b[`*i*`]` is 1 and false otherwise

And there are also operations to convert `bitset`s to integers or strings, together with input and output operations:

- ■ `b.to_ulong()`   the `unsigned long int` represented by the bit string stored in b
- ■ `b.to_string()`   a `string` representation of the bit string stored in b
- ■ `out << b`   output the bitstring stored in b to `ostream out`
- ■ `in >> b`   input a bitstring from `istream in` to be stored in b

One useful application of `bitset`s is to implement *sets*—unordered collections of elements with operations of union, intersection, and complement (as studied in mathematics). The website for this text discusses sets and their implementation using `bitset`s. It uses this implementation to find **prime numbers**—integers greater than 1 whose only divisors are 1 and the number itself—in a given range using the method known as the **Sieve of Eratosthenes**. Prime numbers are important in public-key encryption/decryption methods (see Chapter 5), in random-number generators, in the design of hash tables (which we consider in Section 12.7), and in many other applications of number theory.

Valarrays

We have used arrays in several places: to store list elements in a `List` class in Chapter 6, to store stack elements in a `Stack` class in Chapter 7, and to store queue elements in a `Queue` class in Chapter 8. We have pointed out some of the deficiencies of arrays, especially that they are not self-contained and thus are not consistent with the spirit of object-oriented programming. We indicated that one solution would be to encapsulate an array, its capacity, its size, and other basic operations within a class structure. In Section 9.4 we have seen that this is the approach used by the `vector` class template.

Another important use of arrays is in numeric computation in scientific and engineering applications, for example, in vector processing. In mathematics the term *vector* refers to a sequence (one-dimensional array) of real values on which various arithmetic operations are performed; for example, +, –, scalar multiplication, and dot product. Because much numeric work relies on the use of such vectors, highly-efficient libraries are essential in many fields. For this reason, the standard C++ library provides the **valarray** class template, which is designed to carry out vector operations very efficiently. That is, `valarray`s are (mathematical) vectors that have been highly optimized for numeric computations.

The `valarray` class template is declared in the standard `<valarray>` library, which must be included in any program that uses `valarray`s:

```
#include <valarray>
```

A `valarray` object *v* can then be constructed using one of the following declarations:

```
                        // Initialize v:
valarray<T> v;          //   as empty
valarray<T> v(n);       //   with n default T values
```

```
valarray<T> v(val, n);    // with n copies of val
valarray<T> v(array, n);  // with first n values in array
valarray<T> v(w);         // with copy of w
```

Here, T is a numeric type (typically, `float`, `double`, or `long double`); n is an integer specifying the capacity of v; val is a value of type T; $array$ is an array of T values; and w is a `valarray`. To illustrate, consider the following examples:

```
#include <valarray>
using namespace std;

valarray<double> v0;
valarray<float> v1(100);
valarray<int> v2(999, 100);
const double A[] = {1.1, 2.2, 3.3, 4.4, 5.5};
valarray<double> v3(A, 4);
```

The first declaration creates v0 as an empty `valarray` of `double`s (which can be resized later); the second constructs v1 as a `valarray` that can store 100 `float` values; the third creates v2 as a `valarray` of 100 `int` values, initially 999; and the last declaration constructs v3 as a `valarray` of four `double`s, initially the first four values (1.1, 2.2, 3.3, 4.4) stored in array A.

The basic operations for `valarray`s are as follows:

- the subscript operator [] (can also be used with slices, gslices, masks, and indirect arrays)
- assignment of same-size `valarray`s
- unary operations (applied elementwise): +, -, ~, !
- assignment operators: +=, -=, *=, /=, %=, &=, |=, ^=, <<=, >>=

  If Δ denotes one of these operations, v Δ= x; is equivalent to

  ```
  for (int i = 0; i < v.size(); i++)
     v[i] = v[i] Δ x;
  ```

- `size()`: the number of values stored in the `valarray`
- `resize(n, val)`: reinitialize `valarray` to have n elements with (optional) value val—for example,

  ```
  cin >> n;
  v0.resize(n);
  ```

- `shift(n)` and `cshift(n)`: Shift values in the `valarray` |n| positions left if n > 0, right if n < 0. For `shift`, vacated positions are filled with 0; for `cshift`, values are shifted circularly, with values from one end moving into the other end. For example,

  ```
  v3.shift(2); would change v3 to 3.3, 4.4, 0, 0
  v3.shift(-2); would change v3 to 0, 0, 1.1, 2.2
  v3.cshift(2); would change v3 to 3.3, 4.4, 1.1, 2.2
  ```

There also are several nonmember operations:

- The following binary operators and mathematical functions (from `cmath`):

  ```
  +, -, *, /, %, &, |, ^, <<, >>, &&, ||, ==, !=, <, >, <=, >=,
  atan2(), pow()
  ```

  These operations and functions are applied elementwise. The operands may be

  `valarrays` or a `valarray` and a scalar.

- The following mathematical functions, which are applied elementwise:

  ```
  acos(), asin(), atan(), cos(), cosh(), exp(), log(), log10(),
  sin(), sinh()(), sqrt(), tan(), tanh()
  ```

For example, the assignment statement

```
w = pow(v3, 2);
```

assigns to w the squares of the elements of v3, namely, 1.21, 4.84, 10.89, 19.36.

Some other operations that are useful with `valarrays` are found in the standard `<algorithm>` and `<numeric>` libraries (see Section 10.5). For example, `<numeric>` contains functions for calculating the sum of the elements in a sequence, the inner (dot) product of two sequences, the partial sums of a sequence, and differences of adjacent elements in a sequence.

Slices, Masks, and Indirect Arrays

There are four auxiliary types that specify subsets of a `valarray`:

- `slice_array:`   A **slice** selects every nth element of a `valarray` for some integer n called a *stride*.

- `gslice_array:`   A **gslice** (generalized slice) contains essentially the information of several slices; instead of one stride and one size, there may be several strides and sizes.

- `mask_array:`   A **mask** is a boolean `valarray`, which when used as a subscript of a `valarray`, specifies for each index whether or not that element of the `valarray` is to be included in the subset.

- `indirect_array:`   An `indirect_array` specifies an arbitrary subset and reordering of a `valarray`.

More details about valarrays and these auxiliary types, including examples, can be found on the website for this book.

SUMMARY

Chapter Notes

- A function name may be *overloaded* provided that no two definitions of the function have the same list of parameter types (called its *signature*).

- A *function template* is a *pattern* the compiler can use to construct a function. Type parameters can be used to pass types into the function to declare the types of parameters.

- A *class template is* a pattern the compiler can use to construct a class. Type parameters can be used to pass types into the class to specify the types of its members.

- The Standard Template Library (STL) consists of container class templates, iterators to access and process elements of containers, and function templates to operate on containers.

- STL's vector is an array-based container with a rich set of operations and whose capacity can increase when necessary.

- *Iterators* are generalizations of pointers used to access elements of containers and move from one element to another.

- The stack and queue containers are *adapters* that wrap another container.

- C++'s bitset is an array-based container whose elements are bits; valarray is a numeric-array-based container designed for processing mathematical vectors.

Programming Pointers

1. Every function and class template must be preceded by a template declaration of the form

   ```
   template<typename TypeParam₁, typename TypeParam₂, ...>
   ```

   or

   ```
   template<class TypeParam₁, class TypeParam₂, ...>
   ```

   Note that angle brackets (<>) rather than parentheses are used to enclose the type-parameter list. For a function template, each of the type parameters *must* appear at least once in the regular parameter list of the function if the compiler is to determine the types to bind to them from the arguments in a function call. (See also Appendix D.)

2. Function templates cannot be split into a header file containing their prototypes and a separately compiled file containing their definitions.

3. The following three rules govern the building of class templates:

   - All operations defined outside of the class declaration must be template functions.

   - Any use of the name of a class template as a type must be parameterized.

   - Definitions of operations for a class template must be in the same file as the class declaration at compile time.

4. The subscript operator should not be used to append values to a vector because this updates neither the vector's size nor its capacity; the push_back and insert() operations should be used.

5. The capacity of a vector is doubled each time it is increased.

6. Remember to use a space between the closing angle brackets in declarations of the form

    Type< <T, Container<T> > objectName;

    so that the compiler does not confuse it with the >> operator.

▲ ADT Tips

1. Using a `typedef` to set the type of the elements stored in a container class binds the class to one particular type for the elements.

2. The template mechanism makes it possible to write generic function templates and to develop generic container class templates. It makes it possible for classes and functions to receive not only data values to be stored or operated on via parameters but also to receive the *type* of data via a parameter.

3. The standard C++ containers and algorithms provide generic and very efficient data structures for problem solving and implementing ADTs.

4. Iterators provide a generic way to access elements in a container.

5. A *deque* provides direct access to the items at each end of the list of values it contains.

▣ Programming Problems

Section 9.3

1. Write a driver program that uses the function template in Exercise 1 to find the average of: (a) two `int`s; (b) two `float`s; (c) two `double`s.

2. Write a driver program that uses the function template in Exercise 2 to find the maximum of: (a) two `int`s; (b) two `float`s; (c) two `double`s. (d) Try it with two `complex` values. What happens and why?

3. Write a driver program that uses the function template in Exercise 3 to find the median of: (a) three `int`s; (b) three `float`s; (c) three `double`s. (d) Try it with three `complex` values. What happens and why?

4. Write a driver program that uses the function template `arraySum()` in Exercise 4 to sum the values stored in an array of: (a) `int`s; (b) `float`s; (c) `double`s.

5. Write a driver program that uses the function `arrayMaxMin()` in Exercise 5 to find the maximum and minimum of the values stored in an array of: (a) `int`s; (b) `double`s; (c) `string`s.

6. Write a driver program that uses the function `arraySearch()` in Exercise 6 to search the values stored in an array of: (a) `int`s for a given `int`; (b) `double`s for a given `double`; (c) `string`s for a given `string`.

7. Write a driver program to test the list class template in Exercise 7 in a manner similar to that used for the `Stack` class template in the text.

8. Write a driver program to test the queue class template in Exercise 8 in a manner similar to that used for the `Stack` class template in the text.

9. Write a driver program to test the `CartesianPoint` class template in Exercise 9 by checking it with points whose coordinates are: (a) `int`s; (b) `float`s; (c) `double`s.

Section 9.4

10. Write a driver program to test the ascending-order function of Exercise 15.

11. Write a driver program to test the range function of Exercise 16.

Section 9.6

12. Write a driver program to test the row-sum function of Exercise 1.

13. Write a driver program to test the column-sum function of Exercise 2.

14. Write a driver program to test the row-average function of Exercise 3.

15. Write a driver program to test the row-standard-deviation function of Exercise 4.

16. Write a driver program to test the column-average function of Exercise 5.

17. Write a driver program to test the column-standard-deviation function of Exercise 6.

18. The following table contains data on the noise level (measured in decibels) produced at seven different speeds by six different models of cars. Write a program that will display this table in easy-to-read format, and that will calculate and display the average noise level for each car model, the average noise level at each speed, and the overall average noise level. Store the table in a two-dimensional vector.

	Speed(MPH)						
Car	**20**	**30**	**40**	**50**	**60**	**70**	**80**
0	88	90	94	102	111	122	134
1	75	77	80	86	94	103	113
2	80	83	85	94	100	111	121
3	68	71	76	85	96	110	125
4	77	84	91	98	105	112	119
5	81	85	90	96	102	109	120

19. Storing the entries in a two-dimensional vector, write a program to calculate and display the first ten rows of Pascal's triangle. The first part of the triangle has the form

```
            1
          1   1
        1   2   1
      1   3   3   1
    1   4   6   4   1
```

in which each row begins and ends with 1 and each of the other entries in a row is the sum of the two entries just above it. If this form for the output seems too challenging, you might display the triangle as

```
    1
    1 1
    1 2 1
    1 3 3 1
    1 4 6 4 1
```

20. An automobile dealership sells ten different models of automobiles and employs eight salespersons. A record of sales for each month can be represented by a table in which each row contains the number of sales of each model by a given salesperson, and each column contains the number of sales by each salesperson of a given model. Write a program to input sales data into a two-dimensional `vector` and then produce a monthly sales report, displaying the monthly sales table in a pleasing format. The report should also display the total number of automobiles sold by each salesperson and the total number of each model sold by all salespersons.

21. A certain company has a product line that includes five items that sell for $100, $75, $120, $150, and $35. There are four salespersons working for this company, and the following table gives the sales report for a typical week:

Salesperson Number	Item Number				
	1	2	3	4	5
1	10	4	5	6	7
2	7	0	12	1	3
3	4	9	5	0	8
4	3	2	1	5	6

Storing the report in a two-dimensional `vector`, write a program to do the following:

a. Compute the total dollar sales for each salesperson

b. Compute the total commission for each salesperson if the commission rate is 10 percent

c. Find the total income for each salesperson for the week if each salesperson receives a fixed salary of $200 per week in addition to commission payments.

22. Proceed as in the Programming Problem 6 (demographic study) of Chapter 3, but use a two-dimensional `vector`.

23. Proceed as in the Programming Problem 9 (magic square) of Chapter 3, but use a two-dimensional `vector`.

24. Proceed as in the Programming Problem 10 (temperature in a grid) of Chapter 3, but use a two-dimensional `vector`.

25. Proceed as in the Programming Problem 11 (game of Life) of Chapter 3, but use a two-dimensional `vector`.

26. Write a driver program to test the `Matrix` class of Exercise 7.

Section 9.7

27. Use the `stack` container in a program like that for Programming Problem 2 of Chapter 7 that reads a string, one character at a time, and determines whether the string contains balanced parentheses—that is, for each left parenthesis (if there are any) there is exactly one matching right parenthesis later in the string.

28. Use the `stack` container in a program that determines the prime factorization of a positive integer, displaying the prime factors in descending order. (See Programming Problem 4 of Chapter 7.) For example, for the integer 3960, your program should produce

$$11 * 5 * 3 * 3 * 2 * 2 * 2$$

29. Use the queue and `stack` containers in a program that reverses the elements in a queue.

30. Use the queue container in a memory-recall program that generates a random sequence of letters and/or digits, displays them to the user one at a time for a second or so, and then asks the user to reproduce the sequence. Use a queue to store the sequence of characters.

31. Use the queue and `stack` containers in a program that reads a string of characters, pushing each character onto a stack as it is read and simultaneously adding it to a queue. When the end of the string is encountered, the program should use the basic stack and queue operations to determine if the string is a palindrome (see Exercise 10 of Section 5.2).

32. Redo Problem 31 but use only a deque to store the characters in the string.

CHAPTER 10

ADT Implementation: Recursion, Algorithm Analysis, and Standard Algorithms

CHAPTER CONTENTS

Chapter Objectives

- Review recursion by looking at examples.
- Show how recursion is implemented using a run-time stack.
- Look at the important topic of algorithm efficiency and how it is measured.
- Describe some of the powerful and useful standard C++ function templates in STL.
- (Optional) Introduce briefly the topic of algorithm verification.

Implementations of abstract data types have two major aspects:

1. Find or build storage structures for the data elements in the ADT.
2. Develop algorithms for the basic operations of the ADT.

In the preceding chapters we have looked at several different structures that can be used to organize the data in the problem—compile-time arrays, run-time arrays, linked lists, vectors, and so on. In this chapter we turn our attention to a more careful study of the other aspect of implementing ADTs, concentrating on the development and evaluation of algorithms and also looking at some of the standard algorithms provided in C++.

The algorithms we have considered thus far and the functions that implement them have all been nonrecursive; that is, they do not call themselves, either directly or indirectly. There are some problems, however, for which the most appropriate algorithms are recursive. We begin this chapter by reviewing recursion and how recursive functions are written in C++, and we illustrate recursion with several examples. We also discuss the role of stacks in supporting recursion.

Also, for a given problem, there may be several different algorithms for performing the same task, and it is important that we be able to compare their performance. Thus, we also consider more carefully the analysis of algorithms and introduce some techniques for measuring their efficiency. At the end of this chapter, we introduce some techniques for verifying the correctness of algorithms.

10.1 Recursion

We have seen several examples of functions that call other functions. In this section, we look at functions that call themselves, a phenomenon known as **recursion**. A function is said to be **defined recursively** if its definition consists of two parts:

1. An **anchor** or **base case**, in which the value of the function is specified for one or more values of the parameter(s).
2. An **inductive** or **recursive case**, in which the function's value for the current value of the parameter(s) is defined in terms of previously defined function values and/or parameter values.

The structure is the same as for proofs by *mathematical induction* that you may have studied in mathematics courses: A property $P(n)$ is proved to be true for all nonnegative integers n as follows:

1. Prove a base case ($n = 0$).
2. Prove an inductive case by assuming the property holds for some integer $n = k$—the *induction hypothesis* or *assumption*—and then proving that it holds for $n = k + 1$.

Examples of Recursive Functions

To illustrate recursive functions, we look at two classic examples from mathematics: (1) calculating a power of a real number, and (2) calculating the factorial of a nonnegative integer. Their recursive definitions have the same structure in that the anchor case for each function specifies a particular value of the function, and the inductive case defines its value for an integer n in terms of its value for $n - 1$.

Recursive Power Function   We begin with the problem of calculating x^n, where x is a real value and n is a nonnegative integer. The first definition of x^n that one learns is usually an iterative (nonrecursive) one,

$$x^n = \underbrace{x \times x \times \cdots \times x}_{n \ x's}$$

and later one learns that x^0 is defined to be 1. (For convenience, we assume here that x^0 is 1 also when x is 0, although in this case, it is usually left undefined.)

In calculating a sequence of consecutive powers of some number, however, it would be foolish to calculate each one using this definition—that is, to multiply the number by itself the required number of times; for example,

$$3^0 = 1$$
$$3^1 = 3$$
$$3^2 = 3 \times 3 = 9$$
$$3^3 = 3 \times 3 \times 3 = 27$$
$$3^4 = 3 \times 3 \times 3 \times 3 = 81$$
$$3^5 = 3 \times 3 \times 3 \times 3 \times 3 = 243$$
$$\cdot$$
$$\cdot$$
$$\cdot$$

It is clear that once some power of 3 has been calculated, it can be used to calculate the next power; for example, given the value of $3^3 = 27$, we can use this value to calculate

$$3^4 = 3 \times 3^3 = 3 \times 27 = 81$$

and this value to calculate

$$3^5 = 3 \times 3^4 = 3 \times 81 = 243$$

and so on. Indeed, to calculate any power of 3, we need only know the value of 3^0,

$$3^0 = 1$$

and the fundamental relation between one power of 3 and the next:

$$3^n = 3 \times 3^{n-1}$$

This approach to calculating powers leads to the following recursive definition of the power function:

$$x^0 = 1 \qquad \text{(the anchor or base case)}$$
$$\text{For } n > 0, x^n = x \times x^{n-1} \qquad \text{(the inductive or recursive case)}$$

Recursive Factorial Function Our second example of a function that can be calculated recursively is the factorial function. The first definition of $n!$, the factorial of a nonnegative integer n, that one usually learns is

$$n! = 1 \times 2 \times \cdots \times n, \text{ for } n > 0$$

and that $0!$ is 1. For example,

$$0! = 1$$
$$1! = 1$$
$$2! = 1 \times 2 = 2$$
$$3! = 1 \times 2 \times 3 = 6$$
$$4! = 1 \times 2 \times 3 \times 4 = 24$$
$$5! = 1 \times 2 \times 3 \times 4 \times 5 = 120$$

Once again the value of this function for a given integer can be used to calculate the value for the next integer. For instance, to calculate $5!$, we can simply multiply the value of $4!$ by 5:

$$5! = 4! \times 5 = 24 \times 5 = 120$$

Similarly, we can use $5!$ to calculate $6!$,

$$6! = 5! \times 6 = 120 \times 6 = 720$$

and so on. We need only know the value of 0!,

$$0! = 1$$

and the fundamental relation between one factorial and the next:

$$n! = (n - 1)! \times n$$

This suggests the following recursive definition of $n!$:

$0! = 1$ (the anchor or base case)

For $n > 0$, $n! = (n - 1)! \times n$ (the inductive or recursive case)

Coding Recursive Functions

As we noted in these examples, the recursive definitions are useful in calculating function values $f(n)$ for a sequence of consecutive values of n. Using them to calculate any one particular value, however, requires computing earlier values. For example, consider using the recursive definition of the power function to calculate 3^5. We must first calculate 3^4, because 3^5 is defined as the product of 3 and 3^4. But to calculate 3^4 we must calculate 3^3 because 3^4 is defined as 3×3^3. And to calculate 3^3, we must apply the inductive case of the definition again, $3^3 = 3 \times 3^2$, then again to find 3^2, which is defined as $3^2 = 3 \times 3^1$, and once again to find $3^1 = 3 \times 3^0$. Now we have finally reached the anchor case:

$$3^5 = 3 \times 3^4$$
$$\downarrow$$
$$3^4 = 3 \times 3^3$$
$$\downarrow$$
$$3^3 = 3 \times 3^2$$
$$\downarrow$$
$$3^2 = 3 \times 3^1$$
$$\downarrow$$
$$3^1 = 3 \times 3^0$$
$$\downarrow$$
$$3^0 = 1$$

Since the value of 3^0 is given, we can now backtrack to find the value of 3^1,

$$3^5 = 3 \times 3^4$$
$$\downarrow$$
$$3^4 = 3 \times 3^3$$
$$\downarrow$$
$$3^3 = 3 \times 3^2$$
$$\downarrow$$
$$3^2 = 3 \times 3^1$$
$$\downarrow$$
$$3^1 = 3 \times 3^0 = 3 \times 1 = 3$$
$$\downarrow \quad \nearrow$$
$$3^0 = 1$$

then backtrack again to find the value of 3^2,

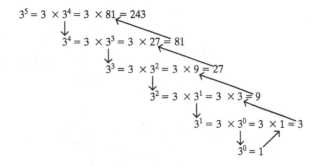

$$3^5 = 3 \times 3^4$$
$$3^4 = 3 \times 3^3$$
$$3^3 = 3 \times 3^2$$
$$3^2 = 3 \times 3^1 = 3 \times 3 = 9$$
$$3^1 = 3 \times 3^0 = 3 \times 1 = 3$$
$$3^0 = 1$$

and so on until we eventually obtain the value 243 for 3^5:

$$3^5 = 3 \times 3^4 = 3 \times 81 = 243$$
$$3^4 = 3 \times 3^3 = 3 \times 27 = 81$$
$$3^3 = 3 \times 3^2 = 3 \times 9 = 27$$
$$3^2 = 3 \times 3^1 = 3 \times 3 = 9$$
$$3^1 = 3 \times 3^0 = 3 \times 1 = 3$$
$$3^0 = 1$$

As this example demonstrates, calculating function values by hand using recursive definitions may require considerable bookkeeping to record information at the various levels of the recursive evaluation, so that after the anchor case is reached, this information can be used to backtrack from one level to the preceding one. Fortunately, in modern high-level languages such as C++, all of the necessary bookkeeping and backtracking is done automatically.

To illustrate, consider the power function again. The recursive definition of this function can be implemented as a recursive function in C++ in a straightforward manner:

```
double power(double x, unsigned n)
/*-----------------------------------------------------------

   Precondition:  None.
   Postcondition: x to the nth power is returned.
   --------------------------------------------------------*/
{
   if (n == 0)
      return 1.0;                    // anchor case
   // else
   return x * power(x, n - 1);   // inductive case (n > 0)
}
```

When this function is called, the inductive case is applied repeatedly, each time with a smaller value of n. Each recursive call, therefore, makes progress toward the anchor case, which ensures that it will eventually be reached, as shown in Figure 10.1.

As this diagram illustrates, when the call power(3.0, 5) is made to calculate 3.0^5, the inductive case is reached, and it needs the value of power(3.0, 4) before it can compute the value to be returned. Consequently, the function power() is called again, but this time with a smaller value for n. The inductive case in this second call to power() is reached again and generates another call power(3.0, 3), which in turn generates another call power(3.0, 2), followed by a call power(3.0, 1), and finally the call power(3.0, 0). Because the anchor condition is now satisfied, no additional calls are generated.

Figure 10.1 Recursive Calls to the Power Function

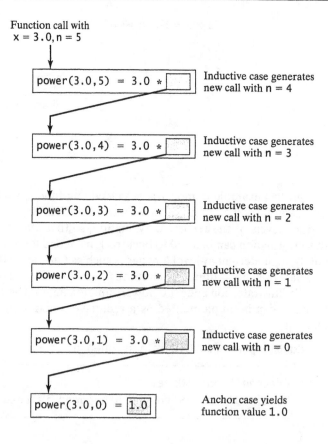

The value 1.0 is returned for power(3.0, 0), which is then used to calculate the value of power(3.0, 1), and so on until the value 243.0 is eventually returned as the value for the original function call power(3.0, 5), as pictured in Figure 10.2.

Figure 10.2 Function Returns for the Recursive Power Function

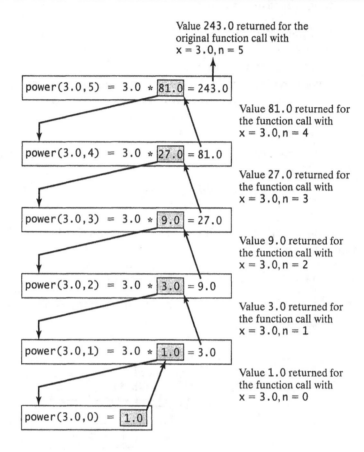

Value 243.0 returned for the original function call with x = 3.0, n = 5

power(3.0,5) = 3.0 * 81.0 = 243.0

Value 81.0 returned for the function call with x = 3.0, n = 4

power(3.0,4) = 3.0 * 27.0 = 81.0

Value 27.0 returned for the function call with x = 3.0, n = 3

power(3.0,3) = 3.0 * 9.0 = 27.0

Value 9.0 returned for the function call with x = 3.0, n = 2

power(3.0,2) = 3.0 * 3.0 = 9.0

Value 3.0 returned for the function call with x = 3.0, n = 1

power(3.0,1) = 3.0 * 1.0 = 3.0

Value 1.0 returned for the function call with x = 3.0, n = 0

power(3.0,0) = 1.0

The recursive definition of the factorial function is also easily implemented as a recursive function in C++. Writing this function and tracing its execution, as we did for the function power(), are left as exercises.

Example of Inappropriate Recursion: Fibonacci Numbers

Each execution of the inductive case in the definitions of the power function and the factorial function generates only one call to the function itself, but recursive definitions of other functions may require more than one such call. To illustrate, consider the sequence of **Fibonacci numbers**,

$$1, 1, 2, 3, 5, 8, 13, 21, 34, 55, \ldots$$

which begins with two 1's and in which each number thereafter is the sum of the two preceding numbers. This infinite sequence is defined recursively as

$$f_1 = 1$$
$$f_2 = 1$$
$$\text{For } n > 2, f_n = f_{n-1} + f_{n-2}$$

where f_n denotes the nth term in the sequence. This definition leads naturally to the following recursive function:

```
unsigned fib(unsigned n)
/*-----------------------------------------------------

  Precondition:  None.
  Postcondition: n-th Fibonacci number is returned.
  -----------------------------------------------------*/
{
   if (n <= 2)
      return 1;                         // anchor case
   // else
   return fib(n - 1) + fib(n - 2);   // inductive case (n > 2)
}
```

If the function call fib(5) is made to obtain the fifth Fibonacci number, the inductive case

```
   return fib(n - 1) + fib(n - 2);
```

immediately generates the call fib(4) with parameter $5 - 1 = 4$:

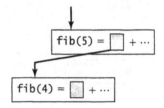

This generates another function call fib(3), which in turn generates the call fib(2):

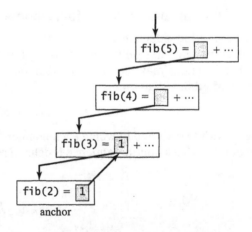

Because the anchor condition is now satisfied, the value 1 is returned for fib(2), and the second call fib(1) needed to calculate fib(3) is generated:

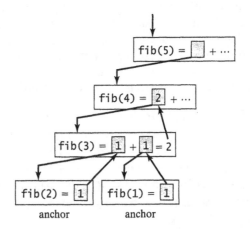

Here again, the value 1 is returned, and the function call fib(3) is completed so that the value 1 + 1 = 2 is returned. The first term in the sum for the call fib(4) thus has been calculated, and the call fib(2) is generated to determine the second term. This process continues until, eventually, the value 5 is returned for fib(5):

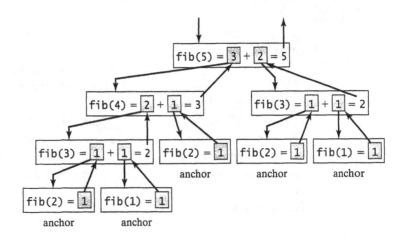

Note the function calls with the same argument in this **recursion tree**; there are two calls with argument 1, three with argument 2, and two with argument 3. These multiple calls suggest that this may not be the most efficient way to calculate Fibonacci numbers, a suspicion that is confirmed by comparing the computing time of this recursive Fibonacci function with a nonrecursive version in Section 10.4.

Example: Binary Search

Recursive functions need not return values via a return statement, but may instead return values via the parameters or may return no values at all. For example, consider the binary search algorithm, which was described in Section 1.4. Although the algorithm given there is an iterative one, the approach of the binary search method is recursive. If the (sub)list we are currently examining is empty, the item for which we are searching is obviously not in the (sub)list, and so we can stop searching (anchor condition 1). If the (sub)list is not empty, we examine its middle element, and if this is the item for which we are searching, we are finished (anchor condition 2). Otherwise, either the sublist of items preceding this middle item or the sublist of items following it is *searched in the same manner* (inductive case).

A recursive binary search function is therefore quite simple:

```
void recBinarySearch(ArrayType a, int first, int last,
                     ElementType item,
                     bool & found, int & loc)
/*------------------------------------------------------------
   Recursively search sub(list) a[first], . . ., a[last]
   for item using a binary search.

   Precondition:  Elements of a are in ascending order;
        item has the same type as the array elements.
   Postcondition: found = true and loc = position of item
        if the search is successful; otherwise, found is
        false.
   ------------------------------------------------------------*/
{
  if (first > last)           // anchor 1 -- empty sublist
    found = false;
  else                        // inductive case:
  {                           //   recursively search:
    loc = (first + last) / 2;
    if (item < a[loc])        //    the first half
      recBinarySearch(a, first, loc - 1, found, loc);
    else if (item > a[loc])   //    the second half
      recBinarySearch(a, loc + 1, last, found, loc);
    else
      found = true;           // anchor 2 -- item found
  }
)
```

To illustrate the action of this function, suppose that the list 11, 22, 33, 44, 55, 66, 77, 88, 99 is stored in positions 0 through 8 of array a and that we wish to search this list for the number 66. We begin with the function call

```
recBinarySearch(a, 0, 8, 66, itemFound, position);
```

where itemFound is a bool variable and position is an int variable. The function calculates loc = 4, and since 66 > a[4] = 55, the second part of the inductive case generates another call with first = 5 and last = 8. This call searches the sublist of elements in positions 5 through 8, as highlighted in the following diagram:

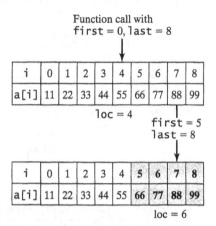

Because the sublist is nonempty, this function call calculates loc = 6, and since 66 < a[6] = 77, the first part of the inductive case generates another function call with first = 5 and last = 5, reducing the search to a one-element sublist:

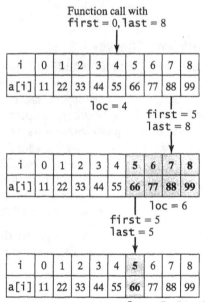

In this third function call, the value loc = 5 is calculated, and since a[5] = 66 is the desired item, the second anchor condition assigns the value true to found. This third execution of recBinarySearch() then terminates and passes the values found = true and loc = 5 back to the second function call. This second execution likewise terminates and passes these same values back to the first execution of recBinary-Search(). The original call to this function is thus completed, and the value true is returned to the argument itemFound and the value 5 to the argument position:

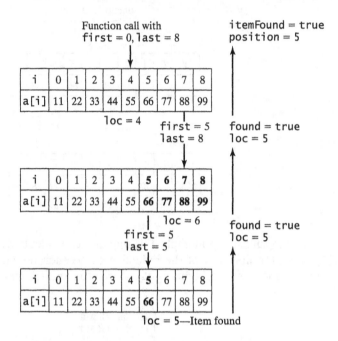

Example: Palindrome Checker

Developing recursive algorithms is difficult for many beginning programmers. Practice, practice, and more practice seems to be the only way to develop the ability to think recursively. So here is one more example of a recursive algorithm to study; more will be given in subsequent chapters.

An integer is said to be a **palindrome** if its value does not change when its digits are reversed; that is, the number reads the same from left to right as it does from right to left. For example, 1, 33, 5665, and 123454321 are palindromes. Now, suppose we wish to develop a boolean-valued function that checks whether a given positive integer is a palindrome, returning true if it is and false otherwise.

Thinking nonrecursively, we might try one of the following:

- Decompose the number into its separate digits and reassemble them in reverse order. Then check if this reversed number is equal to the original number.

- Decompose the number into its separate digits and store them in an array (or vector). Then scan this array from both ends, checking to see if the digits match.

- Decompose the number into its separate digits and push each one onto a stack. Because of a stack's LIFO property, when these digits are popped from the stack, they will appear in the opposite order from that in the original number, and so we can check if the number's reversal is the same as the number.

A more straightforward solution to the problem is a recursive one, obtained simply by analyzing how one would solve this problem by hand. In checking a number such as

$$8507058$$

most people first check the first and last digits and, if they agree, cross them out (perhaps only mentally) and consider the number that remains:

$$\not{8}\, 50705\, \not{8}$$

The resulting number 50705 is then checked *in the same way*, which is a recursive approach to the problem. After two more applications of this inductive case of checking and truncating the first and last digits,

$$\not{5}\, 070\, \not{5}$$

$$\not{0}\, 7\, \not{0}$$

a one-digit number results:

$$7$$

This obviously is a palindrome (anchor case 1). If the original number had an even number of digits, then at this last step, no digits would remain and the number would be a palindrome. If at any point along the way, the first and last digits did not match (anchor case 2), we would stop checking, since the number obviously is not a palindrome.

This leads to the following recursive algorithm:

Recursive Palindrome Checker

/* Check whether nonnegative integer *number* is a palindrome; *number* and *numDigits* (the number of digits in *number*) are received. True is returned if *number* is a palindrome, and *false* otherwise. */

1. If *numDigits* $\leq$ 1   // Anchor case 1
      Return true.
   // Else check if the first and last digits match, and if not, return false
2. Calculate *firstDigit* = *number* / $10^{numDigits-1}$
      and *lastDigit* = *number* % 10.
3. If *firstDigit* $\neq$ *lastDigit*   // Anchor case 2
      Return false.
   // Else the first and last digits match, so check more digits.
4. Apply the algorithm recursively to: // Inductive case
      (*number* % $10^{numDigits-1}$) / 10 and *numDigits* – 2
   // *number* with *firstDigit* and *lastDigit* removed

Implementing this algorithm as a recursive function is straightforward and is left as an exercise.

✔ **Quick Quiz 10.1**

1. _____ is the phenomenon of a function calling itself.

2. Name and describe the two parts of a recursive definition of a function.

3. A nonrecursive function for computing some value may execute more rapidly than a recursive function that computes the same value. (True or false)

4. For the following recursive function, find f(5):

```
int f(int n)
{
   if (n == 0)
      return 0;
   else
      return n + f(n - 1);
}
```

5. For the function in Question 4, find f(0).

6. For the function in Question 4, suppose + is changed to * in the inductive case. Find f(5).

7. For the function in Question 4, what happens with the function call f(-1)?

☙ **Exercises 10.1**

Exercises 1–6 assume ASCII representation of characters and the following function f():

```
void f(char ch)
{
   if (('A' <= ch) && (ch <= 'H'))
   {
      f(ch - 1);
      cout << ch;
   }
   else
      cout << endl;
}
```

Tell what output will be produced by the function call.

1. f('C')

2. f('G')

3. f('3')

4. f('C') if ch - 1 is replaced by ch + 1 in the function

5. f('C') if the output statement and the recursive call to f() are interchanged

6. f('C') if a copy of the output statement is inserted before the recursive call to f()

7. Given the following function f() and assuming ASCII representation of characters, use the method illustrated in this section to trace the sequence of function calls and returns in evaluating f('a', 'e') and f('h', 'c'):

```
int f(char ch1, char ch2)
{
  if (ch1 > ch2)
    return 0;
  if (ch1 + 1 == ch2)
    return 1;
  // else
  return F(ch1 + 1, ch2 - 1) + 2;
}
```

Exercises 8–10 assume ASCII representation of characters and the following function g():

```
void g(char ch, int n)
{
  if (n <= 0)
    cout << endl;
  else
  {
    g(ch - 1, n - 1);
    cout << ch;
    g(ch + 1, n - 1);
  }
}
```

8. What output will be produced by the function call g('M', 4)?
   (*Hint:* First try g('M', 2), then g('M', 3).)

9. How many letters are output by the call g('M', 10)?

10. If the output statement is moved before the first recursive call to g(), what output will be produced by g('M', 4)?

Determine what is calculated by the recursive functions in Exercises 11–15.

11.
```
unsigned f(unsigned n)
{
  if (n == 0)
    return 0;
  // else
    return n * f(n - 1);
}
```

12.
```
unsigned f(double x, unsigned n)
{
  if (n == 0)
    return 0;
```

```
        // else
          return n + f(x, n - 1);
```

13.
```
unsigned f(unsigned n)
{
  if (n < 2)
    return 0;
  // else
    return 1 + f(n / 2);
}
```

14.
```
unsigned f(unsigned n)
{
  if (n == 0)
    return 0;
  // else
    return f(n / 10) + n % 10;
}
```

15.
```
unsigned f(int n)
{
  if (n < 0)
    return f(-n);
  if (n < 10)
    return n;
  // else
    return f(n / 10);
}
```

16–20. Write nonrecursive versions of the functions in Exercises 11–15.

The exercises that follow ask you to write functions. You should test these functions with driver programs as instructed in Programming Problems 1–16 at the end of this chapter.

21. Write a recursive function that returns the number of digits in a nonnegative integer.

22. Write a nonrecursive version of the function in Exercise 21.

23. Write a recursive function `printReverse()` that displays an integer's digits in reverse order.

24. Write a nonrecursive version of the function `printReverse()` in Exercise 23.

25. Modify the recursive exponentiation function in the text so that it also works for negative exponents. One approach is to modify the recursive definition of x^n so that, for negative values of n, division is used instead of multiplication and n

is incremented rather than decremented:

$$x^n = \begin{cases} 1 & \text{if } n \text{ is } 0 \\ x^{n-1} \times x & \text{if } n \text{ is greater than } 0 \\ x^{n+1}/x & \text{otherwise} \end{cases}$$

26. Write a nonrecursive version of the function in Exercise 25 (i.e., a nonrecursive exponential function in which exponents may be 0, positive, or negative).

Assuming declarations of the form

```
const int MAX_CAPACITY = . . .;   // user defined
typedef ElementType = . . . ;     // user defined
typedef ElementType ArrayType[MAX_CAPACITY];
```

write recursive definitions of the functions whose prototypes are given in Exercises 27–29.

27. `void reverseArray(ArrayType a, int first, int last);`
    `/* Reverse the contents of a[first], ..., a[last] */`

28. `int sumArray(ArrayType a, int n);`
    `/* Return the sum of a[0], ..., a[n - 1] */`

29. `int location(ArrayType a, int first, int last, Element elm);`
    `/* Return the location of elm in a[first],`
    `   ..., a[last].  If not found, return 0. */`

30. Using the basic string operations length, concatenate, copy, and find (see Section 5.2), develop a recursive algorithm for reversing a string.

31. Proceed as in Exercise 30, but develop a nonrecursive algorithm.

32. Write a recursive function that implements the algorithm in this section for determining if a number is a palindrome.

33. The *greatest common divisor* of two integers a and b, GCD(a, b), not both of which are zero, is the largest positive integer that divides both a and b. The *Euclidean algorithm* for finding this greatest common divisor of a and b is as follows: Divide a by b to obtain the integer quotient q and the remainder r, so that $a = bq + r$ (if $b = 0$, GCD(a, b) = a). Then GCD(a, b) = GCD(b, r). Replace a with b and b with r and repeat this procedure. Because the remainders are decreasing, eventually a remainder of 0 will result. The last nonzero remainder is GCD(a, b). For example,

$$\begin{array}{ll} 1260 = 198 \cdot 6 + 72 & \text{GCD}(1260, 198) = \text{GCD}(198, 72) \\ 198 = 72 \cdot 2 + 54 & \phantom{\text{GCD}(1260, 198)} = \text{GCD}(72, 54) \\ 72 = 54 \cdot 1 + 18 & \phantom{\text{GCD}(1260, 198)} = \text{GCD}(54, 18) \\ 54 = 18 \cdot 3 + 0 & \phantom{\text{GCD}(1260, 198)} = 18 \end{array}$$

(*Note*: If either a or b is negative, replace them with their absolute values in this algorithm.) Write a recursive greatest common divisor function.

34. Proceed as in Exercise 33, but write a nonrecursive function.

35. *Binomial coefficients* can be defined recursively as follows:

$$\left.\begin{array}{l} \dbinom{n}{0} = 1 \\[2ex] \dbinom{n}{n} = 1 \end{array}\right\} \text{(anchor)}$$

$$\text{For } 0 < k < n, \dbinom{n}{k} = \dbinom{n-1}{k-1} + \dbinom{n-1}{k} \text{ (inductive case)}$$

   a. Write a recursive function to calculate binomial coefficients.

   b. Draw a recursion tree like that in this section showing the function calls

and returns involved in calculating the binomial coefficient $\dbinom{4}{2}$.

36. Binomial coefficients can also be defined as follows:

$$\dbinom{n}{k} = \frac{n!}{k!(n-k)!}$$

Write a nonrecursive function to calculate binomial coefficients using this definition.

10.2 Examples of Recursion: Towers of Hanoi; Parsing

Towers of Hanoi

The Towers of Hanoi problem is a classic example of a problem for which a recursive algorithm is especially appropriate. It can be solved easily using recursion, but a nonrecursive solution is considerably more difficult. The problem is to solve the puzzle shown in Figure 10.3, in which one must move the disks from the left peg to the right peg according to the following rules:

1. When a disk is moved, it must be placed on one of the three pegs.
2. Only one disk may be moved at a time, and it must be the top disk on one of the pegs.
3. A larger disk may never be placed on top of a smaller one.

Figure 10.3 Towers of Hanoi

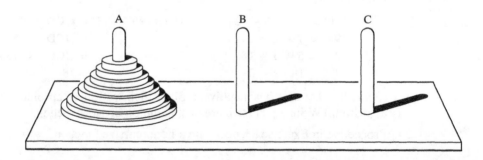

Legend has it that the priests in the Temple of Bramah were given a puzzle consisting of a golden platform with three diamond needles on which were placed 64 golden disks. The priests were to move one disk per day, following these rules, and when they had successfully finished moving the disks to another needle, time would end. (*Question:* If the priests moved one disk per day and began their work in year 0, when would time end?)

Novices usually find the puzzle easy to solve for a small number of disks, but they have more difficulty as the number of disks grows to seven, eight, and beyond. To a computer scientist, however, the Towers of Hanoi puzzle is easy: We begin by identifying a base case, for which the problem is trivial to solve:

If there is one disk, then move it from Peg A to Peg C.

The puzzle is thus easily solved for $n = 1$ disk. We then give an inductive solution for $n > 1$ disks, in which we assume that a solution exists for $n - 1$ disks:

1. *Move the topmost $n - 1$ disks from Peg A to Peg B, using Peg C for temporary storage.*
2. *Move the final disk remaining on Peg A to Peg C.*
3. *Move the $n - 1$ disks from Peg B to Peg C, using Peg A for temporary storage.*

This scheme is implemented by the recursive function move() in Figure 10.4. It also shows a program that uses move() to solve the Hanoi Towers problem, and an execution in which the problem is solved for four disks. Figure 10.5 gives a graphical trace of the solution.

Figure 10.4 Solving the Towers of Hanoi Problem Recursively

```
/*-----------------------------------------------------------------------
   Program to solve the Towers of Hanoi puzzle recursively.

   Input:  numDisks, the number of disks to be moved
   Output: A sequence of moves that solve the puzzle
   -----------------------------------------------------------------------*/

#include <iostream>
#include <iomanip>
using namespace std;

void move(unsigned n, unsigned & moveNumber,
          char source, char destination, char spare);
int main()
{
    const char PEG1 = 'A',              // the three pegs
               PEG2 = 'B',
               PEG3 = 'C';
    unsigned moveNumber = 0;            // counts the moves
```

Figure 10.4 (continued)

```
   cout << "This program solves the Hanoi Towers puzzle.\n\n";
   cout << "Enter the number of disks: ";
   int numDisks;                      // the number of disks to be moved
   cin >> numDisks;
   cout << endl;

   move(numDisks, moveNumber, PEG1, PEG3, PEG2); // the solution
}


void move(unsigned n, unsigned & moveNumber,
          char source, char destination, char spare)
/*-------------------------------------------------------------------
  Recursive function to solve the Towers of Hanoi puzzle with n disks.

  Precondition:  None.
  Postcondition: A message describing the move is output to cout.
  -------------------------------------------------------------------*/
{
  if (n == 1)                        // anchor
  {
    moveNumber++;
    cout << setw(3) << moveNumber
         <<  ". Move the top disk from " << source
         << " to " << destination << endl;
  }
  else
  {                                  // inductive case
    move(n-1, moveNumber, source, spare, destination);
    move(1, moveNumber, source, destination, spare);
    move(n-1, moveNumber, spare, destination, source);
  }
}
```

Execution Trace:
```
  1. Move the top disk from A to B
  2. Move the top disk from A to C
  3. Move the top disk from B to C
  4. Move the top disk from A to B
  5. Move the top disk from C to A
```

Figure 10.4 (continued)

```
 6. Move the top disk from C to B
 7. Move the top disk from A to B
 8. Move the top disk from A to C
 9. Move the top disk from B to C
10. Move the top disk from B to A
11. Move the top disk from C to A
12. Move the top disk from B to C
13. Move the top disk from A to B
14. Move the top disk from A to C
15. Move the top disk from B to C
```

▲

Figure 10.5 Graphical Solution of Towers of Hanoi

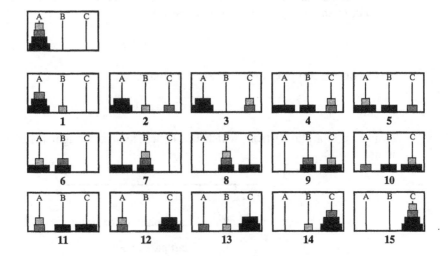

Parsing

All the examples of recursion that we have given thus far have used **direct recursion**; that is, the functions have called themselves directly. **Indirect recursion** occurs when a function calls other functions, and some chain of function calls eventually results in a call to the first function again. For example, function f() may call function g(), which calls function h(), which calls f() again.

To illustrate indirect recursion, we consider the compiler problem of processing arithmetic expressions. In particular, we consider the specific problem of parsing arithmetic expressions, that is, determining whether they are well formed and, if so, what their structure is.

The basic components of a compiler are summarized in the following diagram:

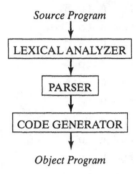

The input to a compiler is a stream of characters that make up the source program. Before the translation can be carried out, this stream of characters must be broken up into meaningful groups, such as identifiers, reserved words, constants, and operators. For example, the arithmetic expression

$$2 \ * \ (a \ + \ b)$$

is read by the compiler as a "stream" of characters

$$2 \cancel{b} * \cancel{b} (a \cancel{b} + \cancel{b} b)$$

(where ⊭ is a blank) from which the lexical analyzer might identify the following units:

2	digit
*	multiplication operator
(	left parenthesis
a	letter
+	addition operator
b	letter
)	right parenthesis

These units are called **tokens**, and the part of the compiler that recognizes these tokens is called the **lexical analyzer**.

The **syntax rules** of a language specify how basic tokens such as identifiers and constructs such as expressions are formed. These syntax rules are commonly stated as **substitution rules**, or **productions**. For very simple arithmetic expressions, the rules might be the following:

1. *expression* → *term* + *term* | *term* – *term* | *term*

2. *term* → *factor* * *factor* | *factor* / *factor* | *factor*

3. *factor* → (*expression*) | *letter* | *digit*

Here the vertical bar (|) is used to separate the various alternatives. For example, the third syntax rule specifies that a factor may be a left parenthesis followed by an expression followed by a right parenthesis, or it may be a single letter or a single digit.

Given a sequence of tokens, it is the task of the **parser** to group these tokens together to form the basic syntactic structures of the language as determined by the syntax rules. For example, for 2 * (a + b) it must recognize that, according to the first syntax rule, an expression can be a term, and by the second rule, a term may have the form *factor* * *factor*. These substitutions can be displayed by the following partially developed **parse tree** for this expression:

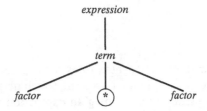

By the third syntax rule, a factor may be a digit; in particular, it may be the digit 2, and the second alternative of the third syntax rule specifies that a factor may be an expression enclosed in parentheses:

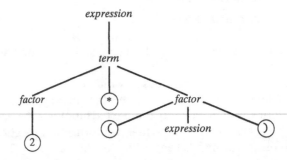

Continued application of these syntax rules produces the following complete parse tree, which shows how 2 * (a + b) can be generated according to the syntax rules and thus demonstrates that it is a valid expression:

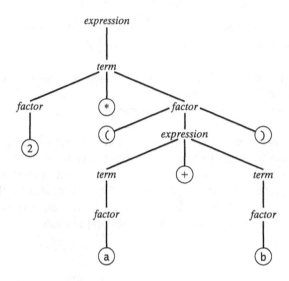

It is clear that these syntax rules for expressions involve indirect recursion. For example, an expression may be a term, which may be a factor, which may be a parenthesized expression, thus defining an expression indirectly in terms of itself. Thus, to implement a parser for these simplified expressions, we could use three functions validExpression(), validTerm(), and validFactor(), which are derived directly from the corresponding syntax rules. For example, consider the function validExpression(). According to the first syntax rule, an expression may have one of the following three forms:

E1. *expression → term + term*

E2. *expression → term - term*

E3. *expression → term*

In each case, it must begin with a term, and so the first action in this function is a call to validTerm().

If validTerm() identifies a valid term by returning true, then the function validExpression() must examine the next symbol to determine which of these three forms is applicable. If the next symbol is + or -, validTerm() must then be called to check for one of the first two forms for an expression; validExpression() then returns true or false according to whether validTerm() returns true or false. If the symbol is not + or -, then an expression of the last form has been identified. The following algorithm summarizes this syntax checking:

Algorithm for `validExpression()`

1. Call `validTerm()` to see if the next part of the expression is a term.
2. If it returns true:
     // Check for syntax rule E2 or E3.
     If the next symbol in the expression is '+' or '−'
         a. Call `validTerm()`
         b. Return the value it returns.
     Else
         Return true   // by syntax rule E1
   Else
       Return false // doesn't begin with a term.

An algorithm for `validTerm()` is also easily derived from the syntax rules

T1. *term → factor * factor*
T2. *term → factor / factor*
T3. *term → factor*

and is very similar to that for `validExpression()`:

Algorithm for `validTerm()`

1. Call `validFactor()` to see if the next part of the expression is a factor.
2. If it returns true:
     // Check for syntax rule T2 or T3.
     If the next symbol in the expression is '*' or '/'
         a. Call `validFactor()`
         b. Return the value it returns.
     Else
         Return true   // by syntax rule T1
   Else
       Return false // doesn't begin with a factor.

The algorithm for `validFactor()` is likewise derived from the syntax rules

F1. *factor → (expression)*
F2. *factor → letter*
F3. *factor → digit*

but has a different structure. Note the recursive call to `validExpression()` in step 2.

Algorithm for `validFactor()`

If the next symbol in the expression is '('
    // Check for syntax rule F1
    Call `validExpression()`. If it returns true:
        If the next symbol in the expression is ')'
            Return true.
        Else
            Return false. // Missing ')' after expression
    Else
        Return false.   // An expression doesn't follow '('
Else   // Check for syntax rule F2 or F3
    If the next symbol is a letter or a digit
        Return true.
    Else
        Return false.

Table 10.1 traces the action of these three functions in parsing the expression a+b.

TABLE 10.1: Parse of a + b

Function	Next symbol	Returns	Action
`validExpression()`			Call `validTerm()`
`validTerm()`			Call `validFactor()`
`validFactor()`	a		Check next symbol
	a	true	Return true to `validTerm()`
`validTerm()`	+		Check next symbol
	+	true	Not * or /, so return true to `validExpression()`
`validExpression()`	+		Check next symbol
	+		It's + or -, so call `validTerm()`
`validTerm()`	+		Call `validFactor()`
`validFactor()`	b		Check next symbol
	b		It's a letter, so return true to `validTerm()`
`validTerm()`	b		Check next symbol (end of expression)
		true	Not * or /, so return true to `validExpression()`
`validExpression()`		true	Return true to calling function

Implementing the preceding algorithms as functions is straightforward. A complete class `ExpressionParser` having these functions members along with a driver program to parse simplified arithmetic expressions can be found on the text's website.

◆ Exercises 10.2

1. Trace the execution of `move(4, moveNumber, 'A', 'B', 'C')` far enough to produce the first five moves in the Towers of Hanoi program. Does your answer agree with the program output in Figure 10.4? Do the same for `move(5, move-Number, 'A', 'B', 'C')`.

Draw parse trees for the expressions in Exercises 2–7.

2. a * b

3. (a * b)

4. (((1)))

5. (a * b) * c

6. a * (b * c)

7. (((a + b) * 2) - (c * d)) * 5

Construct trace tables like that in Table 10.1 for parses of the expressions in Exercises 8–11.

8. a * b

9. (a * b)

10. (a - b) - c

11. a - (b - c)

In Exercises 12–15, assume the following syntax rules for simplified boolean expressions. Draw parse trees for the expressions.

$$bexpression \rightarrow bterm \:||\: bterm \:|\: bterm$$
$$bterm \rightarrow bfactor \:\&\&\: bfactor \:|\: bfactor$$
$$bfactor \rightarrow \:!\: bfactor \:|\: (bexpression) \:|\: letter \:|\: \texttt{true} \:|\: \texttt{false}$$

12. !y && (z || false)

13. x || y && z

14. (false || x) || true

15. !(x || y)

Strings consisting of balanced parentheses can be generated by the productions

$$pstring \rightarrow (pstring) \: pstring \:|\: (\:) \: pstring \:|\: (pstring) \:|\: (\:)$$

Draw parse trees for the strings of balanced parentheses in Exercises 16–18.

16. ( ) ( ) ( )

17. ((( )))

18. ( ) (( ) ( )) ( )

10.3 Implementing Recursion

As we saw in Section 7.4, whenever execution of a function begins, a set of memory locations called an *activation record* is created for it. If execution is interrupted by a call to another (or the same) function, the values of the function's local variables, parameters, the return address, and so on are stored in this activation record. When execution of this program unit resumes, its activation record is used to restore these items to what they were before the interruption.

We also saw that because the last function interrupted is the first one to be reactivated, a stack, called the **run-time stack**, is used to store the activation records so that they can be retrieved in a last-in-first-out order. We illustrated the pushing and popping of this run-time stack with chains of function calls and returns that involved different functions—function f1 calling function f2 calling function f3, and so on. Now we look at it in the context of recursive functions.

Consider again the recursive function of Section 10.1 for calculating powers,

```
         double power(double x, unsigned n)
         {
           if (n == 0)
             return 1.0;                      // anchor case
           // else
/* A */      return x * power(x, n - 1);  // inductive case
         }
```

and suppose that it is called in an assignment statement:

```
         int main()
         {
           . . .
/* B */      z = power(2.0, 3);
           . . .
           return 0;
         }
```

Here we have indicated the return addresses as A and B, that is, the locations of the instructions where execution is to resume when the program or function is reactivated.

When execution of the main() function begins, its activation record is created and pushed onto the run-time stack. This record stores the values of variables, actual parameters, return addresses, and so on for the currently active function, namely, main().

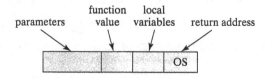

(Here, "OS" indicates that when execution of main() is completed, it returns to the operating system.)

When the function call power(2.0, 3), is encountered, execution of main() is interrupted and the contents of registers and other items needed to restore the current environment are saved in its activation record. The function power() now becomes active, so an activation record storing the parameters 2.0 and 3, the return address (B), and other things is created for it and added to the run-time stack:

top →	x [2.0] n [3]			B	AR for power(2.0, 3)
				OS	AR for main()

When the statement

```
return x * power(x, n - 1);
```

is encountered, execution of power() is interrupted. Key environment items are stored in the current activation record and a new instance of the function power() becomes active so an activation record storing the parameters 2.0 and 2 and return address (A) is created and added to the run-time stack:

top →	x [2.0] n [2]			A	AR for power(2.0, 2)
	x [2.0] n [3]			B	AR for power(2.0, 3)
				OS	AR for main()

Once again, this execution of power() is interrupted when the inductive case is encountered. A new instance of power() with parameters 2.0 and 1 becomes active, and an activation record for it is created and pushed onto the run-time stack:

top →	x [2.0] n [1]			A	AR for power(2.0, 1)
	x [2.0] n [2]			A	AR for power(2.0, 2)
	x [2.0] n [3]			B	AR for power(2.0, 3)
				OS	AR for main()

And again, the inductive case causes another interruption, creating another instance of power() and adding another activation record to the run-time stack:

top →	x [2.0] n [0]			A	AR for power(2.0, 0)
	x [2.0] n [1]			A	AR for power(2.0, 1)
	x [2.0] n [2]			A	AR for power(2.0, 2)
	x [2.0] n [3]			B	AR for power(2.0, 3)
				OS	AR for main()

Execution of power() with parameters 2.0 and 0 terminates with no interruptions and calculates the value 1.0 for power(2.0, 0). The activation record for this call is then popped from the run-time stack, and execution resumes in the previous instance of `power()` at the statement specified by the return address, returning the value 1.0 to this instance of `power()`:

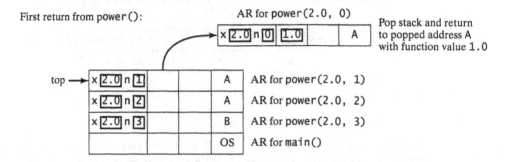

Execution of the preceding call to `power()` with parameters 2.0 and 1 then resumes and terminates without interruption, so that its activation record is popped from the stack, the value 2.0 is returned, and the previous call with parameters 2.0 and 2 is reactivated at statement A:

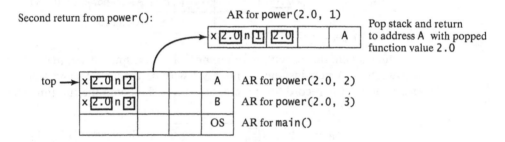

This process continues until the value 8.0 is computed for the original call `power(2.0, 3)`, and execution of the main program is resumed at the statement specified by the return address B in its activation record:

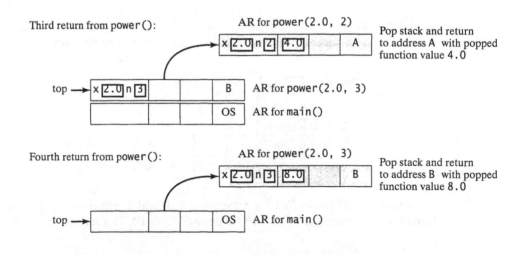

Finally, the statement `return 0;` is encountered in main, and the return value 0 is stored in its activation record, which is popped from the run-time stack. Since the stack is now empty, execution is terminated and the value 0 is returned to the operating system:

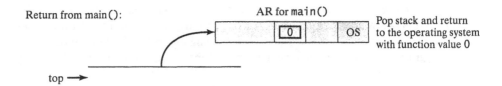

Return from main(): AR for main() Pop stack and return to the operating system with function value 0

`0` OS

top ⟶

In summary, we see that the same mechanism of a run-time stack of activation records that supports nonrecursive function calls makes recursive function calls work. Also, tracing the operation of the run-time stack with recursive functions is an important visual aid that can help with understanding recursion.

10.4 Algorithm Efficiency

An algorithm's efficiency is usually measured according to two criteria. The first is **space utilization**, the amount of memory required to store the data; and the second is **time efficiency**, the amount of time required to process the data. Unfortunately, it is usually not possible to minimize both space and time requirements simultaneously. Algorithms that require the least memory are often slower than those that use more memory. Thus, the programmer is usually faced with a trade-off between space efficiency and time efficiency.

In the early days of computing, when memory (vacuum tubes) and storage devices (magnetic drums and tapes) were expensive, space requirements received primary consideration. The important thing was to get answers to problems, even if it took several hours or perhaps even days. Nowadays, huge amounts of memory and storage are available for very little cost so that, in most cases, an algorithm's time efficiency is considered the most important. But there obviously are some situations when time and space needs are so interrelated that they must both be considered—in space probe control systems, in embedded computers that control automobile anti-lock braking systems, in digital camera microprocessors, to name but a few. In this section, however, we focus our attention on time efficiency and how it can be measured.

An algorithm's execution time is influenced by several factors. Obviously, one factor is the size of the input, since the number of input items usually affects the time required to process these items. For example, the time it takes to sort a list of items surely depends on the number of items in the list. Thus, the execution time T of an algorithm must be expressed as a function $T(n)$ of the size n of the input.

The kinds of instructions and the speed with which the machine can execute them also influence execution time. These factors, however, depend on the particular computer system being used—processor speed, the amount and kind of memory and disk space, the number of users logged in, bandwidth, and so on. Consequently, we cannot expect to express meaningfully the value of $T(n)$ in real time units such as seconds. Instead, $T(n)$ will be an approximate count of the instructions executed.

Another factor that influences computing time is the quality of the source code that implements the algorithm and the quality of the machine code generated from this source code by a compiler. Some languages are better suited than others for certain algorithms; some programmers write faster programs than others; and some compilers generate more efficient code than others. This means, in particular, that $T(n)$ cannot be computed as the number of machine instructions executed, and thus it is taken to be the number of times the instructions in the *algorithm* are executed.

As an example, consider the following algorithm for finding the mean of a set of n numbers stored in an array (the statements have been numbered for easy reference):

Algorithm to Calculate a Mean

/* Algorithm to find the mean of $x[0], \ldots, x[n-1]$. */

1. Initialize *sum* = 0.
2. Initialize index variable $i = 0$.
3. While $i < n$ do the following:
4.   a.   Add $x[i]$ to *sum*.
5.   b.   Increment i by 1.
   End while.
6. Calculate and return *mean* = *sum* / *n*.

Statements 1 and 2 are each executed one time. Statements 4 and 5, which comprise the body of the while loop, are each executed n times, and statement 3, which controls repetition, is executed $n + 1$ times, since one additional check is required to determine that the control variable i is no longer less than the value n. After repetition terminates, statement 6 is then executed one time. This analysis is summarized in the following table:

Statement	# of times executed
1	1
2	1
3	$n + 1$
4	n
5	n
6	1
Total	$3n + 4$

Thus, we see that the computing time for this algorithm is given by

$$T(n) = 3n + 4$$

As the number n of inputs increases, the value of this expression for $T(n)$ grows at a rate proportional to n, so we say that $T(n)$ has "order of magnitude n," which is usually written using "big-O notation" as

$$T(n) \text{ is } O(n)$$

In general, the computing time $T(n)$ of an algorithm is said to have **order of magnitude $f(n)$**, denoted

$$T(n) \text{ is } O(f(n))$$

if there is some constant C such that

$$T(n) \leq C \cdot f(n) \text{ for all sufficiently large values of } n$$

That is, $T(n)$ is bounded above by some constant C times $f(n)$ for all values of n from some point on. The **computational complexity** of the algorithm is said to be $O(f(n))$. For example, the complexity of the preceding algorithm is $O(n)$, since the computing time was found to be

$$T(n) = 3n + 4$$

and since

$$3n + 4 \leq 3n + n \text{ for } n \geq 4$$

we see that

$$T(n) \leq 4n \text{ for } n \geq 4$$

Thus, taking $f(n) = n$ and $C = 4$, we may say that

$$T(n) \text{ is } O(n)$$

Of course, it would also be correct to say $T(n)$ is $O(5280n)$ or $T(n)$ is $O(4n + 5)$ or $T(n)$ is $O(3.1416n + 2.71828)$, but we prefer a *simple* function like n, n^2, or $\log_2 n$ to express an algorithm's complexity. Also, $T(n)$ is $O(n)$ obviously implies that $T(n)$ is $O(n^2)$ as well as $T(n)$ is $O(n^{5/2})$ or $T(n)$ is $O(2^n)$, and in general $T(n)$ is $O(g(n))$ if $g(n) \geq n$ for all n from some point on; but the more slowly the function $g(n)$ grows, the more information it will provide about the computing time $T(n)$.

In this example, the computing time depends only on the size of the input. In other problems, however, it may depend on the arrangement of the input items as well. For example, it may take less time to sort a list of items that are nearly in order initially than to sort a list in which the items are in reverse order. We might then attempt to measure T in the **worst case** or in the **best case**, or we might attempt to compute the **average** value of T over all possible cases. The best-case performance of an algorithm is usually not very informative and the average performance is often difficult to determine. Consequently, $T(n)$ is frequently taken as a measure of the algorithm's performance in the worst case.

As an illustration, consider the following sorting algorithm (again, we have numbered the statements for easy reference):

Simple Selection Sorting Algorithm

/* Algorithm to sort $x[0] \ldots x[n-1]$ into ascending order. */

1. For $i = 0$ to $n - 2$ do the following:
   /* On the ith pass, first find the smallest element in the sublist
   $x[i], \ldots, x[n-1]$. */
2.   a. Set *smallPos* = i.
3.   b. Set *smallest* = $x[smallPos]$.
4.   c. For $j = i + 1$ to $n - 1$ do the following:
5.   If $x[j] < smallest$ then // smaller element found
6.   i. Set *smallPos* = j.
7.   ii. Set *smallest* = $x[smallPos]$.
       End for.
   /* Now interchange this smallest element with the element at the
   beginning of this sublist. */
8.   d. Set $x[smallPos] = x[i]$.
9.   e. Set $x[i]$ = *smallest*.
     End for.

Statement 1 is executed n times (for i ranging from 0 through the value $n - 1$, which causes termination); and statements 2, 3, 8, and 9 each are executed $n - 1$ times, once on each pass through the outer loop.[1] On the first pass through this loop with $i = 0$, statement 4 is executed n times; statement 5 is executed $n - 1$ times, and assuming a worst case (when the items are in descending order), so are statements 6 and 7. On the second pass with $i = 1$, statement 4 is executed $n - 1$ times and each of statements 5, 6, and 7 $n - 2$ times, and so on. Thus, statement 4 is executed a total of $n + (n - 1) + \cdots + 2$ times, and statements 5, 6, and 7 each are executed a total of $(n - 1) + (n - 2) + \cdots + 1$ times. These sums are equal to $n(n + 1)/2 - 1$ and $n(n - 1)/2$, respectively;[2] thus, the total computing time is given by

$$T(n) = n + 4(n - 1) + \frac{n(n + 1)}{2} - 1 + 3\left(\frac{n(n - 1)}{2}\right)$$

---

[1] Statement 1 actually consists of three statements:
    1. Initialize i to 0 (executed once)
    2. While $i < n - 1$ do the following: (executed n times)
    3. Increment i by 1. (executed $n - 1$ times)
  Similarly, statement 4 consists of three statements. For simplicity, however, we will treat these as single statements.

[2] Here we have used the summation formula

$$\sum_{i=1}^{n} i = \frac{n(n + 1)}{2}$$

which simplifies to

$$T(n) = 2n^2 + 4n - 5$$

Since $n \le n^2$ for all $n \ge 0$, we see that

$$2n^2 + 4n - 5 \le 2n^2 + 4n^2 = 6n^2$$

and hence that

$$T(n) \le 6n^2 \text{ for all } n \ge 0$$

Thus, taking $f(n) = n^2$ and $C = 6$ in the definition of big-O notation, we may say that

$$T(n) \text{ is } O(n^2)$$

Determining this big-O estimate in this example involved some nontrivial calculations. However, we can simplify the computation considerably. The only statements that affected the final estimate were those (4, 5, 6, 7) whose execution counts involved n^2. Execution counts of the other statements included terms of lower degree which can be ignored. This means that, *to find a big-O estimate, we need only identity the statement executed most often and determine its execution count*. In our example this was statement 4, which was executed $n(n + 1)/2 - 1 = n^2/2 + n/2 - 1$ times. Since it is only the highest power of n that affects the big-O estimate, we can conclude from this that the computing time is $O(n^2)$.

 It is important to remember that a big-O estimate gives an approximate measure of the computing time of an algorithm *for large inputs*. If two algorithms for performing the same task have different complexities, the algorithm with the lower-order computing time is usually preferred. For example, if the computing time $T_1(n)$ of Algorithm 1 is $O(n)$ and the computing time $T_2(n)$ for Algorithm 2 is $O(n^2)$, then Algorithm 1 is usually considered better than Algorithm 2, since it will perform more efficiently for large values of n. It must be noted, however, that for small values of n, Algorithm 2 might well outperform Algorithm 1. For example, suppose that $T_1(n)$ is $10n$ and $T_2(n)$ is $0.1n^2$. Since $10n > 0.1n^2$ for values of n up to 100, we see that

$$T_1(n) < T_2(n) \text{ only for } n > 100$$

Thus, Algorithm 1 is more efficient than Algorithm 2 only for inputs of size greater than 100.

To illustrate, consider the problem of searching an array of n elements $a[0], \dots, a[n-1]$ to determine whether a specified value *item* appears in this list and, if so, to determine its location. One method is to do a **linear search**, in which we start at the beginning of the list and examine successive elements until either *item* is found or we reach the end of the list. The following is a modification of the algorithm given earlier:

Linear Search Algorithm

/* Algorithm to linear search $a[0], \dots, a[n-1]$ for *item*; *found* = true and *loc* = position of *item* if the search is successful; otherwise, *found* is false */

1. Set *found* = false.
2. Set *loc* = 0.
3. While *loc* < *n* and not *found* do the following:
4.   If *item* == *a*[*loc*] then // *item* found

5.   Set *found* = true.
6.   Else   // keep searching
            Increment *loc* by 1.
        End while.

The worst case is that in which *item* is not in the list. In this case, the statement executed most often is the statement that controls the loop—statement 3—and it is executed $n + 1$ times (once for each of the values $0, 1, \ldots, n$ for *loc*. Thus, if $T_L(n)$ is the worst-case computing time of linear search, we have

$$T_L(n) \text{ is } O(n)$$

If the list being searched has previously been sorted so that the elements are in ascending order, a **binary search** like that described in Section 1.4 can be used instead of a linear search. To locate *item* in such a list, the element $a[mid]$ in the middle of the list is examined. There are three possibilities:

item < $a[mid]$: Search the first half of the list
item > $a[mid]$: Search the last half of the list
item == $a[mid]$: Search is successful

We continue this halving process until either *item* is located or the sublist to search becomes empty. The following algorithm gives the details:

Binary Search Algorithm

/*   Algorithm to binary search $a[0], \ldots, a[n-1]$ for *item*, where the elements are in ascending order; *found* = true and *loc* = position of *item* if the search is successful; otherwise, *found* is false.   */

1. Set *found* = false.
2. Set *first* = 0.
3. Set *last* = $n - 1$.
4. While *first* ≤ *last* and not *found* do the following:
5.   Calculate *loc* = (*first* + *last*) / 2.
6.   If *item* < $a[loc]$ then
7.   Set *last* = *loc* – 1.   // search first half
8.   Else if *item* > $a[loc]$ then
9.   Set *first* = *loc* + 1.   // search last half
10.   Else
            Set *found* = true.   // *item* found
        End while.

To determine the worst-case computing time $T_B(n)$ of this algorithm, we again look at the statement that controls the loop—statement 4. Each pass through this loop reduces by at least one-half the size of the sublist still to be searched. The last pass occurs when the sublist reaches size one. Thus, the total number of iterations of this loop is 1 plus the number k of passes required to produce a sublist of size one. Since the size of the sublist after k passes is at most $n / 2^k$, we must have

$$\frac{n}{2^k} < 2$$

That is,

$$n < 2^{k+1}$$

or equivalently,

$$\log_2 n < k + 1$$

The required number of passes, therefore, is the smallest integer that satisfies this inequality, that is, the integer part of $\log_2 n$. Thus, in the worst case, when *item* is greater than each of $a\,[0], \ldots, a\,[n-1]$, statement 4 is executed no more than $2 + \log_2 n$ times, so that

$$T_B(n) \text{ is } O(\log_2 n)$$

Since the complexity of linear search is $O(n)$ and that of binary search is $O(\log_2 n)$, it is clear that binary search will be more efficient than linear search for large lists. For small lists, however, linear search may—and in fact, does—outperform binary search. Empirical studies indicate that linear search is more efficient than binary search for lists of up to about 20 elements.

In addition to $O(\log_2 n)$, $O(n)$, and $O(n^2)$, other computing times that frequently arise in algorithm analysis are $O(1)$, $O(\log_2\log_2 n)$, $O(n \log_2 n)$, $O(n^3)$, and $O(2^n)$. $O(1)$ denotes a **constant** computing time, that is, one that does not depend on the size of the input. A computing time of $O(n)$ is said to be **linear**, $O(n^2)$ is **quadratic**, $O(n^3)$ is **cubic**, and $O(2^n)$ is **exponential**. Graphs of these computing-time functions are shown in Figure 10.6. Note that, because of the large difference in scales on the axes, the graphs of the lower-order functions look the same in the last two diagrams. Table 10.2 displays the values of these functions for several values of n.

TABLE 10.2: Common Computing Time Functions

$\log_2\log_2 n$	$\log_2 n$	n	$n \log_2 n$	n^2	n^3	2^n
—	0	1	0	1	1	2
0	1	2	2	4	8	4
1	2	4	8	16	64	16
1.58	3	8	24	64	512	256
2	4	16	64	256	4096	65536
2.32	5	32	160	1024	32768	4294967296
2.6	6	64	384	4096	2.6×10^5	1.85×10^{19}
3	8	256	2.05×10^3	6.55×10^4	1.68×10^7	1.16×10^{77}
3.32	10	1024	1.02×10^4	1.05×10^6	$1.07 \text{ v } 10^9$	1.8×10^{308}
4.32	20	1048576	2.1×10^7	1.1×10^{12}	1.15×10^{18}	6.7×10^{315652}

Figure 10.6 Graphs of Common Computing Times

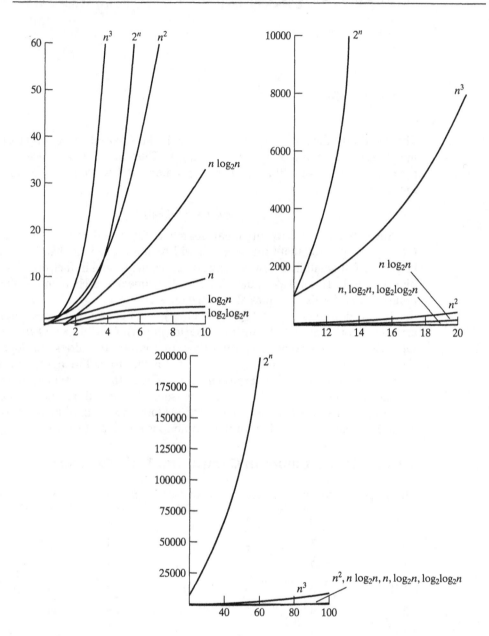

It should be clear from Table 10.2 and the graphs that algorithms with exponential complexity are practical only for solving problems in which the number of inputs is small. To emphasize this, suppose that each instruction in some algorithm can be executed in one microsecond. Table 10.3 shows the time required to execute $f(n)$ instructions for the common complexity functions f with $n = 256$ inputs.

TABLE 10.3: Computing Times for $n = 256$

Statement	# of Times Executed
$\log_2\log_2 n$	3 microseconds
$\log_2 n$	8 microseconds
n	.25 milliseconds
$n \log_2 n$	2 milliseconds
n^2	65 milliseconds
n^3	27 seconds
2^n	3.7×10^{61} centuries

All the algorithms for which we have determined the computing times have thus far been nonrecursive algorithms. The computing time $T(n)$ of a recursive algorithm is naturally given by a **recurrence relation**, which expresses the computing time for inputs of size n in terms of smaller-sized inputs. To illustrate, consider again the recursive function power() of Section 10.1:

```
double power(double x, unsigned n)
// Recursive power function
{
   if (n == 0)
      return 1.0;                    // anchor case
   // else
   return x * power(x, n - 1);   // inductive case (n > 0)
}
```

When power() is called with n > 0, the boolean expression

```
n == 0
```

is first evaluated, and since it is false, the statement in the inductive case

```
return x * power(x, n - 1);
```

is executed. The total computing time, therefore, is 2 plus the time required to compute power(x, n - 1). Thus, $T(n)$ is given by the recurrence relation

$$T(n) = 2 + T(n - 1)$$

Techniques for solving recurrence relations are typically covered in discrete structures courses that you may have taken or will take. One of the techniques, called the **telescoping principle**, is to repeatedly apply the relation until the anchor case is reached. For our example, if $n - 1 > 0$, we can apply the relation with n replaced by $n - 1$,

$$T(n - 1) = 2 + T(n - 2)$$

and substituting this in the original recurrence relation gives

$$T(n) = 2 + 2 + T(n - 2)$$

Continuing this process $n - 2$ more times, we eventually obtain

$$T(n) = 2 + 2 + \cdots + 2 + T(0)$$

The time $T(0)$ to compute x^0 is clearly 2, since the boolean expression n == 0 is evaluated and the anchor statement return 1.0; is executed. Thus, we have

$$T(n) = 2(n + 1)$$

so that

$$T(n) \text{ is } O(n)$$

As we described in Section 10.1, the power function may also be defined iteratively as

$$x^0 = 1$$
$$x^n = \underbrace{x \times x \times \cdots \times x}_{n \ x\text{'s}} \text{ for } n > 0$$

and this definition leads to the following nonrecursive function:

```
double nrPower(double x, unsigned n)
// Nonrecursive power function
{
   double prod = 1.0;      // the product x * x * ... * x
   for (int i = 1; i <= n; i++)
      prod *= x;
   return prod;
}
```

The computing time of this function is easily computed:

$$T_{NR}(n) \text{ is } O(n)$$

Although the computational complexity of the recursive and nonrecursive functions is the same, the overhead involved in manipulating the run-time stack described in the preceding section for a recursive function does produce some inefficiency. Consequently, in cases such as this, in which both a recursive algorithm and a nonrecursive one can be developed with little difference in effort, the nonrecursive solution is usually preferred.

In some cases, the computing time of a recursive algorithm to solve a problem may be much greater than that of a nonrecursive algorithm for the same problem. This is especially true of those like the recursive function fib() for calculating Fibonacci numbers in Section 10.1, in which the inductive case requires more than one call to the function itself:

```
unsigned fib(unsigned n)
// Recursive fibonacci function
```

```
{
    if (n <= 2)
        return 1;                           // anchor case
    // else
    return fib(n - 1) + fib(n - 2); // inductive case (n > 2)
}
```

We noted that multiple function calls with the same parameter indicate that this may not be a particularly efficient method of calculating Fibonacci numbers. Indeed, it is extremely inefficient!

To find the computing time of this function fib(), we observe that for n > 2, the boolean expression n <= 2 is checked, the anchor case is skipped, and the inductive case is executed. The computing time is thus given by the recurrence relation

$$T(n) = 2 + T(n - 1) + T(n - 2)$$

for n > 2. This recurrence relation is considerably more difficult to solve than the one in our earlier example. So, instead, we will use it to obtain a lower bound for $T(n)$ that grows exponentially with n and thus show that $T(n)$ grows exponentially.

If we replace $T(n - 1)$ with $T(n - 2)$ on the right side and drop the 2, we obtain

$$T(n) > 2T(n - 2)$$

for n > 2. If we apply the telescoping principle to this inequality, we will eventually obtain

$$T(n) > 2^{n/2} = (2^{1/2})^n = (\sqrt{2})^n > (1.4)^n \text{ for } n > 2$$

The recursive function fib() thus has computing time that is at least exponential. In fact, it can be shown that

$$T(n) \text{ is } O\left(\left(\frac{1 + \sqrt{5}}{2}\right)^n\right)$$

where $\frac{1 + \sqrt{5}}{2}$ = 1.618034 $\cdots$, called the *golden ratio*, is the value approached by ratios of consecutive Fibonacci numbers.[3]

In contrast, the computing time of the following nonrecursive Fibonacci function is easily seen to grow linearly with n; that is,

$$T_{NR}(n) \text{ is } O(n)$$

```
unsigned nrFib(unsigned n)
// Nonrecursive fibonacci function
{
    unsigned fib1 = 1,   // 3 consecutive Fibonacci numbers
             fib2 = 1,
             fib3;
```

---

[3] The sequence of ratios of consecutive Fibonacci numbers is

$$\frac{1}{1} = 1, \frac{2}{1} = 2, \frac{3}{2} = 1.5, \frac{5}{3} = 1.6666\ldots, \frac{8}{5} = 1.6, \frac{13}{8} = 1.61825, \ldots \rightarrow \frac{1 + \sqrt{5}}{2} = 1.618034\ldots$$

```
for (int i = 3; i <= n; i++)
{
    fib3 = fib1 + fib2;
    fib1 = fib2;
    fib2 = fib3;
}
return fib2;
}
```

On one machine, the time required to compute nrFib(n) for n ≤ 30 was less than 3 milliseconds, whereas the time to compute fib(n) was much greater, as shown by the following table (time is in milliseconds):

n	10	15	20	22	24	26	28	30
Time	6	69	784	2054	5465	14121	36921	96494

Quite obviously, the nonrecursive version is preferable to the recursive one.

In summary, calculating powers and finding Fibonacci numbers are examples of problems that can be solved with nearly equal ease using either a nonrecursive or a recursive algorithm. However, because of the overhead involved in pushing activation records and popping them from a run-time stack (described in the preceding section), nonrecursive functions usually (but not always) execute more rapidly and use memory more efficiently than do the corresponding recursive subprograms. Thus, if the problem can be solved recursively or nonrecursively with little difference in effort, it is usually better to use the nonrecursive version.

✔ Quick Quiz 10.4

1. What two criteria are usually used to measure an algorithm's efficiency?
2. In the early days of computing, which was more important?
3. In most current applications, which is most important?
4. Define what it means to write $T(n)$ is $O(f(n))$.
5. If $T(n) \leq 5000n^3$ for all $n \geq 100000$, then $T(n)$ is $O(n^3)$. (True or false)
6. If $T(n) \leq 5000n^3$ for all $n \geq 100000$, then $T(n)$ is $O(n^4)$. (True or false)
7. If $T(n) > 5000n^3$ for all $n < 100000$, then $T(n)$ cannot be $O(n^3)$. (True or false)
8. The worst case computing time of linear search is $O(\underline{\hspace{1cm}})$.
9. The worst case computing time of binary search is $O(\underline{\hspace{1cm}})$.
10. If the computing time of an algorithm is $O(2^n)$, it should perform acceptably for most large inputs. (True or false)
11. For a recursive algorithm, a(n) _____ relation expresses the computing time for inputs of size n in terms of smaller-sized inputs.

🐟 Exercises 10.4

Which of the orders of magnitude given in this section is the best O notation to describe the computing times in Exercises 1–4?

1. $T(n) = n^3 + 100n \cdot \log_2 n + 5000$

2. $T(n) = 2^n + n^{99} + 7$

3. $T(n) = \dfrac{n^2 - 1}{n + 1} + 8 \log_2 n$

4. $T(n) = 1 + 2 + 4 + \cdots + 2^{n-1}$

5. Give an example of an algorithm with complexity O(1).

6. Explain why, if $T(n)$ is O(n), then it is also correct to say $T(n)$ is O(n^2).

For the code segments in Exercises 7–12, determine which of the orders of magnitude given in this section is the best O notation to use to express the worst-case computing time as a function of n.

7.
```
// Calculate mean
n = 0;
sum  = 0;
cin >> x;
while (x != -999)
{
   n++;
   sum += x;
   cin >> x;
}
mean = sum / n;
```

8.
```
// Matrix addition
for (int i = 0; i < n; i++)
   for (int j = 0; j < n; j++)
      c[i][j] = a[i][j] + b[i][j];
```

9.
```
// Matrix multiplication
for (int i = 0; i < n; i++)
   for (int j = 0; j < n; j++)
   {
      c[i][j] = 0;
      for (int k = 0; k < n; k++)
         c[i][j] += a[i][k] * b[k][j];
   }
```

10.
```
// Bubble sort
for (int i = 0; i < n - 1; i++)
{
   for (int j = 0; j < n - 1; j++)
      if (x[j] > x[j + 1])
```

```
      {
        temp = x[j];
        x[j] = x[j + 1];
        x[j + 1] = temp;
      }
    }
11. while (n >= 1)
      n /= 2;
12. x = 1;
    for (int i = 1; i <= n - 1; i++)
    {
      for (int j = 1; j <= x; j++)
        cout << j << endl;
      x *= 2;
    }
```

13. Write a recurrence relation for the computing time of function move() for the Towers of Hanoi problem in Section 10.2 and solve it to find this computing time.

10.5 Standard Algorithms in C++

As we noted in the preceding chapter, in July of 1994, the Standard Template Library was chosen to be part of standard C++. It is based on work in generic programming done by Alex Stepanov and Meng Lee of the Hewlett-Packard Laboratories. One of the major parts of STL is its collection of more than 80 generic **algorithms**. They are not function members of STL's container classes and do not access containers directly. Rather, they are stand-alone function templates that operate on data by means of iterators. This makes it possible for them to work with various kinds of containers as well as with regular C-style arrays. We illustrate one of these algorithms here.

Example: STL's sort Algorithm

The task of sorting a sequence of values so they are in ascending (or descending) order occurs so often in problems that many different sorting methods have been developed over the years. We described one sorting algorithm in the preceding section—simple selection sort—and noted that it is not very efficient for large data sets.

Because of the frequent need to sort collections of data and to do so efficiently, the developers of STL included a sort algorithm in their library that uses one of the most efficient sorting methods known. This method and several others are described in detail in Chapter 13. This sort algorithm comes in several different forms. We will illustrate two of these forms with examples.

Sort 1: Using < to Compare Elements   STL's sort algorithm requires that a less-than function be defined on the data elements so it can compare items in the list to determine which is smaller. The version of sort in Figure 10.7 assumes that the < operator—that is, the function operator<()—has been defined for the type of items being sorted. We will sort integers stored in a vector<int> and real values stored in a deque<double>.

Figure 10.7 STL's sort **Algorithm—Version 1**

```
/*-------------------------------------------------------------------------
    Program to illustrate use of C++'s standard sort algorithm.

    Output:  A sorted vector of ints and a sorted deque of doubles.
-------------------------------------------------------------------------*/

#include <iostream>
#include <vector>
#include <deque>
#include <algorithm>
using namespace std;

template <typename Container>
void display(const Container & c);

int main()
{
  int ints[] = {555, 33, 444, 22, 222, 777, 1, 66};
  vector<int> v(ints, ints + 5);       // Use only first 5 elements of ints
  sort(v.begin(), v.end());
  cout << "Sorted vector of integers:\n";
  display(v);

  double dubs[] = {55.5, 3.3, 44.4, 2.2, 22.2, 77.7, 0.1};
  deque<double> d(dubs, dubs + 7);     // Use all 7 elements of dubs
  sort(d.begin(), d.end());
  cout << "\nSorted deque of doubles:\n";
  display(d);
}

template <typename Container>
void display(const Container & c)
/*-------------------------------------------------------------------------
  Function template to display elements of any type (for which the output
  operator is defined) stored in a container c (for which [] and size()
  are defined).

  Precondition:  Container is a type parameter.
  Postcondition: Values stored in c are output to out.
-------------------------------------------------------------------------*/
```

Figure 10.7 (continued)

```
{
  for (int i = 0; i < c.size(); i++)
    cout << c[i] << "  ";
  cout << endl;
}
```

Execution Trace:
```
Sorted vector of integers:
22  33  222  444  555

Sorted deque of doubles:
0.1  2.2  3.3  22.2  44.4  55.5  77.7
```

▲

The sort algorithm can also be used with arrays. We pass it a pointer to the beginning of the array—*arrayName*—and a pointer just past the end of the array—*arrayName* + *size*. For example, the int array ints defined in Figure 10.7 by

```
int ints[] = {555, 33, 444, 22, 222, 777, 1, 66};
```

can be sorted with

```
sort(ints, ints + 8);
```

The preceding version of sort can be used to sort a container of any type of elements for which < is defined. The program in Figure 10.8 illustrates this with a vector of stack<int>s, where < is defined for stacks by: s1 < s2 means s1.top() < s2.top(); that is, we simply compare the top stack elements.

Figure 10.8 Sorting a vector of stacks

```
/*-------------------------------------------------------------------
    Use the standard sort algorithm to sort a vector of stack<int>s.
---------------------------------------------------------------------*/
#include <iostream>
#include <vector>
#include <stack>
#include <algorithm>
using namespace std;
```

Figure 10.8 (continued)

```cpp
// Less-than function for stack
template <typename ElementType>
bool operator<(const stack<ElementType> & s1,
               const stack<ElementType> & s2)
{
   return s1.top() < s2.top();
}

// Output a stack
template <typename ElementType>
void dump(stack<ElementType> s);

int main()
{
   vector< stack<int> > s(4);
   s[0].push(90); s[0].push(80);
   s[1].push(10);
   s[2].push(11); s[2].push(22);
   s[3].push(12); s[3].push(56); s[3].push(34);
   cout << "Stacks in original order:\n";
   for (int i = 0; i < 4; i++)
   {
      cout << "Stack #" << i << ": ";
      dump(s[i]);
      cout << endl;
   }

   sort(s.begin(), s.end());
   cout << "\nStacks in sorted order:\n";
   for (int i = 0; i < 4; i++)
   {
      cout << "Stack #" << i << ": ";
      dump(s[i]);
      cout << endl;
   }
}
```

Figure 10.8 (continued)

```
/*-------------------------------------------------------------------
   Display stack elements from top to bottom.

   Precondition:  ElementType is a type parameter.
   Postcondition: Elements of s are output to cout from top to bottom.
   --------------------------------------------------------------------*/
template <typename ElementType>
void dump(stack<ElementType> s)
{
  cout << " Top-->";
  while (!s.empty())
  {
    cout << s.top() << "  ";
    s.pop();
  }
}
```

Execution Trace:

```
Stacks in original order:
Stack #0:   Top-->80   90
Stack #1:   Top-->10
Stack #2:   Top-->22   11
Stack #3:   Top-->34   56   12

Stacks in sorted order:
Stack #0:   Top-->10
Stack #1:   Top-->22   11
Stack #2:   Top-->34   56   12
Stack #3:   Top-->80   90
```

▲

Sort 2: Supplying a "Less-Than" Function to use in Comparing Elements   The sort algorithm may have a third parameter, which is a bool less-than function. Figure 10.9 illustrates.

Figure 10.9 STL's sort Algorithm—Version 2

```
/*-------------------------------------------------------------------
   Program to illustrate use of the standard sort algorithm.

   Output:  A sorted vector of ints and a sorted deque of doubles.
   --------------------------------------------------------------------*/
```

Figure 10.9 (continued)

```
#include <iostream>
#include <vector>
#include <deque>
#include <algorithm>
using namespace std;

template <typename Container>
void display(const Container & c);

// Less-than functions
bool intLessThan(int a, int b)
{ return a > b; }
bool dubLessThan(double a, double b)
{ return a > b; }

int main()
{
  int ints[] = {555, 33, 444, 22, 222, 777, 1, 66};
  vector<int> v(ints, ints + 5);        // Use only first 5 elements of ints
  sort(v.begin(), v.end(), intLessThan);
  cout << "Sorted vector of integers:\n";
  display(v);

  double dubs[] = {55.5, 3.3, 44.4, 2.2, 22.2, 77.7, 0.1};
  deque<double> d(dubs, dubs + 7);     // Use all 7 elements of dubs
  sort(d.begin(), d.end(), dubLessThan);
  cout << "\nSorted deque of doubles:\n";
  display(d);
}

// Add the definition of display() template from Figure 10.8 here
```

Execution Trace:
```
Sorted vector of integers:
555  444  222  33  22

Sorted deque of doubles:
77.7  55.5  44.4  22.2  3.3  2.2  0.1
```

▲

A Sample of STL Algorithms

Like sort(), most of the algorithms in the Standard Template Library are function templates designed to operate on *a sequence of elements*, rather than on a specific container. And most of them designate a sequence by using two iterators:

- An iterator positioned at the first element in the sequence
- An iterator positioned *after* the last element in the sequence

In the descriptions that follow, we will refer to these two iterators as *begin, begin1, begin2, ...* and *end, end1, end2, ...*, respectively.

The Standard Template Library provides over 80 algorithm templates. An in-depth examination of these algorithms is beyond the scope of this text, but Table 10.4 gives a sample of what is available.

TABLE 10.4: Some STL Algorithms

Algorithm	Description
binary_search(*begin*, *end*, *value*)	Return true if *value* is in the sorted sequence; if not present, return false
find(*begin*, *end*, *value*)	Return an iterator to position of *value* in the unsorted sequence; if not present, return *end*
search(*begin1*, *end1*, *begin2*, *end2*)	Find second sequence in the first sequence; if not present, return *end1*
copy(*begin*, *end*, *con*);	Copy a sequence into a container whose first element is pointed to by iterator *con*
count(*begin*, *end*, *value*)	Return how many times *value* occurs in the sequence
equal(*begin1*, *end1*, *begin2*)	Return true if two sequences are identical, false otherwise
fill(*begin*, *end*, *value*);	Assign *value* to every element in the sequence
for_each(*begin*, *end*, *f*);	Apply function *f* to every element in the sequence
lower_bound(*begin*, *end*, *value*)	Return an iterator to the *first* position at which *value* can be inserted and the sequence remains sorted
upper_bound(*begin*, *end*, *value*)	Return an iterator to the *last* position at which *value* can be inserted and the sequence remains sorted
max_element(*begin*, *end*)	Return an iterator to the maximum value in the sequence

TABLE 10.4: Some STL Algorithms (continued)

Algorithm	Description
`min_element(`*begin, end*`)`	Return an iterator to the minimum value in the sequence
`merge` `(`*begin1, end1, begin2, end2, con*`);`	Merge the first sequence with the second and put the resulting sequence in a container whose first element is pointed to by iterator *con*
`next_permutation(`*begin, end*`);`	Shuffle the sequence to its next permutation, and return `true`; if there is none, return `false`
`prev_permutation(`*begin, end*`);`	Shuffle the sequence to its previous permutation, and return `true`; if there is none, return `false`
`random_shuffle(`*begin, end*`);`	Shuffle the values in the sequence randomly
`replace(`*begin, end, old, new*`);`	In the sequence, replace each value *old* with *new*
`reverse(`*begin, end*`);`	Reverse the order of the values in the sequence
`sort(`*begin, end*`);`	Sort the sequence into ascending order
`unique(`*begin, end*`);`	In the sequence, replace any consecutive occurrences of the same value with one instance of that value
Set Algorithms:	
`includes (`*begin, end, begin2, end2*`)`	Return `true` if first sequence is contained in the second, `false` otherwise
	Put in the container whose first element is pointed to by iterator *con* the result of applying the following operation to the first sequence with the second:
`set_union` `(`*begin1, end1, begin2, end2, con*`);`	union
`set_intersection` `(`*begin1, end1, begin2, end2, con*`);`	intersection
`set_difference` `(`*begin1, end1, begin2, end2, con*`);`	difference
`set_symmetric_diference` `(`*begin1, end1, begin2, end2, con*`);`	symmetric difference

Algorithms from the <numeric> Library

The <numeric> library contains function templates that operate on sequential containers in much the same manner as those in <algorithm>. As the library's name suggests, however, these are intended to be used with numeric sequences (for example, with valarrays as described in Section 9.8). Table 10.5 lists these numeric algorithms. As in the descriptions for STL algorithms, *begin, begin1,* and *begin2* refer to iterators positioned at the first element of the sequence; *end* and *end1* refer to iterators positioned just after the sequence's last element.

TABLE 10.5: Numeric Algorithms

Algorithm	Description
accmulate(*begin, end, init*)	Return the sum of the values in the sequence; *init* is the initial value for the sum (e.g., 0 for integers, 0.0 for reals)
inner_product (*begin1, end1, begin2, init*)	Return the inner product of the first sequence with the second; *init* is the initial value for this inner product
partial_sum(*begin, end, con*);	Put in the container whose first element is pointed to by iterator *con* the sequence of partial sums of the sequence
adjacent_difference (*begin, end, con*);	Put in the container whose first element is pointed to by iterator *con* the sequence of differences of adjacent elements in the sequence

Example: Judging Figure Skating

In the judging of certain competitions, a performer's score is obtained by throwing out the high and low scores given by judges to reduce the effect of bias, and then averaging the remaining scores. For example, suppose that a particular figure skater received the following set of scores (each in the range 0 through 10) from the international judges:

$$9.1, 8.8, 9.2, 7.9, 4.5, 8.1, 8.6, 9.9, 7.6, 7.9$$

To determine her score, the low score (4.5) and the high score (9.9) are to be thrown out and the average of the remaining scores computed.

Suppose we store these scores in a vector<double> object named scores. Recall that scores.begin() and scores.end() are iterators that point to the first element of scores and just after scores' last element:

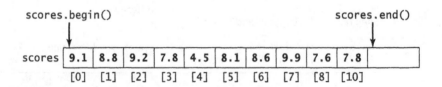

We can use the STL `min_element` algorithm to find the minimum score,

```
vector<double>::iterator it =
              min_element(scores.begin(), scores.end());
```

and then remove it with the `scores` member function `erase()`:

```
scores.erase(it);
```

More simply, we can do this in one step without introducing the iterator `it`:

```
scores.erase(min_element(scores.begin(), scores.end()));
```

We can remove the maximum score in a similar manner:

```
scores.erase(max_element(scores.begin(), scores.end()));
```

The scores 4.5 and 9.9 have been erased from `scores`, the remaining values have been shifted to the left to fill their spaces, and `scores.size()` and `scores.end()` have been updated:

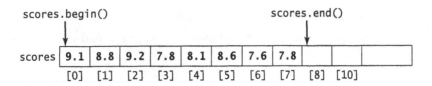

The average score can then be computed using the `accumulate()` algorithm from the `<numeric>` library:

```
double averageScore =
  accumulate(scores.begin(), scores.end(), 0.0) / scores.size();
```

✔ Quick Quiz 10.5

1. The Standard Template Library contains more than 80 function templates known as generic _____.
2. A program that uses the STL algorithms must contain the directive #include _____.
3. Most of the STL algorithms operate on specific containers. (True or false)
4. Most of the STL algorithms designate sequences by two iterators. Where in the sequence are these iterators positioned?
5. The library _____ contains algorithms designed for processing sequences of numbers.

10.6 Proving Algorithms Correct (optional)

In our discussion of software testing in Chapter 1, we gave some examples of errors in software used in defense systems, space travel, and utility networks that had very costly and, in some cases, tragic consequences. Software errors cannot be tolerated in such *safety-critical* systems, where human lives may be at risk. In these situations, simply running a program or system of programs with various sets of test data may not be sufficient, because *testing can show only the presence of errors, not their absence.* A deductive proof of a program's correctness may be required to show that it will produce the correct results (assuming no system malfunction). In this section we describe some of the techniques used in such correctness proofs.

To prove the correctness of an algorithm for solving a given problem, one must prove deductively that the steps of the algorithm correctly process the input given in the problem's specification so that the required output is obtained. Thus, a **proof of correctness** of an algorithm begins with a precondition *Pre* (the "Given:") and a postcondition *Post* (the "To show:"). It then provides a logical argument demonstrating that *Post* follows from *Pre* and execution of the algorithm:

$$Pre \; and \; Algorithm \Rightarrow Post \quad (\text{"}Pre \text{ implies } Post\text{"})$$

It is, therefore, a proof of the theorem:

> *Theorem: Given precondition Pre.*
> *After the algorithm is executed, the postcondition Post holds.*

Example: Calculating the Mean

To illustrate, consider the following algorithm to find the mean of a set of numbers stored in an array:

Algorithm to Calculate a Mean

/* Algorithm to find the mean of $x[0], \ldots, x[n-1]$. */

1. Initialize *sum* = 0.
2. Initialize index variable $i = 0$.
3. While $i < n$ do the following:
   a. Add $x[i]$ to *sum*.
   b. Increment i by 1.
   End while.
4. Calculate and return *mean* = *sum* / *n*.

Here, the precondition might be stated as

> *Pre:* Input consists of an integer $n \geq 1$ and an array x of n real numbers.

and the postcondition as

> *Post:* Execution of the algorithm will terminate, and when it does, the value of the variable *mean* is the mean (average) of $x[0], \ldots, x[n-1]$.

To demonstrate that the postcondition *Post* follows from the precondition *Pre* and the execution of the algorithm, one usually introduces, at several points in the algorithm, intermediate assertions about the state of processing when execution reaches these points. For the preceding algorithm we might use an additional intermediate assertion at the bottom of the while loop that will be true each time execution reaches this point. Such an assertion is called a *loop invariant*:

Pre: Input consists of an integer $n \geq 1$ and an array x of n real numbers.

1. Initialize $sum = 0$.
2. Initialize index variable $i = 0$.
3. While $i < n$ do the following:
    a. Add $x[i]$ to *sum*.
    b. Increment i by 1.
    A: The value of *sum* is the sum of the first i elements of array x and i is the number of times execution has reached this point.
   End while.
4. Calculate and return $mean = sum / n$.

Post: Execution of the algorithm will terminate, and when it does, the value of the variable *mean* is the mean (average) of $x[0], \ldots, x[n-1]$.

The proof then consists of showing that assertion A follows from the precondition *Pre* and then showing that the postcondition *Post* follows from A.

Mathematical induction (see Section 10.1) can be used to establish the loop invariant A. To see this, suppose we let k denote the number of times that execution has reached the bottom of the loop, and let i_k and sum_k denote the values of i and *sum*, respectively, at this time. When $k = 1$, that is, on the first pass through the loop, *sum* will be equal to $x[0]$ since it was initially 0 (step 1), i has the value 0, and $x[i]$ has been added to *sum* (step 3a). The value of i will be 1 since it was initially 0 (step 2) and has been incremented by 1 (step 3b). Thus, i and *sum* have the values asserted in A when $k = 1$.

Now assume that when execution reaches the bottom of the loop for the kth time, the loop invariant A holds:

$$sum_k = x[0] + \cdots + x[k-1] \text{ and } i_k = k$$

We must prove that A is also true when execution continues through the loop for the $k+1$-th time, that is,

$$sum_{k+1} = x[0] + \cdots + x[k] \text{ and } i_{k+1} = k + 1$$

On this $k+1$-th pass through the loop, we will have

$$
\begin{aligned}
sum_{k+1} &= sum_k + x[k] \quad \text{(Step 3a)} \\
&= x[0] + \cdots + x[k-1] + x[k] \quad \text{(Induction assumption)}
\end{aligned}
$$

and the value of i will be incremented by 1 so that

$$
\begin{aligned}
i_{k+1} &= i_k + 1 \quad \text{(Step 3b)} \\
&= k + 1 \quad \text{(Induction assumption)}
\end{aligned}
$$

Thus, i will have the correct value also.

It now follows by mathematical induction that each time execution reaches the bottom of the loop, i and *sum* will have the values asserted in the loop invariant A. In particular, after the nth pass through the loop, *sum* will equal $x[0] + \cdots + x[n-1]$, and i will be equal to n.

Since i will thus eventually have the value n, the boolean expression $i < n$ that controls repetition will become false, and the while loop will terminate. Execution will then continue with statement 4 in the algorithm. This statement correctly calculates the mean of the array elements, and execution will reach the end of the algorithm. Thus, the postcondition is established and the correctness proof is complete; we have proved the following theorem:

Theorem:

Given an integer $n > 1$ and an array x of n real numbers.

When Algorithm to Calculate Mean is executed, it terminates, and when it does, *mean* is the mean of $x[0], \dots, x[n-1]$.

Example: Recursive Power Function

Mathematical induction is also used to prove the correctness of recursive algorithms, because as we saw in Section 10.1, by its very nature, recursion involves an inductive case. As an illustration, consider the recursive power function of Section 10.1:

```
double power(double x, unsigned n)
// Recursive power function
{
    if (n == 0)
        return 1.0;                      // anchor case
    // else
    return x * power(x, n - 1);   // inductive case (n > 0)
}
```

Here the precondition and postcondition are

Pre: Input consists of a real number x and a nonnegative integer n.

Post: Execution of the function terminates and when it does, the value returned by the function is x^n.

We can use mathematical induction on n to show that the postcondition *Post* follows from the precondition *Pre*. If n is 0, the anchor statement

```
return 1.0;
```

is executed immediately, so that execution terminates and the correct value 1.0 is returned for x^0. Now assume that for n = k, execution terminates and returns the correct value for x^n. When it is called with n = k + 1, the inductive case

```
return x * power(x, n-1)
```

is executed. The value of n-1 is k, and thus by the induction assumption, the function call power(x, n-1) terminates and returns the correct value of x^k. It follows that the function call with n = k+1 terminates and returns the value $x * x^k = x^{k+1}$, which is the correct value of x^n. We have thus established that in all cases, the output assertion follows from the input assertion.

Summary

These examples of correctness proof have been rather informal. They could be formalized, however, by using some special notation to state the assertions (such as the predicate calculus or some other formal notation) and a formal deductive system that spells out the rules that can be used to reason from one assertion to the next. For example, a rule governing an assignment statement S of the form $v = e$ might be stated symbolically as

$$Pre \xrightarrow{\ S\ } \{Post = Pre(v, e)\}$$

an abbreviation for "If precondition Pre holds before an assignment statement S of the form $v = e$ is executed, then the postcondition $Post$ is obtained from Pre by replacing each occurrence of the variable v by the expression e." Such formalization is necessary in the design of mechanized "theorem provers," and we leave it to more advanced courses in theoretical computer science, where it more properly belongs.

Also, these proofs were quite simple in that only one intermediate assertion A was used in the first example and none was used in the second. The form of the first proof thus was

$$Pre \Rightarrow A \Rightarrow Post$$

That is, the precondition Pre implies the intermediate assertion A and A implies the postcondition $Post$. For more complex algorithms, it is usually necessary to introduce several intermediate assertions $A_1, A_2, \ldots, A_n$. The algorithm/program is broken down into small segments, each having one of the A_i (or Pre) as a precondition and A_{i+1} (or $Post$) as a postcondition:

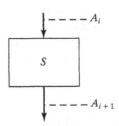

One must show that A_{i+1} follows logically from A_i for each $i = 1, \ldots, n-1$, and thus the structure of the correctness proof is

$$Pre \Rightarrow A_1 \Rightarrow A_2 \Rightarrow \ldots \Rightarrow A_n \Rightarrow Post$$

If one of these program segments is or contains a selection structure, there may be many paths that execution may follow from A_i to A_{i+1}, and because it is necessary to examine *all* such paths, the correctness proof can become quite complex.

Algorithm/program unit verification is an important part of program development, and ideally, the correctness of each program unit should be formally proved. In practice, however, the time and effort required to write out carefully and completely all the details of a correctness proof of a complicated algorithm are usually prohibitive. Nevertheless, it is still a good programming practice to formulate the major assertions that would be used in a correctness proof and then "walk through" the algorithm/program unit, tracing each possible execution path, following the pattern of a deductive proof. This is a more formal and systematic way of desk checking that every good programmer uses in testing algorithms and programs. Although it does not ensure that the algorithm/program unit is absolutely correct, it does increase one's understanding of the algorithm/program unit and one's confidence in its correctness, and it may uncover logical errors that might otherwise go undetected.

▷ Exercises 10.6

1. Consider the following algorithm with precondition *Pre*, intermediate assertion *A*, and postcondition *Post*:

   ### ScanAndCount
   /* Algorithm to find and display a *count* of the elements of an array
   $x[0], ..., x[n-1]$ that exceed a given value *cutoff*. */

   Pre: Input consists of an integer $n \geq 1$, an array x storing n real numbers, and a real number *cutoff*.

   1. Initialize *count* = 0.
   2. Initialize $i = 0$.
   3. While $i < n$ do the following:
       a. Increment i by 1.
       b. If $x[i] > cutoff$
              Add 1 to *count*.
       A: The value of i is the number of times execution has reached this point, and *count* is the number of array elements among $x[0], . . .$ $x[i-1]$ that are greater than *cutoff*.
   End while.
   4. Display *count*.

   Post: The algorithm terminates, and when it does, the value of the variable *count* is the number of elements in array x that are greater than *cutoff*.

   Using the given precondition, intermediate assertions, and postcondition, prove the correctness of this algorithm. Note that on each pass through the loop execution may follow either of two possible paths.

2. Write a nonrecursive version of function power() and prove its correctness.

3. Give an algorithm that finds and returns the largest element in an array x of n elements and prove its correctness.

4. Write a recursive function for calculating $n!$, the factorial of n (see Section 10.1), and prove its correctness.

5. Use mathematical induction to prove that the minimum number of moves required to solve the Towers of Hanoi puzzle with n disks is $2^n - 1$. (See Section 10.2.)

SUMMARY

▨! Chapter Notes

■ A recursive definition of a function has two parts: (1) an *anchor* or *base case* and (2) an *inductive* or *recursive case.*

■ A run-time stack is used to store an activation record for each call to a recursive function. These records store the current environment when execution of an instance of the function is suspended because of a recursive call to the same function, making it possible to resume execution of earlier instances when the recursion unwinds.

■ The two main criteria for evaluating an algorithm's efficiency are *space utilization* and *time efficiency.* Time efficiency is considered the more important and is usually measured as the number of times the algorithm's instructions are executed.

■ STL's algorithms are function templates that efficiently perform common operations (e.g., sorting and searching) on a variety of containers.

■ Verifying an algorithm's correctness consists of giving a deductive proof that the postconditions follow from the preconditions in a problem's specification.

☞ Programming Pointers

1. In a recursive function, one must ensure that each recursive call makes progress towards the anchor case so that it will eventually be reached; otherwise, infinite recursion (resulting in stack overflow) will result.

2. Beware of recursive functions that produce repeated calls to the function with the same argument.

3. *Direct recursion* refers to a function calling itself directly. *Indirect recursion* occurs when a function calls other functions, and some chain of function calls eventually results in a call to the first function.

4. Each recursive call of a function involves pushing/popping of activation records onto/ from the run-time stack.

5. Program testing can show only the *presence* of errors, not the *absence* of errors.

▲ ADT Tips

1. Big-O notation is commonly used to represent an algorithm's efficiency. It gives an upper bound on the algorithm's computing time for large inputs.

2. Algorithm efficiency is usually measured for its *worst-case* performance or, where feasible, its *average-case* performance.

3. Algorithms with exponential complexity are practical only for solving problems with few inputs.

4. If a problem can be solved either recursively or nonrecursively with little difference in effort, it is usually better to use the nonrecursive version.

5. Use standard algorithms to implement operations instead of reinventing the wheel.

Programming Problems

Section 10.1

1. Write a test driver for the recursive digit-counting function in Exercise 21.

2. Write a test driver for the nonrecursive digit-counting function in Exercise 22.

3. Write a test driver for the recursive `printReverse()` function in Exercise 23.

4. Write a test driver for the nonrecursive `printReverse()` function in Exercise 24.

5. Write a test driver for the recursive exponentiation function in Exercise 25.

6. Write a test driver for the nonrecursive exponentiation function in Exercise 26.

7. Write a test driver for the recursive `reverseArray()` function in Exercise 27.

8. Write a test driver for the recursive `sumArray()` function in Exercise 28.

9. Write a test driver for the recursive `location()` function in Exercise 29.

10. Write and test a recursive function for the string-reversal algorithm in Exercise 30.

11. Write and test a nonrecursive function for the string-reversal algorithm in Exercise 31.

12. Write a test driver for the recursive palindrome-checking function in Exercise 32.

13. Write a test driver for the recursive GCD function in Exercise 33.

14. Write a test driver for the nonrecursive GCD function in Exercise 34.

15. Write a test driver for the recursive binomial-coefficient function in Exercise 35.

16. Write a program to compare the computing times of the recursive and nonrecursive functions for calculating binomial coefficients in Exercises 35 and 36.

17. Write a test driver for one of the functions in Exercises 11–15. Add output statements to the function to trace its actions as it executes. For example, the trace displayed for `f(21)` for the function `f()` in Exercise 13 should have a form like

```
f(21) = 1 + f(10)
   f(10) = 1 + f(5)
      f(5) = 1 + f(2)
         f(2) = 1 + f(1)
            f(1) returns 0
         f(2) returns 1
      f(5) returns 2
   f(10) returns 3
f(21) returns 4
```

where the indentation level reflects the depth of the recursion. (*Hint:* This can be accomplished by using a global or static variable `level` that is incremented when the function is entered and decremented when it is exited.)

18. Modify the test driver for `printReverse()` in Problem 3 by adding output statements to the function to trace its actions as it executes. For example, the trace displayed for the function call `printReverse(9254)` should have a form like

```
printReverse(9254):  Output 4 – printReverse(925)
   printReverse(925):  Output 5 – printReverse(92)
      printReverse(92):  Output 2 – printReverse(9)
         printReverse(9):  Output 9 and \n
         printReverse(9) returns
      printReverse(92) returns
   printReverse(925) returns
printReverse(9254) returns
```

where the indentation level reflects the depth of the recursion. (See the hint in Problem 17.)

19. Write a recursive function that displays the lyrics of the song *Bingo*:

> Verse 1: There was a farmer had a dog,
>> And Bingo was his name-o.
>>> B-I-N-G-O!
>>>
>>> B-I-N-G-O!
>>>
>>> B-I-N-G-O!
>>
>> And Bingo was his name-o!
>
> Verse 2: Same as verse 1, but lines 3, 4, and 5 are
>> (Clap)-I-N-G-O!
>
> Verse 3: Same as verse 1, but lines 3, 4, and 5 are
>> (Clap, clap)-N-G-O!
>
> Verse 4: Same as verse 1, but lines 3, 4, and 5 are
>> (Clap, clap, clap)-G-O!
>
> Verse 5: Same as verse 1, but lines 3, 4, and 5 are
>> (Clap, clap, clap, clap)-O!
>
> Verse 6: Same as verse 1, but lines 3, 4, and 5 are
>> (Clap, clap, clap, clap, clap)

Also, write a driver program to test your function.

20. Write a recursive function that displays a nonnegative integer with commas in the correct locations. For example, it should display 20131 as 20,131. Also write a driver program to test your function.

21. Consider a square grid, some of whose cells are empty and others contain an asterisk. Define two asterisks to be *contiguous* if they are adjacent to each other in the same row or in the same column. Now suppose we define a *blob* as follows:

a.   A blob contains at least one asterisk.

b.   If an asterisk is in a blob, then so is any asterisk that is contiguous to it.

c.   If a blob has two or more asterisks, then each asterisk in it is contiguous to at least one other asterisk in the blob.

For example, there are four blobs in the partial grid

seven blobs in

and only one in

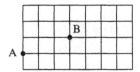

Write a program that uses a recursive function to count the number of blobs in a square grid. Input to the program should consist of the locations of the asterisks in the grid, and the program should display the grid and the blob count.

22. Consider a network of streets laid out in a rectangular grid—for example,

In a *northeast path* from one point in the grid to another, one may walk only to the north (up) and to the east (right). For instance, there are four northeast paths from A to B in the preceding grid:

Write a program that uses a recursive function to count the number of northeast paths from one point to another in a rectangular grid.

23. In Section 7.1 we considered the problem of converting an integer from base-ten to base-two and we used a stack to store the binary digits so that they could be displayed in the correct order. Write a recursive function to accomplish this conversion without using a stack.

24. Write a recursive function to find the prime factorization of an integer, and display these prime factors in descending order. (See Programming Problem 4 of Chapter 7.) Write a driver program to test your function.

25. Develop a recursive function to generate all of the $n!$ permutations of the set $\{1, 2, \ldots, n\}$. (*Hint:* The permutations of $\{1, 2, \ldots, k\}$ can be obtained by considering each permutation of $\{1, 2, \ldots, k - 1\}$ as an ordered list and inserting k into each of the k possible positions in this list, including at the front and at the rear.) For example, the permutations of $\{1, 2\}$ are $(1, 2)$ and $(2, 1)$. Inserting 3 into each of the three possible positions of the first permutation yields the permutations $(3, 1, 2), (1, 3, 2)$, and $(1, 2, 3)$ of $\{1, 2, 3\}$, and using the second permutation gives $(3, 2, 1), (2, 3, 1)$, and $(2, 1, 3)$. Write a program to test your function.

Section 10.2

26. Modify the program in Figure 10.4 to represent the moves graphically, similar to those in Figure 10.5.

27. Write a program that parses simple boolean expressions using the syntax rules preceding Exercise 12.

28. Write a program that reads lines of input, each of which is a (perhaps invalid) C++ statement, and that strips each line of all C++ comments. However, the structure of your program is restricted as follows:

■ The only repetition structure allowed is a loop for reading the input that stops when the end of input occurs. All other repetition must be carried out by using recursion.

■ The characters must be read one at a time, and looking at the next character in the input buffer is not allowed.

29. Write a program that reads a string consisting of only parentheses and that determines whether the parentheses are balanced, as specified by the syntax rules preceding Exercise 16.

30. Proceed as in Problem 29, but design the program to read any string, ignoring all characters other than parentheses.

Section 10.5

In Problems 31–36, use the standard C++ containers and algorithms where possible.

31. The investment company of Pickum & Loozem has been recording the trading price of a particular stock over a 15-day period. Write a program that reads these prices and stores them in a sequential container and then sorts them into increasing order. The program should find and display

a. The trading range (the lowest and the highest prices recorded).

b. A sequence that shows how much the price rose or fell each day.

32. The Rinky Dooflingy Company records the number of cases of dooflingies produced each day over a four-week period. Write a program that reads these production levels and stores them in a container. The program should then find and display

a. The lowest, highest, and average daily production level.

b. A sequence that shows how much the production level rose or fell each day.

c. A sequence that shows for each day the total number of dooflingies produced up to and including that day.

33. The Rinky Dooflingy Company maintains two warehouses, one in Chicago and one in Detroit, each of which stocks at most 25 different items. Write a program that first reads the product numbers of items stored in the Chicago warehouse and stores them in a sequential container Chicago, and then repeats this for the items stored in the Detroit warehouse, storing these product numbers in a sequential container Detroit. The program should then find and display the *intersection* of these two sequences of numbers, that is, the collection of product numbers common to both sequences.

34. Repeat Problem 33 but find and display the *union* of the two sequences, that is, the collection of product numbers that are elements of at least one of the sequences of numbers.

35. The Rinky Dooflingy Company manufactures different kinds of dooflingies, each identified by a product number. Write a program that reads product numbers and prices, and stores these values in a container. The program should then allow the user to select one of the following options:

a. Retrieve and display the price of a product whose number is entered by the user.

b. Determine how many products have a given price.

c. Find all products whose number is the same as that of some other product and remove all but one of them.

    d.   Sort the products so the product numbers are in ascending order.

    e.   Print a table displaying the product number and the price of each item.

    (*Suggestion:* Define a `Product` class where two of its operations are overloaded == and < operators so that standard algorithms can be used on the container of `Product` objects.)

36. a.   Write functions to calculate the mean, variance, and standard deviation of the values stored in a sequential container. (See the grading-on-the-curve program in Programming Problem 1 at the end of Chapter 3 for definitions of these quantities.)

    b.   Write a driver program to test your functions.

    c.   Use your functions in a program for the grading-on-the-curve problem.

CHAPTER 11

More Linking Up with Linked Lists

CHAPTER CONTENTS

Chapter Objectives

- Survey common variants of linked lists and why they are used.
- Study in detail an application of linked lists to implement sparse polynomials.
- Describe doubly-linked lists and how they are used to implement the C++ STL `list` container.
- Build a class that makes it possible to do arithmetic with large integers.
- Look briefly at some other applications of multiply-linked lists.

The linked lists introduced in Chapter 6 and used to implement lists, stacks, and queues in subsequent chapters are characterized by the following properties:

1. Only the first node is directly accessible.
2. Each node consists of a data part and a single link that connects this node to its successor (if there is one).

They are, therefore, linear structures that must be processed sequentially in the order in which the nodes are linked together, and we refer to them as **singly-linked lists**.

In some applications, other kinds of list processing are required, and in these situations, it may be convenient to allow other kinds of access and/or linkages. In this chapter we consider some of these variants of linked lists, such as circular-linked lists, doubly-linked lists, and other multiply-linked lists.

11.1 Some Variants of Singly-Linked Lists

In some list applications, modifications of standard linked lists are used because they make algorithms for some of the basic list operations simpler and more efficient. In this section we consider some of these variants of linked lists.

Linked Lists with Head Nodes

The first node in the linked lists we have considered differs from the other nodes in that it does not have a predecessor. As we saw in Section 6.4, this means that two cases must be considered for some basic list operations such as insertion and deletion. This would not be necessary if we could ensure that every node that stores a list element will have a predecessor. And we can do this simply by introducing a dummy first node, called a **head node**, at the beginning of a linked list. No actual list element is stored in the data part of this head node; instead, it serves as a predecessor of the node that stores the actual first element, because its link field points to this "real" first node. For example, the list of integers 9, 17, 22, 26, 34 can be stored in a linked list with a head node as follows:

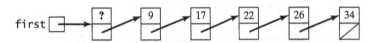

In this implementation, every linked list is required to have a head node. In particular, an empty list has a head node:

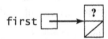

This means that, instead of simply initializing the pointer first to be a null pointer, a constructor for a LinkedList class that uses this implementation would get a head node that is pointed to by first and has a null link. Similarly, a function to check for a list-empty condition must check first->next == 0 rather than first == 0. Also, algorithms for traversing a standard linked list or a part of it remain essentially the same for linked lists that have head nodes; usually, only instructions that set some auxiliary pointer to the first node in the list need to be altered:

```
ptr = first->next;    // instead of ptr = first;
```

The major improvement in adding a head node to a linked list is in the simplifications of the insertion and deletion operations (see Section 6.4) that result from every node in a linked list now having a predecessor. For example, for insertion, we had to consider two cases:

1. Inserting an item after some other element in the list
2. Inserting an item at the beginning of the list.

We get a new node pointed to by `newptr` and store the item to be inserted in its data part. Then, for case 1, we insert this node into the list after some node pointed to by `predptr` as follows:

```
newptr->next = predptr->next;
predptr->next = newptr;
```

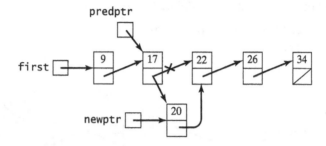

But for case 2, there is no predecessor for the item being inserted and we need to change the pointer to the first node so that it now points to this new first node in the list:

```
newptr->next = first->next;
first = newptr;
```

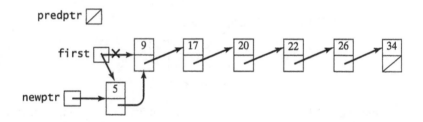

If the list has a head node, however, then inserting at the beginning of the list is not a special case because the head node serves as a predecessor for the new node:

```
newptr->next = predptr->next;
predptr->next = newptr;
```

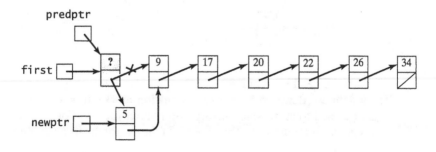

The deletion algorithm simplifies in a similar manner. In our first version of a linked list in Section 6.4, it too required a special case when the first node was deleted:

1. Deleting a list element that has a predecessor in the list.
2. Deleting the element at the beginning of the list.

In the first case, we bypass the node by changing the next link from its predecessor and then deallocating the deleted node:

```
predptr->next = ptr->next;
delete ptr;
```

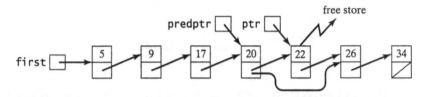

In the second case, there is no predecessor, so we bypass the node by changing the node pointed to by first:

```
first = ptr->next;
delete ptr;
```

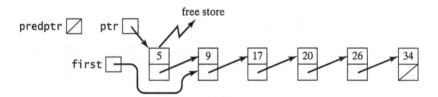

Once again, the second case does not require special treatment if the list has a head node, because the head node serves as a predecessor for the node being deleted:

```
predptr->next = ptr->next;
delete ptr;
```

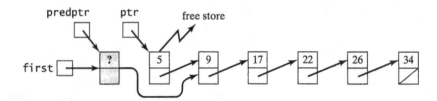

As indicated in the preceding examples, the data part in the head node is usually left undefined (denoted here by the question mark). In some situations, however, it might be used to store some information about the list. For example, in a linked list of integers, we might store the size of the list in the head node. In a list of names of persons, we might store in the head node the name of a team or other organization to which they all belong:

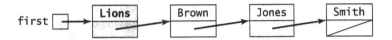

In the linked list representation of polynomials in the next section, the head node could be used to store the degree of the polynomial,

Circular Linked Lists

In Chapter 8 we described an implementation of queues in which the array that stored the elements was thought of as a circular array with the first element following the last. This suggests that an analogous **circular linked list** obtained by setting the link of the last node in a standard linear linked list to point to the first node might also be a useful data structure:

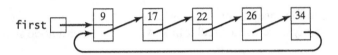

As this diagram illustrates, each node in a circular linked list has a predecessor (and a successor), provided that the list is nonempty. Consequently, as in the case of linked lists with head nodes, the algorithms for insertion and deletion do not require special consideration of nodes without predecessors. For example, item can be inserted as follows:

```
newptr = new Node(item);
if (first == 0)      // list is empty
{
   newptr->next = newptr;
   first = newptr;
}
else                 // nonempty list
{
   newptr->next = predptr->next;
   predptr->next = newptr;
}
```

Note that insertion into an empty list does require special consideration because, in this case, the link in the one-node list that results must point to the node itself:

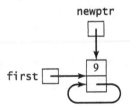

For deletion from a circular list, in addition to an empty list, a one-element list requires special treatment because, in this case, the list becomes empty after this node is deleted. This case is detected by checking whether the node is its own successor—that is, its link field points to itself:

```
if (first == 0)            // list is empty
   cerr << "List is empty\n";
else
{
  ptr = predptr->next;
  if (ptr == predptr)   // one-node list
    first = 0;
  else                     // list with 2 or more nodes
    predptr->next = ptr->next;
  delete ptr;
}
```

As in the case of non-circular linked lists, both the insertion and deletion algorithms simplify if we use a circular linked list with a head node such as the following:

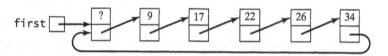

Most of the other algorithms for linked lists must also be modified when applied to circular lists. To illustrate, the traversal algorithm moved a pointer through the list until it became null, signaling that the last node had been processed. For a circular linked list, the link in the last node points to the first node. Thus, a naive attempt to modify this traversal algorithm for a circular list might produce the following:

```
/* INCORRECT attempt to traverse a circular linked list
   with first node pointed to by first, processing
   each list element exactly once. */
ptr = first;
while (ptr != first)
{
  // Process ptr->data;
  ptr = ptr->next;
}
```

Here, the boolean expression ptr != first is false immediately and the while loop is bypassed. Consequently, this algorithm correctly traverses only an empty list!

To obtain an algorithm that correctly traverses all circular linked lists, we can replace the while loop with a do-while loop, provided that we have made sure that the list is not empty:

```
if (first != 0)      // list is not empty
{
  ptr = first;
```

```
        do
        {
          // Process ptr->data;
          ptr = ptr->next;
        }
        while (ptr != first);
      }
```

Both versions of the traversal algorithm will correctly traverse a circular linked list with a head node if the assignment statement before the loop is changed to

```
        ptr = first->next;
```

You should check these revised algorithms for circular lists like the preceding and for one-element lists such as

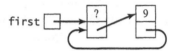

as well as empty lists that consist of only a head node that points to itself:

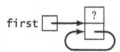

As we noted in Chapter 8, using a pointer to the last node rather than the first works well in some applications:

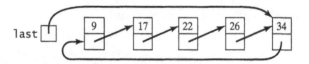

Since we can access the last node directly via last and the first node with last->next, this variation works well when access to both ends of the list is needed (e.g., with linked queues and deques).

✔ Quick Quiz 11.1

1. A dummy node at the beginning of a linked list is called a(n) _____.
2. The purpose of a node as in Question 1 is so that every node in the linked list has a(n) _____.
3. Setting the link of the last node in a standard linear linked list to point to the first node produces a(n) _____ linked list.
4. In a nonempty circular linked list, every node has a successor. (True or false)
5. In a nonempty circular linked list, every node has a predecessor. (True or false)

◆ Exercises 11.1

1. In Section 8.4, a *priority queue* was described as a queue-like structure in which each item has a certain priority and is inserted ahead of all items with a lower priority; normally, it is placed behind all those with an equal or higher priority. Assuming that such a priority queue is implemented as a linked list, develop a `Priority-Queue` class template. You should also test your class template as instructed in Programming Problem 1 at the end of this chapter.

2. Write an algorithm or code segment for searching a circular linked list for a given item.

3. Proceed as in Exercise 2, but assume that the list is ordered so that the elements are in ascending order.

4. Write an algorithm or code segment for locating the *n*th successor of an item in a circular linked list (the *n*th item that follows the given item in the list).

5. Write a class template for deques that uses a circular linked list with a single pointer to the last node to store the deque's elements. You should also test your class template as instructed in Programming Problem 3 at the end of this chapter.

6. The *shuffle-merge* operation on two lists was defined in Exercise 9 of Section 6.4. Write an algorithm to shuffle-merge two circular-linked lists. The items in the lists are to be copied to produce the new circular-linked lists; the original lists are not to be destroyed.

7. Proceed as in Exercise 6, but do not copy the items. Just change links in the two lists (thus destroying the original lists) to produce the merged list.

8. In implementations of linked lists in which the storage pool is maintained as a linked stack, as described in Section 6.6, it is possible to erase any circularly linked list in O(1) time; that is, it is possible to return all of its nodes to the storage pool in constant time, independent of the size of the list. Give such an erase algorithm for a circular-linked list whose computing time is O(1); and show how it works, using the following diagram:

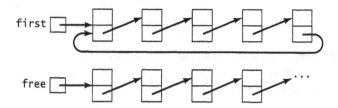

9. In the *Josephus problem*, a group of soldiers is surrounded by the enemy, and one soldier is to be selected to ride for help. The selection is made in the following manner: An integer *n* and a soldier are selected randomly. The soldiers are arranged in a circle and they count off beginning with the randomly selected soldier. When the count reaches *n*, that soldier is removed from the circle, and the counting begins again with the next soldier. This process continues until only one soldier remains, who is the (un)fortunate one selected to ride for help. Write an algorithm to implement this selection strategy, assuming that a circular linked list is used to store the names (or numbers) of the soldiers.

11.2 Linked Implementation of Sparse Polynomials

A **polynomial in one variable** x, $P(x)$, has the form

$$P(x) = a_0 + a_1 x + a_2 x^2 + \cdots + a_n x^n$$

where $a_0, a_1, a_2 \ldots, a_n$ are the **coefficients** of the polynomial. The **degree** of $P(x)$ is the largest power of x that appears in the polynomial with a nonzero coefficient; for example, the polynomial

$$P(x) = 5 + 7x - 8x^3 + 4x^5$$

has degree 5 and coefficients 5, 7, 0 (coefficient on x^2), –8, 0 (coefficient on x^4), and 4. Constant polynomials such as $Q(x) = 3.78$ have degree 0, and the zero polynomial is also said to have degree 0.

A polynomial can be represented as a list of coefficients

$$(a_0, a_1, a_2 \ldots, a_n)$$

which can, in turn, be represented using any of the list implementations we have considered. This was the approach used to build a Polynomial class in the exercises in Section 6.3—one integer data member to store the degree and an array to store the list of coefficients. For example, if we used a static array with capacity 10, the Polynomial object p representing the polynomial $P(x) = 5 + 7x - 8x^3 + 4x^5$, which can also be written

$$P(x) = 5 + 7x + 0x^2 - 8x^3 + 0x^4 + 4x^5 + 0x^6 + 0x^7 + 0x^8 + 0x^9$$

could be pictured as

If the degrees of the polynomials being processed do not vary too much from the upper limit imposed by the array size and do not have a large number of zero coefficients, this representation may be satisfactory. However, for **sparse** polynomials—that is, those that have only a few nonzero terms—this array implementation is not very efficient. For example, the Polynomial object q representing the polynomial

$$Q(x) = 5 + x^{99}$$

or equivalently,

$$Q(x) = 5 + 0x + 0x^2 + 0x^3 + \cdots + 0x^{98} + 1x^{99}$$

would require an array having 2 nonzero elements and 98 zero elements:

The obvious waste of memory caused by storing all of the zero coefficients can be eliminated if only the nonzero coefficients are stored. In such an implementation, however, it is clear that it will also be necessary to store the power of x that corresponds to each coefficient. Thus, rather than representing a polynomial by its list of coefficients, we might represent it as a list of coefficient–exponent pairs—for example,

$$P(x) = 5 + 7x - 8x^3 + 4x^5 \leftrightarrow ((5,0), \ (7,1), \ (-8,3), \ (4,5))$$
$$Q(x) = 5 + x^{99} \leftrightarrow ((5,0), \ (1,99))$$

Note that the pairs are ordered in such a way that the exponents are in increasing order.

Now suppose we represent the coefficient–exponent pairs by a class (or struct) Term, each of which has a coefficient member coef and an exponent member expo, representing one nonzero term of a polynomial:

coef expo

xx yy

Modifying the preceding Polynomial class so that the type of the array elements is Term rather than the coefficient type would give the following objects p and q that represent these sparse polynomials:

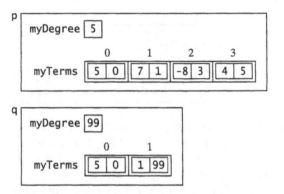

The fixed capacity of an array, however, limits the size of the list and results in considerable waste of memory in applications in which the sizes of the lists—that is, the number of nonzero coefficients in the polynomials—varies considerably from this upper limit. In this case, a linked list implementation is appropriate. Each node will have the form

data

next

in which the data part is of type Term and next is a pointer to the node containing the next term, respectively. For example, if we replace the array in a Polynomial class with a linked list whose nodes have this structure and we use a head node, the following Polynomial objects p and q represent the preceding polynomials $P(x)$ and $Q(x)$:

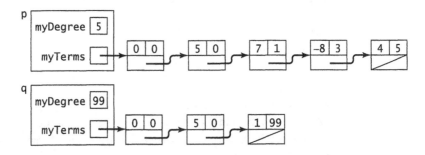

The zero polynomial $0x^0$ will have degree 0 and its myTerms linked list will contain only a head node:

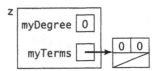

There are various ways we could organize a Polynomial class in this linked implementation so that it encapsulates an integer (myDegree) and a linked list with head node whose elements are of type Term, where Term encapsulates a coefficient of some type CoefType and a nonnegative integer exponent. For simplicity, we will make it a class template with type parameter CoefType and make Term and Node both inner classes:

```
#ifndef POLYNOMIAL
#define POLYNOMIAL

template <typename CoefType>
class Polynomial
{
 private:
  /*** Term class ***/
  class Term
  {
   public:
```

```
      /*** Data members ***/
      CoefType coef;
      unsigned expo;
    }; end class Term

    /*** Node class ***/
    class Node
    {
     public:
      Term data;
      Node * next;

      //-- Node constructor
      // Creates a Node with given initial values
      Node(CoefType co = 0, int ex = 0, Node * ptr = 0)
      {
        data.coef = co;
        data.expo = ex;
        next = ptr;
      }
    }; // end of Node class
    typedef Node * NodePointer;

   public:
    /*** Function members ***/
    // Operations on polynomials

   private:
    /*** Data members ***/
    int myDegree;
    NodePointer myTerms;   // a linked list with head node;
                           // its element type is Term
}; // end of Polynomial class template
#endif
```

To illustrate how the various polynomial operations are implemented, we look at polynomial addition. For example, suppose we wish to add the following polynomials $A(x)$ and $B(x)$:

$$A(x) = 5 + 6x^3 + 2x^5 + x^7$$
$$B(x) = x^3 - 2x^5 + 13x^7 - 2x^8 + 26x^9$$

Recall that this sum is calculated by adding coefficients of terms that have matching powers of x. Thus, the sum of polynomials $A(x)$ and $B(x)$ is

$$C(x) = A(x) + B(x) = 5 + 7x^3 + 14x^7 - 2x^8 + 26x^9$$

Now consider the Polynomial objects a, b, and c that represent these polynomials:

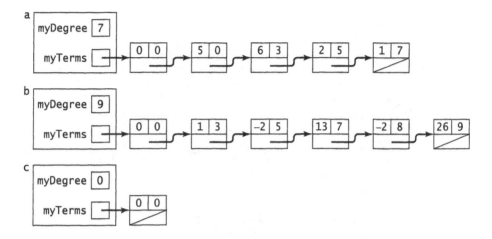

We are assuming that the Polynomial constructor initializes Polynomial objects like c to the zero polynomial.

Three auxiliary pointers, ptra, ptrb, and ptrc, will run through the linked lists in a, b, and c, respectively; ptra and ptrb will point to the current nodes being processed, and ptrc will point to the last node attached to c's linked list. To begin, therefore, ptrA, ptrB, and ptrC are initialized to a.myTerms->next, b.myTerms->next, and c.myTerms, respectively:

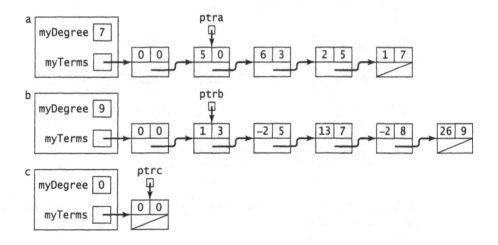

At each step of the computation, we compare the exponents in the nodes pointed to by ptra and ptrb. If they are different, a node containing the smaller exponent and the corresponding coefficient is attached to c, and the pointer for this list and ptrc are advanced:

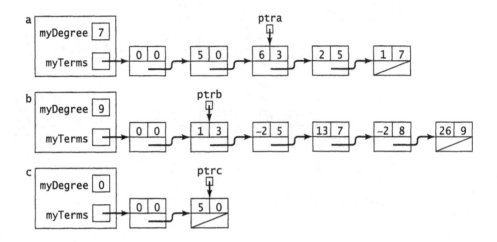

If the exponents in the nodes pointed to by ptra and ptrb match, then the coefficients in these nodes are added. If this sum is not zero, a new node is created with its coefficient part equal to this sum and its exponent part equal to the common exponent, and this node is attached to c. Pointers for all three lists are then advanced:

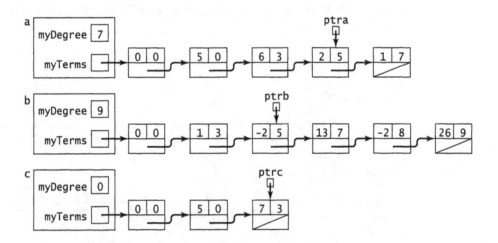

If the sum of the coefficients is zero, then ptra and ptrb are simply advanced and no new node is attached to c:

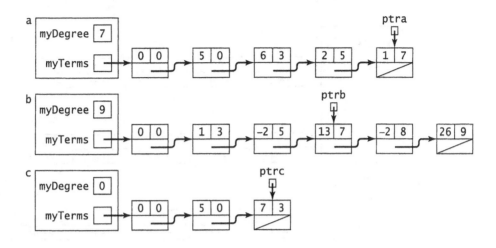

We continue in this manner until the end of a or b is reached, that is, until one of ptra or ptrb becomes null:

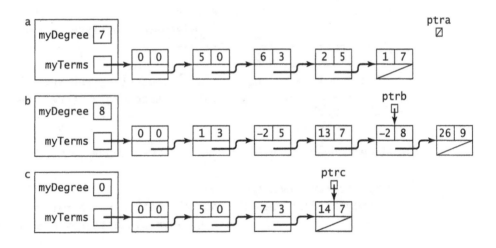

If the end of the other list has not been reached, we simply copy the remaining nodes in it, attaching each to c. Then we complete the construction of the linked list for c by storing the exponent in the last node of c in the myDegree data member:

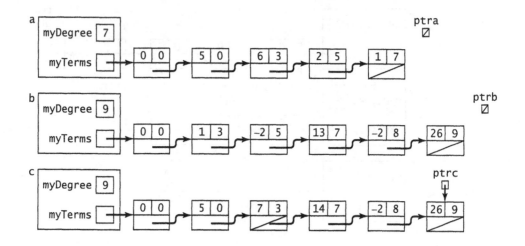

To implement this technique for adding linked polynomials as a function member of the `Polynomial` class template, we could add the following prototype in the public section:

```
Polynomial<CoefType> operator+(
                    const Polynomial<CoefType> & secondPoly);
/*-------------------------------------------------------------
   Precondition:  None
   Postcondition: A polynomial representing the sum of
      the current polynomial and secondPoly is returned.
   ------------------------------------------------------------*/
```

The following definition of this function could be added below the class declaration:

```
template <typename CoefType>
Polynomial<CoefType> Polynomial<CoefType>::operator+(
                    const Polynomial<CoefType> & secondPoly)
{
   Polynomial<CoefType> polySum;
   Polynomial<CoefType>::NodePointer    // pointers to run
      ptra = myTerms->next,             //   thru 1st poly,
      ptrb = secondPoly.myTerms->next,  //   2nd poly,
      ptrc = polySum.myTerms;           //   sum poly
   int degree = 0;
   while (ptra != 0 || ptrb != 0)       // More nodes in
   {                                    //   one of polys
      if ((ptrb == 0) ||               // Copy from 1st poly
          (ptra != 0 && ptra->data.expo < ptrb->data.expo))
```

```
      {
        ptrc->next = new Polynomial<CoefType>::
                          Node(ptra->data.coef, ptra->data.expo);
        degree = ptra->data.expo;
        ptra = ptra->next;
        ptrc = ptrc->next;
      }
      else if ((ptra == 0) ||              // Copy from 2nd poly
        (ptrb != 0 && ptrb->expo < ptra->expo))
      {
        ptrc->next = new Polynomial<CoefType>::
                          Node(ptrb->data.coef, ptrb->data.expo);
        degree = ptrb->data.expo;
        ptrb = ptrb->next;
        ptrc = ptrc->next;
      }
      else                                 // Exponents match
      {
        CoefType sum = ptra->data.coef + ptrb->data.coef;
        if (sum != 0)                      // Nonzero sum --
        {                                  //   add to sum poly
          ptrc->next = new Polynomial<CoefType>::
                            Node(sum, ptra->data.expo);
          degree = ptra->data.expo;
          ptrc = ptrc->next;
        }
        ptra = ptra->next;                 // Move along in
        ptrb = ptrb->next;                 //   1st & 2nd lists
      }
    }
    sumPoly.myDegree = degree;             // Wrapup
    return sumPoly;
  }
```

The code for adding linked polynomials is more complicated than the corresponding code for the array-based implementation described at the beginning of this section, in which the ith coefficient is stored in the ith location of an array. In this case, the loop in the definition of operator+() simplifies to

```
for (int i = 0; i < MAX_DEGREE; i++)
{
  CoefType sum = myCoeffs[i] + second.myCoeffs[i];
  if (sum != 0)
    degree = i;
  sumPoly.myArray[i] = sum;
}
```

(where MAX_DEGREE is the capacity of the arrays in the polynomials.)

Functions for other basic polynomial operations, such as evaluation for a given value of x, multiplication, and so on, are likewise more complicated in the linked implementation than in the array-based implementation. However, in applications in which the polynomials are sparse and of large degree, the memory saved will compensate for the increased complexity of the algorithms.

◆ Exercises 11.2

1. Add an input operation to the `Polynomial` class template.
2. Add an output operation to the `Polynomial` class template that displays a polynomial in the usual mathematical format except that x^n is written as $x \uparrow n$ or $x \wedge n$.
3. Add a subtraction operation to the `Polynomial` class template.
4. Add a function member `value()` to the `Polynomial` class template so that for a `Polynomial` object `p`, `p.value(a)` calculates and returns the value of the polynomial `p` at `a`.
5. The *derivative* of a polynomial $P(x) = a_0 + a_1 x + a_2 x^2 + a_3 x^3 + \cdots + a_n x^n$ of degree n is the polynomial $P(x)$ of degree $n - 1$ defined by

$$P'(x) = a_1 + 2a_2 x + 3a_3 x_2 + \cdots + na_n x^{n-1}$$

    Add a derivative operator to the `Polynomial` class template.
6. Add a multiplication operation to the `Polynomial` class template.

11.3 Doubly-Linked Lists and the Standard C++ `list`

All the lists we have considered up to now are unidirectional, which means that it is possible to move easily from a node to its successor. In many applications, however, some operations require being able to move from a node to its predecessor. In this section we consider how lists that provide this bidirectional movement can be constructed and processed, and we look at how they are used in C++'s standard `list` container. In the next section we show how they can be used to do arithmetic with very large integers.

Doubly-Linked Lists

Bidirectional lists can easily be constructed using nodes that contain, in addition to a data part, two links: a forward link `next` pointing to the successor of the node and a backward link `prev` pointing to its predecessor:

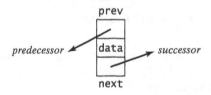

A linked list constructed from such nodes is usually called a **doubly-linked** (or **symmetrically-linked**) list. To facilitate both forward and backward traversal, a pointer (`first`) provides access to the first node and another pointer (`last`) provides access to the last node. For example, a doubly-linked list of integers 9, 17, 22, 26, 34 might be pictured as follows:

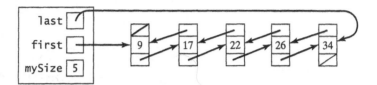

As in the singly-linked case, using head nodes for doubly-linked lists eliminates some special cases (e.g., empty list and first node), and making the lists circular facilitates moving through them in a circular manner. As we shall see later in this section, this is the structure used for the standard C++ `list` type.

Algorithms for the basic list operations are similar to those for the singly-linked case, the main difference being the need to set some additional links. For example, inserting a new node into a doubly-linked list involves first setting its backward and forward links to point to its predecessor and successor, respectively,

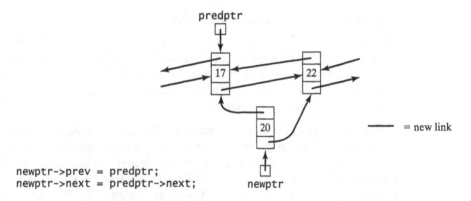

```
newptr->prev = predptr;
newptr->next = predptr->next;
```

and then resetting the forward link of its predecessor and the backward link of its successor to point to this new node:

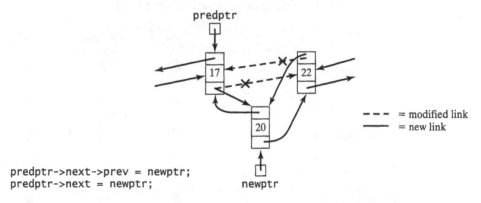

```
predptr->next->prev = newptr;
predptr->next = newptr;
```

It is important that the link changes be done in the correct order. You should look at some examples to see what happens if this order is changed.

A node can be deleted simply by resetting the forward link of its predecessor and the backward link of its successor to bypass the node:

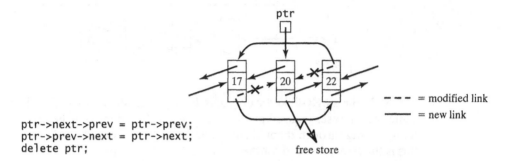

```
ptr->next->prev = ptr->prev;
ptr->prev->next = ptr->next;
delete ptr;
```

Traversals are performed in the same way as for singly-linked lists. Forward traversals follow the `next` links and backward traversals follow the `prev` links. Constructors, destructors, copy constructors, assignment, and several other operations are also straightforward modifications of those for singly-linked lists.

The Standard `list` Class Template

The `list` class template in the Standard Template Library uses a linked list to store the items in a list. The structure of this linked list, however, is a variation of the doubly-linked lists we have been considering. At the end of this section we will take a "look under the hood" at this linked structure. But we will first describe `list`'s basic operations and other important features.

Comparing `list` with Other Containers   We have considered in some detail C-style arrays (and `valarrays`) and the `vector` and `deque` containers from STL. We now describe the `list` container, whose major strength is insertion and deletion at any point in the sequence. Table 11.1 shows how these four containers compare with respect to insertion and deletion, type of access, and the amount of overhead. An ✕ indicates that the container does not have the specified property; the other ratings are ○ (poor), ◐ (good), and ● (excellent).

TABLE 11.1: Comparison of Containers

Property	Array	vector	deque	list
Direct/random access (`[]`)	●	●	◐	✕
Sequential access	●	●	◐	●
Insert/delete at front	○	○	●	●
Insert/delete in middle	○	○	○	●
Insert/delete at end	●	●	●	●
Overhead	lowest	low	low/medium	high

As the table indicates, `list` does not support direct/random access and thus does not provide the subscript operator `[]`.

Iterators   The iterator provided in `list` is called a **bidirectional iterator**, which is weaker than a **random-access iterator** like that in `vector`. Both kinds of iterators have the following operations:

`++`	Moves iterator to the next element (like `ptr = ptr->next`)
`--`	Moves iterator to the preceding element (like `ptr = ptr->prev`)
`*`	Dereferencing operator: to access the value stored at the position to which an iterator points (like `ptr->data`)
`=`	Assignment: For iterators of the same type, `it1 = it2` sets `it1`'s position to the same as `it2`'s
`==` and `!=`	For iterators of the same type, `it1 == it2` is true if `it1` and `it2` are both positioned at the same element and is false otherwise

But bidirectional iterators do *not* have the following "jump" operations: addition (+), subtraction (-), the corresponding assignment operators (+=, -=), and subscript (`[]`). This means that algorithms such as `sort()` that require direct/random access cannot be used with lists. (This is why `list` provides its own `sort()` operation.)

Basic `list` Operations   Table 11.2 gives the most useful operations provided in `list`. In the descriptions, *n* is a nonnegative integer; *value* is of type T; *firstPtr* and *lastPtr* are pointers bound to type T; *pos, pos1, pos2, from, to, first*, and *last* are `list<T>` iterators.

TABLE 11.2: Basic `list` Operations

Operation	Description
Constructors	
`list<T> aList;`	Construct *aList* as an empty `list`
`list<T> aList(n);`	Construct *aList* as a `list` to contain *n* elements (set to default value)
`list<T> aList(n, value);`	Construct *aList* as a `list` to contain *n* copies of *value*
`list<T> aList(firstPtr, lastPtr);`	Construct *aList* as a `list` initialized with the contents of the memory location pointed to by *firstPtr* up to (but not including) that pointed to by *lastPtr*

TABLE 11.2: Basic `list` Operations (continued)

Operation	Description
Copy constructor	
Destructor	
`aList.empty()`	Return true if and only if *aList* contains no values
`aList.size()`	Return the number of values *aList* contains
`aList.push_back(value);`	Append *value* at the end of *aList*
`aList.push_front(value);`	Insert *value* at the front of *aList*
`aList.insert(pos, value)`	Insert *value* into *aList* at iterator position *pos* and return an iterator pointing to the new element's position
`aList.insert(pos, n, value);`	Insert *n* copies of *value* into *aList* at iterator position *pos*
`aList.insert(pos, fPtr, lPtr);`	Insert copies of all the elements in the range [*fPtr*, *lPtr*) into *aList* at iterator position *pos*
`aList.pop_back();`	Erase *aList*'s last element
`aList.pop_front();`	Erase *aList*'s first element
`aList.erase(pos);`	Erase the value in *aList* at iterator position *pos*
`aList.erase(pos1, pos2);`	Erase the values in *aList* from iterator positions *pos1* to *pos2*
`aList.remove(value);`	Erase all elements in *aList* that match *value*, using == to compare items.
`aList.unique()`	Replace all repeating sequences of a single element by a single occurrence of that element
`aList.front()`	Return a reference to *aList*'s first element
`aList.back()`	Return a reference to *aList*'s last element
`aList.begin()`	Return an iterator positioned at *aList*'s first value
`aList.end()`	Return an iterator positioned 1 element past *aList*'s last value

TABLE 11.2: Basic `list` Operations (continued)

Operation	Description
aList.rbegin()	Return a reverse iterator positioned at *aList*'s last value
aList.rend()	Return a reverse iterator positioned 1 element before *aList*'s first value
aList.sort();	Sort *aList*'s elements (using <)
aList.reverse();	Reverse the order of *aList*'s elements
aList1.merge(*aList2*);	Remove all the elements in *aList2* and merge them into *aList1*; that is, move the elements of *aList2* into *aList1* and place them so that the final list of elements is sorted using < (assumes both *aList2* and *aList1* were sorted using <)
aList1.splice(*pos*, *aList2*);	Remove all the elements in *aList2* and insert them into *aList1* at iterator position *pos*
aList1.splice(*to*, *aList2*, *from*);	Remove the element in *aList2* at iterator position *from* and insert it into *aList1* at iterator position *to*
aList1.splice(*pos*, *aList2*, *first*, *last*);	Remove all the elements in *aList2* at iterator positions [*first*, last) and insert them into *aList1* at iterator position *pos*
aList1.swap(*aList2*);	Swap the contents of *aList1* with *aList2*
aList1 = *aList2*	Assign to *aList1* a copy of *aList2*
aList1 == *aList2*	Return true if and only if *aList1* contains the same items as *aList2*, in the same order
aList1 < *aList2*	Return true if and only if *aList1* is lexicographically less than *aList2*

The program in Figure 11.1 is a simple demonstration of several of these operations. Note that it is necessary to use an iterator in the overloaded operator<<() to display the contents of a `list`, because the subscript operator [] is not defined for `lists`.

Figure 11.1 Demonstration of `list` Operations

```cpp
#include <iostream>
#include <list>
#include <algorithm>
using namespace std;

//--- Overload output operator for list<T>
template <typename T>
ostream & operator<<(ostream & out, const list<T> & aList)
{
    for (list<T>::const_iterator it = aList.begin(); it != aList.end(); it++)
        out << *it << " ";
    return out;
}

int main()
{
    // Constructors
    //==============
    list<int> la, lb(4, 111), lc(6);
    int array[] = {2, 22, 222,2222};
    list<int> ld(array, array + 4);

    cout << "la: " << la << " -- size = " << la.size() << endl;
    cout << "lb: " << lb << " -- size = " << lb.size() << endl;
    cout << "lc: " << lc << " -- size = " << lc.size() << endl;
    cout << "ld: " << ld << " -- size = " << ld.size() << endl;

    // Assignment
    //===========
    cout << "\nAssignments la = ld and lc = ld:" << endl;
    la = ld;
    lc = ld;
    cout << "la = " << la << " -- size = " << la.size() << endl;
    cout << "lc = " << lc << " -- size = " << lc.size() << endl;

    // Ways to insert into a list
    //===========================
    cout << "\nInserts in lb:\n";
    list<int>::iterator i;
```

Figure 11.1 (continued)

```
i = lb.begin();
i++; i++;
lb.insert(i, 66666);
cout << lb << endl;
lb.insert(i,3, 555);
cout << lb << endl;
lb.insert(i, array, array + 3);
cout << lb << endl;
lb.push_back(888);
lb.push_front(111);
cout << lb << endl;

// Ways to delete from a list
//============================
cout << "\nErases in lb:\n";
i = find(lb.begin(), lb.end(), 66666);   // find is an algorithm
if (i != lb.end())
{
   cout << "66666 found -- will erase it\n";
   lb.erase(i);
}
else
   cout << "66666 not found\n";
cout << lb << endl;
i = lb.begin(); i++;
list<int>::iterator j = lb.end();
--j; --j; i = --j; i --; i--;
lb.erase(i,j);
cout << lb << endl;
lb.pop_back();
lb.pop_front();
cout << lb << endl;

// Reversing a list
//==================
cout << "\nReverse ld:\n";
ld.reverse();
cout << ld << endl;
```

Figure 11.1 (continued)

```
// Sorting a list
//===============
cout << "\nSort lb and ld:\n";
lb.sort();
ld.sort();
cout << "lb: " << lb << "\nld: " << ld << endl;


// Merging two lists
//==================
cout << "\nMerge lb and ld:\n";
lb.merge(ld);
cout << "lb: " << lb << endl;
cout << "ld: " << ld << endl;


// Splicing a list into another list
//==================================
cout << "\nSplice lc into la at second position:\n";
i=la.begin(); i++;
la.splice(i, lc);
cout << "la: " << la << endl;
cout << "lc: " << lc << endl;


// Global removal of a value
//==========================
cout << "\nRemove 22s from la:\n";
la.remove(22);
cout << la << endl;


// Eliminating duplicates
//=======================
cout << "\nUnique applied to lb:\n";
lb.unique();
cout << lb << endl;
}
```

Execution Trace:
```
la:  -- size = 0
lb: 111 111 111 111  -- size = 4
lc: 0 0 0 0 0 0  -- size = 6
ld: 2 22 222 2222  -- size = 4
```

Figure 11.1 (continued)

Assignments 1a = 1d and 1c = 1d:
1a = 2 22 222 2222 -- size = 4
1c = 2 22 222 2222 -- size = 4

Inserts in 1b:
111 111 66666 111 111
111 111 66666 555 555 555 111 111
111 111 66666 555 555 555 2 22 222 111 111
111 111 111 66666 555 555 555 2 22 222 111 111 888

Erases in 1b:
66666 found -- will erase it
111 111 111 555 555 555 2 22 222 111 111 888
111 111 111 555 555 555 2 111 111 888
111 111 555 555 555 2 111 111

Reverse 1d:
2222 222 22 2

Sort 1b and 1d:
1b: 2 111 111 111 111 555 555 555
1d: 2 22 222 2222

Merge 1b and 1d:
1b: 2 2 22 111 111 111 111 222 555 555 555 2222
1d:

Splice 1c into 1a at second position:
1a: 2 2 22 222 2222 22 222 2222
1c:

Remove 22s from 1a:
2 2 222 2222 222 2222

Unique applied to 1b:
2 22 111 222 555 2222

▲

Example: Internet Addresses

TCP (Transmission Control Protocol) and IP (Internet Protocol) are communication protocols that specify the rules computers use to exchange messages in networks. IP addresses uniquely identify computers in the Internet; for example, `spacelink.msfc.nasa.gov` is the address of NASA Spacelink, which provides educational information related to aeronautics and the space program to teachers, faculty, and students. These addresses are made up of four fields that represent specific parts of the Internet,

> *host.subdomain.subdomain.rootdomain*

which the computer will translate into a unique IP address. This address is a 32-bit value, but it is usually represented in a dotted-decimal notation by separating the 32 bits into four 8-bit fields, expressing each field as a decimal integer, and separating the fields with a period; for example, at the time of this writing, 192.149.89.6 is the IP address of NASA Spacelink.

Suppose connections are made from one network through a gateway to another network, and that each time a connection is made, the IP address of the user's computer is stored in a file. These addresses can be retrieved periodically to monitor who has used the gateway and how many times they have used it.

The program in Figure 11.2 reads these IP addresses from the file and stores them in a linked list of nodes that store an address and the number of times that address appeared in the data file. As each address is read, the program checks to see if it is already in the list. If it is, its count is incremented by 1; otherwise, it is inserted at the end of the list. After all of the addresses in the file have been read, the distinct addresses and their counts are displayed.

The addresses are stored in a `list<AddressCounter>` object `addressList`, where `AddressCounter` is a small class containing two data members (`myAddress` and `myCount`), input and output function members, and a function member `tally()` to increment the count of an address. Also, `operator==()` is overloaded so that STL's `find()` algorithm can be used to search the list.

Figure 11.2 Internet Addresses

```
/*-- Class AddressCounter ----------------------------------------
        Models occurrences of IP addresses in a login file.
 -----------------------------------------------------------------*/


#include <string>
#include <iostream>
using namespace std;


class AddressCounter
{
 public:
  /*** Function Members ***/
```

Figure 11.2 (continued)

```
AddressCounter();
/*------------------------------------------------------------------
  Precondition:  None.
  Postcondition: myAddress is an empty string and myCount is 0.
------------------------------------------------------------------*/

void read(istream & in);
/*------------------------------------------------------------------
  Precondition:  istream in is open.
  Postcondition: Value for AddressCounter object has been read from in.
------------------------------------------------------------------*/

void print(ostream & out) const;
/*------------------------------------------------------------------
  Precondition:  ostream out is open.
  Postcondition: Value of AddressCounter object has been output to out.
------------------------------------------------------------------*/

void tally();
/*------------------------------------------------------------------
  Precondition:  None.
  Postcondition: myCount has been incremented by 1.
------------------------------------------------------------------*/

bool operator==(const AddressCounter & addr);
/*------------------------------------------------------------------
  Precondition:  None.
  Postcondition: True is returned if this address and addr have the
     same address, and false otherwise.
------------------------------------------------------------------*/

private:
 /*** Data Members ***/
 string myAddress;
 int myCount;
}; // end of class declaration

//--- Definition of constructor
inline AddressCounter::AddressCounter()
: myAddress(""), myCount(0)
{ }
```

Figure 11.2 (continued)

```cpp
//--- Definition of read()
inline void AddressCounter::read(istream & in)
{
  in >> myAddress;
  myCount = 1;
}

//--- Definition of print()
inline void AddressCounter::print(ostream & out) const
{
  out << myAddress << "\t occurs " << myCount << " times\n";
}

//--- Definition of tally()
inline void AddressCounter::tally()
{
  myCount++;
}

//--- Definition of == operator
inline bool AddressCounter::operator==(const AddressCounter & addr)
{
  return myAddress == addr.myAddress;
}

/*-----------------------------------------------------------------
   Program to read IP addresses from a file and produce a list of distinct
   addresses and a count of how many times each appeared in the file.
   ----------------------------------------------------------------*/

#include <fstream>
#include <cassert>
#include <list>
#include <algorithm>

int main()
{
   string fileName;                       // name of file of IP addresses
   ifstream inStream;                     // open stream to file of addresses
```

Figure 11.2 (continued)

```
   cout << "Enter name of file containing IP addresses: ";
   cin >> fileName;
   inStream.open(fileName.data());
   assert(inStream.is_open());

   list<AddressCounter> addressList;    // list of AddressCounter objects
   AddressCounter addr;
   for (;;)                             // loop:
   {
      addr.read(inStream);              //    read an address

      if (inStream.eof()) break;        //    if eof, quit

      list<AddressCounter>::iterator    //    check if addr already in list
         it = find(addressList.begin(), addressList.end(), addr);
      if (it != addressList.end())      //    found
         (*it).tally();                 //    increment its count
      else
         addressList.push_back(addr);   //    else add it to the list
   }                                    //    end loop
                                        //    output the list
   cout << "\nList of addresses:\n\n";
   for (list<AddressCounter>::iterator it = addressList.begin();
                                       it != addressList.end(); it++)

      (*it).print(cout);
}
```

Listing of file11-2.dat:
192.149.89.61
123.111.222.333
100.1.4.31
34.56.78.90
120.120.120.120
192.149.89.61
123.111.222.333
123.111.222.333
77.66.55.44
100.1.4.31
123.111.222.333
192.149.89.61

Figure 11.2 (continued)

Execution Trace:
```
Enter name of file containing IP addresses: file11-2.dat

List of addresses:

128.159.4.20      occurs 3 times
123.111.222.333   occurs 4 times
100.1.4.31        occurs 2 times
34.56.78.90       occurs 1 times
120.120.120.120   occurs 1 times
77.66.55.44       occurs 1 times
```

▲

A Look under the Hood at C++'s `list`

STL's `list` stores the list elements in a circular doubly-linked list with a head node. For example, we might picture the three-element list aList constructed by

```
list<int> aList;
aList.push_back(9);
aList.push_back(17);
aList.push_back(22);
```

as follows:

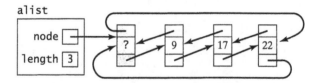

The data member `node` points to the head node and the data member `length` is the number of items in the list.

`list`'s **Memory Management**   On the surface, `list` looks quite simple. However, its allocation/deallocation scheme is significantly more complex than simply using new and `delete` operations. To reduce the inefficiency of using the system's heap manager for large numbers of allocations and deallocations, it does its own management of a free list of available nodes, which is maintained as a linked stack in exactly the way described in Section 6.6. It uses new only when this free list is empty, and then to obtain large memory blocks, which it carves up into nodes of the appropriate size and puts them on a free list. It uses `delete` to return nodes to the system's free store only when the lifetimes of all lists of a particular type are over. The basic algorithm for managing the nodes is as follows:

For each list of a certain type T:

■ When a node is needed:

1. If the free list is empty:
   a. Call the system's heap manager to allocate a block (called a *buffer*) of size (typically) 4K bytes.
   b. Carve it up into pieces of the size required for a node of a list<T>.
   c. Put these nodes on the free list.
2. Allocate a node from the free list,

■ When a node is deallocated,
   Push it onto the free list.

■ When *all* lists of type T have been destroyed,
   Return all buffers to the heap.

Constructor, `size()`, and `empty()`   Implementations of most of the basic list operations are very similar to those we have described in the preceding section for singly-linked lists and in this section for doubly-linked lists. For example, for a list<T> object defined by

    list<T> alist;

the default `list` constructor builds an empty linked list `aList` by obtaining a head node from the free list, storing the address of this node in its node data member, and setting the `length` member to 0:

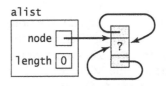

The `size()` function need only

    return length;

and the `empty()` function need only check if the length is 0:

    return length == 0;

Iterators and Pointers   From our discussions of iterators in the preceding two chapters and of pointers from Chapter 2 on, it should be evident that an iterator is an *abstraction* of a pointer, hiding some of its details and eliminating some of its hazards. To illustrate, a `list<T>::iterator` is a class within the `list` class template that contains a data member node, which is a pointer to a list_node (a struct used to describe nodes in the list class template):

```
template<typename T>
class list
{
 // . . .
 public:
  class iterator        // ... some simplification here ...
  {
   protected:
    list_node * node;  // ... and here ...
    // . . .
  };
  // . . .
};
```

The iterator class overloads operator*() so that it returns the value of the data member in the list_node pointed to by the iterator's node member:

```
return node->data;
```

It also overloads operator++() to "increment" the iterator to the next node in the list,

```
// prefix version                 // postfix version
node = node->next;                iterator temp = node;
return *this;                     node = node->next;
                                  return temp;
```

and overloads operator--() similarly to "decrement" the iterator to the previous node in the list.

Two important iterator-valued functions are begin(), which returns an iterator to the first value in the list, and end(), which returns an iterator that points beyond the final value in the list. These functions can be implemented using the pointer members of the head node. More precisely, begin() returns an iterator that contains node->next, which points to the first node in the list:

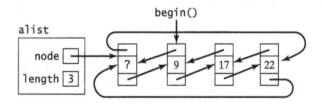

The member function front() that accesses the first value in the list need only dereference the iterator returned by begin():

```
return *begin();
```

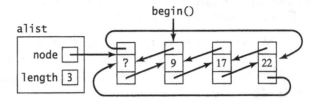

Similarly, `end()` returns an iterator pointing beyond the last node containing a value by returning an iterator containing node, which points to the head node:

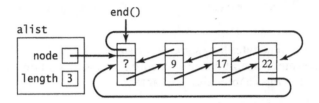

To access the last value in the list, the member function `back()` need only derefer-ence the iterator that results when the iterator returned by `end()` is decremented:

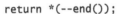

```
return *(--end());
```

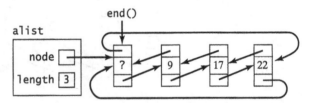

Insertions and Deletions   The `insert()` and `erase()` operations behave in the way we described earlier in this section for doubly-linked lists. The `push_front()` operation essentially uses `insert()` and `begin()` to insert its value at the beginning of the list:

```
insert(begin(), newValue);
```

The `push_back()` operation uses `insert()` and `end()` to insert its value at the end of the list:

```
insert(end(), newValue);
```

Similarly, the `pop_front()` and `pop_back()` operations are implemented using the `erase()` function: `pop_front()` erases the node at position `begin()`,

```
erase(begin());
```

and `pop_back()` erases the node at position `--end()`:

```
erase(--end());
```

Removing values from the list using remove(*value*) can be implemented using erase() and a simple while loop:

```
iterator first = begin(), // begin at first node
         last = end(),    // stop at head node
         next = first;    // save current node address
while (first != last)
{
   ++next;                // save address of next node
   if (*first == value)   // if value in current node
     erase(first);        //    erase it
   first = next;          // reset first to next node
}
```

This illustrates how some of the standard list operations are implemented. Most of the other operations are based on similar operations on linked lists as described earlier in this chapter and in Chapter 6.

✒ Exercises 11.3

Exercises 1–8 assume the following doubly-linked list with the two pointers p1 and p2:

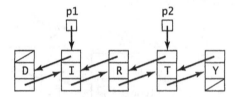

Find the value of each expression.

1. p1->data
2. p1->next->data
3. p1->prev->prev
4. p1->next->next
5. p1->prev->next
6. p2->prev->prev->data
7. p2->prev->prev->prev->prev
8. p2->prev->prev->next->data

In Exercises 9–11, you may use only pointer p1 to access the doubly-linked list preceding Exercise 1. Write statements to do what is asked for.

9. Display the contents of the nodes in alphabetical order.
10. Replace 'D' by 'M' and 'R' by 'S'.
11. Delete the node containing 'T'.

12–14. Repeat Exercises 9–11, but using only pointer p2 to access the list.

15–22. Repeat Exercises 1–8, but for the following circular doubly-linked list:

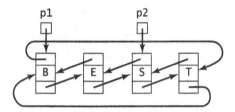

In Exercises 23–25, you may use only pointer p1 to access the preceding circular doubly-linked list. Write statements to do what is asked for.

23. Display the contents of the nodes, in alphabetical order.

24. Insert a node containing 'L' after the node containing 'B' and replace 'E' with 'A'.

25. Delete the node containing 'T'.

26–28. Repeat Exercises 23–25, but using only pointer p2 to access the list.

11.4 Case Study: Large-Integer Arithmetic

Problem

As an application of doubly-linked lists, we consider large-integer arithmetic. Recall that the size of a number that can be stored in computer memory is limited by the number of bits allocated for that type of number. For example, the largest signed integer that can be stored in 32 bits with the usual two's complement representation described in Section 2.2 is $2^{31} - 1 = 2147483647$. In some applications (e.g., keeping track of the U. S. national debt), obviously it is necessary to process integers that are larger than this value. In this section we consider the problem of how to build a C++ BigInt class analogous to Java's BigInteger class that can process integers of any size. For simplicity, we will consider only nonnegative integers and will leave the problem of negative integers as an exercise.

Design

The first step in designing a class for computing with large integers is to select a storage structure to represent these integers. Because the number of digits in these integers may vary considerably, a linked list seems appropriate. Each integer to be processed will be stored in a separate list, with each node storing a block of consecutive digits in the number.

Now consider some of the basic arithmetic operations we will need to implement. To compare two large integers to determine if one is less than the other, we will compare blocks of digits in the list from left to right. But to add two large integers, we will add blocks of digits from right to left. Thus, since it will be necessary to traverse this list in both directions, we will use a doubly-linked list. For example, if we use blocks of length three, make our doubly-linked lists circular, and add a head node, we might store the integer 9,145,632,884 in a doubly-linked list like the following:

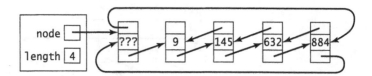

Here, for compatibility with our complete implementation of the BigInt class later that uses a standard list<short int>, we are using a pointer node to the head node and an integer length to store the number of blocks in the large integer.

One of the first operations we need is an input operation. Again, suppose for convenience that a large integer will be entered in three-digit blocks separated by blanks. The input operation must read these blocks and attach a node containing the value of each of these blocks at the end of the doubly-linked list that stores blocks already read. For example, suppose that the input data is

9 145 632 884

and that the first three blocks have already been read and stored, so that the doubly-linked list that stores these blocks is

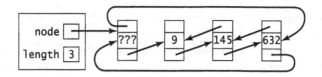

When the block 884 is read, a new node must be created for it and attached to the end of this list:

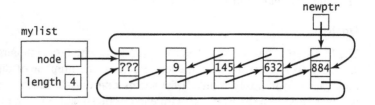

This is done by setting the backward link in this new node to point to the last node in the list,

```
newptr->prev = node->prev;
```

setting the forward link to point to the head node,

```
newptr->next = node;
```

and then setting the forward link in the previous last node and the backward link in the head node to point to this new node:

```
node->prev->next = newptr;
node->prev = newptr;
```

An output operator is simply a traversal of the list from left to right, displaying the block of digits stored in each node (making sure to display leading zeros).

Another operation we need is the addition of two long integers. It must traverse the lists representing these two numbers, from right to left, adding the two three-digit integers in corresponding nodes and the carry digit from the preceding nodes to obtain a three-digit sum and a carry digit. A node is created to store this three-digit sum and is attached at the front of the list representing the sum of the two numbers. The following diagram shows the linked lists corresponding to the computation

carry digits →	1	1	0	1	
			65	313	750
+		999	981	404	873
	1	000	046	718	623

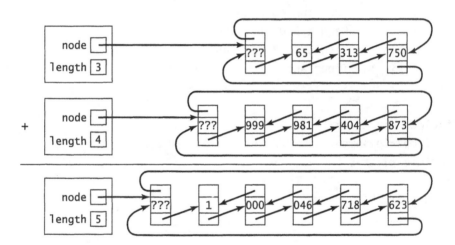

Implementation

We could build a `BigInt` class from scratch using this linked storage structure, but the standard `list` type already uses it and, in addition, provides iterators and a wealth of list operations that are easier to use than the rudimentary pointer operations. So we will use a `list<short int>` data member `myList` in `BigInt` to store the blocks of digits.

As we saw, for the input operator, a node containing the next block of digits from the `BigInt` object being read must be attached to the end of the linked list of those blocks already read. And this is exactly what the `push_back()` operation for a `list` will do. So `operator>>()` need only repeatedly read blocks and use `push_back()` to attach them to the end of `myList`. The output operator can easily be implemented by using an iterator to move through the list and display the blocks of digits.

The definition of operator+() in Figure 11.3 traverses the lists in the two BigInt addends from right to left, using reverse iterators that are moved through the lists synchronously by using the increment operator. The carry digit and the blocks at each position of the iterator are added, the new carry digit and sum block are calculated, and the sum block is inserted at the front of the list in sum using list's push_front() operation.

Figure 11.3 A BigInt Class

```
/*-- BigInt.h --------------------------------------------------------
   This header file defines the data type BigInt for processing
   integers of any size.
   Basic operations are:
      Constructor
      +:         Addition operator
      read():    Read a BigInt object
      display(): Display a BigInt object
      <<, >> :   Input and output operators
   -------------------------------------------------------------------*/

#include <iostream>
#include <iomanip>        // setfill(), setw()
#include <list>

#ifndef BIGINT
#define BIGINT

const int DIGITS_PER_BLOCK = 3;
class BigInt
{
 public:
  /******** Function Members ********/
  /***** Constructor *****/
  // Let the list<short int> constructor take care of this.
```

Figure 11.3 (continued)

```
/***** read *****/
void read(istream & in);
/*------------------------------------------------------------------
   Read a BigInt.

   Precondition:  istream in is open and contains blocks of nonnegative
        integers having at most DIGITS_PER_BLOCK digits per block.
   Postcondition: Blocks have been removed from in and added to myList.
   ------------------------------------------------------------------*/


/***** display *****/
void display(ostream & out) const;
/*------------------------------------------------------------------
   Display a BigInt.

   Precondition:  ostream out is open.
   Postcondition: The large integer represented by this BigInt object
        has been formatted with the usual comma separators and inserted
        into ostream out.
   ------------------------------------------------------------------*/


/***** addition operator *****/
BigInt operator+(BigInt addend2);
/*------------------------------------------------------------------
   Add two BigInts.

   Precondition:  addend2 is the second addend.
   Postcondition: The BigInt representing the sum of the large integer
        represented by this BigInt object and addend2 is returned.
   ------------------------------------------------------------------*/


 private:
  /*** Data Members ***/
  list<short int> myList;
};  // end of BigInt class declaration
```

Figure 11.3 (continued)

```
//------ Input and output operators
inline istream & operator>>(istream & in, BigInt & number)
{
  number.read(in);
  return in;
}

inline ostream & operator<<(ostream & out, const BigInt & number)
{
  number.display(out);
  return out;
}


#endif
```

```
/*-- BigInt.cpp---------------------------------------------------------
               This file implements BigInt member functions.
---------------------------------------------------------------------*/

#include <iostream>
using namespace std;

#include "BigInt.h"

//--- Definition of read()
void BigInt::read(istream & in)
{
  static bool instruct = true;
  if (instruct)
  {
    cout << "Enter " << DIGITS_PER_BLOCK << "-digit blocks, separated by "
         "spaces.\nEnter a negative integer in last block to signal "
         "the end of input.\n\n";
    instruct = false;
  }
  short int block;
  const short int MAX_BLOCK = (short) pow(10.0, DIGITS_PER_BLOCK) - 1;
```

Figure 11.3 (continued)

```cpp
  for (;;)
  {
    in >> block;
    if (block < 0) return;

    if (block > MAX_BLOCK)
      cerr << "Illegal block -- " << block << " -- ignoring\n";
    else
      myList.push_back(block);
  }
}


//--- Definition of display()
void BigInt::display(ostream & out) const
{
   int blockCount = 0;
   const int BLOCKS_PER_LINE = 20;    // number of blocks to display per line

   for (list<short int>::const_iterator it = myList.begin(); ; )
   {
      out << setfill('0');
      if (blockCount == 0)
         out << setfill(' ');

      if (it == myList.end())
         return;

      out << setw(3) << *it;
      blockCount++ ;

      it++;
      if (it != myList.end())
      {
         out << ',';
         if (blockCount > 0 && blockCount % BLOCKS_PER_LINE == 0)
            out << endl;
      }
   }
}
```

Figure 11.3 (continued)

```cpp
//--- Definition of operator+()
BigInt BigInt::operator+(BigInt addend2)
{
   BigInt sum;
   short int first,              // a block of 1st addend (this object)
            second,              // a block of 2nd addend (addend2)
            result,              // a block in their sum
            carry = 0;           // the carry in adding two blocks

   list<short int>::reverse_iterator // to iterate right to left
      it1 = myList.rbegin(),         //   through 1st list, and
      it2 = addend2.myList.rbegin(); //   through 2nd list

   while (it1 != myList.rend() || it2 != addend2.myList.rend())
   {
      if (it1 != myList.rend())
      {
         first = *it1;
         it1++ ;
      }
      else
         first = 0;
      if (it2 != addend2.myList.rend())
      {
         second = *it2;
         it2++ ;
      }
      else
         second = 0;

      short int temp = first + second + carry;
      result = temp % 1000;
      carry = temp / 1000;
      sum.myList.push_front(result);
   }

   if (carry > 0)
      sum.myList.push_front(carry);

   return sum;
}
```

▲

Figure 11.4 shows a driver program that tests the BigInt class and shows the results of several addition computations with various small and large integers.

Figure 11.4 Driver Program for BigInt Class

```
//--- Program to test BigInt class.

#include <iostream>
using namespace std;

#include "BigInt.h"

int main()
{
   char response;
   do
   {
      BigInt number1, number2;
      cout <<"Enter a big integer:\n";
      cin >> number1;
      cout <<"Enter another big integer:\n";
      cin >> number2;

      cout << "The sum of\n\t"
           << number1 << "\nand\n\t" << number2
           << "\nis\n\t" << number1 + number2 << endl;

      cout << "\nAdd more integers (Y or N)? ";
      cin >> response;
   }
   while (response == 'y' || response == 'Y');
}
```

Execution Trace:
```
Enter a big integer:
Enter 3-digit blocks, separated by spaces.
Enter a negative integer in last block to signal the end of input.

999 888 777 666 555
-1
```

Figure 11.4 (continued)

```
Enter another big integer:
111 222 333 444
-1
The sum of
        999,888,777,666,555
and
        111,222,333,444
is
        999,999,999,999,999

Add more integers (Y or N)? Y
Enter a big integer:
1
-1
Enter another big integer:
999 999 999 999 999 999 999 999 999 999
-1
The sum of
           1
and
        999,999,999,999,999,999,999,999,999,999
is
          1,000,000,000,000,000,000,000,000,000,000

Add more integers (Y or N)? Y
Enter a big integer:
1
-1
Enter another big integer:
2
-2
The sum of
           1
and
           2
is
           3

Add more integers (Y or N)? N
```

▲

This example illustrates the power of the standard C++ containers such as `list`. It was relatively easy to get a working version of the `BigInt` class up and running by taking advantage of the features of the `list` container. Any container that provides iterators and basic insert operations could be used for storage. The main disadvantage of using `list` or another STL container is the overhead of all the extra features that aren't used. However, it isn't overly difficult to change this first implementation of the new class into a "lean and mean" version that uses only a linked list built from pointers and nodes as the basic storage structure. Building such a version of the `BigInt` class is left as an exercise.

◆ Exercises 11.4

Exercises 1–5 ask you to modify the `BigInt` class in various ways. For each modification, you should test the resulting class as called for in Programming Problems 13–18 at the end of this chapter.

1. Add the < operation to class `BigInt` to determine whether one `BigInt` object is less than another.

2. Add the == operation to class `BigInt` to determine whether one `BigInt` object is equal to another.

3. Add the subtraction operation − to class `BigInt`: `int1` − `int2` should return 0 if `int1` is less than `int2`.

4. Add the multiplication operation * to class `BigInt`.

5. Modify the class `BigInt` to process both positive and negative large integers.

6. Build your own doubly-linked list container class to replace the standard `list` class, including only those features that are needed to implement the `BigInt` class. Then test the modified `BigInt` class using the driver program in Figure 11.4.

11.5 Other Multiply-Linked Lists

We have seen that doubly-linked lists are useful data structures in applications in which it is necessary to move in either direction in a list. In this section, we consider an assortment of other kinds of list processing in which linked lists whose nodes contain more than one link are useful. Such structures are usually considered in detail in advanced data structures courses and so are only previewed here.

Multiply-Ordered Lists

Building and maintaining an *ordered linked list* in which the nodes are arranged so that the data items (or values in some key field of the data items) stored in the nodes are in ascending (or descending) order is quite straightforward. In some applications, however, it is necessary to maintain a collection ordered in two or more different ways. For example, we might wish to have a collection of student records ordered by both name and id number.

One way to accomplish such multiple orderings is to maintain separate ordered linked lists, one for each of the desired orders. But this is obviously inefficient, especially for large records, because multiple copies of each record are required. A better approach is to use a single list in which multiple links are used to link the nodes together in the different orders. For example, to store a collection of records containing student names and id numbers, with the names in alphabetical order and the id numbers in ascending order, we might use the following multiply-linked list having two links per node:

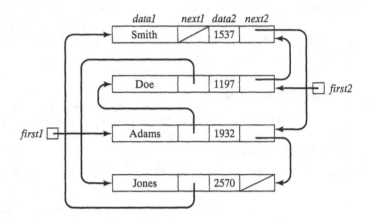

If this list is traversed and the data fields are displayed by using *first1* to point to the first node and following the pointers in the field *next1*, the names will be in alphabetical order:

>   Adams 1932
>   Doe   1197
>   Jones 2570
>   Smith 1537

A traversal using *first2* to point to the first node and following the pointers in the field *next2* gives the id numbers in ascending order:

>   Doe   1197
>   Smith 1537
>   Adams 1932
>   Jones 2570

This list is ordered, therefore, in two different ways.

Sparse Matrices

An $m \times n$ **matrix** is a rectangular array containing m rows and n columns. The usual storage structure for matrices is thus quite naturally a two-dimensional array as described in Section 3.3 (or a two-dimensional vector described in Section 9.6), especially since arrays are provided in nearly every programming language.

In some applications, however (e.g., in solving differential equations), it is necessary to process very large matrices having few nonzero entries. Using a two-dimensional array to store all the entries (including zeros) of such **sparse matrices** is not very efficient. They can be stored more efficiently using a linked structure analogous to that for sparse polynomials described in Section 11.2.

One common linked implementation is to represent each row of the matrix as a linked list, storing only the nonzero entries in each row. In this scheme, the matrix is represented as an array of pointers $A[1], A[2], \ldots, A[m]$, one for each row of the matrix. Each array element $A[i]$ points to a linked list of nodes, each of which stores a nonzero entry in that row and the number of the column in which it appears, together with a link to the node for the next nonzero entry in that row:

For example, the 4×5 matrix

$$A = \begin{bmatrix} 9 & 0 & 0 & 8 & 0 \\ 7 & 0 & 0 & 0 & 0 \\ 0 & 0 & 0 & 0 & 0 \\ -1 & 6 & 0 & -8 & 0 \end{bmatrix}$$

can be represented by the following array of circular linked lists:

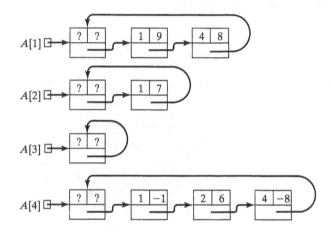

Although this is a useful linked storage structure for matrices, the size of the array limits the number of rows that such matrices may have. Moreover, for smaller matrices or those having a large number of rows with all zero entries, many of the elements in this array will be wasted.

An alternative implementation is to create a single linked list. Each node contains a row number, a column number, the nonzero entry in that row and column, and a link to the next node:

row col value next

| rr | cc | XXX | → |

These nodes are usually arranged in the list so that traversing the list visits the entries of the matrix in rowwise order. For example, the preceding 4×5 matrix can be represented by the following circular linked list, which uses a head node to store the dimensions of the matrix:

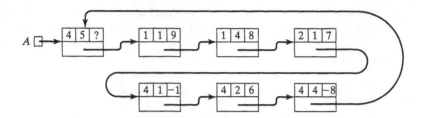

In this implementation, however, we lose direct access to each row of the matrix. If rowwise processing is important to a particular application, such as the addition of matrices, it might be better to replace the array of pointers with a linked list of row head nodes, each of which contains a pointer to a nonempty row list. Each row head node will also contain the number of that row and a pointer to the next row head node, and these row head nodes are ordered so that the row numbers are in ascending order. In this implementation, the preceding 4×5 matrix might be represented by the following linked structure:

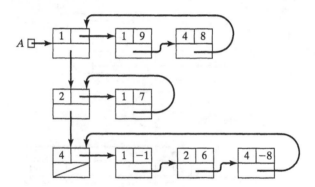

One drawback of all of these linked implementations is that it is difficult to process a matrix columnwise as required, for example, when multiplying two matrices. One linked structure that provides easy access to both the rows and the columns of a matrix is known as an **orthogonal list**. Each node stores a row number, a column number, and the nonzero entry in that row and column, and it appears in both a row list and a column list. This is accomplished by using two links in each node, one pointing to its successor in the row list and the other pointing to its successor in the column list:

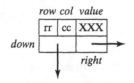

Usually each of the row lists and column lists is a circular list with a head node, and these head nodes are linked together to form circular lists with a master head node. For example, the orthogonal list representation of the preceding 4 × 5 matrix might be as shown in Figure 11.5. Here ∞ denotes some value larger than any valid row or column index (e.g., INT_MAX in C++).

Figure 11.5 Orthogonal Linked-List Representation of a Matrix

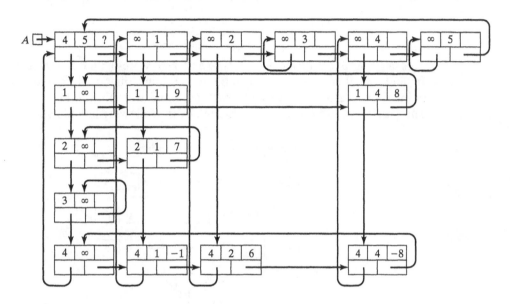

Generalized Lists

In nearly all of our examples of lists thus far, the list elements have been *atomic*, which means that they themselves are not lists. We considered, for example, lists of integers and lists of student records. However, we just described a representation of sparse matrices that is a list of row lists. On several occasions, we also considered lists of strings, and a string is itself a list. In fact, a string might be stored in a linked list of characters and a linked list of strings would then be a linked list of linked lists. For example, the list S of names AL, FRED, JOE would be represented as

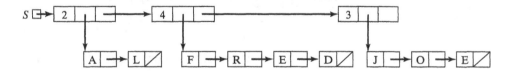

Lists in which the elements are allowed to be lists are called **generalized lists**. As illustrations, consider the following examples of lists:

$$A = (4, 6)$$
$$B = ((4, 6), 8)$$
$$C = (((4)), 6)$$
$$D = (2, A, A)$$

A is an ordinary list containing two atomic elements, the integers 4 and 6. *B* is also a list of two elements, but the first element (4, 6) is itself a list with two elements. *C* is also a list with two elements; its first element is ((4)), which is a list of one element (4), and this element is itself a list having one element, namely, the integer 4. *D* is a list with three elements in which the second and third are themselves lists.

Generalized lists are commonly represented as linked lists in which the nodes have a *tag field* in addition to a data part and a link part:

tag   data   next

This tag is used to indicate whether the data field stores an atom or a pointer to a list. It can be implemented as a single bit, with 0 indicating an atom and 1 indicating a pointer, or as a boolean variable, with false and true playing the roles of 0 and 1. Thus, lists *A*, *B*, and *C* can be represented by the following linked lists:

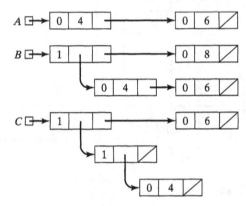

Of course, linked lists with head nodes, circular lists, and other variations may also be used.

Two implementations of *D* are possible. Because *A* is the list (4, 6), we can think of *D* as the list

$$(2, (4, 6), (4, 6))$$

and represent it as

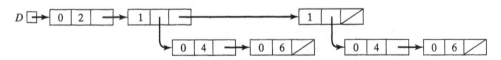

The second possibility is to allow **shared lists** and represent *D* and *A* as follows:

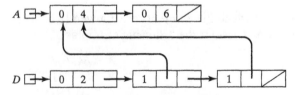

Note that in this case, modifying *A* also changes *D*.

In Section 11.2 we described a linked implementation of polynomials in a single variable. Polynomials in more than one variable can be represented as generalized lists and can thus be implemented using linked structures similar to these. For example, consider the following polynomial $P(x, y)$ in two variables:

$$P(x, y) = 3 + 7x + 14y^2 + 25y^7 - 9x^2y^7 + 18x^6y^7$$

This can be written as a polynomial in y whose coefficients are polynomials in x:

$$P(x, y) = (3 + 7x) + 14y^2 + (25 - 9x^2 + 18x^6)y^7$$

If we use nodes of the form

tag	coef	expo	next
b	CCC	EEE	→

where $tag = 0$ indicates that the *field coef* stores a number and $tag = 1$ indicates that it stores a pointer to a linked list representing a polynomial in x, we can represent the polynomial $P(x, y)$ as

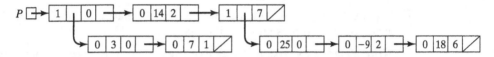

In this section we introduced several kinds of multiply-linked structures and noted some of their applications. There are many other problems in which multiply-linked structures can be used effectively. Several of these applications, including the study of trees and graphs, are considered in detail in later chapters.

✎ Exercises 11.5

For Exercises 1–4, beginning with the multiply-ordered linked list of names and id numbers pictured in the text, show the linked list that results from each of the operations or sequence of operations.

1. Insert Brown with id number 2250.

2. Delete Smith with id number 1537.

3. Insert Zzyzk with id number 1025.

4. Insert Evans with id number 1620; insert Harris with id number 1750; and delete Adams with id number 1932.

5. Write appropriate declarations for a multiply-ordered linked list of names and id numbers like that described in the text.

6. Suppose that the following sparse matrix is implemented by an array of pointers to row lists:

$$A = \begin{bmatrix} 1 & 0 & 0 & 0 & 8 & 0 & 0 \\ -5 & -6 & 0 & 0 & 0 & 0 & 0 \\ 0 & 0 & 0 & 0 & 0 & 0 & 10 \\ 0 & 0 & 0 & 0 & 0 & 0 & 0 \\ 9 & 8 & 7 & 0 & 0 & 0 & 0 \end{bmatrix}$$

Give a diagram of the resulting linked lists similar to that in the text.

7. Repeat Exercise 6, but implement the matrix as a circular linked list having a head node that stores its dimensions.

8. Repeat Exercise 6, but implement the matrix as a linked list of head nodes containing pointers to linked row lists, as described in the text.

9. Repeat Exercise 7, but give an orthogonal list representation like that described in this section.

10–13. Write the declarations needed to store a sparse matrix of integers using the implementations in Exercises 6–9.

14. Write a function to add two sparse matrices, assuming the array of linked row lists implementation described in this section.

15. Repeat Exercise 14, but assume that each matrix is implemented as a circular linked list having a head node that stores its dimensions.

16. Repeat Exercise 14, but assume that each matrix is implemented as a linked list of head nodes containing pointers to linked row lists as described in the text.

17. Repeat Exercise 14, but assume that each matrix is implemented using an orthogonal list representation like that described in this section.

18. Write a class for sparse matrices that uses one of the linked-list implementations described in this section, has an input operation, and has an output operation that displays the matrix in its usual tabular format. You should also write a driver program to test your class as instructed in Programming Problem 23 at the end of this chapter.

19. Extend the class in Exercise 18 to add two matrices.

For Exercises 20–23, give a diagram of the linked-list implementation of the generalized list

20. $(1, (2, 3))$

21. $((1, 2), (3, 4), 5)$

22. $(1, (2, 3), (\ ), 4)$ [$(\ )$ denotes an empty list.]

23. $((1, (2, 3)), ((4)))$

For Exercises 24 and 25, give a diagram of the linked-list implementation of the polynomials in two variables:

24. $P(x, y) = 7 + 3xy + 5x^3y - 17y^2$

25. $P(x, y) = 6 - 5x + 4x^2 - 2x^3y^4 + 6x^5y^4 - x^9y^4 + y^8$

26. Describe how a polynomial $P(x, y, z)$ in three variables can be implemented as a linked list, and illustrate your implementation for the polynomial

$$P(x, y, z) = 6 - 5x + 4x^2 - 2x^3y^4 + 6x^5y^4z^3 - x^9y^4z^3 + y^8z^3 + z^7$$

SUMMARY

🖥 Chapter Notes

- Some variants of standard linked lists make algorithms for some of the basic list operations simpler and more efficient. These include:
  - use of a head node
  - circular linked lists
  - doubly-linked lists
- A linked-list implementation of sparse polynomials eliminates wasted storage of zero coefficients in an array-based implementation, but does result in more complicated algorithms for operations.
- STL's list container provides a large collection of efficient list-processing operations. It uses a circular doubly-linked list with a head node as the basic storage structure.
- Adding several links to the nodes in a linked list can facilitate list-processing in some situations, such as keeping a list ordered in various ways.

☞ Programming Pointers

1. Beware of infinite loops in processing circular linked lists. Also, algorithms that look correct may in fact work only for empty lists.
2. Be careful in changing links in a doubly-linked list. Making changes in the wrong order may result in dangling pointers and marooned sections of the list.

▲ ADT Tips

1. Most of the ADT tips at the end of Chapter 6 that deal with singly-linked lists also pertain to variations and to multiply-linked lists.
2. Using a head node for a linked list will simplify some algorithms, such as those for insertions and deletions, because every node has a predecessor.
3. In a circular linked list, every node has a predecessor and a successor.
4. Deletion from a one-element circular list requires special treatment, because it becomes empty after this node is deleted.
5. A circular linked list with a pointer to the last node works well for implementing lists such as deques and queues in which it is necessary to access repeatedly the elements at the ends of the list.
6. Doubly-linked lists are useful when bidirectional movement in a list is important.
7. STL's list class template stores list elements in a circular doubly-linked list with a head node.
8. Multiply-linked lists are useful for maintaining multiply-ordered lists, sparse matrices, and generalized lists.

Programming Problems

Section 11.1

1. Write a driver program to test the priority queue class template in Exercise 1.

2. Write a driver program to test the circular-linked-list version of a deque class template in Exercise 5.

3. Write a program to solve the *Josephus problem* described in Exercise 9. Use output statements to trace the selection process, showing the contents of the list at each stage.

Section 11.2

4. Use the `Polynomial` class template in a menu-driven program for processing polynomials. The menu of options should (at least) include reading a polynomial, printing a polynomial using the usual mathematical format described in Exercise 2, evaluating the polynomial for a given value of x as described in Exercise 4, and polynomial addition.

5. Extend the menu of options in Problem 4 to include subtraction (see Exercise 3).

6. Extend the menu of options in Problem 4 to include calculating the derivative of a polynomial (see Exercise 5).

7. Extend the menu of options in Problem 4 to include multiplication (see Exercise 6).

8. A *root* of a polynomial $P(x)$ is a number c for which $P(c) = 0$. The *bisection method* is one scheme that can be used to find an approximate root of $P(x)$ in some given interval $[a, b]$, where $P(a)$ and $P(b)$ have opposite signs (thus guaranteeing that $P(x)$ has a root in $[a, b]$). In this method, we begin by bisecting the interval $[a, b]$ and determining in which half $P(x)$ changes sign, because P must have a root in that half of the interval. Now bisect this subinterval and determine in which half of this subinterval $P(x)$ changes sign. Repeating this process gives a sequence of smaller and smaller subintervals, each of which contains a root of $P(x)$, as pictured in the following diagram. The process can be terminated when a small subinterval—say, of length less than 0.0001—is obtained or when $P(x)$ has the value 0 at one of the endpoints:

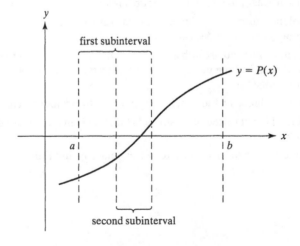

Add and test a member function `root()` to the `Polynomial` class template so that, for a `Polynomial` object p, `p.root(a,b)` returns an approximate root of the polynomial in the interval [a, b] (if there is one), using the *bisection method*.

9. Another method for finding a root of a polynomial $P(x)$ is *Newton's method*. This method consists of taking an initial approximation x_1 and constructing a tangent line to the graph of $P(x)$ at that point. The point x_2 where this tangent line crosses the x axis is taken as the second approximation to the root. Then another tangent line is constructed at x_2, and the point x_3 where this tangent line crosses the x axis is the next approximation. The following diagram shows this process:

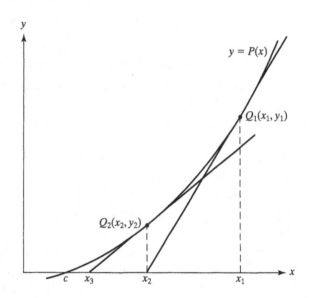

If c is an approximation to the root of $P(x)$, then the formula for obtaining the new approximation is

$$\text{new approximation} = c - \frac{P(c)}{P'(c)}$$

where $P'(x)$ is the derivative of $P(x)$ (see Exercise 5). The process should terminate when a value of $P(x)$ is sufficiently small in absolute value or when the number of iterations exceeds some upper limit. Repeat Problem 8, but use Newton's method.

Section 11.3

10. In a multi-user environment, jobs with various memory requirements are submitted to the computer system, and the operating system allocates a portion of memory to each job, using some memory-management scheme. One popular scheme maintains a circular doubly-linked list of free memory blocks. When a memory request is received, this list is searched to locate the first available block that is large enough to satisfy the request. An appropriate portion of this block is allocated to the job, and any remaining portion remains on the free list.

   Write and test a function to implement this *first-fit* memory-management scheme. Assume that memory blocks are represented as classes (or structs) that contain the beginning address of an available block and its size, together with the links necessary to maintain a circular doubly-linked list. The function should return the address of the allocated block or an indication that the request cannot be satisfied.

11. Another common memory-allocation strategy is the *best-fit* scheme, in which the free list is scanned and the memory block that best fits the request is allocated. This block is either the first block whose size is equal to the request or the block whose size least exceeds the request. Rewrite and test the function in Problem 10 to use this best-fit scheme.

Section 11.4

12. The sequence of *Fibonacci numbers* begins with the integers

$$1, 1, 2, 3, 5, 8, 13, 21, 34, 55, 89, \ldots$$

where each number after the first two is the sum of the two preceding numbers. Write a program that uses class `BigInt` to calculate and display large Fibonacci numbers.

13. Write a driver program to test your modified class `BigInt` with the < and == operations added in Exercises 1 and 2.

14. Write a driver program to test your modified class `BigInt` with the subtraction operation – added in Exercise 3.

15. Write a driver program to test your modified class `BigInt` with the multiplication operation * added in Exercise 4.

16. Use the modified class `BigInt` from Problem 15 in a program that calculates large factorials.

17. Write a driver program to test your modified class `BigInt` for processing both positive and negative large integers as described in Exercise 5.

18. Write a driver program to test your modified class `BigInt` from Exercise 6.

19. Write a program to read the records from the file `StudentFile` (described at the end of Chapter 4) and construct five linked lists of records containing a student's name, number, and cumulative GPA, one list for each class. Store these records in a `vector` of `lists`. After the lists have been constructed, sort each list and then print each of them with appropriate headings. *Note*: If aList is a `list<T>` object, then `alist.sort()`; will sort aList provided < is defined for type T objects. In this exercise, you must overload operator<() to define what it means for one student record to be less than another.

20. The number of elements in a list may grow so large that finding a value in the list is not efficient. One way to improve efficiency is to maintain several smaller linked lists. Write a program to read several lines of uppercase text and to produce a text concordance, which is a list of all distinct words in the text. Store distinct words beginning with A in one linked list, those beginning with B in another, and so on. After all the text lines have been read, sort each list (see Problem 19) and then print a list of all these words in alphabetical order.

21. Modify the program of Problem 20 so that the concordance also includes the frequency with which each word occurs in the text.

22. In addition to the words in a section of text, a concordance usually stores the numbers of selected pages on which there is a significant use of the word. Modify the program of Problem 20 so that the numbers of all lines in which a word appears are stored along with the word itself, but don't list the same line number more than once for a word. The program should display each word together with its associated line numbers in ascending order.

23. Write a "quiz-tutor" program, perhaps on a topic from one of the early chapters, or some other topic about which you are knowledgeable. The program should read a question, possible answers, and the correct answer from a file, display the question and possible answers, and accept an answer from the user. If the answer is correct, the program should go on to the next question. If it is incorrect, store the question in a list. When the file of questions is exhausted, the questions that were missed should be displayed again (in their original order). Keep a count of the correct answers and display the final count. Also, display the correct answer, when necessary, in the second round of questioning.

24. Suppose that jobs entering a computer system are assigned a job number and a priority from 0 through 9. The numbers of jobs awaiting execution by the system are kept in a *priority queue*. A job entered into this queue is placed ahead of all jobs of lower priority but after all those of equal or higher priority. Write a program that uses a list to store the jobs and allows the user to select one of the following menu options: R (remove), A (add), or L (list). For R, read a job number and remove it from the priority queue; for A, read a job number and priority and then add it to the priority queue in the manner just described; and for L, list all the job numbers in the priority queue.

Section 11.5

25. Write a program to read the records from StudentFile (described at the end of Chapter 4) and store them in a multiply-ordered list with two link fields, in which one link is used to order the nodes so that the id numbers are in ascending order and another link orders the nodes so that the names are in alphabetical order. Note that the records in StudentFile are already arranged in order of ascending id numbers. Then search this list for a given student id or a given student name, and display the other information in the record.

26. Extend the program in Problem 25 so that new records can be inserted or existing records can be deleted.

27. Write a driver program to test the sparse-matrix class of Exercise 18.

28. Extend the program in Problem 27 to test the sparse-matrix class of Exercise 19.

CHAPTER 12

Searching: Binary Trees and Hash Tables

Chapter Objectives

- Look at ways to search collections of data, beginning with a review of linear and binary search.
- Introduce trees in general and then focus on binary trees, looking at some of their applications and implementations.
- See how binary trees can be viewed as recursive data structures and how this simplifies algorithms for some of the basic operations.
- Develop a class to implement binary search trees using a linked storage structure for the data items.
- (Optional) Look briefly at how threaded binary search trees facilitate traversals.
- Introduce the basic features of hash tables and examine some of the ways they are implemented.

In the last sections of the preceding chapter we considered linked lists in which the nodes were connected by two or more links. For example, the nodes in doubly-linked lists have two links, one pointing in the forward direction from a node to its successor and the other pointing backward from a node to its predecessor. The nodes in a multiply-ordered linked list may have to be connected by several links, depending on how many logical orderings are desired. There are several other important multiply-linked structures, and in this chapter we consider one of these, binary trees.

One important application of binary trees is to organize data in a two-dimensional linked structure so that it can be searched more efficiently than if it is stored in a linked list. Thus, we begin by reviewing some of the search algorithms we have already considered. This will lead to the study of binary trees and, in particular, binary search trees, and how they can be used to organize data so that it can be searched efficiently.

Another important structure we consider in this chapter is the hash table. Its approach to searching a collection of data values for an item is quite different from the others and it is usually very efficient.

12.1 Review of Linear Search and Binary Search

In many applications, the collection of data items to be searched is organized as a list,

$$x_1, x_2, \ldots, x_n$$

This list is to be searched to determine whether one of the x_i's has a specified value. In our review of the searching problem in this section, we assume that the equality (==) operator has been defined for the type of the x_i's, and for binary search, that less than (<) has also been defined. Thus, when the list elements are records with different types of information, as is often the case, and the search is based on some *key field* in these records, the appropriate relational operators must be defined on these records to compare these key fields.

Linear Search

The most straightforward searching scheme is **linear search**, in which we begin with the first list element and then search the list sequentially until either we find the specified item or we reach the end of the list. An algorithm for linear search was given in Section 10.4 for a list of elements stored in an array or `vector`:

Linear Search Algorithm—Array/Vector Version

/*   Linear search the list $a[0], \ldots, a[n-1]$ for *item*; *found* = true and
     loc = position of *item* if the search is successful; otherwise, *found* is false.   */

1. Set *found* = false.
2. Set *loc* = 0.
3. While *loc* < *n* and not *found* do the following:
       If *item* == *a* [*loc*] then   // *item* found
           Set *found* = true.
       Else   // keep searching
           Increment *loc* by 1.
   End while

A linear-search algorithm for a linked list is very similar. Instead of varying an index *loc* over the positions of the array or `vector`, we initialize a pointer *locptr* to the first node and advance it from one node to the next by following the *next* links:

 ## Linear Search Algorithm—Linked List Version

/* Linear search a linked list with first node pointed to by *firstNode* for *item*; *found* = true and *locptr* = pointer to a node containing *item* if the search is successful; otherwise, *found* is false. */

1. Set *found* = false.
2. Set *locptr* = *firstNode*.
3. While *locptr* ≠ null and not *found* do the following:
   If *item* == *locptr->data*   // *item* found
      Set *found* = true.
   Else   // keep searching
      Set *locptr* = *locptr->next*.
   End while

This linked-list version of linear search is essentially how the find() algorithm in the standard <algorithm> library searches a sequential container. A call to it has the form

```
find(begin, end, item)
```

where *begin* and *end* are iterators positioned at the first element and just beyond the last element, respectively. It returns an iterator positioned at the location of *item* if the search is successful, and an iterator positioned beyond the end of the list if the search is unsuccessful. An iterator-based version of linear search is as follows:

 ## Linear Search Algorithm—Iterator Version

/* Linear search a sequential container with iterators *begin* and *end* positioned at the first element and just beyond the last element for *item*; *locIter* is positioned at *item* if the search is successful; otherwise, *locIter* == *end*. */

1. Set iterator *locIter* = *begin*.
2. While (*locIter* ≠ *end*) and (**locIter* ≠ *item*) do the following:
   ++*locIter*
   End while

The worst case for linear search is obviously that in which the item for which we are searching is not in the list, because in this case, each of the *n* items in the list must be examined. The worst-case computing time for linear search is thus $O(n)$. If the list elements are arranged in ascending (or descending) order, searching can be terminated as soon as a list element is encountered that is greater than (less than) the item. For example, when searching the list

10, 20, 30, 40, 50, 60, 70, 80, 90, 100

for the value 35, there is no need to search beyond the list element 40, because it—and, therefore, all the list elements that follow it—are greater than 35. The worst-case computing time is still O(n), however, since n comparisons are required if the item being sought is greater than all items in the list.

Binary Search

An alternative scheme for searching an ordered list is **binary search**, also described in Section 10.4.

Binary Search Algorithm—Array/Vector Version

/* Linear search the list $a[0], \ldots, a[n-1]$, whose elements are in ascending order, for *item*; *found* = true and *loc* = position of *item* if the search is successful; otherwise, *found* is false.   */

1. Set *found* = false.
2. Set *first* = 0.
3. Set *last* = $n-1$.
4. While *first* ≤ *last* and not *found* do the following:
       a. Calculate *loc* = (*first* + *last*) / 2.
       b. If *item* < $a\,[loc]$ then
           Set *last* = *loc* − 1.   // search first half
         Else if $a\,[loc]$ < *item* then
           Set *first* = *loc* + 1.   // search last half
         Else
           Set *found* = true.   // *item* found
     End while

Here the middle list element is examined first, and if it is not the desired item, the search continues with either the first half or the last half of the list. Thus, on each pass through the loop, the size of the sublist being searched is reduced by one-half. We showed in some detail in Section 10.4 that it follows from this observation that the worst-case computing time for binary search is O($\log_2 n$). It is, therefore, more efficient than linear search for large n ($n \geq 20$, as indicated by empirical studies). For example, if n = 8,000,000 (the approximate population of New York City in the 2000 census), linear search would require 8,000,000 comparisons to determine that an item wasn't in the list, whereas binary search would require only 23.

Binary search is also the kind of search performed by the `binary_search()` algorithm in C++'s standard `<algorithm>` library. A call to it has the form

    `binary_search(begin, end, item)`

where *begin* and *end* are iterators positioned at the first list element and just beyond the last list element, respectively. It returns `true` for a successful search and `false` for an unsuccessful one. Notice that, unlike `find()`, it does not return an iterator positioned at the location of `item` if the search is successful.

The preceding algorithm for binary search is iterative, but it is also natural to view binary search recursively, as noted in Chapter 10. The basic idea at each stage is to examine the middle element of the (sub)list and if it is not the desired item, then search one of the two halves of the (sub)list *in exactly the same way.* The computing time of a recursive binary search function also is $O(\log_2 n)$ but does have the extra overhead of pushing activation records onto and popping them from the run-time stack (see Section 10.3).

For binary search to be efficient, however, it does require a direct-access storage structure to be efficient. It is not appropriate for linked lists because locating the middle element requires traversing the sublist of elements that precede it. This means that we would have to modify the preceding algorithm by adding to the instruction that calculates *loc* a loop that moves a pointer *locPtr* from the first element of the sublist to the middle element:

Binary Search Algorithm—Linked List Version

1. Set *found* = false.
2. Set *first* = 0.
3. Set *last* = $n - 1$.
4. Set *locptr* = *firstNode.*
5. While *first* ≤ *last* and not *found* do the following:
    a. Calculate *loc* = (*first* + *last*) / 2.
    b. For *i* ranging from *first* to *loc* – 1 do the following:
        locptr = *locptr->next.*
       End for.
    c. If *item* < *locptr->data* then
            Set *last* = *loc* – 1.   // search first half
        Else if *locptr->data* < *item* then
            Set *first* = *loc* + 1.   // search last half
        Else
            Set *found* = true.   // *item* found
   End while

In the worst case, when item is greater than all elements in the list, the for loop will move the pointer *locptr* through the entire list, which means that the computing time is $O(n)$ instead of $O(\log_2 n)$.

Our study of the many linked list variants in the preceding chapter raises the question of whether it might be possible to binary search one of them in $O(\log_2 n)$ time. To see what is needed, consider the following ordered list of integers:

13, 28, 35, 49, 62, 66, 80

The first step in binary search requires examining the middle element in the list. Direct access to this element is possible if we maintain a pointer to the node storing it:

At the next stage, one of the two sublists, the left half or the right half, must be searched and must, therefore, be accessible from this node. This is possible if we maintain two pointers, one to each of these sublists. Since these sublists are searched in the same manner, these pointers should point to nodes containing the middle elements in these sublists:

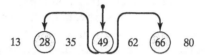

By the same reasoning, pointers from each of these "second-level" nodes are needed to access the middle elements in the sublists at the next stage:

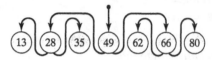

The resulting structure is usually drawn with rigid pointers, giving it an upside-down tree-like shape:

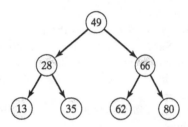

It is called a **binary search tree** and is a special kind of **binary tree**, which is the data structure studied in the rest of this chapter.

◆ Exercises 12.1

Exercises 1–5 use the following array `critter`:

i	0	1	2	3	4	5	6	7	8
critter[i]	auk	bat	cow	eel	elk	fox	gnu	pig	rat

Give the indices of the elements of `critter` in the order that the components are examined during a binary search for

1. gnu   2. eel   3. fly
4. ant   5. yak

Most of the following exercises ask you to write various search functions. You should also test your functions with driver programs as instructed in Programming Problems 1–10 at the end of this chapter.

6. The performance of function `linearSearch()` can be improved slightly if the item being searched for is added at the end of the list. This makes it possible to replace the compound boolean expression in the first `if` inside the `for` loop by a simple one. Write this improved version of `linearSearch()`.

7. Modify the array-based linear search algorithm to make it more efficient for ordered lists.

8. Write a recursive version of the array-based linear search algorithm.

9. Write a recursive version of the linked-list-based linear search algorithm.

10. In many cases of list searching, certain items in the list are retrieved more frequently than others. The performance of linear search in such cases improves if these frequently sought items are placed at the beginning of the list. One data structure that allows this is a self-organizing list, in which list elements are rearranged so that frequently accessed items move to or toward the front of the list. Write a linear search function for such a **self-organizing list** using a *move-to-the-front* strategy, in which the item being retrieved is moved to the front of the list. Assume that the list is stored in an array or a `vector`.

11. Repeat Exercise 10, but for a linked list.

12. Proceed as in Exercise 10, but use a *move-ahead-one* strategy in which the item being retrieved is interchanged with its predecessor.

13. Repeat Exercise 12, but for a linked list.

14. In binary search, *probes* are always made at the middle of the (sub)list. In many situations, however, we have some idea of approximately where the item is located; for example, in searching a telephone directory for "Doe, John," we might estimate that this name is approximately 1/6 of the way through the list. This idea is the basis for **interpolation search**, in which probes of a sublist of size k are made at position $first + f * k$ for some fraction f (not necessarily 1/2). Write a function to implement interpolation search for an ordered list of integers stored in an array or a `vector` using the fraction f given by

$$f = \frac{item - x_{first}}{x_{last} - x_{first}}$$

12.2 Introduction to Binary Trees

We have seen that a linked list is a useful structure for processing dynamic lists whose maximum sizes are not known in advance and that change frequently because of repeated insertions and deletions. We noted in the preceding section that although binary search is not efficient for linked lists, it can be used for a *binary search tree*. This is a special kind of *binary tree*, which is a special instance of a more general structure called a *tree*.

Tree Terminology

A **tree** consists of a finite set of elements called **nodes**, or **vertices**, and a finite set of **directed arcs** that connect pairs of nodes.[1] If the tree is nonempty, then one of the nodes, called the **root**, has no incoming arcs, but every other node in the tree can be reached from it by following a *unique* **path**, which is a sequence of consecutive arcs.

Trees derive their names from the treelike diagrams that are used to picture them. For example,

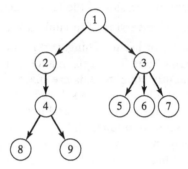

shows a tree having nine vertices in which vertex 1 is the root. As this diagram indicates, trees are usually drawn upside down, with the root at the top and the **leaves**—that is, vertices with no outgoing arcs—at the bottom. Nodes that are directly accessible from a given node (by using only one directed arc) are called the **children** of that node, and a node is said to be the **parent** of its children. For example, in the preceding tree, vertex 3 is the parent of vertices 5, 6, and 7, and these vertices are the children of vertex 3 and are called **siblings**:

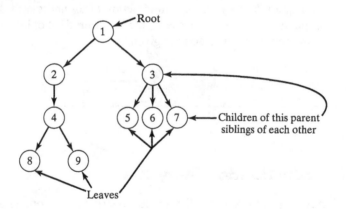

---

[1] If we stopped the definition here, we would have defined a **digraph** (**directed graph**). See Chapter 16 for more information about graphs and digraphs.

Nodes that can be reached by following a path from another node are called **descendants** of that node, which is an **ancestor** of those nodes. For example, nodes 8 and 9 are descendants of node 2 and are also descendants of node 1. Node 1 is an ancestor of all of the other nodes in the tree. For each node in a tree, a **subtree** of that node is formed by selecting one of its children and all descendants of that child. For example, for the preceding tree, node 1 has two subtrees: a left subtree and a right subtree:

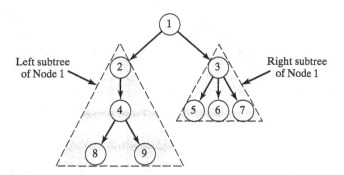

Node 2 has only one subtree and node 3 has three subtrees, each containing only one node:

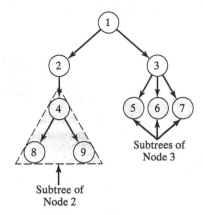

In this chapter, we will restrict our attention to trees in which each node has at most two children and thus has at most two nonempty subtrees. Such trees are called **binary trees**. More general trees like those in the preceding diagrams are considered in Chapter 15.

Some Examples of Binary Trees

As was noted in the introduction to this chapter, binary trees can be used to solve a variety of problems. Binary trees are useful in modeling processes in which some experiment is performed repeatedly and there are two possible outcomes at each stage (e.g., off or on, 0 or 1, false or true, head or tail). For example, the following tree might be used to represent the possible outcomes of flipping a coin three times:

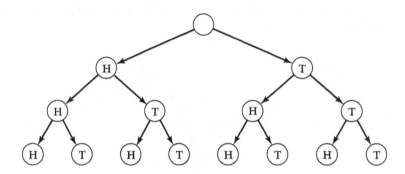

Each path from the root to one of the leaf nodes corresponds to a particular sequence of outcomes, such as HTH, a head followed by a tail followed by another head, as highlighted in the diagram.

Decision trees have a similar structure; each node contains information that requires a yes–no decision between its two subtrees. For example, the following diagram, might be part of a decision tree in an animal-guessing game:

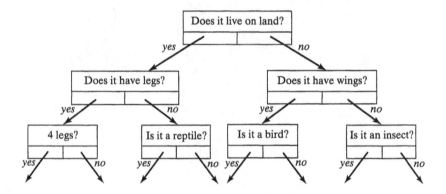

Decision trees similar to these are used to develop knowledge bases for programs called **expert systems** that exhibit expertise through the use of the knowledge base. Examples of such systems range from experts that control welding robots in an automotive assembly line to legal experts that can help draw up standard legal documents and medical experts that diagnose medical problems. The study of expert systems is a branch of artificial intelligence.

A binary tree can also be used in coding problems such as in encoding and decoding messages transmitted in Morse code, a scheme in which characters are represented as sequences of dots and dashes, as shown in the following table:

A · —	M — —	Y — · — —
B — · · ·	N — ·	Z — — · ·
C — · — ·	O — — —	1 · — — — —
D — · ·	P · — — ·	2 · · — — —
E ·	Q — — · —	3 · · · — —
F · · — ·	R · — ·	4 · · · · —
G — — ·	S · · ·	5 · · · · ·
H · · · ·	T —	6 — · · · ·
I · ·	U · · —	7 — — · · ·
J · — — —	V · · · —	8 — — — · ·
K — · —	W · — —	9 — — — — ·
L · — · ·	X — · · —	0 — — — — —

In this case, the nodes in a binary tree are used to represent the characters, and each arc from a node to its children is labeled with a dot or a dash, according to whether it leads to a left child or to a right child, respectively. Thus, the following is part of the tree for Morse code (completing it is left as an exercise):

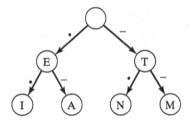

The sequence of dots and dashes labeling a path from the root to a particular node corresponds to the Morse code for that character; for example, · · is the code for I and — · is the code for N. In Section 15.1 we use a similar tree to construct another kind of code known as *Huffman code*.

Array Representation of Binary Trees

An array (or vector) can be used to store binary trees. We simply number the nodes in the tree from the root down, numbering the nodes on each level from left to right,

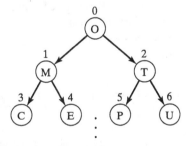

and store the contents of the ith node in the ith location of the array:

i	0	1	2	3	4	5	6	···
$t[i]$	O	M	T	C	E	P	U	···

This implementation works very well for **complete** trees, in which each level of the tree is completely filled, except possibly the bottom level, but there the nodes are in the leftmost positions. For example, the trees in the following diagram are complete:

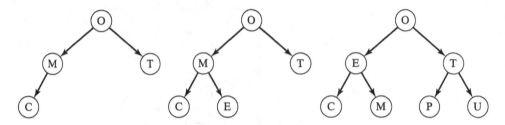

But the trees that follow are not complete; in the first, the nodes in the bottom level are not in the leftmost positions and in the other two, the upper levels are not completely filled:

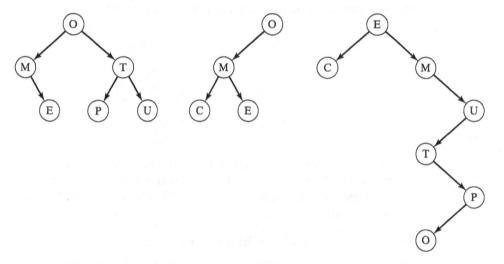

The completeness property guarantees that the data items will be stored in consecutive locations at the beginning of the array. It should be obvious, however, that this implementation may not be space efficient for other kinds of binary trees. For example, consider the last tree in the preceding diagram. It contains the same characters as the complete tree we represented by an array earlier, but this tree requires 58 array positions for storage:

i	0	1	2	3	4	5	6	7	8	9	10	11	12	13	14	15	16	17	18	19
$t[i]$	E	C	M				U							T						

20	21	22	23	24	25	26	27	28	29	30	31	32	33	34	35	36	37	38	39
								P										

40	41	42	43	44	45	46	47	48	49	50	51	52	53	54	55	56	57	⋯
																	O	⋯

This tree not only fails to be complete, but it is also unbalanced. **Balanced trees** are binary trees with the property that for each node, the height of its left subtree and the height of its right subtree differ by at most one, where a tree's **height** is the number of levels in the tree. For the preceding tree, there are many violations of this balance requirement. For example, the left subtree of the root has height 1 and the right subtree has height 5; the left subtree of the node containing U has height 3 and the right subtree has height 0 (because it is empty). As we will see later, in addition to having inefficient array representations, unbalanced binary trees like this also cannot be searched efficiently.

Linked Representation of Binary Trees

For more efficient storage and to provide additional flexibility, binary trees are usually implemented as linked structures in which each node has two links, one pointing to the left child of that node (if there is one) and the other pointing to the right child (if there is one):

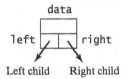

The two link fields `left` and `right` in a node are pointers to nodes representing its left and right children, respectively, or are null pointers if the node does not have a left or right child. A leaf node is thus characterized by having null values for both `left` and `right`:

With this implementation, the following binary tree can be represented by the linked tree at the right:

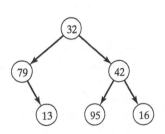

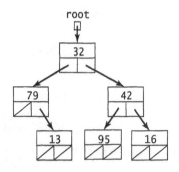

We will use such a linked tree representation in the class template for binary search trees that we will build later in this chapter. Like our classes for linked lists, linked stacks, and linked queues in earlier chapters, this class will have an inner class to implement the node structure:

```
class BinNode
{
 public:
  DataType data;
  BinNode * left;
  BinNode * right;

  // BinNode constructors
  // Default -- data is default DataType value;
  //         -- both links are null
  BinNode()
  : left(0), right(0)
  {}

  // Explicit Value -- data part contains item;
  //                -- both links are null
  BinNode(DataType item)
  : data(item), left(0), right(0)
  {}
};// end of class BinNode declaration
```

This class has three public data members (so they are accessible to binary tree operations):

- data of type DataType, which is a type parameter passed to the enclosing binary-search-tree class; and
- pointers left and right to nodes that are the roots of the left and right subtrees, respectively, and which are null for empty subtrees.

Two BinNode constructors are provided: a default constructor that sets the left and right links to null pointers and an explicit-value constructor that receives a data value, stores it in the data part, and sets the left and right links to null pointers.

✔ Quick Quiz 12.2

1. A(n) _____ consists of nodes (or vertices) and directed arcs that connect pairs of nodes.

2. A node that has no incoming arcs but from which every other node in the tree can be reached by following a unique sequence of consecutive arcs is called a(n) _____.

3. Nodes with no outgoing arcs are called _____.

4. Nodes that are directly accessible from a given node (by using only one directed arc) are called the _____ of that node, which is said to be the _____ of these nodes.

5. Binary trees are trees in which each node has _____.

Questions 6–10 refer to the following binary tree:

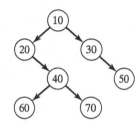

6. Which node is the root?
7. List all the leaves.
8. Is this binary tree complete? If not, explain why it isn't.
9. Find the height of the tree.
10. Is this binary tree balanced? If not, explain why it isn't.
11. Show the array used to represent this binary tree.

✏ Exercises 12.2

1. Complete the binary tree for Morse code that was begun in this section.

Questions 2–7 refer to the following binary tree:

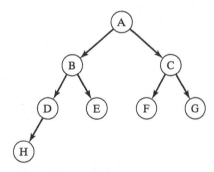

2. List all the leaves.
3. Is this binary tree complete? If not, explain why it isn't.
4. Find the height of the tree.
5. For each of the nodes, find the height of its left subtree and the height of its right subtree.
6. Is this binary tree balanced? If not, explain why it isn't.
7. Show the array used to represent this binary tree.

Questions 8–12 refer to the following binary tree:

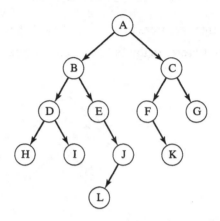

8. List all the leaves.
9. Is this binary tree complete? If not, explain why it isn't.
10. Find the height of the tree.
11. Is this binary tree balanced? If not, explain why it isn't.
12. Show the array used to represent this binary tree.

12.3 Binary Trees as Recursive Data Structures

A binary tree can be defined as a **recursive data structure** in a very natural way. As an illustration, consider the binary tree of the preceding section:

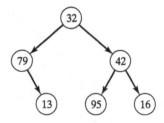

Its root node contains the integer 32 and has pointers to the nodes containing 79 and 42, each of which is itself the root of a binary subtree:

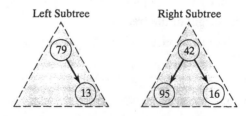

Now consider the left subtree. Its root node contains the integer 79 and has a right child but no left child. Nevertheless, we can still regard this node as having pointers to two binary subtrees, a left subtree and a right subtree, provided that we allow empty binary trees:

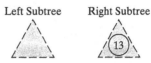

Left Subtree   Right Subtree

Both the left and right subtrees of the one-node tree containing 13 are thus empty binary trees.

This leads to the following recursive definition of a binary tree:

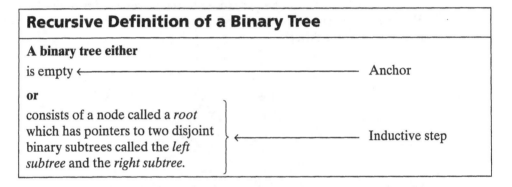

Recursive Definition of a Binary Tree

A binary tree either

is empty ⟵——————————————— Anchor

or

consists of a node called a *root* which has pointers to two disjoint binary subtrees called the *left subtree* and the *right subtree*. ⟵——————————————— Inductive step

Because of the recursive nature of binary trees, many of the basic operations on them can be carried out most simply and elegantly using recursive algorithms. These algorithms are typically anchored by the special case of an empty binary tree, and the inductive step specifies how a binary tree is to be processed in terms of its root and either or both of its subtrees. In this section we will focus our attention on traversals and leave other operations to the next section.

Traversals

Traversing a tree involves moving through a tree such as the preceding one, visiting each node exactly once. Suppose for now that the order in which the nodes are visited is not relevant. What is important is that we visit each node, not missing any, and that the information in each node is processed exactly once.

One simple recursive scheme is to traverse the binary tree as follows:

1. Visit the root and process its contents.
2. Traverse the left subtree.
3. Traverse the right subtree.

Thus, in our example, if we simply display a node's contents when we visit it, we begin by displaying the value 32 in the root of the binary tree. Next, we must traverse the left subtree; after this traversal is finished, we then must traverse the right subtree; and when this traversal is completed, we will have traversed the entire binary tree:

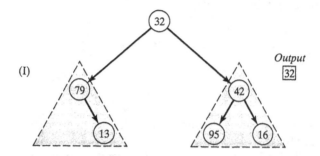

(I)   *Output*
                                                                   32

The problem has now been reduced to the traversal of two smaller binary trees. We consider the left subtree and visit its root. Next we must traverse its left subtree and then its right subtree:

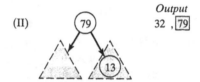

(II)   *Output*
                                                               32 , 79

The left subtree is empty, and so we have reached the anchor case of the recursive definition of a binary tree, and to complete the traversal algorithm, we must specify how an empty binary tree is to be traversed. But this is easy: we do nothing.

Because no action is required to traverse the empty left subtree, we turn to traversing the right subtree. We visit its root and then must traverse its left subtree followed by its right subtree:

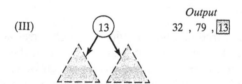

(III)   *Output*
                                                             32 , 79 , 13

As both subtrees are empty, no action is required to traverse them. Consequently, traversal of the binary tree in diagram III is complete, and since this was the right subtree of the tree in diagram II, traversal of this tree is also complete.

This means that we have finished traversing the left subtree of the root in the original binary tree in diagram I, and we finally are ready to begin traversing the right subtree. This traversal proceeds in a similar manner. We first visit its root, displaying the value 42 stored in it, then traverse its left subtree, and then its right subtree:

Output

(IV)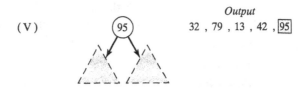

32 , 79 , 13 , 42

The left subtree consists of a single node with empty left and right subtrees and is traversed as described earlier for a one-node binary tree:

Output

(V) 95

32 , 79 , 13 , 42 , 95

The right subtree is traversed in the same way:

Output

(VI)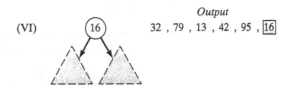

32 , 79 , 13 , 42 , 95 , 16

This completes the traversal of the binary tree in diagram IV and thus also completes the traversal of the original tree in diagram I.

As this example demonstrates, traversing a binary tree recursively requires three basic steps, which we shall denote V, L, and R:

V   Visit a node.
L   Traverse the left subtree of a node.
R   Traverse the right subtree of a node.

We performed these steps in the order listed here, but in fact, there are six different orders in which they can be carried out:

LVR
VLR
LRV
VRL
RVL
RLV

For example, the ordering LVR corresponds to the following recursive traversal algorithm:

> If the binary tree is empty   // anchor
> > Do nothing
>
> Else do the following: // inductive step
> > L: Traverse the left subtree.
> > V: Visit the root.
> > R: Traverse the right subtree.

To obtain an algorithm for any of the other traversals, one need only rearrange the three instructions labeled L, V, and R appropriately.

The first three orders, in which the left subtree is traversed before the right, are the most important of the six traversals and are commonly called by other names:

LVR ↔ **Inorder**

VLR ↔ **Preorder**

LRV ↔ **Postorder**

For the preceding binary tree, these three traversals visit the nodes as follows:

Inorder: 79, 13, 32, 95, 42, 16
Preorder: 32, 79, 13, 42, 95, 16
Postorder: 13, 79, 95, 16, 42, 32

To see why these names are appropriate, consider the following **expression tree**, a binary tree used to represent the arithmetic expression

$$A - B * C + D$$

by representing each operand as a child of a parent node representing the corresponding operator (see also Section 7.5):

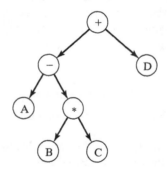

An inorder traversal of this expression tree produces the *infix* expression

$$A - B * C + D$$

A preorder traversal gives the *prefix* expression (see Exercise 53 in Section 7.5)

$$+ - A * B C D$$

And a postorder traversal yields the *postfix* (RPN) expression (see Section 7.5)

$$A B C * - D +$$

✔ Quick Quiz 12.3

Questions 1–3 refer to the following binary tree:

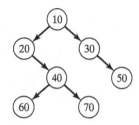

1. Perform an inorder traversal of this binary tree.
2. Perform a preorder traversal of this binary tree.
3. Perform a postorder traversal of this binary tree.

Questions 4–6 refer to the following binary tree:

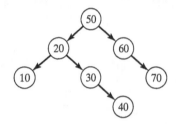

4. Perform an inorder traversal of this binary tree.
5. Perform a preorder traversal of this binary tree.
6. Perform a postorder traversal of this binary tree.

◆ Exercises 12.3

Exercises 1–3 refer to the following binary tree:

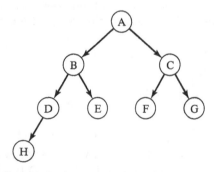

1. Perform an inorder traversal of this binary tree.
2. Perform a preorder traversal of this binary tree.

3. Perform a postorder traversal of this binary tree.

4–6. Repeat Exercises 1–3 for the following binary tree:

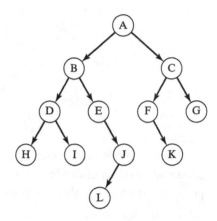

7–9. Repeat Exercises 1–3 for the following binary tree:

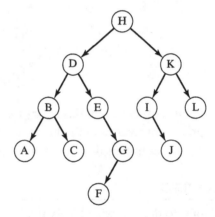

For the arithmetic expressions in Exercises 10–14, draw a binary tree that represents the expression, and then use tree traversals to find the equivalent prefix and postfix expressions.

10. $(A - B) - C$

11. $A - (B - C)$

12. $A / (B - (C - (D - (E - F))))$

13. $((((A - B) - C) - D) - E) / F$

14. $((A * (B + C)) / (D - (E + F))) * (G / (H / (I * J)))$

15. A preorder traversal of a binary tree produced A D F G H K L P Q R W Z, and an inorder traversal produced G F H K D L A W R Q P Z. Draw the binary tree.

16. A postorder traversal of a binary tree produced F G H D A L P Q R Z W K, and an inorder traversal gave the same result as in Exercise 15. Draw the binary tree.

17. Show by example that knowing the results of a preorder traversal and a postorder traversal of a binary tree does not uniquely determine the tree; that is, give an example of two different binary trees for which a preorder traversal of each gives the same result, and so does a postorder traversal.

12.4 Binary Search Trees

At first glance, the following binary tree doesn't look much different from those we considered in the preceding section:

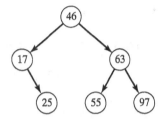

However, it has one property that makes it very different: the value in each node is greater than the values in its left subtree (if there are any) and less than the values in its right subtree (if there are any). A binary tree having this property is called a **binary search tree (BST)** because, as we noted at the end of Section 12.1, it can be searched using an algorithm much like the binary search algorithm for lists. This is one of the key operations of a BST as an abstract data type.

Binary Search Tree (BST) ADT

Collection of Data Elements

A binary tree that satisfies the **BST property**: For each node x, values in left subtree of x < value in x < values in right subtree of x

Basic Operations

- Construct an empty BST.
- Determine if the BST is empty.
- Search the BST for a given item.
- Insert a new item in the BST and maintain the BST property.
- Delete an item from the BST and maintain the BST property.
- Traverse the BST visiting each node exactly once. At least one of the traversals (an *inorder traversal*) must visit the values in the nodes in ascending order.

Implementing BSTs

In this section we will build a class template to implement binary search trees. (The finished product is in Figure 12.7.) As we know, any node in a tree can be accessed if we maintain a pointer to the root of the tree, so our class template needs only one data member, a pointer myRoot to the root of the binary tree. The BST constructor will then simply initialize myRoot to a null pointer and an empty operation need only check whether this pointer is null. We also need a structure for the nodes of the tree, and for this we will use the two-linked node described in Section 12.2:

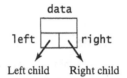

There we also described a class BinNode to represent such nodes, so we can begin building our class template as shown in Figure 12.1.

Figure 12.1 A Binary Search Tree (BST) Class Template

```
/* BST.h contains the declaration of class template BST.
   Basic operations:
     Constructor: Constructs an empty BST
     empty:       Checks if a BST is empty
     ... and others to be added ...
------------------------------------------------------------*/


#include <iostream>

#ifndef BINARY_SEARCH_TREE
#define BINARY_SEARCH_TREE

template <typename DataType>
class BST
{
 public:
  /***** Function Members *****/
  BST();
  /*-----------------------------------------------------------

    Construct a BST object.

    Precondition:  None.
    Postcondition: An empty BST has been constructed.
   ------------------------------------------------------------*/


  bool empty() const;
  /*-----------------------------------------------------------
    Check if BST is empty.
```

Figure 12.1 (continued)

```
     Precondition:   None.
     Postcondition: Returns true if BST is empty and false otherwise.
     ------------------------------------------------------------------*/

private:
 /***** Node class *****/
 class BinNode
 {
  public:
    DataType data;
    BinNode * left;
    BinNode * right;

    // BinNode constructors
    // Default -- data part is default DataType value; both links are null.
    BinNode()
    : left(0), right(0)
    {}

    // Explicit Value -- data part contains item; both links are null.
    BinNode(DataType item)
    : data(item), left(0), right(0)
    {}

  };// end of class BinNode declaration

  typedef BinNode * BinNodePointer;

 /***** Data Members *****/
  BinNodePointer myRoot;

}; // end of class template declaration

//--- Definition of constructor
template <typename DataType>
inline BST<DataType>::BST()
: myRoot(0)
{}
```

Figure 12.1 (continued)

```
//--- Definition of empty()
template <typename DataType>
inline bool BST<DataType>::empty() const
{ return myRoot == 0; }


#endif
```

▲

BST Traversals

In the last section we described various ways to traverse a binary tree and singled out three of them: inorder, preorder, and postorder. A recursive function to implement any of the algorithms for these traversals (or others we considered) is easy. One need only attempt to write a correct nonrecursive version to appreciate the simple elegance of the functions in Figures 12.2 and 12.7.

There is one problem, however. To illustrate it, suppose we want to do an inorder traversal of some binary tree. For a nonempty tree, this requires the following steps:

L: Recursively traverse the left subtree of the root.
V. Visit the root.
R. Recursively traverse the right subtree of the root.

The L operation requires a recursive call of the form

traverse(subtreeRoot->left);

and the R operation requires one of the form

traverse(subtreeRoot->right);

But such function calls are not appropriate for users of our BST class who know nothing about pointers to nodes or the -> operation, since these are hidden implementation details.

The solution is to use two functions. The first is a public method that one can use to send a message to a BST object to do an inorder traversal of itself:

```
binTreeObj.inorder(argument_list);
```

The inorder() method can then pass this request on to a private auxiliary method inorderAux() that can access BinNodes and pointers within these nodes:

```
void inorder(parameter_list) const
{ inorderAux(parameter_list, myRoot); }


void inorderAux(parameter_list,
            BST<DataType>::BinNodePointer subtreeRoot) const
```

```
    {
      if (subtreeRoot != 0)
      {
        inorderAux(param_list, subtreeRoot->left);     // L
        // Visit the node pointed to by subTreeRoot     // V
        inorderAux(param_list, subtreeRoot->right);    // R
      }
    }
```

Functions for any of the other traversals are obtained simply by changing the order of the statements representing the L, V, and R operations. Figure 12.2 shows the prototypes and definitions for the preceding inorder-traversal functions in which the parameter list is an ostream reference to which output is to be directed during the traversal.

    It should be noted that *an inorder traversal visits the nodes in a BST in ascending order*. The reason is that in a binary search tree, for each node, all of the values in the left subtree are smaller than the value in this node, which is less than all values in its right subtree. Because an inorder traversal is an LVR traversal, it follows that it must visit the nodes in ascending order.

Figure 12.2 BST Inorder Traversals

Add the following prototype to the public function prototypes of the BST class template:

```
void inorder(ostream & out) const;
/*------------------------------------------------------------------
   Inorder traversal of BST.

   Precondition:  ostream out is open.
   Postcondition: BST has been inorder traversed and values in nodes
      have been output to out.
   Note: inorder uses private auxiliary function inorderAux().
   ------------------------------------------------------------------*/
```

Add the following to a private section of private function members of the BST class template:

```
private:
  /***** Private Function Members *****/
  void inorderAux(ostream & out,
              BST<DataType>::BinNodePointer subtreePtr) const;
  /*------------------------------------------------------------------
     Inorder traversal auxiliary function.
```

Figure 12.2 (continued)

```
      Precondition:  ostream out is open; subtreePtr points to a subtree
         of this BST.
      Postcondition: Subtree with root pointed to by subtreePtr has been
         output to out.
   -----------------------------------------------------------------------*/
```

Add the following to the function definitions that follow the BST class template declaration:

```
//--- Definition of inorder()
template <typename DataType>
inline void BST<DataType>::inorder(ostream & out) const
{
   inorderAux(out, myRoot);
}


//--- Definition of inorderAux()
template <typename DataType>
void BST<DataType>::inorderAux(ostream & out,
                  BST<DataType>::BinNodePointer subtreeRoot) const
{
   if (subtreeRoot != 0)
   {
      inorderAux(out, subtreeRoot->left);    // L operation
      out << subtreeRoot->data << "  ";      // V operation
      inorderAux(out, subtreeRoot->right);   // R operation
   }
}
```

▲

Some interesting and useful output is obtained by doing an RVL traversal, with *param_list* an ostream to which output is to go and an integer parameter that produces an indent with each recursive call. This is illustrated by the function members of the BST class template in Figure 12.3. Sending a message

```
      aBST.graph(cout);
```

produces a somewhat primitive graphical representation of a binary tree that is useful for visualizing the result of various BST operations. For example, if aBST is the binary tree pictured earlier or in the diagram that follows Figure 12.3, the output produced

will be

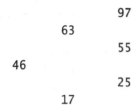

The root is at the left and the children of each node are indented 8 more spaces with the right child above it and its left child below. Supplying the links from each node to its children (perhaps only mentally) gives the following:

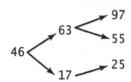

Figure 12.3 BST Graphic Output

Add the following prototype to the public function prototypes of the BST class template:

```
void graph(ostream & out) const;
/*-----------------------------------------------------------------
   Graphic output of BST.

   Precondition:  ostream out is open.
   Postcondition: Graphical representation of BST has been output to out.
   Note: graph() uses private auxiliary function graphAux().
-----------------------------------------------------------------*/
```

Add the following to a private section of private function members of the BST class template:

```
private:
   /***** Private Function Members *****/
   void graphAux(ostream & out, int indent,
                    BST<DataType>::BinNodePointer subtreeRoot) const;
/*-----------------------------------------------------------------
   Graph auxiliary function.
```

Figure 12.3 (continued)

```
    Precondition:  ostream out is open; subtreePtr points to a subtree
        of this BST.
    Postcondition: Graphical representation of subtree with root pointed
        to by subtreePtr has been output to out, indented indent spaces.
    ----------------------------------------------------------------------*/
```

Add the following to the function definitions that follow the BST class template declaration:

```
//--- Definition of graph()
template <typename DataType>
inline void BST<DataType>::graph(ostream & out) const
{ graphAux(out, 0, myRoot); }


//--- Definition of graphAux()
#include <iomanip>

template <typename DataType>
void BST<DataType>::graphAux(ostream & out, int indent,
                    BST<DataType>::BinNodePointer subtreeRoot) const
{
  if (subtreeRoot != 0)
    {
      graphAux(out, indent + 8, subtreeRoot->right);
      out << setw(indent) << " " << subtreeRoot->data << endl;
      graphAux(out, indent + 8, subtreeRoot->left);
    }
}
```

▲

Searching a BST

Recursive Search   We have viewed binary trees, and BSTs in particular, as recursive data structures and have seen how easily traversal can be implemented by recursive functions. It is natural, therefore, to see whether similar recursive implementations of the other basic operations are also easy. We begin by considering how to search a BST like the following:

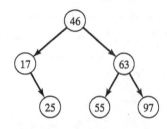

The search begins at the root. If it is the desired item, the search is finished; if the item we wish to find is less than the value in the root, we move down to the left subtree and search it; and if it is greater, we descend to the right subtree and search it. If the subtree we select is empty, we conclude that the item is not in the tree; otherwise, we search this subtree *in exactly the same manner* as we did the original tree.

For example, suppose that we are searching this BST for 55. Since 55 > 46, the value in the root, we search the right subtree of the root:

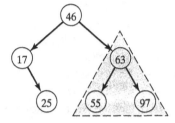

We compare the value we are searching for with the root 63 of this smaller subtree, and because 55 < 63 we search the left subtree of the node containing 63:

Since the root of this one-node subtree contains the value 55 we are searching for, we can terminate our search.

Had we been searching for the value 56 instead of 55, our search would not be over. Since 56 is greater than the value in this subtree with root containing 55, we would examine its right subtree:

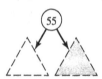

But since this subtree is empty, we can conclude that the value 56 is not in the tree and terminate our search.

To implement this search operation as a function member of our BST class template, we need two functions for the same reasons as for traversals: a `search()` function that calls a recursive helper function `searchAux()`. The function `searchAux()` assumes that the relational operators < and > have been defined for the type `DataType`:

```
//--- Definition of search()
template <typename DataType>
inline bool BST<DataType>::search(const DataType & item) const
{ return searchAux(myRoot, item); }
```

```
//--- Definition of searchAux()
template <typename DataType>
bool BST<DataType>::searchAux(
                  BST<DataType>::BinNodePointer subtreeRoot,
                  const DataType & item) const
{
  if (subtreeRoot == 0)                    // empty subtree
    return false;
  // else there is a nonempty subtree
  if (item < subtreeRoot->data)      // search left subtree
    return searchAux(subtreeRoot->left, item);
  else if (subtreeRoot->data < item) // search right subtree
    return searchAux(subtreeRoot->right, item);
  else                                     // item is found
    return true;
}
```

A nonrecursive function for searching a BST is also easy to write. We begin with a pointer locptr positioned at the root of the BST and then repeatedly replace it with the left or right link of the current node, according to whether the item for which we are searching is less than or greater than the value stored in this node. This process continues until either the desired item is found or locptr becomes null, indicating an empty subtree, in which case the item is not in the tree. This iterative definition is given in Figure 12.4.

Search can be implemented either iteratively or recursively with little difference of effort. And neither version is really simpler or more understandable than the other version. As we noted in Section 10.4, it is common to opt for the iterative version since the recursive version involves the overhead of pushing and popping the run-time stack with the various function calls. The complete version of the BST class template in Figure 12.7 uses the iterative version.

Figure 12.4 Searching a BST

Add the following prototype to the public function prototypes of the BST class template:

```
bool search(const DataType & item) const;
/*-----------------------------------------------------------------------
  Search the BST for item.

  Precondition:  None.
  Postcondition: Returns true if item found, and false otherwise.
  -----------------------------------------------------------------------*/
```

Figure 12.4 (continued)

Add the following to the function definitions that follow the BST class template declaration:

```
//--- Definition of search()
template <typename DataType>
bool BST<DataType>::search(const DataType & item) const
{
   BST<DataType>::BinNodePointer locptr = myRoot;
   bool found = false;
   while (!found && locptr != 0)
   {
      if (item < locptr->data)          // descend left
         locptr = locptr->left;
      else if (locptr->data < item)   // descend right
         locptr = locptr->right;
      else                              // item found
         found = true;
   }
   return found;
}
```

▲

Inserting into a BST

A binary search tree can be built by repeatedly calling a function to insert elements into a BST that is initially empty (myRoot is a null pointer). As we will now see, the method used to determine where an element is to be inserted in a BST is similar to that used to search the tree.

The insert operation can be implemented either recursively or nonrecursively. Here we will begin with the iterative version because most beginning programmers find it easier to understand than the recursive method and because it is an easy modification of the search operation. In fact, we basically need only change search() to maintain a pointer to the parent of the node currently being examined as we descend the tree, looking for a place to insert the item.

To illustrate, suppose that the following BST has already been constructed and we wish to insert the letter 'R'. We begin a search for 'R' at the root:

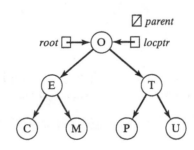

Since 'R' >'O', we set *parent* = *locptr* and then descend to the right subtree:

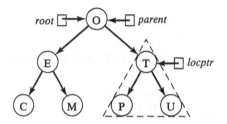

After comparing 'R' with 'T' stored in the root of this subtree pointed to by *locptr*, we descend to the left subtree, since 'R' < 'T', but first set *parent* = *locptr*:

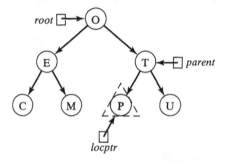

Since 'R' >'P', we set *parent* = *locptr* and then descend to the right subtree of this one-node subtree containing 'P':

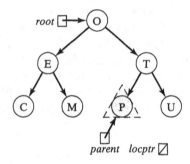

The fact that this right subtree is empty (*locptr* is null) indicates that 'R' is not in the BST and should be inserted as a right child of its parent node:

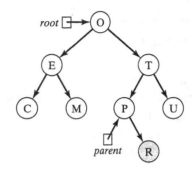

The insert() function member in Figure 12.5 uses this modified version of search() to locate where a given item is to be inserted (or is found). The pointer parent that trails the search pointer locptr down the tree keeps track of the parent node so that the new node can be attached to the BST in the proper place.

Figure 12.5 Insert Operation

Add the following prototype to the public function prototypes of the BST class template:

```
void insert(const DataType & item);
/*-------------------------------------------------------------------
   Insert item into BST.

   Precondition:  None.
   Postcondition: BST has been modified with item inserted at proper
       position to maintain BST property.
   -------------------------------------------------------------------*/
```

Add the following to the function definitions that follow the BST class template declaration:

```
//--- Definition of insert()
template <typename DataType>
void BST<DataType>::insert(const DataType & item)
{
   BST<DataType>::BinNodePointer
        locptr = myRoot,    // search pointer
        parent = 0;         // pointer to parent of current node
   bool found = false;      // indicates if item already in BST
```

Figure 12.5 (continued)

```
while (!found && locptr != 0)
{
    parent = locptr;
    if (item < locptr->data)         // descend left
        locptr = locptr->left;
    else if (locptr->data < item)    // descend right
        locptr = locptr->right;
    else                             // item found
        found = true;
}
if (!found)
{                                    // construct node containing item
    locptr = new BST<DataType>::BinNode(item);
    if (parent == 0)                 // empty tree
        myRoot = locptr;
    else if (item < parent->data )   // insert to left of parent
        parent->left = locptr;
    else                             // insert to right of parent
        parent->right = locptr;
}
else
    cout << "Item already in the tree\n";
}
```

▲

A recursive function for the insertion operation is a bit easier than the iterative version. The obvious anchor is an empty BST, and we must specify how to insert an item into such a tree; otherwise, we can proceed recursively by inserting an item into the left subtree or the right subtree of the current node, according to whether the item is less than or greater than the value in this node.

Again we need two functions. Note that in insertAux(), the parameter subtreeRoot is a reference parameter, so that when item is inserted into one of its subtrees, it is actually being inserted into a subtree of the corresponding argument. Because the first call to insertAux() is with myRoot, this means that each of the subtreeRoot pointers is actually one of the links in the tree whose root is pointed to by myRoot.

```
//--- Definition of insert()
template <typename DataType>
void BST<DataType>::insert(const DataType & item)
{ insertAux(myRoot, item); }
```

```
//--- Definition of insertAux()
template <typename DataType>
void BST<DataType>::insertAux(
                    BST<DataType>::BinNodePointer & subtreeRoot,
                    const DataType & item)
{
  if (subtreeRoot == 0)                    // empty tree
    subtreeRoot = new BST<DataType>::BinNode(item);
  // else there is a nonempty tree.  Insert into:
  else if (item < subtreeRoot->data)  //  left subtree
    insertAux(subtreeRoot->left, item);
  else if (subtreeRoot->data < item)  //  right subtree
    insertAux(subtreeRoot->right, item);
  else
    cerr << "Item already in the tree\n";
}
```

Removing a Node from a BST

To remove a node x from a BST, we consider three cases:

1. x is a leaf.
2. x has one child.
3. x has two children.

The first case is very easy. We simply make the appropriate pointer in x's parent a null pointer; this is the left or right pointer according to whether x is the left or the right child of its parent. For example, to delete the leaf node containing D in the following BST, we can simply make the right pointer in its parent C a null pointer and then return x to the free store:

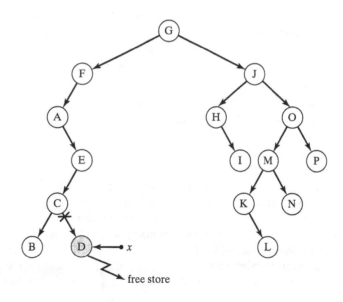

The second case, where the node x has exactly one child, is just as easy. Here we need only bypass the node to be deleted by setting the appropriate pointer in x's parent to point to x's child. For example, we can delete the node containing E in the BST of our example by simply setting the right pointer of its parent A to point to the node containing C and then dispose of x:

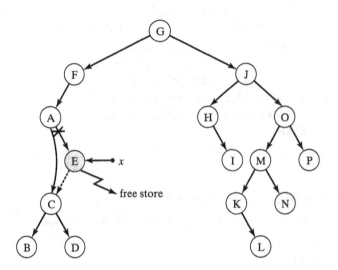

These two cases can be combined into one case in which x has at most one nonempty subtree. If the left pointer of x is null, we set the appropriate pointer of x's parent to point to the right subtree of x (which may be empty—an, example of case 1); otherwise, we set it to point to the left subtree of x. The following statements handle both cases:

```
subtree = x->left;      // pointer to a subtree of x
if (subtree == 0)
   subtree = x->right;
if (parent == 0)        // root being deleted
   root = subtree;
else if (parent->left == x)
   parent->left = subtree;
else
   parent->right = subtree;
```

The third case, in which x has two children, can be reduced to one of the first two cases if we replace the value stored in node x by its inorder successor (or predecessor) and then delete this successor (predecessor). The inorder successor (predecessor) of the value stored in a given node of a BST is its successor (predecessor) in an inorder traversal of the BST.

To illustrate this case, consider again the following binary search tree and suppose we wish to delete the node containing J. As we just noted, we can replace it with either its inorder successor or its inorder predecessor. We will illustrate here with its successor. We can locate this inorder successor by starting at the right child of x and then descending left as far as possible. In our example, this inorder successor is the node containing K:

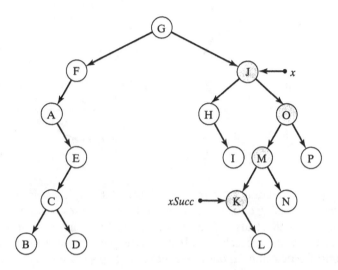

We replace the contents of x with this inorder successor:

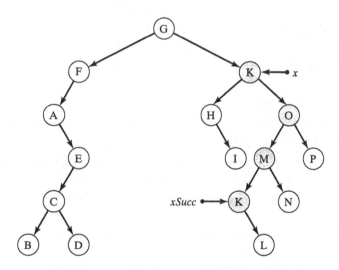

Now we need only delete the node pointed to by *xSucc*. We do this as described for cases 1 and 2, since this node will always have an empty left subtree (and perhaps an empty right subtree as well):

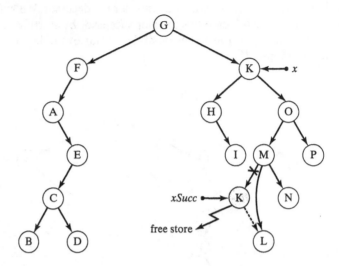

The function `remove()` in Figure 12.6 implements the delete operation for all cases, reducing case 3 to one of the first two cases, when necessary, in the manner we have just illustrated. It also is possible to design a recursive function for deletion from a binary search tree. In this case, the necessary searching can be incorporated into the deletion function. We leave writing a recursive delete function as an exercise.

Figure 12.6 Delete Operation

Add the following prototype to the public function prototypes of the BST class template:

```
void remove(const DataType & item);
/*--------------------------------------------------------------------
   Remove item from BST.

   Precondition:  None.
   Postcondition: BST has been modified with item removed (if present);
      BST property is maintained.
   Note: remove uses auxiliary function search2() to locate the node
         containing item and its parent.
   --------------------------------------------------------------*/
```

Add the following to the private function prototypes of the BST class template:

```
void search2(const DataType & item, bool & found,
             BinNodePointer & locptr, BinNodePointer & parent) const;
/*--------------------------------------------------------------------
   Locate a node containing item and its parent.
```

Figure 12.6 (continued)

```
Precondition:  None.
Postcondition: locptr points to node containing item or is null if
    not found, and parent points to its parent.
----------------------------------------------------------------------*/
```

Add the following to the function definitions that follow the BST class template declaration:

```
//--- Definition of remove()
template <typename DataType>
void BST<DataType>::remove(const DataType & item)
{
   bool found;                        // signals if item is found
   BST<DataType>::BinNodePointer
      x,                              // points to node to be deleted
      parent;                         //    "     " parent of x and xSucc
   search2(item, found, x, parent);

   if (!found)
   {
      cout << "Item not in the BST\n";
      return;
   }
   //else
   if (x->left != 0 && x->right != 0)
   {                                  // node has 2 children
      // Find x's inorder successor and its parent
      BST<DataType>::BinNodePointer xSucc = x->right;
      parent = x;
      while (xSucc->left != 0)        // descend left
      {
         parent = xSucc;
         xSucc = xSucc->left;
      }

      // Move contents of xSucc to x and change x
      // to point to successor, which will be removed.
      x->data = xSucc->data;
      x = xSucc;
   } // end if node has 2 children
```

Figure 12.6 (continued)

```cpp
   // Now proceed with case where node has 0 of 1 child
   BST<DataType>::BinNodePointer
      subtree = x->left;              // pointer to a subtree of x
   if (subtree == 0)
      subtree = x->right;
   if (parent == 0)                    // root being removed
      myRoot = subtree;
   else if (parent->left == x)         // left child of parent
      parent->left = subtree;
   else                                // right child of parent
      parent->right = subtree;
   delete x;
}


//--- Definition of search2()
template <class DataType>
void BST<DataType>::search2(const DataType & item, bool & found,
                            BST<DataType>::BinNodePointer & locptr,
                            BST<DataType>::BinNodePointer & parent) const
{
   locptr = myRoot;
   parent = 0;
   found = false;
   while (!found && locptr != 0)
   {
      if (item < locptr->data)        // descend left
      {
         parent = locptr;
         locptr = locptr->left;
      }
      else if (locptr->data < item)   // descend right
      {
         parent = locptr;
         locptr = locptr->right;
      }
      else                            // item found
         found = true;
   }
}
```

▲

Figure 12.7 shows the contents of the complete BST class template; the complete version, including documentation can be found in the folder *Fig12.1-8* for Chapter 12 source code on the website for this text. Additional operations that should be added are described in the exercises: destructor, copy constructor, and assignment operator. Others that might be added are preorder and postorder traversals, a level finder, and a level-by-level traversal. These also are described in the exercises.

Figure 12.7 The Complete Binary Search Tree (BST) Class Template

```
/* BST.h contains the declaration of class template BST.
   Basic operations:
     Constructor: Constructs an empty BST
     empty:       Checks if a BST is empty
     search:      Search a BST for an item
     insert:      Inserts a value into a BST
     remove:      Removes a value from a BST
     inorder:     Inorder traversal of a BST -- output the data values
     graph:       Output a graphical representation of a BST
   Private utility helper operations:
     search2:     Used by delete
     inorderAux:  Used by inorder
     graphAux:    Used by graph
   Other operations described in the exercises:
     destructor
     copy constructor
     assignment operator
     preorder, postorder, and level-by-level traversals
     level finder
   Note: Execution terminates if memory isn't available for a new BST node.
-------------------------------------------------------------------------*/

#include <iostream>
#include <new>

#ifndef BINARY_SEARCH_TREE
#define BINARY_SEARCH_TREE

template <typename DataType>
class BST
{
 public:
```

Figure 12.7 (continued)

```
/***** Function Members *****/
//--- See Figures 12.1-12.6 for documentation
BST();
bool empty() const;
bool search(const DataType & item) const;
void insert(const DataType & item);
void remove(const DataType & item);
void inorder(ostream & out) const;
void graph(ostream & out) const;

private:
 /***** Node class *****/
 class BinNode
 {
  public:
   DataType data;
   BinNode * left;
   BinNode * right;

   // BinNode constructors
   // Default -- data part is default DataType value; both links are null.
   BinNode()
   : left(0), right(0)
   {}

   // Explicit Value -- data part contains item; both links are null.
   BinNode(DataType item)
   : data(item), left(0), right(0)
   {}
 };// end of class BinNode declaration

 typedef BinNode * BinNodePointer;

 /***** Private Function Members *****/
 void search2(const DataType & item, bool & found,
              BinNodePointer & locptr, BinNodePointer & parent) const;
 void inorderAux(ostream & out, BinNodePointer subtreePtr) const;
```

Figure 12.7 (continued)

```
  void graphAux(ostream & out, int indent, BinNodePointer subtreeRoot) const;

 /***** Data Members *****/
  BinNodePointer myRoot;

}; // end of class template declaration

//--- Definition of constructor -- Insert from Figure 12.1

//--- Definition of empty() -- Insert from Figure 12.1

//--- Definition of search() -- Insert from Figure 12.4

//--- Definition of insert() -- Insert from Figure 12.5

//--- Definition of remove() -- Insert from Figure 12.6

//--- Definition of inorder() -- Insert from Figure 12.2

//--- Definition of graph() -- Insert from Figure 12.3

//--- Definition of search2() -- Insert from Figure 12.5

//--- Definition of inorderAux() -- Insert from Figure 12.2

//--- Definition of graphAux() -- Insert from Figure 12.3

#endif
```

▲

Figure 12.8 shows a driver program to test BST and a sample execution. Remember that the function member graph() displays a binary tree with its root at the left and subtrees to the right. A version of this driver program (treetester.cpp) in the folder *Fig12.1-8* for Chapter 12 source code on the website contains extra program sections that can be uncommented and used to test other BST operations that can be added.

Figure 12.8 Testing a Binary Search Tree (BST) Class Template

```cpp
/*----- treetester.cpp --------------------------------------------
            Program for testing class template BST.
   -----------------------------------------------------------*/

#include <iostream>
using namespace std;

#include "BST.h"

int main()
{
   // Testing Constructor and empty()
   BST<int> intBST;                // test the class constructor
   cout << "Constructing empty BST\n";
   cout << "BST " << (intBST.empty() ? "is" : "is not") << " empty\n";

   // Testing inorder
   cout << "Inorder Traversal of BST: \n";
   intBST.inorder(cout);

   // Testing insert
   cout << "\nNow insert a bunch of integers into the BST."
           "\nTry items not in the BST and some that are in it:\n";
   int number;
   for (;;)
   {
      cout << "Item to insert (-999 to stop): ";
      cin >> number;
      if (number == -999) break;
      intBST.insert(number);
   }
   intBST.graph(cout);

   cout << "BST " << (intBST.empty() ? "is" : "is not") << " empty\n";
   cout << "Inorder Traversal of BST: \n";
   intBST.inorder(cout);

   cout << endl;
```

Figure 12.8 (continued)

```cpp
// Testing search()
cout << "\n\nNow testing the search() operation."
        "\nTry both items in the BST and some not in it:\n";
for (;;)
{
   cout << "Item to find (-999 to stop): ";
   cin >> number;
   if (number == -999) break;
   cout << (intBST.search(number) ? "Found" : "Not found") << endl;
}

// Testing remove()
cout << "\nNow testing the remove() operation."
        "\nTry both items in the BST and some not in it:\n";
for (;;)
{
   cout << "Item to remove (-999 to stop): ";
   cin >> number;
   if (number == -999) break;
   intBST.remove(number);
   intBST.graph(cout);
}
cout << "\nInorder Traversal of BST: \n";
intBST.inorder(cout);
cout << endl;
}
```

Execution Trace:
```
Constructing empty BST
BST is empty
Inorder Traversal of BST:

Now insert a bunch of integers into the BST.
Try items not in the BST and some that are in it:
Item to insert (-999 to stop): 55
Item to insert (-999 to stop): 66
Item to insert (-999 to stop): 88
```

Figure 12.8 (continued)

```
Item to insert (-999 to stop): 77
Item to insert (-999 to stop): 20
Item to insert (-999 to stop): 10
Item to insert (-999 to stop): 30
Item to insert (-999 to stop): -999
                88
                            77
        66
  55
                30
        20
                10
BST is not empty
Inorder Traversal of BST:
10  20  30  55  66  77  88



Now testing the search() operation.
Try both items in the BST and some not in it:
Item to find (-999 to stop): 66
Found
Item to find (-999 to stop): 44
Not found
Item to find (-999 to stop): 10
Found
Item to find (-999 to stop): 11
Not found
Item to find (-999 to stop): -999

Now testing the remove() operation.
Try both items in the BST and some not in it:
Item to remove (-999 to stop): 10
                88
                            77
        66
  55
                30
        20
```

Figure 12.8 (continued)

```
Item to remove (-999 to stop): 66
        88
                77
 55
                30
        20
Item to remove (-999 to stop): 55
        88
 77
                30
        20
Item to remove (-999 to stop): -999

Inorder Traversal of BST:
20   30   77   88
```

▲

Problem of Lopsidedness

The order in which items are inserted into a BST determines the shape of the tree. For example, inserting the letters O, E, T, C, U, M, P into a BST of characters in this order gives the nicely *balanced* tree

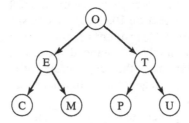

but inserting them in the order C, O, M, P, U, T, E yields the unbalanced tree

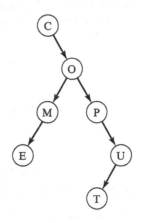

and inserting them in alphabetical order, C, E, M, O, P, T, U, causes the tree to degenerate into a linked list:

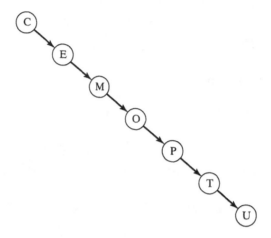

The time required to carry out most of the basic operations on a BST quite clearly depends on the "shape" of the tree. If it is balanced so that the left and right subtrees of each node contain approximately the same number of nodes, then as a search pointer moves down the tree from one level to the next, the size of the subtree to be examined is reduced by about one-half. Using an analysis like that used for binary search in Section 10.4, it is easy to show that the computing time for each of search(), search2(), insert(), and delete() is $O(\log_2 n)$ in this case. As the BST becomes increasingly unbalanced, however, the performance of these functions deteriorates. For trees that degenerate into linked lists as in the last example, the search operations degenerate into linear search, so that the computing time is $O(n)$ for such BSTs.

Preordering data items so that inserting them into a BST will result in a balanced tree is often not possible or at least not practical. The usual solution is to rebalance the tree after each new element is inserted using rebalancing algorithms. One common rebalancing scheme is described in Chapter 15.

✔ Quick Quiz 12.4

For Questions 1–3, draw the BST that results when the C++ keywords are inserted in the order given

1. if, do, goto, case, switch, while, for

2. do, case, for, if, switch, while, goto

3. while, switch, goto, for, if, do, case

Questions 4–9 refer to the following binary search tree:

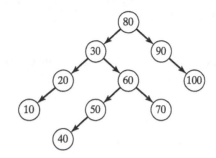

4. Perform an inorder traversal of this BST.
5. Perform a preorder traversal of this BST.
6. Perform a postorder traversal of this BST.
7. Show the BST that results when the node containing 20 is deleted from the given BST.
8. Show the BST that results when the node containing 30 is deleted from the given BST.
9. Show the BST that results when the root is deleted from the given BST.

▶ Exercises 12.4

For each of the lists of letters in Exercises 1–5, do the following:

    a. Draw the BST that results when the letters are inserted in the order given.
    b. Perform inorder, preorder, and postorder traversals of the tree that results and show the sequence of letters that results in each case.

1. A, C, R, E, S
2. R, A, C, E, S
3. C, A, R, E, S
4. S, C, A, R, E
5. C, O, R, N, F, L, A, K, E, S

For each of the lists of C++ keywords in Exercises 6–11, do the following:

    a. Draw the BST that results when the words are inserted in the order given.
    b. Perform inorder, preorder, and postorder traversals of the tree that results and show the sequence of words that results in each case.

6. `new, const, typedef, if, main, bool, float`
7. `break, operator, return, char, else, switch, friend`
8. `double, long, namespace, class, public, int, new`

9. `while`, `using`, `static`, `private`, `enum`, `case`

10. `break`, `operator`, `if`, `typedef`, `else`, `case`, `while`, `do`, `return`, `unsigned`, `for`, `true`, `double`, `void`

11. `struct`, `class`

For Exercises 12–21, use the following binary search tree:

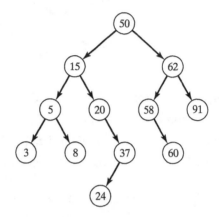

In each of Exercises 12–16, *begin with this tree* and show the BST that results after the operation or sequence of operations is performed on this tree.

12. Insert 7.

13. Insert 7, 1, 55, 29, and 19.

14. Delete 8.

15. Delete 8, 37, and 62.

16. Insert 7, delete 8, insert 59, delete 60, insert 92, delete 50.

17. Display the output produced by an inorder traversal.

18. Display the output produced by a preorder traversal.

19. Display the output produced by a postorder traversal.

20. Display the output produced by the following function, where `root` points to the root of the given binary tree:

```
void traceInorder(BST<DataType>::BinNodePointer root)
{
  if (myRoot != 0)
  {
    cout << 'L';       // left
    traceInorder(root->left);
    cout << '/' << root->data << endl;
    cout <<'R';        // right
    traceInorder(root->right);
```

```
        }
        cout << 'U';          // up
    }
```

21. The function member `graph()` in the BST class template displays a binary tree graphically. A useful alternative is to generate a table that displays enough information about a BST to reconstruct the tree. Write a function `displayPreorder()` that displays, in preorder, the data part of a node, its left child, and its right child. For example, the output of `displayPreorder()` for the given tree should be:

Node.data	LChild.data	RChild.data
50	15	62
15	5	20
5	3	8
3	–	–
.	.	.
.	.	.
.	.	.
58	–	60
60	–	–
91	–	–

You should also write a driver program to test your function as instructed in Programming Problem 13 at the end of this chapter.

The following exercises ask you to write functions for BST operations. You should also write driver programs to test these functions as instructed in Programming Problems 15–20 at the end of this chapter.

22. Write a recursive function member `level()` for class template BST that determines the *level* in the BST at which a specified item is located. The root of the BST is at level 0, its children are at level 1, and so on.

23. Proceed as in Exercise 23, but write a nonrecursive function.

24. The worst-case number of comparisons in searching a BST is equal to its *height*, that is, the number of levels in the tree. Write a recursive function member `height()` for class template BST to determine the height of the BST.

25. Write a recursive function member `leafCount()` for class template BST to count the leaves in a binary tree. (*Hint:* How is the number of leaves in the entire tree related to the number of leaves in the left and right subtrees of the root?)

26. Write a nonrecursive version of `inorder()` to perform inorder traversal. (Use a stack of pointers to eliminate the recursion.)

27. Write a function `levelByLevel()` to traverse a tree level by level; that is, first visit the root, then all nodes on level 1 (children of the root), then all nodes on level 2, and so on. Nodes on the same level should be visited in order from left to right. (*Hint:* Write a nonrecursive function, and use a queue of pointers.)

28. Write a recursive version of the `remove()` operation for the BST class template.

12.5 Case Study: Validating Computer Logins

Problem

Consider the problem of organizing a collection of computer user-ids and passwords. Each time a user logs in to the system by entering his or her user-id and a secret password, the system must check the validity of this user-id and password to verify that this is a legitimate user. Because this user validation must be done many times each day, it is necessary to structure this information in such a way that it can be searched rapidly. Moreover, this must be a dynamic structure because new users are regularly added to the system.

Design

One of the objects in this problem is the user information—id and password, which are strings. For this we will build a class `UserInfo`. And we need a collection of `UserInfo` objects. We will use a BST for this, because it can be searched rapidly and it is a dynamic structure. Thus, the major operations we need are provided in the BST class:

> Build a BST of `UserInfo` objects
>
> Search the BST for a given `UserInfo` object entered from the keyboard
>
> Display a message indicating if the user is a valid user

Our class `UserInfo` will have the user-id and password (both strings) as data members. Since searching and inserting into a BST requires being able to compare the values stored in it with < and ==, we must overload these operators for `UserInfo`. And we also need an input operation, so we will overload >> for it:

An algorithm for using these objects and operations is straightforward:

Algorithm for Computer Login Validation

/*   Algorithm to read user-ids and passwords and check if they are valid. */

// First, create the initial BST of valid `UserInfo` objects.

1. Open a stream to a file containing the valid user information.
2. Create an empty BST with elements of type `UserInfo`.
3. Read the `UserInfo` objects from the file and insert them into the BST.

// Now process logins.

4. Repeat the following until shutdown:
   a. Read a `UserInfo` object.
   b. Search the BST for this object.
   c. If it is found, display a "valid" message.
      Else display a "not valid" message
   End repeat.

Coding

The program in Figure 12.9 implements the preceding algorithm. The class `UserInfo` also is shown.

Figure 12.9 Validating Computer Logins

```cpp
#include <iostream>
#include <fstream>
#include <string>
using namespace std;


/*-------------------------------------------------------------------------
  Program to validate computer user-ids and passwords.  A list of valid
  ids and passwords is read from UsersFile and is stored in a BST.  When
  user-ids and passwords are entered during execution, this BST is
  searched to determine whether they are legal.

   Input (file):    UserInfo records for valid users
   Input (keyboard): Ids and passwords of users logging in
   Output (screen):  Messages indicating whether user-ids and passwords
                     are valid
  -------------------------------------------------------------------------*/


//----- Class containing user information -----//
//      with >>, ==, and < operators
class UserInfo
{
 public:
  // ***** Function Members and Friends ***** //
  //--- id accessor
  string id() const { return myId; }

  //--- input function
  void read(istream & in)
  {
    in >> myId >> myPassword;
  }

  //--- equals operator
  bool operator==(const UserInfo & user) const
  { return myId == user.myId &&
          myPassword == user.myPassword; }
```

Figure 12.9 (continued)

```
//--- less-than operator
bool operator<(const UserInfo & user) const
{ return myId < user.myId ||
        myId == user.myId && myPassword < user.myPassword; }


private:
// ***** Data Members ***** //
string myId,
       myPassword;
};


//--- Definition of input operator
istream & operator>>(istream & in, UserInfo & user)
{
  user.read(in);
}



#include "BST.h"

int main()
{
   // Open stream to file of legal user-ids and password
   string userFile;
   cout << "Enter name of user-info file: ";
   getline(cin, userFile);
   ifstream inStream(userFile.data());
   if (!inStream.is_open())
   {
      cerr << "Cannot open " << userFile << "\n";
      exit(1);
   }

   // Build the BST of user records
   BST<UserInfo> userTree;    // BST of user records
   UserInfo user;             // a user record
```

Figure 12.9 (continued)

```
for(;;)
{
   inStream >> user;
   if (inStream.eof()) break;

   userTree.insert(user);
}

// Validate logins
cout << "Enter Q Q to stop processing.\n";
for (;;)
{
   cout << "\nUser id & password: ";
   cin >> user;
   if (user.id() == "Q") break;
   if (userTree.search(user))
      cout << "Valid user\n";
   else
      cout << "Not a valid user\n";
}
}
```

Listing of *File12-9.dat* used in sample run:
```
GEORGEWASH CHERRY31416
BINARYBABE 11011100101
NATURALLOG E271828
PALINDROME ABC3CBA
EINSTEIN EISMC**2
LUMBERMAN 2X4X8FT
WATERBOY H2O4U
```

Execution Trace:
```
Enter name of user-info file: File11-9.dat
Enter Q Q to stop processing.
```

Figure 12.9 (continued)

```
User id & password: NATURALLOG E271828
Valid user


User id & password: GEORGEWASH CHERRY31416
Valid user


User id & password: EINSTEIN E=MCSQUARED
Not a valid user


User id & password: WATERBOY H2O4U
Valid user


User id & password: Q Q
```

▲

12.6 Threaded Binary Search Trees (Optional)

For most of the binary tree operations in the preceding sections, we gave both recursive and nonrecursive versions. Exceptions were the traversal operations, for which we gave only recursive versions. In this section we show how special links called *threads* make simple and efficient *nonrecursive traversal* algorithms possible by essentially incorporating into the tree a run-time stack to handle the recursive calls.

If a binary tree has n nodes, then the total number of link fields in the tree is $2n$. Since each node except the root has exactly one incoming arc, it follows that only $n - 1$ of these links point to nodes; the remaining $n + 1$ links are null. Thus, more than one-half of the links in the tree are not used to point to other nodes. **A threaded binary search tree** is obtained when these unused links are used to point to certain other nodes in the tree in such a way that traversals or other tree operations can be performed more efficiently.

To illustrate, suppose that we wish to thread a BST such as the following to facilitate inorder traversal:

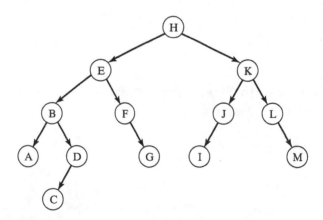

The first node visited in an inorder traversal is the leftmost leaf, that is, the node containing A. Since A has no right child, the next node visited in this traversal is its parent, the node containing B. We can use the right pointer of node A as a thread to its parent to make this backtracking in the tree easy. This thread is shown as the dashed line from A to B in the following diagram:

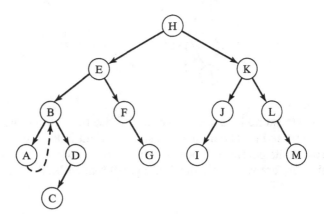

The next node visited is C, and since its right pointer is null, it also can be used as a thread to its parent D. And since the right pointer in node D also is null, it can be used as a thread to its successor, which in this case is the node containing E:

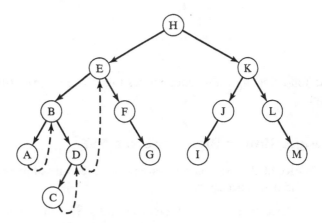

The next nodes visited are E, F, and G, and since G has a null right pointer, we replace it with a thread to its successor, the node containing H:

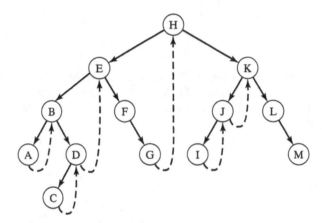

We next visit node H and then node I. Since the right pointer of I is null, we replace it with a thread to its parent J, and since its right link is null, we replace this link with a thread to its parent K. Since no other nodes except the last one visited (M) have null right pointers, we obtain the final **right-threaded BST**:

The following algorithm summarizes this process of right-threading a binary search tree:

 ### Algorithm to Right-Thread a BST

/* Right-thread a binary search tree. Each thread links a node to its inorder successor. */

Perform an inorder traversal of the BST. Whenever a node x with a null right pointer is encountered, replace this right link with a thread to the inorder successor of x. The inorder successor of such a node x is its parent if x is a left child of its parent; otherwise, it is the nearest ancestor of x that contains x in its left subtree.

An iterative algorithm for traversing a right-threaded binary search tree is now straightforward:

Algorithm for Inorder Traversal of a Right-Threaded BST

/*   Carry out an inorder traversal of a right-threaded BST in which each thread connects a node and its inorder successor.   */

1. Initialize a pointer *ptr* to the root of the tree.
2. While *ptr* is not null:
   a. While *ptr->left* is not null,
         Replace *ptr* by *ptr->left*.
   b. Visit the node pointed to by *ptr*.
   c. While *ptr->right* is a thread do the following:
      i. Replace *ptr* by *ptr->right*
      ii. Visit the node pointed to by *ptr*.
   d. Replace *ptr* by *ptr->right*.
   End while.

Note that this algorithm requires being able to distinguish between right links that are threads and those that are actual pointers to right children. This suggests adding a boolean field `rightThread` in the node declarations like those in Section 12.2:

```
/*** Node class ***/
class BinNode
{
 public:
  DataType data;
  bool rightThread;
  BinNode * left;
  BinNode * right;
  // BinNode constructors
  // Default -- data part is default DataType value;
  //         -- rightThread is false; both links are null
  BinNode ()
  : rightThread(false), left(0), right(0)
  {}

  //Explicit Value -- data part contains item; rightThread
  //                -- is false; both links are null
  BinNode(DataType item)
  : data(item), rightThread(false), left(0), right(0)
  {}
};// end of class BinNode declaration
```

While the tree is being threaded, `rightThread` will be set to true if the right link of a node is a thread and will be set to false otherwise. Functions to implement the algorithms given in this section for threading a BST and traversing a threaded BST are quite straightforward and are left as exercises.

✔ Quick Quiz 12.6

1. What is a thread in a right-threaded BST?
2. What is the purpose of threading a BST?

For Questions 3–6, show the right-threaded BST that results from inserting the characters in the order shown.

3. A, C, R, E, S
4. R, A, C, E, S
5. C, A, R, E, S
6. S, C, A, R, E

⬥ Exercises 12.6

For Exercises 1–7, show the threaded BST that results from right-threading the binary search tree.

1. The BST preceding Exercise 12 in Section 12.4.
2. The BST obtained by inserting the following C++ keywords in the order given: `int, short, char, bool, void, unsigned, long, double`
3. The BST obtained by inserting the following C++ keywords in the order given: `bool, char, double, int, long, short, unsigned, void`
4. The BST obtained by inserting the following C++ keywords in the order given: `void, unsigned, short, long, int, double, char, bool`
5. The BST obtained by inserting the following C++ keywords in the order given: `enum, bool, if, typename, case, else, while, do, return, unsigned, void, for, double, throw`

Exercises 6 and 7 ask you to write functions for right-threaded BSTs. You should also test your functions with driver programs as instructed in Programming Problems 28 and 29 at the end of this chapter.

6. Write a function to implement the inorder traversal algorithm for a right-threaded BST given in the text.
7. Write a function to implement the right-threading algorithm for a BST given in the text.
8. Give an algorithm similar to that in the text for threading a binary tree, but to facilitate preorder traversal.

9-13. For the binary trees in Exercises 1–5, show the binary tree threaded as described in Exercise 8.

14. Give an algorithm for carrying out a preorder traversal of a binary tree threaded as described in Exercise 8.

15. Consider a binary tree that is threaded to facilitate inorder traversal. Give an algorithm for finding the preorder successor of a given node in such an inorder-threaded binary tree. Do *not* rethread the tree to facilitate preorder traversal as described in Exercise 8.

16. Proceeding as in Exercise 15, give an algorithm for carrying out a preorder traversal of an inorder-threaded binary tree.

17. The right-threading algorithm given in the text right-threads an existing BST. It is also possible to construct a right-threaded BST by inserting an item into a right-threaded BST (beginning with an empty BST) in such a way that the resulting BST is right-threaded. Give such an insertion algorithm.

18. Trace the algorithm in Exercise 17 using the C++ keywords given in Exercise 2. Show the right-threaded BST after each word is inserted.

19. Repeat Exercise 18 for the words in Exercise 4.

20. Give an algorithm to delete a node from a right-threaded BST so that the resulting BST is also right-threaded.

Exercises 21–28 deal with *fully-threaded* BSTs, in which not only are null right links replaced with threads to inorder successors, as described in the text, but also null left links are replaced with threads to inorder predecessors.

21–25. Show the fully-threaded BST for the BSTs in Exercises 1–5.

26. Give an algorithm to fully thread a BST.

27. Write an algorithm to insert a node into a fully threaded BST so that the resulting BST is also fully threaded.

28. Write an algorithm to find the parent of a given node in a fully-threaded BST.

12.7 Hash Tables

The search algorithms considered in this chapter search for an item in a list or binary search tree by "rummaging around" among the data values according to some systematic policy, comparing them with the item being sought. For a list of n items, linear search requires $O(n)$ comparisons, whereas for binary search, $O(\log_2 n)$ comparisons are required. And as we have seen, for a balanced binary search tree, the search operation requires $O(\log_2 n)$ but becomes $O(n)$ for very unbalanced trees.

In some situations, however, even faster searching is needed. For example, calls to an emergency response system require fast retrieval of information from a database that may be very large. A *symbol table* constructed by a compiler stores identifiers and information about them, and the speed with which this table can be constructed and searched is critical to the speed of compilation. In this section we look at a search method known as *hashing*, designed for these and other applications in which fast data storage and retrieval, are essential.

The problem with the search methods considered thus far is the time it takes for them to go through the sequence of trial-and-error comparisons needed to locate an item. The approach in hashed searching is very different. A function, called a **hash function**, is applied to an item (or more commonly, to some key field in the item) and computes its location in a table, called a **hash table**:

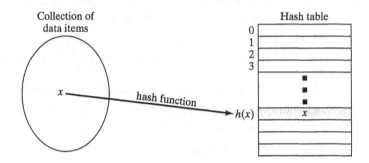

Under ideal circumstances, the time required to locate an item in a hash table is O(1); that is, it is constant and does not depend on the number of items stored.

Hash Functions

As an illustration, suppose that up to 31 integers—one for each day of a month—in the range 0 through 999 are to be stored in a hash table. This hash table can be implemented as an integer array *table* in which each array element is initialized with some dummy value, such as –1. If we use each integer i in the set as an index, that is, if we store i in *table*[i], then to determine whether a particular integer *number* has been stored, we need only check if *table*[*number*] is equal to *number*. The function h defined by $h(i) = i$ that determines the location of an item i in the hash table is called a **hash function**.

The hash function in this example works perfectly because the time required to search the table for a given value is constant; only one location needs to be examined. This scheme is thus very time efficient, but it is surely not space efficient. Only about 3 percent of the available space is used and 97 percent is wasted!

Because it is possible to store 31 values in 31 locations, we might try improving space utilization by using an array *table* with capacity 31. Obviously, the original hash function $h(i) = i$ can no longer be used. Instead, we might use

$$h(i) = i \bmod 31$$

or, in C++ syntax,

```
int h(int i)
{ return i % 31; }
```

because this function always produces an integer in the range 0 through 30. The integer 64 thus is stored in *table*[2], since $h(64) = 64 \% 31 = 2$. Similarly, 128, 620,

277, and 61 are stored in locations 4, 0, 29, and 30, respectively. The following table illustrates:

Hash table

table[0]	620	$h(620) = 620 \% 31 = 0$
table[1]	−1	
table[2]	64	$h(64) = 64 \% 31 = 2$
table[3]	−1	
table[4]	128	$h(128) = 128 \% 31 = 4$
table[5]	−1	
⋮	⋮	
table[29]	277	$h(277) = 277 \% 31 = 29$
table[30]	61	$h(61) = 61 \% 31 = 30$

Collision Strategies

There is an obvious problem with the preceding hash table, namely, that **collisions** may occur. For example, if 95 is to be stored, it should be placed at location $h(95) = 95 \% 31 = 2$, but this location is already occupied by 64. In the same way, many other values may collide at a given position, for example, 2, 33, 188; and, in fact, all integers of the form $31k + 2$ hash to location 2. Obviously, some strategy is needed to resolve such collisions.

One simple strategy for handling collisions is known as **linear probing**. In this scheme, a linear search of the table begins at the location where a collision occurs and continues until an empty slot is found in which the item can be stored. Thus, in the preceding example, when 95 collides with the value 64 at location 2, we simply put 95 in position 3; to insert 188, we follow the **probe sequence** consisting of locations 2, 3, 4, and 5 to find the first available location and thus store 188 in *table*[5]. If the search reaches the bottom of the table, we continue at the first location. For example, 339 is stored in location 1, since it collides with 277 at location 29, and the probe sequence 29, 30, 0, 1 locates the first empty slot at position 1:

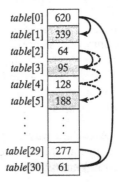

If there are no deletions from the hash table, then searching this hash table for a specified value is straightforward. We apply the hash function to compute the position at which this value should be found. There are three cases to consider. First, if this location is empty, we can conclude immediately that the value is not in the table. Second, if this location contains the specified value, the search is immediately successful. In the third case, this location contains a value other than the one for which we are searching, because of the way that collisions were resolved in constructing the table. In this case, we begin a "circular" linear search at this location and continue until either the item is found or we reach an empty location or the starting location, indicating that the item is not in the table. Thus, the search time in the first two cases is constant, but in this last case, it is not. If the table is nearly full, we may, in fact, have to examine almost every location before we find the item or conclude that it is not in the table.

If deletions of items are permitted, then the third case needs to be modified, because the linear search will stop prematurely when it encounters a location that was occupied, but now is empty because the item there was removed. One solution is to mark this location differently when the item is deleted; for example, use –1 for locations that were never occupied and –2 for those that were occupied but now are not. In this case, the linear search continues through locations that are now or were occupied until the item is found or an empty (never occupied) location is encountered.

Improvements

There seem to be three things we might do to improve performance:

1. Increase the table capacity.
2. Use a different strategy for resolving collisions.
3. Use a different hash function.

Hash Table Capacity   Making the table capacity equal to the number of possible items, as in our first example, is usually not practical, but using any smaller table leaves open the possibility of collisions. In fact, even though the table is capable of storing considerably more items than necessary, collisions may be quite likely. For example, for a hash table with 365 locations in which 23 randomly selected items are to be stored, the probability that a collision will occur is greater than 0.5! (This is related to the *birthday problem*, whose solution states that in a room containing 23 people, there is a greater than 50 percent chance that two or more of them will have the same birthday.) Thus, it is clearly unreasonable to expect a hashing scheme to prevent collisions completely. Instead, we must be satisfied with hash tables in which reasonably few collisions occur. Empirical studies suggest using tables whose capacities are approximately $1\frac{1}{2}$ to 2 times the number of items that must be stored. Also, *for hash functions such as the one we used earlier that use modular arithmetic, the table capacity should be a prime number to produce the maximum amount of "hashing," thus reducing the number of collisions.*

Collision Strategies   A second way to improve performance is to design a better method for handling collisions. In the linear probe scheme, elements colliding at the same hash table location generate clusters of entries, and eventually these clusters merge forming larger clusters. This results in more collisions and longer search time. This phenomenon is known as **primary clustering**.

Linear probing is an example of what is known as an *open-addressing* strategy for resolving collisions. Other open-addressing schemes attempt to break up the clusters that form from linear probing by using a different probe sequence. For example, *quadratic probing* uses $i + 1^2, i - 1^2, i + 2^2, i - 2^2, i + 3^2, i - 3^2, \ldots$ with all operations done modulo the table size; that is, jump ahead 1, jump back 1, jump ahead 4, jump back 4, and so on, where these jumps are done circularly as before. The following illustrates how various collisions are handled, using a hash table of capacity 31 and the earlier hash function:

```
h(620) = 620 % 31 = 0
h(64)  = 64 % 31 = 2
h(128) = 128 % 31 = 4
h(467) = 467 % 31 = 2 → 2 + 1 = 3
h(777) = 777 % 31 = 2→ 2 + 1 = 3 → 2 - 1 = 1
h(35)  = 35 % 31 = 4 → 4 + 1 = 5
h(127) = 127 % 31 = 3 → 3 + 1 = 4 → 3 - 1 = 2 → 3 + 4 = 7
h(282) = 282 % 31 = 3 → 3 + 1 = 4 → 3 - 1 = 2 → 3 + 4 = 7 → 3 - 4 = 30
```

(Note that for the last value, $3 - 4$ produces 30 because all the computations are done mod 31.) The following table results:

table[0]	620
table[1]	777
table[2]	64
table[3]	467
table[4]	128
table[5]	35
table[6]	−1
table[7]	127
⋮	⋮
table[30]	282

As this example demonstrates, primary clustering is avoided, but clusters can still develop as items are inserted. This is known as **secondary clustering**.

One way to combat clustering is to use different probe sequences for different items, rather than the same one for all items, as in linear and quadratic probing. This is called **double hashing**, because it uses a second hash function to determine the probe sequence. To insert an item x into the table, we apply a first hash function to compute a table index for x: $h_1(x) = i$. If there is a collision at this location, we apply a second hash function to obtain an increment for the probe sequence: $h_2(x) = k$. This gives $i, i + k, i + 2k, \ldots$ as the probe sequence for this item x.

To illustrate, for the hash function we have been using,

$$h_1(x) = x \text{ \% } 31$$

we might use the secondary hash function[2]

$$h_2(x) = 17 - (x \ \% \ 17)$$

As we have seen, 64, 467, and 777 all hash to location 2. However, they all have different probe sequences. Since $h_2(64) = 4$, the probe sequence for it is

2, 6, 10, 14, 18, 22, 26, 30, 3, 7, 11, 15, 19, 23, 27,
0, 4, 8, 12, 16, 20, 24, 28, 1, 5, 9, 13, 17, 21, 25, 29

But $h_2(467) = 9$, so its probe sequence is

2, 11, 20, 29, 7, 16, 25, 3, 12, 21, 30, 8, 17, 26, 4,
13, 22, 0, 9, 18, 27, 5, 14, 23, 1, 10, 19, 28, 6, 15, 24

And $h_2(777) = 5$, so its probe sequence is

2, 7, 12, 17, 22, 27, 1, 6, 11, 16, 21, 26, 0, 5, 10, 15,
20, 25, 30, 4, 9, 14, 19, 24, 29, 3, 8, 13, 18, 23, 28

With any open-addressing strategy, however, whenever collisions occur, the colliding values are stored in locations that should be reserved for items that hash directly to these locations. This approach of "robbing Peter to pay Paul" makes subsequent collisions more likely, thus compounding the problem. A different approach, known as **chaining**, uses a hash table that is an array or `vector` of linked lists that store the items. To illustrate, suppose we wish to store a collection of names. We might use an array *table* of 26 linked lists, initially empty, and the simple hash function $h(name) = name[0] -$ 'A'; that is, $h(name)$ is 0 if *name*[0] is 'A', 1 if *name*[0] is 'B', . . . , 25 if *name*[0] is 'Z'.[3] Thus, for example, "Adams, John" and "Doe, Mary" are stored in nodes pointed to by *table*[0] and *table*[3], respectively.

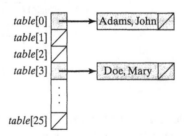

When a collision occurs, we simply insert the new item into the appropriate linked list. For example, since $h(\text{"Davis, Joe"}) = h(\text{"Doe, Mary"}) = $ 'D' $-$ 'A' $= 3$, a collision

---

[2] To ensure that the probe sequence goes through all of the table locations, the second modulus should be chosen to be relatively prime to the table size; that is, it has no factors in common with it.

[3] Remember that in C and C++, chars are identified with their numeric codes (e.g., ASCII) so the arithmetic operators can be applied to them. Thus, in ASCII, if the char variable ch has the value 'D', then ch - 'A' = 68 − 65 = 3.

occurs when we attempt to store the name "Davis, Joe", and thus we add a new node containing this name to the linked list pointed to by *table*[3]:

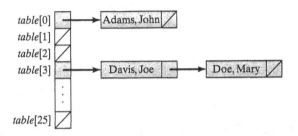

Searching such a hash table is straightforward. We simply apply the hash function to the item being sought and then use one of the search algorithms for linked lists. Deleting an item also is easy. We search to find to which linked list it belongs and then remove it from that list as described in Chapter 6. Note that unlike the open-addressing strategies, deletion does not necessitate any changes in how the table is searched.

The Hash Function   A third factor in the design of a hash table is the selection of the hash function. An ideal hash function is one that is simple to evaluate and that scatters the items throughout the hash table, thus minimizing the probability of collisions. This is one reason why using modulo arithmetic as in our earlier examples is common. The function is easy to compute and making the table capacity a prime number facilitates scattering of data values throughout the table.

In the preceding example, the function used for hashing names is not a good choice because some letters occur much more frequently than others as first letters of names. Thus the linked list of names beginning with 'S' tends to be much longer than that containing names that begin with 'Z'. This clustering effect results in longer search times for S-names than for Z-names. A better hash function that distributes the names more uniformly throughout the hash table might be the "average" of the first and last letters in the name,

$$h(name) = (firstLetter + lastLetter) / 2$$

or one might use the "average" of all the letters. The hash function must not, however, be so complex that the time required to evaluate it makes the search time unacceptable.

Although no single hashing method performs perfectly in all situations, one popular method known as **random hashing** uses a simple random number generation technique to scatter the items "randomly" throughout the hash table.[4] The item is first transformed into a large random integer using a statement of the form

```
randomInt = ((MULTIPLIER * item) + ADDEND) % MODULUS;
```

---

[4] Details of the technique used here for generating random numbers and other techniques can be found in Donald Knuth, *The Art of Computer Programming: Seminumerical Algorithms*, vol. 2 (Reading, MA.: Addison-Wesley, 1981). The choices of MULTIPLIER, ADDEND, and MODULUS must be chosen with care. For 32-bit arithmetic, appropriate choices are MULTIPLIER = 25173, ADDEND = 13849, and MODULUS = 65536.

If the item is not an integer, it must first be represented by an integer before using this formula; for example, a name might be encoded as the sum of the ASCII codes of some or all of its letters. The resulting value is then reduced modulo the table's capacity to determine the location of the item:

```
location = randomInt % CAPACITY;
```

✔ Quick Quiz 12.7

1. In a(n) _____, the location of an item is determined directly by applying a function to the item. The function is called a(n) _____ function.
2. The case of two items needing to be placed at the same location in hash table is called a(n) _____.
3. What is linear probing?
4. What is quadratic probing?
5. Describe dual hashing?
6. A collision strategy in which the hash table is an array or vector of linked lists that store the items is known as _____.

For Questions 5 and 6, assume a hash table with 7 locations and the hashing function $h(i) = i \% 7$. Show the hash table that results when the integers are inserted in the order given.

7. 5, 11, 18, 23, 28, 13, 25, with collisions resolved using linear probing.
8. 5, 11, 18, 23, 28, 13, 25, with collisions resolved using quadratic probing.
9. 5, 11, 18, 23, 28, 13, 25 with collisions resolved using chaining.

➤ Exercises 12.7

1. Using a hash table with eleven locations and the hashing function $h(i) = i \% 11$, show the hash table that results when the following integers are inserted in the order given: 26, 42, 5, 44, 92, 59, 40, 36, 12, 60, 80. Assume that collisions are resolved using linear probing.
2. Repeat Exercise 1, but assume that collisions are resolved using quadratic probing.
3. Repeat Exercise 1, but use double hashing to resolve collisions with the following secondary hash function:

$$h_2(x) = \begin{cases} 2x \ \% \ 11 & \text{if this is nonzero} \\ 1 & \text{otherwise} \end{cases}$$

4. Repeat Exercise 1, but assume that collisions are resolved using chaining.
5. Suppose that the following character codes are used: 'A' = 1, 'B' = 2, ..., 'Y' = 25, 'Z' = 26. Using a hash table with eleven locations and the hashing function $h(identifier) = average \% 11$, where *average* is the average of the codes of the first and last letters in *identifier*, show the hash table that results when the following identifiers are inserted in the order given, assuming that collisions are resolved using linear probing: BETA, RATE, FREQ, ALPHA, MEAN, SUM, NUM, BAR, WAGE, PAY, KAPPA.

6. Repeat Exercise 5, but assume that collisions are resolved using quadratic probing.

7. Repeat Exercise 5, but use double hashing to resolve collisions with the secondary hash function

$$h_2(x) = 7 - (x \% 7)$$

8. Repeat Exercise 5, but assume that collisions are resolved using chaining.

9. Design a class template for the ADT *HashTable*, using the implementation described in this section. The basic operations should include (at least) constructors, a destructor, a copy constructor, inserting an item into a hash table, searching for an item in the hash table, and deleting an item from the hash table. Use random hashing for the hash function and chaining to resolve collisions. You should also write a driver program to test your class template as instructed in Programming Problem 32 at the end of this chapter.

SUMMARY

📖 Chapter Notes

- Linear search can be used for both array-based and linked lists, but binary search is appropriate only for array-based lists, since it requires direct access to the list elements to be efficient.

- In most cases, binary trees should be implemented by two-dimensional linked structures; array-based implementations are appropriate for *complete trees*—all levels are full except possibly the bottom, for which the nodes are in the leftmost positions.

- Recursive algorithms for some binary tree operations are simpler than nonrecursive ones because binary trees can be viewed as recursive data structures.

- Threading a binary search tree makes it easy to do traversals nonrecursively.

- Three significant factors in the performance of a hash table are the table capacity, the hash function, and the strategy for resolving collisions. The hash function should be easy to compute and should scatter items in the hash table. Open addressing and chaining are common collision-resolution strategies.

📝 Programming Pointers

Most of the programming pointers that apply to the linked lists described in Chapters 6 and following also apply to trees, since trees are also linked structures.

1. When implementing an object using a class, keep the implementation details hidden by declaring them in a private (or protected) section of the class. In class BST, the BinNode class used to represent the tree's nodes is such a detail.

2. Take twice as much care when implementing binary trees, since their nodes contain two pointer members. With two pointers to keep track of in every node instead of one, making logical errors is twice as easy. The ease with which one can write tree operations that compile correctly but that generate run-time errors is notorious.

3. Always make certain that a tree is not empty before processing it. The same holds true for subtrees. In most recursive tree-processing algorithms, the empty tree provides the anchor case for the recursion. As a result, checking whether a tree is empty makes it possible to avoid:
   - dereferencing a null pointer
   - generating an infinite recursion

▲ ADT Tips

1. The worst- and average-case computing times for linear search is $O(n)$. Linear search is used by `find()` in `<algorithm>`.

2. The worst- and average-case computing times for binary search is $O(\log_2 n)$. Binary search is used by `binary_search()` in `<algorithm>`.

3. The array-based implementation works very well for complete binary trees, but it becomes increasingly less space efficient as the tree becomes more lopsided.

4. A binary tree can be defined as a recursive data structure in a very natural way and several of the operations on a binary tree can thus be implemented most easily by recursive functions.

5. An inorder traversal of a binary search tree visits the nodes in ascending order of the values stored in them.

6. The computing time for searching and inserting into a balanced binary search tree is $O(\log_2 n)$. As BSTs become increasingly unbalanced, their performance deteriorates. In the worst case, the BST degenerates into a linked list and the complexity of these operations becomes $O(n)$. Rebalancing methods such as those described in Chapter 15 are required to keep this from happening.

7. Deletion from a binary search tree can also cause it to become unbalanced.

8. Hash tables are designed for fast (constant-time) searches, insertions, and deletions.

▣ Programming Problems

Section 12.1

1. Write a driver program to test the improved `linearSearch()` function in Exercise 6.

2. Write a driver program to test the `linearSearch()` function for ordered lists in Exercise 7.

3. Write a driver program to test the recursive `linearSearch()` function from Exercise 8.

4. Write a driver program to test the recursive `linearSearch()` function from Exercise 9.

5. Write a driver program to test the linear search function for move-to-the-front self-organizing array-based lists in Exercise 10.

6. Write a driver program to test the linear search function for move-to-the-front self-organizing linked lists in Exercise 11.

7. Write a driver program to test the linear search function for move-ahead-one self-organizing array-based lists in Exercise 12.

8. Write a driver program to test the linear search function for move-ahead-one self-organizing linked lists in Exercise 13.

9. Write a driver program to test the interpolation-search function in Exercise 14.

10. Linear search is not practical for large lists because the search time becomes unacceptably large. In a dictionary, this problem is alleviated by providing thumb cutouts that allow direct access to the beginnings of sublists, which can then be searched. Imitating this approach, we might break a long list into a number of sublists and construct an *index array* of these sublists. Write a program to read records from StudentFile (described at the end of Chapter 4) and store them in an array of sublists of names beginning with 'A', 'B', 'C', ... The program should then accept a name and retrieve the record for this student.

11. Linear search outperforms binary search for small lists. Write a program to compare the computing times of linear search and binary search.

12. Repeat Problem 11, but also include interpolation search (see Exercise 14).

Section 12.4

13. Write a driver program to test the function displayPreOrder() in Exercise 21.

14. Write a definition for the following function generateBST() for generating a binary search tree containing uppercase letters inserted in a random order:

```
BST<char> generateBST();
/*-----------------------------------------------------------
    Generate a BST with uppercase letters 'A'-'Z' inserted
    in random order.

    Precondition:  None.
    Postcondition: A BST containing uppercase letters inserted
        in random order has been generated and returned.
    ----------------------------------------------------------*/
```

15. Test the function level() in Exercise 22 by using generateBST() of Problem 14 to generate BSTs and then determine the level of 'A', 'B', . . . , 'Z' in each tree.

16. Proceed as in Problem 15, but for the recursive function level() in Exercise 23.

17. Test the function height() of Exercise 24 by using generateBST() of Problem 14 to generate BSTs and then determine the height of each tree.

18. Test the function leafCount() from Exercise 25. Generate binary trees using the function generateBST() in Problem 14, display them using displayPreOrder() (see Exercise 21), and then count the leaves using leafCount().

19. Test the function inorder() of Exercise 26. Generate binary trees using the function generateBST() in Problem 14, and then traverse them using inorder().

20. Test the function levelByLevel() of Exercise 27. Generate binary trees using the function generateBST() in Problem 14, and then traverse them using levelByLevel().

21. In this section, binary search trees were implemented using pointers, but it also is possible to use an array-based implementation, similar to that for linked lists described in Section 6.6. In this implementation, each node is represented as a class BinNode and the BST is stored in an array of BinNodes. Each BinNode object contains three data members: one to store data and two link members that point to the left and the right child, respectively,

by storing their indices in the array. Imitating the array-based implementation of linked lists in Section 6.6, do the following:

a. Write appropriate declarations for this array-based implementation of binary search trees.

b. Design and test a class for maintaining a storage pool of available nodes, with operations to initialize it, to get a node from it, and to return a node to it.

22. Assuming the array-based implementation of BSTs in Problem 21, write and test a function member `search()` for searching a BST.

23. Assuming the array-based implementation of BSTs in Problem 21, write and test a function member `insert()` for inserting an item into a BST.

24. Write a program to process a BST whose nodes contain characters. The user should be allowed to select from the following menu of options:

I followed by a character: To insert a character
S followed by a character: To search for a character
TI: for inorder traversal
TP: for preorder traversal
TR: for postorder traversal
QU: to quit

25. Write a *spell checker*, that is, a program that reads the words in a piece of text and looks up each of them in a *dictionary* to check its spelling. Use a BST to store this dictionary, reading the list of words from a file. While checking the spelling of words in a piece of text, the program should print a list of all words not found in the dictionary.

26. Programming Problems 20–22 at the end of Chapter 11 ask for a program to construct a *text concordance*, which is an alphabetical listing of all the distinct words in a piece of text. The basic storage structure for such a concordance was an array of ordered linked lists, one for words beginning with A, another for words beginning with B, and so on. Write a program that reads a piece of text, constructs a concordance that contains the distinct words that appear in the text and, for each word, the line (or page) number of its first occurrence, and then allows the user to search for this concordance. Use an array of BSTs as storage for the concordance.

27. Extend the program in Problem 26, so that an ordered linked list of *all* occurrences of each word is stored. When the concordance is searched for a particular word, the program should display the line (or page) numbers of all occurrences of this word. The data structure used for the concordance is thus constructed from a good sample of those we have been studying: an *array* of *binary search trees*, each of whose nodes is a *class*, one of whose members is a *string* and whose other member is an *ordered linked list*.

Section 12.6

28. Write a driver program to test the traversal function for right-threaded BSTs in Exercise 6.

29. Write a driver program to test the function for right-threading a BST in Exercise 7.

30. Write a program that uses the techniques described in this section to construct a BST, threads it using the function of Exercise 7, and then traverses it using the function of Exercise 6.

31. Proceed as in Problem 30, but implement the insertion algorithm of Exercise 17 and use this to construct the threaded BST.

Section 12.7

32. Write a driver program to test the hash table class template from Exercise 9.

33. Write a program that reads a collection of computer user-ids and passwords and stores them in a hash table. The program should then read two strings representing a user's id and password and then check whether this is a valid user of the computer system by searching the hash table for this id and password.

34. Suppose that integers in the range 1 through 100 are to be stored in a hash table using the hashing function $h(i) = i \% n$, where n is the table's capacity. Write a program that generates random integers in this range and inserts them into the hash table until a collision occurs. The program should carry out this experiment 100 times and should calculate the average number of integers that can be inserted into the hash table before a collision occurs. Run the program with various values for the table's capacity.

Sorting

CHAPTER CONTENTS

Chapter Objectives

- Describe three kinds of sorting methods: selection, exchange, and insertion.
- Look at examples of each kind of O(n^2) sorts: simple selection sort, bubble sort, and insertion sort.
- Study heaps, show how they can be used to develop an efficient selection sort called heapsort, and also look at an implementation of priority queues that uses heaps.
- Study quicksort in detail as an example of using a divide-and-conquer strategy to develop an efficient exchange sort.
- Study mergesort as an example of a sort that can be used for sequential files.
- Look at radix sort as an example of a non-comparison-based sort.

In this chapter we consider the problem of sorting a list,

$$x_1, x_2, \ldots, x_n$$

that is, arranging the list elements so that they (or some key fields in them) are in ascending order,

$$x_1 \leq x_2 \leq \cdots \leq x_n$$

or in descending order,

$$x_1 \geq x_2 \geq \cdots \geq x_n$$

Like searching a collection of data, this is one of the fundamental problems in processing data. We may need to arrange a list of mailing labels with zip codes in increasing order; or output a list of student records with the names in alphabetical order; or output a list of interest rates for various types of financing in descending order; and the examples go on and on. And, as we have seen, some common list-processing algorithms—for example, binary search—require that the list has been sorted.

There are many different sorting methods and they can be classified in various ways. One classification is based on where the data to be sorted is stored:

- *Internal* sorts are designed for data stored in main memory.
- *External* sorts are designed for data stored in secondary memory (e.g., on disk).

Most of the sorting methods we consider here are internal sorts, but one popular external method is described in the last section.

Another classification is based on the general approach used to carry out the sorting. Three categories that we will consider are *selection*, *exchange*, and *insertion*. They will be described and illustrated in the first section. Although these sorts are, for the most part, fairly easy to understand and to implement, they are not very efficient, especially for large data sets. Thus, in later sections and exercises, we also describe some of the more efficient sorting schemes such as heapsort and quicksort.

13.1 Some $O(n^2)$ Sorting Schemes

We begin our discussion of sorting algorithms by considering one simple sorting scheme from each of the three categories listed in the introduction: selection, exchange, and insertion. These are sorting methods that are typically studied in introductory programming courses because they are relatively easy to understand and *not* because they are the best.

 Also, it should be noted that, for simplicity, we are assuming that the lists to be sorted have elements for which the relational operators (< and ==, in particular) are defined and that are to be arranged so that they themselves are in ascending or descending order. In practice, sorting deals with lists of objects that represent records containing several different items of information of various types. In this case, sorting is based on some **key** field within these records. The algorithms we give for sorting can easily be modified to compare keys in list elements rather than entire elements.

Selection Sorts

The basic idea of a **selection sort** of a list is to make a number of passes through the list or a part of the list and, on each pass, select one element to be correctly positioned. For example, on each pass through a sublist, the smallest element in this sublist might be found and then moved to its proper location.

As an illustration, suppose that the following list is to be sorted into ascending order:

67, 33, 21, 84, 49, 50, 75

We scan the list to locate the smallest element and find it in position 3:

$$67 \, , \, 33 \, , \, \boxed{21} \, , \, 84 \, , \, 49 \, , \, 50 \, , \, 75$$

We interchange this element with the first element and thus properly position the smallest element at the beginning of the list:

$$\boxed{67} \, , \, 33 \, , \, 21 \, , \, 84 \, , \, 49 \, , \, 50 \, , \, 75$$

We now scan the sublist consisting of the elements from position 2 on to find the smallest element

$$21 \, , \, \boxed{33} \, , \, 67 \, , \, 84 \, , \, 49 \, , \, 50 \, , \, 75$$

and exchange it with the second element (itself in this case), thus properly positioning the next-to-smallest element in position 2:

$$21 \, , \, \boxed{33} \, , \, 67 \, , \, 84 \, , \, 49 \, , \, 50 \, , \, 75$$

We continue in this manner, locating the smallest element in the sublist of elements from position 3 on and interchanging it with the third element, then properly positioning the smallest element in the sublist of elements from position 4 on, and so on until we eventually do this for the sublist consisting of the last two elements:

$$21 \, , \, 33 \, , \, \boxed{49} \, , \, 84 \, , \, 67 \, , \, 50 \, , \, 75$$

$$21 \, , \, 33 \, , \, 49 \, , \, \boxed{50} \, , \, 67 \, , \, 84 \, , \, 75$$

$$21 \, , \, 33 \, , \, 49 \, , \, 50 \, , \, \boxed{67} \, , \, 84 \, , \, 75$$

$$21 \, , \, 33 \, , \, 49 \, , \, 50 \, , \, 67 \, , \, \boxed{75} \, , \, 84$$

Positioning the smallest element in this last sublist obviously also positions the last element correctly and thus completes the sort.

An algorithm for this **simple selection sort** was given in Section 10.4 for lists stored in arrays or vectors:

Simple Selection Sort Algorithm—Array-Based

/* Use selection sort to sort $x[1], \ldots, x[n]$ into ascending order.
    Note: For consistency with other sorting methods, $x[0]$ is reserved
           for special purposes. */

For $i = 1$ to $n - 1$ do the following:
    // Find the smallest element in the sublist $x[i] \ldots x[n]$.
    a. Set *smallPos* = i and *smallest* = $x[smallPos]$.
    b. For $j = i + 1$ to $n - 1$ do the following:
        If $x[j] < smallest$:   // smaller element found
            Set *smallPos* = j and *smallest* = $x[smallPos]$.
    End for
    // Now interchange *smallest* with $x[i]$, first element of this sublist.
    c. Set $x[smallPos] = x[i]$ and $x[i] = smallest$.
End for.

A version that can be used for linked lists is just as easy. We need only replace the indices i and j with pointers that move through the list and sublists. Using the notation introduced in Section 6.4 for abstract linked lists, we can express this algorithm as follows:

Simple Selection Sort Algorithm for Linked Lists

/* Use selection sort to sort the elements in a linked list into ascending order.
    Note: $p{\rightarrow}data$ and $p{\rightarrow}next$ denote the data part and the next part,
           respectively, of the node pointed to by p. */

1. Initialize pointer p to the first node.
2. While p is not null do the following:

    // Find the smallest element in the sublist pointed to by p.
    a. Set pointer *smallPtr* = p, *smallest* = $p{\rightarrow}data$.
    b. Set pointer $q = p{\rightarrow}next$.
    c. While q is not null do the following:
        i. If $q{\rightarrow}data < smallest$ // smaller element found
            Set *smallPtr* = q and *smallest* = $q{\rightarrow}data$.
        ii. Set $q = q{\rightarrow}next$.
    End while.
    // Now interchange *smallest* with element in the first node of this sublist.
    d. Set *smallPtr*${\rightarrow}data = p{\rightarrow}data$ and $p{\rightarrow}data = smallest$.
    e. Set $p = p{\rightarrow}next$.
End while.

Note that although we have given iterative algorithms for simple selection sort, its fundamental approach is recursive:

If the list has only 1 element   // anchor

    Stop—list is sorted.

Else do the following: // inductive step

    a. Find the smallest element and put it at the front of the list.
    b. Sort the rest of the list.

In Section 10.4 we derived a worst-case computing time of O(n^2) for this sorting method. This is, in fact, the computing time for all cases. On the first pass through the list, the first item is compared with each of the $n - 1$ elements that follow it; on the second pass, the second element is compared with the $n - 2$ elements following it; and so on. The total number of comparisons is

$$(n-1) + (n-2) + \cdots + 2 + 1 \ = \ \frac{n(n-1)}{2}$$

from which it follows that the computing time is O(n^2) in all cases.

Exchange Sorts

Unlike selection sorts, in which some element is selected and then moved to its correct position in the list, an **exchange sort** systematically interchanges pairs of elements that are out of order until eventually no such pairs remain and the list is therefore sorted. One example of an exchange sort is **bubble sort**. Although this sorting scheme is too inefficient to be recommended, it is quite easy to understand and has, therefore, been taught in many introductory programming courses.

To illustrate bubble sort, consider again the list

$$67 , 33 , 21 , 84 , 49 , 50 , 75$$

On the first pass, we compare the first two elements, 67 and 33, and interchange them because they are out of order:

67 , 33 , 21 , 84 , 49 , 50 , 75

33 , 67 , 21 , 84 , 49 , 50 , 75

Now we compare the second and third elements, 67 and 21 and interchange them:

33 , 67 , 21 , 84 , 49 , 50 , 75

33 , 21 , 67 , 84 , 49 , 50 , 75

Next we compare 67 and 84 but do not interchange them because they are already in the correct order:

$$33\,,21\,,67\,,84\,,49\,,50\,,75$$
$$\downarrow\quad\downarrow$$
$$33\,,21\,,67\,,84\,,49\,,50\,,75$$

Next, 84 and 49 are compared and interchanged:

$$33\,,21\,,67\,,84\,,49\,,50\,,75$$
$$\times$$
$$33\,,21\,,67\,,49\,,84\,,50\,,75$$

Then 84 and 50 are compared and interchanged:

$$33\,,21\,,67\,,49\,,84\,,50\,,75$$
$$\times$$
$$33\,,21\,,67\,,49\,,50\,,84\,,75$$

Finally 84 and 75 are compared and interchanged:

$$33\,,21\,,67\,,49\,,50\,,84\,,75$$
$$\times$$
$$33\,,21\,,67\,,49\,,50\,,75\,,84$$

The first pass through the list is now complete.

We are guaranteed that on this pass, the largest element in the list will "sink" to the end of the list, since it will obviously be moved past all smaller elements:

$$33\,,21\,,67\,,49\,,50\,,75\,\boxed{,84}$$

But notice also that some of the smaller items have "bubbled up" toward their proper positions nearer the front of the list.[1] We now scan the list again, but this time we leave out the last item because it is already in its proper position. The comparisons and interchanges that take place on this pass are summarized in the following diagram:

---

[1] To some algorithmists, larger elements "bubble up" toward the end and smaller ones "sink" to the front. Take your pick!

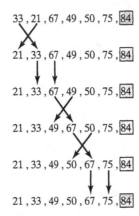

On this pass, the last element involved in an interchange was in position 5, which means that this element and all those that follow it have been properly positioned and can thus be omitted on the next pass.

On the next pass, therefore, we consider only the sublist consisting of the elements in positions 1 through 4:

$$21, 33, 49, 50, \boxed{67}, \boxed{75}, \boxed{84}$$

In scanning this sublist, we find that no interchanges are necessary, and so we conclude that the sorting is complete.

The details of this sorting scheme are given in the following algorithm:

 Bubble Sort Algorithm

/* Use bubble sort to sort $x[1], \ldots, x[n]$ into ascending order.
Note: For consistency with other sorting methods, $x[0]$ is reserved
for special purposes. */

1. Initialize *numCompares* to $n - 1$. // number of comparisons on next pass
2. While *numCompares* $\neq 0$, do the following:
   a. Set *last* = 1.   // location of last element involved in a swap
   b. For $i = 1$ to *numCompares*:
      If $x_i > x_{i+1}$
         Swap x_i and x_{i+1} and set *last* = *i*.
   c. Set *numCompares* = *last* – 1.
   End while.

The worst case for bubble sort occurs when the list elements are in reverse order because in this case, only one item (the largest) is positioned correctly on each pass through the list. On the first pass through the list, $n - 1$ comparisons and interchanges are made, and only the largest element is correctly positioned. For example, after 8 comparisons and interchanges, the list

$$90, 80, 70, 60, 50, 40, 30, 20, 10$$

becomes

$$80, 70, 60, 50, 40, 30, 20, 10, 90$$

On the next pass, the sublist consisting of the first $n - 1$ elements is scanned; there are $n - 2$ comparisons and interchanges; and the next largest element sinks to position $n - 1$. For example, after 7 comparisons and interchanges, the preceding list becomes

$$70, 60, 50, 40, 30, 20, 10, 80, 90$$

This continues until a sublist of two elements is to be scanned:

$$20, 10, 30, 40, 50, 60, 70, 80, 90$$

And on this pass, there is one comparison and interchange:

$$10, 20, 30, 40, 50, 60, 70, 80, 90$$

Thus, a total of $(n - 1) + (n - 2) + \cdots + 1 = n(n - 1) / 2$ comparisons and interchanges is required; for our example, this is $8 + 7 + 6 + 5 + 4 + 3 + 2 + 1 = (8 \times 7)/2 = 28$. The instructions that carry out these comparisons and interchanges are the instructions in the algorithm executed most often. It follows that the worst-case computing time for bubble sort is $O(n^2)$. The average computing time is also $O(n^2)$, but this is considerably more difficult to show.

Insertion Sorts

Insertion sorts are based on the idea of repeatedly inserting a new element into a list of already sorted elements so that the resulting list is still sorted. The method used is similar to that used by a card player when putting cards into order as they are dealt. To illustrate, suppose that the first card dealt is a 7. (We will ignore all other attributes, such as suit or color.) This card is trivially in its proper place in the hand:

When the second card is dealt, it is inserted into its proper place, either before or after the first card. For example, if the second card is a 2, it is placed to the left of the 7:

When the third card is dealt, it is inserted into its proper place among the first two cards so that the resulting three-card hand is properly ordered. For example, if it is a 4, the 7 is moved to make room for the 4, which must be inserted between the 2 and the 7:

This process continues. At each stage, the newly dealt card is inserted into the proper place among the cards already in the hand, so that the newly formed hand is ordered:

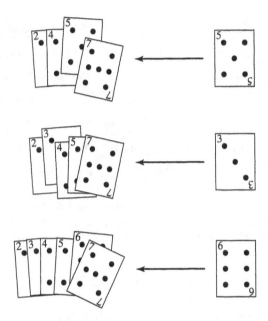

The following algorithm describes this procedure for lists stored in arrays. At the ith stage, x_i is inserted into its proper place among the already sorted $x_1, x_2, \ldots, x_{i-1}$. We do this by comparing x_i with each of these elements, starting from the right end, and shifting them to the right as necessary. We use array position 0 to store a copy of x_i to prevent "falling off the left end" in these right-to-left scans.

Linear Insertion Sort

/*   Use linear insertion sort to sort $x[1], \ldots, x[n]$ into ascending order.
Note: Position 0 is used to store the list element being inserted.   */
For $i = 2$ to n do the following:

    // Insert $x[i]$ into its proper position among $x[1], \ldots, x[i-1]$
    a. Set *nextElement* = $x[i]$ and $x[0]$ = *nextElement*.
    b. Set $j = i$.

c. While *nextElement* < *x*[*j* – 1] do the following:
    // Shift element to the right to open a spot
    Set *x*[*j*] equal to *x*[*j* – 1] and decrement j by 1.
  End while.
// Now drop *nextElement* into the open spot.
d. Set *x*[*j*] equal to *nextElement*.
End for.

The following sequence of diagrams demonstrates this algorithm for the list 67, 33, 21, 84, 49, 50, 75. The sorted sublist produced at each stage is highlighted and the arrows show the elements being shifted to the right to make room for the new item being inserted.

67,	33,	21,	84,	49,	50,	75	Initial sorted sublist of 1 element
33,	67,	21,	84,	49,	50,	75	Insert 33 to get 2-element sorted sublist
21,	33,	67,	84,	49,	50,	75	Insert 21 to get 3-element sorted sublist
21,	33,	67,	84,	49,	50,	75	Insert 84 to get 4-element sorted sublist
21,	33,	49,	67,	84,	50,	75	Insert 49 to get 5-element sorted sublist
21,	33,	49,	50,	67,	84,	75	Insert 50 to get 6-element sorted sublist
21,	33,	49,	50,	67,	75,	84	Insert 75 to get 7-element sorted sublist

The worst case for linear insertion sort is once again the case in which the list elements are in reverse order. Inserting *x*[2] requires two comparisons (with *x*[1] and then with *x*[0]), inserting *x*[3] requires three, and so on. The total number of comparisons is thus

$$2 + 3 + \cdots + n = \frac{n(n+1)}{2} - 1$$

so the computing time is again O(n^2). This is also the average case computing time, since one would expect that on the average, the item being inserted must be compared with one-half the items in the already sorted sublist.

Linear insertion sort can also be used with linked lists. For singly-linked lists, however, the algorithm obviously is different from the preceding one because we have direct access to only the first element. It is not difficult, however, and is left as an exercise.

Evaluation of These Sorting Schemes

All of the sorting algorithms that we have considered have the same computing time, O(n^2), in the worst and average cases, and so this measure of efficiency provides no basis for choosing one over the others. More careful analysis together with empirical studies, however, reveals that their performance is not the same in all situations.

The primary virtue of simple selection sort is its simplicity. It is too inefficient, however, for use as a general sorting scheme, especially for large lists. The source of this inefficiency is that it requires O(*n*) time to search for the next item to be selected and positioned. A better selection sort, known as **heapsort**, uses a more efficient search algorithm, which gives this sorting scheme a computing time of $O(n \log_2 n)$. Heapsort is described in the next section. One weakness of both of these selection sorts, however, is that they perform no better for lists that are almost sorted than they do for random lists. Many applications involve lists that are already partially sorted, and for such applications, therefore, other sorting schemes may be more appropriate.

Bubble sort (as described here) does perform better for partially sorted lists because it is able to detect when a list is sorted and does not continue making unnecessary passes through the list. As a general sorting scheme, however, it is very inefficient because of the large number of interchanges that it requires, especially when the items being sorted are large records. In fact, it is the least efficient of the sorting schemes we have considered and has virtually nothing to recommend its use. A two-way version described in the exercises performs only slightly better. The exchange sort known as **quicksort**, which is described in Section 13.3, has average computing time $O(n \log_2 n)$ and is one of the most efficient general-purpose sorting schemes.

Linear insertion sort also is too inefficient to be used as a general-purpose sorting scheme. However, the low overhead that it requires makes it better than simple selection sort and bubble sort. In fact, empirical studies indicate that of all the sorting schemes we consider, it is the best choice for small lists (with up to 20 or so elements) and for lists that are already partially sorted. Two more efficient insertion sorts, **binary insertion sort** and **Shell sort**, are described in the exercises—binary insertion sort in Exercise 11 and Shell sort in Exercise 12.

 In summary, *there is no such thing as one universally good sorting scheme*. For small lists, linear insertion sort performs well. For lists in general, quicksort, Shell sort, or heapsort is the method of choice. Table 13.1 demonstrates this for randomly generated lists of size 500. The results were taken from a 1970s video *Sorting Out Sorting*,[2] generally accepted as the beginning of algorithm animations. The actual times are very slow compared to what they would be on today's machines, of course, but relative to each other, these times clearly indicate which of the sorts are the more efficient ones.

Indirect Sorting

Each of the sorting schemes described in this section requires moving list elements from one position to another. If these list elements are large objects such as employee records that contain many pieces of information, then the time required for such data transfers may be unacceptable. For such lists of large objects, an alternative is to do an **indirect sort** that uses an **index table** to store the positions of the

---

[2] *Sorting Out Sorting* is a classic 30-minute video created by Ronald Baecker and Dave Sherman of the University of Toronto that provides a fascinating visual comparison of the performance of nine sorting algorithms, three selection sorts, three exchange sorts, and three insertion sorts. A recap of the film can be found at http://www.dgp.toronto.edu/people/RMB/video/sos_recap.mov and the famous race among these nine algorithms, all sorting the same large random array of numbers, with which the video ends at http://www.dgp.toronto.edu/people/RMB/video/sos_dotclouds.mov. For more modern graphical comparisons of sorting algorithms, see some of the many algorithm animation sites on the Internet; for example, http://www.cs.ubc.ca/spider/harrison/Java/sorting-demo.html and "The Complete Collection of Algorithm Animation" at http://www.cs.hope.edu/~alganim/ccaa/index.html.

TABLE 13.1: Sort Timings

Sorting Algorithm	Type of Sort	Sorting Time (sec)
Simple selection	Selection	69
Heapsort	Selection	18
Bubblesort	Exchange	165
Two-way bubble sort	Exchange	141
Quicksort	Exchange	6
Linear insertion	Insertion	66
Binary insertion	Insertion	37
Shell sort	Insertion	11

objects and moves the entries in this index table rather than the objects themselves. For example, for an array $x[1], \ldots, x[5]$ of employee records, an array *index* is initialized with $index[1] = 1, index[2] = 2, \ldots, index[5] = 5$. If it is necessary while sorting these records to interchange the first and third records as well as the second and fifth, we interchange the first and third elements and the second and fifth elements of the index table to obtain $index[1] = 3, index[2] = 5, index[3] = 1, index[4] = 4, index[5] = 2$. At this stage, the records are arranged in the *logical* order $x[index[1]], x[index[2]], \ldots, x[index[5]]$, that is, $x[3], x[5], x[1], x[4], x[2]$. Modifying one of the sorting schemes so it sorts indirectly is left as an exercise (see Programming Problem 8 at the end of this chapter).

✔ Quick Quiz 13.1

1. Describe how selection sorts work.
2. Simple selection sort performs better for partially sorted lists than for random lists. (True or false)
3. Describe how exchange sorts work.
4. Bubble sort performs better for partially sorted lists than for random lists. (True or false)
5. Describe how insertion sorts work.
6. Linear insertion sort performs better for partially sorted lists than for random lists. (True or false)
7. Linear insertion sort performs well for small lists (with 15–20 elements). (True or false)
8. A(n) _____ sort uses an index table that stores the positions of items to be sorted and moves the entries in this index rather than the records themselves.

◈ Exercises 13.1

1. For the following array x, show x after each of the first two passes of simple selection sort to arrange the elements in ascending order:

i	1	2	3	4	5	6
$x[i]$	30	50	70	10	40	60

2. a. For the following array x, show x after each of the first two passes of bubble sort to arrange the elements in descending order:

i	1	2	3	4	5	6
$x[i]$	60	50	70	10	40	20

   b. How many passes will bubble sort make altogether?
   c. In what situations will bubble sort make the most interchanges?

3. a. Linear insertion sort has just correctly positioned $x[3]$ in the following array x:

i	1	2	3	4	5	6
$x[i]$	20	40	60	30	10	50

   Show x after each of $x[4]$ and $x[5]$ is correctly positioned.
   b. In what situation will linear insertion sort make the fewest interchanges?

   Several of the following ask you to write functions for some sorting method. You should also test these functions by writing driver programs as instructed in Programming Problems 1–6 at the end of this chapter.

4. The basic operation in the simple selection sort algorithm is to scan a list $x_1, \ldots, x_n$ to locate the smallest element and to position it at the beginning of the list. A variation of this approach is to locate both the smallest and the largest elements while scanning the list and to position them at the beginning and the end of the list, respectively. On the next scan this process is repeated for the sublist $x_2, \ldots, x_{n-1}$, and so on.

   a. Using the array x in Exercise 1, show x after the first two passes of this double-ended simple selection sort.
   b. Write a function to implement this double-ended simple selection sort.
   c. Determine its computing time.

5. The double-ended selection sort algorithm described in Exercise 4 can be improved by using a more efficient method for determining the smallest and largest elements in a (sub)list. One such algorithm is known as *Min-Max Sort*.[3]

---

[3] Narayan Murthy, "Min-Max Sort: A Simple Method," *CSC '87 Proceedings* (Association of Computing Machinery, 1987).

Consider a list $x_1, \ldots, x_n$, where n is even.

1. For i ranging from 1 to $n/2$, compare x_i with x_{n+1-i} and interchange them if $x_i > x_{n+1-i}$. This establishes a "rainbow pattern" in which $x_1 \leq x_n, x_2 \leq x_{n-1}, x_3 \leq x_{n-2}$, and so on and guarantees that the smallest element of the list is in the first half of the list and that the largest element is in the second half.

2. Repeat the following for the list $x_1, \ldots, x_n$, then for the sublist $x_2, \ldots, x_{n-1}$, and so on:

   i. Find the smallest element x_S in the first half and the largest element in the second half X_L, and swap them with the elements in the first and last positions of this (sub)list, respectively.

   ii. Restore the rainbow pattern by comparing x_S with x_{n+1-S} and x_L with x_{n+1-L}, interchanging as necessary.

a. For the following array x, show x after Step 1 is executed, and then after each pass through the loop in Step 2:

i	1	2	3	4	5	6	7	8	9	10
$x[i]$	30	80	90	20	60	70	10	100	50	40

b. Write a function to implement this sorting algorithm.

6. Write a recursive function to implement simple selection sort.

7. Write a recursive function to implement bubble sort.

8. Write a bubble sort algorithm that is appropriate for a linked list.

9. A variation of bubble sort called *two-way bubble sort* alternates left-to-right scans with right-to-left scans of the unsorted sublists. On left-to-right scans, x_i is interchanged with x_{i+1} if $x_i > x_{i+1}$ so that larger elements are moved toward the right end of the sublist. On the right-to-left scans, x_{i+1} is interchanged with x_i if $x_{i+1} < x_i$ so that smaller elements are moved toward the left end of the sublist. Scans are repeated until no interchanges are made on one of these scans.

   a. For the array x in Exercise 5, show x at the end of each left-to-right pass and each right-to-left pass through the list.

   b. Write an algorithm to implement this two-way bubble sort and determine its computing time.

10. Write an insertion sort algorithm for a linked list.

11. In **binary insertion sort**, a binary search is used instead of a linear search to locate the position in the sorted sublist $x[1], x[2], \ldots, x[i-1]$ where the next item $x[i]$ is to be inserted.

   a. Write an algorithm for binary insertion sort.

   b. For the following array x, show x after each of the elements $x[i], i = 2, 3, \ldots,$ 10 is inserted into the sorted sublist $x[1], \ldots, x[i-1]$ using binary insertion sort. Keep a count of how many times array elements are compared.

i	1	2	3	4	5	6	7	8	9	10
$x[i]$	100	90	60	70	40	20	50	30	80	10

    c. Repeat (b), but use linear insertion sort.

12. Linear insertion sort performs best for small lists or partially sorted lists. **Shell sort** (named after Donald Shell) is an insertion sort that uses linear insertion sort to sort small sublists to produce larger partially ordered sublists. Specifically, one begins with a "gap" of a certain size g and then uses linear insertion to sort sublists of elements that are g apart, first $x[1]$, $x[1 + g]$, $x[1 + 2g]$, ..., then the sublist $x[2]$, $x[2 + g]$, $x[2 + 2g]$, ..., then $x[3]$, $x[3 + g]$, $x[3 + 2g]$, ..., and so on. Next, the size of the gap g is reduced, and the process is repeated. This continues until the gap g is 1, and the final linear insertion sort results in the sorted list.

    a. For the array x in Exercise 11, show x after each of the sublists of elements that are g apart has been sorted using linear insertion sort. Use $g = 4$ and then reduce it to $g = 1$.

    b. Write a function to sort a list of items using this Shell sort method, beginning with a gap g of the form $\dfrac{3^k - 1}{2}$ for some integer k and reducing it by 3 at each stage.

13. A binary search tree can also be used to sort a list. We simply insert the list elements into a BST, initially empty, and then use an inorder traversal to copy them back into the list. Write an algorithm for this **treesort** method of sorting, assuming that the list is stored in

    a. an array.

    b. a linked list.

14. Write a function to implement the treesort algorithm of Exercise 13.

13.2 Heaps, Heapsort, and Priority Queues

In the preceding section we looked at three sorting algorithms, simple selection sort, bubble sort, and linear insertion sort, all of which have worst-case and average-case computing time $O(n^2)$, where n is the size of the list being sorted. As we noted, there are other schemes with computing time $O(n \log_2 n)$ and thus, in most cases, are more efficient than these three. In fact, *it can be shown that any sorting scheme based on comparisons and interchanges like those we are considering must have a worst-case computing time of at least* $O(n \log_2 n)$. In this section we describe one of these, known as **heapsort**, which, as we mentioned, is a selection sort. It was discovered by John Williams in 1964 and uses a new data structure called a *heap* to organize the list elements in such a way that the selection can be made efficiently.[4]

Heaps

As an ADT, a **heap** is defined as follows:

Heap ADT

Collection of Data Elements

A binary tree with the following attributes:

- It is *complete*; that is, each level of the tree is completely filled, except possibly the bottom level, and in this level, the nodes are in the leftmost positions.

- It satisfies the *heap-order property*: The data item stored in each node is greater than or equal to the data items stored in its children. (If the data items are records, then some key field in these records must satisfy this condition.)

Note: This is sometimes called a **maxheap**; replacing "greater than" by "less than" in the heap-order property and "largest" by "smallest" in the basic operations gives a **minheap**.

Basic Operations

- Construct an empty heap
- Check if the heap is empty
- Insert an item
- Retrieve the largest element
- Remove the largest element

For example, before reading on, determine which of the following binary trees are heaps:

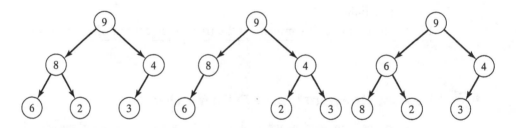

The first binary tree is a heap; the second binary tree is not, because it is not complete; the third binary tree is complete, but it is not a heap because the heap-order condition is not satisfied.

To implement a heap as a class, we could use a linked structure like that for binary search trees to store the items, but an array or a **vector** can be used more

---

[4] J. W. J. Williams, "Algorithm 232: Heapsort," *Communication of the Association of Computing Machinery* 7 (1964): 347–348.

effectively. We simply number the nodes in the heap from top to bottom, numbering the nodes on each level from left to right,

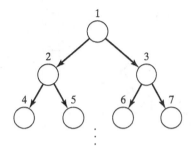

and store the data in the ith node in the ith location of the array. (Because a heap will serve as the basis for a sorting method, we will not store a list element in location 0 of the array or `vector` for consistency with the other sorting algorithms.) The complete-ness property of a heap guarantees that these data items will be stored in consecutive locations at the beginning of the array. If *myArray* is the name of the array or `vector` data member, the items in the heap

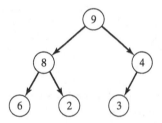

are then stored as follows: $myArray[1] = 9, myArray[2] = 8, myArray[3] = 4, myArray[4] = 6, myArray[5] = 2, myArray[6] = 3$. If we are using an array instead of a vector, we would also add a *mySize* data member to store the number of items in the heap.

Note that in such an array-based implementation, it is easy to find the children of a given node: The children of the ith node are at locations $2*i$ and $2*i + 1$. Similarly, the parent of the ith node is easily seen to be in location $i / 2$.

Basic Heap Operations

Constructor and Empty Implementing the constructor consists simply of setting *mySize* to 0 (and allocating the array if we are using a dynamic array). The empty operation also is easy since it need only check whether *mySize* is 0.

Retrieve Max Item Retrieval of the max element in the heap is also straightfor-ward. We need only return the root of the binary tree, which is stored in *myArray*[1].

Delete Max Item Deleting this max element requires a little more work. To illustrate it, consider the following heap:

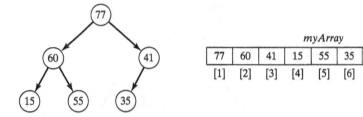

The max element is at the root, and we remove it by replacing it with the last node in the tree and decrementing *mySize* by 1:

myArray[1] = *myArray*[*mySize*];
mySize--;

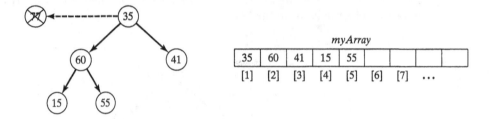

The resulting tree is called a **semiheap**, because it is complete and both subtrees are heaps, and the only reason it is not a heap is that the root item is not greater than or equal to both of its children.

The first step in converting this semiheap into a heap is to interchange the root with the larger of its two children, in this case, the left child:

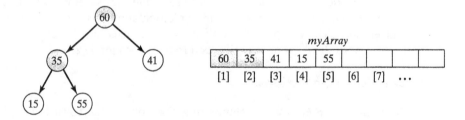

This guarantees that the new root will be greater than both of its children and that one of its subtrees, the right one in this case, will still be a heap. The other subtree may or may not be a heap. If it is, the entire tree is a heap, and we are finished. If it is not, as in this example, we simply repeat this "percolate down" procedure on this subtree:

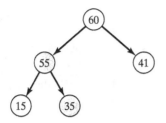

myArray

60	55	41	15	35			
[1]	[2]	[3]	[4]	[5]	[6]	[7]	...

This process is repeated until at some stage, both subtrees of the node being examined are heaps or we reach the bottom of the tree.

An algorithm for this percolate-down process is as follows:

percolate_down Algorithm

/* *myArray*[*r*], ..., *myArray*[*n*] stores a semiheap—only the value in *heap*[*r*] may fail the heap-order condition. This semiheap is to be converted into a heap. */

1. Set *c* = 2 * *r*.   // *c* is location of left child
2. While *r* ≤ *n* do the following:
    a. If *c* < *n* and   // If *r* has two children and
       myArray[*c*] < *myArray*[*c* + 1]   //   right child is the larger,
       Increment *c* by 1.   //   make *c* the right child

    // Swap node and largest child if necessary, and
    // move down to the next subtree.
    b. If *myArray*[*r*] < *myArray*[*c*]   // Parent fails heap-order cond.
       i. Swap *myArray*[*r*]   //   So fix it.
          and *myArray*[*c*].
       ii. Set *r* = *c*.   //   But we may have messed up
       iii. Set *c* = 2 * *c*.   //   binary tree at *c*, so check it.
    Else   // Heap-order condition holds
        Terminate repetition.   //   so we can stop.
    End while.

Since each pass through the while loop moves *c* down the tree one level, the maximum number of repetitions is the height of the tree. Since a tree with *k* levels has at most $1 + 2 + 4 + \cdots + 2^{k-1} = 2^k - 1$ nodes, it follows by an analysis similar to that for binary search in the preceding chapter and in Section 10.4, that the worst-case computing time for this algorithm is $O(\log_2 n)$.

Inserting an Item Inserting a new item into a heap amounts essentially to running the percolate-down operation in reverse. To illustrate it, suppose we want to insert 50 into the preceding heap. We add it as the last node of the tree,

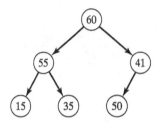

and then percolate it up the tree by interchanging it with its parent so long as it is greater than its parent. When this process terminates, the result is a heap:

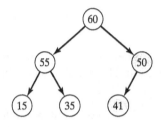

An algorithm for this percolate-up process is as follows:

percolate_up Algorithm

/* *myArray*[1], ... , *myArray*[*mySize*] stores a heap and an item is to be added to the array so that the result is still a heap. */

1. Increment *mySize*.   // Add *item* at end of tree
2. Set *myArray*[*mySize*] = *item*.
3. Set *loc* = *mySize* and *parent* = (*loc* – 1) / 2.
4. While *parent* ≥ 1 and *myArray*[*loc*] > *myArray*[*parent*]
   do the following:
      a. Interchange *myArray*[*loc*] and *myArray*[*parent*].
      b. Set *loc* = *parent* and *parent* = (*loc* – 1) / 2.
   End while.

By the same analysis as for *percolate_down*, the worst-case computing time for *percolate_up* is O(log$_2 n$).

This completes our implementation of the basic operations of a heap ADT. We leave the actual coding of a Heap class template as an exercise.

Heapsort

Now that we know about heaps, we can show how they can be used to develop an efficient selection sort algorithm. To illustrate, suppose the following list is to be sorted:

$$35, 15, 77, 60, 22, 41$$

We think of the array storing these items as a complete binary tree:

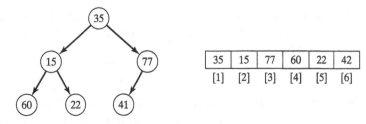

First, we must convert this tree to a heap. One way to do this is to repeatedly use the heap-insert algorithm, but there is a more efficient procedure. We begin at the last node that is not a leaf, apply the percolate-down procedure to convert to a heap the subtree rooted at this node, move to the preceding node and percolate down in that subtree, and so on, working our way up the tree until we reach the root of the given tree. The following sequence of diagrams illustrates this "heapify" process, with the subtree that is heapified at each stage highlighted:

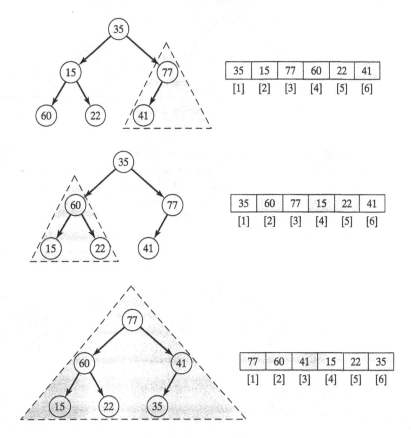

The algorithm for converting a complete binary tree to a heap is as follows:

heapify Algorithm to Convert a Complete Binary Tree into a Heap

/* *myArray*[1], ... , *myArray*[n] stores a complete binary tree. Convert it to a heap. */

For $r = n / 2$ down to 1:   // start at last nonleaf
    Apply *percolate_down* to the subtree in *myArray*[r], ... , *myArray*[n].
End for.

This puts the largest element in the list at the root of the tree—that is, at position 1 of the array. We now use the strategy of a selection sort and correctly position this largest element by swapping it with the element at the end of the list and turn our attention to sorting the sublist consisting of the first five elements. In terms of the tree, we are exchanging the root element and the rightmost leaf element and then "pruning" this leaf from the tree, as indicated by the dotted arrow in the following diagram:

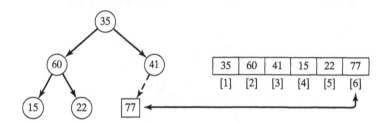

Quite obviously, the tree that results when we perform this root–leaf exchange followed by pruning the leaf is not usually a heap. In our example, the five-node tree that corresponds to the sublist 35, 60, 41, 15, 22 is not a heap. However, since we have changed only the root, the tree is a semiheap. Thus, we can use the *percolate-down* algorithm rather than the more time-consuming *heapify* algorithm to convert this tree to a heap:

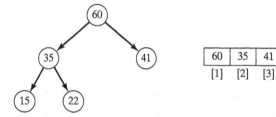

Again we swap the root with the rightmost leaf to correctly position the second largest element in the list and then prune this leaf from the tree to prepare for the next stage:

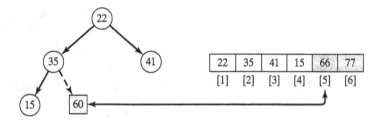

22	35	41	15	66	77
[1]	[2]	[3]	[4]	[5]	[6]

Now we use *percolate_down* to convert to a heap the tree corresponding to the sublist consisting of the first four elements,

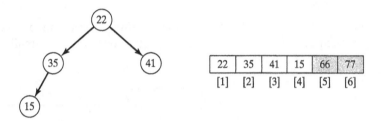

22	35	41	15	66	77
[1]	[2]	[3]	[4]	[5]	[6]

and do the root–leaf exchange and the leaf pruning to correctly position the third largest element in the list:

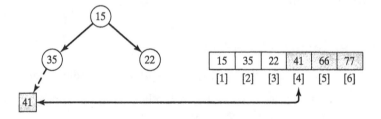

15	35	22	41	66	77
[1]	[2]	[3]	[4]	[5]	[6]

Next, the three-node tree corresponding to the sublist 15, 35, 22 is converted to a heap using *percolate_down*,

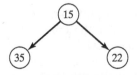

15	35	22	41	66	77
[1]	[2]	[3]	[4]	[5]	[6]

and the roof–leaf exchange and pruning operations are used to correctly position the next largest element in the list:

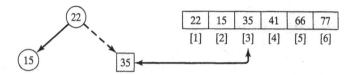

Finally, the two-node tree corresponding to the two-element sublist 22, 15 is converted to a heap,

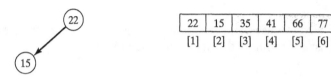

and one last root–leaf swap and leaf pruning are performed to correctly position the element 22, which obviously also correctly positions the smallest element 15 at the beginning of the list:

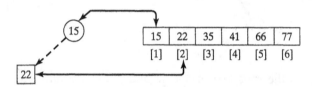

The following algorithm summarizes this simple but efficient sorting scheme, known as *heapsort*:

 Heapsort Algorithm

/* Use heapsort to sort $x[1], \ldots , x[n]$ into ascending order.

Note: For consistency with other sorting methods, position 0 in x is reserved for special purposes. */

1. Consider x as a complete binary tree and use *heapify* to convert this tree to a heap.
2. For $i = n$ down to 2:
   // Do a root–leaf exchange
   a. Interchange $x[1]$ and $x[i]$, thus putting the largest element in the sublist $x[1], \ldots , x[i]$ at the end of the sublist.
   // Prune the leaf and percolate down
   b. Apply *percolate_down* to convert the binary tree corresponding to the sublist stored in positions 1 through $i - 1$.
   End for.

In the introduction to this section the claim was made that the computing time of heapsort is $O(n \log_2 n)$. To see why, we must first analyze the *heapify* algorithm in step 1. Since *percolate_down* is an $O(\log_2 n)$ algorithm and *heapify* executes *percolate_down* $n/2$ times, its worst-case computing time is $O(n\log_2 n)$. *Heapsort* executes *heapify* one time and *percolate_down* $n - 1$ times in the loop in step 2; consequently, its worst-case computing time is $O(n \log_2 n)$.

Heap Algorithms in STL

In Chapter 10, we described the standard C++ library `<algorithm>`, which is a collection of algorithms (function templates), and we considered several of them. This library also contains the four algorithms for heap operations listed in Table 13.2, which carry out the *heapify*, *insert*, *delete*, and *heapsort* operations, respectively. In these descriptions, *begin* and *end* are iterators (or pointers).

TABLE 13.2: STL Heap Algorithms

Algorithm	Description
make_heap(*begin*, *end*)	Converts the sequence in locations *begin* through *end* - 1 into a heap (ala *heapify*).
push_heap(*begin*, *end*)	Insert operation for a heap: If the sequence in locations from *begin* up to (but not including) *end* - 1 is a heap, the element at location *end* - 1 is added to produce a heap.
pop_heap(*begin*, *end*)	Delete operation for a heap: Removes the element at location *begin* and restores the heap property.
sort_heap(*begin*, *end*)	Sorts the heap using heapsort.

The program in Figure 13.1 illustrates these operations. It uses the function templates `displayTree()` and `displayOneRow()` to display the heaps in a tree-like format.

Figure 13.1 Heap Algorithms in STL

```
/*-----------------------------------------------------------------------
        Demonstration of the heap algorithms in STL.
   -----------------------------------------------------------------------*/

#include <iostream>
#include <cmath>
#include <iomanip>
#include <algorithm>
using namespace std;
```

Figure 13.1 (continued)

```
template <typename DataType>
void displayTree(DataType x[], int n);

template <typename DataType>
void displayOneLevel(DataType x[], int numRows,
                     int row, int row_begin, int row_end);

int main()
{
   int x[11] = {87, 35, 74, 67, 79, 84, 76, 73, 81, 32};
   make_heap(x, x + 10);
   displayTree(x, 10);

   x[10] = 83;
   push_heap(x, x + 11);
   cout << "\nAfter push_heap(83):\n\n";
   displayTree(x, 11);

   pop_heap(x, x+11);
   cout << "\nAfter pop_heap( ):\n\n";
   displayTree(x, 10);

   sort_heap(x, x+10);
   cout << "\nAfter sort_heap( ), array contains:\n\n";
   for (int i = 0; i < 10; i++)
      cout << x[i] << "  ";
   cout << endl;
}

template <typename DataType>
void displayTree(DataType x[], int n)
/*-----------------------------------------------------------------
   Display a binary tree stored in an array in tree format.

   Precondition:  Binary tree is stored in an array x; n is the
      number of nodes in the tree.
   Postcondition: The binary tree has been displayed.
-----------------------------------------------------------------*/
```

Figure 13.1 (continued)

```
{
   int beginIndex = 0,   // index of first node on some level
       endIndex = 0,     //     "    " last node on this level
       rowLength,        // length of current row
       numLevels = int(ceil(log(float(n)) / log(2.0)));  // Number of levels

   for (int level = 0; level < numLevels; level++)
   {
      displayOneLevel(x, numLevels, level, beginIndex, endIndex);
      rowLength = endIndex - beginIndex + 1;
      beginIndex = endIndex + 1;
      endIndex = min(endIndex + 2*rowLength, n - 1);
   }
}


template <typename DataType>
void displayOneLevel(DataType x[], int numRows,
                int level, int beginIndex, int endIndex)
/*-------------------------------------------------------------------
   Display nodes on one level of a binary tree stored in an array.

   Precondition:  Binary tree is stored in an array x; numRows is the
      number of rows used to display the entire tree, level is the
      current level being displayed; and beginIndex and endIndex are
      the indices in x of the first and last nodes on this level.
   Postcondition: Nodes on this level of binary tree have been
      displayed.
   ----------------------------------------------------------------*/
{
   int skip = int(pow(2.0, numRows - level) - 1);
                                   // space between items in row
   for (int i = beginIndex; i <= endIndex; i++)
   {
      cout << setw(skip) << " ";
      cout << setw(2) << x[i];
      cout << setw(skip) << " ";
   }
   cout << "\n\n";
}
```

Figure 13.1 (continued)

Execution Trace:

```
                87

        81              84

     73      79      74      76

   35  67  32
```

After push_heap(83):

```
                87

        83              84

     73      81      74      76

   35  67  32  79
```

After pop_heap( ):

```
                84

        83              79

     73      81      74      76

   35  67  32
```

After sort_heap( ), array contains:

```
32   35   67   73   74   76   79   81   83   84
```

▲

Heaps and Priority Queues

In this section we have emphasized the role of heaps in sorting, but they also play other important roles as data structures. They provide a viable alternative to binary search trees in organizing some collections of data and, unlike BSTs, they do not become lopsided as items are inserted or removed. Heaps can also be used to implement priority queues, which were introduced in Section 8.4 in the discussion of CPU scheduling. And it is this role that we describe here.

Priority Queue ADT

Collection of Data Elements

A collection of data elements (all of the same type) in which a certain priority is associated with each data item, and these items are to be stored in such a way that those with higher priority are removed before those of lower priority.

Basic Operations

* Construct an empty priority queue
* Insert an item
* Find, return, and remove the largest (or smallest) element

  Other operations are important in some applications; most of them can be implemented using the preceding basic operations:

* *Construct* a priority queue from n given items
* *Replace* largest (smallest) item with a new item (unless new item is larger)
* *Change* the priority of an item
* *Delete* a specified item
* *Join* two priority queues into one larger one

There are two natural ways to implement a priority queue. One is to use a list (stored in an array or `vector` or linked list). Implementations of the two basic operations and their computing times are as follows:

Insert: Just add the item at the end (or front)—O(1)

Remove max: Traverse the list to find the max, swap it with the front (or end) item, and remove the front (or end) item—O(n)

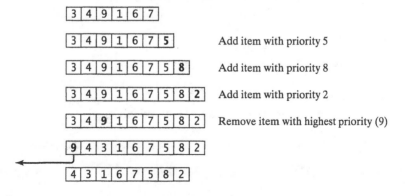

A second implementation is to use an ordered list (stored in an array or `vector` or linked list), ordered by priority. Implementations of the two basic operations and their computing times are as follows:

Insert: As in linear insertion sort—O(n)
Remove max: Just remove the item at the front—O(1)

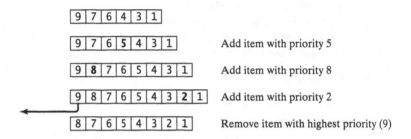

The best implementation is to *use a heap*, where the priorities determine when one element is greater than another. The insert and remove-max operations for a priority queue are simply the corresponding operations for the heap. As we have seen for heaps, the basic operations can be done in O($\log_2 n$) time.

This is the implementation used in most implementations of the Standard Template Library's `priority_queue` adapter. In a `priority_queue<T, C<T> >` declaration, `C` may be a `vector`, a `deque`, or a `list`. If no container is specified, `vector` *is the default container*; that is, declarations of the form

```
priority_queue<T> pq;
```

are equivalent to

```
priority_queue<T, vector<T> > pq;
```

The basic operations for the `priority_queue` container are given in Figure 13.2.

The default operator used to compare elements of a `priority_queue` is <, but we can also supply an alternative for comparison as a second template argument. This argument must be a **function object** that is declared by enclosing a function named `operator()` within a class declaration; for example,

```
// function object
class lessIsMore
{
public:
  bool operator() (double x, double y)
  { return x > y; }
};
```

If we defined pq by

```
priority_queue<int, lessIsMore> pq;
```

then the elements of pq would be ordered using `lessIsMore()`; that is, smaller integers would be considered to have higher priority than larger ones.

Figure 13.2 Basic `priority_queue` Operations

Operation	Description
Constructors	
`priority_queue<T, C<T> > pq;` `priority_queue<T, C<T>, compare> pq;`	Construct an empty priority queue pq using a container C (default vector) to store the elements; < is used to compare T values in the first form and function object `compare` in the second.

`priority_queue<T, C<T> >`
`            pq(first, last);`
`priority_queue<T, C<T>, compare>`
`            pq(first, last);`
	Construct a priority queue pq as before, but initialize it with elements in memory locations [*first*, *last*); < is used to compare T values in the first form and function object `compare` in the second.

`pq.empty()`	Return `true` if and only if pq contains no values
`pq.size()`	Return the number of values pq contains
`pq.push(item)`	Add *item* to pq
`pq.top()`	Return largest item in pq
`pq.pop()`	Remove largest item from pq

✔ Quick Quiz 13.2

1. What is the heap-order property?
2. An array or **vector** can be used to store a heap efficiently because a heap is a(n) _____ binary tree.
3. The complexity of the insert and delete-max operations for a heap are O(_____).
4. The complexity of heapsort is O(_____).
5. Describe how items must be stored in a priority queue.
6. (True or false) A heap can be used to implement a priority queue efficiently.

◘ Exercises 13.2

In Exercises 1–3, convert the binary tree to a heap using the *heapify* algorithm, or explain why it is not possible.

1.

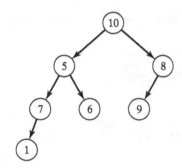

2.

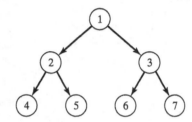

3.

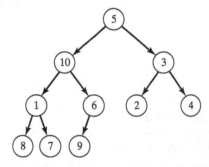

In Exercises 4–7, show the heap that results when the items are inserted into the heap, starting with one that is empty.

4.   7, 1, 6, 5, 4, 2, 3

5.   1, 7, 2, 6, 3, 5, 4

6.   7, 6, 5, 4, 3, 2, 1

7.   1, 2, 3, 4, 5, 6, 7

8–11. Using diagrams like those in this section, trace the action of heapsort on the lists in Exercises 4–7.

12. Four calls to *percolate_down* must be made to heapify the following array *x*:

i	1	2	3	4	5	6	7	8	9
$x[i]$	20	15	31	10	67	50	3	49	26

Show *x* after each of the first two calls.

13. For the following array *x*, show the contents of *x* after each of the first two iterations of the loop:

For $i = 8$ down to 2:
1. *Interchange* $x[1]$ and $x[i]$.
2. Apply *percolate_down* to the subtree in $x[1], \ldots, x[i-1]$.

i	1	2	3	4	5	6	7	8
$x[i]$	99	88	55	77	22	33	44	66

Exercises 14–16 ask you to build class templates. You should also write driver programs to test your class template as instructed in Programming Problems 10, 11, and 13 at the end of this chapter

14. Design a class template for the *Heap* ADT, using the implementation described in this section. The basic operations should include (at least) the basic operations given in the definition of a heap as an ADT.

15. Add a delete operation to the *Heap* ADT that can be used to delete an item anywhere in the heap.

16. Design a class template for the ADT *Priority_Queue*, using the heap-based implementation described in this section. The basic operations should include (at least) the basic operations given in the definition of a priority queue as an ADT.

13.3 Quicksort

In Section 13.1 we noted that an exchange sort repeatedly interchanges elements in lists and sublists until no more interchanges are possible. In the case of bubble sort, consecutive items are compared and possibly interchanged on each pass through the list, which means that many interchanges may be needed to move an element to its correct position. In this section we consider an exchange sort, developed by C. A. R. Hoare and refined significantly by Robert Sedgewick. It is known as **quicksort** and is more efficient than bubble sort because a typical exchange involves elements that are far apart so that fewer interchanges are required to correctly position an element.

Quicksort uses a **divide-and-conquer** strategy. This is an approach to problem solving in which the original problem is partitioned into simpler subproblems, each of which can be considered independently. Some or all of these subproblems may still be fairly complicated, and this divide-and-conquer approach can be repeated for them, continuing until subproblems are obtained that are sufficiently simple that they can be solved (i.e., conquered).

With quicksort, the divide-and-conquer approach chooses some element called a **pivot** and then performs a sequence of exchanges so that all elements that precede the pivot are less than or equal to the pivot and all elements that follow it are greater than the pivot. This correctly positions the pivot and divides the (sub)list into two smaller sublists, each of which may then be sorted independently in the *same* way. Repeating this approach will eventually produce small lists that are sorted or can easily be sorted. This leads naturally to the following recursive sorting algorithm:

Quicksort Algorithm

/* Use quicksort to sort $x[1], \ldots, x[n]$ into ascending order.

Note: For consistency with other sorting methods, position 0 in x is reserved for special purposes. */

If the list has 0 or 1 elements, do nothing. // the list is sorted
Else do the following.
   a. Pick an element in the list to use as the *pivot*.
   b. Split the remaining elements into two disjoint groups:
      SmallerThanPivot = {all elements ≤ *pivot*}
      LargerThanPivot = {all elements > *pivot*}
   c. Return the list rearranged as:
      quicksort(*SmallerThanPivot*), *pivot*, *quicksort*(*LargerThanPivot*).

As an illustration, consider the following list of test scores:

75, 70, 65, 84, 98, 78, 100, 93, 55, 61, 81, 68

Suppose, for simplicity, that we select the first number 75 as the pivot. *SmallerThanPivot* consists of 70, 65, 55, 61, and 68, and *LargerThanPivot* consists of 84, 98, 78, 100, 93, and 81. We must rearrange the list so that the numbers in *SmallerThanPivot* come before 75 (but not necessarily in the order listed here) and the numbers in *LargerThanPivot* come after 75:

SmallerThanPivot | 75 | *LargerThanPivot*

The only thing we require of this rearrangement is that all the numbers in the sublist to the left of 75 are less than or equal to 75 and that those in the right sublist are greater than 75. We do not care how the elements in each of these sublists are themselves ordered. And it is precisely this flexibility that makes it possible to do this rearrangement very efficiently.

The Split Operation

We carry out two searches, one from the right end of the list for elements less than or equal to the pivot 75 and the other from the left end for elements greater than 75. In our example, the first element located on the search from the right is 68, and that on the search from the left is 84:

$$\boxed{75}, 70, 65, \boxed{84}, 98, 78, 100, 93, 55, 61, 81, \boxed{68}$$

These elements are then interchanged:

$$\boxed{75}, 70, 65, \boxed{68}, 98, 78, 100, 93, 55, 61, 81, \boxed{84}$$

The searches are then resumed, from the right to locate another element less than or equal to 75 and from the left to find another element greater than 75

$$\boxed{75}, 70, 65, 68, \boxed{98}, 78, 100, 93, 55, \boxed{61}, 81, 84$$

and these elements, 61 and 98, are interchanged:

$$\boxed{75}, 70, 65, 68, \boxed{61}, 78, 100, 93, 55, \boxed{98}, 81, 84$$

A continuation of the searches next locates 78 and 55

$$\boxed{75}, 70, 65, 68, 61, \boxed{78}, 100, 93, \boxed{55}, 98, 81, 84$$

and interchanging them yields

$$\boxed{75}, 70, 65, 68, 61, \boxed{55}, 100, 93, \boxed{78}, 98, 81, 84$$

Now, when we resume our search from the right, we locate the element 55 that was found on the previous search from the left:

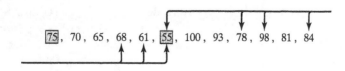

The "pointers" for the left and right searches have thus met, and this signals the end of the two searches. We now interchange 55 and the pivot 75

$$55, \ 70, \ 65, \ 68, \ 61, \ \boxed{75}, \ 100, \ 93, \ 78, \ 98, \ 81, \ 84$$

Note that all elements to the left of 75 are less than 75 and that all those to its right are greater than 75, and thus the pivot 75 has been properly positioned.

The left sublist

$$55, \ 70, \ 65, \ 68, \ 61$$

and the right sublist

$$100, \ 93, \ 78, \ 98, \ 81, \ 84$$

can now be sorted *independently, using any sorting scheme desired.* Quicksort uses the same scheme we have just illustrated for the entire list; that is, these sublists must themselves be split by choosing and correctly positioning one pivot element in each of them. The following function template split() can be used for this. It assumes that the list is stored in an array and uses a swap() function template (see Section 9.2) to interchange two list elements.

```
template <typename ElementType>

int split (ElementType x[], int first, int last)
/*-----------------------------------------------------------
   Rearrange x[first], ... , x[last] to position pivot.

   Precondition:  < and == are defined for ElementType;
       first <= last.  Note that this version of split()
       chooses pivot = x[first]; better pivot choices
       are described later in this section.
   Postcondition: Elements of sublist are rearranged and
       pos returned so x[first],..., x[pos-1] <= pivot
                 and pivot < x[pos+1],..., x[last].
   -----------------------------------------------------------*/
{
   ElementType pivot = x[first]; // pivot element
   int left = first,             // index for left search
       right = last;             // index for right search
   while (left < right)
   {
      while (pivot < x[right])     // Search from right for
         right--;                  //    element <= pivot
                                   // Search from left for
      while (left < right &&       //    element > pivot
            (x[left] < pivot || x[left] == pivot))
         left++;
```

```
     if (left < right)              // If searches haven't met
        swap(x[left], x[right]);    //   interchange elements
   }
   // End of searches; place pivot in correct position
   int pos = right;
   x[first] = x[pos];
   x[pos] = pivot;
   return pos;
}
```

Quicksort

A recursive function to sort a list using quicksort is now easy to write:

```
template <typename ElementType>
void quicksort(ElementType x[], int first, int last)
/*-------------------------------------------------------
   Quicksort array elements x[first], ..., x[last] so
   they are in ascending order.

   Precondition:  < and == are defined for ElementType.
      Note: Client programs call quicksort with first = 1
      and last = n, where n is the list size.
   Postcondition: x[first], ..., x[last] is sorted.
   --------------------------------------------------------*/
{
   int pos;                         // pivot's final position
   if (first < last)                // list size is > 1
   {
      pos = split(x, first, last);  // Split into 2 sublists
      quicksort(x, first, pos - 1); // Sort left sublist
      quicksort(x, pos + 1, last);  // Sort right sublist
   }
   // else list has 0 or 1 element and requires no sorting
}
```

As the note in the documentation indicates, this function is called with a statement of the form

```
   quicksort(x, 1, n);
```

where $x[1], x[2], \ldots, x[n]$ is the list of elements to be sorted.

The sequence of treelike diagrams that follows traces the action of quicksort() as it sorts the following list of integers:

8, 2, 13, 5, 14, 3, 7

In each tree, a circle indicates an element that has been correctly positioned at an earlier stage and a shaded circle indicates the current pivot. Rectangles represent sublists to be sorted, and a highlighted rectangle indicates the next sublist to be sorted.

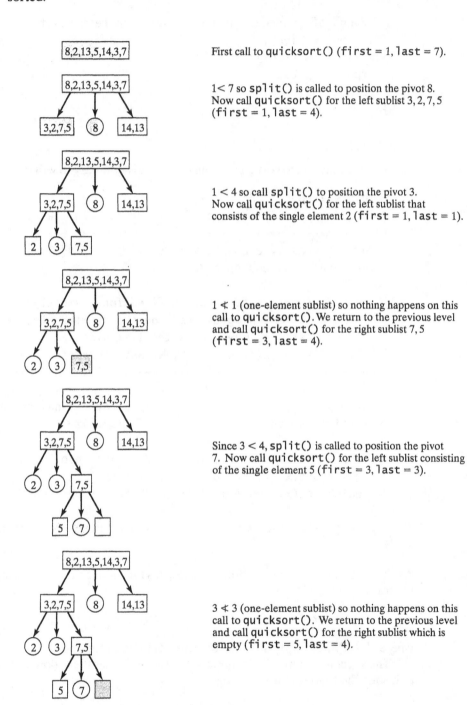

First call to quicksort() (first = 1, last = 7).

1 < 7 so split() is called to position the pivot 8. Now call quicksort() for the left sublist 3, 2, 7, 5 (first = 1, last = 4).

1 < 4 so call split() to position the pivot 3. Now call quicksort() for the left sublist that consists of the single element 2 (first = 1, last = 1).

1 ≮ 1 (one-element sublist) so nothing happens on this call to quicksort(). We return to the previous level and call quicksort() for the right sublist 7, 5 (first = 3, last = 4).

Since 3 < 4, split() is called to position the pivot 7. Now call quicksort() for the left sublist consisting of the single element 5 (first = 3, last = 3).

3 ≮ 3 (one-element sublist) so nothing happens on this call to quicksort(). We return to the previous level and call quicksort() for the right sublist which is empty (first = 5, last = 4).

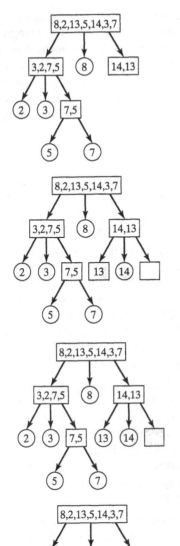

5 ≮ 4 (empty sublist) so again nothing happens on this call to quicksort(). We return to the previous level and find the call to quicksort() for sublist 7, 5 is complete. So we back up to the previous level and call quicksort() for the right sublist 14,13 at this level (first = 6, last = 7).

Since 6 < 7, split() is called to position the pivot 14. Now quicksort() is called for the resulting left sublist that consists of the single element 13 (first = 6, last = 6).

6 ≮ 6 (one-element sublist) so nothing is done on this call to quicksort(). We return to the previous level and call quicksort() for the right sublist, which is empty (first = 8, last = 7).

8 ≮ 7 (empty sublist), so do nothing on this call to quicksort(); simply return to the previous level. But this completes the call to quicksort() for the sublist 14, 13, and we return to the previous level. Now we find that the original call to quicksort() is complete.

The worst case for quicksort occurs when the list is already ordered or the elements are in reverse order (see Exercises 4 and 5). The worst-case computing time is $O(n^2)$, and the average-case computing time is $O(n \log_2 n)$. Although a rigorous derivation of these computing times is rather difficult, we can see intuitively why they are correct by considering the treelike diagrams used to describe the action of quicksort(). At each level of the tree, the function split() is applied to several sublists, whose total size is, of course, at most n; hence, each of the statements in the while loop of split() is executed at most n times on each level. The computing time for quicksort is thus $O(n \cdot L)$, where L is the number of levels in the tree. In the worst case, one of the sublists produced by split() is always empty, so that the tree has n levels. It follows that the worst-case computing time is $O(n^2)$. If, however, the two sublists produced by split() are approximately the same size, the number of levels will be approximately $\log_2 n$, thus giving $O(n \log_2 n)$ as the computing time in the average case.

Improvements

A number of changes can be made in quicksort to improve its performance, several of which are due to Robert Sedgewick. We will look at two of them here.

Choice of Pivot   Until now we have simply selected the first element in the list. However, this is acceptable only for random input. If the list is partially sorted (or in reverse order), it gives a poor partition; virtually all the elements go into either *SmallerThanPivot* or *LargerThanPivot*. And this happens consistently through the recursive calls. Quicksort takes quadratic time to do essentially nothing at all.

One common method for selecting the pivot is the **median-of-three rule**, which selects the median of the first, middle, and last elements in each sublist as the pivot. In practice, it is often the case that the list to be sorted is already partially ordered, and then it is likely that the median-of-three rule will select a pivot closer to the middle of the sublist than will the "first-element" rule.

Small Sublists   For small files ($n \leq 20$), quicksort is worse than insertion sort; and small files occur often because of recursion. So a common solution is to use an efficient sort (e.g., insertion sort) for small files. A better idea is simply to ignore all small subfiles, and when execution of the quicksort algorithm terminates, the file will not be sorted. It will only be slightly unsorted, however, in that it will contain small unordered groups of elements, but all of the elements in each such group will be smaller than those in the next group. One then simply sorts the list using insertion sort which works well, since it is efficient for nearly sorted files.

STL's sort()   The sort() function template in the C++ standard library <algorithm> uses quicksort. Most implementations will use modifications of quicksort like those just described to improve its performance.

✔ Quick Quiz 13.3

1. Describe the divide-and-conquer approach to problem solving.
2. Describe how quicksort uses a divide-and-conquer sorting strategy.
3. The item properly positioned on each call to quicksort is called a(n) _____.
4. The worst-case complexity of quicksort is O(_____), and the average-case complexity is O(_____).
5. Using the first list element as pivot works well for partially-sorted lists. (True or false)
6. The _____ rule selects the median of the first, middle, and last elements in each sublist as the pivot.
7. The C++ standard sort() algorithm uses quicksort. (True or false)

◆ Exercises 13.3

1. For the following array x, show the contents of x after the function call `splitPos = split(x, 1, 10);` is executed, and give the value of the array index `splitPos`:

i	1	2	3	4	5	6	7	8	9	10
x[i]	45	20	50	30	80	10	60	70	40	90

For Exercises 2–5, draw a sequence of trees like those in the text to illustrate the actions of `split()` and `quicksort()` while sorting the given list.

2. E, A, F, D, C, B

3. A, B, C, F, E, D

4. F, E, D, C, B, A

5. A, B, C, D, E, F

6. One of the lists in Exercises 2–5 shows why the compound boolean condition is needed to control the search from the left in function `split()`. Which list is it? What would happen if we were to omit the boolean expression `left < right`?

For the following exercises, you should write functions and test them with driver programs as instructed in Programming Problems 14–19 at the end of the chapter.

7. Modify `quicksort()` to use insertion sort if the sublist has fewer than LOWER_BOUND elements for some constant LOWER_BOUND and use quicksort otherwise.

8. The preferred alternative to the approach in Exercise 7 suggested in the text was to ignore all sublists with fewer than LOWER_BOUND elements, not splitting them further. When execution of the quicksort algorithm terminates, simply sort the list using insertion sort. Modify `quicksort()` to incorporate this modification.

9. Modify the function `split()` to use the median-of-three rule to select the pivot. (The median of three numbers a, b, and c arranged so that $a \leq b \leq c$ is the middle number b.)

10. As we saw in Section 10.3, recursion is usually implemented using a stack; parameters, local variables, and return addresses are pushed onto the stack when a recursive subprogram is called, and values are popped from the stack upon return from the subprogram. Generally, we can transform a recursive subprogram into a nonrecursive one by maintaining such a stack within the subprogram itself. Use this approach to design a nonrecursive version of function `quicksort()`; use a stack to store the first and last positions of the sublists that arise in quicksort.

11. The *median* of a set with an odd number of elements is the middle value if the data items are arranged in order. An efficient algorithm to find the median that does not require first ordering the entire set can be obtained by modifying the quicksort algorithm. We use function `split()` to position a pivot element. If this pivot is positioned at location $(n + 1)/2$, it is the median; otherwise, one of the two sublists produced by `split()` contains the median, and that sublist can be processed recursively. Write a function to find the median of a list using this method.

12. The technique described in Exercise 11 for finding the median of a set of data items can easily be modified to find the kth smallest element in the set. Write such a function.

13.4 Mergesort

Sorting schemes can be classified as **internal** or **external**, according to whether they are designed for a collection of data items stored in main memory or in secondary memory. The sorting schemes described in the preceding sections are used almost exclusively as internal sorts. They are not practical for sequential files because they require direct access to the list elements, which is not possible for sequential files. Also, some of them make many passes through the list. This too is not practical for files because they must be reset before each pass and large numbers of data transfers from disks take too much time, especially when large records are being sorted. In this section we describe two versions of a popular sorting scheme known as **mergesort** that can be used both as an internal and an external sort. We will describe it as an external sort, because this is how it is most often used. You should pay special attention to whether direct access is needed and to the number of passes made through the lists.

Merging Lists

As the name suggests, the basic operation in mergesort is **merging**—that is, combining two lists that have previously been sorted so that the resulting list is also sorted. As a simple illustration, suppose that *File1* contains eight integers in increasing order

File1: 15 20 25 35 45 60 65 70

and *File2* contains five integers in increasing order

File2: 10 30 40 50 55

In practice, of course, files contain many more items, and each item is usually a record containing several different types of information, and as we have commented before, sorting is then based on some key field within these records.

To merge files *File1* and *File2* to produce sorted *File3*, we read one element from each file, say, *x* from *File1* and *y* from *File2*:

File1: [15] 20 25 35 45 60 65 70
↑
x

File2: [10] 30 40 50 55
↑
y

We compare these items and write the smaller, in this case y, to *File3*,

File3: 10

and then read another value for y from *File2*:

File1: 15 20 25 35 45 60 65 70
      ↑
      x

File2: 10 30 40 50 55
         ↑
         y

Now x is smaller than y, so it is written to *File3*, and a new value for x is read from *File1*:

File1: 15 20 25 35 45 60 65 70
         ↑
         x

File2: 10 30 40 50 55
         ↑
         y

File3: 10 15

Again, x is less than y, so it is written to *File3*, and a new value for x is read from *File1*:

File1: 15 20 25 35 45 60 65 70
            ↑
            x

File2: 10 30 40 50 55
         ↑
         y

File3: 10 15 20

Continuing in this manner, we eventually read the value 60 for x and 55, the last value of *File2*, for y:

File1: 15 20 25 35 45 60 65 70
                  ↑
                  x

File2: 10 30 40 50 55
                ↑
                y

File3: 10 15 20 25 30 35 40 45 50

Because $y < x$, we write y to *File3*:

File3:   10   15   20   25   30   35   40   45   50   55

Because the end of *File2* has been reached, we simply copy the remaining items in *File1* to *File3* to complete the merging:

File3:   15   20   25   30   35   40   45   50   55   60   65   70

The following is a general algorithm for merging two sorted files:

 ## Merge Algorithm

/*   Merge sorted (in ascending order) *File1* and *File2* to produce sorted *File3*.   */

1. Open *File1* and *File2* for input, *File3* for output.
2. Read the first element x from *File1* and the first element y from *File2*.
3. While neither the end of *File1* nor the end of *File2* was encountered:
   If $x < y$, then
      a. Write x to *File3*.
      b. Read a new x value from *File1*.
   Otherwise:
      a. Write y to *File3*.
      b. Read a new y value from *File2*.
   End while.
4. If the end of *File1* was encountered, copy any remaining elements from *File2* into *File3*. If the end of *File2* was encountered, copy the rest of *File1* into *File3*.

Binary Mergesort

To see how the merge operation can be used in sorting a file, consider the following file *F* containing 16 integers:

F: 75   55   15   20   85   30   35   10   60   40   50   25   45   80   70   65

We begin by copying the elements of *F* alternatively into two other files *F1* and *F2*:

F1:   75   15   85   35   60   50   45   70

F2:   55   20   30   10   40   25   80   65

We now merge the first one-element "subfile" of *F1* with the first one-element subfile of *F2* to give a sorted two-element subfile of *F*:

$$F1: \boxed{75} \ 15 \ 85 \ 35 \ 60 \ 50 \ 45 \ 70$$

$$F2: \boxed{55} \ 20 \ 30 \ 10 \ 40 \ 25 \ 80 \ 65$$

$$F: \boxed{55 \ \ 75}$$

Next the second one-element subfile of *F1* is merged with the second one-element subfile of *F2* and is written to *F*:

$$F1: 75 \ \boxed{15} \ 85 \ 35 \ 60 \ 50 \ 45 \ 70$$

$$F2: 55 \ \boxed{20} \ 30 \ 10 \ 40 \ 25 \ 80 \ 65$$

$$F: 55 \ 75 \ \boxed{15 \ \ 20}$$

This merging of corresponding one-element subfiles continues until the end of either or both of the files *F1* and *F2* is reached. If either file still contains a subfile, it is simply copied into *F*:

$$F: \boxed{55 \ \ 75} \ \boxed{15 \ \ 20} \ \boxed{30 \ \ 85} \ \boxed{10 \ \ 35} \ \boxed{40 \ \ 60} \ \boxed{25 \ \ 50} \ \boxed{45 \ \ 80} \ \boxed{65 \ \ 70}$$

As the highlighted blocks indicate, the file *F* now consists of a sequence of two-element sorted subfiles. We again split it into files *F1* and *F2*, copying these two-element subfiles alternately to *F1* and *F2*:

$$F1: \boxed{55 \ \ 75} \ \boxed{30 \ \ 85} \ \boxed{40 \ \ 60} \ \boxed{45 \ \ 80}$$

$$F2: \boxed{15 \ \ 20} \ \boxed{10 \ \ 35} \ \boxed{25 \ \ 50} \ \boxed{65 \ \ 70}$$

Now we merge corresponding subfiles in *F1* and *F2* to produce four-element sorted subfiles in *F*:

$$F: \boxed{15 \ \ 20 \ \ 55 \ \ 75} \ \boxed{10 \ \ 30 \ \ 35 \ \ 85} \ \boxed{25 \ \ 40 \ \ 50 \ \ 60} \ \boxed{45 \ \ 65 \ \ 70 \ \ 80}$$

Now, using four-element subfiles, we again split *F* by copying subfiles alternately to *F1* and *F2*:

$$F1: \boxed{15 \ \ 20 \ \ 55 \ \ 75} \ \boxed{25 \ \ 40 \ \ 50 \ \ 60}$$

$$F2: \boxed{10 \ \ 30 \ \ 35 \ \ 85} \ \boxed{45 \ \ 65 \ \ 70 \ \ 80}$$

and then merge corresponding four-element subfiles to produce eight-element sorted subfiles in F:

F: | 10 15 20 30 35 55 75 85 | 25 40 45 50 60 65 70 80 |

The next splitting into files $F1$ and $F2$ produces

$F1$: | 10 15 20 30 35 55 75 85 |

$F2$: | 25 40 45 50 60 65 70 80 |

and merging corresponding 8-element subfiles in $F1$ and $F2$ produces one sorted 16-element sorted subfile in F so that F has now been sorted:

F: | 10 15 20 25 30 35 40 45 50 55 60 65 70 75 80 85 |

In this example, the size of F is a power of 2, so that all the subfiles produced by the split and merge operations have the same size, and this size is also a power of 2. In general, this will be true for all of the subfiles except possibly the last one, which may have fewer elements. Although this means that some care must be exercised in checking for the ends of files and subfiles in this version of mergesort, known as **binary mergesort**, it does not present any serious difficulties in designing the required split and merge algorithms.

Natural Mergesort

A more serious criticism of binary mergesort is that it restricts itself to subfiles of sizes $1, 2, 4, 8, \ldots, 2^k$, where $2^k \geq$ size of F and must, therefore, always go through a series of k split–merge phases. If sorted subfiles of other sizes are allowed, the number of phases can be reduced in those situations where the file contains longer "runs" of elements that are already in order. A version of mergesort that takes advantage of these "natural" sorted subfiles (in contrast to the "artificial" sizes and subfiles created by binary mergesort) is called **natural mergesort**, naturally.

As an illustration of natural mergesort, consider again the file F used to demonstrate binary mergesort:

F: 75 55 15 20 85 30 35 10 60 40 50 25 45 80 70 65

Notice that several segments of F consist of elements that are already in order,

F: | 75 | 55 | 15 20 85 | 30 35 | 10 60 | 40 50 | 25 45 80 | 70 | 65 |

and that these sorted subfiles subdivide F in a natural way.

We begin as before by copying subfiles of F alternately to two other files, $F1$ and $F2$, but using these natural subfiles rather than requiring that at each stage, their sizes be a power of 2:

$F1$: | 75 | 15 20 85 | 10 60 | 25 45 80 | 65 |

$F2$: | 55 | 30 35 | 40 50 | 70 |

We now identify the natural sorted subfiles in each of $F1$ and $F2$:

$F1$: | 75 | 15 20 85 | 10 60 | 25 45 80 | 65 |

$F2$: | 55 | 30 35 40 50 70 |

Notice that, although the subfiles of $F1$ are the same as those copied from F, the last three subfiles written to $F2$ have combined to form a larger subfile.

Now, proceeding as in binary mergesort, we merge the first subfile of $F1$ with the first one in $F2$ to produce a sorted subfile in F,

F: | 55 75 |

and then merge the second subfiles:

F: | 55 75 | 15 20 30 35 40 50 70 85 |

Since we have now reached the end of $F2$, we simply copy the remaining subfiles of $F1$ back to F:

F: | 55 75 | 15 20 30 35 40 50 70 85 | 10 60 | 25 45 80 | 65 |

Now, we again split F, alternately copying sorted subfiles to $F1$ and $F2$:

$F1$: | 55 75 | 10 60 | 65 |

$F2$: | 15 20 30 35 40 50 70 85 | 25 45 80 |

This time we see that two subfiles of $F1$ combine to form a larger subfile:

$F1$: | 55 75 | 10 60 65 |

$F2$: | 15 20 30 35 40 50 70 85 | 25 45 80 |

As before, we merge corresponding subfiles of $F1$ and $F2$, writing the results back to F:

F: | 15 20 30 35 40 50 55 70 75 85 | 10 25 45 60 65 80 |

In the next phase, splitting F produces files $F1$ and $F2$, each of which contains only one sorted subfile, and thus they are themselves completely sorted files:

$F1$: | 15 20 30 35 40 50 55 70 75 85 |

$F2$: | 15 20 30 35 40 50 |

Consequently, when we perform the merge operation in this phase, F will be a sorted file:

F: | 10 15 20 25 30 35 40 45 50 55 60 65 70 75 80 85 |

Notice that one fewer split–merge phase was required here than in binary mergesort.

The splitting operation in natural mergesort is carried out by the following algorithm:

Split Algorithm for Natural Mergesort

/* Split file F into files $F1$ and $F2$ by copying natural sorted subfiles of F alternately to $F1$ and $F2$. */

1. Open F for input and $F1$ and $F2$ for output.
2. While the end of F has not been reached:
   a. Copy a sorted subfile of F into $F1$ as follows: Repeatedly read an element of F and write it into $F1$ until the next element in F is smaller than this copied item or the end of F is reached.
   b. If the end of F has not been reached, copy the next sorted subfile of F into $F2$ in a similar manner.
   End while.

And the following algorithm implements the merge operation illustrated in the example:

Merge Algorithm for Natural Mergesort

/* Merge corresponding sorted subfiles from files $F1$ and $F2$ to produce file F.

1. Open $F1$ and $F2$ for input, F for output.
2. Initialize *numSubfiles* to 0.
3. While neither the end of $F1$ nor the end of $F2$ has been reached:
   a. While no end of a subfile in $F1$ or in $F2$ has been reached:
      If the next element in $F1$ is less than the next element in $F2$
         Copy the next element from $F1$ into F.
      Else
         Copy the next element from $F2$ into F.
      End while.

b. If the end of a subfile in *F1* has been reached
    Copy the rest of the corresponding subfile in *F2* to *F.*
Else
    Copy the rest of the corresponding subfile in *F1* to *F.*
c. Increment *numSubfiles* by 1.
End while.
4. Copy any subfiles remaining in *F1* or *F2* to *F,* incrementing *numSubfiles* by 1
for each.

An algorithm for natural mergesort consists of simply calling these two algorithms
repeatedly until the file is sorted:

 ## Natural Mergesort

/* Use natural mergesort to sort file *F.* */

Repeat the following until *numSubfiles* is equal to 1:

1. Call the *Split* algorithm to split *F* into files *F1* and *F2*.
2. Call the *Merge* algorithm to merge corresponding subfiles in *F1* and *F2*
back into *F.*

Mergesort can also be used as an internal sorting method for lists. The split and
merge algorithms can easily be modified to use arrays or vectors or linked lists in
place of the files *F, F1,* and *F2*.

The worst case for natural mergesort occurs when the items are in reverse order.
In this case, natural mergesort functions in exactly the same manner as binary mergesort, using subfiles of sizes 1, 2, 4, 8, and so on. It follows that to sort a file or list of n
items, $\log_2 n$ split and merge operations are required and each of the n items must be
examined in each of them. Hence, in the worst case, and as can be shown for the
average case also, the computing time of natural mergesort is $O(n \log_2 n)$.

✔ Quick Quiz 13.4

1. Sorting methods are classified as _____ or_____ according to whether they
are used for lists stored in main memory or for lists stored in secondary memory.
2. What are some reasons a sorting method may not be appropriate for files?
3. Why is mergesort so named?
4. The worst- and average-case complexities of mergesort are O(_____).

✪ Exercises 13.4

For Exercises 1–5, use diagrams like those in the text to show the various splitting–
merging stages of binary mergesort for the following lists of numbers:

1. 13, 57, 39, 85, 70, 22, 64, 48
2. 13, 57, 39, 85, 99, 70, 22, 48, 64
3. 13, 22, 57, 99, 39, 64, 57, 48, 70

4. $13, 22, 39, 48, 57, 64, 70, 85$

5. $85, 70, 65, 57, 48, 39, 22, 13$

6–10. Give diagrams as in Exercises 1–5, but use natural mergesort.

The following exercises ask you to write functions. You should also test these functions with driver programs as instructed in Programming Problems 20–25 at the end of this chapter.

11. Write functions to implement the *split, merge*, and *mergesort* algorithms for files.

12. Proceed as in Exercise 11, but for a list stored in an array or `vector`.

13. Proceed as in Exercise 11, but for a linked list.

14. One variation of the mergesort method is to modify the splitting operation as follows: Copy some fixed number of elements into main memory, sort them using an internal sorting method such as quicksort, and write this sorted list to *F1*; then read the same number of elements from *F* into main memory, sort them internally, and write this sorted list to *F2*; and so on, alternating between *F1* and *F2*. Write a function for this modified mergesort scheme, using quicksort to sort internally the sublists containing *SIZE* elements for some constant *SIZE*.

15. Write a function to carry out a *three-way merge*—that is, a procedure that merges three sorted files to form another sorted file.

13.5 Radix Sort

All the sorts we have considered thus far have a common pattern: rummage around in the list, comparing elements, and moving them here and there according to some specific rules. We conclude our study of sorts with one that is very different: **radix sort**. There are several versions of radix sort, but their common characteristic is that they are based on examining the digits in some base-b numeric representation of the items (or numeric keys of records).[5]

One simple version is sometimes called a *least-significant-digit radix sort*, because it processes the digits from right to left. It is also known as *card sort*, because it was used in the early days of computing to sort old-style punched cards. Program instructions in early programming languages such as Fortran and COBOL were punched on 80-column cards, with the source code in columns 1–72; columns 73–80 were used to number the cards. Since each program statement was on a separate card, a large program could require a large deck of hundreds of cards. Accidentally dropping the deck was the nightmare that threatened every beginning programmer, because of the time and effort required to rearrange the cards in the correct order, especially if the cards had not been numbered!

If the cards were numbered and a machine called a *card sorter* was available, the programmer could place the cards in its hopper, set the machine to sort on column 80 (the least significant digit of the numbers), and the cards would be distributed into ten bins. One would then collect them in order, from bin 0 to bin 9, put them in the hopper again, set the machine to sort on column 79, and again the cards would be distributed into the 10 bins. Repeating this procedure for each of columns 78 down to 73 restored the cards to their original order.

---

[5] The term *radix* is another term used in mathematics for the base of a number system.

This is the basic idea of radix sort. To illustrate it, suppose the numbers we are sorting are expressed in base ten and have at most 3 digits, for example,

64, 8, 216, 512, 27, 729, 199, 550, 343, 125, 93, 666

To help with understanding radix sort, we will write them all with three digits, padding with 0s to the left where necessary:

064, 008, 216, 512, 027, 729, 199, 550, 343, 125, 093, 666

We first distribute them into 10 bins labeled 0, 1, ..., 9, according to their rightmost digit:

| | | | 093 | | | 666 | | | 199 |
550	011	512	343	064	125	216	027	008	729
0	1	2	3	4	5	6	7	8	9

Now we collect them together from left to right, bottom to top,

550, 011, 512, 343, 093, 064, 125, 216, 666, 027, 008, 729,199

and then distribute them again, this time using the second digit:

| | 216 | 729 | | | | 666 | | | 199 |
| | 512 | 027 | | | | | | | |
008	011	125		343	550	064			093
0	1	2	3	4	5	6	7	8	9

Collecting them together produces

008, 011, 512, 216, 125, 027, 729, 343, 550, 064, 666, 093, 199

Now we distribute them one last time, using the leftmost digit:

093									
064									
027									
011	199				550				
008	125	216	343		512	666	729		
0	1	2	3	4	5	6	7	8	9

This time, collecting them produces the sorted list:

008, 011, 027, 064, 093, 125, 199, 216, 343, 512, 550, 666, 729

Here is the preceding procedure as an algorithm:

Radix Sort

/*   Use radix sort to sort a list $x[1], \ldots, x[n]$ of numbers, each having
     NUM_DIGITS digits, into ascending order. Note: For consistency with
     other sorting methods, position 0 in x is reserved for special purposes.
     (Also, the algorithm can easily be modified for a linked list.)   */

1. Create 10 containers $c[0], \ldots, c[9]$ for the list elements (e.g., an array of
   10 linked lists of integers).
2. For $d = NUM\_DIGITS$ down to 1 do the following:
   a. Clear each container $c[0], \ldots, c[9]$ so it is empty.
   // Distribute values into the containers.
   b. For $i = 1$ through n do the following:
      i. Set *nextDigit* = d^{th} digit of $x[i]$.
      ii. Add $x[i]$ at the end of $c[nextDigit]$.
   // Now copy the containers back into x.
   d. Set *nextPos* = 1.
   e. For *dig* = 0 to 9 do the following:
      i. Copy elements of $c[dig]$ into the next $c[dig].size()$ positions of x
         starting at position *nextPos*.
      ii. Increase the value of *nextPos* by $c[dig].size()$.
   End for.

As noted in step 1 of the algorithm, each of the containers can be a linked list.
This is an efficient data structure to use since one has no idea how many items will be
placed in each container. Also, as the opening documentation states, the items need
not be stored in an array or `vector`; a linked-list version of the algorithm is straightforward and is left as an exercise.

Radix sort can be used with numbers expressed in any base b. We need only
replace 10 by b and 9 by $b - 1$ in the preceding algorithm. It can also be used with
strings if we use one container for each possible character in the string. For example,
strings of all lower case letters would require 27 containers, one for blanks used to
pad strings on the right and one for each of the letters 'a' through 'z'.

Determining the computing time of radix is straightforward. The instructions
in the inner loop that distributes values into the containers are the ones encountered most often and they are executed n times each time this loop is encountered.
Since the outer loop is executed *NUM_DIGITS* times, we see that each of these
instructions is executed *NUM_DIGITS* * n times. It follows that this is an $O(n)$
algorithm.

◆ Exercises 13.5

For Exercises 1–5, trace the execution of radix sort using diagrams like those in the text for each of the following lists of integers:

1. 29, 778, 11, 352, 233, 710, 783, 812, 165, 106

2. 38, 399, 892, 389, 683, 400, 937, 406, 316, 5

3. 353, 6, 295, 44, 989, 442, 11, 544, 209, 46

4. 8745, 7438, 15, 12, 8501, 3642, 8219, 6152, 369, 6166, 8583, 7508, 8717, 8114, 630

5. 9001, 78, 8639, 252, 9685, 3754, 4971, 888, 6225, 9686, 6967, 6884, 2, 4370, 131

Using the modification of radix sort for strings, trace its execution using diagrams like those in the text for each of the following lists of strings of lowercase characters. You need only show containers for those letters (and blanks) that appear in one of the words.

6. `for, if, do, else, case, int, main`

7. `while, if, for, break, float, bool`

Suppose that we sort a list of records in which some of the values in the key field may be the same. A sorting scheme is said to be *stable* if it does not change the order of such records. For example, consider a list of records containing a person's name and age that is to be sorted so that the ages are in ascending order. Suppose that

comes before

in the original list (with possibly several records between them). For a stable sorting scheme, Doe's record still comes before Smith's after the list is sorted. In Exercises 8–15, determine whether the sorting method is stable.

8. Simple selection sort

9. Bubble sort

10. Linear insertion sort

11. Heapsort

12. Quicksort

13. Binary mergesort

14. Natural mergesort

15. Radix sort

Exercises 16–18 ask you to write functions. You should also test these functions with driver programs, as instructed in Programming Problems 30–32 at the end of this chapter.

16. The radix search algorithm for lists of integers given in the text. Use `list<int>`s for the containers.

17. Proceed as in Exercise 16 for lists of base-*b* integers, where the base *b* is entered by the user.

18. Proceed as in Exercise 16, but for lists of strings of lowercase letters (and blanks) as described in the text.

SUMMARY

▦ Chapter Notes

- Three categories of sorts are *selection*, *exchange*, and *insertion*. Selection sorts make a number of passes through a list or part of a list and, on each pass, select one element to be correctly positioned. Exchange sorts systematically interchange pairs of elements that are out of order until no such pairs remain and the list is sorted. Insertion sorts repeatedly insert a new element into a list of already sorted elements so that the resulting list is still sorted.

- Simple selection sort, bubble sort, and insertion sort are $O(n^2)$ sorts and do not perform well for large lists. For small lists, linear insertion sort performs well. Bubblesort is inefficient in almost every situation and should not be used as a general sorting scheme.

- Many applications involve lists that are already partially sorted, and a good sorting method should take advantage of this.

- There is no such thing as one universally good sorting scheme. For lists in general, quicksort, Shell sort, or heapsort are the methods of choice.

- An *indirect sort* uses an index table that stores the positions of the list elements and moves the entries in this index rather than the elements themselves, which is more efficient than moving large objects.

- Heapsort is an $O(n \log_2 n)$ selection sort that is based on storing the items in a *heap*.

- Quicksort is a divide-and-conquer sorting method with average complexity $O(n \log_2 n)$. Industrial-strength versions, such as the `sort()` algorithm in STL, use a nontrivial pivot selection strategy such as the median-of-three rule, and use some other sorting method such as insertion sort to sort small sublists.

- Mergesort is an $O(n \log_2 n)$ sorting method that can be used either as an internal or external sort. Natural mergesort takes advantage of partially sorted lists and is thus preferred over binary mergesort.

- Radix sort is different from the preceding sort methods in that it is not based on comparing list elements. It groups elements together based on each digit in their (or their key's) numeric representation and is thus limited to lists that have such representations.

☞ Programming Pointers

1. The Standard Template Library provides algorithms for processing heaps: `make_heap()`, `push_heap()`, `pop_heap()`, and `sort_heap()`.

2. C++ provides *function objects*, which are defined by enclosing a function named `operator()` within a class declaration. They are used to pass functions into class templates.

3. *Divide-and-conquer* is a problem-solving approach that divides the original problem into simpler subproblems, perhaps repeatedly, until subproblems are obtained that are sufficiently simple that they can be solved (i.e., conquered).

▲ ADT Tips

1. A *heap* (or *maxheap*) organizes list elements in such a way that insertions and removal of the largest (or smallest for a *minheap*) element can be done in $O(\log_2 n)$ time. It is a complete binary tree that satisfies the *heap-order property*: Each node stores a value that is greater than (less than) or equal to the values in its children.

2. Because a heap is a complete binary tree, it can be stored efficiently in an array.

3. Unlike a binary search tree, a heap cannot become lopsided as items are inserted or removed.

4. Each data item in a *priority queue* has a priority associated with it, and these items are stored in such a way that those with higher priority are removed before those of lower priority.

5. One of the most efficient implementations of a priority queue uses a heap.

▣ Programming Problems

Section 13.1

For each of Problems 1–6, write a driver program to test the given function.

1. The double-ended selection-sort function in Exercise 4.

2. The Min-Max-Sort function in Exercise 5.

3. The recursive simple-selection-sort function in Exercise 6.

4. The recursive bubblesort function in Exercise 7.

5. The Shell-sort function in Exercise 12.

6. The treesort function in Exercise 14.

7. Write a program that reads a collection of student numbers and names and then uses the treesort function of Exercise 14 to sort them so that the student numbers are in ascending order.

8. Write a program that reads the records in `UserIdFile` (described at the end of Chapter 4) and stores them in an array or `vector`. Then sort the records so that the resources used to date are in descending order, using one of the sorting schemes in this section as an indirect sort.

9. Write a program that compares the execution times of various $O(n^2)$ sorting algorithms described in this section for randomly generated lists of integers.

Section 13.2

10. Write a driver program to test the *Heap* class template of Exercise 14.

11. Write a driver program to test the modified *Heap* class template of Exercise 15.

12. Write a program that reads records containing an employee number and an hourly rate for several employees and stores these in a heap, using the employee number as the key.

The program should then allow the user to insert or delete records and, finally, use heap-sort to sort the updated list so that the employee numbers are in ascending order, and display this sorted list.

13. Write a driver program to test the *Priority_Queue* class template of Exercise 16.

Section 13.3

For each of Problems. 14–20, write a driver program to test the given function.

14. The modified `quicksort()` function in Exercise 7.

15. The modified `quicksort()` function in Exercise 8.

16. The modified `split()` function in Exercise 9.

17. The nonrecursive `quicksort()` function in Exercise 10.

18. The function for finding the median of a list in Exercise 11.

19. The function for finding the kth smallest element of a set in Exercise 12.

Section 13.4

For each of Problems 20–22, write a driver program to test the given functions.

20. The *split*, *merge*, and *mergesort* functions for files in Exercise 11.

21. The *split*, *merge*, and *mergesort* functions for lists stored in arrays or `vectors` in Exercise 12.

22. The *split*, *merge*, and *mergesort* functions for linked lists in Exercise 13.

23. Suppose that a file contains employee records containing the following items of information in the order given:

> Id number
> Last name, first name, and middle initial
> Street address
> City, state, and zip (or postal) code
> Phone number
> Gender
> Age
> Number of dependents
> Department category (factory, office, sales)
> Indicator of whether employee is a union member
> An hourly pay rate

Write a program to read these employee records and sort them using mergesort so that the id numbers are in ascending order.

24. Write a driver program to test the function for the modified mergesort scheme in Exercise 14.

25. Write a driver program to test the three-way merge function in Exercise 15.

26. Use the function in Exercise 15 to merge three files of records containing names and phone numbers, sorted so that the names are in alphabetical order. For duplicate entries in the files, put only one entry in the final file.

27. Use the function in Exercise 15 in a program that performs a *ternary mergesort*, which differs from binary mergesort in that three files rather than two are used to split a given file.

28. Write a program to compare the computing times of binary mergesort and natural mergesort for files of randomly generated integers.

29. **Polyphase sort** is another external sorting scheme of the mergesort variety. A simple version of it begins by merging one-element subfiles in two files, *F1* and *F2*, forming sorted subfiles of size 2 in a third file, *F3*. However, only enough subfiles are merged to empty one of *F1 and F2*—say, *F1*. The remaining one-element subfiles in *F2* are then merged with the two-element subfiles in *F3* to produce subfiles of length 3 and are written to *F1* until *F2* becomes empty. The remaining two-element subfiles of *F3* are then merged with three-element subfiles of *F2* to form subfiles of length 5 in *F1* until the end of *F3* becomes empty. This process continues until the sorting is complete.

    Note that the sequence of subfile lengths in polyphase sort is 1, 1, 2, 3, 5, 8, 13, 21, 34, ..., the sequence of *Fibonacci numbers* (see Section 10.1). The final subfile length (which is also the size of the original file *F3* to be sorted) must therefore be some Fibonacci number f_n. It also follows that the sizes of the initial files *F1* and *F2* must be the two Fibonacci numbers f_{n-1} and f_{n-2}, which precede f_n. Rewrite the program in Problem 28 to sort the file of employee records using polyphase sort, adding "dummy" subfiles to either *F1* or *F2* if necessary to make their sizes two consecutive Fibonacci numbers and removing them when sorting is completed.

Section 13.5

For each of Problems 30–32, write a driver program to test the given functions.

30. The function for radix sorting lists of integers in Exercise 16.

31. The function for radix sorting lists of base-*b* integers in Exercise 17.

32. The function for radix sorting lists of strings in Exercise 18.

14

OOP and ADTs

CHAPTER CONTENTS

Chapter Objectives

■ Study the basic properties of object-oriented programming: encapsulation, inheritance, and polymorphism.

■ Discuss object-oriented design and the role inheritance plays in it.

■ Describe how inheritance is implemented in C++.

■ Look at examples of inheritance and class hierarchies.

■ Describe the need for polymorphism and how it is accomplished in C++ by means of virtual functions and late binding.

A major objective of object-oriented programming is *reusability*. Some of the ways this is accomplished in C++ that we have described are the following:

■ Encapsulating code within *functions*

■ Building *classes* to represent the nontrivial objects in a problem

■ Storing class and function definitions in *separately-compiled libraries*

■ Converting functions into *type-parameterized function templates*

■ Converting classes into *type-parameterized class templates*

Up to now, most of the classes and class templates we have developed were built "from scratch." In this chapter we introduce the important OOP concept of *inheritance*, which makes another level of reusability possible:

■ Reuse the work done in building one class (or class template) to build another class (or class template).

If we invest time and effort in building a class and then need to build another one that is a variation of the first, we should be able to capitalize on our investment.

The focus of this chapter will be on how inheritance can facilitate the design and development of abstract data types. We will study in detail how one class can be derived from another class. We will then look at an important new aspect of inheritance—*polymorphism*—and at how virtual functions in C++ make it possible to extend the "A" in ADT—that is, how some abstract data types can be made still more abstract (i.e., separate from any implementations). In the same way that class templates and function templates make it possible to "abstract away" the *types* of elements in an ADT, virtual functions make it possible to abstract away the *operations*.

14.1 A Brief History and Overview of OOP and ADTs

The features built into imperative programming languages such as Pascal and C facilitate the development of *structured* programs. As we noted in Chapter 1, structured programs are easier to develop and maintain than unstructured ones, and as a result, structured programming techniques were widely used in program development for several years. As the complexity of software systems increased, however, it became necessary to divide them into simpler modules that could be developed, compiled, and tested separately before they were integrated to form larger systems. This led to the introduction of new structures into programming languages, such as modules in Modula-2, units in Pascal, libraries in Fortran and C, and packages in Ada. As the number and complexity of software systems continued to increase, it became clear that development cost could be reduced if portions of existing software could be extended and reused in developing new systems. These notions of software *extensibility* and *reusability* together with the techniques of structured and modular programming are fundamental concepts in object-oriented programming. Its goals are to improve programmer productivity by making it easier to reuse and extend software and to manage its complexity, thereby reducing the cost of developing and maintaining software.

The term *object-oriented programming* was first used to describe the programming environment for Smalltalk, one of the earliest true object-oriented programming languages. As OOP methods became more widely available with the development of languages such as C++ and Java, the popularity of the object-oriented approach increased to the point where it has become a major modus operandi in programming and system development

In the introduction to OOP in Chapter 1, we listed three important properties that characterize object-oriented programming:

■ *Encapsulation*

■ *Inheritance*

■ *Polymorphism*, with the related concept of *dynamic* or *late binding*

In this section, we consider again and illustrate each of these fundamental characteristics.

Encapsulation

A central theme of this text is the study of abstract data types, but we also are interested in the data structures provided in programming languages for implementing ADTs—that is, in features provided for converting *abstract data types* into *concrete data types*. One of the trademarks of an ADT is its *encapsulation* of data and basic operations for processing this data within a single entity. The structures provided in programming languages for defining concrete data types should reflect this property by making it possible to encapsulate both data and operations. This was not one of the strengths of early imperative languages, but it became possible with the introduction of units, modules, libraries, and packages.

Another key feature of *abstract* data types is that they are defined independently of implementations, and some of the concrete realizations of ADTs reflect this *definition–implementation separation*. For example, units in Pascal have an interface part in which the definition of an ADT can be expressed and an implementation part to contain the functions and procedures for the basic operations. Similarly, modules in Modula-2 have a definition part and an implementation part; and packages in Ada consist of a specification part and a body (implementation part). In each case, the interface or definition part contains *public* information that is accessible to outside clients, and the implementation part contains *private* information that is accessible only within the structure. This separation of a concrete data type's definition from its implementation makes it possible to hide the private implementation details so that a user of the data type is forced to process the data items using only the basic operations defined for that type. Another benefit of this separation is that the implementation may be changed without having to change the programs, subprograms, modules, or units that use the data type.

In object-oriented programming languages, ADTs can be implemented with *classes*, which have the encapsulation property together with the public–private separation that it entails. An ADT's data items are stored in a class's data members, and its operations are implemented by a class's *function members* or *methods*. The process of calling one of these function members to modify the data stored in an object is referred to as *sending a message* to the object. For example, if Stack is one of the several stack classes (or templates) we have studied and s is an object of type Stack, then to remove the top element of s, we send a message to s instructing it to pop its top element. Similarly, to add a new element to this stack, we send a message to s telling it to push an element onto itself. In non-OOP languages, we would send the stack s to some procedure or function that performs an operation on s. In the OOP approach, we send a message to the object (data) s asking it to *perform an operation on itself*. Object-oriented programming thus focuses on the data to be processed rather than on the subprograms that do the processing.

Inheritance

Classes also provide the second important property of object-oriented programming, *inheritance*. A class can be derived from another class, and this new class then inherits the data members and function members of the original class, thus making it possible to reuse them in another class.

To illustrate, suppose that a problem requires the usual stack operations, but also requires some other operations not provided in a Stack class; for example, suppose that we need to be able to determine the smallest and the largest values in the stack at any time. There are several ways we might approach building a new class that provides the additional min() and max() operations.

The first approach is simply to add function members min() and max() to the Stack class:

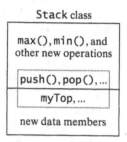

Stack class

This is not a good way to proceed, however, because we are tampering with a tested and operational class and may mess it up so that client programs that use this class no longer work correctly after we add our new operations. In fact, it may not even be possible to use this approach, because the source code for the class may not be accessible to the programmer.

A second approach is an *adapter* approach in which we build a new RevStack class that contains a Stack object as a data member:

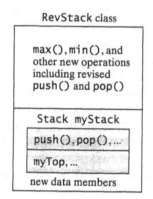

RevStack class

This inclusion technique works, but it is not good design, because we cannot say that a RevStack object *is a* Stack; only that it *has a* Stack. A RevStack should be a special kind of Stack.

 Design should reflect reality not implementation.

A third approach is a *copy-&-paste* approach: we build a new RevStack class, copying and pasting the data members and function members of Stack into RevStack:

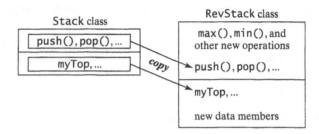

This is almost right, but these are separate independent classes. Updating Stack (e.g., changing from an array to a linked list for the stack elements) does not automatically update RevStack.

The object-oriented approach is to derive a new class RevStack from the Stack class, which is called its *parent class* or *base class* or *superclass*. RevStack is called a *child class* or *derived class* or *subclass*. The following are some of the reasons why this is the best method:

- A derived class inherits all members of its parent class (including its operations); it *reuses* the members inherited from the parent class. A RevStack *is a* Stack.

- Modifying the Stack class automatically updates the RevStack class.

- Mistakes made in building the RevStack class will be local to it; the original Stack class remains unsoiled, and client programs that use it are not affected.

Polymorphism and Dynamic Binding

Polymorphism (from the Greek, meaning "many forms") and the related concept of *dynamic* (or *late*) *binding* is the third important property of object-oriented programming. We have already seen examples of a kind of polymorphic behavior in functions:

- A function name can be overloaded to denote several different functions.

- A function template can be a pattern for many different actual functions.

We have also seen a similar kind of polymorphic behavior in connection with classes:

- A class template can be a pattern for many different classes.

In each case, the compiler determines the correct function or instance of a class to use.

In object-oriented programming, however, polymorphism has a different meaning. We will describe it more precisely later, but for now we will simply illustrate it with an example. Both of the classes Stack and RevStack could have an output function named display(), but it might perform differently for each of them; for example, for a Stack object, it displays the elements of the stack, but for a RevStack object it might display the stack elements and also identify the largest and the smallest elements. We could, of course, use different names for this function, but we would prefer using the same name such as display(). This function is an example of a *polymorphic function*; it has the same prototype in both class declarations, but it can result in different actions for the two classes. It performs one way for a RevStack object and in a different manner for a Stack object.

In the examples of polymorphic behavior of functions given earlier, the compiler can select which is the correct version of the function to use wherever the function is called. This is referred to as **static** (or **early**) **binding** of the code for a function to the function call. However, there are times when the decision of which version of a polymorphic function like display() to use for a function call cannot be made until run time. For example, as we will see later, a pointer variable declared by

```
Stack * sptr;
```

can point to either a Stack object,

```
sptr = new Stack;
```

or a RevStack object,

```
sptr = new RevStack;
```

Now, what we want is that a message to the object pointed to by sptr,

```
sptr->display(cout);
```

will use the display() function from the Stack class in the first case, but in the second case, it will use the display() function from the RevStack class. The compiler cannot determine this; it cannot bind this function call to a particular version of display(). This decision must be deferred until execution of this statement, which is what is meant by **dynamic** (or **late**) **binding**. Although this is automatic in some OOP languages such as Java, C++ requires the use of *virtual functions*, which we will study in Section 14.5.

✔ Quick Quiz 14.1

1. Name and define the three fundamental concepts of object-oriented programming.
2. The _____ of data and basic operations within a single entity is one of the key properties of ADTs.
3. Calling a member function in an object is referred to as sending a(n) _____ to the object.
4. A derived class _____ the members of the parent class.
5. The word _____ means "many forms."
6. _____ binding is done at compile time; _____ binding is done at run time.

14.2 Inheritance and Object-Oriented Design

In a first programming course that uses some programming language such as C++ or Java that supports OOP, beginning students might use a simplified object-centered problem-solving approach like the following in designing their first programs:

    1. Identify the *objects* in the problem's specification and their types.
    2. Identify the *operations* needed to solve the problem.
    3. Arrange the problem's objects and operations in a sequence of steps, called an *algorithm*, that solves the problem.

This solution is then coded in the programming language being used, tested, debugged, and executed.

As the course proceeds, various inadequacies in this approach are discovered. The first inadequacy is in step 2: the required operations may not be available. Once functions have been introduced, step 2 is modified as follows:

2. Identify the *operations* needed to solve the problem.
If an operation is not available, define a function to perform that operation.

The next shortcoming has to do with step 1: the required types may not be available. The introduction of classes leads to a modification of step 1:

1. Identify the *objects* in the problem's specification and their types.
If a type is not available, design a new type using classes.

Inheritance leads to the final enhancement to this design methodology, producing true **Object-Oriented Design (OOD)**, which is the focus of this chapter. In the preceding section, we briefly described the inheritance mechanism and illustrated how it makes it possible to derive a new class from a class already available so that the derived class inherits the function members and data members of the base class. Object-oriented design exploits this capability to build objects in which shared attributes are stored in a base class, and attributes unique to a given object are stored in a derived class.

Object-oriented design (OOD) is to engineer one's software as follows:

1. Identify the objects in the problem.

2. Carefully analyze the objects to determine if there is commonality in them.

3. Where commonality exists, group the common attributes together:

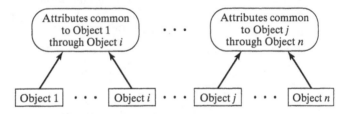

Then repeat this approach upwards as appropriate:

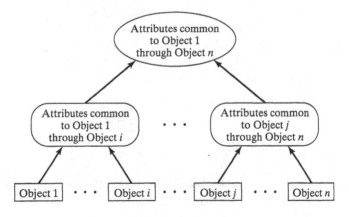

4. *Once no more commonality is found, do the following:*
Proceeding from the top down, build the general base class(es) and from them derive the less-general classes, continuing until classes for the actual objects in the system result.

Thus, we see that this leads to **class hierarchies**, which are usually pictured as a tree, but with arrows drawn from a derived class to its base class. *Each non-root class inherits the members of its ancestor classes. This means that an attribute needs to be defined only once at the appropriate level, allowing a programmer to reuse the (one) definition many times.*

Example 1: Licenses

Suppose we work for the state licensing bureau and we want to model various kinds of licenses: deer-hunting license, bear-hunting license, pheasant-hunting license, fishing license, trout-fishing license, chauffeur's license, automobile-operator license, motorcycle license, marriage license, dog license, cat license, and so on. We could design a separate class for each possible license independently, but this would involve a lot of code duplication, since licenses have many attributes in common. So we begin with the important question in OOD:

What attributes do the objects (licenses) in this problem have in common?

After analyzing the various kinds of licenses we have to consider, we would probably find that we can form several groups of licenses that have common features. For example, we might identify a group of licenses—those to drive an automobile, operate a motorcycle, a taxi cab, and so on—that all pertain to licenses that permit a person to drive some vehicle. Then we might encapsulate these common attributes in a drivers-license class that will serve as a base class from which we will derive the specialized licenses to operate cars, motorcycles, and so on.

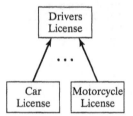

In a similar way, licenses to hunt deer, to hunt bear, to hunt pheasants, and so on all pertain to hunting licenses and they all have certain properties in common; for example, each might store the kind of prey being hunted, the beginning and end of the hunting season, and what kind of weapon may be used. Another group of licenses might be those that permit a person to own a pet. And there may be several other license groups that one can identify:

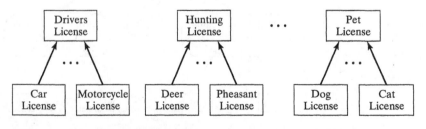

Once we have identified the various groups of licenses, we would probably discover that all of them store some of the same information about a person: an identification number, name, age, birthday, and so on. After we have identified these common properties, we might encapsulate them in a higher-level license class that could serve as a base class for the license groups we identified earlier:

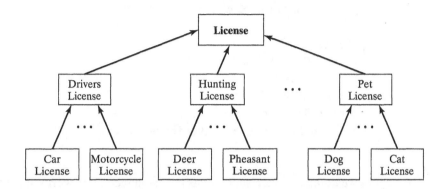

Eventually we reach a point at which it seems there is no more commonality to be found and we terminate this bottom-up design of our class hierarchy. Now we begin the top-down process of building the actual classes in our hierarchy.

We begin at the root of the tree and build a general License class to store the attributes and operations that all licenses have in common:

```
class License         // base class
{
 public:
  /***** Function Members *****/
  void display(ostream & out) const;
  void read(istream & in);
  // ... and other operations ...

 private:
  /***** Data Members *****/
  long myIdNumber;
  string myLastName,
         myFirstName;
  char myMiddleInitial;
  int myAge;
  Date myBirthDay;  // where Date is a user-defined class
  // ... and perhaps other attributes ...
};
```

Now, as we described in the preceding section, there are various ways we could design the classes for the different kinds of licenses. Some programmers who are not familiar with inheritance or who are perhaps working in a non-OOP language will *include* a data member of type License in each class and then add new members for each particular kind of license; for example:

```
class DriversLicense
{
 public:
  /***** Function Members *****/

 private:
  /***** Data Members *****/
  License common;
  int myVehicleType;
  char myRestrictionsCode;
  //... other relevant attributes ...
};
```

But as we noted before, although this inclusion technique works, it is bad design! The structure of these classes says that a DriversLicense object *has a* License as one of its members but it *is not a* License. What is needed is a mechanism by which DriversLicense, HuntingLicense, and PetLicense objects *are* automatically also License objects.

This mechanism is *inheritance*. We *derive* more specialized license classes from the *base class* License, and add new members to store and operate on their specialized attributes:

```
class DriversLicense : public License
{
 public:
  /***** New function members *****/

 private:
  /***** New data members *****/
  int myVehicleType;
  char myRestrictionsCode;
  //... other relevant attributes ...
};

class HuntingLicense : public License
{
 public:
  /***** New function members *****/

 private:
  /***** New data members *****/
```

```
    string thePrey;
    Date seasonBegin,
         season End;
    string myWeapon;
    //... other relevant attributes ...
};

class PetLicense : public License
{
 public:
  /***** New function members *****/

 private:
  /***** New data members *****/
  string myAnimalType;
  //... other relevant attributes ...
};
```

Classes like HuntingLicense, DriversLicense, and PetLicense are said to be **child classes** or **derived classes** or **subclasses,** and the class License from which they are derived is called the **parent class** or **base class** or **superclass.**

Of course, the classes HuntingLicense, DriversLicense, and PetLicense can also serve as parent classes for other classes. For example, the class for deer-hunting licenses could be derived from HuntingLicense:

```
class DeerLicense : public HuntingLicense
{
 public:
  /***** New function members *****/

 private:
  /***** New data members *****/
  int deerLimit;
  string myRegion;
  //... other relevant attributes ...
};
```

The class DeerLicense is called a **descendant** of the class License, which is then an **ancestor** of DeerLicense.

Public, Private, and Protected Sections

Up to now, we have considered only two kinds of sections in a class: public and private. But C++ also provides a **protected section**. The kind of section is specified by preceding it with one of the following three modifiers:

public: Members of a public section can be accessed by any function.

> **private:** Members of a private section can be accessed only by function members and friends of the class.
>
> **protected:** Members of a protected section can be accessed only by function members and friends of the class and its descendants.

Specifying a section to be protected thus provides an intermediate level of access to members between private and public.

The Form of Derived Classes

The general form of a declaration of a derived class is as follows:

Declaration of a Derived Class

Form:

```
DerivedClassName : kind BaseClassName
{
 public:
  /* New function members for derived class */
 private:          // or protected:
  /* New data members for derived class */
};
```

where *kind* is one of the following keywords:

public for **public inheritance**

private for **private inheritance**

protected for **protected inheritance**

The Fundamental Property of Derived Classes

A derived class inherits all the members of a base class (and thus inherits the members of all ancestor classes). It cannot access private members of a base class, and the kind of access it has to public and protected members depends on the kind of inheritance:

Kind of inheritance	Kind of access in the derived class to the public and protected members of the base class
public	public and protected, respectively
private	private
protected	protected

   Public inheritance is the most important and most commonly used kind of inheritance and we will use it in all of our examples. It makes it possible for a derived class to *use public and protected members of the base class just as though they were declared within the derived class itself; a derived-class object is a parent-class object.*

The Is-a, Has-a, and Uses-a Relationships Between Classes

The primary idea governing the use of public inheritance is the **is-a relationship**: If a class is derived from a base class

```
class BaseClass : public DerivedClass
{
    // ... members of DerivedClass  ...
};
```

then a *DerivedClass* object inherits all of the members of *BaseClass*. Conceptually (and as far as the C++ compiler is concerned),

> A derived-class object *is a* base-class object.

For example,

> A HuntingLicense *is a* License
>
> A DeerLicense *is a* HuntingLicense
>
> A DeerLicense *is a* License

Public inheritance should be used when and only when analysis of the problem reveals that an is-a relationship exists between objects, that is, when one object is a special case of another object; it should not be used otherwise. It would not be proper, for example, to derive a class PedigreeCertificate from the class License even though it might have data members much like those in PetLicense, because a pedigree certificate *is not a* license. *Using public inheritance merely to avoid some code writing is not acceptable.*

Other relationships besides *is-a* may exist between objects in a problem. For example, one of the data members of class License is myBirthdate of type Date, which is a user-defined class; that is, a License *has a* Date object as one of its members. This is an example of a **has-a relationship** between classes (also called an **inclusion** or **containment** relationship or **class composition**). We might picture it in our class-hierarchy diagram by using a different kind of arrow connecting classes License and Date:

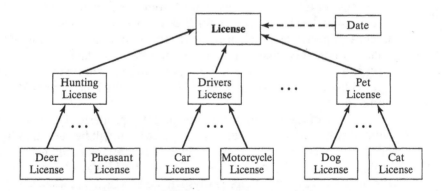

The property that derived classes inherit the members of ancestor classes can easily be misused. For example, it is bad design to derive an AirlinePilot class from the `License` class just to get the members of one class into another class:

Not Acceptable:

```
class AirlinePilot : public License // NO!!!
{ . . . };
```

Rather, an airline pilot *has a* license, so including a data member of type `License` in class `AirlinePilot` is appropriate for implementing this *has-a* relationship:

Acceptable:

```
class AirlinePilot
{
  . . .
 private:
  /***** Data members *****/
  License myPilotsLicense;
  . . .
};
```

Public inheritance should not be used for has-a relationships between classes.

A third kind of relationship between classes is the **uses-a relationship**. A class might simply use another class. For example, one of the operations in a class `AutoInsurance` might need information from a person's drivers license. To obtain this information, an object of type `DriversLicense` might be passed to this operation. The class `AutoInsurance` therefore *uses* the `DriversLicense` class, but it is not a `DriversLicense` nor does it have a `DriversLicense` data member.

Sometimes, however, it is not so easy to determine which of these relationships (if any) hold between objects in a problem. Two other tests are sometimes helpful in this regard.[1] Suppose that we are trying to decide whether to derive a class *B* from a class *A*. One test is to look at the operations in the objects.

1. Do the operations of the proposed base class *A* behave properly in the proposed derived class *B*?

If the answer is "Yes," then deriving *B* from *A* is probably appropriate. For example, in designing the class hierarchy for licenses, one would most likely find that all of the `License` operations perform properly for hunting licenses. It may be necessary, of course, to modify some of them to process new data members; for example, a `License` output operation will output correct information for `HuntingLicense` objects but will need to be extended to output the kind of prey, the hunting season, and so on.

If some of the operations do not perform properly, then one must question the suitability of deriving *B* from *A*. In some cases, it will be clear that inheritance is not appropriate. For example, most pet license operations would not work correctly with pedigree certificates, so deriving `PedigreeCertificate` from `PetLicense` is out of the question. However, there always will be borderline cases in which one must evaluate just how well *A* operations work with *B* objects.

---

[1] Thanks to Ralph Ewton for passing these along.

A second test that is useful in determining whether a class for *B* objects should be derived from a class for *A* objects is a *need-a . . . use-a* test:

2. If all you need is an *A* object, can you use a *B* object?

For example, if all you need is a license to pay for groceries with a check, board an airplane, and so on, can you use a drivers license? Yes, so the class `DriversLicense` class can be derived from the `License` class. If all you need is a pet license, can you use a dog license? Yes, so the `DogLicense` class can be derived from the `PetLicense` class. If all you need is a license, can you use a pedigree certificate? No, so deriving a class `PedigreeCertificate` from a class `License` is not appropriate. If all you need is a license, can you use an airline pilot? No, so one should not derive a class `AirlinePilot` from the class `License`.

✔ Quick Quiz 14.2

1. The method of achieving reusability that most distinguishes OOP from other approaches is based on _____.

2. List the main steps in OOD.

3. Members of a base class declared as _____ cannot be accessed in a derived class.

4. Members of a base class declared as _____ can be accessed in a derived class but not by other classes or programs.

5. Protected inheritance is the most common kind of inheritance. (True or false)

6. The primary idea governing the use of public inheritance is the _____ relationship.

⌨ Exercises 14.2

1. Contrast public, private, and protected inheritance.

2. Contrast the *is-a*, *has-a*, and *uses-a* relationships between classes.

For Exercises 3–18, determine which of the following best describes the relationship between the given objects: *is-a*, *has-a*, *uses-a*, none of the preceding.

3. Lines and rectangles

4. Squares and rectangles

5. Triangles and rectangles

6. Students at Universal University and GPAs

7. Students and the library at Universal University

8. Professors and employees at Universal University

9. Employees and persons at Universal University

10. Stacks and queues

11. Stacks and ADTs

12. Binary trees and trees

13. Binary trees and binary search trees

14. `vectors` and containers

15. Computers and electronic equipment

14.3 Building Derived Classes

There are several issues that arise from implementing in code an object-oriented design that involves a class hierarchy. We will address them in this section and in Section 14.5. The first two stem from the property stated in the Fundamental Property of Derived Classes that, even though a derived class inherits all the members of its parent class, the private members it inherits cannot be accessed by function members of the derived class.

Derived Class Constructors

The first issue deals with constructors in a derived class. They can initialize data members added to the derived class, but how can they initialize the private data members inherited from the parent class when they are not permitted to access them? The solution is to access them through the public constructors provided by the parent class.

Specifically, we use the parent class's constructors to initialize the base class members, and use derived class constructors to initialize new data members in the derived class. A constructor of a derived class can invoke a constructor of its parent class in its member-initializer list. For example, the DriversLicense class constructor could be defined as follows:

```
DriversLicense::DriversLicense
    ( unsigned idNumber, string lastName, string firstName,
      char midInitial, int age, Date birth,
      int vehicleCode, char restriction )
  : License(idNumber, lastName, firstName,
            midInitial, age, birth),
    myVehicleCode(vehicleCode),
    myRestrictionsCode(restriction)
{ }
```

The first six initial values in the parameter list are passed as arguments to the License constructor, which uses them to initialize its data members; then the DriversLicense constructor uses the remaining initial values to initialize the new data members myVehicleCode and myRestrictionsCode.

Accessing Inherited Data Members

The second issue arises when a class needs to access or modify a data member it inherits from some ancestor class. If the ancestor class declares this data member to be public, then the descendant can modify it, but so can any other user of the class. If the ancestor declares the data members to be private, then users of the class are prevented from accessing them, but so are descendant classes.

A simple solution used by some programmers is simply to change the sections containing these data members from private sections to protected sections in classes that serve as base classes. This makes it possible for function members and friends of derived classes and their descendants to access and modify these data members, but they are still protected from all other functions. But it also means that some descendant class can change a data member in an ancestor class without the new value being validated, which may result in a violation of the class invariant for that ancestor. For example, a DeerLicense object could put an invalid id number in its inherited myIdNumber data member.

A preferred solution, and the one that we will use, is to always *keep data members in a private section, and if changes to some data member by derived classes and their descendants is to be permitted, then provide a protected mutator for it.* For example, if we wanted to allow classes DriversLicense, HuntingLicense, DeerLicense, and other descendants of the License class to modify the id number of one of these licenses, we could add a protected section to the License class that declares a mutator setIdNumber():

```
class License          // base class
{
 public:
  /***** Function Members *****/
  void display(ostream & out) const;
  void read(istream & in);
  // ... and other operations ...

 protected:
  void setIdNumber(long newNumber);
  /* This will check if newNumber is a legal id number */

 private:
  /***** Data Members *****/
  long myIdNumber;
  string myLastName,
         myFirstName;
  char myMiddleInitial;
  int myAge;
  Date myBirthDay;  // where Date is a user-defined class
  // ... and perhaps other attributes ...
};
```

By requiring a descendant class to access private data through a mutator, we can ensure the validity of any new value by having the mutator check it.

Reusing Operations

A derived class inherits the members of its ancestor classes and adds new members for the specialized characteristics of the objects being modeled. Although the inherited data members usually should not be modified in the derived class, the inherited member functions can be redefined if necessary. A member function in a derived class might *extend* a member function from an ancestor class so that it performs additional tasks or it might *replace* an ancestor member function so that it performs different tasks.[2]

In extending a member function f() of an ancestor class, a descendant class can reuse the work of this function by using a qualified call of the form Ancestor::f(). To illustrate, suppose that class License has an output member function named display():

```
void License::display(ostream & out) const
{
    out << myIdNum << " "
        << myFirstName << " " << myMiddleInitial << ". "
        << myLastName
        << "\nAge: " << myAge << "  Birthdate: "
        << myBirthDate;    // assumes << defined for Date
}
```

For example, if aLicense is of type License, the message aLicense.display(cout); might produce the following output:

```
101011 Betty B. Binary
Age: 36  Birthdate: 6/6/1968
```

Then, in our derived classes, we can extend display() with new definitions that reuse the display() function of class License:

```
void HuntingLicense::display(ostream & out) const
{
    License::display(out);          // inherited members
    out << "\nPrey: " << thePrey    // local members
        << "\nSeason: "
        << seasonBegin << " - " << seasonEnd
        << "\nWeapon: " << myWeapon;
}
```

```
void DeerLicense::display(ostream & out) const
{
    HuntingLicense::display(out);    //inherited members
    out << "\nLimit: " << deerLimit  //local members
        << "Region: " << myRegion;
}
```

---

[2] Some programming languages do not allow replacement of member functions. Some programmers frown on any modification of inherited member functions because it changes the *is-a* relationship of a derived class to its base class; they argue that virtual functions (described in Section 14.5) were invented for this purpose.

The messages

```
aHuntingLicense.display(cout);
cout << endl;
aDeerLicense.display(cout);
cout << endl;
```

will then produce output like the following:

```
392766 David W. Goliath
Age: 11  Birthdate:  8/18/1994
Prey: Giants
Season: 1/1 - 12/31
Weapon: Sling

1781 Buck C. Doe
Age: 20  Birthdate:  9/9/1984
Prey: Deer
Season: 2/16 - 2/22
Weapon: Bow and Arrow
Limit: 2
Region: Northwest
```

The problem that remains is that if a variable licPtr, a pointer variable of type License *, can refer to any of these three kinds of objects, which of the three versions of display() is to be used? We will address this issue in Section 14.5.

Example: Stacks and Bounded Stacks

In analyzing some problems, we may encounter borderline cases in which the relationship between some of the problem's objects is not clear; is it *is-a, has-a, uses-a*, or none of these? To illustrate, suppose that some application requires the use of stacks having a limited capacity and we must design a class template BoundedStack for these objects. We already have at our disposal STL's stack container along with several stack classes that we have developed in earlier chapters. But what is the relationship of a bounded stack to stacks?

Is a bounded stack also a stack? If so we can derive BoundedStack from one of these stack classes. A bounded stack will obviously need the same data members as a stack and a new data member for the bound on the stack size. Also, the empty, top, and pop operations are the same for bounded stacks as for stacks, but the push operation is not. If the bounded stack becomes full, there is no room to push a new item onto it, and so we will need a different push operation. Because of this difference, some might argue that a bounded stack is not a stack, and inheritance is therefore not a good idea.

On the other hand, push is the only stack operation that will be different in bounded stacks and the required modification can be viewed as an extension of the stack push operation rather than a wholesale replacement:

If the bounded stack is not full,
    Push the item onto the bounded stack using the stack push operation.
Otherwise
    Display an overflow message.

One could thus argue that a bounded stack is a stack with special properties and inheritance is therefore appropriate.

We will opt for the second approach and derive a class template BoundedStack from a class template version of our linked stack in Section 7.3. (This version is available in the source code for Chapter 14 on the text's website—see *Chap14/ Figure14.1*.) BoundedStack will then inherit the data members (including the underlying default deque container) and the function members from Stack. We will add a new data member myLimit to store the limit on the size of a bounded stack, and this means that we will also need a BoundedStack constructor to initialize it. We will also need to revise the push() operation. Figure 14.1 shows the BoundedStack class template.

Figure 14.1 BoundedStack—Interface

```
#include <iostream>
#include "LStackT.h"          // A class template version of our
                              // linked stack class from Section 7.3
#ifndef BOUNDED_STACK
#define BOUNDED_STACK
template <typename ElementType>
class BoundedStack : public Stack<ElementType>
{
 public:
  /***** Function Members *****/
  BoundedStack(int limit = 0);
. /* --- Constructor ------------------------------------------------
    Precondition:  limit (default 0) is an upper bound on the size of the
        bounded stack.
    Postcondition: A BoundedStack has been constructed as an empty stack
        with mySize initialized to 0 and myLimit initialized to limit
        (default 0).
    ------------------------------------------------------------------*/

  void push(const ElementType & value);
  /*--- Add a value to the stack if there is room ----------------------
    Precondition:  None.
    Postcondition: value was added at the top of this BoundedStack and
        mySize was incremented by 1 provided there was room; if there
        wasn't, an overflow message was displayed.
    ------------------------------------------------------------------*/
```

Figure 14.1 (continued)

```
private:
  /***** Data Members *****/
    int mySize,
        myLimit;
};   // end of class template declaration

//--- Definition of Constructor ---
template <typename ElementType>
inline BoundedStack<ElementType>::BoundedStack(int limit)
: Stack<ElementType>(), mySize(0), myLimit(limit)
{ }

//--- Definition of push() ---
template <typename ElementType>
inline void BoundedStack<ElementType>::push(const ElementType & value)
{
  if (mySize < myLimit)
  {
    Stack<ElementType>::push(value);
    mySize++;
  }
  else
    cerr << "*** Bounded stack overflow ***\n";
}

#endif
```

▲

To illustrate the use of this derived class BoundedStack, we consider a modification of the base-conversion problem in Section 7.1 of converting positive integers from their decimal representation to binary representation. The algorithm for carrying out this conversion uses repeated division by 2 with the successive remainders giving the binary digits in the base-two representation from right to left. A stack is used to store these remainders so they can be displayed in the correct order once the conversion is complete.

Now consider the modified problem of converting integers to binary, but in which there is a limit on the number of bits allowed in the base-two representation. For example, we may be interested in binary representations that will fit in 2 bytes—that is, representations with at most 16 bits. This means that if the size of the stack used to store the digits of the base-two representation exceeds this limit, an overflow occurs. A BoundedStack is therefore an appropriate container to use for these bits. Figure 14.2 shows the program that results by replacing a Stack in the program in Figure 7.2 with a BoundedStack.

Figure 14.2 Conversion from Base 10 to Base 2 Using a BoundedStack

```
/*-------------------------------------------------------------------------
  Program to convert the base-ten representation of a positive integer to
  base two.  A BoundedStack stores the remainders produced by the repeated-
  division algorithm.
  -----------------------------------------------------------------------*/

#include <iostream>
using namespace std;
#include "BoundedStack.h"

int main()
{
  const int STACK_BOUND = 16;          // bound on number of stack elements
  unsigned number,                     // the number to be converted
           remainder;                  // remainder of number divided by 2
  char response;                       // user response
  do
  {
    BoundedStack<short int>
      stackOfRemainders(STACK_BOUND);  // bounded stack of remainders
    cout << "Enter positive integer to convert: ";
    cin >> number;
    while (number != 0)
    {
      remainder = number % 2;
      stackOfRemainders.push(remainder);
      number /= 2;
    }
    cout << "Base-two representation: ";
    while (!stackOfRemainders.empty())
    {
      remainder = stackOfRemainders.top();
      stackOfRemainders.pop();
      cout << remainder;
    }
    cout << endl;
```

Figure 14.2 (continued)

```
    cout << "WARNING:  If a bounded stack overflow occurred,\n"
            "                some bits are missing in the representation.\n";

    cout << "\nMore (Y or N)? ";
    cin >> response;
  }
  while (response == 'Y' || response == 'y');
}
```

Execution Trace:

```
Enter positive integer to convert: 999
Base-two representation: 1111100111
WARNING:  If a bounded stack overflow occurred,
          some bits are missing in the representation.

More (Y or N)? Y
Enter positive integer to convert: 9999
Base-two representation: 10011100001111
WARNING:  If a bounded stack overflow occurred,
          some bits are missing in the representation.

More (Y or N)? Y
Enter positive integer to convert: 99999
*** Bounded stack overflow ***
Base-two representation: 1000011010011111
WARNING:  If a bounded stack overflow occurred,
          some bits are missing in the representation.

More (Y or N)? N
```

▲

14.4 Case Study: Payroll

One of the standard examples used to illustrate class hierarchies and the basic ideas of object-oriented programming is modeling the payroll for a company with various kinds of employees.

Problem

Dooflingy, Inc. has several categories of employees—hourly employees, salaried employees, salespersons paid on commission, contract workers, to name but a few—and biweekly pay is computed differently for each category. We have been asked to develop a payroll system for this company.

Design

Following the steps of object-oriented design, we might proceed as follows:

1. Identify the objects in the problem. We will begin with just two employee categories:

   - Salaried employees
   - Hourly employees

2. Look for *commonality* in those objects. What attributes do they share? Initially, we will use only the following three attributes:

   - Id number
   - Name
   - Department

3. Define a *base class* containing the common data members (see Figure 14.3 for definitions of the functions):

```
class Employee
{
 public:
  //--- Constructor
  Employee(long id = 0, string last = "",
           string first = "", char initial = ' ',
           int dept = 0);
  //--- Output
  void display(ostream & out) const;

  // ... Other employee operations ...

 private:
  long myIdNum;              // Employee's id number
  string myLastName,         //     "       last name
         myFirstName;        //     "       first name
  char myMiddleInitial;      //     "       middle initial
  int myDeptCode;            //     "       department code
  // ... other attributes common to all employees
};
```

4. From the *base* class, *derive* classes containing special attributes. Inheritance is appropriate here because, obviously, a salaried employee *is an* employee and an hourly employee *is an* employee. (See Figure 14.3 for definitions of the functions.)

   - A salaried employee class:

```
class SalariedEmployee : public Employee
{
 public:
   //--- Constructor
```

```
SalariedEmployee (long id = 0, string last = "",
                  string first = "", char initial = ' ',
                  int dept = 0, double salary = 0);
//--- Output
void display(ostream & out) const;

// ... Other salaried employee operations ...

private:
 double mySalary;
};
```

- An hourly employee class:

```
class HourlyEmployee : public Employee
{
 public:
  //--- Constructor
  HourlyEmployee (long id = 0, string last = "",
                  string first = "",char initial = ' ',
                  int dept = 0, double weeklyWage = 0,
                  double hoursWorked = 0,
                  double overTimeFactor = 1.5);
  //--- Output
  void display(ostream & out) const;

  // ... Other hourly employee operations ...

 private:
  double myWeeklyWage,
         myHoursWorked,
         myOverTimeFactor;
};
```

Eventually, we would add derived classes for the other employee categories, and probably the categories we have used might lead to other categories, resulting in a class hierarchy like the following:

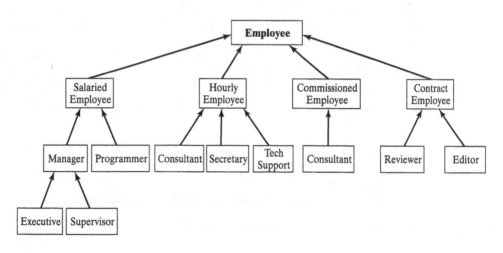

Each of the classes that has `Employee` as an ancestor inherits all of the data members and function members from the base class `Employee`. For example, each `HourlyEmployee` and `Manager` object is an `Employee` object so each contains the members `myIdNum`, `myLastName`, `myFirstName`, and so on. So, if `Employee` has a public operation to extract `myIdNum`,

```
long Employee::getIdNumber() const { return myIdNum; }
```

then it can be used by hourly employees and managers:

```
HourlyEmployee hourlyEmp;
Manager managerEmp;
cout << hourlyEmp.getIdNumber() << endl
     << managerEmp.getIdNumber() << endl;
```

Figure 14.3 shows all of the three classes `Employee`, `SalariedEmployee`, and `HourlyEmployee`, including definitions of their constructors and output functions. Also shown is a small driver program to test the classes and the output produced by it. Note how the `SalariedEmployee` and `HourlyEmployee` constructors use the `Employee` constructor in the manner described in the preceding section to initialize the data members they inherit from their parent: `myIdNum`, `myLastName`, `myFirst-Name`, `myMiddleInitial`, and `myDeptCode`. For example, here is the definition of the `SalariedEmployee` constructor:

```
inline SalariedEmployee::SalariedEmployee(
                    long id, string last, string first,
                    char initial, int dept, double sal)
  : Employee(id, last, first, initial, dept),
    mySalary(sal)
{ }
```

The values of the parameters `id`, `last`, `first`, `initial`, and `dept` are passed to the `Employee` constructor in the function call in the initializer list, which will use those values to initialize the data members `myIdNum`, `myLastName`, `myFirstName`, `myMid-dleInitial`, and `myDeptCode`, respectively. The only task for the constructor in `SalariedEmployee` is to initialize its new member `mySalary`, which it does in the usual way.

Also note how `Employee`'s `display()` is reused in the `display()` functions of the `SalariedEmployee` and `HourlyEmployee` classes to output the data members they inherit from `Employee`. The method for doing this also was described in the preceding section. For example, here is the definition of `SalariedEmployee`'s `display()` member:

```
void SalariedEmployee::display(ostream & out) const
{
  Employee::display(out);            //inherited members
  out << "$" << mySalary << endl;   //local members
}
```

Figure 14.3 Employee Class Hierarchy—Version 1

```
/* Employee.h ------------------------------------------------------------
   Header file for a class Employee that encapsulates the attributes common
   to all employees.
   Operations are:  A constructor and an output operation.
   ---------------------------------------------------------------------*/

#include <iostream>

#ifndef EMPLOYEE
#define EMPLOYEE

class Employee
{
 public:
   Employee(long id = 0, string last = "", string first = "",
            char initial = ' ', int dept = 0);
  /*------------------------------------------------------------------
    Employee constructor.
    Preconditions:  None.
    Postconditions: myIdNum is initialized to id (default 0), myLastName
        to last (default empty string), myFirstName to first (default
        empty string), myMiddleInitial to initial (default blank char),
        and myDeptCode to dept (default 0).
    ----------------------------------------------------------------*/

   void display(ostream & out) const;
  /*------------------------------------------------------------------
    Output function member.
    Precondition:  ostream out is open.
    Postcondition: A text representation of this Employee object has
        been output to out.
    ----------------------------------------------------------------*/

   // ... Other employee operations ...

 private:
   long myIdNum;            // Employee's id number
   string myLastName,       //    "      last name
          myFirstName;      //    "      first name
   char myMiddleInitial;    //    "      middle initial
```

Figure 14.3 (continued)

```
  int myDeptCode;                //     "      department code
  // ... other attributes common to all employees
};


//--- Definition of Employee's Constructor
inline Employee::Employee(long id, string last, string first,
                          char initial, int dept)
  : myIdNum(id), myLastName(last), myFirstName(first),
    myMiddleInitial(initial), MyDeptCode(dept)
  { }

//--- Definition of Employee's display()
inline void Employee::display(ostream & out) const
{
  out << myIdNum << ' ' << myLastName << ", "
      << myFirstName << ' ' << myMiddleInitial << "   "
      << myDeptCode << endl;
}

//--- Definition of output operator <<
inline ostream & operator<<(ostream & out, const Employee & emp)
{
  emp.display(out);
  return out;
};

#endif
```

▬▬▬▬▬▬▬▬▬▬▬▬▬▬▬▬▬▬▬▬▬▬▬▬▬▬▬▬▬▬▬▬▬▬▬▬▬▬▬

```
/* SalariedEmployee.h ------------------------------------------------
   Header file for a class SalariedEmployee derived from Employee that
   adds the attributes unique to salaried employees.
   Operations are:  A constructor and an output operation.
   --------------------------------------------------------------------*/
#include "Employee.h"
```

Figure 14.3 (continued)

```
#ifndef SALARIED_EMPLOYEE
#define SALARIED_EMPLOYEE

class SalariedEmployee : public Employee
{
 public:
   SalariedEmployee (long id = 0, string last = "",
                     string first = "", char initial = ' ',
                     int dept = 0, double salary = 0);
  /*-----------------------------------------------------------------
    Salaried Employee constructor.
    Preconditions:  None.
    Postconditions: Data members myIdNum, myLastName, myFirstName,
       myMiddleInitial, and myDeptCode are initialized by the Employee
       constructor; mySalary is initialized to salary (default 0).
    ----------------------------------------------------------------*/

   void display(ostream & out) const;
  /*-----------------------------------------------------------------
    Output function member.
    Precondition:   ostream out is open.
    Postcondition: A text representation of this SalariedEmployee
       object has been output to out.
    ----------------------------------------------------------------*/

   // ... Other salaried employee operations ...

 private:
  double mySalary;
};

//--- Definition of SalariedEmployee's Constructor
inline SalariedEmployee::SalariedEmployee
                  (long id, string last, string first, char initial,
                   int dept, double sal)
: Employee(id, last, first, initial, dept),
  mySalary(sal)
{ }
```

Figure 14.3 (continued)

```
//--- Definition of SalariedEmployee's display()
inline void SalariedEmployee::display(ostream & out) const
{
  Employee::display(out);              //inherited members
  out << "$" << mySalary << endl;      //local members
}
#endif
```

```
/* HourlyEmployee.h -------------------------------------------------
    Header file for a class HourlyEmployee derived from Employee that
    adds the attributes unique to hourly employees.
    Operations are:  A constructor and an output operation.
    --------------------------------------------------------------*/
#include "Employee.h"

#ifndef HOURLY_EMPLOYEE
#define HOURLY_EMPLOYEE

class HourlyEmployee : public Employee
{
 public:
   HourlyEmployee (long id = 0, string last = "", string first = "",
                   char initial = ' ', int dept = 0, double weeklyWage = 0,
                   double hoursWorked = 0, double overTimeFactor = 1.5);
   /*-------------------------------------------------------------
     Hourly Employee constructor.
     Preconditions:  None.
     Postconditions: Data members myIdNum, myLastName, myFirstName,
        myMiddleInitial, and myDeptCode are initialized by the Employee
        constructor; myWeeklyWage is initialized to weeklyWage (default
        0), myHoursWorked to hoursWorked (default 0), and
        myOverTimeFactor to overTimeFactor (default 1.5).
     -------------------------------------------------------------*/

   void display(ostream & out) const;
   /*-------------------------------------------------------------
     Output function member.
```

Figure 14.3 (continued)

```
        Precondition:  ostream out is open.
        Postcondition: A text representation of this HourlyEmployee
            object has been output to out.
        ------------------------------------------------------------------*/


    // ... Other hourly employee operations ...

 private:
   double myWeeklyWage,
          myHoursWorked,
          myOverTimeFactor;
};


//--- Definition of HourlyEmployee's Constructor
inline HourlyEmployee::HourlyEmployee
                    (long id, string last, string first, char initial,
                     int dept, double weeklyWage, double hoursWorked,
                     double overTimeFactor)
 : Employee(id, last, first, initial, dept),
   myWeeklyWage(weeklyWage), myHoursWorked(hoursWorked),
   myOverTimeFactor(overTimeFactor)
{ }


//--- Definition of HourlyEmployee's display()
inline void HourlyEmployee::display(ostream & out) const
{
   Employee::display(out);                   //inherited members
   out << "$" << myWeeklyWage << endl    //local members
       << myHoursWorked << endl
       << myOverTimeFactor << endl;
}
#endif
```

```
/*------------------------------------------------------------------
   Driver program to test Employee class and derived classes
   SalariedEmployee and HourlyEmployee.
   ------------------------------------------------------------------*/

#include <iostream>
using namespace std;
```

Figure 14.3 (continued)

```
#include "Employee.h"
#include "SalariedEmployee.h"
#include "HourlyEmployee.h"

int main()
{
  Employee emp(11111, "Doe", "John", 'J', 11);
  SalariedEmployee empSal(22222, "Smith", "Mary", 'M', 22, 59900);
  HourlyEmployee empHr(33333, "Jones", "Jay", 'J', 33, 15.25, 40);

  emp.display(cout); cout << endl;
  empSal.display(cout); cout << endl;
  empHr.display(cout); cout << endl;
}
```

Execution Trace:

```
11111 Doe, John J   11

22222 Smith, Mary M   22
$59900

33333 Jones, Jay J   33
$15.25
40
1.5
```

▲

14.5 Polymorphism, Virtual Functions, and ADTs

The third characteristic of object-oriented programming is *polymorphism*. We gave a rather imprecise description of it in the first section of this chapter, because we had not yet described the inheritance mechanism in C++. Now, however, we can explain what polymorphism is, why it is needed, and how it is accomplished.

Why Polymorphism is Needed: a Binding Problem

The Employee class of the preceding section has two function members: a constructor and a display() function. If you examine the code in Figure 14.3 more closely, however, you will note that we also overloaded the output operator for this class:

```
//--- Definition of output operator <<
inline ostream & operator<<(ostream & out,
                                 const Employee & emp)
{
  emp.display(out);
  return out;
};
```

You may be curious about why we didn't use it in the driver program; that is, why we used

```
emp.display(cout); cout << endl;
empSal.display(cout); cout << endl;
empHr.display(cout); cout << endl;
```

to display the values of the Employee object emp, the SalariedEmployee object empSal, and the HourlyEmployee object empHr instead of the more convenient

```
cout << emp << endl << empSal << endl << empHr << endl;
```

One might first think that a compile-time error would result because we did not overload the output operator for the derived classes SalariedEmployee and Hour-lymployee. But this does not happen because of the *is-a* relationship. Every Sala-riedEmployee object *is an* Employee object, which means that because << can output Employee objects, it can also output SalariedEmployee objects such as emp-Sal. Similarly, every HourlyEmployee object *is an* Employee object, which means that << can also output HourlyEmployee objects such as empHr. But there is a problem. If this replacement is made in the driver program of Figure 14.3, the output produced is

```
11111 Doe, John J   11

22222 Smith, Mary M   22

33333 Jones, Jay J   33
```

instead of the correct output

```
11111 Doe, John J   11

22222 Smith, Mary M   22
$59900

33333 Jones, Jay J   33
$15.25
40
1.5
```

None of the values of the new data members in `empSal` or `empHr` were displayed, but only the values of the data members inherited from `Employee`.

This happens because the definition of `operator<<()` for the `Employee` class in Figure 14.3 sends the `display()` message to an `Employee` object:

```
inline ostream & operator<<(ostream & out,
                                    const Employee & emp)
{
  emp.display(out);
  return out;
};
```

As a result, the compiler *binds* this function call `emp.display(out);` to the definition of `display()` for the `Employee` class. Any call to `operator<<()` for a SalariedEmployee object, an `Hourlymployee` object, a `Manager` object, or any other object whose type is a descendant of `Employee` must use this same code, which means that the wrong version of `display()` is being used.

Based on what we have learned about C++, it seems that we have no recourse but to reinvent the wheel many times and overload `<<` for each class in the hierarchy. The code in each case would be almost identical, the only difference being the type of the parameter `emp`. Fortunately, there is an alternative: make the output operator `<<` behave in different ways for the various kinds of objects—that is, make it *polymorphic*. Accomplishing this requires a new feature of C++.

Virtual Functions and Dynamic Binding

What is needed is a mechanism that will use the appropriate version of `display()` when it is called in `operator<<()`. For an `Employee` object we want `Employee::display()` to be used, but for a `SalariedEmployee` object, we want `SalariedEmployee::display()` to be used and for an `HourlyEmployee` object, we want `HourlyEmployee::display()` to be used; for a `Manager`, we want `Manager::display()` to be used; and so on. This means, however, that a specific definition of `display()` cannot be bound at compile time to the call to `display()` that is in `operator<<()`. Rather, this must be *deferred until run time*; that is, the selection of which version of `display()` to use must be made *during execution*, when the type of the object can be determined.

This **dynamic (or late) binding** is accomplished in C++ by using **virtual functions**. One common way this is done is to have the compiler create a **virtual function table** (**vtbl**) for each object containing virtual functions; this is a table of pointers to the actual code for these functions. When execution reaches a call to a virtual function for some object, the index for this function in the object's vtbl is used to find the pointer to the correct function code for that type of object.

What is needed to make the function `operator<<()` work correctly is to make `display()` a virtual function in the base class `Employee`. In C++, a member function is declared to be virtual simply by preceding its prototype in the class declaration with the keyword **virtual**. Figure 14.4 shows the modified class `Employee` and driver program.

Figure 14.4 Employee Class Hierarchy—Version 2

```
/* Employee.h --------------------------------------------------------
                    See Figure 14.3 for documentation
   ------------------------------------------------------------------*/
#include <iostream>

#ifndef EMPLOYEE
#define EMPLOYEE

class Employee
{
 public:
   Employee(long id = 0, string last = "", string first = "",
        char initial = ' ', int dept = 0);
   //-- See Figure 14.3 for documentation

   virtual void display(ostream & out) const;
   //-- See Figure 14.3 for documentation

   // ... Other employee operations ...

 private:
   long myIdNum;              // Employee's id number
   string myLastName,         //     "       last name
          myFirstName;        //     "       first name
   char myMiddleInitial;      //     "       middle initial
   int myDeptCode;            //     "       department code
   // ... other attributes common to all employees
};


//--- Definition of Employee's Constructor
inline Employee::Employee(long id, string last, string first,
                        char initial, int dept)
  : myIdNum(id), myLastName(last), myFirstName(first),
    myMiddleInitial(initial), MyDeptCode(dept)
  { }
```

Figure 14.4 (continued)

```cpp
//--- Definition of Employee's display()
void Employee::display(ostream & out) const
{
   out << myIdNum << ' ' << myLastName << ", "
       << myFirstName << ' ' << myMiddleInitial << "   "
       << myDeptCode << endl;
}


//--- Definition of output operator <<
inline ostream & operator<<(ostream & out, const Employee & emp)
{
   emp.display(out);
   return out;
};


#endif
```

```
/* In this example, SalariedEmployee.h and HourlyEmployee.h can be
   the same as in Figure 14.3.  In practice, however, their display()
   function members are usually also declared to be virtual so that
   classes derived from them will perform correctly. */
```

```cpp
/*------------------------------------------------------------------
   Driver program to test Employee class and derived classes
   SalariedEmployee and HourlyEmployee.
 -------------------------------------------------------------*/
#include <iostream>
using namespace std;
#include "Employee.h"
#include "SalariedEmployee.h"
#include "HourlyEmployee.h"

int main()
{
   Employee emp(11111, "Doe", "John", 'J', 11);
   SalariedEmployee empSal(22222, "Smith", "Mary", 'M', 22, 59900);
   HourlyEmployee empHr(33333, "Jones", "Jay", 'J', 33, 15.25, 40);
```

Figure 14.4 (continued)

```
  cout << emp << endl << empSal << endl << empHr << endl;
}
```

Execution Trace:

```
11111 Doe, John J   11

22222 Smith, Mary M   22
$59900

33333 Jones, Jay J   33
$15.25
40
1.5
```

▲

From the trace of the execution of the driver program, we see that the output statement

```
    cout << emp << endl << empSal << endl << empHr << endl;
```

produces the correct output. It uses

> `Employee::display()` for `Employee` objects
> `SalariedEmployee::display()` for `SalariedEmployee` objects
> `HourlyEmployee::display()` for `HourlyEmployee` objects

Here we clearly see polymorphism ("many forms") in action: The same function call can cause different effects at different times, based on the function definition to which the call is bound.

We see that, thanks to public inheritance, virtual functions, and dynamic binding, we can use << for derived class objects without explicitly overloading it for each of those classes! The definitions of `display()` in the derived classes **override** the virtual version in the base class `Employee`, and applying << to derived class objects will select the correct versions of `display()`. We should also note that this is an advantage of defining `operator<<()` so that it calls some output function member of a class rather than making it a friend function.

If no definition of `display()` is provided in a derived class, then the definition from the base class `License` will be used. In general, we have the following property of virtual functions:

> *The definition of a virtual function in a base class serves as a default definition. It will be used in any derived class in which the definition is not overridden.*

Example 1: Using Handles

A **handle** for an object is a variable whose value is the address of that object; that is, it is a pointer variable. Instead of having the object as its value, it refers to the object *indirectly*. For example, the value of the variable emp declared by

```
Employee emp;
```

is an Employee object, whereas, the statement

```
Employee * eptr;
```

defines eptr as a handle for an Employee object; dereferencing this handle with *eptr yields the actual object itself.

The important property of handles in the context of class hierarchies is the following:

> *A handle for a class object can also refer to any derived class object; that is, a pointer declared by ClassName * ptr can point to any object of type ClassName or any descendant of ClassName.*

This means that eptr can point to any Employee object,

```
eptr = new Employee(11111, "John", "Doe", 'J', 11);
```

to any SalariedEmployee object,

```
eptr = new SalariedEmployee(22222, "Smith", "Mary", 'M',
                            22, 59900);
```

to any HourlyEmployee object,

```
eptr = new HourlyEmployee(33333, "Jones", "Jay", 'J',
                          33, 15.25, 40);
```

to any Manager object,

```
eptr = new Manager(44444, "Brown", "Betty", 'B', 25,
                   60000, 13)
```

and so on.

For the function call

```
eptr->display(cout);
```

to work correctly, Employee::display(cout) must be used when eptr points to an Employee object; SalariedEmployee::display(cout) must be used when eptr points to a SalariedEmployee object; HourlyEmployee::display(cout) must be used when eptr points to a HourlyEmployee object; Manager::display(cout) must be used when eptr points to a Manager object; and so on. Here is another instance, therefore, where display() must be a virtual function so that this function call can be bound to different function definitions at different times. We will use this feature in the linked-list example of the next section.

Example 2: Stacks and Bounded Stacks

As another illustration of a problem in which virtual functions are needed, suppose we wish to add a new operation repeatedPush() to each of the class templates Stack and BoundedStack from Section 14.3, which can be used to push more than one copy of an element onto an object of one of these types. The code for this function template is the same for each class:

```
template <typename TypeParam>
inline void ClassName::repeatedPush(
                      const TypeParam & value, int number)
{
  for (int i = 1; i <= number; i++)
    push(value);
}
```

So we might add this function template to the base Stack class and let the derived class BoundedStack inherit it:

```
// Add to public function members of class Stack in LStackT.h

void repeatedPush(const StackElement & value, int number);

//--- Add to function definitions in LStackT.h
template <typename StackElement>
inline void Stack<StackElement>::repeatedPush(
                      const StackElement & value, int number)
{
  for (int i = 1; i <= number; i++)
    push(value);
}
```

As we might expect from the employee example, this does not work. To demonstrate this, we consider a variation of the base-conversion problem of the preceding section, in which all of the binary representations must have the same number of bits; for example, 16 bits are commonly used to store short integers and 32 bits are used for long integers. The program in Figure 14.2 can easily be modified to obtain such representations. We need only count the bits as they are generated and then use repeatedPush() to push the required number of leading zeros onto the stack of remainders, by sending the message

```
stackOfRemainders.repeatedPush(0, numBits - count)
```

where count is the number of bits generated and stored in the bounded stack and numBits is the total number of bits in the binary representation. The program in Figure 14.5 uses this approach to obtain such representations.

Figure 14.5 Conversion from Base 10 to Base 2 Using a BoundedStack—Version 3

```
/*------------------------------------------------------------------
   Program to convert the base-ten representation of a positive integer
   to base two.  A BoundedStack stores the remainders produced by the
   repeated-division algorithm.
   ----------------------------------------------------------------*/
#include <iostream>
using namespace std;
#include "BoundedStack.h"

int main()
{
  const int STACK_BOUND = 16;     // bound on number of stack elements
  int numBits;                    // number of bits in binary rep.
  cout << "How many bits do you want in the binary representations? ";
  cin >> numBits;
  unsigned number,                // the number to be converted
           remainder;             // remainder of number divided by 2
  char response;                  // user response
  do
  {
    BoundedStack<unsigned>        // bounded stack of remainders
      stackOfRemainders(STACK_BOUND);
    cout << "Enter positive integer to convert: ";
    cin >> number;
    int count = 0;                // counts bits in binary representation
    while (number != 0)
    {
      remainder = number % 2;
      stackOfRemainders.push(remainder);
      count++;
      number /= 2;
    }
    stackOfRemainders.repeatedPush (0, numBits - count);
    cout << "Base-two representation: ";
```

Figure 14.5 (continued)

```
    while (!stackOfRemainders.empty() )
    {
      remainder = stackOfRemainders.top();
      stackOfRemainders.pop();
      cout << remainder;
    }
    cout << endl;
    cout << "WARNING:  If a bounded stack overflow occurred,\n"
            "                 some bits are missing in the representation.\n";

    cout << "\nMore (Y or N)? ";
    cin >> response;
  }
  while (response == 'Y' || response == 'y');
}
```

Execution Trace:

```
How many bits do you want in the binary representations? 16
Enter positive integer to convert:  63
Base-two representation:  0000000000111111
WARNING:  If a bounded stack overflow occurred,
          some bits are missing in the representation.

More (Y or N)?  N
```

▲

Based on the execution trace in Figure 14.5, we may be tempted to conclude that the program and the class templates Stack and BoundedStack are correct. However, this is not the case, as the following execution shows:

```
How many bits do you want in the binary representations? 24
Enter positive integer to convert:  63
Base-two representation:  000000000000000000111111
WARNING:  If a bounded stack overflow occurred,
          some bits are missing in the representation.

More (Y or N)?  N
```

In the program, BITS_LIMIT was set at 16, which means that no more than 16 elements can ever be pushed onto the BoundedStack object stackOfRemainders. The output clearly indicates, however, that 24 bits were somehow pushed onto the stack, even though the capacity of the stack was exceeded. This happened because the definition of repeatedPush() for the Stack class uses the function push() from this class and consequently, the code generated by the compiler and bound to repeated-Push() contains the code for the function push() in Stack. Any reference to repeatedPush() in the derived class BoundedStack must use this same code, which means that the wrong version of push() is being used, so that the stack limit is ignored when pushing elements onto the stack.

To make the function repeatedPush() work correctly, we need to make push() a virtual function in the base class template Stack:

```
virtual void push(const ElementType & value);
```

If we make this change, then the following output is produced by the program in Figure 14.5:

Execution Trace:

```
How many bits do you want in the binary representations? 24
Enter positive integer to convert: 63
*** Bounded stack overflow ***
*** Bounded stack overflow ***
*** Bounded stack overflow ***
*** Bounded stack overflow ***
*** Bounded stack overflow ***
*** Bounded stack overflow ***
*** Bounded stack overflow ***
*** Bounded stack overflow ***
Base-two representation: 0000000000111111
WARNING:  If a bounded stack overflow occurred,
          some bits are missing in the representation.

More (Y or N)? N
```

This output shows that repeatedPush() for objects of type BoundedStack now uses the definition of push() for this derived class. When repeatedPush() attempted to push 18 leading zeros onto the bounded stack stackOfRemainders, the function push() for bounded stacks was called 18 times, and the last 8 calls produced a message that the stack limit was exceeded. The 16 bits in the final base-two representation rather than the 24 bits obtained before also demonstrate that the correct method push() has been used.

Pure Virtual Functions and Abstract Classes

Most classes like those we have been considering—License, Employee, and Stack—have the property that they themselves model real-world things, and objects of these types are useful for processing such entities. But these classes can also serve as base classes from which other useful classes can be derived. Sometimes, however, it is convenient to have *classes for which no objects can exist*. They represent only abstract concepts and are thus called *abstract classes*. They can *only* serve as base classes from which other classes can be derived. For example, in a hierarchy of classes for drawing geometric figures, we might have a base class Figure containing some of the common operations such as draw, rotate, move, and so on for these figures. We do not intend, however, for Figure objects to exist. Instead, we derive concrete classes for specific figures such as circles, rectangles, and triangles from Figure. The abstract base class Figure serves as an interface for all of these derived classes.

An **abstract class** is one in which no definition is provided for one or more of the function members, which are called **pure virtual functions**. In C++, a virtual function is specified to be a pure virtual function by appending the initializer = 0 to its prototype. A class derived from an abstract class *must* provide definitions of these pure virtual functions or else it also is an abstract class.

As a simple illustration, we might create an abstract class Document that contains some of the common operations for documents—for example, input and output operations:

```
class Document
{
 public:
  /***** Function Members *****/
  virtual void display(ostream & out) const = 0;
  virtual void read(istream & in) = 0;
  //--- Other operations on documents ---
 private:
  /***** Data Members *****/
}; // end of abstract-class declaration
// Output operator
inline ostream & operator<<(ostream & out, const Document & doc)
{ doc.display(out); return out; }
// Input operator
inline istream & operator>>(istream & in, Document & doc)
{ doc.read(in); return in; }
```

We could then derive the class License from it as follows:

```
class License : public Document
{
  public:
   /***** Function Members *****/
   virtual void display(ostream & out) const;
   //--- Other operations on licenses ---
  private:
   /***** Data Members *****/
}; // end of class declaration
// Definition of display
```

```
void License::display(ostream & out) const
{
   out << myIdNum << " " << myFirstName << " "
      << myMiddleInitial << ". " << myLastName
      << "\nAge: " << myAge << "  Birthdate: "
      << myBirthDate;    // assumes << defined for Date
}
void License::read(istream & in)
{
  in >> myIdNum >> my FirstName >> myMiddleInitial
     >> myLastName >> myAge >> myBirthDate;
}                        // assumes << defined for Date
```

Base classes for other class hierarchies might also be derived from Document:

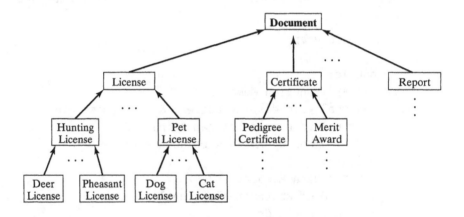

The abstract class Document thus serves as a common interface for all of the classes in this hierarchy. Defining the input and output operators for Document makes it available for input and output of an object of any of the derived classes in this hierarchy (provided they use public inheritance).

✔ Quick Quiz 14.5

1. What is polymorphism?

2. Tying the code for a function to a function call at compile time is called _____ binding.

3. _____ functions are used to accomplish _____ binding, which means that the selection of the code to use for a function is deferred until run time.

4. Vtbl stands for _____.

5. A(n) _____ class is a class for which there are no objects. It must have at least one _____ function.

▶ Exercises 14.5

The following exercises ask you to develop classes or class templates. You should also write driver programs to test them as instructed in the programming problems at the end of this chapter.

1. Administrative employees are paid a salary, but they also receive a bonus at regular intervals during the year. Add a class `Administrator` to the `Employee` class hierarchy described in the text.

2. Factory workers are paid a certain amount for each unit they make and their total pay is the number of units produced times the pay per unit. Add a class `FactoryEmployee` to the `Employee` class hierarchy described in the text.

3. Salespersons are paid a salary plus a commission on their sales; their total pay, therefore, is their salary plus the amount of their sales times the commission rate. Add a class `SalesPerson` to the `Employee` class hierarchy described in the text.

4. Add the abstract class `Document` to the `Employee` class hierarchy as described in the text.

5. Design `LookAheadStack` as a class template derived from a `Stack` class template. A look-ahead stack differs from a standard stack only in the push operation. An item is added to the stack by the push method only if it is different from the top stack element.

14.6 Case Study: A Heterogeneous Data Structure

In Section 14.4, we described how a fairly large employee hierarchy might evolve in designing a payroll system for a company. We built an `Employee` class that contained common employee information and served as the base class for the entire hierarchy. We also derived two classes from it—`SalariedEmployee` for salaried employees and `HourlyEmployee` for hourly employees—and also mentioned how a `Manager` class could be derived from `SalariedEmployee`.

Suppose now that we want to process a list `empList` of employees:

Because each value in the list has the same type (`Employee`), such a list is called a **homogeneous** structure. All of the data structures we have studied thus far have been homogeneous.

If we declare `empList` as

```
List<Employee> empList;
```

where `List` is a class template for implementing lists like those we have considered in several earlier chapters, or we can use the standard `list` class template as in Figure 14.6. Then each element of `empList` must be an `Employee` object and cannot be a

SalariedEmployee or an HourlyEmployee. For this, we would need a **heterogeneous** structure that *can store objects of different types.*

What makes it possible to build such structures is the property of handles for objects in a class hierarchy that we described in the preceding section:

A handle for a class object can also refer to any derived class object.

In particular,

A pointer to the base class in a class hierarchy can also point to any object whose type is another class in that hierarchy.

From this we see that if instead of a list of Employee objects, we declare empList as a list of Employee *pointers,*

```
List<Employee *> L;
```

then each node of empList can refer to any Employee object or to any object whose type is derived from class Employee. Thus, salaried and hourly employees can be intermixed in the same list:

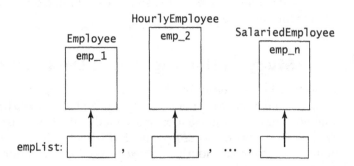

Being able to build such heterogeneous storage structures is an important benefit provided by an OOP language's inheritance mechanism.

The Need for Virtual Functions

Suppose that, as in Section 14.4, the Employee base class has an output member function display() and that each descendant class has a new definition of display() that extends that of its parent class to output the new data members (see Figure 14.6). Now consider statements such as the following to traverse empList and output the employee information for each element with a statement of the form

```
element->display(cout);
```

For this to work correctly, when *element* points at an Employee object, the function Employee::display() within that object must be called; when *element* points at a SalariedEmployee object, the function SalariedEmployee::display() within that object must be called; when *element* is a pointer to an HourlyEmployee object, the function HourlyEmployee::display() within that object must be called. Again we need polymorphic behavior: *The same function call produces different results in different contexts.*

As we saw in Section 14.5, this is possible if we make the version of display() in each class that serves as a base class a virtual function (see Figure 14.4). Figure 14.6 also shows a Manager class derived from SalariedEmployee and a driver program that creates a list of Employee handles and outputs the employee information in objects in this list. Listings of all the classes in the employee hierarchy and this driver program can be found in source code for Chapter 14 on the text's website—see *Chap14/Figure14.6.*

Figure 14.6 A Heterogeneous Data Structure

```
// See Figure 14.4 for Employee.h, SalariedEmployee.h, and HourlyEmployee.h.


/* Manager.h ----------------------------------------------------------------
    Header file for a class Manager derived from SalariedEmployee that adds
    the attributes unique to managers.
    Operations are:  A constructor and a virtual output operation.
    ----------------------------------------------------------------------*/
#include "SalariedEmployee.h"


#ifndef MANAGER
#define MANAGER


class Manager : public SalariedEmployee
{
 public:
  Manager(long id = 0, string last = "", string first = "",
    char initial = ' ', int dept = 0, double sal = 0, int numEmps = 0);
  /*-----------------------------------------------------------------
    Manager constructor.
    Preconditions:  None.
    Postconditions: Data members myIdNum, myLastName, myFirstName,
       myMiddleInitial, myDeptCode, mySalary are initialized by the
       SalariedEmployee constructor; myNumEmps is initialized to
       numEmps (default 0).
    ----------------------------------------------------------------*/


  virtual void display(ostream & out) const;
  /*-----------------------------------------------------------
    Output function member.
    Precondition:  ostream out is open.
```

Figure 14.6 (continued)

Postcondition: A text representation of this Manager object has been
output to out.
--*/

// ... Other Manager operations ...

```cpp
private:
  int myNumEmps;
};

//--- Definition of Manager's Constructor
inline Manager::Manager(long id, string last, string first, char initial,
                        int dept, double sal, int numEmps)
: SalariedEmployee(id, last, first, initial, dept, sal),
  myNumEmps(numEmps)
{}

//--- Definition of Manager's display()
inline void Manager::display(ostream & out) const
{
  SalariedEmployee::display(out);
  out << myNumEmps << endl;
}
#endif
```

```cpp
/*------------------------------------------------------------------
        Driver program to process a list of pointers to employee objects.
------------------------------------------------------------------*/


#include <iostream>
#include <list>
using namespace std;
#include "Employee.h"
#include "SalariedEmployee.h"
#include "HourlyEmployee.h"
#include "Manager.h"
```

Figure 14.6 (continued)

```
int main()
{
  Employee * ptr;
  list<Employee*> empList;
  ptr = new Employee(11111, "Doe", "John", 'J', 11);
  empList.push_back(ptr);
  ptr = new SalariedEmployee(22222, "Smith", "Mary", 'M', 22, 59900);
  empList.push_back(ptr);
  ptr = new HourlyEmployee(33333, "Jones", "Jay", 'J', 33, 15.25, 40);
  empList.push_back(ptr);
  ptr = new Manager(22222, "Brown", "Betty", 'B', 25, 60000, 13);
  empList.push_back(ptr);

  for (list<Employee*>::iterator it = empList.begin();
                          it!= empList.end(); it++)
  {
    ptr = *it;
    cout << *ptr << endl;
  }

}
```

Execution Trace:
```
11111 Doe, John J   11

22222 Smith, Mary M   22
$59900

33333 Jones, Jay J   33
$15.25
40
1.5

22222 Brown, Betty B   25
$60000
13
```

▲

SUMMARY

▣ Chapter Notes

■ The basic approach in object-oriented design (OOD) is as follows:
   a. Identify the objects in the problem.
   b. Analyze the objects to determine if there is *commonality* among them.
   c. While there is commonality, *define base classes that contain this commonality.*
   d. *Derive classes that inherit commonality from a base class.*

■ A class declaration of the form `class Derived : public Base {...};` specifies that the class `Derived` is derived from the class `Base` and inherits all of its members. Alternatives to public inheritance are private and protected inheritance.

■ Polymorphism is implemented in C++ by means of virtual functions.

☞ Programming Pointers

1. Only public and protected members of a base class are accessible in a derived class; private members are not.

2. Access to inherited public and protected members in a derived class is determined by the kind of inheritance—public, private, or protected.

3. Two useful tests for determining whether one object *B* should be publicly derived from another object *A* are the following:
   ■ *Operation Test*: Do *A*'s public member functions behave properly in *B*?
   ■ *Need-a ... Use-a Test*: If all you need is an *A* object, can you just use a *B* object?

4. A function is declared to be virtual by preceding its prototype with the keyword `virtual`.

5. To specify that it is purely virtual, attach the initializer `= 0`:
   `virtual function-heading = 0;`

6. A base-class pointer can point to any derived class object.

7. Nonvirtual function members of a class, as well as virtual member functions that are not pure, must be defined for that class.

8. The definition of a virtual function in a base class serves as a default definition. It will be used in any derived class in which the definition is not overridden.

9. A class that has at least one pure virtual function is an *abstract class.* There are no objects for such classes. They serve only as base classes for other classes.

10. Pure virtual function members of an abstract base class may not be defined for that class. Definitions must be given in derived classes (or those classes will also be abstract).

▲ ADT Tips

1. Reusability that is unique to object-oriented design is reusing a class (via inheritance) to build another class.

2. Three properties that characterize object-oriented programming are the following:
   ■ *Encapsulation* of data and basic operations

■ *Inheritance*: Deriving one class from another class so that the new class inherits all the members of the original class

■ *Polymorphism*: A function call being bound to different functions for different kinds of objects.

3. Public inheritance is the most important and most commonly used kind of inheritance.

4. Public inheritance should be used only when an *is-a* relationship exists between a problem's objects.

5. Other relationships between classes are *has-a* and *uses-a*. Public inheritance should not be used for either of these.

6. Data structures that can store objects of different types are called *heterogeneous* data structures. Inheritance and polymorphism make it possible to design such structures.

Programming Problems

Section 14.5

1. Write a driver program to test the Administrator class from Exercise 1.

2. Write a driver program to test the FactoryEmployee class from Exercise 2.

3. Write a driver program to test the SalesPerson class from Exercise 3.

4. Write a complete payroll program for a company in which each employee falls into one of the five categories described in the text and in Exercises 1–3—salaried, hourly, administrative, factory, or salesperson.

5. Write a driver program to test the Document class from Exercise 4.

6. Write a driver program to test the LookAheadStack class from Exercise 5.

7. In an ordered list, all operations that modify the list are designed to ensure that the elements remain in ascending order. Build and test an OrderedList class template derived from class List that exhibits this characteristic.

Section 14.6

8. Write a program that processes a heterogeneous list of the five different kinds of employees in Problem 4. Instead of the simple creation of list elements in the driver program in Figure 14.6, use other list operations to input the list, output the list, add to the list, remove from the list, search the list, and sort the list so that id-numbers are in ascending order.

9. Proceed as in Problem 8 but for a heterogeneous stack of employees. Allow stack operations to be performed—push, top, pop, and output.

10. Proceed as in Problem 9 but for a heterogeneous queue of employees and operations enqueue, front, dequeue, and output.

11. Proceed as in Problem 8 for for a BST of employees where *employee1* < *employee2* means that *employee1*'s id-number is less than that for *employee2*. Allow various BST operations to be performed such as inorder traversal, search, insert, and delete.

Trees

CHAPTER CONTENTS

Chapter Objectives

- Show how binary trees can be used to develop efficient codes.
- Study the problem of binary search trees becoming unbalanced and look at one of the classical approaches (AVL) for solving this problem.
- Look at other kinds of trees, including 2-3-4 trees, red–black trees, and B-trees.
- Introduce the associative containers in STL and see how red–black trees are used in their implementations.

In Chapter 12 we studied binary search trees in some detail, but we also mentioned several other applications of binary trees. We begin this chapter by looking at their use in encoding and decoding problems. More specifically, we will describe Huffman codes, which can be used for data compression, and show how binary trees are used in building these codes. Other applications of binary trees and other kinds of trees will be described in later sections.

There also is a problem of binary search trees that was left unresolved in Chapter 12, namely, the deterioration of search efficiency as the tree becomes lopsided. In this chapter we will look at one important way to keep BSTs from becoming unbalanced using AVL trees, and we will then look at some other alternatives to binary trees that produce efficient search trees: 2-3-4 trees, red–black trees, and B-Trees. The last section takes a quick look at the associative containers in STL, which use trees as storage structures. Our descriptions of all these topics are quite brief, however, because these structures are usually covered in detail in more advanced data structures courses.

15.1 Case Study: Huffman Codes

In Section 12.2 we showed part of a binary tree for the Morse code, which represents each character by a sequence of dots and dashes:

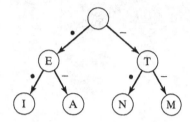

Unlike ASCII, EBCDIC, and Unicode schemes, in which the length of the code is the same for all characters, Morse code uses variable-length sequences. For example, · is the code for E, – · is the code for N, and – – · · is the code for Z. In this section we consider another coding scheme, Huffman coding, that uses variable-length codes.

Variable-Length Codes

The basic idea in a variable-length coding scheme is to use shorter codes for characters that occur more frequently and longer codes for those used less frequently. For example, 'E' in Morse code is a single dot, whereas – – · · is used to represent 'Z'. The objective is to minimize the expected length of the code for a character. This reduces the number of bits that must be sent when transmitting encoded messages. These variable-length coding schemes are also useful when compressing data because they reduce the number of bits that must be stored.

To state the problem more precisely, suppose that some character set $\{C_1, C_2, \ldots, C_n\}$ is given, and certain weights $w_1, w_2, \ldots, w_n$ are associated with these characters; w_i is the weight attached to character C_i and is a measure (e.g., probability or relative frequency) of how frequently this character occurs in messages to be encoded. If $l_1, l_2, \ldots, l_n$ are the lengths of the codes for characters $C_1, C_2, \ldots, C_n$, respectively, then the **expected length** of the code for any one of these characters is given by

$$\text{expected length} = w_1 l_1 + w_2 l_2 + \cdots + w_n l_n = \sum_{i=1}^{n} w_i l_i$$

As a simple example, consider the five characters A, B, C, D, and E, and suppose they occur with the following weights (probabilities):

character	A	B	C	D	E
weight	0.2	0.1	0.1	0.15	0.45

In Morse code, with a dot replaced by 0 and a dash by 1, these characters are encoded as follows:

Character	Code
A	01
B	1000
C	1010
D	100
E	0

Thus, the expected length of the code for each of these five letters in this scheme is

$$0.2 \times 2 + 0.1 \times 4 + 0.1 \times 4 + 0.15 \times 3 + 0.45 \times 1 = 2.1$$

Immediate Decodability

Another useful property of some coding schemes is that they are **immediately decodable**. This means that no sequence of bits that represents a character is a prefix of a longer sequence for some other character. Consequently, when a sequence of bits is received that is the code for a character, it can be decoded as that character immediately, without waiting to see whether subsequent bits change it into a longer code for some other character. Note that the preceding Morse code scheme is not immediately decodable because, for example, the code for E (0) is a prefix of the code for A (01), and the code for D (100) is a prefix of the code for B (1000). (For decoding, Morse code uses a third "bit," a pause, to separate letters.) A coding scheme for which the code lengths are the same as in the preceding scheme and that is immediately decodable is as follows:

Character	Code
A	01
B	1000
C	0001
D	001
E	1

Huffman Codes

The following algorithm, given by D. A. Huffman in 1952, can be used to construct coding schemes that are immediately decodable and for which each character has a minimal expected code length:

Huffman's Algorithm

/* Construct a binary code for a given set of characters for which the expected length of the bit string for a given character is minimal.

A set of n characters $\{C_1, C_2, \ldots, C_n\}$ is received as is a set of weights $\{w_1, w_2, \ldots, w_n\}$, where w_i is the weight of character C_i. A collection of n bit strings representing codes for the characters is returned. */

1. Initialize a list of one-node binary trees containing the weights $w_1, w_2, \ldots, w_n$, one for each of the characters $C_1, C_2, \ldots, C_n$.
2. Do the following $n - 1$ times:
   a. Find two trees T' and T'' in this list with roots of minimal weights w' and w''.
   b. Replace these two trees with a binary tree whose root is $w' + w''$, and whose subtrees are T' and T'', and label the pointers to these subtrees 0 and 1, respectively:

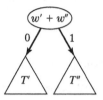

3. The code for character C_i is the bit string labeling a path in the final binary tree from the root to the leaf for C_i.

As an illustration of Huffman's algorithm, consider again the characters A, B, C, D, and E, with the weights given earlier. We begin by constructing a list of one-node binary trees, one for each character:

The first two trees to be selected are those corresponding to letters B and C, since they have the smallest weights, and these are combined to produce a tree having weight $0.1 + 0.1 = 0.2$ and having these two trees as subtrees:

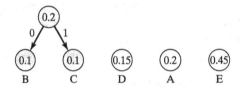

From this list of four binary trees, we again select two of minimal weights, the first and the second (or the second and the third), and replace them with another tree having weight $0.2 + 0.15 = 0.35$ and having these two trees as subtrees:

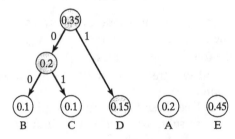

From this list of three binary trees, the first two have minimal weights and are combined to produce a binary tree having weight 0.35 + 0.2 = 0.55 and having these trees as subtrees:

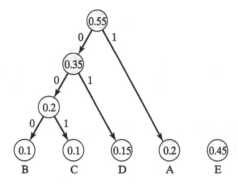

The resulting binary tree is then combined with the one-node tree representing E to produce the final Huffman tree:

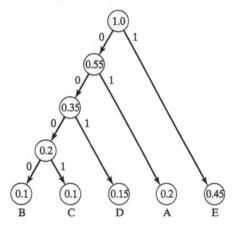

The Huffman codes obtained from this tree are as follows:

Character	Huffman Code
A	01
B	0000
C	0001
D	001
E	1

As we calculated earlier, the expected length of the code for each of these characters is 2.1.

A different assignment of codes to these characters for which the expected length is also 2.1 is possible because at the second stage, we had two choices for trees of minimal weight:

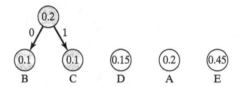

We selected the first and second trees from this list, but we could have used the second and third:

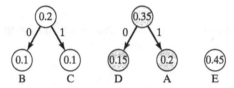

At the next stage, the resulting list of two binary trees would have been

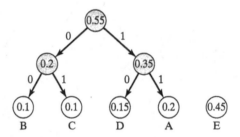

and the final Huffman tree would be

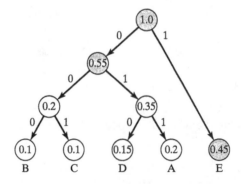

The assignment of codes corresponding to this tree is

Character	Huffman code
A	011
B	000
C	001
D	010
E	1

The immediate decodability property of Huffman codes is clear. Each character is associated with a leaf node in the Huffman tree, and there is a unique path from the root of the tree to each leaf. Consequently, no sequence of bits that is the code for some character can be a prefix of a longer sequence of bits for some other character.

Because of this property of immediate decodability, a decoding algorithm is easy:

 ## Huffman Decoding Algorithm

/* Decode a message encoded using a Huffman tree.
A Huffman tree and a bit string representing some message that was encoded using the Huffman tree is received and the decoded message is output. */

1. Initialize pointer p to the root of the Huffman tree.
2. While the end of the message string has not been reached, do the following:
   a. Let x be the next bit in the string.
   b. If x is 0 then
      Set p = its left child pointer.
   Else
      Set p = its right child pointer.
   c. If p points to a leaf then
      i. Display the character associated with that leaf.
      ii. Reset p to the root of the Huffman tree.
   End while.

As an illustration, suppose that the message string 0101011010 is received and that this message was encoded using the second Huffman tree constructed earlier. The pointer follows the path labeled 010 from the root of this tree to the letter D and is then reset to the root:

$$\boxed{0\ 1\ 0}\ 1\ 0\ 1\ 1\ 0\ 1\ 0$$
$$\text{D}$$

The next bit, 1, leads immediately to the letter E:

$$\boxed{0\ 1\ 0}\boxed{1}\ 0\ 1\ 1\ 0\ 1\ 0$$
$$\text{D}\quad\text{E}$$

The pointer p next follows the path 011 to the letter A:

$$\boxed{0\ 1\ 0}\boxed{1}\boxed{0\ 1\ 1}\ 0\ 1\ 0$$
$$\quad\ \text{D}\qquad\ \text{E}\quad\ \text{A}$$

Finally, the path 010 leads to the letter D again:

$$\boxed{0\ 1\ 0}\boxed{1}\boxed{0\ 1\ 1}\boxed{0\ 1\ 0}$$
$$\quad\ \text{D}\qquad\ \text{E}\quad\ \text{A}\qquad\ \text{D}$$

Implementing the preceding algorithms for building a Huffman tree and using it to decode strings is straightforward. A HuffmanCode class that does this and a simple driver program for it are available on the website for this text (see *Chap15/ HuffmanCode*).

Exercises 15.1

1. Demonstrate that Morse code is not immediately decodable by showing that the bit string 100001100 can be decoded in more than one way.

Using the first Huffman code given in this section (A = 01, B = 0000, C = 0001, D = 001, E = 1), decode the bit strings in Exercises 2–5.

2. 000001001

3. 001101001

4. 000101001

5. 00001010011001

6. Construct the Huffman code for the C++ keywords and weights given in the following table:

Words	Weight
int	.30
main	.30
while	.05
if	.20
for	.15

7. Repeat Exercise 6 for the following table of letters and weights:

Character	Weight
a	.20
b	.10
c	.08
d	.08
e	.40
f	.05
g	.05
h	.04

8. Using the Huffman code developed in Exercise 7, encode the message "feed a deaf aged hag".

9. Repeat Exercise 3 for the following table of C++ keywords and weights (frequencies):

Words	Weight
case	2
class	20
do	5
else	10
false	4
for	20
goto	1
if	20
int	22
main	22
static	2
struct	3
switch	2
true	4
while	15

15.2 Tree Balancing: AVL Trees

Binary search trees are designed to facilitate fast searching of the items stored in the tree. As we observed in Section 12.4, however, the order in which items are inserted into a binary search tree determines the shape of the tree and how efficiently this tree can be searched. If it grows in such a way that it fills in approximately level by level, then it can be searched much more efficiently in a binary-search manner than if it becomes lopsided.

Example: A BST of State Abbreviations

To illustrate the problem, consider the BST that results when the abbreviations of states NY, IL, GA, RI, MA, PA, DE, IN, VT, TX, OH, and WY are inserted into an empty tree in this order:

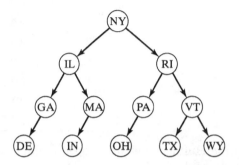

For such nicely balanced trees, the search time is $O(\log_2 n)$, where n is the number of nodes in the tree. If the abbreviations are inserted in the order DE, GA, IL, IN, MA, MI, NY, OH, PA, RI, TX, VT, WY, however, the BST degenerates into a linked list for which the search time is $O(n)$:

In this section we describe a technique developed in the 1960s by the two Russian mathematicians, Georgii Maksimovich Adel'son-Vel'skii and Evgenii Mikhailovich Landis, for keeping a binary search tree balanced as items are inserted into it. The trees that result are commonly called *AVL trees*, in their honor.

As an ADT, an **AVL** (or **height-balanced**) **tree** is a special kind of BST:

AVL Tree ADT

Collection of Data Elements

A binary search tree in which the balance factor of each node is 0, 1, or –1, where the **balance factor** of a node x is the height of the left subtree of x minus the height of x's right subtree. (Recall that the height of a tree is the number of levels in it.)

Basic Operations

- Construction, empty, search, and traverse as for BSTs
- Insert a new item in the AVL tree in such a way that the height-balanced property is maintained
- Delete an item from the AVL tree in such a way that the height-balanced property is maintained

For example, the following are AVL trees; the balance factor of each node is shown in the node:

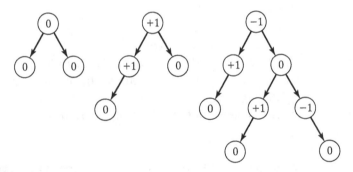

The following are not AVL trees, and the nodes whose balance factors are different from 0, 1, or –1 are highlighted:

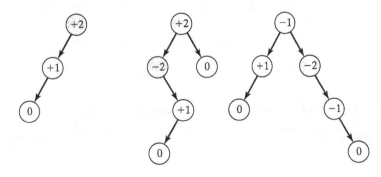

We can implement an AVL tree as a linked structure in much the same way as we did for binary trees in Section 12.2. For nodes, we simply add a data member to store the balance factor:

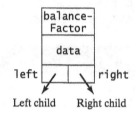

left   right

Left child   Right child

```
template <typename DataType>
class AVLTree
{
 public:
  /***** AVLTree Function Members *****/
 private:
  /***** Node class *****/
  class AVLNode
  {
   public:
    DataType data;
    short int balanceFactor;
    AVLNode * left;
    AVLNode * right;
    // AVLNode constructors
    // Default -- data is default DataType value;
    //         -- balance factor 0; both links null
    AVLNode()
    : balanceFactor(0), left(0), right(0)
    { }

    // Explicit Value -- data part contains item;
    //                 -- balance factor 0; both links null
    AVLNode(DataType item)
    : balanceFactor(0), data(item), left(0), right(0)
    { }
  }; // end of class AVLNode declaration

  typedef AVLNode * AVLNodePointer;

  /***** AVLTree Data Members *****/
}; // end of class AVLTree declaration
```

The constructor, empty, search, and traverse operations for AVL trees can then be implemented in the same way as for BSTs. Here we will concentrate on the insertion operation.

To illustrate how to insert items into an AVL tree, beginning with an empty AVL tree, we consider again the example of a BST containing state abbreviations. As we will see, each time the tree becomes unbalanced as signaled by a balance factor of ±1 for at least one node, its AVL condition can be restored by applying one of four *rotations*.

Suppose that the first abbreviation inserted is RI, giving the following balanced tree:

If the next abbreviation is inserted in PA, the result is still a balanced tree:

If DE is inserted next, an unbalanced tree results. To remedy the lopsideness to the left in this tree, we perform a **right rotation** (clockwise) of the tree rooted at the node RI:

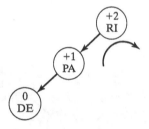

This produces the following balanced tree:

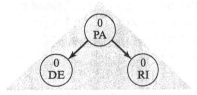

Inserting GA next does not unbalance the tree:

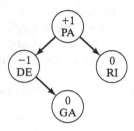

But an unbalanced tree results if OH is inserted next. Since the subtree rooted at DE is lopsided to the right, we perform a **left rotation** (counterclockwise) of its nodes:

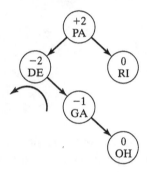

And this rebalances the entire tree:

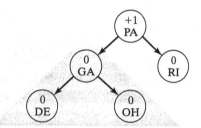

Inserting MA next produces another unbalanced tree. But removing the imbalance in this tree is more complicated because it arose from descending to the left subtree of the node containing PA (where the balance factor is 2) and then to the right subtree of the node containing GA. To cancel these out we use a double *left-right rotation*. We first perform a left rotation of the nodes in the left subtree of PA:

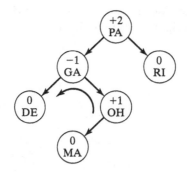

This gives the following tree, and we now apply a right rotation to the tree rooted at PA:

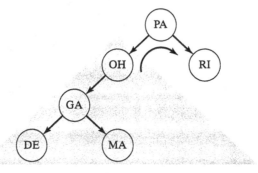

Once again, we obtain a balanced tree:

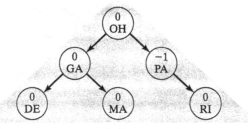

Inserting IL and then MI does not unbalance the tree,

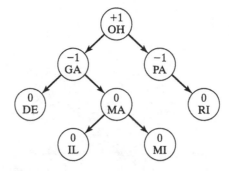

but inserting IN does. In this case, a double **right-left rotation** rebalances the tree. We first perform a right rotation of the nodes in the right subtree of GA:

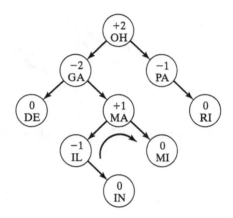

This gives the following tree, to which we apply a left rotation of the subtree rooted at GA:

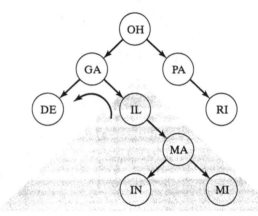

Once again, we obtain a balanced tree:

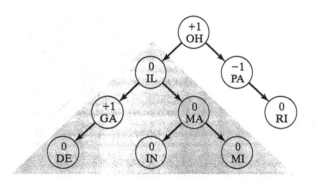

Inserting NY produces an unbalanced tree that requires a double left-right rotation for rebalancing. We first do a left rotation of the nodes in the left subtree of OH,

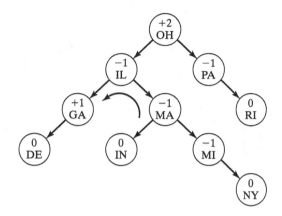

which produces the following tree. Now we perform by a right rotation of the nodes in the tree rooted at OH

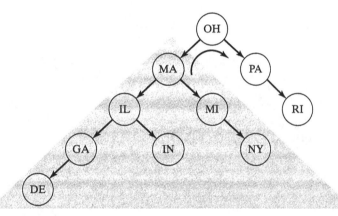

and obtain the following balanced tree:

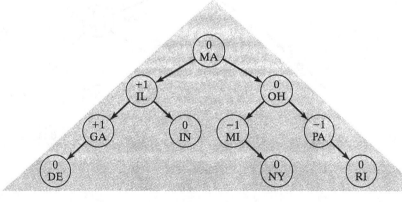

Inserting VT next causes an imbalance, but it is easily removed. A simple left rotation of the subtree rooted at PA,

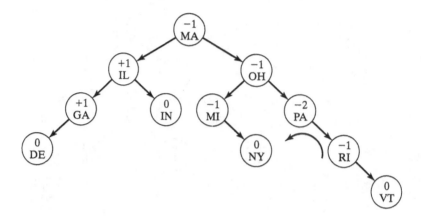

easily rebalances the tree:

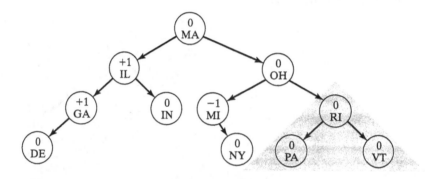

Insertion of the last two abbreviations, TX and WY, does not unbalance the tree, and the final AVL tree obtained is

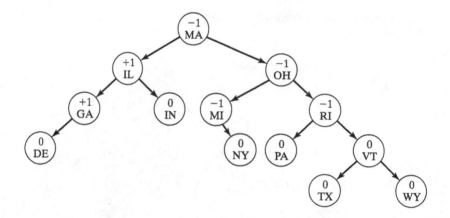

The Basic Rebalancing Rotations

As this example demonstrates, when insertion of a new item causes an imbalance in a binary tree, the tree can be rebalanced by *applying a rotation to the subtree whose root has balance factor ±2 and is the nearest ancestor of the inserted node.* The four types of rotations are:

1. *Simple right rotation*: Use when the inserted item is in the left subtree of the left child of the nearest ancestor with balance factor +2.

2. *Simple left rotation*: Use when the inserted item is in the right subtree of the right child of the nearest ancestor with balance factor –2.

3. *Left-right rotation*: Use when the inserted item is in the right subtree of the left child of the nearest ancestor with balance factor +2.

4. *Right-left rotation*: Use when the inserted item is in the left subtree of the right child of the nearest ancestor with balance factor –2.

Each of these rotations can be carried out by simply resetting some of the links. For example, consider a simple right rotation. If we let A denote the nearest ancestor of the inserted item that has balance factor +2, and let B denote its left child, then a simple right rotation can be accomplished by simply resetting three links:

1. Reset the link from the parent of A to B.

2. Set the left link of A equal to the right link of B.

3. Set the right link of B to point A.

The following sequence of diagrams illustrates these link changes:

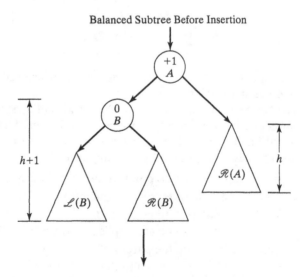

Balanced Subtree Before Insertion

Unbalanced Subtree After Insertion

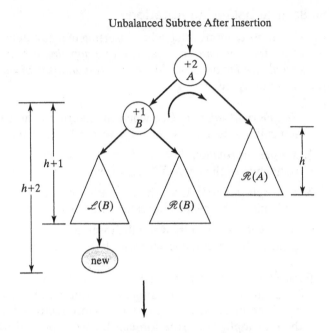

Rebalanced Subtree After Simple Right Rotation

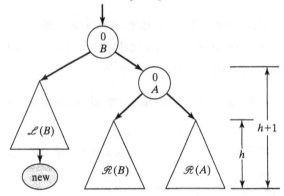

The corresponding simple left rotation can also be carried out by resetting three links and is left as an exercise.

The double rotations can be carried out with at most five link changes. For example, consider a left-right rotation, which is used when the item is inserted in the right subtree of the left child B of the nearest ancestor A with balance factor +2. The left rotation can be accomplished by resetting three links:

1. Set the left link of A to point to the root C of the right subtree of B.

2. Set the right link of B equal to the left link of C.

3. Set the left link of C to point to B.

The right rotation can also be accomplished by resetting three links:

4. Reset the link from the parent of A to point to C.

5. Set the left link of A equal to the right link of C.

6. Set the right link of C to point to A.

Note that the link change in Step 5 cancels that in step 1, so that in fact only five links are reset.

The diagrams that follow show two of the three possible cases for this left-right rotation: (1) B has no right child before the new node is inserted, and the new node becomes the right child C of B; (2) B has a right child C, and the new node is inserted in the left subtree of C; and (3) B has right child C, and the new node is inserted in the right subtree of C. (A diagram for Case 3 is similar to that for Case 2 and is left as an exercise.)

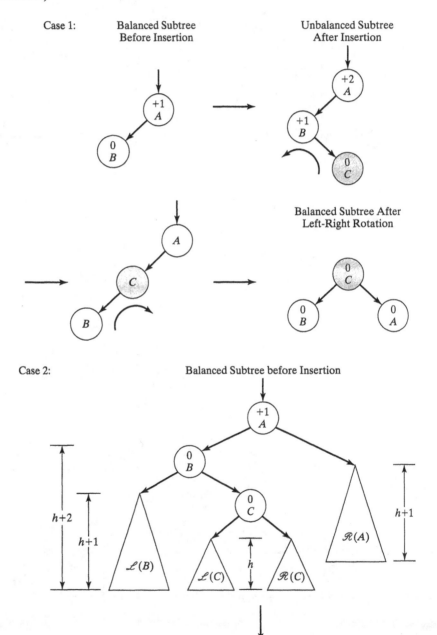

Unbalanced Subtree after Insertion

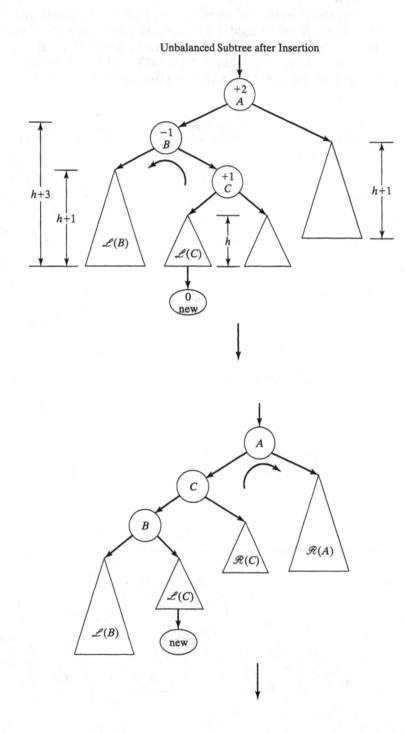

Balanced Subtree after Left–Right Rotation

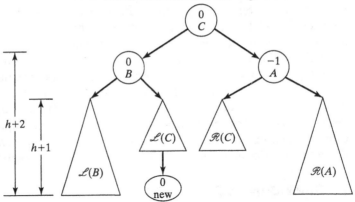

The corresponding right-left rotations can also be accomplished with at most five link changes and are left as exercises.

Deleting an item from an AVL tree can obviously also cause an imbalance. For example, for the one of the trees of state abbreviations considered earlier,

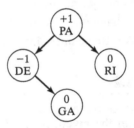

removing RI produces an unbalanced tree:

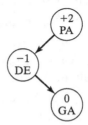

A left-right rotation will again produce a balanced tree:

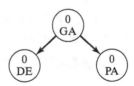

In general, imbalances caused by deletions from AVL trees can be removed using rotations, but the algorithms are more difficult than those for insertions, because the deletion can occur anywhere in the tree. We leave the study of these algorithms to more advanced data structures courses.

Using an AVL tree to store data items, rather than allowing the binary tree to grow haphazardly when new items are inserted, guarantees that the search time will be $O(\log_2 n)$. There is obviously some overhead involved in rebalancing, but if the number of search operations is sufficiently greater than the number of insertions, the faster searches will compensate for the slower insertions. Empirical studies have indicated that, on the average, rebalancing is required for approximately 45 percent of the insertions. Roughly one-half of these require double rotations.

✔ Quick Quiz 15.2

1. Define balance factor.
2. Define AVL tree as an ADT.
3. Another name for an AVL tree is a(n) _____-balanced tree.
4. Show the AVL tree that results from inserting the letters S, P, E, C, I, A, L, T, Y in this order.
5. How many link changes are needed to carry out a simple rotation?
6. How many link changes are needed to carry out a double rotation?
7. Searching an AVL tree can be done in O(_____) time.

⬧ Exercises 15.2

For Exercises 1–5, trace the construction of the AVL tree that results from inserting the C++ keywords in the given order. Show the tree and balance factors for each node before and after each rebalancing.

1. `long, const, typedef, bool, public, break, else`
2. `bool, new, return, struct, while, case, enum`
3. `do, long, new, and, operator, int, namespace`
4. `unsigned, short, long, int, double, char`
5. `bool, enum, if, this, else, case, void, do, return, unsigned, false, true, double, while`

Proceed as in Exercises 1–5, but for the following collections of numbers:

6. 22, 44, 88, 66, 55, 11, 99, 77, 33
7. 11, 22, 33, 44, 55, 66, 77, 88, 99
8. 99, 88, 77, 66, 55, 44, 33, 22, 11
9. 55, 33, 77, 22, 11, 44, 88, 66, 99
10. 50, 45, 75, 65, 70, 35, 25, 15, 60, 20, 41, 30, 55, 10, 80
11. Draw diagrams for a simple left rotation similar to those in the text for the simple right rotation. Also describe what links must be reset to accomplish this rotation.

12. Draw diagrams for Case 3 of the left-right rotation described in the text.

13. Draw diagrams for a right-left rotation similar to those in the text for the left-right rotation. Also describe what links must be reset to accomplish this rotation.

14. Design and test an AVLTree class template.

15.3 2-3-4 Trees, Red–Black Trees, B-Trees, and Other Trees

Until now we have confined our attention to binary trees, those in which each node has at most two children. In many applications, however, allowing more than two children is necessary or at least desirable. For example, in a **genealogical tree** such as the following, it is not the case that each person has a maximum of two children:

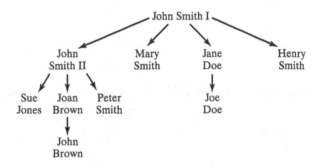

Game trees that are used to analyze games and puzzles also do not have the binary property. The following tree, showing the various configurations possible in the Tower of Hanoi problem with two disks (see Section 10.2), is a simple illustration of such a game tree:

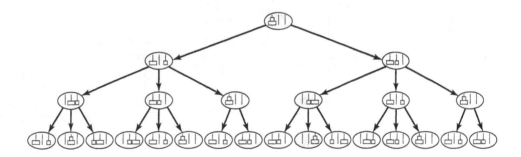

Parse trees constructed during the compilation of a program are used to check the program's syntax. Most of these do not have the binary property. For example, in

Section 10.2 we considered the parse tree for the expression $2 * (a + b)$:

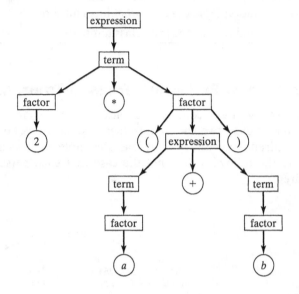

And the following tree could be the parse tree constructed by a C++ compiler for the statement

```
if (x < 0)
    flag = 1;
```

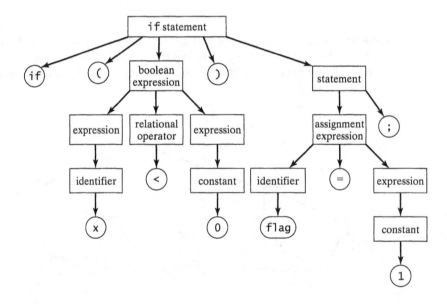

2-3-4 Trees

The searching technique used for binary search trees has been extended to trees in which nodes may have more than two children. In the search of a BST for a particular item, the search path descends to the left subtree of a particular node if the item is less than the data value in that node; otherwise, it descends to the right subtree. These are the only two options. For other trees, however, at a given node, there may be several different directions that a search path may follow; and in general, this results in shorter search paths because there are fewer levels in the tree. We will illustrate this first for 2-3-4 trees, in which all non-leaf nodes have 2, 3, or 4 children.

Giving a precise definition of a 2-3-4 tree is easiest if we first make the following definition: An ***m*-node** in a search tree stores $m - 1$ data values $k_1 < k_2 < \ldots < k_{m-1}$ and has links to m subtrees $T_1, \ldots, T_m$, where for each i,[1]

$$\text{all data values in } T_i < k_i \le \text{all data values in } T_{i+1}$$

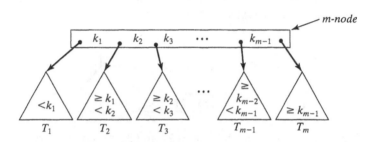

Thus, a binary search tree has all 2-nodes.

Now we can define a **2-3-4-tree**.

2-3-4 Tree ADT

Collection of Data Elements

A tree with the following properties:

1. Each node stores at most 3 data values.
2. Each non-leaf node is a 2-node, a 3-node, or a 4-node.
3. All the leaves are on the same level.

Basic Operations

- Construction, empty, and search
- Insert a new item in the 2-3-4 tree so the result is a 2-3-4 tree
- Delete an item from the 2-3-4 tree so the result is a 2-3-4 tree

---

[1] We use k for the data values to remind ourselves that the data values are usually records, and comparisons are made using *keys* in these records.

For example, the following tree is a 2-3-4 tree that stores integers:

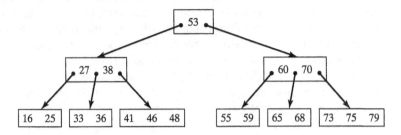

To search this tree for the value 36, we begin at the root and compare 36 with the data items stored in the root. In this 2-3-4 tree, the root contains only 53, and 36 is less than 53, so we next search the left subtree:

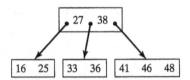

Comparing 36 with the data items 27 and 38 stored in the root of this subtree, we find that 36 is between these values, indicating that 36 is in the middle subtree:

33	36

Examining the data items in this one-node subtree, we locate the value 36.

Notice that the preceding 2-3-4 tree is nicely balanced. This is a result of how it was constructed and would most likely not have been the case if we had imitated the approach used for binary search trees in Section 12.4. That is, if we searched the tree, starting at the root, comparing the item to be inserted with the data values in each node to determine which link to follow, we would eventually either find a node with room for the item or we would create a new node at the bottom of the tree for the item. This could lead to very lopsided trees. For example, inserting 10, 20, 30, 40, 50, 60, 70, 80, 90, 100 in this order would produce

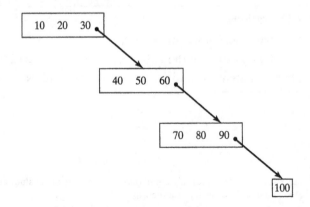

The key to building a balanced 2-3-4 tree is to add new nodes at the top of the tree when a node becomes full, rather than at the bottom. More precisely, we proceed as follows:

Building a Balanced 2-3-4 Tree

If the tree is empty,

> Create a 2-node containing *item*, which is the initial root of the tree.

Otherwise do the following:

1. Find the leaf node where *item* should be inserted by repeatedly comparing *item* with the values in a node and following the appropriate link to one of the children.
2. If there is room in the leaf node,

> Add *item* to it.

Otherwise:

> a. Split this 4-node into two nodes, one storing the items less than the median value in the node and the other storing those greater than the median. The median itself is moved to a parent having these two nodes as children.
> b. If the parent has no room for the median, split that 4-node in the same manner, continuing until either a parent is found that has room or we reach the root of the tree and it is full.
> c. In the case that the root is a 4-node, split it into two nodes and create a new parent 2-node, which also serves as a new root.

As an illustration, we describe how the preceding 2-3-4 tree can be constructed. If the first integer inserted is 53, we create a 2-node for it, which is the current root of our one-node 2-3-4 tree:

$$\boxed{53}$$

If 27 is inserted next, it is added to this node to the left of 53, creating a 3-node:

$$\boxed{27 \quad 53}$$

If 75 is now inserted next, it is added to this node to the right of 53, creating a 4-node root. Note that the values in each node are arranged in ascending order:

$$\boxed{27 \quad 53 \quad 75}$$

Now, suppose the next item to be inserted is 25. Because the root node is full, it must be split, and a new root containing the median 53 must be created with its left child containing the values 25 and 27, which are less than the median 53, and the right child containing the value 75, which is greater than the median:

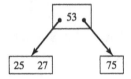

Next 70 and 41 can be inserted into the leaves:

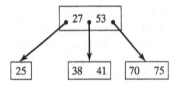

If 38 is inserted, the leftmost leaf must be split by moving the median, 27, into the parent node, with its left child storing values (25) that are less than 27 and the right child storing values (38 and 41) that are greater than 27:

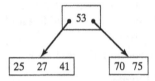

Now 16, 59, and 36 can be inserted into leaves; no splitting is necessary:

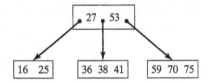

The insertion of 73 forces a splitting of the rightmost leaf, with the median 70 moved to the root:

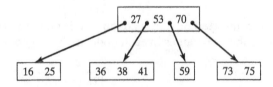

Now 65 and 60 can be inserted into the second leaf from the right with no splitting, but the insertion of 46 causes the second leaf from the left to split. When the median

38 is inserted into the parent node, which is the root, it also must be split, with the median 53 moving to a new root node; the resulting 2-3-4 tree is

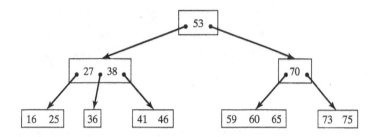

Inserting 55 causes a split in the second leaf from the right, and the median 60 is moved to the parent node:

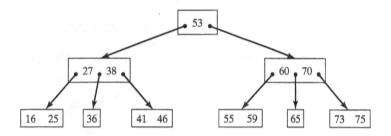

Finally, 33, 68, 79, and 48 can be inserted into leaf nodes without splitting any nodes:

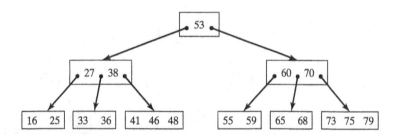

In this example, when we inserted 46, the leaf node where it was to be put was a 4-node, so we had to split it; but its parent was also a 4-node, so we had to split it as well before we could move 38 up one level. In general, the grandparent node might also be a 4-node that will need to be split before we can move a key from the parent node up one level, and so on. There may be a long sequence of splits all the way up to the root.

To avoid this, a better alternative to this *bottom-up insertion* is to use *top-down insertion*, in which we do not allow any parent nodes to become 4-nodes. Instead, as we follow the search path to locate where a new item is to be inserted, we split all 4-nodes along this path as they are encountered. For this, there are two basic cases, depending on whether the parent of the node to be split is a 2-node or a 3-node—we need not worry about the parent being a 4-node since we automatically split them as we descend the tree:

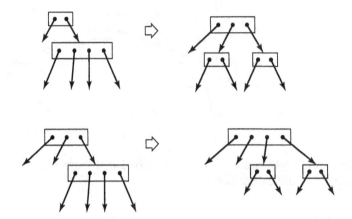

Also, since the root has no parent, it is simpler to split it as soon as it becomes a 4-node and not wait until the next insertion.

To illustrate, in the preceding example, after we had inserted 73, the 2-3-4 tree was

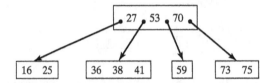

so we would split the root node immediately before inserting any other values:

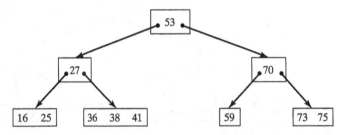

The insertion of 46 then causes a split of only the leaf node; no nodes above it need to be split.

As this example illustrates, *2-3-4 trees stay balanced during insertions.* This is also the case for deletion, which is left as an exercise.

We turn now to the problem of implementing 2-3-4 trees. We could use nodes having three data fields and four links:

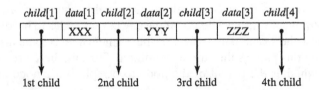

```
class Node234
{
 public:
  DataType data[3];  // type of data items in nodes
  Node234 * child[4];
  // Node234 operations
};
typedef Node234 * Pointer234;
```

The difficulty with this representation is that each node must have one link for each possible child, even though most of the nodes will not use all of these links. In fact, the amount of "wasted" space may be quite large. To demonstrate this, suppose that a 2-3-4 tree has n nodes. The linked representation will thus require n nodes, each having 4 links, for a total of $4n$ links. In such a tree, however, there are only $n - 1$ directed arcs, and thus only $n - 1$ of these links are used to connect the nodes. This means that $4n - (n - 1) = 3n + 1$ of the links are null; thus, the fraction of unused links is $(3n + 1) / 4n$, which is approximately 3/4; that is, approximately 75 percent of the links are null.

As we will see later in this section, there is a general method for representing any tree by a binary tree, but these trees typically don't stay balanced. However, for 2-3-4 trees, there is a special kind of binary tree called a *red–black tree* that can be used, and we will consider it next.

Red–Black Trees

Before we can show how **red–black trees** can be used to implement 2-3-4 trees, we must first say what they are.

Red–Black Tree ADT

Collection of Data Elements

A binary search tree with two kinds of links, red and black, which satisfy the following properties:

1. Every path from the root to a leaf node has the same number of black links.
2. No path from the root to a leaf node has two or more consecutive red links.

Basic Operations

- Construction, empty, search, and traverse as for BSTs
- Insert a new item in the red–black tree in such a way that the red–black properties are maintained
- Delete an item from the red–black tree in such a way that the red–black properties are maintained

There are two methods one could use to implement the nodes in a red–black tree. One is to add two new data members to store the colors of the links to the children.

An alternative and more common method is to add just one data member that stores the color of the link from the parent:

```
enum ColorType {RED, BLACK};
class RedBlackTreeNode
{
 public:
  DataType data;
  ColorType parentColor;   // RED if link from parent is red,
                           // BLACK otherwise
  RedBlackTreeNode * parent;
  RedBlackTreeNode * left;
  RedBlackTreeNode * right;
};
```

This is the approach used in the standard C++ library for the class rb_tree.

For the empty, search, and traverse operations, we can use the usual BST operations—we simply ignore the colors of the links. Here, we will concentrate on the insert operation and, in particular, how we can construct a red–black tree to represent a 2-3-4 tree. Deletion is left as an exercise.

2-3-4 trees are represented by red–black trees as follows:

Make a link black if it is a link in the 2-3-4 tree.

Make a link red if it connects nodes containing values in the same node of the 2-3-4 tree.

This means that we transform 2-, 3-, and 4-nodes and links in a 2-3-4 tree into nodes and links of a red–black tree by using the following transformations (*note that because red was not used in typesetting this text, black links will be represented by black arrows and red links by dashed colored arrows*):

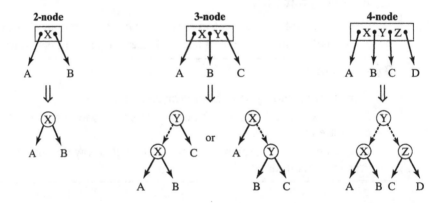

For example, the 2-3-4 tree

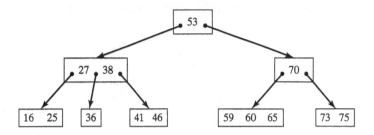

can be represented by the following red–black tree:

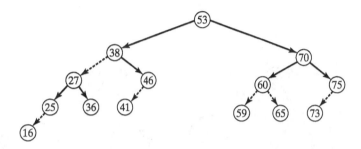

Note that the properties in the definition of a red–black tree do hold. Notice also that the tree is balanced.

Although AVL trees have been replaced in many applications by more modern data structures such as 2-3-4 trees and red–black trees, the basic AVL rotations are still used to keep a red–black tree balanced. To construct a red–black tree, we can simply do top-down insertion as it was described for 2-3-4 trees, splitting 4-nodes when they are encountered:

1. Search for a place to insert the new node. (Keep track of its parent, grandparent, and great grandparent.)
2. Whenever a 4-node q is encountered along the search path, split it as follows:
   a. Change both links of q to black.
   b. Change the link from the parent to red:

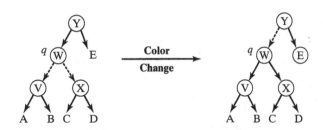

3. If there now are two consecutive red links (from grandparent gp to parent p to q), perform the appropriate AVL-type rotation determined by the direction (left-left, right-right, left-right, right-left) from $gp \rightarrow p \rightarrow q$; for example,

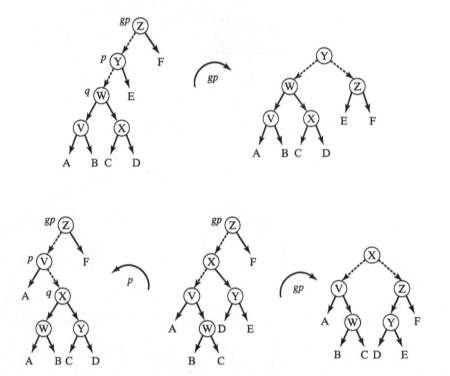

To illustrate, the following diagrams show the first 12 insertions in the 2-3-4 tree given earlier:

Insert 53:

Insert 27:

Insert 75:

Insert 25, 70, 41:

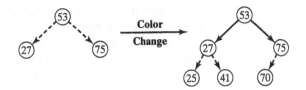

Insert 38:

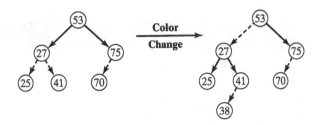

Insert 16:

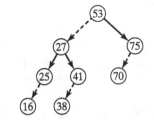

Insert 59:

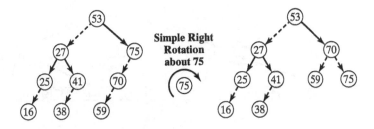

Insert 36:

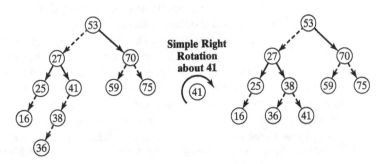

B-Trees

BSTs, 2-3-4 trees, and red–black trees are data structures used in *internal* searching schemes—that is, those in which the data set being searched is small enough that it can be stored in main memory. A B-tree is one data structure that is useful in *external* searching, where the data is stored in secondary memory. We will leave a detailed study of B-trees to an advanced data structures course and give only a very brief introduction to them here.

A **B-tree of order** m is a generalization of 2-3-4 trees:

B-Tree of Order *M* ADT
Collection of Data Elements A tree with the following properties: **1.** Each node stores at most $m - 1$ data values. **2.** Each non-leaf node is a 2-node, a 3-node, . . . , or an m-node. **3.** All the leaves are on the same level.
Basic Operations • Construction, empty, and search • Insert a new item in the B-tree so the result is a B-tree • Delete an item from the B-tree so the result is a B-tree

Thus, a 2-3-4 tree is a B-tree of order 4, and the following is a B-tree of order 5:

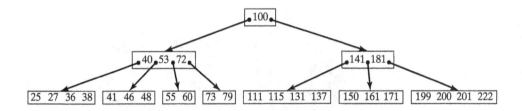

The algorithms for the basic operations are modifications of those for 2-3-4 trees.

As we noted, B-trees are useful for organizing data sets stored in secondary memory, such as files and databases stored on disk. In such applications, nodes in the B-tree typically store one file block, the maximum amount of information that can be retrieved in one access. This maximizes the number of data items stored in each node and the number of children. This in turn minimizes the height of the B-tree and hence the length of a search path. Because one disk access is required at each level along the search path, the number of data transfers from the disk is also minimized.

A natural question to ask, therefore, is what value to use for the order m. It is clear that the larger the value of m, the more values that can be stored in B-trees with a given height. The following table gives a few values:

height	m = 2	m = 4	m = 10	m = 100
0	1	3	9	99
1	3	15	99	9999
2	7	63	999	999999
3	15	255	9999	99999999

Empirical studies have shown that the best performance is achieved for values of m in the range 50 to 400.

In practice, when the data items are large records, modified B-trees in which only the leaves store complete records can be used; the other nodes store certain key values from these records because only the key values are used in searching. Also, the leaves may be linked together to reduce still further the number of disk accesses required.

Representing Trees and Forests as Binary Trees

Because general trees arise in a variety of applications, we must consider what structures might be used to implement them. We have already considered using nodes with four links for 2-3-4 trees, and in general, we might use any number of links,

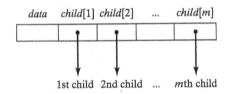

where m is the maximum number of children that a node may have. Declarations for such nodes would thus have the form

```
const int MAX_CHILDREN = ... ;
                  // maximum number of children per node
class TreeNode
{
 public:
  DataType data;   // type of data items in nodes
  TreeNode * child[MAX_CHILDREN];
  //-- TreeNode operations
};


typedef TreeNode * TreePointer;
```

As we saw before, the problem with this linked representation is that each node must have one link for each possible child, even though most of the nodes will not use all of these links. This can result in a large amount of wasted space. For example, an analysis like that for 2-3-4 trees would show that, for a tree with up to 100 links per node, the fraction of unused links is

$$\frac{99n + 1}{100n}$$

which is approximately 99 percent!

It is possible, however, to represent any tree using nodes that have only two links—that is, by a binary tree. We use one of these links to connect siblings together (that is, all the children of a given node) in the order in which they appear in the tree, from left to right. The other link in each node points to the first node in this linked list of its children. For example, the tree

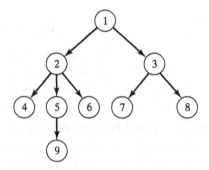

can be represented by the binary tree

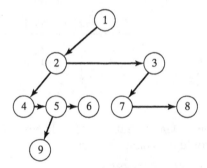

or, drawn in the more customary manner,

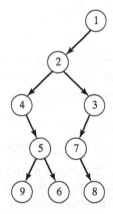

In this binary tree, *node x is a left child of node y if x is the leftmost child of y in the given tree; and x is the right child of y if x is the next sibling of y in the original tree.*

When a binary tree is used in this manner to represent a general tree, the right pointer in the root is always null because the root never has a right child. (Why?) This allows us to use a binary tree to represent not merely a single tree but an entire **forest**, which is a collection of trees. We simply set the right pointer of the root to the root of the binary tree for the next tree in the forest. For example, the forest

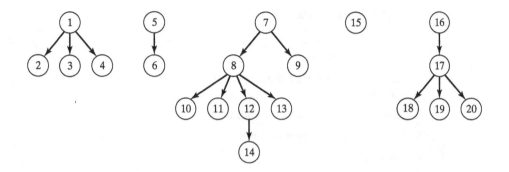

can be represented by the single binary tree

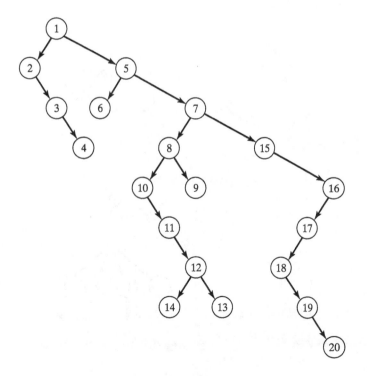

One especially attractive feature of this representation of general trees is that we have studied binary trees in some detail and have developed algorithms for processing them. These algorithms can thus be used to process general trees, as described in the exercises; in particular, the traversal algorithms can be used to traverse general trees and forests.

A third representation of general trees is based on the fact that trees are special cases of a more general structure known as a *directed graph*. Directed graphs are considered in the next chapter, and any of the implementations described there can also be used for trees.

✔ Quick Quiz 15.3

1. Draw a picture of (a) a 2-node, (b) a 3-node, and (c) a 4-node, and tell what must be true for each.

2. Show the 2-3-4 tree that results from inserting the letters S, P, E, C, I, A, L, T, Y, in this order.

3. Draw the red–black tree that represents the 2-3-4 tree in Question 2.

4. A(n) _____-tree is commonly used for external searching.

5. A B-tree of order _____ is a 2-3-4 tree.

6. Draw the B-tree of order 5 that results from inserting the letters S, P, E, C, I, A, L, T, Y, in this order. When it is necessary to split a 5-node, use the second value in the node as the median.

Give the binary-tree representation of each of the general trees in Questions 7 and 8.

7.

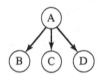

8.

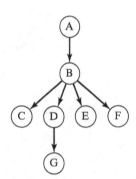

Exercises 15.3

For Exercises 1–6, draw the 2-3-4 tree that results when the values are inserted in the order given:

1. 55, 66, 44, 77, 33, 88, 22, 99, 11
2. 55, 66, 77, 88, 99, 11, 22, 33, 44
3. 11, 22, 33, 44, 55, 66, 77, 88, 99
4. 99, 88, 77, 66, 55, 44, 33, 22, 11
5. B, E, A, N, S
6. C, O, R, N, F, L, A, K, E, S

7–12. Draw the red–black trees for the 2-3-4 trees in Exercises 1–6.

13–18. Repeat Exercises 1–6, but use B-trees of order 5.

19. Construct the B-tree of order 5 that results when the following integers are inserted in the order given: 261, 381, 385, 295, 134, 400, 95, 150, 477, 291, 414, 240, 456, 80, 25, 474, 493, 467, 349, 180, 370, 257.

20. Give the binary-tree representation of the following tree:

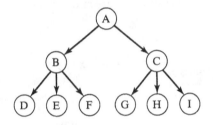

21. Give the binary-tree representation of the following forest:

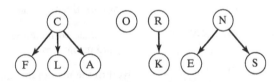

22. Give an algorithm to delete a node from a 2-3-4 tree.

23. Give an algorithm to delete a node from a red–black tree.

Exercises 24–26 ask you to develop class templates for various trees. You should also write driver programs to test your answers as instructed in Programming Problems 4–6 at the end of this chapter.

24. Develop a class template for red–black trees.

25. Develop a class template for B-trees that uses nodes with more than two links as described in the text to store the nodes of the B-tree.

26. Develop a class template for general search trees that uses a binary tree to represent the tree as described in the text.

15.4 Associative Containers in STL—maps (optional)

In Chapter 9 we described the **sequential containers** in C++'s Standard Template Library:

```
vector
deque
list
stack
queue
priority_queue
```

The **associative containers** provided in STL are

```
set
multiset
map
multimap
```

These associative containers are similar in the operations they provide, which include the following:

Function Member	Description
Constructors	Construct container *c* to be:
c()	empty
c(*compare*)	empty, using *compare* function to compare keys
c(*first*, *last*)	initialized with elements in the range [*first*, *last*)
c(*first*, *last*, *compare*)	initialized with elements in the range [*first*, *last*) and using *compare* function to compare keys
c.max_size()	Return the maximum number of locations *c* can ever have
c.size()	Return the number of values currently stored in *c*
c.empty()	Return true if and only if *c* contains no values (i.e., *c*'s size is 0)
c.count(*key*)	Return number of elements in *c* that match *key*
c.find(*key*)	Return iterator positioned at element in *c* matching *key*; at end() if none.
c.lower_bound(*key*)	Return iterator positioned at first position in *c* where *key* can be inserted and ordering maintained. If none, return iterator at end().

Function Member	Description
c.upper_bound(*key*)	Same, but find last position
c.begin()	Return an iterator positioned at *c*'s first element
c.end()	Return an iterator positioned past *c*'s last element
c.rbegin()	Return a reverse iterator positioned at c's last element
c.rend()	Return a reverse iterator positioned before *c*'s first element
c.insert(*first*, *last*);	Insert elements in the range [*first*, *last*)
c.insert(*it*,*key*);	Insert a copy of *key* if there is none, using *it* as a hint on where to start searching
c.insert(*key*);	Insert a copy of *key* if there is none and return $$pair<it, boolean>$$ where *it* is positioned at the new element and *boolean* is true or *it* is positioned at an existing element and boolean is false. *Note:* **pair<T1, T2>** is a class template that contains two objects, the first of type T1 and the second of type T2. It is defined in <utility>. Its constructor has the form pair(a, b) (no default constructor). Operations are: == and <. There are 2 *public* data members: first and second
c.erase(*it*);	Erase the value in c at iterator position *it*
c.erase(*it1*, *it2*);	Erase the values in c from iterator positions *it1* to *it2*
c.erase(*key*);	Erase element(s) that match *key*
c[*key*]	Access the element of c (a map) whose index is *key*
c1 = c2	Assign a copy of *c2* to *c1*
c1.swap(c2)	Swap *c1*'s contents with *c2*'s
c1 == c2	Return true if and only if *c1* has the same values as *c2*
c1 < c2	Return true if and only if *c1* is lexicographically less than *c2*

The associative containers are also quite similar in their implementations—they all use red–black trees to store their elements. They differ in whether both keys and their associated data are stored (map and multimap) or only keys are stored (set and multiset); also, the multi- containers allow multiple instances of keys, whereas the other containers do not.

Like several of the other topics in this chapter, a detailed study of these containers is beyond the level of this introductory text and is left to more advanced courses in data structures. We will give one example of maps, however, because they provide one operation that makes them especially useful, namely, the subscript operator []:

$m[key]$:   Returns a reference to the T value associated with *key*; a default T-value if there is none, where T is the type of the elements in *m*.

([] is not provided for the other containers.) It allows us to use **associative arrays** in which *the index type may be any type*, as illustrated by the program in Figure 15.1.

A common form of map declarations is

```
map<KeyType, DataType, less<KeyType>) obj;
```

(with similar declarations for the other associative containers). The less-than operator (<) must be defined for elements of type *KeyType*. The map object obj then operates in essentially the same manner as an array whose indices are of type *KeyType* and whose elements are of type *DataType*. For example, the definition of map object a1 in the program is equivalent to

```
map<string, Student, less<string> > a1;
```

For any string object name,

```
a1[name]
```

is a Student object, where Student is the class defined in the program. The declaration of map object a2 is equivalent to

```
map<Student, string, less<Student> > a2;
```

For any Student object aStudent,

```
a2[aStudent]
```

is a string. Note that < is defined for type Student.

Figure 15.1 Examples of maps

```
#include <iostream>
#include <string>
#include <map>
using namespace std;

class Student
{
 public:
  //--- Constructor
  Student (int id = 0, double gpa = 0);
  //--- Output operator
  friend ostream & operator<<(ostream & out, const Student & s);
  //--- Input operator
  friend istream & operator>>(istream & in, Student & s);
```

Figure 15.1 (continued)

```cpp
    //--- Less-than operator
    friend bool operator<(const Student & a, const Student & b);
  private:
    //--- Data members
    int myId;
    double myGPA;
};   // end of class Student

//--- Definition of constructor
inline Student::Student(int id, double gpa)
  : myId(id), myGPA(gpa)
{ }

//--- Definition of input operator
inline istream & operator>>(istream & in, Student & s)
{
  in >> s.myId >> s.myGPA;
}

//--- Definition of output operator
inline ostream & operator<<(ostream & out, const Student & s)
{ out << "id = " << s.myId << "  GPA = " << s.myGPA;
  return out;
}

//--- Definition of less-than operator
inline bool operator<(const Student & a, const Student & b)
{ return a.myId < b.myId; }

//=================================================================

int main()
{
  typedef map<string, Student, less<string> > map1;
  typedef map<Student, string, less<Student> > map2;

  map1 a1;    // associative array of Student, index type is string
  map2 a2;    // associative array of string, index type is Student
```

Figure 15.1 (continued)

```
        Student s;
        s = Student(12345, 3.3);  a1["Fred"] = s;    a2[s] = "Fred";
        s = Student(32322, 3.9);  a1["Al"] = s;      a2[s] = "Al";
        s = Student(13131, 2.5);  a1["Joan"] = s;    a2[s] = "Joan";
        s = Student(22121, 4.0);  a1["Barb"] = s;    a2[s] = "Barb";
        s = Student(28888, 2.9);  a1["George"] = s;  a2[s] = "George";
        s = Student(19981, 3.0);  a1["Dot"] = s;     a2[s] = "Dot";
        s = Student(20012, 2.9);  a1["Sue"] = s;     a2[s] = "Sue";
        string name;
        cout << "Enter a name: ";
        cin >> name;
        map1::iterator it1 = a1.find(name);
        cout << name << " has ";
        if (it1== a1.end())
          cout << "no info";
        else
          cout << a1[name];
        cout << endl;

        Student aStudent;
        cout << "Enter a Student's id and GPA: ";
        cin >> aStudent;
        map2::iterator it2 = a2.find(aStudent);
        cout << "Student " << aStudent << " is ";

        if (it2 == a2.end())
          cout << "no info";
        else
          cout << a2[aStudent];
        cout << endl;
}
```

Execution Traces:
```
Enter a name: Fred
Fred has id = 12345  GPA = 3.3
Enter a Student's id and GPA: 12345 3.3
Student id = 12345  GPA = 3.3 is Fred
```

Figure 15.1 (continued)

```
Enter a name: Hank
Hank has no info
Enter a Student's id and GPA: 22121 4.0
Student id = 22121  GPA = 4 is Barb
```

▲

As we noted earlier, the associative containers use red–black trees for storing their elements. For example, the red–black tree used to store the map a1 is

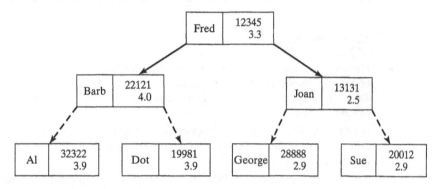

and that for a2 is

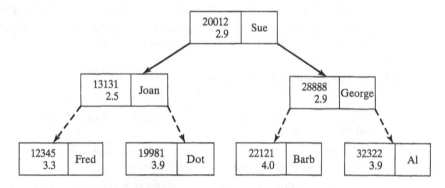

Declarations of the nodes for these red–black trees used to implement maps are declared inside class rb_tree and have the following form:

```
enum color_type {red, black};
struct rb_tree_node
{
  color_type color_field;
  void_pointer parent_link, left_link, right_link;
  Value value_field;
};
```

✔ Quick Quiz 15.4

1. Name the sequential containers in STL.
2. Name the associative containers in STL.
3. For which of the associative containers is [] defined?
4. How is an associative array different from ordinary arrays?
5. The elements in an associative container are stored in a(n) _____ tree.

SUMMARY

🖾 Chapter Notes

- *Huffman codes* are an examples of codes that can be used for data compression. They use codes of different lengths for characters to minimize the expected length of the code for any character. They are also instantly decodable. One way of constructing them makes use of binary trees.

- An *AVL tree* is one of the earliest examples of binary trees that stay height-balanced—the difference between the heights of left and right subtrees of each node is at most 1—during insertions and deletions.

- *2-3-4 trees* store at most 3 data items per node and have at most 4 children. They stay balanced during insertions and deletions.

- *Red–black trees* are binary trees with one link designated red and the other black. They are commonly used to implement 2-3-4 trees as well as STL's associative containers.

- *B-trees* are generalizations of 2-3-4 trees that are commonly used to search data on disk. Using an order between 50 and 400 seems to work best.

☞ Programming Pointers

1. AVL rotations can be accomplished by resetting at most 5 links—3 for simple rotations and 5 for double rotations.

2. AVL rotations are always carried out about the last ancestor along the search path to the point of insertion whose balance factor becomes 2 or –2.

3. Top-down insertion with splitting of 4-nodes is best for 2-3-4 trees, since it prevents the proliferation of node splitting upward from one level to the next.

4. Using nodes with multiple links—*m* links, where *m* is the maximum number of children any node may have—can waste much space because of all the unused links in the leaves.

5. STL's associative containers have the same operations, except that map has a subscript operator that can be used to form *associative arrays* whose indices may be *any* type.

▲ ADT Tips

1. An AVL tree is a height-balanced tree in which the difference between the height of the left subtree and the height of the right subtree (called the *balance factor*) at every node is always 0, +1, or –1.

2. 2-3-4 trees and B-trees are generalized search trees in which, for each value (key) in each node, the items in its left subtree are smaller than that value, and those in its right subtree are greater.

3. 2-3-4 trees are usually implemented with red–black trees.

4. Every tree and forest can be represented by a binary tree using a *left-leftmost-child right-next-sibling* representation; that is, the leftmost child of a node in the original tree or forest becomes the left child of that node in the binary tree, and its next sibling is the right child of that node.

5. STL's associative containers use red–black trees to store their elements.

Programming Problems

Section 15.1

1. Write a function that reads a table of letters and their weights and constructs a Huffman code for these letters. Use the function in a program that encodes a message that the user enters.

2. (Project) Write a program to compress a file using a Huffman code and to decompress a file generated using this code. The program should first read through the file and determine the number of occurrences of each character in the file and the total number of characters in the file. The weight of each character will be the frequency count for that character. The program should then use these weights to construct the Huffman codes for the characters in the file. It should then read the file again and encode it using these Huffman codes and generate a file containing this encoded data. Compute the compression ratio, which is the number of bits in the compressed file divided by the total number of bits in the original file (eight times the number of characters in the file). The program should also provide the option of decompressing a file that was encoded using this Huffman code.

Section 15.2

3. Write a driver program to test your AVLTree class template from Exercise 14.

Section 15.3

4. Write a driver program to test your red–black tree class template from Exercise 24.

5. Write a driver program to test your B-tree class template from Exercise 25.

6. Write a driver program to test your general-tree class template from Exercise 26.

7. Use your B-tree class template from Exercise 26 in a program that reads words and constructs a B-tree to store these words. The program should then allow the user to enter a word and should search the B-tree for this word.

16

Graphs and Digraphs

CHAPTER CONTENTS

Chapter Objectives

- Introduce directed graphs (digraphs) and look at some of the common implementations of them.
- Study some of the algorithms for searching and traversing digraphs.
- See how searching is basic to traversals and shortest-path problems in digraphs.
- Introduce undirected graphs and some of their implementations.

As we noted in Chapter 12 and in the preceding chapter, a tree is a special case of a more general structure known as a *directed graph*, or simply *digraph*. Directed graphs differ from trees in that they need not have a root node and there may be several (or no) paths from one vertex to another. They are useful in modeling communication networks and other networks in which signals, electrical pulses, and the like flow from one node to another along various paths. In other networks, there may be no direction associated with the links, and these can be modeled using *graphs*, which are sometimes called *undirected graphs*. In this chapter we consider how both directed and undirected graphs can be represented, and we look at algorithms for some of the basic operations such as searching and traversal.

16.1 Directed Graphs

As a mathematical structure, a **directed graph**, or **digraph**, like a tree, consists of a finite set of elements called **vertices** or **nodes**, together with a finite set of **directed arcs** or **edges** that connect pairs of vertices.

For example, a directed graph having six vertices numbered 1, 2, 3, 4, 5, 6 and ten directed arcs joining vertices 1 to 2, 1 to 4, 1 to 5, 2 to 3, 2 to 4, 3 to itself, 4 to 2, 4 to 3, 6 to 2, and 6 to 3, can be pictured as

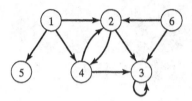

Trees are special kinds of directed graphs and are characterized by the fact that one of their nodes, the root, has no incoming arcs and every other node can be reached from the root by a unique path, that is, by following one and only one sequence of consecutive arcs. In the preceding digraph, vertex 1 is a "rootlike" node having no incoming arcs, but there are many different paths from vertex 1 to various other nodes—for example, to vertex 3:

$$1 \longrightarrow 2 \longrightarrow 3$$

$$1 \longrightarrow 4 \longrightarrow 3$$

$$1 \longrightarrow 4 \longrightarrow 2 \longrightarrow 3$$

$$1 \longrightarrow 4 \longrightarrow 2 \longrightarrow 4 \longrightarrow 3 \longrightarrow 3 \longrightarrow 3$$

Also, there is no path from vertex 1 to vertex 6.

Applications of directed graphs are many and varied. They are used to analyze electrical circuits, develop project schedules, find shortest routes, analyze social relationships, and construct models for the analysis and solution of many other problems. For example, the following directed graph illustrates how digraphs might be used to plan the activities that must be carried out and the order in which they must be done for a (simplified) construction project:

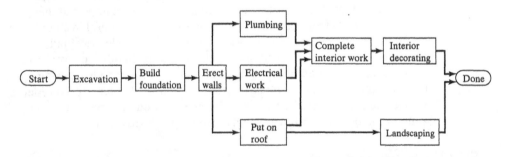

As abstract data types, digraphs also differ from trees. For example, the insertion operation for a tree adds a node to the tree, and adding a link to that node from its parent is part of this operation. For digraphs, however, we may insert a node, but no edges to or from it; or we may insert an edge between two existing nodes. Similarly, the deletion operation may apply either to nodes or edges. The following description of a digraph as an ADT includes some of the most common operations on digraphs:

Directed Graph ADT

Collection of Data Elements
A *finite* set of elements called *nodes* or *vertices*, and a finite set of *directed arcs* or *edges* that connect pairs of nodes.

Basic Operations
Construct an empty directed graph
Check if it is empty
Destroy a directed graph
Insert a new node
Insert a directed edge between two existing nodes or from a node to itself
Delete a node and all directed edges to or from it
Delete a directed edge between two existing nodes
Search for a value in a node, starting from a given node

Other operations, such as the following, are important in some applications: traversal, determining whether one node is reachable from another node, determining the number of paths from one node to another, or finding a shortest path between two nodes.

Adjacency-Matrix Representation

There are several common ways of implementing a directed graph using data structures already known to us. One of these is the **adjacency matrix** of the digraph. To construct it, we first number the vertices of the digraph 1, 2, ... , n; the adjacency matrix is the $n \times n$ matrix *adj*, in which the entry in row i and column j is 1 (or true) if vertex j is **adjacent** to vertex i (that is, if there is a directed arc from vertex i to vertex j), and is 0 (or false) otherwise. (*Note: In mathematics, the rows and columns are usually numbered beginning with 1.*) For example, the adjacency matrix for the digraph

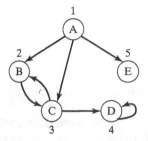

with nodes numbered as shown is

$$adj = \begin{bmatrix} 0 & 1 & 1 & 0 & 1 \\ 0 & 0 & 1 & 0 & 0 \\ 0 & 1 & 0 & 1 & 0 \\ 0 & 0 & 0 & 1 & 0 \\ 0 & 0 & 0 & 0 & 0 \end{bmatrix}$$

For a **weighted digraph** in which some "cost" or "weight" is associated with each arc (e.g., in a digraph modeling a communication network), the cost of the arc from vertex i to vertex j is used instead of 1 in the adjacency matrix.

This matrix representation of a directed graph is straightforward and is useful in a variety of graph problems. For example, with this representation, it is easy to determine the **in-degree** and the **out-degree** of any vertex, which are the number of edges coming into or emanating from that vertex, respectively. The sum of the entries in row i of the adjacency matrix is obviously the out-degree of the ith vertex, and the sum of the entries in the ith column is its in-degree.

The matrix representation of a digraph is also useful in path-counting problems. For example, suppose we wish to count the number of paths of length 2 from vertex i to vertex j in a digraph G. Such a path will exist if and only if there is some vertex k such that there is an edge from vertex i to vertex k and an edge from vertex k to vertex j:

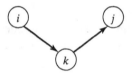

This means that if adj is the adjacency matrix of G, $adj_{i,k}$, *the* entry in row i and column k, and $adj_{k,j}$, the entry in row k and column j, must be 1. The i, j entry of adj^2 is the sum of all the products $adj_{i,k} \cdot adj_{k,j}$ for all possible values of k (see Programming Problem 8 at the end of Chapter 3). These products will contribute 1 to the sum only when both of these entries are 1—that is, only when there is a path of length 2 from vertex i to vertex j running through vertex k. It follows that the i, j entry of adj^2 will be the total number of paths of length 2 from vertex i to vertex j.

In general, the i, j entry of the mth power of adj, adj^m, indicates the number of paths of length m from vertex i to vertex j. For example, for the preceding digraph,

$$adj^3 = \begin{bmatrix} 0 & 1 & 1 & 2 & 0 \\ 0 & 0 & 1 & 1 & 0 \\ 0 & 1 & 0 & 2 & 0 \\ 0 & 0 & 0 & 1 & 0 \\ 0 & 0 & 0 & 0 & 0 \end{bmatrix}$$

The entry in position $(1, 4)$ is 2, indicating that there are 2 paths of length 3 from vertex 1 (A) to vertex 4 (D): A→B→C→D and A→C→D→D.

There are, however, some deficiencies in this representation. One is that it does not store the data items in the vertices of the digraph, the letters A, B, C, D, and E in our example. But this difficulty is easily remedied; we need only create an auxiliary array *data* and store the data item for the *i*th vertex in *data*[*i*]. For our example, therefore, the two arrays

$$adj = \begin{bmatrix} 0 & 1 & 1 & 0 & 1 \\ 0 & 0 & 1 & 0 & 0 \\ 0 & 1 & 0 & 1 & 0 \\ 0 & 0 & 0 & 1 & 0 \\ 0 & 0 & 0 & 0 & 0 \end{bmatrix} \qquad data = \begin{bmatrix} A \\ B \\ C \\ D \\ E \end{bmatrix}$$

completely characterize the digraph.

Adjacency-List Representation

Another deficiency of the adjacency-matrix representation is that this matrix is often **sparse**, that is, it has many zero entries, and thus considerable space is "wasted" in storing these zero values. We can alleviate this problem by adapting one of the representations of sparse matrices described in Section 11.5. For example, modifying the representation of a sparse matrix as an array of pointers to linked row-lists gives rise to the **adjacency-list representation** for digraphs. The directed graph is represented by an array or vector $v[1], v[2], \ldots, v[n]$, one element for each vertex in the digraph. Each $v[i]$ stores the data stored in vertex i together with a linked list of the numbers of all vertices adjacent to vertex i. For example, the adjacency-list representation of the digraph

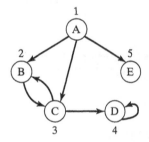

can be pictured as follows:

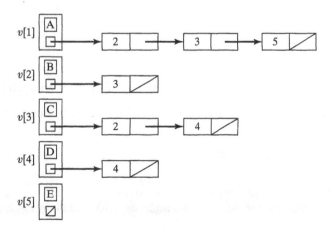

Note that the numbers in the list nodes are the numbers of the columns in the adjacency matrix in which 1's appear. These nodes thus play the same role as the nodes in the row lists of the sparse matrix representation considered in Section 11.5.

This adjacency-list representation of a digraph can be implemented as a class template in C++ with declarations like the following:

```
#include <list>
#include <vector>

template <typename DataType>
class Digraph
{
 public:
  /***** Functions for digraph operations *****/

 private:
  /***** Class for data and adjacency lists *****/
  class VertexInfo
  {
   public:
    DataType data;
    list<int> adjacencyList;
  };

  /***** Data members *****/
  vector<VertexInfo> v;
};
```

In the next section we use this adjacency-list representation in a program to find the shortest path joining two specified nodes in a directed graph.

✔ Quick Quiz 16.1

1. What are some ways a directed graph differs from a tree?

2. In a digraph, it may not be possible to get from one vertex to another. (True or false)

3. In a digraph, vertex w is said to be _____ to vertex v if there is a directed arc from v to w.

4. In a digraph, the number of edges coming into a vertex is called the _____ of that vertex and the number of edges emanating from a vertex is called its _____.

For Questions 5–8, use the following directed graphs:

A.

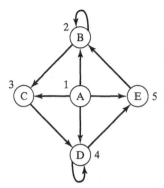

B.

5. Give the adjacency matrix *adj* and the data matrix *data* for digraph A.
6. Give the adjacency matrix *adj* and the data matrix *data* for digraph B.
7. Give the adjacency-list representation of digraph A.
8. Give the adjacency-list representation of digraph B.

Exercises 16.1

For Exercises 1–4, find the adjacency matrix *adj* and the data matrix *data* for the given digraph.

1.

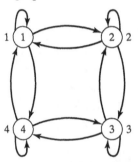

2.

3.

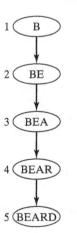

4.

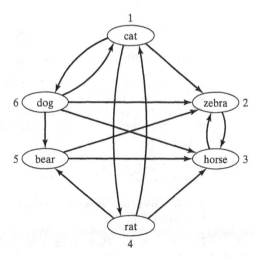

For Exercises 5–8, draw the directed graph represented by the given adjacency matrix *adj* and the data matrix *data*.

5. $adj = \begin{bmatrix} 0 & 1 & 0 & 1 & 0 \\ 1 & 1 & 1 & 0 & 0 \\ 0 & 0 & 0 & 0 & 1 \\ 0 & 1 & 0 & 0 & 1 \\ 0 & 0 & 0 & 0 & 0 \end{bmatrix}$, $data = \begin{bmatrix} A \\ B \\ C \\ D \\ E \end{bmatrix}$

6. $adj = \begin{bmatrix} 0 & 1 & 1 & 1 \\ 0 & 0 & 1 & 1 \\ 0 & 0 & 0 & 1 \\ 0 & 0 & 0 & 0 \end{bmatrix}$, $data = \begin{bmatrix} \text{CAT} \\ \text{RAT} \\ \text{BAT} \\ \text{DOG} \end{bmatrix}$

7. $adj = \begin{bmatrix} 1 & 1 & 1 \\ 1 & 1 & 1 \\ 1 & 1 & 1 \end{bmatrix}$, $data = \begin{bmatrix} 111 \\ 222 \\ 333 \end{bmatrix}$

8. $adj = \begin{bmatrix} 1 & 0 & 0 & 1 & 0 & 0 & 1 \\ 0 & 0 & 1 & 1 & 1 & 0 & 0 \\ 0 & 0 & 1 & 1 & 0 & 0 & 1 \\ 1 & 1 & 1 & 1 & 1 & 1 & 1 \\ 0 & 0 & 0 & 0 & 0 & 0 & 0 \\ 0 & 0 & 0 & 1 & 0 & 0 & 1 \\ 1 & 0 & 0 & 0 & 0 & 1 & 0 \end{bmatrix}$, $data = \begin{bmatrix} \text{Alpha} \\ \text{Beta} \\ \text{Gamma} \\ \text{Delta} \\ \text{Mu} \\ \text{Pi} \\ \text{Rho} \end{bmatrix}$

9–12. Give the adjacency-list representation of the directed graphs in Exercises 1–4.

13–16. Give the adjacency-list representation of the directed graphs in Exercises 5–8.

An alternative to the adjacency-list representation for a directed graph is a *linked adjacency-list* representation that uses a linked list instead of an array or vector, one list node for each vertex in the digraph. A list node stores the data stored in a vertex together with a linked list of the numbers of all vertices adjacent to that vertex.

17–20. Give the linked adjacency-list representation of the directed graphs in Exercises 1–4.

21–24. Give the linked adjacency-list representation of the directed graphs in Exercises 5–8.

In Exercises 25–30, draw the directed graph represented by the adjacency-list.

25.

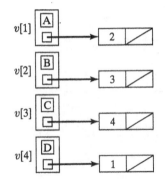

26.

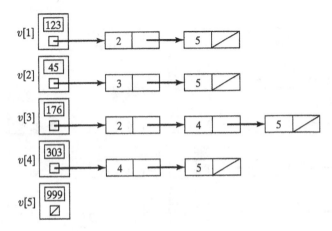

27.

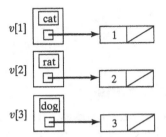

28.

$v[1]$ cat ⊘

$v[2]$ rat ⊘

$v[3]$ dog ⊘

29.

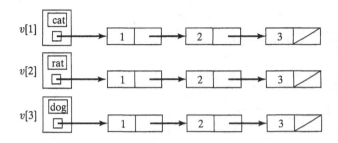

30.

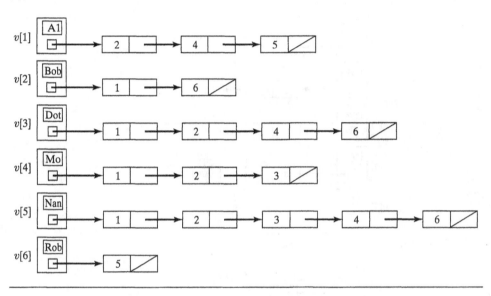

16.2 Searching and Traversing Digraphs

One of the basic operations we considered for trees was traversal, visiting each node exactly once, and we described three standard traversal orders for binary trees: inorder, preorder, and postorder. Traversal of a tree is always possible if we begin at the root, because every other node is reachable from this root via a sequence of consecutive arcs. In a general directed graph, however, there may not be a vertex from which every other vertex can be reached, and thus it may not be possible to traverse the entire digraph, regardless of the start vertex. Consequently, we must first look at the problem of determining which nodes in a digraph are reachable from a given node. Two standard methods of searching for such vertices are **depth-first search** and **breadth-first search**. We illustrate these methods first for trees.

To illustrate depth-first search, consider the following tree:

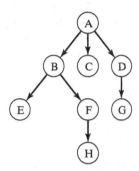

If we begin at the root, we first visit it and then select one of its children, say B, and then visit it. Before visiting the other children of A, however, we visit the descendents of B in a depth-first manner. Thus, we select one of its children, say E, and visit it:

    A, B, E

Again, before visiting the other child of B, we must visit the descendents of E. Because there are none, we backtrack to B and visit its other child F and then visit the descendents of F:

    A, B, E, F, H

Because all of B's descendants have now been visited, we can now backtrack to the last previously visited node along this search path, namely A, and begin visiting the rest of its descendants. We might select C and its descendants (of which there are none):

    A, B, E, F, H, C

Finally, we visit D and its descendants:

    A, B, E, F, H, C, D, G

The following diagram summarizes the different probes and backtracks:

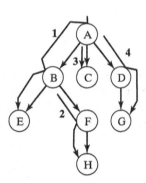

    One question that must be addressed is how to do the required **backtracking**. It is important in many problems wherever it is necessary to process some values and later return to some that were already processed or that were skipped over on an earlier pass. For example, in Section 12.6, we saw how threads could be used to make back-tracking possible in carrying out an inorder traversal of a binary search tree. The usual solution in these problems is to store the items in a *stack* as they are encountered.

Then, when it is necessary to return to an earlier item, we simply pop one from the stack. As one might guess, this makes recursion a natural technique for such problems, because a stack is automatically maintained to make backtracking possible.

In contrast to depth-first search, a breadth-first search of the given tree, beginning at the root, first visits the root

$\underline{A}$

and then each of its children, say, from left to right:

A, <u>B, C, D</u>

The children of these first-level nodes are then visited:

A, B, C, D, <u>E, F, G</u>

Finally, the children of the second-level nodes E, F, and G are visited:

A, B, C, D, E, F, G, <u>H</u>

The following diagram summarizes this search:

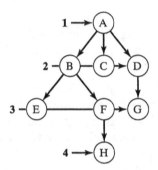

Here we are visiting the nodes level by level, and while visiting each node on some level, we must store it so we can return to it after completing this level, so that the nodes adjacent to it can be visited. Because the first node visited on this level should be the first one to which we return, a *queue* is an appropriate data structure for storing the nodes.

Depth-First Search

A depth-first search of a general directed graph from a given start vertex is similar to that for trees. We visit the start vertex and then follow directed arcs as "deeply" as possible to visit the vertices reachable from it that have not already been visited, backtracking when necessary. For example, a depth-first search of the digraph

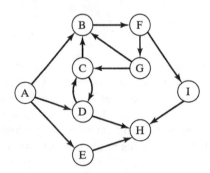

beginning at vertex A might first visit vertices

A, B, F, I, H

We then backtrack to I, the last node visited on this search path, but no unvisited nodes are reachable from it. So we backtrack to F and from there visit G, from which we can reach vertices C and D (as well as B, F, I, and H—but they have already been visited):

A, B, F, I, H, <u>G, C, D</u>

We backtrack to C, but no unvisited nodes are reachable from it, so we backtrack to G. Finding no unvisited nodes reachable from it, we backtrack to F and then to B; there are no unvisited nodes reachable from either of these vertices. Finally, we backtrack to A, from which we can reach the last unvisited vertex E. We have visited the vertices in the order

A, B, F, I, H, G, C, D, <u>E</u>

The following diagram summarizes the probes and backtracks:

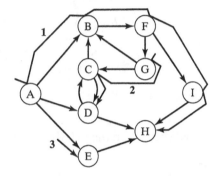

If we start a depth-first search from some vertices, we may not be able to reach all of the other vertices. For example, a depth-first search starting at B will visit the vertices

B, F, I, H, G, C, D

but cannot reach vertices A and E.

The following is a recursive algorithm for depth-first search. At each stage, after visiting a vertex, we select some unvisited vertex adjacent to it (if there are any) and use it as the start vertex for a depth-first search.

 Depth-first Search Algorithm

/*   Depth-first search a digraph to find all vertices reachable
     from a given start vertex.   */

1. Visit the start vertex *v*.

2. For each vertex *w* adjacent to *v* do the following:
   If *w* has not been visited, apply the depth-first search algorithm
   with *w* as the start vertex.
   End for.

One implementation of this algorithm is in the Digraph class template given later in this section (see Figure 16.1).

Breadth-First Search

In a breadth-first search of the preceding directed graph

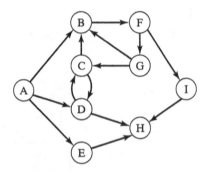

beginning at A, we visit A and then all those vertices adjacent to A:

   A, B, D, E

We then select B, the first vertex adjacent to A, and visit all unvisited vertices adjacent to it:

   A, B, D, E, F

We repeat this for D, the next vertex adjacent to A, and visit all unvisited vertices adjacent to it:

   A, B, D, E, F, C, H

Then we do the same for E, the last vertex adjacent to A, for which the only adjacent vertex is H, which was already visited.

   Having finished with B, D, and E, the nodes adjacent to A, we now repeat this approach for the unvisited vertices adjacent to them: F, then C, and then H. G and I are adjacent to F, so we visit them:

   A, B, D, E, F, C, H, G, I

A, B, and D are adjacent to C, but these vertices have already been visited, and no vertices are adjacent to H. Since all of the vertices have been visited, the search terminates. The following diagram summarizes this search:

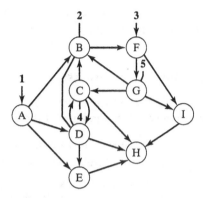

As was true for depth-first search, a breadth-first search from some vertices may fail to locate all vertices. For example, a breadth-first search from B might first visit B and F, then G and I, followed by H and C, and finally, D:

> B, F, G, I, H, C, D

Because A and E are not reachable from B, the search terminates.

As we noted in looking at breadth-first search for trees, a queue is an appropriate data structure to store the vertices as they are visited. The following algorithm uses a queue in this manner:

 Breadth-first Search Algorithm

/* Breadth-first search a digraph to find all vertices reachable from a given start vertex.   */

1. Visit the start vertex.
2. Initialize a queue to contain only the start vertex.
3. While the queue is not empty do the following:
   a. Remove a vertex v from the queue.
   b. For all vertices w adjacent to v do the following:
      If w has not been visited then:
      i. Visit w.
      ii. Add w to the queue.
      End for.
   End while.

Traversal and Shortest-Path Problems

Search algorithms such as those for depth-first and breadth-first searches are basic to many other algorithms for processing directed graphs. For example, to traverse a digraph, we can repeatedly apply one of these searches, selecting new start vertices when necessary, until all of the vertices have been visited. Thus, one possible traversal algorithm is the following:

Digraph Traversal Algorithm

/* Traverse a digraph, visiting each vertex exactly once.
    A depth-first search is the basis of the traversal.   */

1. Initialize an array or `vector` *unvisited* with *unvisited*[*i*] true for each vertex *i*.
2. While some element of *unvisited* is true, do the following:
   a. Select an unvisited vertex *v*.
   b. Use the depth-first search algorithm to visit all vertices reachable from *v*.
   End while.

Another class of problems that require search algorithms for their solutions are **routing problems**, in which one must find an optimal path in a network—a shortest path in a graph or a digraph, a cheapest path in a weighted graph or digraph, and so on. The Dutch computer scientist Edsger Dijkstra is well known for his algorithms used in many such problems.

As a simple example of a routing problem, consider a directed graph that models an airline network in which the vertices represent cities and the directed arcs represent flights connecting these cities. We may be interested in determining the most direct route between two cities—that is, the route with the fewest intermediate stops. In terms of a digraph modeling such a network, we must determine the length of a shortest path, one composed of a minimum number of arcs, from a start vertex to a destination vertex. An algorithm for determining such a shortest path is an easy modification of the breadth-first search algorithm:

A Shortest-path Algorithm

/* Find a shortest path from a *start* vertex to a *destination* vertex in a digraph.
    The vertices on a shortest path from *start* to *destination* are displayed or
    a message indicating that *destination* is not reachable from *start*.   */

1. *Visit start* and label it with 0.
2. Initialize *distance* to 0.
3. Initialize a queue to contain only *start*.
4. While *destination* has not been visited and the queue is not empty,
   do the following:
   a. Remove a vertex *v* from the queue.
   b. If the label of *v* is greater than *distance*, increment *distance* by 1.
   c. For each vertex *w* adjacent to *v*:
      If *w* has not been visited, then
         i. Visit *w* and label it with *distance* + 1.
         ii. Add *w* to the queue.

End for.
End while.
5. If *destination* has not been visited then
    Display "Destination not reachable from start vertex."
    Else find the vertices $p[0], \ldots, p[distance]$ on the shortest path as follows:
    a. Initialize $p[distance]$ to *destination*.
    b. For each value of k ranging from *distance* – 1 down to 0:
        Find a vertex $p[k]$ adjacent to $p[k + 1]$ with label k.
    End for.

The following table traces the execution of the first part of this algorithm as it finds the shortest path from vertex A to vertex H in the digraph given earlier:

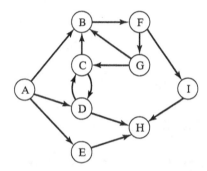

Step(s)	v	distance	Queue	Labels for:	A	B	C	D	E	F	G	H	I
1, 2, 3		0	A		0								
4	A	0	BDE		0	1		1	1				
4	B	1	DEF		0	1		1	1	2			
4	D	1	EFCH		0	1	2	1	1	2		2	
4	E	1	FCH		0	1	2	1	1	2		2	
4	F	2	CHGI		0	1	2	1	1	2	3	2	3
4	C	2	HGI		0	1	2	1	2	2	3	2	3
4	H	2	GI		0	1	2	1	2	2	3	2	3

Step 5 then determines a sequence of vertices on a path from A to H, for example, $p[2] = \text{'H'}, p[1] = \text{'D'}, p[0] = \text{'A'}$.

The shortestPath() method in the Digraph class template in Figure 16.1 implements this algorithm.

Figure 16.1 Digraph Class Template

```
/*--- Digraph.h ---------------------------------------------------
                Header file for Digraph Class Template
  ------------------------------------------------------------------*/


#include <list>
#include <vector>
#include <queue>
#include <iostream>
#include <fstream>

template <typename DataType>
class Digraph
{
 public:
  /***** Function Members *****/
  DataType data(int k) const;
  /*------------------------------------------------------------
     Retrieve data value in a given vertex.

     Precondition:  k is the number of a vertex.
     Postcondition: Data value stored in vertex k is returned.
    ------------------------------------------------------------*/


  void read(ifstream & inStream);
  /*------------------------------------------------------------
     Input operation.

     Precondition:  ifstream inStream is open.  The lines in the file to
         which it is connected are organized so that the data item in a
         vertex is on one line and on the next line is the number of
         vertices adjacent to it followed by a list of these vertices.
     Postcondition: The adjacency list representation of this digraph
         has been stored in myAdjacencyLists.
    ------------------------------------------------------------*/


  void display(ostream & out);
  /*------------------------------------------------------------
     Output operation.

     Precondition:  ostream out is open.
```

Figure 16.1 (continued)

```
      Postcondition: Each vertex and its adjacency list have
          been output to out.
    ----------------------------------------------------------------*/


void depthFirstSearch(int start);
/*-------------------------------------------------------------
   Depth first search of digraph via depthFirstSearchAux(), starting
   at vertex start.

   Precondition:  start is a vertex.
   Postcondition: Digraph has been depth-first searched from start.
   ----------------------------------------------------------------*/


vector<int> shortestPath(int start, int destination);
/*-------------------------------------------------------------
   Find a shortest path in the digraph from vertex start to vertex
   destination.

   Precondition:  start and destination are vertices.
   Postcondition: A vector of vertices along the shortest path from
          start to destination is returned.
   ----------------------------------------------------------------*/


private:
 /***** "Head nodes" of adjacency lists *****/
  class VertexInfo
  {
   public:
     DataType data;
     list<int> adjacencyList;
  }; // end of VertexInfo class

 /***** Data Member *****/
  vector<VertexInfo> myAdjacencyLists;

 /***** Private Function Member *****/
  void depthFirstSearchAux(int start, vector<bool> & unvisited);
  /*-------------------------------------------------------------
     Recursive depth first search of digraph, starting at vertex start.
```

Figure 16.1 (continued)

```
        Precondition:  start is a vertex;  unvisited[i] is true if vertex i has
            not yet been visited, and is false otherwise.
        Postcondition: Vector unvisited has been updated.
        --------------------------------------------------------------------*/

}; // end of Digraph class template declaration

//--- Definition of data()
template <typename DataType>
inline DataType Digraph<DataType>::data(int k) const
{
  return myAdjacencyLists[k].data;
}

//--- Definition of read()
template <typename DataType>
void Digraph<DataType>::read(ifstream & inStream)
{
  Digraph<DataType>::VertexInfo vi;
  int n,           // number of vertices adjacent to some vertex
      vertex;      // the number of a vertex

  // Put a garbage 0-th value so indices start with 1, as is customary
  myAdjacencyLists.push_back(vi);

  // Construct adjacency list representation
  for (;;)
  {
    inStream >> vi.data;
    if (inStream.eof()) break;

    inStream >> n;
    list<int> adjList;      // construct empty list
    for (int i = 1; i <= n; i++)
    {
      inStream >> vertex;
      adjList.push_back(vertex);
    }
```

Figure 16.1 (continued)

```
      vi.adjacencyList = adjList;
      myAdjacencyLists.push_back(vi);
   }
}


//--- Definition of display()
template <typename DataType>
void Digraph<DataType>::display(ostream & out)
{
  out << "Adjacency-List Representation: \n";
  for (int i = 1; i < myAdjacencyLists.size(); i++)
  {
    out << i << ": " <<  myAdjacencyLists[i].data << "--";
    for (list<int>::iterator
         it = myAdjacencyLists[i].adjacencyList.begin();
         it != myAdjacencyLists[i].adjacencyList.end(); it++)
      out << *it << "   ";
    out << endl;
  }
}


//-- Definitions of depthFirstSearch() and depthFirstSearchAux()
template <typename DataType>
inline void Digraph<DataType>::depthFirstSearch(int start)
{
  vector<bool> unvisited(myAdjacencyLists.size(), true);
  depthFirstSearchAux(start, unvisited);
}


template <typename DataType>
void Digraph<DataType>::depthFirstSearchAux(
                                int start, vector<bool> & unvisited)
{
  // Add statements here to process myAdjacencyLists[start].data
  cout << myAdjacencyLists[start].data << endl;

  unvisited[start] = false;
  // Traverse its adjacency list, performing depth-first
  // searches from each unvisited vertex in it.
```

Figure 16.1 (continued)

```
  for (list<int>::iterator
       it = myAdjacencyLists[start].adjacencyList.begin();
       it != myAdjacencyLists[start].adjacencyList.end(); it++)
    // check if current vertex has been visited
    if (unvisited[*it])
      // start DFS from new node
      depthFirstSearchAux(*it, unvisited);
}


//--- Definition of shortestPath()
template<typename DataType>
vector<int> Digraph<DataType>::shortestPath(int start, int destination)
{
  int n = myAdjacencyLists.size(); // number of vertices (#ed from 1)
  vector<int> distLabel(n,-1),     // distance labels for vertices, all
                                   // marked as unvisited (-1)
              predLabel(n);        // predecessor labels for vertices
  // Perform breadth first search from start to find destination,
  // labeling vertices with distances from start as we go.
  distLabel[start] = 0;
  int distance = 0,                // distance from start vertex
      vertex;                      // a vertex
  queue<int> vertexQueue;          // queue of vertices
  vertexQueue.push(start);
  while (distLabel[destination] < 0 && !vertexQueue.empty())
  {
    vertex = vertexQueue.front();
    vertexQueue.pop();
    if (distLabel[vertex] > distance)
      distance++;
    for (list<int>::iterator
         it = myAdjacencyLists[vertex].adjacencyList.begin();
         it != myAdjacencyLists[vertex].adjacencyList.end(); it++)
      if (distLabel[*it] < 0)
      {
        distLabel[*it] = distance + 1;
```

Figure 16.1 (continued)

```
      predLabel[*it] = vertex;
      vertexQueue.push(*it);
    }
  }
  distance++;


  // Now reconstruct the shortest path if there is one
  vector<int> path(distance+1);
  if (distLabel[destination] < 0)
    cout << "Destination not reachable from start vertex\n";
  else
  {
    path[distance] = destination;
    for (int k = distance - 1; k >= 0; k--)
      path[k] = predLabel[path[k+1]];
  }

  return path;
}
```

▲

Figure 16.2 shows a program that uses Digraph to solve the airline network problem described earlier. The adjacency-list representation of the network is input from networkFile. Each city is identified by both number and name, and the *i*th line of the file contains the name of the *i*th city followed by the numbers of all vertices adjacent to the *i*th vertex. The user then enters the name of a start city and the name of a destination, and the function member short-estPath() of class template Digraph is used to find the shortest path from the start vertex to the destination vertex, if there is one.

Figure 16.2 Shortest Paths in a Network

```
/*-------------------------------------------------------------------------
   Program to find the most direct route in an airline network from a given
   start city to a given destination city.  A digraph represented by its
   adjacency-list implementation is used for the network, and the
   information needed to construct it is read from networkFile.
   -----------------------------------------------------------------------*/
```

Figure 16.2 (continued)

```cpp
#include <iostream>
#include <fstream>
#include <iomanip>
#include <string>
#include <vector>
using namespace std;

#include "Digraph.h"

int main()
{
  cout << "Enter name of network file: ";
  string networkFile;
  cin >> networkFile;
  ifstream inFile(networkFile.data());
  if (!inFile.is_open())
  {
    cerr << "*** Cannot open " << networkFile << " ***\n";
    exit(-1);
  }

  Digraph<string> d;
  d.read(inFile);
  cout << "The Digraph's ";
  d.display(cout);
  cout << endl;

  int start, destination;
  char response;
  do
  {
    cout << "Number of start city? ";
    cin >> start;
    cout << "Number of destination? ";
    cin >> destination;

    vector<int> path = d.shortestPath(start, destination);
    cout << "Shortest path is:\n";
```

Figure 16.2 (continued)

```
    for (int k = 0; k < path.size()-1; k++)
    {
      cout << setw(3) << path[k] << ' ' << d.data(path[k]) << endl;
      cout << "        |\n"
              "        v\n";
    }
    cout << setw(3) << destination << ' ' << d.data(destination) << endl;
    cout << "\nMore (Y or N)?";
    cin >> response;
  }
  while (response == 'y' || response == 'Y');
}
```

Listing of *NetworkFile*:
```
Los_Angeles
3 3 4 6
San_Francisco
3 1 3 4
Denver
3 1 2 3
Chicago
2 3 8
Boston
2 4 6
New_York
3 4 7 8
Miami
3 8 3 5
New_Orleans
2 1 7
```

Execution Trace:
```
Enter name of network file: NetworkFile
The Digraph's Adjacency-List Representation:
1: Los_Angeles--3  4  6
2: San_Francisco--1  3  4
3: Denver--1  2  3
4: Chicago--3  8
```

Figure 16.2 (continued)

```
5: Boston--4  6
6: New_York--4  7  8
7: Miami--8  3  5
8: New_Orleans--1  7
Number of start city? 5
Number of destination? 1
Shortest path is:
  5 Boston
    |
    v
  4 Chicago
    |
    v
  3 Denver
    |
    v
  1 Los_Angeles

More (Y or N)?N
```

▲

NP-Complete Problems

A classic routing problem that is of both practical and theoretical interest is the **traveling salesman problem**. In this problem, a weighted digraph with vertices representing cities and the cost of an arc representing the distance between the cities must be traversed using a path of minimal total cost. The practical importance of this problem should be obvious.

The traveling salesman problem belongs to the large collection of problems known as **NP**, which stands for *nondeterministic polynomial*. These are problems for which a solution can be guessed and then checked with an algorithm whose computing time is $O(P(n))$ for some polynomial $P(n)$. No particular strategy is required (or known) for guessing—thus the nondeterminism. This is in contrast to the collection **P**, which stands for *(deterministic) polynomial time*. These problems can be solved by algorithms in polynomial time.

One of the most important problems in computer science theory is the following:

> *Are there **NP** problems that are not **P** problems?*

No one has ever found such a problem, but neither has anyone been able to prove that one does not exist.

The traveling salesman problem is in fact a special kind of NP problem known as **NP-complete**. These problems have the property that, if a polynomial time algorithm that solves *any one* of these problems can be found—for example, for the traveling salesman problem—then the existence of polynomial time algorithms for *all* NP problems is guaranteed; that is NP = P.

✔ Quick Quiz 16.2

1. What is backtracking?
2. For the digraph labeled A in Quick Quiz 16.1, which nodes can be reached using a depth-first search from vertex 1? from vertex 2?
3. For the digraph labeled B in Quick Quiz 16.1, which nodes can be reached using a depth-first search from vertex 1?
4. For a breadth-first search of the digraph labeled A in Quick Quiz 16.1 starting from vertex 1, which nodes will be visited next?
5. What are NP problems? P problems? NP-complete problems?

◆ Exercises 16.2

For Exercises 1–5, construct a trace table for the algorithm, using the digraph in Exercise 1 of Section 16.1. Whenever a new vertex to visit must be selected and there is more than one possibility, use the vertex labeled with the smallest number.

1. Depth-first search starting at vertex 1.
2. Depth-first search starting at vertex 2.
3. Breadth-first search starting at vertex 1.
4. Breadth-first search starting at vertex 2.
5. Shortest path from vertex 2 to vertex 4.

For Exercises 6–10, proceed as in Exercises 1–5, but use the digraph in Exercise 4 of Section 16.1.

6. Depth-first search starting at vertex 1.
7. Depth-first search starting at vertex 2.
8. Breadth-first search starting at vertex 1.
9. Breadth-first search starting at vertex 2.
10. Shortest path from vertex 4 to vertex 6.

For Exercises 11–19, proceed as in Exercises 1–5, but use the following digraph. Whenever a new vertex to visit must be selected and there is more than one possibility, use the vertex containing the letter that comes earliest in the alphabet.

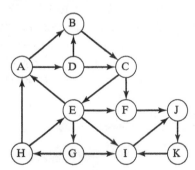

11. Depth-first search starting at vertex A.

12. Depth-first search starting at vertex F.

13. Breadth-first search starting at vertex A.

14. Breadth-first search starting at vertex F.

15. Shortest path from vertex A to vertex E.

16. Shortest path from vertex A to vertex H.

17. Shortest path from vertex G to vertex C.

18. Shortest path from vertex J to vertex I.

19. Shortest path from vertex J to vertex A.

The following exercises ask you to write functions. You should also write driver programs to test them, as instructed in Programming Problems 1–4 at the end of this chapter.

20. Add a function member to the `Digraph` class template for doing a breadth-first search from some start vertex.

21. If A is an $n \times n$ adjacency matrix for a directed graph, then the entry in the ith row and jth column of A^k is equal to the number of paths of length k from the ith vertex to the jth vertex in this digraph. The *reachability matrix* R of a digraph is the $n \times n$ matrix defined by

$$R = I + A + A^2 + \cdots + A^{n-1}$$

where I is the $n \times n$ identity matrix having ones on the diagonal (from upper left corner to lower right corner) and zeros off. In the digraph, there is a path from vertex i to vertex j if and only if the entry in row i and column j of R is nonzero. Write a function to find the reachability matrix for a directed graph.

22. An alternative to the method of Exercise 21 for determining reachability is to use "boolean multiplication and addition," that is, *bitwise and* (&) and *bitwise or* (|) operations, in carrying out the matrix computations ($0 = false$, $1 = true$). Rewrite the function in Exercise 21 to find this form of the reachability matrix.

23. *Warshall's algorithm* provides a more efficient method for calculating the boolean form of the reachability matrix described in Exercise 21:

    a. Initialize R to A and k to 1.

    b. While $k \leq n$ and R is not all ones do the following:

        i. For i ranging from 1 to n with $i \neq k$:

            If the entry in the ith row and kth column of R is 1,
            then replace row i with (row i) | (row k).

        ii. Increment k by 1.

    End while.

Use Warshall's algorithm to find the reachability matrix for the following digraph:

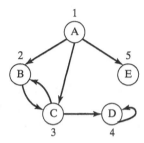

24. Write a function to find the reachability matrix of a digraph using Warshall's algorithm.

16.3 Graphs

A **graph**, sometimes called an **undirected graph**, is like a digraph except that no direction is associated with the edges. Also, no edges joining a vertex to itself are allowed. For example, the following diagram shows a graph having five vertices with edges joining vertices 1 and 2, 1 and 4, 1 and 5, 2 and 4, 3 and 4, and 4 and 5:

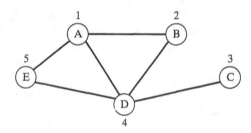

Such graphs are useful in modeling electrical circuits, structures of chemical compounds, communication systems, and many other networks in which no direction is associated with the links.

As ADTs, graphs and digraphs have basically the same operations:

Graph ADT

Collection of Data Elements

A *finite* set of elements called *nodes* or *vertices*, and a finite set of *edges* that connect pairs of distinct nodes.

Basic Operations

Construct an empty graph
Check if it is empty
Destroy a graph
Insert a new node
Insert an edge between two existing nodes
Delete a node and all edges having it as an endpoint
Delete an edge between two existing nodes
Search for a value in a node, starting from a given node

Most of the other operations described for digraphs—traversals, finding shortest paths, and so forth—are also important in applications of graphs.

Adjacency-Matrix and Adjacency-List Representations

Like digraphs, graphs can be represented by either adjacency matrices or adjacency lists. For example, the adjacency matrix for the preceding graph is

$$adj = \begin{bmatrix} 0 & 1 & 0 & 1 & 1 \\ 1 & 0 & 0 & 1 & 0 \\ 0 & 0 & 0 & 1 & 0 \\ 1 & 1 & 1 & 0 & 1 \\ 1 & 0 & 0 & 1 & 0 \end{bmatrix}$$

where a 1 in row i and column j (numbered from 1) indicates the existence of an edge joining the ith and jth vertices. Because these edges are undirected, there also is a 1 in row j and column i; thus, the adjacency matrix for an undirected graph is always **symmetric**. This means that the entries on one side of the diagonal (from the upper-left corner to the lower-right corner) are redundant. Also, since undirected graphs have no edges from a vertex to itself, all entries on the diagonal of the adjacency matrix are 0. Consequently, the adjacency matrix is not a very efficient representation of an undirected graph (unless we use a *jagged* two-dimensional table as described in Section 9.6).

The following is the adjacency-list representation for the preceding graph:

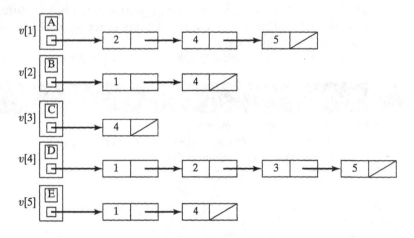

Like the adjacency matrix, this representation is also not very efficient because redundant information is stored. If an edge joins vertices i and j, then a vertex node containing vertex i appears in the adjacency list for vertex j, and a vertex node containing vertex j appears in the adjacency list for vertex i.

Edge-List Representation

A more efficient representation of a graph uses **edge lists.** Each **edge node** in one of these lists represents one edge in the graph and has the form

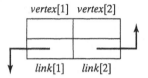

where $vertex[1]$ and $vertex[2]$ are vertices connected by an edge, $link[1]$ points to another edge node having $vertex[1]$ as one endpoint, and $link[2]$ points to another edge node having $vertex[2]$ as an endpoint. The edge-list representation then consists of an array or `vector` v of classes (or structs), one for each vertex, with each class containing a data member and a pointer to an edge node having that vertex as one of its endpoints. For example, the edge-list representation for the graph

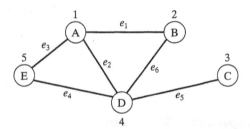

where we have labeled the edges $e_1, e_2, \ldots, e_6$ as indicated, is pictured in Figure 16.3.

Depth-first search, breadth-first search, traversal, and other algorithms for processing graphs are similar to those for digraphs. Figure 16.4 shows a class template Graph with function members that implement these algorithms as well as some other operations. And other function members for Graph are described in the exercises. This version of Graph uses the edge-list representation of graphs just described.

Connectedness

One important property of a graph is whether it is **connected**—that is, whether there is a path from each vertex to every other vertex. One of the function members in the Graph class template in Figure 16.4 is isConnected(), which checks a graph for connectedness. It does so by using a depth-first search, marking all vertices that are reachable from vertex 1. The program in Figure 16.5 uses this function member of Graph to determine whether a graph entered by the user is connected. If it is not, the program provides a list of all vertices that cannot be reached from the start vertex specified by the user.

Figure 16.3 Edge-list Representation of a Graph

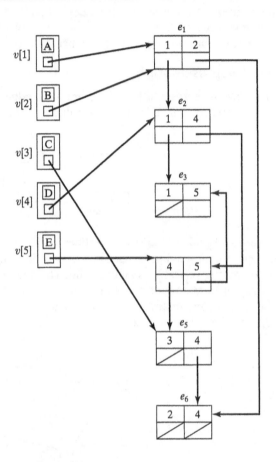

Figure 16.4 Graph Class Template

```
/*--- Graph.h -----------------------------------------------------
                Header file for Graph Class Template
----------------------------------------------------------------*/


#include <vector>
#include <iostream>

template <typename DataType>
class Graph
{
 public:
  /***** Function Members *****/
```

Figure 16.4 (continued)

```
DataType data(int k) const;
/*------------------------------------------------------------------
  Retrieve data value in a given vertex.

  Precondition:  k is the number of a vertex.
  Postcondition: Data value stored in vertex #k is returned.
  ----------------------------------------------------------------*/

void read(istream & in, int numVertices, int numEdges);
/*------------------------------------------------------------------
  Input operation.

  Precondition:  istream in is open; numVertices and numEdges are the
      number of vertices and edges in the graph, respectively.
  Postcondition: The vertices and edges of the graph have been read
      from in and the edge-list representation of this graph stored
      in myEdgeLists.
  ----------------------------------------------------------------*/


void depthFirstSearch(int start, vector<bool> & unvisited);
/*------------------------------------------------------------------
  Depth first search of graph via depthFirstSearchAux(), starting
  at vertex start.

  Precondition:  start is a vertex.
  Postcondition: Graph has been depth-first searched from start.
  ----------------------------------------------------------------*/


bool isConnected();
/*------------------------------------------------------------------
  Check if graph is connected.

  Precondition:  None.
  Postcondition: True is returned if graph is connected, false if not.
  ----------------------------------------------------------------*/


private:
/***** Edge Nodes *****/
```

Figure 16.4 (continued)

```cpp
  class EdgeNode
  {
   public:
    int vertex[3];          // Use 1 and 2 for indices
    EdgeNode * link[3];     //   as is customary
  }; // end of EdgeNode class

  typedef EdgeNode * EdgePointer;

/***** "Head nodes" of edge lists *****/
  class VertexInfo
  {
   public:
    DataType data;          // data value in vertex
    EdgePointer first;      // pointer to first edge node
  }; // end of VertexInfo class

/***** Data Members *****/
  vector<VertexInfo> myEdgeLists;

/***** Private Function Member *****/
  void depthFirstSearchAux(int start, vector<bool> & unvisited);
  /*-------------------------------------------------------------
    Recursive depth first search of graph, starting at vertex start.

    Precondition:  start is a vertex; unvisited[i] is true if vertex i has
        not yet been visited, and is false otherwise.
    Postcondition: Vector unvisited has been updated.
    -----------------------------------------------------------*/

}; // end of Graph class template declaration

//--- Definition of data()
template <typename DataType>
inline DataType Graph<DataType>::data(int k) const
{
  return myEdgeLists[k].data;
}
```

Figure 16.4 (continued)

```
//--- Definition of read()
template <typename DataType>
void Graph<DataType>::read(istream & in, int numVertices, int numEdges)
{
  Graph<DataType>::VertexInfo vi;

  // Put a garbage 0-th value so indices start with 1, as is customary
  myEdgeLists.push_back(vi);

  // Create "head nodes"
  cout << "Enter label of vertex:\n";
  for (int i = 1; i <= numVertices; i++)
  {
    cout << "  " << i << ": ";
    in >> vi.data;
    vi.first = 0;
    myEdgeLists.push_back(vi);
  }

  int endpoint;        // endpoint of an edge
  // Create edge lists
  cout << "Enter endpoints of edge\n";
  for (int i = 1; i <= numEdges; i++)
  {
    cout << "  " << i << ": ";
    EdgePointer newPtr = new EdgeNode;
    for (int j = 1; j <= 2; j++)
    {
      in >> endpoint;
      // insert new edge node at beginning
      // of edge list for endpoint
      newPtr->vertex[j] = endpoint;
      newPtr->link[j] = myEdgeLists[endpoint].first;
      myEdgeLists[endpoint].first = newPtr;
    }
  }
}
```

Figure 16.4 (continued)

```
/*--- Utility function to check if all nodes have been visited.
   Precondition:  unvisited tells which nodes have not been
         visited
   Postcondition: true is returned if all vertices, false if not.
   ----------------------------------------------------------------*/
bool anyLeft(const vector<bool> & unvisited)
{
  for (int i = 1; i < unvisited.size(); i++)
    if (unvisited[i])
      return true;
  return false;
}


//-- Definition of depthFirstSearch()
template <typename DataType>
void Graph<DataType>::depthFirstSearch(int start, vector<bool> & unvisited)
{
  // --- Insert statements here to process visited node
  // Mark start visited, and initialize pointer
  // to its first edge node to begin DFS.
  unvisited[start] = false;

  Graph<DataType>::EdgePointer ptr = myEdgeLists[start].first;
  while(anyLeft(unvisited) && ptr != 0)
  {
    // Determine which end of edge is start
    int startEnd = 1,
        otherEnd = 2;
    if (ptr->vertex[1] != start)
    { startEnd = 2; otherEnd = 1;}

    // Start new (recursive) DFS from vertex at other end
    // if it hasn't already been visited
```

Figure 16.4 (continued)

```
    int newStart = ptr->vertex[otherEnd];
    if (unvisited[newStart])
      depthFirstSearch(newStart, unvisited);
    // Move to next edge node
    ptr = ptr->link[startEnd];
  }
}


//-- Definition of isConnected()
template <typename DataType>
inline bool Graph<DataType>::isConnected()
{
  vector<bool> unvisited(myEdgeLists.size(), true);
  depthFirstSearch(1, unvisited);
  return !anyLeft(unvisited);
}
```

▲

Figure 16.5 Graph Connectedness

```
/*------------------------------------------------------------------------
  Program to determine if a graph is connected. If the graph is not
  connected, a list of unreachable vertices from the start vertex is
  provided to the user.
  ------------------------------------------------------------------------*/

#include <iostream>
using namespace std;

#include "Graph.h"
```

Figure 16.5 (continued)

```cpp
int main()
{
  int numVertices,         // number of vertices in the graph
      numEdges;            //     "       "   edges    "   "    "

  cout << "Enter number of vertices and number of edges in graph: ";
  cin >> numVertices >> numEdges;
  Graph<char> g;
  g.read(cin, numVertices, numEdges);

  cout << "Graph is ";
  if (g.isConnected())
    cout << "connected.\n";
  else
  {
    cout << "not connected.\n"
            "Would you like to see which vertices are not\n"
            "reachable from vertex 1 ("
         << g.data(1) << ") -- (Y or N)? ";
    char response;
    cin >> response;
    if (response == 'y' || response == 'Y')
    {
      cout << "They are the following: \n";
      vector<bool> unreachable(numVertices + 1, true);
      g.depthFirstSearch(1, unreachable);
      for (int i = 1; i < unreachable.size(); i++)
        if (unreachable[i])
          cout << "Vertex " << i << " (" << g.data(i) << ")\n";
    }
    cout << endl;
  }
}
```

Figure 16.5 (continued)

Execution Trace 1:
Enter number of vertices and number of edges in graph: 5 6
Enter label of vertex:
  1: A
  2: B
  3: C
  4: D
  5: E
Enter endpoints of edge
  1: 1 2
  2: 1 4
  3: 1 5
  4: 2 4
  5: 3 4
  6: 4 5
Graph is connected.

Execution Trace 2:
Enter number of vertices and number of edges in graph: 5 2
Enter label of vertex:
  1: A
  2: B
  3: C
  4: D
  5: E
Enter endpoints of edge
  1: 1 4
  2: 5 4
Graph is not connected.
Would you like to see which vertices are not
reachable from vertex 1 (A) -- (Y or N)? Y
They are the following:
Vertex 2 (B)
Vertex 3 (C)

✔ Quick Quiz 16.3

1. Give two ways that a graph differs from a digraph?

For Questions 2–7, use the following graphs:

A.

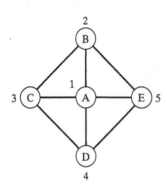

B.

2. Give the adjacency matrix *adj* and the data matrix *data* for graph A.
3. Give the adjacency matrix *adj* and the data matrix *data* for graph B.
4. Give the adjacency-list representation of graph A.
5. Give the adjacency-list representation of graph B.
6. Give the edge-list representation of graph A.
7. Give the edge-list representation of graph B.
8. For graph A, which nodes can be reached using a depth-first search from vertex 1? from vertex 2?
9. For graph B, which nodes can be reached using a depth-first search from vertex 1?
10. For a breadth-first search of graph A starting from vertex 1, which nodes will be visited next?
11. Which of graphs A and B are connected?

⟐ Exercises 16.3

For Exercises 1–4, give the adjacency-matrix representation of the graph.

1.

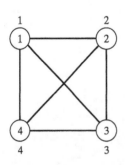

2.

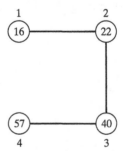

3.

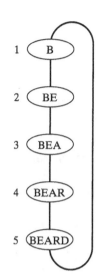

4.

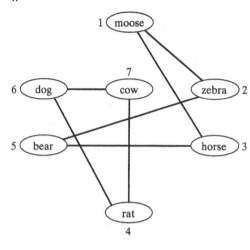

5–8. Proceed as in Exercises 1–4, but give the adjacency-list representation.

9–12. Proceed as in Exercises 1–4, but give the edge-list representation.

13–16. The linked adjacency-list representation for directed graphs described in the paragraph preceding Exercise 17 of Section 16.1 can also be used for undirected graphs. Give the linked adjacency-list representation for the graphs in Exercises 1–4.

In Exercises 17–20, draw the graph represented by the adjacency matrices; assume that the data value stored in vertex i is the integer i.

17. $adj = \begin{bmatrix} 0 & 1 & 0 & 1 & 0 \\ 1 & 0 & 1 & 0 & 0 \\ 0 & 1 & 0 & 0 & 1 \\ 1 & 0 & 0 & 0 & 1 \\ 0 & 0 & 1 & 1 & 0 \end{bmatrix}$

18. $adj = \begin{bmatrix} 0 & 1 & 1 & 1 \\ 1 & 0 & 1 & 1 \\ 1 & 1 & 0 & 1 \\ 1 & 1 & 1 & 0 \end{bmatrix}$

19. $adj = \begin{bmatrix} 0 & 0 & 0 \\ 0 & 0 & 0 \\ 0 & 0 & 0 \end{bmatrix}$

20. $adj = \begin{bmatrix} 0 & 0 & 1 & 0 & 0 & 0 & 1 \\ 0 & 0 & 1 & 1 & 1 & 0 & 0 \\ 1 & 1 & 0 & 1 & 0 & 0 & 1 \\ 0 & 1 & 1 & 0 & 1 & 1 & 1 \\ 0 & 1 & 0 & 1 & 0 & 0 & 0 \\ 0 & 0 & 0 & 1 & 0 & 0 & 1 \\ 1 & 0 & 1 & 1 & 0 & 1 & 0 \end{bmatrix}$

For Exercises 21–26, draw the graph represented by the adjacency lists.

21.

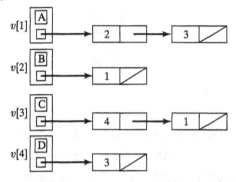

22.

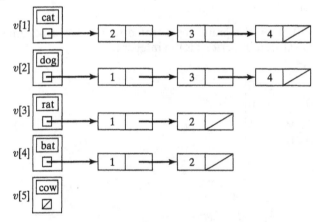

23.

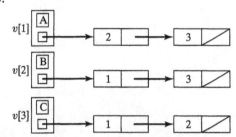

24.

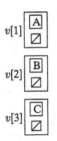

25.

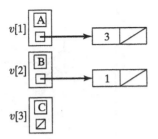

26.

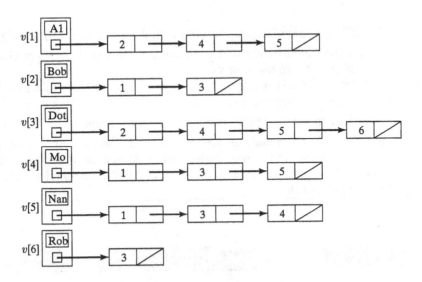

27–32. Give the edge-list representation for the graphs whose adjacency lists are given in Exercises 21–26.

For Exercises 33–39, using one of the representations for graphs described in this section, including that in Exercises 13–16, or devising one of your own, give an algorithm or function to implement the operations. Programming Problems 7–14 at the end of this chapter ask you to write and test functions for the algorithms.

33. Insert a new vertex, given a specification of all vertices adjacent to it.

34. Search a graph for a vertex that stores a given data item, and retrieve information about that item and/or update the information.

35. Delete a vertex containing a given data item and all edges incident to it.

36. Find all vertices adjacent to a given vertex.

37. Determine whether a graph contains a *cycle*—that is, a path connecting some vertex to itself.

38. A *spanning tree T* for a graph *G* is a subgraph of *G* containing all the vertices of *G* but containing no cycles (see Exercise 37). (A *subgraph* of a graph *G* has a vertex set and an edge set that are subsets of the vertex set and the edge set of *G*, respectively.) For example, the following are some of the possible spanning trees for the graph in Exercise 1.

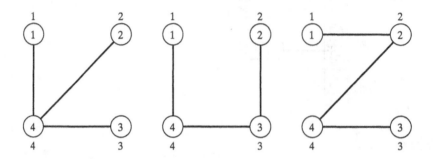

The following algorithm can be used to find a spanning tree *T* for a graph *G*:

a. Initialize the vertex set V_T of *T* equal to the vertex set V_G of *G* and the edge set E_T of *T* to the empty set.

b. While there is an edge *e* in the edge set E_G of *G* such that $E_T \cup \{e\}$ forms no cycle in *T*, add *e* to E_T.

Write a function to find a spanning tree for a graph.

39. *Kruskal's algorithm* finds the spanning tree of minimal cost in a weighted graph. It is a simple modification of the algorithm in Exercise 38. In Step 2, add the edge *e* of minimal cost that does not create a cycle. Write a function that implements Kruskal's algorithm.

SUMMARY

▣ Chapter Notes

■ Directed graphs (digraphs) are useful in modeling networks in which flow from one node to another is directional. (Undirected) graphs are useful when there is no direction associated with the flow.

■ Routing problems involve finding a shortest path in a graph or digraph.

☞ Programming Pointers

1. Search and traversal functions for digraphs and graphs must take into account that some nodes are not reachable from others.

2. Depth-first searches are most easily done recursively.

3. Breadth-first search can be implemented using a queue to store visited nodes (instead of the run-time stack of recursion).

4. For *connected* graphs it is always possible to get from one node to another.

▲ ADT Tips

1. Adjacency matrices and adjacency lists are common representations for digraphs.

2. Adjacency matrices and adjacency lists are not spacewise efficient for graphs. Each piece of information about an edge (its presence/absence or its weight) is stored twice.

3. Edge-list representations work well for graphs.

▣ Programming Problems

Section 16.2

1. Write a program to test the breadth-first search function in Exercise 20.

2. Write a program to test the reachability-matrix function in Exercise 21.

3. Write a program to test the boolean reachability-matrix function in Exercise 22.

4. Write a program to test the reachability-matrix function in Exercise 24 that implements Warshall's algorithm.

5. Modify the class template Digraph in Figure 16.1 to use the adjacency-matrix representation for the digraph.

6. Modify the class template Digraph in Figure 16.1 to use the linked adjacency-list representation described in the paragraph preceding Exercise 17 of Section 16.1.

Section 16.3

7. Write and test a function for the vertex-insertion algorithm in Exercise 33.

8. Write and test a function for the search-and-retrieve algorithm in Exercise 34.

9. Write and test a function for the vertex-deletion algorithm in Exercise 35.

10. Write and test a function for the adjacent-vertices algorithm in Exercise 36.

11. Write and test a function for the cycle-detection algorithm in Exercise 37.

12. Write and test a function for the spanning-tree algorithm in Exercise 38.

13. Write and test a function for Kruskal's spanning-tree algorithm in Exercise 39.

14. Revise the Graph class template in Figure 16.4 so that it uses an adjacency-matrix representation for the graph.

15. Proceed as in Problem 14, but use the adjacency-list representation.

16. Proceed as in Problem 14, but use the linked adjacency-list representation described in Exercises 13–16.

17. Write a program that reads and stores the names of persons and the names of job positions in the vertices of a graph. Two vertices will be connected if one of them represents a person and the other a job position for which that person is qualified. The program should allow the user to specify one of the following options:

a. Insert (a) a new applicant or (b) a new job position into the graph.

b. Delete (a) an applicant or (b) a job position from the graph.

c. List all persons qualified for a specified job position.

d. List all job positions for which a specified person is qualified.

Use the functions developed in Problems 7–10 to implement these operations.

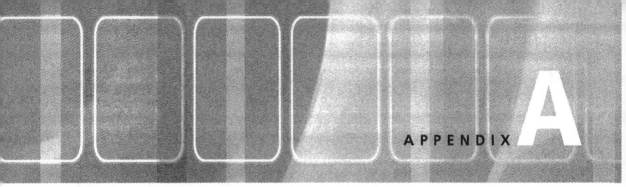

ASCII Character Set

ASCII Codes of Characters

Decimal	Octal	Character	Decimal	Octal	Character
0	000	NUL (Null)	19	023	DC3 (Device control 3)
1	001	SOH (Start of heading)	20	024	DC4 (Device control 4)
2	002	STX (Start of text)	21	025	NAK (Negative ACK)
3	003	ETX (End of text)	22	026	SYN (Synchronous)
4	004	EOT (End of transmission)	23	027	ETB (EOT block)
5	005	ENQ (Enquiry)	24	030	CAN (Cancel)
6	006	ACK (Acknowledge)	25	031	EM (End of medium)
7	007	BEL (Ring bell)	26	032	SUB (Substitute)
8	010	BS (BackSpace)	27	033	ESC (Escape)
9	011	HT (Horizontal tab)	28	034	FS (File separator)
10	012	LF (Line feed)	29	035	GS (Group separator)
11	013	VT (Vertical tab)	30	036	RS (Record separator)
12	014	FF (Form feed)	31	037	US (Unit separator)
13	015	CR (Carriage return)	32	040	SP (Space)
14	016	SO (Shift out)	33	041	!
15	017	SI (Shift in)	34	042	"
16	020	DLE (Data link escape)	35	043	#
17	021	DC1 (Device control 1)	36	044	$
18	022	DC2 (Device control 2)	37	045	%

Decimal	Octal	Character	Decimal	Octal	Character
38	046	&	67	103	C
39	047	' (Single quote)	68	104	D
40	050	(	69	105	E
41	051	)	70	106	F
42	052	*	71	107	G
43	053	+	72	110	H
44	054	, (Comma)	73	111	I
45	055	- (Hyphen)	74	112	J
46	056	. (Period)	75	113	K
47	057	/	76	114	L
48	060	0	77	115	M
49	061	1	78	116	N
50	062	2	79	117	O
51	063	3	80	120	P
52	064	4	81	121	Q
53	065	5	82	122	R
54	066	6	83	123	S
55	067	7	84	124	T
56	070	8	85	125	U
57	071	9	86	126	V
58	072	:	87	127	W
59	073	;	88	130	X
60	074	<	89	131	Y
61	075	=	90	132	Z
62	076	>	91	133	[
63	077	?	92	134	\
64	100	@	93	135	]
65	101	A	94	136	^
66	102	B	95	137	_ (Underscore)

Decimal	Octal	Character	Decimal	Octal	Character
96	140	`	112	160	p
97	141	a	113	161	q
98	142	b	114	162	r
99	143	c	115	163	s
100	144	d	116	164	t
101	145	e	117	165	u
102	146	f	118	166	v
103	147	g	119	167	w
104	150	h	120	170	x
105	151	i	121	171	y
106	152	j	122	172	z
107	153	k	123	173	{
108	154	l	124	174	|
109	155	m	125	175	}
110	156	n	126	176	~
111	157	o	127	177	DEL

Number Systems

The number system that we are accustomed to using to represent numeric values is a **decimal** or **base-ten number system**, which uses the digits 0, 1, 2, 3, 4, 5, 6, 7, 8, and 9. The significance of these digits in a numeral depends on the positions they occupy in that numeral. For example, in the numeral 427, the digit 4 is interpreted as 4 hundreds, the digit 2 as 2 tens, and the digit 7 as 7 ones. Thus, the numeral 427 represents the number four-hundred twenty-seven and can be written in **expanded form** as

$$4 \times 100 + 2 \times 10 + 7 \times 1$$

or

$$4 \times 10^2 + 2 \times 10^1 + 7 \times 10^0$$

The digits that appear in the various positions of a decimal (base-ten) numeral thus are coefficients of powers of ten.

Similar positional number systems can be devised using numbers other than ten as a base. The **binary** number system uses two as the base and has only two digits, 0 and 1. As in a decimal system, the significance of the bits in a binary numeral is determined by their positions in that numeral. For example, the binary numeral

$$111010$$

can be written in expanded form (using decimal notation) as

$$(1 \times 2^5) + (1 \times 2^4) + (1 \times 2^3) + (0 \times 2^2) + (1 \times 2^1) + (0 \times 2^0)$$

That is, the binary numeral 111010 has the decimal value

$$32 + 16 + 8 + 0 + 2 + 0 = 58$$

When necessary, to avoid confusion about which base is being used, it is customary to write the base as a subscript for nondecimal numerals. Using this convention, we could indicate that 58 has the binary representations just given by writing

$$58 = 111010_2$$

Two other nondecimal numeration systems are important in the consideration of computer systems: **octal** and **hexadecimal**. The octal system is a base-eight system and uses the eight digits 0, 1, 2, 3, 4, 5, 6, and 7. In an octal numeral such as

$$1703_8$$

the digits are coefficients of powers of eight; this numeral is, therefore, an abbreviation for the expanded form

$$(1 \times 8^3) + (7 \times 8^2) + (0 \times 8^1) + (3 \times 8^0)$$

and thus has the decimal value

$$512 + 448 + 0 + 3 = 963$$

A hexadecimal system uses a base of sixteen and the digits 0, 1, 2, 3, 4, 5, 6, 7, 8, 9, A (10), B (11), C (12), D (13), E (14), and F (15).[1] The hexadecimal numeral

$$5E4_{16}$$

has the expanded form

$$(5 \times 16^2) + (14 \times 16^1) + (4 \times 16^0)$$

which has the decimal value

$$1280 + 224 + 4 = 1508$$

In C++, *an integer literal is taken to be a decimal integer unless it begins with* 0. In this case,

- A sequence of digits that begins with 0 is interpreted as an octal integer
- A sequence of digits preceded by 0x is interpreted as a hexadecimal integer
- Any other digit sequence is a decimal (base-ten) integer

Table B.1 shows how the integer constants $0, 1, \ldots, 20$ can be represented in C++.

TABLE B.1: C++ Integer Literals

Decimal	Octal	Hexadecimal
0	0	0x0
1	01	0x1
2	02	0x2
3	03	0x3
4	04	0x4
5	05	0x5
6	06	0x6
7	07	0x7
8	010	0x8
9	011	0x9
10	012	0xA

---

[1] Lowercase letters a, b, c, d, e, and f are also commonly allowed for these last six digits.

TABLE B.1: C++ Integer Literals (continued)

Decimal	Octal	Hexadecimal
11	013	0xB
12	014	0xC
13	015	0xD
14	016	0xE
15	017	0xF
16	020	0x10
17	021	0x11
18	022	0x12
19	023	0x13
20	024	0x14

Exercises

Find the decimal value represented by the octal numerals in Exercises 1–6.

1. 321_8
2. 2607_8
3. 100000_8
4. 7777_8
5. 6.6_8
6. 432.234_8

Find the decimal value represented by the hexadecimal numerals in Exercises 7–12.

7. 45_{16}
8. $3A0_{16}$
9. ABC_{16}
10. FFF_{16}
11. $7.C_{16}$
12. $FE.DC_{16}$

13–18. Conversion from octal to binary (base-two) is easy; we need only replace each octal digit by its 3-bit binary equivalent. For example to convert 714_8 to binary, replace 7 by 111, 1 by 001, and 4 by 100, to obtain 111001100_2. Convert the octal numerals in Exercises 1–6 to binary numerals.

19–24. Imitating the conversion scheme in Exercises 13–18, convert each of the hexadecimal numerals in Exercises 7–12 to binary numerals.

To convert a binary numeral to octal, group the digits in groups of three, starting from the binary point (or from the right end if there is none), and replace each group with the corresponding octal digit. For example,

$$11110101_2 = (11\ 110\ 101)_2 = 365_8$$

Convert the binary numerals in Exercises 25–30 to octal numerals.

25. 101010
26. 1011
27. 10000000000
28. 01111111111111111111
29. 11.1
30. 10101.10101

31–36. Imitating the conversion scheme in Exercises 25–30, convert the binary numerals given there to hexadecimal numerals.

One method for finding the *base-b representation* of a positive integer represented in base-ten notation is to divide the number by b repeatedly until a quotient of zero results. The successive remainders are the digits from right to left of the base-b representation. For example, the base-two representation of 26 is 11010_2, as the following computation shows:

$$
\begin{array}{l}
0\ \text{R}\ 1 \\
2\overline{)1}\ \text{R}\ 1 \\
2\overline{)3}\ \text{R}\ 0 \\
2\overline{)6}\ \text{R}\ 1 \\
2\overline{)13}\ \text{R}\ 0 \\
2\overline{)26}
\end{array}
$$

Convert the base-ten numerals in Exercises 37–39 to base two.

37. 99

38. 2571

39. 5280

40–42. Convert the base-ten numerals in Exercises 37–39 to base eight.

43–45. Convert the base-ten numerals in Exercises 37–39 to base sixteen.

To convert a decimal fraction to its base-b equivalent, repeatedly multiply the fractional part of the number by b. The integer parts are the digits from left to right of the base-b representation. For example, the decimal numeral .6875 corresponds to the base-two numeral $.1011_2$, as the following computation shows:

$$
\begin{array}{r|l}
 & .6875 \\
 & \times\,2 \\
\hline
1 & .375 \\
 & \times\,2 \\
\hline
0 & .75 \\
 & \times\,2 \\
\hline
1 & .5 \\
 & \times\,2 \\
\hline
1 & .0
\end{array}
$$

Convert the base-ten numerals in Exercises 46–48 to base two.

46. .5   47. .6875   48. 13.828125

49–51. Convert the base-ten numerals in Exercises 46–48 to base eight.

52–54. Convert the base-ten numerals in Exercises 46–48 to base sixteen.

As noted in the text, even though the base-ten representation of a fraction may terminate, its representation in some other base need not terminate; for example,

$$0.7 = (0.10110011001100110011\ldots)_2 = 0.\,1\overline{0110}_2$$

where the "overline" in the last notation indicates that the bit string 0110 is repeated indefinitely.

```
       |.7
       |× 2
      ‾‾‾‾‾
   1 |.4 ←┐
       |× 2
      ‾‾‾‾‾
   0 |.8
       |× 2
      ‾‾‾‾‾
   1 |.6
       |× 2
      ‾‾‾‾‾
   1 |.2
       |× 2
      ‾‾‾‾‾
   0 |.4 ──┘
```

Convert the base-ten numerals in Exercises 55–57 to base two.

55. 0.6   56. 0.05   57. $0.3 = 0.\overline{3}3333\cdots = 1/3$

58–60. Convert the base-ten numerals in Exercises 55–57 to base eight.

61–63. Convert the base-ten numerals in Exercises 55–57 to base sixteen.

Basic C++

C.1 C++ Program Structure

A program is basically a collection of *functions*, one of which must be named **main()**. Program execution begins with main(). Figure C.1 is an example of a simple program that contains only this main function. Note that *each statement must be terminated by a semicolon* (;).

The contents of the files inserted by the #include directives together with items that are declared or defined ahead of main()—for example, function prototypes—are *global*; they are accessible in what follows, unless the same identifier is used for some other purpose.

Figure C.1 Example of a C++ Program

```
/*-------------------------------------------
   Program to greet its user.
   Input:  The name of the user                    }  Opening
   Output: A personalized greeting                     documentation
   ----------------------------------------*/

#include <iostream>    // cin, cout, <<, >>     }  Compiler directives that
#include <string>      // string                   insert the contents of files
using namespace std; ←                             Use libraries from namespace std
                     ←                             Declarations and definitions
                                                   of other items could go here
int main() ←                                       Execution begins here
{
   cout << "Please enter your first name: ";
   string firstName;                               Program statements that make
   cin >> firstName;                               up the body of the main
                                                   function
   cout << "\nWelcome to the world of C++, "
        << firstName << "!\n";
}←                                                 Execution stops here or when a
                                                   return statement is executed

                                                   More #includes could go here.
                     ←                             Also, function definitions can go
                                                   here if their prototypes are above
```

C.2 Compiler Directives

The most commonly used compiler directives are the **#include directives**. These are instructions to the preprocessor to insert the contents of the specified files at this point:

```
#include <filename>    For standard libraries
#include "filename"    For other (programmer-defined) libraries
```

The files included are called **header files** (often with names of the form *filename*.h); they contain *declarations* of functions, constants, variables, and so on. **Implementation files** (with names of the form *filename*.cpp or *filename*.cc) contain *definitions* of the items declared (but not defined) in the corresponding header file. They are usually compiled separately and then *linked* with the program to produce a binary executable.

C.3 Standard Libraries

Normally, we want to use the standard libraries in the namespace named std. (Namespaces are described later in this appendix.) The line following the #include directives in the program in Figure C.1 informs the compiler of this. Without it, we would have to *qualify* each item such as cout from these libraries with the prefix std::; for example,

```
std::cout << "Please enter your first name: ";
```

The following are some of the commonly used **standard libraries** provided in C++:

Name	What it provides
iostream	Basic interactive i/o (see Appendix D and Section 5.1)
iomanip	Format manipulators (see Appendix D and Section 5.1)
fstream	File i/o (see Appendix D and Section 5.1)
string	Standard C++ string type (see Appendix D and Section 5.2)
cassert	The assert mechanism
cctype	Character functions (see Appendix D)
cfloat	Max and min values of real types
climits	Max and min values of integer types
cmath	Math library
cstdlib	Standard C library
cstring	C's string library (see Appendix D)

Libraries whose names begin with 'c' are C libraries. (Their names in C do not have this added 'c' at the beginning but instead have ".h" appended; for example, math.h instead of cmath.) Other libraries such as valarray, bitset, sstream, and the Standard Template Libraries such as vector, list, algorithm, and numeric, are described in the text. Some of the most useful items in the C libraries are described in the following lists or in Appendix D:

---

cassert

void assert(bool expr)	Tests the boolean expression expr and if it is true, allows execution to proceed. If it is false, execution is terminated and an error message is displayed.

---

cfloat

The following constants specify the minimum value in the specified floating-point type:

FLT_MIN ($\leq$ –1E+37)	float
DBL_MIN ($\leq$ –1E+37)	double
LDBL_MIN ($\leq$ –1E+37)	long double

The following constants specify the maximum value in the specified floating-point type:

FLT_MAX ($\geq$ 1E+37)	float
DBL_MAX ($\geq$ 1E+37)	double
LDBL_MAX ($\geq$ 1E+37)	long double

The following constants specify the smallest positive value representable in the specified floating-point type:

FLT_EPSILON ($\leq$ 1E–37)	float
DBL_EPSILON ($\leq$ 1E–37)	double
LDBL_EPSILON ($\leq$ 1E–37)	long double

---

climits

The following constants specify the minimum and maximum values for the specified type:

SCHAR_MIN ($\leq$ –127)	signed char
SCHAR_MAX ($\geq$ 127)	signed char
UCHAR_MAX ($\geq$ 255)	unsigned char
CHAR_MIN (0 or SCHAR_MIN)	char
CHAR_MAX (SCHAR_MAX or USHRT_MAX)	char

climits	
SHORT_MIN (≤ -32767)	short int
SHORT_MAX (≥ 32767)	short int
USHRT_MAX (≥ 65535)	unsigned short int
INT_MIN (≤ -32767)	int
INT_MAX (≥ 32767)	int
UINT_MAX (≥ 65535)	unsigned int
LONG_MIN (≤ -2147483647)	long int
LONG_MAX (≥ 2147483647)	long int
ULONG_MAX (≥ 4294967295)	unsigned long int

cmath	
double acos(double x)	Returns the angle in $[0, \pi]$ (in radians) whose cosine is x
double asin(double x)	Returns the angle in $[-\pi/2, \pi/2]$ (in radians) whose sine is x
double atan(double x)	Returns the angle in $(-\pi/2, \pi/2)$ (in radians) whose tangent is x
double atan2(double y, double x)	Returns the angle in $(-\pi, \pi]$ (in radians) whose tangent is y/x
double ceil(double x)	Returns the least integer $\geq$ x
double cos(double x)	Returns the cosine of x (radians)
double cosh(double x)	Returns the hyperbolic cosine of x
double exp(double x)	Returns e^x
double fabs(double x)	Returns the absolute value of x
double floor(double x)	Returns the greatest integer $\leq$ x
double fmod(double x, double y)	Returns the integer remainder of x/y
double frexp(double x, int & ex)	Returns value v in $[1/2, 1]$ and passes back ex such that $x = v * 2^{ex})$
double ldexp(double x, int ex)	Returns x $* 2^{ex}$
double log(double x)	Returns natural logarithm of x

cmath	
`double log10(double x)`	Returns base-ten logarithm of x
`double modf(double x,` `            double & ip)`	Returns fractional part of x and passes back ip = the integer part of x
`double pow(double x,` `           double y)`	Returns x^y
`double sin(double x)`	Returns the sine of x (radians)
`double sinh(double x)`	Returns the hyperbolic sine of x
`double sqrt(double x)`	Returns the square root of x (provided $x \geq 0$)
`double tan(double x)`	Returns the tangent of x (radians)
`double tanh(double x)`	Returns the hyperbolic tangent of x

cstdlib	
`int abs(int i)` `long abs(long li)`	`abs(i)` and `labs(li)` return the `int` and `long int` absolute value of `i` and `li`, respectively

`double atof(char s[])`
`int atoi(char s[])`
`long atol(char s[])`
	`atof(s)`, `atoi(s)`, and `atol(s)` return the value obtained by converting the character string s to `double`, `int`, and `long int`, respectively

`void exit(int status)`	Terminates program execution and returns control to the operating system; `status` = 0 signals normal termination and any nonzero value signals abnormal termination
`int rand()`	Returns a pseudorandom integer in the range 0 to `RAND_MAX`
`RAND_MAX`	An integer constant (≥ 32767) which is the maximum value returned by `rand()`
`void srand(int seed)`	Uses seed to initialize the sequence of pseudorandom numbers returned by `rand()`
`int system(char s[])`	Passes the string s to the operating system to be executed as a command and returns an implementation-dependent value.

C.4 Comments

Two kinds of **comments** are allowed in C++:

```
// comment -- continues to end of the line
/* comment -- may extend over several lines ... */
```

C.5 Identifiers and Keywords

Identifiers consist of a letter followed by any number of letters, underscores, and digits. C++ is *case sensitive*; thus, for example, Sum, sum, and SUM are all different identifiers. Identifiers may not be any of the **keywords** in Table C.1.

TABLE C.1: C++ Keywords

Keyword	Description of Its Usage
asm	Declare information to be passed directly to the assembler
auto	Declare entities whose lifetime is the block containing their declaration
bool	A boolean type whose values are true or false
break	Terminate processing of a switch statement or loop
case	Specify a match for the expression in a switch statement
catch	Specify actions to be taken when an exception occurs (see throw, try)
char	A type for characters
class	Construct new types encapsulating data and operations (default private); also, declare a type parameter in a template declaration
const	Declare entities whose values should not change during execution
const_cast	Add or remove the const or volatile property of a type
continue	Transfer control to the beginning of a loop statement
default	Handle expression values not specified using case in a switch statement
delete	Deallocate memory allocated at run time, returning it to the free store
do	Mark the beginning of a do-while statement
double	A type for (double precision) real numbers
dynamic_cast	Cast pointer or reference types in a class hierarchy
else	Mark the section in an if statement to be executed if the condition is false
enum	Define an enumeration type
explicit	Prevent constructors from being called implicitly for type conversions

TABLE C.1: C++ Keywords (continued)

Keyword	Description of Its Usage
extern	Declare objects whose definitions are external to a local block
false	A bool literal
float	A type for (single precision) real numbers
for	Mark the beginning of a for statement
friend	Allow non-member function to access members of a class' private section
goto	Transfer control to a labeled statement
if	Mark the beginning of an if statement
inline	Specify that code of a function's definition may be substituted for a call to that function
int	A type for integers
long	A type for long integers, or with double for long double precision reals
mutable	Declare a class data member as modifiable even in a const object
namespace	Control the scope of global names (to avoid name conflicts)
new	Request memory allocation during program execution
operator	Overload an operator with a new declaration
private	Declare class members to be inaccessible from outside of the class
protected	Like private, except access is permitted for derived classes
public	Declare class members to be accessible outside of the class
register	Declare entities whose values are to be kept in registers
reinterpret_cast	Perform type conversions on unrelated types
return	Stop function execution, usually returning a value to calling function
short	A type for short integers
signed	Declare that one bit of an integer's representation is to store its sign
sizeof	Find the size (in bytes) of an object, or of the representation of a type

TABLE C.1: C++ Keywords (continued)

Keyword	Description of Its Usage
static	Declare entities whose lifetime is the duration of the program
static_cast	Convert one type to another type
struct	Construct new types encapsulating data and operations (default public)
switch	Mark the beginning of a switch statement
template	Declare type-independent classes or functions
this	A pointer whose value is the address of an instance of that class
throw	Generate an exception (see catch, try)
true	A bool literal
try	Mark the beginning of a block containing exception handlers (see catch)
typedef	Declare a name as a synonym for an existing type
typeid	Obtain type information during run time
typename	Declare a type parameter in a template declaration; (alternative of class)
union	Declare a structure whose members share memory
unsigned	Declare that no bits of an integer's representation are used for a sign
using	Allow members of a namespace to be accessed without qualification
virtual	Declare that calls to a class function member will not be bound to a definition of that function until run-time
void	Declare the absence of any type
volatile	Declare entities whose values may be modified by means undetectable to the compiler (such as shared memory objects of concurrent processes)
w_char	A type for wide characters
while	Mark the beginning of a while statement, as well as the end of a do-while statement

C.6 Fundamental Data Types

The most important data types are the following:

Integers: `int`

Integer variations: `short` (or `short int`), `long` (or `long int`), `unsigned` (or `unsigned int`)

Reals: `float`, `double`, `long double`

Complex numbers: The library `<complex>` provides the types `complex<float>`, `complex<double>`, `complex<long double>` for complex values with components of type `float`, `double`, `long double`, respectively.

Characters: `char` (and less commonly used variations `signed char` and `unsigned char`), `wchar_t` for wide characters

Booleans (logical values `true` and `false`): `bool`

Absence of type: `void`

Some of their properties are as follows:

- `char` values are stored in 1 byte; `char` is considered to be an integer type, because values are stored using numeric codes (e.g., ASCII).

- `short` values require at least as many bytes as `char` values, `int` values at least as many as `short` values, and `long` values at least as many as `int` values.

- `double` values require at least as many bytes as `float` values and `long double` values at least as many as `double` values.

- Real values are stored as `double`s (except for real literals with suffix F attached), so it is common to always use `double`.

- The size of memory locations used for `bool` values is implementation dependent; `true` is defined as 1 and `false` as 0; any nonzero value will be interpreted as true and any zero value as false.

- `sizeof` operator: `sizeof(type)` or `sizeof(expression)` returns the number of bytes used for this type object. The parentheses are not required in the second form.

- If two operands in an expression have different types, the shorter one is converted (*promoted*) to the longer type. This can also be done explicitly with type conversions described later.

C.7 Literals

Integer: Use the usual decimal representation.

Octal representations begin with 0, which is followed by octal digits

Hexadecimal representations begin with 0x, which is followed by hexadecimal digits

Real: Use the usual decimal representation and e or E representations. A suffix F can be appended to specify a (single precision) `float` literal.

Character: Single characters are enclosed in single quotes (apostrophes).

Escape sequences are used for special character constants:

\n (new line)	\r (carriage return)
\t (horizontal tab)	\v (vertical tab)
\b (backspace)	\f (form feed)
\a (alert)	\\ (backslash)
\' (single quote)	\" (double quote)
\? (question mark)	\x*hhh* (with hexadecimal code *hhh*)
ooo (with octal code *ooo*)	

Character literals of the form L'*x*', where *x* consists of one or more characters, are *wide-character literals* and are used to represent alternate character sets (e.g., 16-bit Unicode).

String: Strings are enclosed in double quotes.

Complex: Complex values have the form (*a*, *b*), where *a* and *b* are real values.

C.8 Declarations

Variable declarations have the form

```
type list;
```

where each item in *list* has the form

```
variable_name        or        variable_name = init_expression
```

Variables are usually declared near their first use.

Constant declarations have the form

```
const type list;
```

where each item in *list* has the form

```
CONSTANT_NAME = constant_value
```

C.9 Operators and Expressions

In expressions that contain several operators, the order in which the operators are applied depends on operator **priority** (or **precedence**) and **associativity**:

- Higher-priority operators are applied before lower-priority ones.
- If operators have equal priority, they are applied
  - From left to right if they are *left associative*
  - From right to left if they are *right associative*
- A semicolon appended to an expression changes the expression into a *statement*.

Table C.2 lists the C++ operators, ordered by their precedence levels, from highest to lowest. Operators in the same horizontal band of the table have equal precedence. The table also gives each operator's associativity, whether they can be overloaded, their arity (number of operands), and a brief description.

TABLE C.2: C++ Operators

Operator	Associativity	Overloadable	Arity	Description
::	right	no	unary	global scope
::	left	no	binary	class scope
.	left	no	binary	direct member selection
->	left	yes	binary	indirect member selection
[]	left	yes	binary	subscript (array index)
()	left	yes	n/a	function call
()	left	yes	n/a	type construction
++	right	yes	unary	post increment
--	right	yes	unary	post decrement
typeid	left	no	unary	type identification
static_cast	left	no	unary	compile-time checked conversion
dynamic_cast	left	no	unary	run-time checked conversion
reinterpret_cast	left	no	unary	unchecked conversion
const_cast	left	no	unary	const conversion
sizeof	right	n/a	unary	size (in bytes) of an expression or type
++	right	yes	unary	pre increment
--	right	yes	unary	pre decrement
~	right	yes	unary	bitwise NOT
!	right	yes	unary	logical NOT
+	right	yes	unary	plus(sign)
-	right	yes	unary	minus (sign)
*	right	yes	unary	pointer dereferencing
&	right	yes	unary	get address of an object
new	right	yes	unary	memory allocation
delete	right	yes	unary	memory deallocation
()	right	yes	binary	type conversion (cast)

TABLE C.2: C++ Operators (continued)

Operator	Associativity	Overloadable	Arity	Description
.*	left	no	binary	direct member pointer selection
->*	left	yes	binary	indirect member pointer selection
*	left	yes	binary	multiplication
/	left	yes	binary	division
%	left	yes	binary	modulus (remainder)
+	left	yes	binary	addition
-	left	yes	binary	subtraction
<<	left	yes	binary	output; also bit-shift left
>>	left	yes	binary	input; also bit-shift right
<	left	yes	binary	less than
<=	left	yes	binary	less than or equal
>	left	yes	binary	greater than
>=	left	yes	binary	greater than or equal
==	left	yes	binary	equal
!=	left	yes	binary	not equal
&	left	yes	binary	bitwise AND
^	left	yes	binary	bitwise XOR
|	left	yes	binary	bitwise OR
&&	left	yes	binary	logical AND
||	left	yes	binary	logical OR
=	right	yes	binary	assignment
+=	right	yes	binary	addition-assignment shortcut
-=	right	yes	binary	subtraction-assignment shortcut
*=	right	yes	binary	multiplication-assignment shortcut
/=	right	yes	binary	division-assignment shortcut

TABLE C.2: C++ Operators (continued)

Operator	Associativity	Overloadable	Arity	Description
%=	right	yes	binary	modulus-assignment shortcut
&=	right	yes	binary	bitwise-AND-assignment shortcut
|=	right	yes	binary	bitwise-OR-assignment shortcut
^=	right	yes	binary	bitwise-XOR-assignment shortcut
<<=	right	yes	binary	bitshift-left-assignment shortcut
>>=	right	yes	binary	bitshift-right-assignment shortcut
? :	left	no	ternary	conditional expression
throw	right	yes	unary	throw an exception
,	left	yes	binary	expression separation

The following are some of the important properties of several of these operators:

Division   If a and b are integers, a / b is the *integer quotient* and a % b the *integer remainder* when a is divided by b. If a and b are reals, a / b is the *real quotient* and a % b is *an error.*

Assignment   An assignment of the form *variable* = *expression*

1. Stores the value of *expression* in *variable*; and
2. Returns the value of *expression* as its result.

This, along with the right associativity of = allows assignments to be chained:

var_1 = var_2 = ... = var_n = *expression*

An **assignment statement** is an assignment expression followed by a semicolon:

variable = *expression*;

In place of the assignment *variable* = *variable* + 1; we can use the **increment operator ++**,

++*variable*; (Prefix form)

or

variable++; (Postfix form)

The **decrement operator** -- can be used in a similar manner to subtract 1 from a variable. These forms are equivalent when used as stand-alone statements, but they differ when they are used as part of an expression:

Prefix Form: Increment (or decrement) and then use the new value; for example, b = ++a; means a = a + 1; b = a;

Postfix Form: Use old value and then increment (or decrement); for example, b = a++; means b = a; a = a + 1;

Assignment shortcuts can be used to simplify assignments in which a variable appears on both sides. For example, var_1 = var_1 + var_2; can be simplified to var_1 += var_2; and similarly for -=, *=, /=, and %=.

Boolean Expressions   Don't use = when == is intended; for example,

    if (x = 0) ...

will assign 0 to x and the value of (x = 0) is 0 (false);

    if (x = 9) ...

will assign 9 to x and the value of (x = 9) is 9 (true). Also, be careful to use && and || for the logical operators *and* and *or*, not & and |, which are bitwise operators.

The operator ?: is a *ternary* operator. The value of

    $boolean\text{-}expr_1$? $expr_2$: $expr_3$

is $expr_2$ if $boolean\text{-}expr_1$ is true (nonzero), $expr_3$ if $boolean\text{-}expr_1$ is false (zero).

Input/Output Expressions   I/O is carried out using **streams** connecting the program and i/o devices or files. Input expressions use the **input** (or **extraction**) **operator** >>. The expression *inStream* >> *variable*

1. Extracts a value of the type of *variable* (if possible) from *inStream*,
2. Stores that value in *variable*, and
3. Returns *inStream* as its result (if successful, else 0).

This last property along with the left associativity of >> makes it possible to chain input expressions:

    $inStream$ >> var_1 >> var_2 >> ... >> var_n

Output expressions use the **output** (or **insertion**) **operator** <<. The expression *outStream* << *value*

1. Inserts *value* into *outStream*, and
2. Returns *outStream* as its result.

This last property along with the left-associativity of << makes it possible to chain output expressions:

    $outStream$ << $expr_1$ << $expr_2$ << ... << $expr_n$

See Appendix D for more information about input and output.

Type Conversions   If intVal is an integer variable and doubleVal is a double variable, then either of the expressions

    double(intVal) and static_cast<double>(intVal)

produces the double value equivalent to intVal. Similarly, either of

int(doubleVal) and static_cast<int>(doubleVal)

will truncate the fractional part and produce the integer part of doubleVal as its value. More generally, the type of an expression can be explicitly converted to a different type as follows:

type(expression)
static_cast<*type*>(*expression*)
(*type*) *expression*

The type of the value produced by *expression* is converted to *type* (if possible). The first form is sometimes referred to as *functional notation* and the last form as (C-style) *cast notation*.

Function Call Operator **The function call operator ()** is used to pass an argument list to a function:

functionName(argument_list)

Subscript Operator The **subscript operator []** provides access to the elements of an array:

arrayName[index]

See Section 3.2.

Dot Operator The **dot operator .** is used to select a member of a struct or class object:

classObject.memberName

See Secs. 3.5 and 4.2.

Scope Operator The **scope operator ::** is used to identify a component within a class:

ClassName::componentName

See Section 4.3.

Bitwise Operators These operators provide bit-level control:

Expression	Produces the result of:
x & y	ANDing the bits of x with those of y
x | y	ORing the bits of x with those of y
x ^ y	XORing the bits of x with those of y
~x	Inverting (complementing) the bits of x ($0 \rightarrow 1$ and $1 \rightarrow 0$)
x << y	Shifting the bits of x to the *left* y positions
x >> y	Shifting the bits of x to the *right* y positions

Shortcut versions (with assignment) are also provided: &=, |=, ^=, !=, <<=, >>=. *Note*: << and >> are classic examples of *overloaded* operators.

C.10 Control Structures

Control structures are language constructs that allow a programmer to control the flow of execution through a program. There are three main categories: **sequence**, **selection**, and **repetition**.

Sequence   Sequential execution is implemented by **compound statements** (also called **blocks**). They consist of statements enclosed between curly braces ({ and }):

```
{
    statement₁
    statement₂          ← (Remember: Statements end with ; )
    ...
    statementₙ
}
```

Selection   Selective execution is implemented by one of the following statements:

1. **if Statement**

```
if (boolean_expression)
    statement₁
else
    statement₂
```

- The *boolean_expression* must be enclosed in parentheses.
- *statement₁* and *statement₂* may be compound.
- *Remember*: nonzero = true, 0 = false.

2. **switch Statement**

```
switch(integer_expression)
{
    case_list₁ : statement_list₁
    case_list₂ : statement_list₂
    ...
    default     : statement_listₙ
}
```

- The `default` part is optional.
- Each *case_listᵢ* is a sequence of distinct case labels of the form

```
case constant :
```

- Semantics:

    a. Evaluate *integer_expression*.
    b. If value of *integer_expression* is in *case_listᵢ*:
        i. Begin executing statements in *statement_listᵢ*.
        ii. Continue until a `break` statement, a `return` statement, or the end of the `switch` statement is reached. (Usually, a `break` or a `return` statement is used as the last statement in each statement list, except for the default case, where it is not needed.)

c. If value of *integer_expression* is in no *case_list_i*:
Execute statements in default part if there is one; else skip the `switch` statement.

Repetition Repetitive execution is implemented by one of the following statements:

1. While Loops

```
while(boolean_expression)
   statement
```

Like while loops in other languages, this is a **pretest (zero-trip)** loop, in which *boolean_expression*, which constitutes the termination test for repetition, is evaluated *before* execution of *statement*, called the **body of the loop**. The loop body is, therefore, not executed if *boolean_expression* is false initially. Normally, *statement* is a compound statement.

2. Do-While Loops

```
do
   statement
while (boolean_expression);   ← Note the semicolon.
```

This is like do-while or repeat-until loops in other languages, which are **post-test (one-trip)** loops, in which *boolean_expression*, which constitutes the termination test for repetition, is evaluated *after* execution of the body of the loop. The loop body is, therefore, always executed at least once.

3. For Loops

```
for (initializing_expr; boolean_expr; step_expr)
   statement
```

where any of *initializing_expr, boolean_expr, step_expr* may be omitted. This is equivalent to the following:

```
initializing_expr;
while (boolean_expr)
{
   statement
   step_expr;
}
```

A common use is to construct *counting loops*:

```
for (int counter = 1; counter <= n; counter++)
   statement
```

4. Indeterminate (or Forever) Loops

```
for(;;)          or        while(true)
   statement                  statement
```

This is an *infinite loop*. We usually use forever loops to build *test-in-the-middle* loops:

```
for(;;)
{
```

```
          StatementList₁
          if (boolExpr) break;    or  if (boolExpr) return;
          StatementList₂
       }
```

Note: A **break statement** terminates execution of a switch statement containing it or the innermost loop containing it. A **continue statement** terminates only the current iteration of the loop and continues execution of the
loop at the top of the loop.

 Examples   The programs in Figures C.2–C.6 illustrate several of these control structures. Complete versions of them are available on the text's website (see *AppC* in the
source files).

Figure C.2 Using a Forever Loop

```
/*----------------------------------------------------------------
   Program to compute the volumes of spheres of various radii.
   Written at Doofus Univ. by Joe Somebody for CPSC 31416.


   Input:  Radii of spheres
   Output: Volumes of spheres
----------------------------------------------------------------*/
#include <iostream>
#include <cmath>
using namespace std;
int main()
{
  const double PI = 3.14159265359;
  double radius;                      // radius of a sphere
  int count = 0;                      // number of spheres processed
  for (;;)                            // loop:
  {
    cout << "Enter radius of sphere (0 to stop): ";
    cin >> radius;                    //    get next radius
    if (radius == 0) break;           //    terminate loop if end of data
    count++;                          //    count the data
                                      //    find the volume
    double volume = 4.0 * PI * pow(radius, 3)/ 3.0;
                                      //    output the results
    cout << "Volume of sphere of radius " << radius
         << " is " << volume << " cubic inches.\n\n";
  }                                   // end loop
```

Figure C.2 (continued)

```
   // Output data count
   cout << endl << count << " spheres processed\n";
}
```

Execution Trace:
```
Enter radius of sphere (0 to stop): 2
Volume of sphere of radius 2 is 33.5103 cubic inches.

Enter radius of sphere (0 to stop): 1
Volume of sphere of radius 1 is 4.18879 cubic inches.

Enter radius of sphere (0 to stop): 0

2 spheres processed
```

▲

Figure C.3 Using a Do-While Loop

```
//--- Insert #include directives from Figure C.2
int main()
{
  //--- Insert declarations from Figure C.2
  char  response;                        // user response to "More data?"
  do
  {
    cout << "Enter radius of sphere: ";
    cin >> radius;                    // get next radius
    //--- Insert statements from Figure C.2 to compute and output volume
                                  // query user if more data
    cout << "More data (Y or N)? ";
    cin >> response;
  }
  while (response == 'Y' || response == 'y');

  // Output data count
  cout << endl << count << " spheres processed\n";
}
```

Figure C.3 (continued)

Execution Trace:
```
Enter radius of sphere: 2
Volume of sphere of radius 2 is 33.5103 cubic inches.

More data (Y or N)? Y
Enter radius of sphere: 1
Volume of sphere of radius 1 is 4.18879 cubic inches.

More data (Y or N)? N

2 spheres processed
```

▲

Figure C.4 Using a While Loop

```
//--- Insert #includes, start of main() with declarations from Figure C.2
  cout << "Enter radius of sphere (0 to stop): ";
  cin >> radius;                        // get first radius
  while (radius > 0)                    // while not end-of-data
  {
    //--- Insert statements from Figure C.2 to compute and output volume
    cout << "Enter radius of sphere (0 to stop): ";
    cin >> radius;                      // get next radius
  } //end while

  // Output data count
  cout << endl << count << " spheres processed\n";
}
```

▲

Figure C.5 Using Format Manipulators

```
//--- Insert #include directives from Figure C.2
#include <iomanip>

int main()
{
  //--- Insert declarations from Figure C.2
  cout << showpoint << fixed<< setprecision(3) ;
```

Figure C.5 (continued)

```
  //--- Insert loop and other statement from one of Figures C.2-C.4
}
```

Execution Trace:
```
Enter radius of sphere (0 to stop): 2
Volume of sphere of radius 2.000 is 33.510 cubic inches.

Enter radius of sphere (0 to stop): 1
Volume of sphere of radius 1.000 is 4.189 cubic inches.

Enter radius of sphere (0 to stop): 0

2 spheres processed
```

▲

Figure C.6 Using End-of-File Mark

```
//--- Insert #include directives from Figure C.2
#include <string>

int main()
{
  //--- Insert declarations from Figure C.2
  string END_OF_FILE_MARK = "Control-D";   // for Unix systems
  ...
  for (;;)
  {
    cout << "Enter radius of sphere (("
         << END_OF_FILE_MARK << " to stop): ";
    cin >> radius;
    if (cin.eof()) break;                    // end of data
    //--- Insert statements from Figure C.2 to compute and output volume
  }

  // Output data count
  cout << endl << count << " spheres processed\n";
}
```

▲

C.11 Functions

We write functions:

- To implement an *operation not provided* in C++
- When a piece of code will be used several times in a program (to *avoid duplication*)
- When a piece of code is likely to be useful in the future (for *software reusability*); in this case it may be put in a library
- To modularize programs (A rule of thumb used by some programmers is that no function should exceed one page in length.)

Function Definitions   The definition of a function has the form

```
return_type name(param_declaration_list) ← Function heading
{
    statement_list  ←─────────────────────── Function body
}
```

where

return_type is the type of value returned by the function or is **void** if no value is returned

param_declaration_list is a list of declarations of variables, which are the function's parameters, or is empty if there are none

Values passed to a function when it is called are **arguments**, and variables in the function heading used to hold these values are **parameters**.

Functions return values with statements of the form

```
return expression;
```

`void` functions cannot return values, but they may contain

```
return;
```

statements to cause an immediate return from the function to the calling function.

Function Prototypes (Declarations)   Before a function can be used, it must be **declared**. This can be done by giving its **prototype:**

```
return_type name(param_declaration_list); ← Note the semicolon
```

The list of parameter declarations is called the **signature** of the function. The following are some examples of function prototypes:

```
double wages(int dependents, double hours, double rate);
void instruct();
void printWages(int empNum, double grossPay);
```

Function prototypes are usually placed at the beginning of the file containing the source program, following the compiler directives.

The list of parameter declarations may consist of just the *types* of the parameters (possibly empty). For example, the first function prototype could be written

```
double wages(int, double, double);
```

However, it a good practice to include the parameter names also to provide additional documentation. Also, the prototype is then simply the function heading followed by a semicolon.

Parameter-Passing Mechanisms   There are three ways that parameters can be passed in C++:

1. **Call by Value.** If the declaration of a parameter has the form

   `type parameter_name`

   that parameter is a **value** parameter, which has the following properties:

   - A value parameter is allocated *different* memory locations than the corresponding argument.
   - The value of the corresponding argument is *copied* to a value parameter.
   - Changing a value parameter *does not change* the corresponding argument.

   For example, in the function call `printWages(empId, grossPay);` the value of the argument `empId` will be copied to the parameter `empNum` and the value of the argument `grossPay` will be copied to the parameter `grossPay`; the parameters will occupy different locations than the arguments.

2. **Call by Reference.** If the declaration of a parameter has the form

   `type & parameter_name`

   that parameter is a **reference** parameter, which has the following properties:

   - A reference parameter is simply an *alias* for the corresponding argument.
   - A reference parameter is allocated ***the same*** memory locations as the corresponding argument
   - Changing a reference parameter *changes* the corresponding argument.

   Reference parameters make it possible for *functions to return multiple values*; for example:

```
void computeNetPay(double grossPay, int dependents,
                   double & tax, double & netPay);
{ ...
  tax = . . .
  netPay = . . .
}
void getEmployeeInfo(int & empNumber, int & dependents,
                     double & hours, double & rate,
                     bool & done)
{ ...
  cin >> empNumber >> ...
}
```

3. const **Reference Parameters.** These are parameters whose declarations have the form

   `const type & parameter_name`

They are used when copying values of all the arguments each time a function is called is too inefficient, but we do want to protect the arguments. A compile-time error results if a function tries to change the value of a constant reference parameter.

Example   The functions in the program in Figure C.7 illustrate these parameter passing mechanisms:

instruct() has no parameters and returns no values.

printEmpInfo() has all value parameters and returns no values.

grossWages() has all value parameters and returns a double value.

getEmployeeInfo() has all reference parameters and returns no values, but it does pass back each of the parameter values to the corresponding arguments.

computeNetPay() has two value parameters and two reference parameters and returns no values, but it does pass back the values of the reference parameters to the corresponding arguments.

Figure C.7 Using Functions

```
/*-------------------------------------------------------------------------
   Program to compute wages for several employees.
   Written at Doofus Univ. by Joe Somebody for CPSC 31416.

   Input:   Id-number, number of dependents, hours worked, and hourly rate
               for each of several employees
   Output: Id-number, hours worked, gross pay, taxes withheld, and net pay
   ----------------------------------------------------------------------*/
#include <iostream>
#include <iomanip>
using namespace std;

// FUNCTION PROTOTYPES

void instruct();
void getEmployeeInfo(int & empNumber, int & dependents,
                     double & hours, double & rate, bool & done);
double grossWages(int dependents, double hours, double rate);
void computeNetPay(double grossPay, int dependents,
                   double & tax, double & netPay);
void printEmpInfo(int idNumber, double hours, double grossPay,
                  double taxes, double netPay);
```

Figure C.7 (continued)

```cpp
int main()
{
  int idNumber,           // employee's id-number
      numDependents;      //   number of dependents
  double hoursWorked,     //   hours worked for this pay period
         hourlyRate,      //   dollars per hour
         grossPay,        //   gross pay (before taxes)
         taxWithheld,     //   amount of tax withheld
         netPay;          //   grossPay - taxWithheld
  bool endOfData;         // signals end of data
  instruct();
  for (;;)
  {
    getEmployeeInfo(idNumber, numDependents,
                    hoursWorked, hourlyRate, endOfData);
    if (endOfData) break;
    grossPay = grossWages(numDependents, hoursWorked, hourlyRate);
    computeNetPay(grossPay, numDependents, taxWithheld, netPay);
    printEmpInfo(idNumber, hoursWorked, grossPay, taxWithheld, netPay);
  }
}
// FUNCTION DEFINITIONS
//    If these were placed before main(), the prototypes could be
//    omitted. This is not usually done, however.

void instruct()
/*-----------------------------------------------------------------
  Display instructions to the user.

  Output: Instructions
  ---------------------------------------------------------------*/
{
  cout
    << "This program computes gross pay, tax withheld, and net pay for "
    << "employees.\nWhen prompted, enter employee's id-number (enter "
    << "0 to stop).  Then enter:"
    << "\n\t# of dependents   hours worked   hourly rate:"
    << "\nseparated by spaces.\n";
}
```

Figure C.7 (continued)

```cpp
void getEmployeeInfo(int & empNumber, int & dependents,
                     double & hours, double & rate, bool & finis)
/*-------------------------------------------------------------------
  Get employee information and/or signal there is no more.

  Input:     Id-number, # of dependents, hours worked, and hourly rate
  Pass back: The four input values (via parameters)
             done is true if end of data was signaled, false otherwise
  ------------------------------------------------------------------*/
{
  cout << "\nEnter employee number (0 to stop): ";
  cin >> empNumber;                         // get employee number
  finis = (empNumber == 0);
  if (finis) return;                        // if end of data, return
                                            // else get other info
  cout << "Enter # of dependents, hours worked, and hourly rate for "
       << empNumber << ": ";
  cin >> dependents >> hours >> rate;
}


double grossWages(int dependents, double hours, double rate)
/*-------------------------------------------------------------------
  Compute gross wages as determined by number of hours employee worked
  plus a dependency allowance for each dependent.

  Receive:  Number of dependents, hours worked, hourly rate
  Return:   Gross wages
  ------------------------------------------------------------------*/
{
  const double DEP_ALLOWANCE = 100; // bonus per dependent
  double wages;                     // wages earned
  if (hours <= 40)                  // no overtime
    wages = hours * rate;
  else                              // overtime
    wages = 40 * rate + 1.5 * rate * (hours - 40);

                                    // return wages + allowance for deps
  return wages + DEP_ALLOWANCE * dependents;
}
```

Figure C.7 (continued)

```cpp
void computeNetPay(double grossPay, int dependents,
                   double & tax, double & netPay)
/*---------------------------------------------------------------------
   Compute taxes withheld and net pay as gross pay minus taxes withheld.

   Receive:  Gross pay and number of dependents
   Return:   Taxes withheld and net pay (via parameters)
   ------------------------------------------------------------------*/
{
  const double
    DEDUCTION = 25.00,          // deduction per dependent
    TAX_RATE = 0.12;            // withholding rate
  tax = TAX_RATE * (grossPay - DEDUCTION * dependents);
  if (tax < 0)                  // check if any tax to be withheld
    tax = 0;

  netPay = grossPay - tax;      // compute net pay
}


void printEmpInfo(int idNumber, double hours, double grossPay,
                  double taxes, double netPay)
/*---------------------------------------------------------------------
   Display employee information

   Receive:  Employee's id number, hours worked, gross pay, taxes withheld,
             and net pay
   Output:   These values with appropriate labels.
   ------------------------------------------------------------------*/
{
  cout << setprecision(2) << setiosflags(ios::showpoint | ios::fixed)
       << "Employee " << idNumber << ":\n"
       << "\tHours worked:   " << setw(6) << hours << endl
       << "\tGross Pay:     $" << setw(6) << grossPay << endl
       << "\tTaxes withheld: $" << setw(6) << taxes << endl
       << "\tNet Pay:       $" << setw(6) << netPay << endl;
}
```

Figure C.7 (continued)

Execution Trace:
When prompted, enter employee's id-number (enter 0 to stop).   Then enter:
         # of dependents   hours worked   hourly rate:
separated by spaces.

Enter employee number (0 to stop): 12345
Enter # of dependents, hours worked, and hourly rate for 12345: 0 40 8
Employee 12345:
         Hours worked: 40.00
         Gross Pay: $320.00
         Taxes withheld: $ 38.40
         Net Pay: $281.60

Enter employee number (0 to stop): 0

▲

Default Values for Parameters   The last (trailing, rightmost) parameters in a parameter list may be assigned **default values**. These will be used as values if the function call does not provide arguments for these parameters. For example, we might assign default values to the parameters hours and rate in function grossWages() as follows:

```
double grossWages(int dependents,   double hours = 0.0,
                        double rate = 4.50);
```

This cannot be done in both the prototype and the definition and is usually done in its prototype.

Inline Functions   Preceding a function declaration with the keyword **inline** allows the compiler to replace each call of the function with the function body (with arguments substituted for parameters). This (usually) speeds execution; but do this only for simple functions. (See Section 4.3 for more information about inlined functions.)

Function Overloading   Two different functions may have the same name provided they have different signatures; that is, their parameter lists must differ in the number and/or types of parameters. The compiler uses the arguments in a function call to determine which function to use. (See Section 4.4 for more information about overloading functions.)

C.12 Lifetimes, Scopes, and Namespaces

Object Lifetime   An object has

- a name,
- memory allocated to it, and
- a value.

Constructing an object consists of

■ binding its name to a memory location, and

■ storing an initial value (possibly an undefined "garbage" value) in the memory locations.

An object is *destroyed* when it is no longer bound to a memory location.

The **lifetime** of an object is the time it exists—from its construction to its destruction. Most objects are **auto** (automatic) objects, which are created when execution enters the block containing their declarations and are destroyed when execution leaves the block. If we precede the declaration of an object with the keyword `static`,

```
static type object_name = init_expression;
```

then it is created when execution of the program begins and is destroyed when execution terminates. The following are some properties of auto and static objects:

1. Auto objects are initialized each time execution passes through their declaration. Static objects are initialized once—when program execution begins.

2. Objects declared in functions are auto unless declared to be static.

3. As auto objects, a function's parameters and local variables are created each time the function is called and are destroyed when the function terminates.

4. A static local variable's value *persists* between calls to a function and can thus be used to store data that is needed from one function call to the next.

Scope An object's lifetime indicates its existence at *run time*. An object's **scope** indicates its existence at *compile time*; it is the portion of the program in which that object can be accessed. The scope of an identifier depends on where the identifier is declared. The following are basic scope rules:

1. If an identifier is declared within a block, then its scope runs from its declaration to the end of the block. It can be accessed only within that block.

2. If an identifier is declared in the initialization expression of a for loop, then its scope runs from its declaration to the end of the loop. It can be accessed only within that for loop.

3. If an identifier is declared outside all blocks, then its scope runs from its declaration to the end of the file. It can be used anywhere within that file following its declaration (except when the identifier used for that object is also used for some other object).

4. If an identifier is a parameter of a function, then its scope is the body of the function. It can be accessed only within that function.

5. The scope of a member identifier in a struct or class is that struct or class. It cannot be accessed outside the struct or class just by giving its name; rather, the dot operator or the scope operator (::)must be used.

6. The scope of an identifier declared or defined in a namespace block is that namespace block.

Note that an identifier's scope always begins at some point following its declaration. This observation can be summarized in the following single rule:

An identifier must be declared before it can be used.

Namespaces   One of the newer additions to C++ is the **namespace** mechanism. If *name* is declared or defined in a namespace declaration of the form

```
namespace Something
{
   // declarations and definitions
}
```

then the scope of an identifier *name* declared inside this namespace block is this block. It can be accessed outside of the namespace only in the following ways:

1. By its fully qualified name:

   Something::*name*

2. By its unqualified name *name*, if a **using declaration** of the form

   using namespace *Something*::*name*;

or a **using directive** of the form

   using namespace *Something*;

has already been given, provided that no other item has the same name (in which case qualification is required as described in 1). A using directive makes all names in the namespace available. This is why we add the directive using namespace std; with the #includes of standard libraries—so that the names declared and defined in them can be used without qualification.

C.13 Files

Files are processed using ifstreams, ofstreams, and fstreams, which connect a program and a file on disk; ofstreams are used only for output to a file, and writing to an ofstream actually writes to the file to which it is connected; ifstreams are used only for input from a file and reading from an ifstream actually reads from the file to which it is connected; fstreams can be used for both input and output.

Opening File Streams   File streams are declared by using the types ifstream, ofstream, and fstream; for example,

```
ifstream in;    // input stream
ofstream out;   // output stream
```

These types are declared in <fstream>, so it must be #included in the program:

```
#include <fstream>
```

Declaring a file stream only declares the name to be used for that stream. Before it can actually be used, it must be *opened*, which establishes a connection to an actual disk file. This can be done in two ways:

1. Use the open() member function:

   stream.open(*disk_filename*)

where *disk_filename* has a string constant as its value—for example,

```
in.open("/home/cs/186/xyz.dat");
```

```
string outFileName;
cin >> outFileName;
out.open(outFileName.data());
```

or

```
out.open(outFileName.c_str());
```

In the last few examples, we must use the `string` function member `data()` or `c_str()` to extract the string constant stored in `outFileName`.

2. Attach (*disk_filename*) to the file stream's name in its declaration:

```
ifstream in(disk_filename);
ofstream out(disk_filename);
```

for example,

```
ifstream in("/home/cs/123/xyz.dat");
ofstream out(outFileName.data());
```

or

```
ofstream out(outFileName.c_str());
```

We can also use a second *mode* argument in either of these methods that specifies how the file is being opened—for input (`ios::in`), for output (`ios::out`), for appending (`ios::app`). Opening a file for output destroys any previous contents of the file unless `ios::app` is used.

It is always a good idea to check that a file was opened successfully before proceeding. For this, we can use the member function `is_open()`; for example,

```
assert(in.is_open());
```

or

```
if (!in.is_open())
{
  cerr << "Error opening file\n";
  exit(1);
}
```

Closing File Streams   After processing of a file is complete, the stream to that file should be **closed**, which disconnects it from the file:

```
stream.close();
```

If necessary, the file stream can be reopened (using `open()`). For example, one might open a file for output, write some data to it, then close it, reopen it for input, and then read and process this data.

I/O with Files   It is important to remember that class `ifstream` is derived from class `istream` and class `ofstream` is derived from class `ostream`, so *they inherit all of the operations from these base classes* such as `eof()`, `fail()`, `ignore()`, `>>`, `<<`, and get(). These functions and operations can therefore also be used with file streams and format manipulators can be used with ofstreams. (See Appendix D for more information.)

Example The program in Figure C.8 illustrates the use of files. It reads permanent employee information from a file and current information is entered from the keyboard. A complete version is available on the text's website (see *AppC* in the source files).

Figure C.8 Using Files

```
/*---------------------------------------------------------------
  A modification of the program in Fig. C.7 for computing wages for
  several employees.  Permanent employee information is read from a file.

  Input (file):     Id-number, number of dependents, and hourly rate
                      for each of several employees
  Input (keyboard): Hours worked by employees
  Output (screen):  Prompts to user, including id-numbers.
  Output (file):    Id-numbers, hours worked, gross pay, taxes withheld
                      and net pay
---------------------------------------------------------------*/

#include <iostream>
#include <fstream>
#include <iomanip>
#include <string>
using namespace std;

void instruct();
void getEmployeeInfo(ifstream & in, int & empNumber, int & dependents,
                     double & hours, double & rate, bool & done);
double grossWages(int dependents, double hours, double rate);
void computeNetPay(double grossPay, int dependents,
                   double & tax, double & netPay);
void printEmpInfo(ofstream & out, int idNumber, double hours,
                  double grossPay, double taxes, double netPay);
int main()
{
  string inFilename,
         outFilename;
```

Figure C.8 (continued)

```cpp
   cout << "Enter names of input and output files: ";
   cin >> inFilename >> outFilename;
   ifstream inStream(inFilename.data());
   ofstream outStream(outFilename.data());
   int idNumber,               // employee's id-number
         numDependents;        //   number of dependents
   double hoursWorked,         //   hours worked for this pay period
          hourlyRate,          //   dollars per hour
          grossPay,            //   gross pay (before taxes)
          taxWithheld,         //   amount of tax withheld
          netPay;              //   grossPay - taxWithheld
   bool endOfData;             // signals end of data
   instruct();
   for (;;)
   {
     getEmployeeInfo(inStream, idNumber, numDependents,
                     hoursWorked, hourlyRate, endOfData);
     if (endOfData) break;
     grossPay = grossWages(numDependents, hoursWorked, hourlyRate);
     computeNetPay(grossPay, numDependents, taxWithheld, netPay);
     printEmpInfo(outStream, idNumber, hoursWorked, grossPay,
                  taxWithheld, netPay);
   }
}


void instruct()
/*-------------------------------------------------------------------
  Display instructions to the user.

  Output: Instructions
  --------------------------------------------------------------------*/
{
  cout <<
        "This program computes gross pay, tax withheld, and net pay for "
        "employees.\n\tWhen prompted, enter hours worked and hourly rate"
        "\n\t(separated by spaces) for the indicated employee.\n\n";
}
```

Figure C.8 (continued)

```cpp
void getEmployeeInfo(ifstream & in, int & empNumber, int & dependents,
                     double & hours, double & rate, bool & done)
/*-----------------------------------------------------------------
   Get employee information and/or signal there is no more.

     Receive:           ifstream
     Input (file):      Id-number, number of dependents, and hourly rate
     Input (keyboard):  Hours worked by employee
     Output (screen):   Prompts to user, including id-number
     Pass back:         Modified ifstream, the four input values, done is
                        true if end of data was signaled, false otherwise
   -----------------------------------------------------------------
*/
{
  in >> empNumber;                    // get employee number from file
  done = in.eof();
  if (done) return;                   // if end of file, return
                                      // else
  in >> dependents >> rate;           // get other info from file
  cout << "Enter hours worked by " << empNumber << ": ";
  cin >> hours;                       // get hours worked from user
}


//--- Insert definitions of grossWages() and computeNetPay() from Figure C.7

void printEmpInfo(ofstream & out, int idNumber, double hours,
                  double grossPay, double taxes, double netPay)
/*-----------------------------------------------------------------
   Write employee information to a file.

     Receive:   ofstream, employee's id number, hours worked, gross pay,
                taxes withheld, and net pay
     Pass back: the modified ofstream
   -----------------------------------------------------------------
*/
{
  out << setprecision(2) << setiosflags(ios::showpoint | ios::fixed)
      << "Employee " << idNumber << ":\n"
      << "\tHours worked:   " << setw(6) << hours << endl
      << "\tGross Pay:     $" << setw(6) << grossPay << endl
```

```
        << "\tTaxes withheld: $" << setw(6) << taxes << endl
        << "\tNet Pay:        $" << setw(6) << netPay << endl;
}
```

Figure C.8 (continued)

Execution Trace:
```
Enter names of input and output file: employee.dat payinfo
This program computes gross pay, tax withheld, and net pay for employees.
        When prompted, enter hours worked and hourly rate
        (separated by spaces) for the indicated employee.

Enter hours worked by 12345: 40
Enter hours worked by 22244: 45
Enter hours worked by 33333: 42.5
```

Listing of input file *employee.dat*:
```
12345 0 8.00
22244 1 9.00
33333 2 10.00
```

Listing of output file *payinfo*:
```
Employee 12345:
        Hours worked:     40.00
        Gross Pay:      $320.00
        Taxes withheld: $ 38.40
        Net Pay:        $281.60
Employee 22244:
        Hours worked:     45.00
        Gross Pay:      $527.50
        Taxes withheld: $ 60.30
        Net Pay:        $467.20
Employee 33333:
        Hours worked:     42.50
        Gross Pay:      $637.50
        Taxes withheld: $ 70.50
        Net Pay:        $567.00
```

▲

Other C++ Features

D.1 Stream Operations

Several I/O operations were listed in Section 5.1. This section describes them in more detail.

Input

In the following operations and functions, `in_stream` is an `istream`, an `ifstream`, or an `istringstream`:

`in_stream >> variable`

> Tries to extract a sequence of characters corresponding to a value of the type of `variable` from `in_stream` and assign it to `variable`; for a char array of capacity n, it reads at most n – 1 characters and adds a terminating null character. If there are no characters, it *blocks execution* from proceeding until characters are entered. If the **noskipws manipulator** is used in an input statement,
>
> > `... >> noskipws >> ...`
>
> then in all subsequent input, white-space characters will not be skipped. The **skipws manipulator** can be used to reactivate white-space skipping, which is the default condition:
>
> > `... >> skipws >> ...`
>
> `>>` returns `in_stream`.

`in_stream.width(n)`

> Sets the maximum number of characters to be read from `in_stream` by the next `>>` to n – 1.

`in_stream.get()`
`in_stream.get(char_variable);`

> Reads the next character from `in_stream` regardless of whether or not it is a white-space character. The first form returns this character; the second form assigns it to `char_variable`.

`in_stream.get(char_array, n);`
`in_stream.get(char_array, n, terminator);`

Extracts characters from `in_stream` and stores them in `char_array` until one of the following occurs:

1. n – 1 characters have been read.
2. The end of file occurs.
3. `terminator` is encountered (which is not extracted from `in_stream`). In the second case, `'\n'` is used.

A terminating null character is then added.

```
in_stream.getline(char_array, n);
in_stream.getline(char_array, n, terminator);
```

Same as `get()`, but removes the terminating character.

```
in_stream.read(char_array, n);
```

Extracts characters from `in_stream` and stores them in `char_array` until one of the following occurs:

1. n characters have been read.
2. The end of file occurs.

No terminating null character is added.

```
in_stream.readsome(char_array, n);
```

Like `read()`, but returns the number of characters extracted.

```
in_stream.gcount()
```

Returns the number of characters extracted by the last unformatted input—`get()`, `getline()`, `read()`, `readsome()`—from `in_stream`.

```
in_stream.peek()
```

Returns next character to be read but doesn't remove it from `in_stream`.

```
in_stream.ignore(n, stopChar);
```

Extracts and discards characters from `in_stream` until one of the following occurs:

1. n characters have been extracted; default is 1.
2. `stopChar` is encountered and removed from `in_stream`; default terminator is the end of file.

```
in_stream.putback(ch);
```

Put character ch back into `in_stream`.

```
in_stream.unget(ch);
```

Put most recently read character back into `in_stream`.

```
in_stream.seekg(n);
in_stream.seekg(offset, base);
```

For the first form, move the read position to nth character in `in_stream`. For the second form, move the read position `offset` bytes from base, where base is one of `ios::beg` (beginning of stream), `ios::cur` (current position), or `ios::end` (end of stream).

`in_stream.tellg()`

Return the offset of the read position within `in_stream`.

`in_stream.sync();`

Flush `in_stream`; return 0 if successful; return –1 and set `badbit` if not successful.

Output

In the following operations and functions, `out_stream` is an `ostream`, an `ofstream`, or an `ostringstream`:

`out_stream << expression`

Insert string of characters representing the value of `expression` into `out_stream`; returns `out_stream`.

`out_stream.put(ch);`

Insert character ch into `out_stream`.

`out_stream.write(char_array, n);`

Insert first n characters of `char_array` into `out_stream`.

`out_stream.seekp(n);`
`out_stream.seekp(offset, base);`

Same as `seekg`, but for setting the write position in `out_stream`.

`out_stream.tellp()`

Return the offset of the write position within `out_stream`.

`out_stream.flush();`

Flush `out_stream`.

Files

In the following operations and functions, `file_stream` is an `ifstream`, an `ofstream`, or an `fstream`:

`fstream.open(name);`
`fstream.open(name, mode);`

Connect `fstream` to the file with specified name. In the second form, mode is one of the following:

`ios::in`	The default mode for `ifstream` objects. Open a file for input nondestructively with the read position at the file's beginning.
`ios::trunc`	Open a file and delete any contents it contains (i.e., *truncate* it).
`ios::out`	The default mode for `ofstream` objects. Open a file for output, using `ios::trunc`.

`ios::app`	Open a file for output, but nondestructively, with the write position at the file's end (i.e., for *appending*).
`ios::ate`	Open an existing file with the read position (`ifstream` objects) or write position (`ofstream` objects) at the end of the file.
`ios::nocreate`	Open a file only if it already exists.
`ios::noreplace`	Open a file only if it does not already exist.
`ios::binary`	Open a file in binary mode.

`fstream.is_open()`

Returns `true` if a file was opened successfully and `false` otherwise.

`fstream.close();`

Disconnect `fstream` from the file to which is is currently connected.

Stream States

`ios::badbit`	1 if an unrecoverable error occurred, 0 otherwise.
`ios::failbit`	1 if a recoverable error occurred, 0 otherwise.
`ios::eofbit`	1 if the end-of-file mark was read, 0 otherwise.
`stream.setstate(sBit);`	Set the status bit `sBit` to 1, where `sBit` is one or more of `ios::badbit`, `ios::failbit`, `ios::eofbit`.
`stream.good()`	Returns `true` if and only if the good bit is set (1).
`stream.fail()`	Returns `true` if and only if the fail bit is set (1).
`stream.bad()`	Returns `true` if and only if the bad bit is set (1).
`stream.eof()`	Returns `true` if and only if the eof bit is set (1).
`stream.clear()`	Resets the good bit to 1, all other status bits to 0.

Format Manipulators

`boolalpha`	Use strings `true` and `false` for I/O of boolean values.
`noboolalpha`	Use integers 1 and 0 for I/O of boolean values.
`scientific`	Use floating-point (scientific) notation.
`fixed`	Use fixed-point notation.
`showpoint`	Show decimal point and trailing zeros for whole real numbers.
`noshowpoint`	Hide decimal point and trailing zeros for whole real numbers.
`showpos`	Display positive values with a + sign.
`noshowpos`	Display positive values without a + sign.
`dec`	Display integer values in base 10.
`oct`	Display integer values in base 8.
`hex`	Display integer values in base 16.
`showbase`	Display integer values indicating their base (e.g., 0x for hex).
`noshowbase`	Display integer values without indicating their base.

uppercase	In hexadecimal, use symbols A–F; in scientific, use E.
nouppercase	In hexadecimal, use symbols a–f; in scientific, use e.
skipws	Skip white space on input.
noskipws	Don't skip white space on input.
flush	Write contents of stream to screen (or file).
endl	Insert newline character and flush the stream.
left	Left-justify displayed values, pad with fill character on right.
right	Right-justify displayed values (except strings), pad with fill character on left.
internal	Pad with fill character between sign or base and value.
setprecision(num)	Set the number of decimal digits to be displayed to num.
setw(num)	Display the next value in a field whose width is num.
setfill(ch)	Set the fill character to ch (blank is the default).

The iomanip library must be included for the last three format manipulators. It also provides the following, which can be used for formatting:

setiosflags(flaglist)	Sets the flags in flaglist
resetiosflags(flaglist)	Resets the flags in flaglist to their defaults,

where the form of flaglist is $flag_1$ | $flag_2$ | ... | $flag_n$, with the flags selected from the following list: ios::showpoint, ios::fixed, ios::scientific, ios::left, ios::right, ios::skipws.

D.2 String Operations

Many of the string operations described in Section 5.2 are implemented by C-style functions provided in the C++ library <cstring>.[1] Table D.1 lists these functions; s, s1, and s2 are char arrays, ch is a character, and n is an integer. Other useful string-processing functions are the conversion functions in <cstdlib> listed in Table D.2 and the character-processing functions from <cctype> listed in Table D.3. Many of these C string-processing functions use the null character to detect the end of a string and cannot be expected to perform correctly if it is not present.

TABLE D.1: Functions in <cstring>

Operation	Description
strcat(s1, s2)	Appends s2 to s1.
strncat(s1, s2, n)	Appends at most n characters of s2 to s1.
strcpy(s1, s2)	Copies s2 into s1.
strncpy(s1, s2, n)	Copies first n characters of s2 into s1.

---

[1] The C++ standard specifies that a library provided in C with a name of the form <lib.h> be renamed in C++ as <clib> in which the prefix c is attached and the extension .h is dropped. In particular, C's string library <string.h> is renamed <cstring>. Many versions of C++ support both names.

TABLE D.1: Functions in `<cstring>` (continued)

Operation	Description
`strlen(s)`	Returns length of s (not counting the terminating null character).
`strcmp(s1, s2)`	Compares s1 with s2—returns an integer less than, equal to, or greater than 0, according to whether s1 is less than, equal to, or greater than s2.
`strncmp(s1, s2, n)`	Same as `strcmp`, but compare first n characters of s1 and s2.
`strchr(s, c)`	Returns a pointer to the, first occurrence of c in s, null if not found.
`strrchr(s, c)`	Like `strchr`, but locates last occurrence of c in s.
`strstr(s1, s2)`	Returns a pointer to the first occurrence in s1 of s2, null if not found.
`strpbrk(s1, s2)`	Returns a pointer to the first occurrence in s1 of any character of s2, null if none found.
`strspn(s1, s2)`	Returns the number of characters in s1 before any character in s2.
`strcspn(s1, s2)`	Returns the number of characters in s1 before a character not in s2.

TABLE D.2: Conversion Functions in `<cstdlib>`

Operation	Description
`double atof(s)`	`atof(s)`, `atoi(s)`, and `atol(s)` return the value obtained
`int atoi(s)`	by converting the character string s to `double`, `int`, and
`long atol(s)`	`long int`, respectively

TABLE D.3: Functions in `<cctype>`

Operation	Description
`isalnum(c)`	Returns true if c is a letter or a digit, false otherwise.
`isalpha(c)`	Returns true if c is a letter, false otherwise.
`iscntrl(c)`	Returns true if c is a control character, false otherwise.
`isdigit(c)`	Returns true if c is a decimal digit, false otherwise.
`isgraph(c)`	Returns true if c is a printing character, except space, false otherwise.
`islower(c)`	Returns true if c is lowercase, false otherwise.

TABLE D.3: Functions in <cctype> (continued)

Operation	Description
isprint(c)	Returns true if c is a printing character, including space, false otherwise.
ispunct(c)	Returns true if c is a punctuation character (not a space, an alphabetic character, or a digit), false otherwise.
isspace(c)	Returns true if c is a white-space character (space, '\f', '\n', '\r', '\t', or '\v'), false otherwise.
isupper(c)	Returns true if c is uppercase, false otherwise.
isxdigit(c)	Returns true if c is a hexadecimal digit, false otherwise.
tolower(c)	Returns lowercase equivalent of c (if c is uppercase).
toupper(c)	Returns the uppercase equivalent of c (if c is lowercase).

The string class, which was described in Chapter 5, is defined by

```
typedef basic_string<char> string;
```

The unsigned integer type **size_type** is defined in this class as is an integer constant **npos**, which is some integer that is usually greater than the number of characters in a string. Table D.4 gives a list of the major operations defined on a string object s; pos, pos1, pos2, n, n1, and n2 are of type size_type; str, str1, and str2 are of type string; charArray is a character array; ch and delim are of type char; istr is an istream; ostr is an ostream; it1 and it2 are iterators; and inpIt1 and inpIt2 are input iterators. All of these operations except >>, <<, +, the relational operators, getline(), and the second version of swap() are member functions.

TABLE D.4: Operations on C++ strings

Operation	Description
Constructors:	
string s;	This declaration invokes the default constructor to construct s as an empty string.
string s(charArray);	This declaration initializes s to contain a copy of charArray.
string s(charArray, n);	This declaration initializes s to contain a copy of the first n characters in charArray.
string s(str);	This declaration initializes s to contain a copy of string str.

TABLE D.4: Operations on C++ `strings` (continued)

Operation	Description
`string s(str, pos, n);`	This declaration initializes s to contain a copy of the n characters in string `str`, starting at position pos; if n is too large, characters are copied only to the end of `str`.
`string s(n, ch);`	This declaration initializes s to contain n copies of the character ch.
`string s(inpIt1, inpIt2);`	This declaration initializes s to contain the characters in the range [`inpIt1, inpIt2`).
`getline(istr, s, delim)`	Extracts characters from `istr` and stores them in s until `s.max_size()` characters have been extracted, the end of file occurs, or `delim` is encountered, in which case `delim` is extracted from `istr` but is not stored in s.
`getline(istr, s)`	Inputs a string value for s as in the preceding function with `delim = '\n'`.
`istr >> s`	Extracts characters from `istr` and stores them in s until `s.max_size()` characters have been extracted, the end of file occurs, or a white-space character is encountered, in which case the white-space character is not removed from `istr`; returns `istr`.
`ostr << s`	Inserts characters of s into `ostr`; returns `ostr`.
`s = val`	Assigns a copy of `val` to s; `val` may be a string, a character array, or a character.
`s += val`	Appends a copy of `val` to s; `val` may be a string, a character array, or a character.
`s[pos]`	Returns a reference to the character stored in s at position pos, provided `pos < s.length()`.
`s + t` `t + s`	Returns the result of concatenating s and t; t may be a string, a character array, or a character.

`s < t,  t < s`
`s <= t,  t <= s`
`s > t,  t > s`
`s >= t,  t >= s`
`s == t, t == s`
`s != t, t != s`
	Returns `true` or `false`, as determined by the relational operator; t may be a string or a character array.

`s.append(str)`	Appends string `str` at the end of s; returns s.

TABLE D.4: Operations on C++ strings (continued)

Operation	Description
`s.append(str, pos, n)`	Appends at the end of s a copy of the n characters in `str`, starting at position pos; if n is too large, characters are copied only until the end of `str` is reached; returns s.
`s.append(charArray)`	Appends `charArray` at the end of s; returns s.
`s.append(charArray, n)`	Appends the first n characters in `charArray` at the end of s; returns s.
`s.append(n, ch)`	Appends n copies of ch at the end of s; returns s.
`s.append(inpIt1, inpIt2)`	Appends copies of the characters in the range [`inpIt1, inpIt2`) to s; returns s.
`s.assign(str)`	Assigns a copy of `str` to s; returns s.
`s.assign(str, pos, n)`	Assigns to s a copy of the n characters in `str`, starting at position pos; if n is too large, characters are copied only until the end of `str` is reached; returns s.
`s.assign(charArray)`	Assigns to s a copy of `charArray`; returns s.
`s.assign(charArray, n)`	Assigns to s a string consisting of the first n characters in `charArray`; returns s.
`s.assign(n, ch)`	Assigns to s a string consisting of n copies of ch; returns s.
`s.assign(inpIt1, inpIt2)`	Assigns to s a string consisting of the characters in the range [`inpIt1, inpIt2`); returns s.
`s.at(pos)`	Returns `s[pos]`.
`s.begin()`	Returns an iterator positioned at the first character in s.
`s.c_str()`	Returns (the base address of) a char array containing the characters stored in s, terminated by a null character.
`s.capacity()`	Returns the size (of type `size_type`) of the storage allocated in s.
`s.clear()`	Removes all the characters in s; return type is `void`.
`s.compare(str)`	Returns a negative value, 0, or a positive value according as s is less than, equal to, or greater than `str`.

TABLE D.4: Operations on C++ `strings` (continued)

Operation	Description
`s.compare(charArray)`	Compares s and charArray as in the preceding function member.
`s.compare(pos, n, str)`	Compares strings s and str as before, but starts at position pos in s and compares only the next n characters.
`s.compare(pos, n, charArray)`	Compares string s and charArray as in the preceding function member.
`s.compare(pos1, n1, str, pos2, n2)`	Compares s and str as before, but starts at position pos1 in s, position pos2 in str, and compares only the next n1 characters in s and the next n2 characters in str.
`s.compare(pos1, n1, charArray, n2)`	Compares strings s and charArray as before, but using only the first n2 characters in charArray.
`s.copy(charArray, pos, n)`	Replaces the string in s with n characters in charArray, starting at position pos or at position 0, if pos is omitted; if n is too large, characters are copied only until the end of charArray is reached; returns the number (of type size_type) of characters copied.
`s.data()`	Returns a char array containing the characters stored in s.
`s.empty()`	Returns true if s contains no characters, false otherwise.
`s.end()`	Returns an iterator positioned immediately after the last character in s.
`s.erase(pos, n)`	Removes n characters from s, beginning at position pos (default value 0); if n is too large or is omitted, characters are erased only to the end of s; returns s.
`s.erase(it)`	Removes the character at the position specified by it; returns an iterator positioned immediately after the erased character.
`s.find(str, pos)`	Returns the first position $\geq$ pos such that the next str.size() characters of s match those in str; returns npos if there is no such position; 0 is the default value for pos.
`s.find(ch, pos)`	Searches s as in the preceding function member, but for ch.

TABLE D.4: Operations on C++ `strings` (continued)

Operation	Description
`s.find(charArray, pos)`	Searches s as in the preceding function member, but for the characters in charArray.
`s.find(charArray, pos, n)`	Searches s as in the preceding function member, but for the first n characters in charArray; the value pos must be given.
`s.find_first_not_of(str, pos)`	Returns the first position ≥ pos of a character in s that does not match any of the characters in str; returns npos if there is no such position; 0 is the default value for pos.
`s.find_first_not_of(ch, pos)`	Searches s as in the preceding function member, but for ch.
`s.find_first_not_of (charArray, pos)`	Searches s as in the preceding function member, but for the characters in charArray.
`s.find_first_not_of (charArray, pos, n)`	Searches s as in the preceding function member, but using the first n characters in charArray; the value pos must be given.
`s.find_first_of(str, pos)`	Returns the first position ≥ pos of a character in s that matches any character in str; returns npos if there is no such position; 0 is the default value for pos.
`s.find_first_of(ch, pos)`	Searches s as in the preceding function member, but for ch.
`s.find_first_of (charArray, pos)`	Searches s as in the preceding function member, but for the characters in charArray.
`s.find_first_of (charArray, pos, n)`	Searches s as in the preceding function member, but using the first n characters in charArray; the value pos must be given.
`s.find_last_not_of (str, pos)`	Returns the highest position ≤ pos of a character in s that does not match any character in str; returns npos if there is no such position; npos is the default value for pos.
`s.find_last_not_of (ch, pos)`	Searches s as in the preceding function member, but for ch.
`s.find_last_not_of (charArray, pos)`	Searches s as in the preceding function member, but using the characters in charArray.
`s.find_last_not_of (charArray, pos, n)`	Searches s as in the preceding function member, but using the first n characters in charArray; the value pos must be given.

TABLE D.4: Operations on C++ strings (continued)

Operation	Description
s.find_last_of(str, pos)	Returns the highest position ≤ pos of a character in s that matches any character in str; returns npos if there is no such position; npos is the default value for pos.
s.find_last_of(ch, pos)	Searches s as in the preceding function member, but for ch.
s.find_last_of (charArray, pos)	Searches s as in the preceding function member, but using the characters in charArray.
s.find_last_of (charArray, pos, n)	Searches s as in the preceding function member, but using the first n characters in charArray; the value pos must be given.
s.insert(pos, str)	Inserts a copy of str into s at position pos; returns s.
s.insert(pos1, str, pos2, n)	Inserts a copy of n characters of str starting at position pos2 into s at position pos; if n is too large, characters are copied only until the end of str is reached; returns s.
s.insert(pos, charArray, n)	Inserts a copy of the first n characters of charArray into s at position pos; inserts all of its characters if n is omitted; returns s.
s.insert(pos, n, ch)	Inserts n copies of the character ch into s at position pos; returns s.
s.insert(it, ch)	Inserts a copy of the character ch into s at the position specified by it and returns an iterator positioned at this copy.
s.insert(it, n, ch)	Inserts n copies of the character ch into s at the position specified by it; return type is void.
s.insert(it, inpIt1, inpIt2)	Inserts copies of the characters in the range [inpIt1, inpIt2) into s at the position specified by it; return type is void.
s.length()	Returns the length (of type size_type) of s.
s.max_size()	Returns the maximum length (of type size_type) of s.
s.rbegin()	Returns a reverse iterator positioned at the last character in s.
s.rend()	Returns a reverse iterator positioned immediately before the first character in s.

TABLE D.4: Operations on C++ `strings` (continued)

Operation	Description
`s.replace(pos1, n1, str)`	Replaces the substring of s of length n1 beginning at position pos1 with `str`; if n1 is too large, all characters to the end of s are replaced; returns s.
`s.replace(it1, it2, str)`	Same as the preceding but for the substring of s consisting of the characters in the range [`it1`, `it2`); returns s.
`s.replace(pos1, n1,` `         str, pos2, n2)`	Replaces a substring of s as in the preceding reference, but using n2 characters in `str`, beginning at position pos2; if n2 is too large, characters to the end of `str` are used; returns s.
`s.replace(pos1, n1,` `         charArray, n2)`	Replaces a substring of s as before, but with the first n2 characters in `charArray`; if n2 is too large, characters to the end of `charArray` are used; if n2 is omitted, all of `charArray` is used; returns s.
`s.replace(it1, it2,` `         charArray, n2)`	Same as the preceding, but for the substring of s consisting of the characters in the range [`it1`, `it2`); returns s.
`s.replace(pos1, n1,` `         n2, ch)`	Replaces a substring of s as before, but with n2 copies of ch.
`s.replace(it1, it2,` `         n2, ch)`	Same as the preceding, but for the substring of s consisting of the characters in the range [`it1`, `it2`); returns s.
`s.replace(it1, it2,` `         inpIt1, inpIt2)`	Same as the preceding, but replaces with copies of the characters in the range [`inpIt1`, `inpIt2`); returns s.
`s.reserve(n)`	Changes the storage allocation for s so that `s.capacity()` $\geq$ n, 0 if n is omitted; return type is `void`
`s.resize(n, ch)`	If n $\leq$ `s.size()`, truncates rightmost characters in s to make it of size n; otherwise, adds copies of character ch to end of s to increase its size to n, or adds a default character value (usually a blank) if ch is omitted; return type is `void`.
`s.rfind(str, pos)`	Returns the highest position $\leq$ pos such that the next `str.size()` characters of s match those in `str`; returns npos if there is no such position; npos is the default value for pos.

TABLE D.4: Operations on C++ strings (continued)

Operation	Description
s.rfind(ch, pos)	Searches s as in the preceding function member, but for ch.
s.rfind(charArray, pos)	Searches s as in the preceding function member, but for the characters in charArray.
s.rfind(charArray, pos, n)	Searches s as in the preceding function member, but for the first n characters in charArray; the value pos must be given.
s.size()	Returns the length (of type size_type) of s.
s.substr(pos, n)	Returns a copy of the substring consisting of n characters from s, beginning at position pos (default value 0); if n is too large or is omitted, characters are copied only until the end of s is reached.
s.swap(str)	Swaps the contents of s and str; return type is void.
swap(str1, str2)	Swaps the contents of str1 and str2; return type is void.

D.3 Exceptions

In Chapter 4 we looked at some ways of handling errors in class design. The programmer can write code to *detect* errors, but may not know how to *handle* them. In our examples, usually we have simply issued an error message or aborted execution by means of the exit() function or assert() function. In some cases, however, it would be better to simply signal the error and let the user of the class take appropriate action, and exceptions are designed to make this possible.

When a function detects an error, it can **throw an exception**, which is usually an error-message string or a class object that conveys information to the *exception handler*, which will **catch the exception** and take appropriate action. If there is no handler for that type of exception, execution terminates. The set operation in the Time class in Section 4.3 illustrates:

```
if (hours >= 1 && hours <= 12 &&
    minutes >= 0 && minutes <= 59 &&
    (am_pm == 'A' || am_pm == 'P'))
{
    . . .
}
else
{
```

```
    char illegal_Time_Error[] =
        "*** Can't set time with these values ***\n";
    throw illegal_Time_Error;
}
```

A program or function that calls a function that may throw an exception encloses the function call and associated code in a **try block** of the form

```
try
{
    ... statements that may cause error
}
```

This is followed by one or more **catch blocks**, each of which specifies an exception type and contains code for handling that exception. They have the form

```
catch(exception_type optional_parameter_name)
{
    ... the exception handler
}
```

For example, the following code attempts to use the set operation in a Time object mealTime and catches the exception thrown in set():

```
try
{
    mealTime.set(13, 30, 'P');
    cout << "This is a valid time\n";
}
catch (char badTime[])
{
    cout << "ERROR: " << badTime << endl;
    exit(1);
}
cout << "Proceeding. . .\n";
```

When the code in the try clock is executed and no exceptions are thrown, all catch blocks are skipped and execution continues with the statement after the last one. If an exception is thrown, execution leaves the try block and the attached catch blocks are searched for one whose parameter type matches the type of exception. If one is found, its exception handler is executed; otherwise, the catch blocks of any enclosing try blocks are searched. If none are found, execution terminates.

The types of exceptions that a function can throw can be declared by attaching an **exception specification** of the form throw(exception_list):

```
ReturnType name(parameterlist) throw(exc1, exc2, ...);
```

This function can throw only the exceptions listed and exceptions derived from them. If it attempts to do otherwise, the function std::unexpected() is called, which will terminate execution (unless unexpected() is redefined by calling set_unexpected()) or which will throw bad_exception if std::bad_exception is included in the list of exceptions.

There are several standard exceptions provided in C++. They are listed in Table D.5. They are all derived from the class exception provided in <stdexcept>, which in addition to member function throw(), also has a virtual member function what().

TABLE D.5: Standard Exceptions

Exception	Thrown by
bad_alloc	new()
bad_cast	dynamic_cast()
bad_typeid	typeid()
bad_exception	exception specification
out_of_range	at() and [] in bitset
invalid_argument	bitset constructor
overflow_error	to_ulong() in bitset
ios_base::failure	ios_base::clear ()

In Section 3.4, we gave several examples of bad_alloc exceptions thrown by the new operator when it is unable to satisfy requests for dynamic memory allocations. And in Section 9.4, we described the out-of-range exception thrown by the at member function of vector if the index gets out of range. The following is a modification of the example given there:

```
vector<int> v(4, 99);

try
{
  for (int i = 0; i < 5; i++)
    cout << v.at(i) << endl;
}
. . .
catch(out_of_range ex)
{
  cout << "Exception occurred: "
       << ex.what() << endl;
}
```

The member function what() used in the output statement returns a string describing the exception. In one version of C++, the output produced was

```
99
99
99
99
Exception occurred: vector::at out of range
```

D.4 More About Function Templates

In Section 9.2 we concentrated on function templates having a single type parameter, but we noted that more type parameters are allowed,

> template <typename $TypeParam_1$, ..., typename $TypeParam_n$>
> *function*

where $TypeParam_1, ..., TypeParam_n$ are type parameters. To illustrate this more general function template, consider the generic conversion function and the test-driver program in Figure D.1.

Figure D.1 Using a Function Template to Convert Types—Version 1

```
#include <iostream>
using namespace std;

template <typename Type1, typename Type2>
void convert(Type1 value1, Type2 & value2)
/*-------------------------------------------------------------
   Function template to convert a Type1 value to a Type2 value.
   Receive:    Type parameters Type1 and Type2
               value1 of Type 1
   Pass back: value2 of Type2
--------------------------------------------------------------*/
{
  value2 = static_cast<Type2>(value1);
}

int main()
{
  char a = 'a';
  int ia;
  convert(a, ia);
  cout << a << "   " << ia << endl;
  double x = 3.14;
  int ix;
  convert(x, ix);
  cout << x << "   " << ix << endl;
}
```

Execution Trace:

a   97

3.14   3

▲

Note that in the function template convert(), each of the type parameters Type1 and Type2 appears in the parameter list of the function heading. This is necessary if the compiler is to figure out what types to bind to the type parameters from the types of the arguments in a function call.

To illustrate, suppose we modify the function template convert() to return its value by means of a return statement rather than via a reference parameter, which is more natural when only a single value is being returned:

```cpp
template <typename Type1, typename Type2>
Type2 convert(Type1 value1)  // Note--Type2 not used in
{                            // parameter list
  return static_cast<Type2>(value1);
}
```

Here, however, the type parameter Type2 does not appear in the parameter list of convert(). So the compiler will not be able to bind an actual type to it from a function call of the form convert(arg) because it uses only the types of the arguments in a function call to determine what types to associate with the type parameters.

One solution is to use **explicit specification** in the function call,

```cpp
ia = convert<char, int>(a);
```

as illustrated in Figure D.2. Here the actual types char and int are associated explicitly with the type parameters Type1 and Type2.

Figure D.2 Using a Function Template to Convert Types—Version 2

```cpp
#include <iostream>
using namespace std;

template <typename Type1, typename Type2>
Type2 convert(Type1 value1)
/*-------------------------------------------------------------------
  Function template to convert a Type1 value to a Type2 value.
  Receive:  Type parameters Type1 and Type2
            value1 of Type 1
  Return:   value1 converted to Type2
-------------------------------------------------------------------*/
{
  return static_cast<Type2>(value1);
}

int main()
{
  char a = 'a';
  int ia = convert<char, int>(a);
```

Figure D.2 (continued)

```
  cout << a << "   " << ia << endl;


  double x = 3.14;
  int ix = convert<double, int>(x);
  cout << x << "   " << ix << endl;
}
```

Execution Trace:

```
a   97
3.14   3
```

▲

D.5 Other Applications of Pointers

In Chapters 3 and 6 we focused on how pointers are used to construct run-time arrays and linked lists. There are also several other applications of pointers that C++ has inherited from C. Two of these are described here.

Command-Line Arguments

In Section 3.4 we noted that command-line arguments can be passed to a main function main() via two parameters, which are usually named argc and argv:

- argc (the **arg**ument **c**ount): an int whose value is the number of strings on the command line when the command to execute the binary executable containing this function is given

- argv (the **arg**ument **v**ector): an array of pointers to chars; for $i = 0, 1, \ldots,$ argc-1, argv[i] is the address of the ith character string on the command line

The program in Figure D.3 and the sample runs demonstrate this. The compiled version of the program is stored in a file named comm, and comm is executed by entering the command

```
  comm
```

which produces the output

```
  There are 1 strings on the command line:
      argv[0] contains: comm
```

Thus, within comm, argc has the value 1, and argv[0] refers to the character string comm. When comm is executed by entering the command

```
  comm Computer Science 112
```

the output produced is

```
  There are 4 strings on the command line:
      argv[0] contains: comm
      argv[1] contains: Computer
      argv[2] contains: Science
      argv[3] contains: 112
```

Figure D.3 Parameters for `main()`

```
/*---------------------------------------------------------------
   Program to demonstrate main parameters argc and argv.

   Receive: A sequence of command-line strings
   Output:  The value of argc, followed by each string in argv
   ------------------------------------------------------------*/

#include <iostream>
using namespace std;

int main(int argc, char * argv[])
{
   cout << "There are " << argc
        << "strings on the command line:\n";
   for (int i = 0; i < argc; i++)
     cout << "   argv[" << i << "] = "  << argv[i] << endl;
}
```

Execution Traces (in Unix):
```
% g++ commandline1.cc -o comm
% comm
There are 1 strings on the command line:
   argv[0] contains: comm

% comm Computer Science 112
There are 4 strings on the command line:
   argv[0] contains: comm
   argv[1] contains: Computer
   argv[2] contains: Science
   argv[3] contains: 112
```

▲

Figure D.4 shows a program for implementing a system file-copy command. If the compiled version of the program is saved with the name copy, a command of the form

  copy file1 file2

can then be given to copy one file to another.

Figure D.4 Program for a System Command

```
/*-------------------------------------------------------------------------
   Program to implement a copy command.  If it is compiled and saved under
   the name copy, a command of the form
                        copy file1 file2
   will copy the contents of file1 to file2.

   Receive:       A sequence of command-line strings
   Input(file):   A text file
   Output(file):  Contents of the text file
-----------------------------------------------------------------------*/

#include <iostream>
#include <fstream>
#include <cassert>
using namespace std;

int main(int argc, char * argv[])
{
  if (argc != 3)
    cerr << "Usage:  copy file1 file2 \n\n";
  else
  {
    ifstream in(argv[1]);
    assert(in.is_open());
    ofstream out(argv[2]);
    assert (out.is_open());
    char ch;
    while (!in.eof())
    {
      in.get(ch);
      out.put(ch);
    }
    cout << "File copy completed\n\n";
  }
}
```

Figure D.4 (continued)

Execution Traces (in Unix):
```
% g++ commandline2.cc -o copy
CS:% copy
Usage:  copy file1 file2

% copy fileD-3A fileD-3B
% File copy completed
```

▲

Functions as Arguments

In Section 3.4 we noted that the *value of a function name is the starting address of that function*, that is, a function is a pointer. This means that if we can declare a type `FunctionPtr` capable of storing the address of a function and then declare a variable `fPtr` of that type,

```
FunctionPtr fPtr;
```

then the assignment statement

```
fPtr = f;
```

can be used to store the starting address of function `f()` in the variable `fPtr`. Because the value of `fPtr` is a valid address, `fPtr` can be dereferenced using the indirection operator (`*`), just like any other pointer variable. Thus, the expression

```
(*fPtr)(argument_list)
```

dereferences `fPtr`, which (since function `f()` is at that address) calls function `f()`, passing it `argument_list`.[2] In fact, we need not even use the indirection operator, since attaching an argument list to `fPtr` *automatically dereferences* `fPtr`,

```
fPtr(argument_list)
```

(much like attaching subscripts to a pointer to an array).

Similarly, we can declare `fPtr` as a parameter of a function `g()` and then use `fPtr` to call `f()` from within `g()`:

```
void g(FunctionPtr fPtr)
{
    ...
    fPtr(argument_list);
    ...
}
```

Then, we could call `g()` and pass the name of function `f()` as an argument

```
g(f);
```

and `g()`, when it dereferences its parameter `fPtr`, will call function `f()`.

---

[2] The parentheses around `*fPtr` are necessary because the dereferencing operator `*` has lower priority than the function-call operation (). See Appendix C for a table of operator priorities.

The `typedef` mechanism can be used to declare `FunctionPtr` as a type whose objects can store the address of a function,

```
typedef ReturnType (*FunctionPtr)(parameter_type_list);
```

which declares the name `FunctionPtr` as a type whose objects can store the address of any function whose return type is *ReturnType*, and whose parameters match those in *parameter_type_list*. For example, the program in Figure D.5 uses the declaration

```
typedef double (*FunctionPtr)(double);
```

to declare `FunctionPtr` as a pointer to a function that has a `double` parameter and that returns a `double` value. The function `bisector()` in this program has a function parameter of type `FunctionPtr` and uses the bisection method described in Programming Problem 8 of Chapter 11 to find an approximate zero of this function. A solution of the equation

$$f(x) = x^3 + x - 5 = 0$$

is found by passing the function `f()` to `bisect()`.

Figure D.5 Bisection method—Functions as Arguments

```
/*---------------------------------------------------------------------
   Find an approximate solution of the equation f(x) = 0 in a given
   interval, using the bisection method.

   Input:   Desired accuracy of approximation, endpoints of an
            interval containing a solution
   Output:  Prompts to the user and the approximate solution

   Notes:
   1. The solution will be within desiredAccuracy of the exact
      solution.
   2. To find the solution for a different f(x), redefine f() below.
---------------------------------------------------------------------*/

#include <iostream>
using namespace std;

double f(double x)
{
    return x*x*x + x - 5;        // the function f for which the
}                                // equation f(x) = 0 is being solved

//---------------------------------------------------------------
```

Figure D.5 (continued)

```
typedef double (* FunctionPointer)(double);

double bisector(FunctionPointer fPtr,
                double left, double right, double accuracy);

int main()
{
  cout << "\nThis program uses the bisection method to find an"
          "\napproximate solution to the equation f(x) = 0.\n";
  double desiredAccuracy;   // the accuracy desired

  cout << "\nEnter the accuracy desired (e.g. .001): ";
  cin >> desiredAccuracy;
  double left,              // left and right endpoints
         right;             //   of (sub)interval containing a solution
  do                        // get the interval containing a solution
  {
    cout << "Enter the x-values of interval containing solution: ";
    cin >> left >> right;
  }
  while (f(left) * f(right) >= 0.0);

  double                    // find the approximate solution
     solution = bisector(f, left, right, desiredAccuracy);
  cout << "\n--> "<< solution
       << " is an approximate solution of f(x) = 0, to within "
       << desiredAccuracy << endl;
}

double bisector(FunctionPointer fPtr,
                double left, double right, double accuracy)
/*---------------------------------------------------------------------
  Function to perform the bisection algorithm.

  Receive:  FPtr, (a pointer to) a function for which a zero is to be found.
            left, the left endpoint of the original interval
            right, the right endpoint of the original interval
            accuracy, the desired accuracy of the approximation
  Return:   midPt, the middle of the final interval
  -------------------------------------------------------------------*/
```

Figure D.5 (continued)

```
{
  double width = right - left,     // the interval width
        midPt,                     // the midpoint of the interval
        f_Mid;                     // value of fPtr at midpoint
  while (width/2.0 > accuracy)
  {
    midPt = (left + right) / 2.0;  //   compute midpoint
    f_Mid = fPtr(midPt);           //   compute function at midpoint
    if (fPtr(left) * f_Mid < 0.0 ) //   solution is in left half
      right = midPt;

    else                           //   solution is in right half
      left = midPt;

    width /= 2.0;                  //   split the interval
  }

  return midPt;
}
```

Execution Trace:

This program uses the bisection method to find an approximate solution to the equation f(x) = 0.

Enter the accuracy desired (e.g. .001): .001
Enter the x-values of interval containing solution: 0 1
Enter the x-values of interval containing solution: 1 2

--> 1.51758 is an approximate solution of f(x) = 0, to within 0.001

▲

From Java to C++

E.1 Program Structure

C++

A progam is a collection of functions (see Figure C.7). Execution starts with a main() function.

```
int main()
{ . . .
}
```

Java

A progam is a collection of classes. Execution starts with a class that has a main() method.

```
class Something {
  public static void main(String args[])
  { . . .
  }
```

E.2 using and Compiler Directives

C++

- A using clause makes the contents of a namespace usable without qualification (e.g., cin instead of std::cin).
- Source code is preprocessed—to strip comments and process compiler directives that begin with #.
- #include is used to include the contents of libraries (see §C.2-3). Important standard libraries are <iostream>, <fstream>, <string>, <cassert>, <cmath>, <cctype>, and <iomanip>.

```
#include <iostream>
using namespace std;
#include "MyClass"
```

Java

- `import` makes names of items in classes and packages usable without qualification (e.g., `Date today;` instead of `java.util.Date today;`).

  ```
  import java.util.*;
  ```

E.3 Input and Output (§C.9, §C.13, & §D.1)

Screen Output in C++

- The output operator `<<` from the `<iostream>` library can be used to output values to `cout` (buffered) or `cerr` (unbuffered), which are `ostream` objects connecting a program to the screen.
- `'\n'` advances to a new line; `endl` advances to a new line and flushes the output buffer; interactive input (`cin >> ...`) also flushes the output buffer.

  ```
  cout << "Hello";
  cout << " There" << endl;
  cerr << "Bad Value\n";
  ```

- Format manipulators can be used to format output; use `#include <iomanip>` for `setprecision()` and `setw()` (see Section D.1).

  ```
  cout << fixed << showpoint << setprecision(2)
       << "Wages = $" << setw(10) << wages << endl;
  ```

Screen Output in Java

- Use `System.out`'s `print()` and `println()` methods to output strings; they assume availability of a `toString()` method to convert other objects to strings.
- `"\n"` advances to a new line; `println()` also causes a line advance after output.

  ```
  System.out.print("Hello");
  System.out.println(" There");
  ```

- Formatting output requires use of special classes such as `DecimalFormat`.

Keyboard Input in C++

- The input operator `>>` from the `<iostream>` library can be used to read values from `cin`, an `istream` object from the keyboard to a program. `>>` skips leading white space and stops reading characters at white space; for numeric variables, `>>` will stop at the first character that cannot belong to a value of that type; in both cases, the stop character is left in the stream.

  ```
  double wage;
  cin >> wage;
  int idNumber, zip;
  char code;
  cout << "Enter ID, code, wage, zipCode: ";
  cin >> idNumber >> code >> wage >> zip;
  ```

```
// Input:  12345 X 456.78 49546
string aWord;
cin >> aWord;
```

■ getline(cin, str) can be used to read an entire line of characters for string variable str, up to an end-of-line character, which is removed from the stream. Be careful, however, with using both >> and getline(), because >> stops at an end-of-line character and leaves it in the stream; getline() will stop at this end-of-line character immediately.

■ get(cin, ch) or ch = get(cin) can be used to read any character and assign to a char variable ch.

Keyboard Input in Java

■ Use System.in. It is common to wrap an InputStreamReader around it followed by a BufferedReader for efficiency.

■ Strings can be read with the readLine() method. For numeric input, the string that is read must be parsed—for example, with parseInt() or parseDouble().

```
BufferedReader in =
 new BufferedReader(new InputStreamReader(System.in));
String dubStr = in.readLine();
double dub = Double.parseDouble(dubStr);
```

■ Several values can be read from a line of input by reading the line into a String and then using the StringTokenizer class to break it up into tokens, which can then be parsed.

File Input in C++

■ The input operator >> as well as the getline() or get() functions can be used with an ifstream object that has been connected to a file as follows:

1. Get the name of the file.

2. Open an ifstream with an initialized declaration of an ifstream object:

● Use string's data() or c_str() method to extract the actual (C-style) char array.

```
string inFileName;
cin >> inFileName;  // or getline(cin, inFilename);
ifstream fin(inFileName.data());
```

● Or use uninitialized declaration of an ifstream object and then use it's open() method:

```
ifstream fin;
fin.open(inFileName.data());
```

3. Check that the stream was opened successfully:

```
assert(fin.is_open());    // #include <cassert>
```

■ ifstream is a subclass of istream, so it inherits all of its input features, including >>, getline(), and get.

   ● Also, the good() and fail() methods can be used to check for input errors.

   ● Use the clear() method to reset failure flags in the stream, and ignore(n, stopChar) to remove the next n characters or until stop-Char is encountered from an inStream object, whichever comes first. The default value of stopChar is '\n'.

   ● Use eof() to check if end of file was encountered while attempting to read a value.

■ Close an ifstream object with close().

```
double wage;
int idNumber, zip;
char code;
for (;;)
{
   fin >> idNumber >> code>> wage >> zip;
   if (fin.eof()) break;
   if (fin.fail())
   {
      cerr << "BAD DATA\n";
      fin.clear();
      fin.ignore(1024, '\n');
   }
   // Process input data
}
fin.close();
```

File Input in Java

■ It is common to wrap a BufferedReader around a FileReader to create file-input objects. Strings can then be read from them with readLine(); parse them for numeric values as described for keyboard input.

■ Do these in a try block, because exceptions can be thrown.

```
try {
   BufferedReader fin =
      new BufferedReader(
         new FileReader(fileName) );
   String dubStr = fin.readLine();
   double dub = Double.parseDouble(dubStr);
   . . .
}
catch {
   . . .
}
```

File Output in C++

■ Open an ofstream object from the program to an output file in the same manner as for input, but here it will create the output file if it doesn't exist or erase its contents if it does. A second argument ios::app can be used to open an output file for appending.

```
string outFileName;
cin >> outFileName;   // or getline(cin, outFilename);
ofstream fout(outFileName.data());
```

- ofstream is a subclass of ostream, so it inherits all of its output features, including << and format manipulators:

```
fout << fixed << showpoint << setprecision(2)
     << "Wages = $" << setw(10) << wages << endl;
```

File Output in Java

- It is common to wrap a PrintWriter around a BufferedWriter that wraps a FileWriter. Use print() and println() methods for output:

```
PrintWriter fout = new PrintWriter(
        new BufferedWriter(new FileWriter(fileName)));
fout.println("Wages " + wages);
```

E.4 Data Types

C++	Java
The data types in C++ are similar to those in Java, but there are some differences:	
■ The range of numeric types such as int is machine dependent.	■ Sizes of types are specified; they are machine independent.
■ There are short and unsigned types.	■ No short type; and there are only signed integers.
■ Boolean type is bool, but it behaves basically like an enumeration enum bool {false, true}; false is basically the same as 0, true as 1 (or any nonzero value).	■ A true boolean type with literals false and true.
• bool values are input/output as integers unless the boolalpha format manipulator is used.	• I/O uses false and true.
• Zero is interpreted as false and nonzero as true in boolean expressions. For example, in if (x = 0)... the assignment returns 0, so the condition is always false.	• Not allowed.

- char: ASCII representation is used for characters.

  - They are treated as integers in arithmetic expressions; for example, the following assigns 'B' to ch2:

    ```
    char ch1 = 'A', ch2;
    ch2 = ch1 + 1;
    ```

  - w_char is for wide characters.

- C++ string type is the string class; must #include <string>.

  - string objects can be modified.

  - + concatenates strings.

  - Compare with relops (<, >, ==, <=, >=, !=).
  - Access individual characters with [].
  - Large number of operations (see §D.2).

- Has enumerations.

- Unicode representation is used.

  - There is no such automatic type conversion.

- Use String and StringBuffer classes

  - String objects can't be modified; StringBuffer objects can.
  - + can concatenate objects onto strings.
  - Use equals, compareTo.

  - Use charAt().

- Added in Java 1.5.

E.5 Variables and Constants

C++

- No check is made whether local variables are initialized before they are used. Value of an uninitialized variable can be some default value or some "garbage value" represented by the bit string in its memory location. Forgetting to initialize variables is a common source of errors.

- Variables can be declared outside functions and classes. These global variables can be accessed from any function in a program, which makes them difficult to manage. They should not be used.

- Constants can be declared anywhere.

- Declaration uses keyword const:

  ```
  const int YEAR = 2004;
  ```

Java

- Checked in Java.

- Only in classes.

- Must be a static member of a class.

- Uses final:

  ```
  final int YEAR = 2004;
  ```

- An object variable holds an actual value, not a reference to it. The new operator need not be used when constructing an object in its declaration; instead, supply the constructor arguments (if any) after the variable name:

  ClassName
      objectName(args_to_constructor);

- An object variable holds a reference to (address of, pointer to) the actual object. new is used to construct an object in its declaration.

  ClassName objectName =
      new *ClassName*
              (args_to_constructor);

E.6 Functions

Stand-Alone Functions in C++

- C++ supports methods in classes—both instance methods and static methods—but it also permits stand-alone functions that are not part of any class—*global functions.*

- C++ supports procedural abstraction by putting information about *what* a function does (its *prototype* or *declaration*) in one place and *how* it does it (its *definition*) in another.

- A C++ program is a collection of stand-alone functions, in which execution begins with the global function main().

  ```
  #include declarations
  //--- Function prototypes
  double interest(double amount, double rate, int years);

  int main()
  { ...
    double earn = interest(wages, .05, YEAR - 2000);
    ...
  }
  //--- Function definitions
  #include <cmath>
  double interest(double amount, double rate, int years)
  {
    return amount*(1 + pow(rate, years));
  }
  ```

  - Command-line arguments can be passed to main main() via an integer parameter (argc), which is the number of strings on the command line, and an array parameter (argv) of character strings — see §D.5.
  - main() returns zero if the program completes successfully, a nonzero integer otherwise.

- *Note*: Prototypes need not list parameter names—for example,

  ```
  double interest(double, double, int);
  ```

  but it is good to include them for documentation.

■ Functions can be stored in a library:

- Put prototypes in a *header file*: myLib.h.
- Put definitions in an *implementation file*: myLib.cpp.
- Use #include "myLib.h" in both myLib.cpp and client programs.
- Client program and myLib.cpp can be compiled separately—but not myLib.h; it gets compiled automatically when included in a client program or implementation file. For example, in gnu C++,

```
g++ -c prog.cpp
g++ -c myLib.cpp
```

compiles prog.cpp and myLib.cpp (and the included Lib.h), creating the object files prog.o and myLib.o. These can then be linked together to produce a binary executable:

```
g++ prog.o myLib.o -o prog
```

(The default name of the binary executable is a.out if -o prog is omitted.)

Stand-Alone Functions in Java

■ Every method must be in a class; there are no stand-alone methods.

■ main() is a void method.

■ Command-line arguments can be passed to main() via an array parameter (args) of String values.

Function Members (Methods) of a Class in C++

■ Prototypes are usually placed inside the class declaration in *ClassName*.h.

■ Definitions of nontrivial functions are usually placed in *ClassName*.cpp.

■ Simple functions are often inlined and put in *ClassName*.h below the class declaration.

Function Members (Methods) of a Class in Java

■ Methods are not separated into prototypes and definitions. Method definitions are put inside the class declaration.

Parameter Passing in C++

■ There are several parameter-passing mechanisms:

- *Call by value*
- *Call by reference*
- *Call by constant reference*

■ For an argument passed by value (which is the default), the function receives a copy of the actual argument. Modifying this copy in the function does not change the argument. This is the case for all types of arguments, including objects.

■ For an argument passed by reference, its address is passed so the parameter receives (a copy of) this reference, making it an alias for the actual argument. Thus, it can be modified by changing the parameter in the function.

A reference parameter is specified by an ampersand (&) after the parameter type.

```
void update(double & wage, double increase)
{ wage *= increase; }

void display(ostream & out, Color c)
{
  if (c == RED)
    out << "RED";
  else if  . . .
}

void read(istream & in, Color & c)
{ . . . }
```

- Using a constant reference avoids the copying that happens with call by value (which is expensive for large objects), but prevents the function from modifying the parameter. Indicate these by adding const before the parameter's type and & after.

```
void display(ostream & out, const vector<int> & v)
{
  for (int i = 0; i < v.size(); i++)
    out << v[i] << "  ";
  out << endl;
}
```

Parameter Passing in Java

- There is only one parameter-passing mechanism.

- Arguments are passed by value. However, although this prevents arguments of primitive types from being modified by a method, modifying an object in a method will change the corresponding argument because it is a reference, so the parameter receives (a copy of) this reference, making it an alias for the actual argument.

- Objects are automatically passed by reference. Primitive types can't be; the corresponding wrapper classes can be used instead.

E.7 Operator Overloading

C++

- A C++ operator Δ can be overloaded for a new type by defining a function with the name operatorΔ(). For example, to overload + for type Color, we use a function whose prototype is

```
Color operator+(Color c1, Color c2);
```

and whose definition defines what Color value c1 + c2 should be. Then statements like the following can be used:

```
Color a = RED, b = YELLOW, c;
c = a + b;
```

- The output operator << and the input operator >> can be overloaded by defining operator<<() and operator>>(). For example, to overload the output operator for type Color, use:

  In Color.h,

  ```
  ostream & operator<<(ostream & out, Color col);
  ```

  Note: A reference to the ostream is returned so << can be chained—for example,

  ```
  cout << aColor << endl;
  ```

  In Color.cpp,

  ```
  ostream & operator<<(ostream & out, Color col)
  {
    // Color-to-string converter ala toString() in Java
    switch (col)
    {
      case RED:    out << "RED";   break;
      // ...
    }
    return out;
  }
  ```

Overloading the input operator is similar:

In Color.h:

```
istream & operator>>istream & in, Color & col);
```

In Color.cpp:

```
istream & operator>>(istream & out, Color & col)
{
  // Read name of color into a local string variable
  // Note:  Must #include <string>

  // Convert it to all uppercase a character at a time
  // using toupper() from <cctype>

  // String-to-color converter:  set col to Color
  // value corresponding to input string; return in;
}
```

E.8 Things the Same in Both C++ and Java

Since Java grew out of C++, much of the syntax is the same. This includes:

- control structures:
  - if and switch
  - for, while, and do-while loops
  - recursion
- Arithmetic operations and relational operators
- Assignment operations, increment/decrement operations

- Dot operator to access class members
- Comments (excluding javadoc)

E.9 More Differences Between C++ and Java

There are several other differences between C++ and Java, most of which are described at some point in this text. The following is a list of some of the major ones.

- Enumerations in C++ are not provided in earlier versions of Java; they were added in Java 1.5.
- Default arguments for parameters are allowed in C++ functions.
- Arrays in C++ are not classes.
- Pointers to any type can be declared in C++. In Java, any variable whose type is a class is a *handle* for (i.e., a pointer to) an object of that type.
- Dynamic memory allocation is done somewhat differently in the two languages.
- Dynamic memory deallocation is automatic in Java; it must be done explicitly (via the `delete` operator) in C++ to avoid memory leaks.
- C++ provides function templates and class templates; generics were added in Java 1.5.
- The Standard Template Library (STL) with its containers (e.g., `vector`, `list`, `stack`, `queue`, and `deque`), iterators, and powerful function templates called *algorithms* is a standard part of C++.
- Exceptions are somewhat different in the two languages.
- C++ allows multiple inheritance; Java does not. In its place, Java provides interfaces, which C++ does not have.
- Polymorphism in C++ is achieved through the use of virtual functions; it is automatic in Java.

Answers to Quick Quizzes

Quick Quiz 1.5

1. software engineering
2. Problem analysis and specification
   Design
   Coding
   Testing, execution, and debugging
   Maintenance
3. waterfall
4. specification
5. false
6. preconditions, postconditions
7. top-down
8. OOD
9. UML (Unified Modeling Language)
10. data, function
11. pseudocode
12. sequence, selection, and repetition
13. coding
14. false

15. Verification refers to checking that documents, program modules, and the like that are produced are correct and complete and that they are consistent with one another and with those of the preceding phases. Validation is concerned with checking that these products match the problem's specification.

16. Syntax errors are caused by not obeying the syntax rules of the programming languages such as bad punctuation. Run-time errors are caused by some unexpected event (such as division by 0) occurring during program execution. Logic errors are errors in designing the algorithm for solving the problem or in not coding the algorithm correctly.

17. In black-box testing, the outputs produced for various inputs are checked for correctness without considering the structure of the program unit itself. In white-box testing, the performance of the program unit is tested by examining its internal structure.

18. true

Quick Quiz 2.2

1. A collection of data items together with basic operations and relations on them.
2. Storage structures for the data items and algorithms for the basic operations and relations.

3. data abstraction

4. bit, byte

5. overflow

6. 23

7. 5.75

8. mantissa or fractional part

9. underflow

10. true

11. false

Quick Quiz 2.3

1. `typedef bool logical;`

2. `English`

3. enumerator

4. 3

5. 3

6. 6

7. 0

8. 8

9. 4

10. true

11. false

12. `enum WeekDays {SUNDAY = 1, MONDAY, TUESDAY, WEDNESDAY,`
    `                THURSDAY, FRIDAY, SATURDAY};`

Quick Quiz 2.4

1. address

2. &

3. *

4. *

5. address

6. `double` value

7. address

8. address

9. `double` value

10. `double` value

11. null

12. `1.1`

13. `3.3`

14. new, address

15. anonymous

Quick Quiz 3.2

1. A fixed-size sequence of elements, all of the same type, with the basic operation of direct access to each element so that values can be retrieved from and stored in this element.

2. direct

3. true

4. 1, 0, 0, 0, 0

5. null

6. subscript

7. base address, pointer

8. true

9. false

10. (1) Their capacity cannot change during program execution.

    (2) They are not self-contained objects.

Quick Quiz 3.3

1. false
2. false
3. true

4. $\begin{bmatrix} 1\ 2\ 3\ 4 \\ 5\ 6\ 7\ 8 \end{bmatrix}$

5. $\begin{bmatrix} 1\ 2 \\ 3\ 4 \\ 5\ 6 \\ 7\ 8 \end{bmatrix}$

6. A $3 \times 2 \times 2$ array with `array[0]` $= \begin{bmatrix} 1\ 2 \\ 3\ 4 \end{bmatrix}$, `array[1]` $= \begin{bmatrix} 5\ 6 \\ 7\ 8 \end{bmatrix}$, and `array[2]` $= \begin{bmatrix} 9\ 10 \\ 11\ 12 \end{bmatrix}$

Quick Quiz 3.4

1. new, address
2. anonymous
3. throw a bad_alloc exception
4. return the null address (0)
5. delete
6. 66
7. false
8. `delete [] dubarray;`
9. `argc, argv`
10. true

Quick Quiz 3.5

1. false
2. dot
3. `x.m = 100;`
4. `cin >> x.m >> x.n;`
5. `cout << x.m << "   " << x.n;`
6. `(*p).m` and `p->m`
7. `cin >> p->m >> p->n;`
8. `cout << p->m << "   " << p->n;`

Quick Quiz 4.1

1. procedural programming
2. object-oriented programming
3. procedural programming, object-oriented programming
4. procedural programming
5. object-oriented programming

Quick Quiz 4.2

1. Members of a class by default are private, but members of a struct by default are public.
2. data, function
3. An object carries its own operations around with it.
4. header
5. implementation
6. compiling and linking

7. object, object
8. linked
9. object

Quick Quiz 4.5

1. Declaring data members of a class to be private.
2. So that client programs cannot access the data members directly, but rather must interact with objects via public function members.
3. scope (::)
4. inline
5. class invariant
6. (1) Allocate memory for it
   (2) Initialize it
7. default, explicit-value
8. signatures
9. initialization, assignment
10. operatorΔ
11. true
12. friend
13. conditional

Quick Quiz 5.1

1. `istream` and `ostream`
2. `istream`
3. `ostream`
4. `istream`, `cin`
5. `ostream`, `cout` (or `cerr` or `clog`)
6. good, bad, fail
7. `good()`
8. `clear()`
9. `ignore()`
10. true
11. false
12. `endl`
13. false
14. `ifstream`
15. `ofstream`
16. false
17. `ifstream inputStream;`
    `inputStream.open(empFileName.data());`
18. `ifstream inputStream(empFileName.data());`
19. `ofstream outputStream;`
    `onputStream.open(reportFileName.data());`
20. `ofstream outputStream(reportFileName.data());`
21. false
22. true
23. `assert(inputStream.is_open());`
24. `inputStream.close();`

Quick Quiz 5.2

1. char, null character
2. empty
3. `stringstream`
4. 0, 3, 13

5. The
6. The cat in the hat
7. neuroses are red
8. e
9. neutron
10. roses are colored

11. rose
12. noses are red
13. 7
14. 3
15. true
16. some positive value

Quick Quiz 6.3

1. A finite sequence of data items with basic operations: construct an empty list, check if list is empty, traverse the list or part of it, insert and delete at any point in the list.
2. n
3. n
4. false
5. C(const C & original);
6. ~C();
7. false
8. true
9. default
10. When a class contains a data member that is a pointer to dynamically-allocated memory, because the default copy constructor does not make a distinct copy of the contents of that memory location.
11. memory leak
12. destructor
13. When a class contains a data member that is a pointer to dynamically-allocated memory, because the default destructor will not reclaim that memory, resulting in marooned memory blocks.
14. When a class contains a data member that is a pointer to dynamically-allocated memory, because the default assignment operator will simply do a pointer assignment, resulting in two pointers to the same memory location and not to distinct ones. A memory leak also results.

Quick Quiz 6.4

1. nodes
2. data, next
3. null
4. 1
5. 1
6. false

Quick Quiz 7.2

1. first, LIFO (last-in-first-out)
2. A sequence of data items that can be accessed at only one end, called the top of the stack. Basic operations are: construct an empty stack, check if stack is empty, push a value onto the top of the stack, retrieve the top value, and remove the top value.

3.   myTop = 0; myArray[0] = 123, myArray[1] = 789; other elements are undefined

4.   myTop = 1; myArray[0] = 111, myArray[1] = 111; other elements are undefined

5.   myTop = 2; myArray[0] = 0, myArray[1] = 2, myArray[2] = 4, myArray[3] = 6, myArray[4] = 8

Quick Quiz 7.4

1.   activation record

2.   run-time

3.   pushed onto

4.   popped from

5.   activation record

Quick Quiz 7.5

1.   postfix

2.   infix

3.   prefix

4.   postfix

5.   5

6.   a b c - - d *

7.   (a - b - c) * d

Quick Quiz 8.2

1.   last, FIFO (first-in-first-out)

2.   A sequence of data items that can be removed only at one end, called the front, and can be added only at the other end, called the back. Basic operations are: construct an empty queue, check if queue is empty, add a value at the back, retrieve the front value, and remove the front value.

3.   myFront = 2, myBack = 3; myArray[0] = 123, myArray[1] = 456, myArray[2] = 789; other elements are undefined

4.   myFront = 1, myBack = 3; myArray[0] = 111, myArray[1] = 222, myArray[2] = 111, other elements are undefined

5.   myFront = 2, myBack = 4; myArray[0] = 0, myArray[1] = 2, myArray[2] = 4, myArray[3] = 6, myArray[4] is undefined. Queue becomes full when i is 3, so 8 is not added to it.

Quick Quiz 8.3

1.   The link in the last node points to the first node.

2.   One has direct access to the last node and almost direct access to the first node (by following the linkfrom the last node).

3.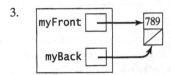

4.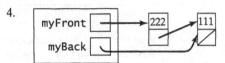

5.

Quick Quiz 8.4

1. spool
2. buffer
3. deque
4. scroll

5. priority queue
6. ready
7. resident
8. suspended

Quick Quiz 9.3

1. overloaded
2. true
3. false

4. templates
5. typename or class
6. instantiation

7. (1) Changing the typedef is a change to the header file, which means that any program or library that uses the class must be recompiled. (2) A name declared using typedef can have only one meaning at a time.

8. (1) All operations defined outside of the class declaration must be template functions.

   (2) Any use of the name of a class template as a type must be parameterized.

   (3) Definitions of operations on a class template must be available to the compiler whenever the class template is used. One common way to do this is to put them in the same file as the class template declaration, following the class declaration.

9. Standard Template Library
10. true
11. containers, algorithms, and iterators
12. iterators

Quick Quiz 9.4

1. int
2. 0,0
3. 5,5
4. 5,5
5. 10,7
6. 1 1
7. 0 88
8. true
9. false
10. true

11. 1 1 1 1 1
12. 0 0 0 0 0 77
13. 0
14. behind 88
15. 20
16. true
17. 0, 0.5, 1.0, 1.5, 2.0
18. 1, 1, 1, 1, 1, 0, 3, 4, 7, 8
19. 1, 1, 1, 1, 1, 2, 2, 2, 2, ?
20. 1, 1, 2, 2, 2

Quick Quiz 9.7

1. double-ended queue

2. A sequence of data items with the property that items can be added and removed only at the ends. Basic operations are: construct an empty deque, check if deque is empty, add to front or rear of deque, retrieve from front or rear of deque, remove from front or rear of deque.

3. false

4. true

5. false

6. adapter

7. interface

8. Need space between >s: `stack< vector<double> > st;`

9. `stack and queue`

Quick Quiz 10.1

1. recursion

2. (1) An anchor or base case that specifies the value of the function for one or more values of the parameter(s).

   (2) An inductive or recursive step that defines the function's value for the current value of the parameter(s) in terms of previously defined function values and/or parameter values.

3. true

4. 15

5. 0

6. 0

7. infinite recursion

Quick Quiz 10.4

1. time and space

2. space

3. time

4. There is some constant C such that $T(n) \leq C \cdot f(n)$ for all sufficiently large values of n.

5. true

6. true

7. false

8. n

9. $\log_2 n$

10. false

11. recurrence

Quick Quiz 10.5

1. algorithms
2. <algorithm>
3. false

4. first element, and just past the last element
5. <numeric>

Quick Quiz 11.1

1. head node
2. predecessor
3. circular

4. true
5. true

Quick Quiz 12.2

1. tree (or directed graph)
2. root
3. leaves
4. children, parent
5. at most 2 children

6. 10
7. 50, 60, 70
8. No, the third level is not full
9. 3

10. No. For node 20, the left subtree has height 0, but the right subtree has height 2.

11.

i	0	1	2	3	4	5	6	7	8	9	10	...
$t[i]$	10	20	30	?	40	?	50	?	?	60	70	...

Quick Quiz 12.3

1. 20, 60, 40, 70, 10, 30, 50
2. 10, 20, 40, 60, 70, 30, 50
3. 60, 70, 40, 20, 50, 30, 10

4. 10, 20, 30, 40, 50, 60, 70
5. 50, 20, 10, 30, 40, 60, 70
6. 10, 40, 30, 20, 70, 60, 50

Quick Quiz 12.4

1.

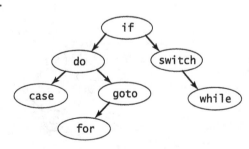

2.

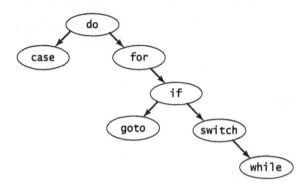

3.

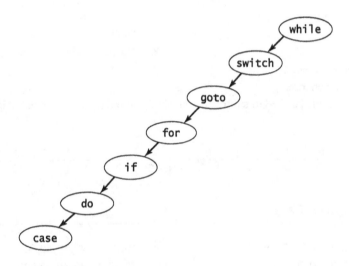

4.   10, 20, 30, 40, 50, 60, 70, 80, 90, 100
5.   80, 30, 20, 10, 60, 50, 40, 70, 90, 100
6.   10, 20, 40, 50, 70, 60, 30, 100, 90, 80

7.

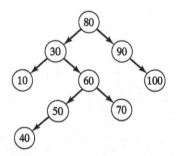

8.

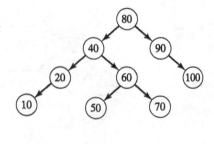

9.

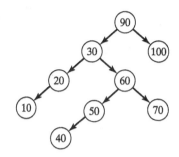

Quick Quiz 12.6

1. A link from node to its inorder successor.
2. So that traversals or other tree operations can be performed more efficiently.

3.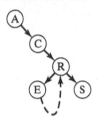

4.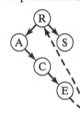

5.

6.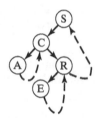

Quick Quiz 12.7

1. hash table, hash

2. collision

3. If a collision occurs at index i, examine the locations $i + 1, i + 2, i + 3, \ldots$ with all operations done modulo the table size, continuing until an empty slot is found where the item can be stored.

4. If a collision occurs at index i, examine the locations $i + 1^2, i - 1^2, i + 2^2, i - 2^2, i + 3^2, i - 3^2, \ldots$ with all operations done modulo the table size, continuing until an empty slot is found where the item can be stored.

5. Find the location $i = h_1(x)$ of an item x in the hash table with a first hash function h_1. If a collision occurs, compute an increment $k = h_2(x)$ using a second hash function h_2, and then examine the locations $i + k, i + 2k, i + 3k, \ldots$, with all operations done modulo the table size, continuing until an empty slot is found where the item can be stored.

6. chaining

7.

	Table
0	28
1	13
2	23
3	25
4	11
5	5
6	18

8.

	Table
0	28
1	25
2	23
3	18
4	11
5	5
6	13

9.   Table

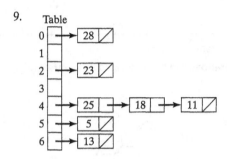

Quick Quiz 13.1

1. Make a number of passes through the list or a part of the list, and on each pass, select one element to be correctly positioned.

2. false

3. Systematically interchange pairs of elements that are out of order until eventually no such pairs remain and the list is therefore sorted.

4. true

5. Repeatedly insert a new element into a list of already sorted elements so that the resulting list is still sorted.

6. true

7. true

8. indirect

Quick Quiz 13.2

1. The data item stored in each node is greater than or equal to the data item stored in each of its children.

2. complete

3. $\log_2 n$

4. $n \log_2 n$

5. So that those with higher priority are removed before those of lower priority.

6. true

Quick Quiz 13.3

1. A problem is repeatedly partitioned into simpler subproblems, each of which can be considered independently, continuing until subproblems are obtained that are sufficiently simple that they can be solved (i.e., conquered).

2. Select an element, called a pivot, and then perform a sequence of exchanges so that all elements that are less than or equal to this pivot are to its left and all elements that are greater than the pivot are to its right. This correctly positions the pivot and divides the (sub)list into two smaller sublists, each of which may then be sorted independently in the same way.

3. pivot
4. $n^2, n\log_2 n$
5. false

6. median-of-three
7. true

Quick Quiz 13.4

1. internal, external
2. It requires direct access to the list elements. It may make many passes through the list.
3. The basic operation involved is merging: combining two lists that have previously been sorted so that the resulting list is also sorted.
4. $n\log_2 n$

Quick Quiz 14.1

1. Encapsulation: Wrapping the data and basic operations used for processing this data within a single entity.

   Inheritance: A class can be derived from another class, and this derived class then inherits the members of the parent class.

   Polymorphism: The property of a derived class D and an ancestor class A having a function member with the same prototype, but that behaves differently for A objects than for D objects.

2. encapsulation
3. message
4. inherits

5. polymorphism
6. static (or early), dynamic (or late)

Quick Quiz 14.2

1. inheritance
2. (1) Identify the objects in the problem.

   (2) Analyze the objects to determine if there is commonality in them.

   (3) Where there is commonalty:

       a. Define base classes that contain this commonality.

       b. Derive classes that inherit this commonality from the base class.

3. private

4. protected
5. false
6. is-a

Quick Quiz 14.5

1. The property of a derived class D and an ancestor class A having a function member with the same prototype, but that behaves differently for A objects than for D objects.
2. static (or early)
3. virtual, dynamic (or late)
4. virtual table
5. abstract, pure virtual

Quick Quiz 15.2

1. The height of the left subtree of a node minus the height of its right subtree.
2. A binary search tree in which the balance factor of each node is 0, 1, or –1. Basic operations are: construction, empty, search, and traverse as for BSTs; insert and delete items in such a way that the height-balanced property is maintained.
3. height

4.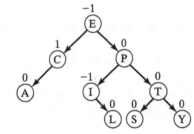

5. 3
6. 5
7. $\log_2 n$

Quick Quiz 15.3

1. (a) 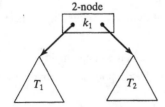 (b)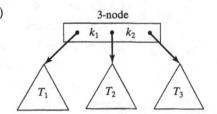

(c)

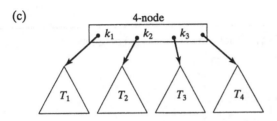

(a) 2-node: all values in $T_1 < k_1 \leq$ all values in T_2

(b) 3-node: all values in $T_1 < k_1 \leq$ all values in $T_2 < k_2 \leq$ all values in T_3

(c) 4-node: all values in $T_1 < k_1 \leq$ all values in $T_2 < k_2 \leq$ all values in $T_3 < k_3 \leq$ all values in T_4

2.

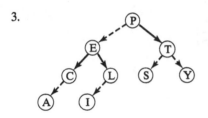

3.

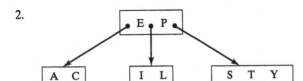

4. B

5. 4

6.

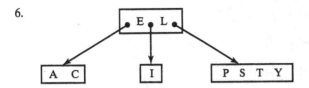

7.

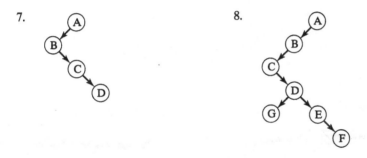

8.

Quick Quiz 15.4

1. `vector, deque, list, stack, queue, priority_queue.`
2. `set, multiset, map, multimap`
3. `map`
4. The index type may be any type.
5. red-black

Quick Quiz 16.1

1. Digraphs need not have a root node and there may be several (or no) paths from one vertex to another.
2. true
3. adjacent
4. in-degree, out-degree

5. $adj = \begin{bmatrix} 0 & 1 & 1 & 1 & 1 \\ 0 & 1 & 1 & 0 & 0 \\ 0 & 0 & 0 & 1 & 0 \\ 0 & 0 & 0 & 1 & 1 \\ 0 & 1 & 0 & 0 & 0 \end{bmatrix}$ $data = \begin{bmatrix} A \\ B \\ C \\ D \\ E \end{bmatrix}$

6. $adj = \begin{bmatrix} 0 & 0 & 0 & 0 \\ 0 & 0 & 0 & 0 \\ 0 & 0 & 0 & 0 \\ 0 & 0 & 0 & 0 \end{bmatrix}$ $data = \begin{bmatrix} 1 \\ 2 \\ 3 \\ 4 \end{bmatrix}$

7.

8.

Quick Quiz 16.2

1. When processing some values, it becomes necessary to return to some that were already processed or that were skipped over on an earlier pass.

2. From vertex 1: all of them; from vertex 2: 2, 3, 4, 5

3. Only 1 itself

4. 2, 3, 4, 5

5. NP: Problems for which a solution can be guessed and then checked with an algorithm whose computing time is $O(P(n))$ for some polynomial $P(n)$.

   P: Problems that can be solved by algorithms in polynomial time.

   NP-Complete: Problems with the property that if a polynomial time algorithm that solves any one of these problems can be found, then the existence of polynomial-time algorithms for all NP problems is guaranteed.

Quick Quiz 16.3

1. No direction is associated with the edges. No edge may join a vertex to itself.

2. $adj = \begin{bmatrix} 0 & 1 & 1 & 1 & 1 \\ 1 & 0 & 1 & 0 & 1 \\ 1 & 1 & 0 & 1 & 0 \\ 1 & 0 & 1 & 0 & 1 \\ 1 & 1 & 0 & 1 & 0 \end{bmatrix} \qquad data = \begin{bmatrix} A \\ B \\ C \\ D \\ E \end{bmatrix}$

3. $adj = \begin{bmatrix} 0 & 0 & 0 & 0 \\ 0 & 0 & 0 & 0 \\ 0 & 0 & 0 & 0 \\ 0 & 0 & 0 & 0 \end{bmatrix} \qquad data = \begin{bmatrix} 1 \\ 2 \\ 3 \\ 4 \end{bmatrix}$

4.
   v[1] ⊡→ A ⊡→ 2 ⊡→ 3 ⊡→ 4 ⊡→ 5 ⊠

   v[2] ⊡→ B ⊡→ 1 ⊡→ 3 ⊡→ 5 ⊠

   v[3] ⊡→ C ⊡→ 1 ⊡→ 2 ⊡→ 4 ⊠

   v[4] ⊡→ D ⊡→ 1 ⊡→ 3 ⊡→ 5 ⊠

   v[5] ⊡→ E ⊡→ 1 ⊡→ 2 ⊡→ 4 ⊠

5.
   v[1] ⊡→ 1 ⊠

   v[2] ⊡→ 2 ⊠

   v[3] ⊡→ 3 ⊠

   v[4] ⊡→ 4 ⊠

6.

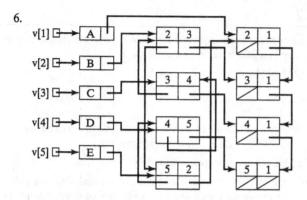

7. Same answer as 5.

8. all of them in each case

9. Only 1 itself

10. 2, 3, 4, 5

11. Only A

Index